THE KINGDOM OF GOD HAS NO BORDERS

The Kingdom of God Has No Borders

A GLOBAL HISTORY OF AMERICAN EVANGELICALS

Melani McAlister

OXFORD
UNIVERSITY PRESS

OXFORD

UNIVERSITY PRESS

Oxford University Press is a department of the University of Oxford. It furthers
the University's objective of excellence in research, scholarship, and education
by publishing worldwide. Oxford is a registered trade mark of Oxford University
Press in the UK and certain other countries.

Published in the United States of America by Oxford University Press
198 Madison Avenue, New York, NY 10016, United States of America.

© Oxford University Press 2018

CIP data is on file at the Library of Congress
ISBN 978-0-19-021342-8

9 8 7 6 5 4 3 2 1

Printed by Sheridan Books, Inc, United States of America

To my father, Gene McAlister, and in loving memory of my mother, Katie Slater McAlister (1937–2016), for their love and patient support.

Contents

Figures

ix

Abbreviations

KJV	King James Version (Bible translation)
LAOS	Laymen's Overseas Service
MARC	Missions Advanced Research Center
NAE	National Association of Evangelicals
NBEA	National Black Evangelical Association
NGO	Non-governmental organization
NIV	New International Version (Bible translation)
OLS	Operation Lifeline Sudan
PEPFAR	President's Emergency Fund for AIDS Relief
RSV	Revised Standard Version (Bible translation)
SACC	South African Council of Churches
SADF	South African Defence Forces
SBC	Southern Baptist Convention
SPLA	Southern People's Liberation Army (Sudan)
STA	Short Terms Abroad
STM	Short-term mission
TEAM	The Evangelical Alliance Mission
UDF	United Democratic Front (South Africa)
UFM	Unevangelized Fields Mission
UNHCR	UN High Commissioner for Refugees
USAID	US Agency for International Development
USCIRF	US Commission on International Religious Freedom
VOM	Voice of the Martyrs
WCC	World Council of Churches
WEA	World Evangelical Alliance
WMU	Women's Missionary Union (of the Southern Baptist Convention)
YWAM	Youth with a Mission
WWJD	What Would Jesus Do?
ZCC	Zion Christian Church (South Africa)

THE KINGDOM OF GOD HAS NO BORDERS

Introduction

IT WAS A hot December afternoon in Otalla, a remote village of five hundred people in Sudan (now South Sudan), near the Ethiopian border. But it was dark and cool in the thatched-roof hut that served as the church where Dick Robinson was preaching. Dick was the senior associate pastor at a largely white megachurch outside Milwaukee. I had joined him and a small team from the church who had come to Sudan for a week to, as Dick put it, "visit our friends and to learn." A group of about fifty people, mostly women and children, sat on the dirt floor of the church or on gazelle skins they had brought. Dick's sermon was relatively simple. Its heart was a humorous parable that drew heavily on his experience growing up as a missionary kid across the border in Congo. Speaking in short sentences punctuated by rhythmic repetitions, he told the villagers about himself. "I grew up just near here," he said, "just fifty miles away." "Just over there," he said again, pointing out the door. "I was born in Africa; my parents died in Africa."

Dick didn't say that his parents were missionaries, or discuss their complicated relationship to Congo. He didn't tell the audience that they had escaped under fire during the 1961 missionary evacuations (they returned a few months later). Instead, he told what he called "an African story." When Dick was young, he and his brothers once found some crocodile eggs. "Crocodile eggs are beautiful," he said. And the boys decided to take them back home, just to look at them. They figured that they could return them to the river bank the following day. But, then the eggs hatched while the family was all asleep. They woke up surrounded by baby crocodiles—small but dangerous, threatening them all. The overt message was simple: what seems beautiful can be dangerous. You have to look at the heart of things, not be deceived by appearance or wrong teaching. But there was another message too: I grew up in Congo, Dick was saying to the Sudanese in the church. We are not so different, you and I.

I had met Dick the previous summer at Wheaton College, where he was the featured speaker at a conference for missionary organizations. Dick does not look like a preacher. He is a big man, with a white beard that gives him a passing resemblance to Jerry Garcia. His wardrobe was built almost entirely around jeans and hiking boots. He had come to the conference, he told the audience, on his Harley-Davidson motorcycle.

For three evenings Dick spoke about his vision of a global church community. The story he told was "based on facts," he said, but "much of it is still a dream." He imagined a young American couple who leave the United States to work and live in Nairobi. The young man, who has a degree in international relations, gets a job with the US State Department. Once in Kenya, he and his wife—that she would follow him was assumed—join a thriving church. The church, Dick imagined, was led by a Kenyan pastor "who had studied business in India and theology in Australia." The fantasy congregation was international. It included, perhaps, Chinese people who had come temporarily to Africa for work; the Chinese would join the worship service, "singing in English and Swahili, with the sermon translated for them into Mandarin." And every year, Americans would arrive in Nairobi as part of missions and outreach teams, where they would work with local churches and "luxuriate in the vibrant, healing worship of Africa."

Dick clearly longed for this "postmodern" church family, with American Christians circulating through the halls of power, traversing borders, and worshipping in multiple languages. But he also recognized that American sojourns in the global South might be problematic: "The question is, I suppose, are they present [overseas] . . . for Kingdom reasons, or simply to advance the interests of the American empire?"[1]

It was a good question.

The Kingdom of God Has No Borders explores how American evangelicals have engaged the world beyond their borders over the past fifty years, particularly in the Middle East and Africa. In the early twenty-first century, journalists and scholars, as well as evangelicals themselves, have begun to describe a new form of evangelical internationalism that encompasses everything from lobbying for more US aid for Africa to organizing around international religious freedom. The evangelical activists with an internationalist bent did not always espouse the kind of deeply conservative politics that one might expect. But it turns out that these "new" stances are not in fact so new. They could be traced back at least to the nineteenth century, but took their modern shape in the years after World War II, when evangelicals began operating on the world stage in ways that went well beyond missionary work.[2]

Until very recently, the standard story of late twentieth-century evangelicalism has focused on the "rise of the religious Right."[3] According to legend, after World War II a group of Christians led by Billy Graham broke with fundamentalists, who had retreated from the world. These "neo-evangelicals," as they called themselves, marched out of the churches and into the voting booths, transforming American politics. There is some truth to that story. But those believers did not stop at the voting booth—or at the borders. They marched out across the globe and became enmeshed in global politics. That is why the history of American evangelicalism cannot be fully understood through a domestic lens. This book rethinks the history of evangelical Christians in the United States by recontextualizing that history on international terrain. It looks beyond the nation to account for the institutions, emotional attachments, and cross-border ties that pushed American evangelicals toward greater interest in humanitarianism, human rights, and economic justice than anyone—most evangelicals included—would have imagined in 1945.[4]

The world evangelicals operated in was shaped by three major forces. One was the dramatic expansion of the US military's reach during and after the Cold War. The postwar world was forged in part by the long arm of American power. US wars, hot and cold, sometimes opened new places to evangelize. At the same time, those wars often created anti-American sentiment that made evangelizing much more difficult. In many parts of the world, evangelicals were never able to fully escape the reality of US hegemony; often, they did not want to.

The US state could be a powerful protector when Christians went abroad. This did not mean, however, that American believers were puppets of the US government. Evangelicals, like other Christians overseas, sometimes did serve as agents or background support for the United States, championing the expansion of US influence. Yet, there was no simple, unilateral endorsement for American military power or US policy per se. Evangelicals of various stripes at times pushed for changes in US foreign policy, challenging, for instance, US relations with the rapacious Belgian rule over Congo in the early twentieth century, or calling for more support for southern Sudan in the early twenty-first. American evangelicals might see their country as a force for good in the world, but they also sometimes insisted that US foreign policy had gone dangerously wrong and needed to reform.

Equally important was the broad reach of American economic and cultural power. American films, commodities, and businesses shaped both material desires and cultural values around the world. This was a complex process, and it is clear that people on the "receiving end" of US exports—whether sewing machines or movies—were far from passive receptors of a predetermined meaning. But the dominance of American culture meant that evangelicals abroad were perceived as emissaries of a prosperous—they might say "blessed"—nation. By the middle of the century it had become difficult, in sociologist Robert Wuthnow's words, "to disentangle the Christian message from images of US wealth and power."[5]

The third force was a countervailing one. Millions of Latin Americans, Africans, and Asians converted to some form of Protestantism during the twentieth century. In 2010, almost 70 percent of the world's evangelicals lived outside the United States and Europe.[6] Starting in the 1970s, many US Christians (and others) became acutely conscious of—and increasingly engaged with—the evangelical churches of the global

South. And the members of those churches made their presence felt—attending conferences, publishing books, posting on Facebook, taking on denominational leadership roles, and sending missionaries to the rest of the world, including to the United States. At the same time, immigration transformed the religious landscape within the United States, so that American evangelicalism came to include African-born ministers, Latino congregants, Caribbean deacons, and TV preachers from across the globe. In that context, non-Western believers taught their fellow Christians much about economic realities, medical crises, and political instabilities that shaped their daily lives.

The Kingdom of God Has No Borders focuses primarily, although not exclusively, on US evangelicals' encounters with the Middle East and Africa. Both areas were important to US foreign policy after 1960. The significance of the Middle East is obvious, with multiple wars and high-stakes oil politics. Africa has been less central but its importance is increasing. In the wake of rising awareness about the HIV/AIDS crisis in Africa in the 1980s, and in the context of various crises in Somalia, Congo, Rwanda, and Sudan in the 1990s, Africa has become a new frontier of US foreign policy and humanitarian interest. With the rise of Islamist movements in Africa in the 2000s, it also became a new frontier for the US "war on terrorism."

Africa and the Middle East also offer useful contrasts. For evangelicals interested in the Middle East, politics have been front and center, from support for Israel to the impact of September 11 and the Iraq war. The Middle East is also a source of deep frustration; perhaps more than anywhere else on earth, it has been an area of intense but often failed missionary activity. Overall, Christians are only 4 percent of the population there, although local percentages range from a high of 38 percent in Lebanon to a low of fewer than 1 percent in Iraq. Of these Christians, most are Catholic or Orthodox.[7]

Africa is a different story. For more than half a century, it has been the site of the most explosive growth of Christianity in the world. In eight African countries, more than 70 percent of people say they are "born again," ranging from the Democratic Republic of Congo (71 percent) to Liberia (87 percent).[8] African Christians have been a primary force in pivoting Christianity toward the global South, and their political concerns—from global poverty to gender politics—are now on the agenda of international evangelicalism.

The Kingdom of God Has No Borders analyzes American evangelicals' decades-long endeavor to define how and under what terms they would engage the non-Western world. Through interaction with evangelicals in Africa, the Middle East, Asia, Eastern Europe, and Latin America, some conservative Protestants in the United States came to understand themselves differently, as part of a truly global community. Globalizing views were not always liberal, certainly, but they were influential, reshaping the moral map for many believers. Other US evangelicals did not have a particularly internationalist tilt, or, if they did, it was built primarily around fears of Islam as a global force. In the twenty-first century, America-first evangelicalism remains alive and well, as the election of Donald Trump made clear. The story told in this book is one of contest and transformation, a struggle to shape US evangelicals' views of themselves, and their God, in the world.

The category of "evangelical" is broad and often messy. Like most historians of evangelicalism, I begin with a theological definition. Evangelicals generally share many of the doctrines that are held by almost all Christians, such as the Trinity (Father, Son, and Holy Ghost) and the divinity of Jesus. But they believe other things as well. First is the centrality of the Bible as authoritative truth—the word of God. Of course, the question of just what "authoritative" means is a matter of great debate. Still, they are bibliocentric: the Bible is central, foundational, believable—and true.[9] Second, evangelicals believe in the inherent sinfulness of humans and, thus, the necessity of personal salvation. They affirm that the only path to salvation is accepting that humans are sinners in need of atonement, recognizing that Jesus died on the cross for humanity's sins. In short, we are forgiven only when we accept, by faith, that Jesus died for us. The final tenet follows from the others: evangelicals believe passionately in evangelizing the world. They are committed to teaching others about their faith. "Therefore go and make disciples of all the nations, baptizing them in the name of the Father and of the Son and of the Holy Spirit," Jesus says in the book of Matthew (28:19, NIV), and this "Great Commission" has shaped Christianity from its beginnings. A useful shorthand is that evangelicals emphasize the Bible, the cross, personal salvation, and evangelism.[10]

There are problems with defining any religion by its beliefs alone, however, since people experience religious identity through rituals and the construction of community as much as through clarifying their doctrines. In 1960, Harold Ockenga made this point in an essay in *Christianity Today*. Ockenga was an evangelical luminary, part of that group of conservative Protestants who in the postwar period began to describe themselves as "neo" evangelicals, different than old-style fundamentalists. Ockenga argued that, yes, evangelicals were defined primarily by what they believed, but that they could be identified by something else as well. Evangelicals, he said, are "in a special sense, spiritually minded and zealous for practical Christian living, distinguished from merely orthodox."[11] Being an evangelical, Ockenga insisted, was a matter of passion. While many religious people claim that their subgroup comprises the best and most thoroughgoing of believers, there is value in Ockenga's notion of evangelicals as being distinctively "zealous for practical Christian living." His approach encourages us to see evangelicalism as not just a form of believing but as a way of operating in the world. Indeed, American evangelicals are not only zealous, but also have tended to be entrepreneurial and populist, with decentralized denominations and innovative independent organizations. They have a penchant for frequent renewal and revival, with a focus on individual experiences of faith, a transformed life, and the presence and active involvement of God in the world.[12]

How many American evangelicals are there? Some polls today tell us that 35 percent of the US population is evangelical. Perhaps that is true, if we use the broadest definition and count anyone who says they are "born again." But maybe the number is closer to 30 percent, if we ask people to agree to a concrete statement of faith adopted in 2015 by the National Association of Evangelicals. Some pollsters claim that as few as 9 percent of Americans are evangelical; those lower numbers come when polls ask respondents to accede to a long and clear list of doctrines.[13] Some people do not include Pentecostal Christians among evangelicals; they share many beliefs but traditionally had different modes of worship—more emotive, charismatic, and oriented toward "gifts of the spirit" such as healing and speaking in tongues. These days, however, the lines are blurring. Counting evangelicals on a global scale is even more complicated, since polling is less common and less standardized, and the terms people use for their religious identity have different connotations.[14] I take a broad approach, counting as evangelical any Protestants, including Pentecostals, who answer yes when they are asked whether they are evangelical or born-again—about 30 percent of the US population.

My definition of evangelicals includes people of color who fit those criteria. This is increasingly common among scholars, although it is still the case that most polls and many histories separate out "white evangelicals" from everybody else. Those studies often distinguish African American believers in particular, isolating the "black church" from both evangelicalism and mainline Protestantism. There are good reasons for this. African Americans themselves have traditionally been wary of the evangelical label. Decades ago, William Bentley, the long-time leader of the National Black Evangelical Association (NBEA), pointed out that African Americans were often evangelical in theology. "Bible-believers" were everywhere in African American communities, he said, but they saw "evangelical" as a term for white people. In some ways, not much has changed: a recent survey by the National Association of Evangelicals (NAE) found that only 25 percent of African Americans who hold evangelical beliefs consider themselves evangelical Christians.[15]

It is crucial to recognize this reality, but I also believe it makes sense to include African American "Bible believers" in a study of evangelicals. When asked by Gallup if they are "born again" or evangelical, more than 70 percent of black Protestants said yes. Although only about 15 percent of African Americans are members of self-defined evangelical churches, many more attend Baptist or African Methodist Episcopal (AME) churches that have evangelical statements of faith. Other black churches, like the Church of God in Christ (COGIC), are Pentecostal, with no significant theological differences from other Pentecostals.[16] They often disagree politically with white evangelicals, and that is an important part of the story I tell.

The evangelical community is not just white and black, of course. It includes Latinos, Asian Americans, Arab Americans, and many others who are migrants or immigrants. Eleven percent of US evangelicals are Latino, and their numbers are growing. Asian Americans are only 2 percent of the US evangelical population, but some subsections of the Asian American community, such as Korean Americans, are largely Christian and significantly evangelical.[17] Asians and Latinos are far less important in shaping US evangelical relationships with Africa and the Middle East than white or black evangelicals, so I focus less on them. But they too embody the reality of US evangelicalism, where diversity is genuine and prized, but race and racism remain highly charged points of contention.

When we look beyond US borders, we see how little of global evangelicalism is comprised of Europeans or European Americans; in other words, how very non-white it is. In Africa, evangelical churches include not only the Nigerian Baptists, who have the third largest Baptist Convention in the world, but also South Africans who gather in small African Methodist Episcopal churches in their villages. In Latin America, especially Brazil, Pentecostalism has seen explosive growth. The same is true in some parts of Asia, particularly South Korea, the Philippines, and China. Overall, the global evangelical community is racially diverse, dispersed across the planet (although not evenly so), and increasingly linked through media, travel, and interpersonal networks.

US evangelical life is structured by gender as well as race. Gender is at once silent and deafening in the evangelical world, where men are almost uniformly the megachurch pastors, the most prominent televangelists, the editors of journals, and the presidents of denominations. Most conservative Protestants, in the United States and beyond, believe that only men can serve as primary pastors for congregations or as deacons within the church. There is, however, an anxiety at the center of the valorization of male power and authority among theological conservatives. In the United States, Christianity has been deeply identified with the heart, and thus with the supposedly more emotional activities of women. How does traditional male power operate within a religion that speaks so frequently of love, forgiveness, and non-violence?[18]

In the 1910s, the nation's most popular evangelist, Billy Sunday, addressed the common anxiety among men that Christianity had become too "feminized," that the church—much like US life overall—did not value manly qualities. "Lord save us," Sunday preached, "from offhanded, flabby-cheeked, brittle-boned, weak-kneed, thin-skinned, pliable, plastic, spineless, effeminate, sissified, three-caret Christianity." In the ensuing century, one commentator after another has tried to rescue Jesus from the assumption that he was passive or weak, and Christianity from any association with the "women's sphere" of excessive feeling.[19]

Despite efforts to masculinize the church, women have been neither silent nor silenced. In the local church, they are almost always the majority of parishioners, and they are engines of Sunday school, youth choir, and prayer groups. In the early twentieth century, as Billy Sunday was preaching his manly gospel, Aimee Semple McPherson began her storied career as a Pentecostal evangelist and radio preacher, building a denomination that today claims eight million members.[20] In the 1930s, Mary McLeod Bethune pointedly critiqued a colleague who had written a male-centered history of the black church. "Throughout its growth, the untiring effort, the unflagging enthusiasm, the sacrificial contribution of time, effort, and cash earnings of the black woman have been the most significant factors, without which the modern Negro church would have no history worth the writing."[21] More recently, evangelical women at the national and international level have held important roles as Bible teachers, lecturers, and increasingly, authors and televangelists. Women's prayer and worship groups, such as Pentecostal Aglow International, provide a space for women to create community, pray for each other, and cultivate their own leadership.[22]

Starting in the 1990s, a number of leading US evangelicals began to make their reputations on discussions of gender and sexuality. Megachurch pastor T.D. Jakes became one of the bestselling Christian authors in the country on the basis of his massively successful advice book, *Woman, Thou Art Loosed!*, which was adapted into a play and movie. Jakes attracts a large audience of both black and white women who attend his "Woman Thou Art Loosed!" conferences. Recognizing that many women have suffered loss, abuse, poverty, or other hardships, Jakes argues that women can heal the wounds of their past, becoming the person God wants them to be by embracing their God-given roles in the family. Jakes's views are empowering for many women, but are built on the idea of fundamental, essential differences between the genders. Jakes's "complementarian" model of gender is not unusual among evangelicals, who often argue that women and men each have distinct roles—roles that require women to accept men's leadership, while also seeing themselves as central to God's plan.[23]

A number of women televangelists and authors have become globally recognized by embracing precisely this combination of promoting empowerment through emotional healing and affirming notions of women's subservience to men. Paula White, Joyce Meyers, and Juanita Bynum all have global audiences for their preaching, in which they emphasize their histories of suffering, sexual abuse, and, ultimately, recovery through their faith in Jesus. Their narratives of trauma and healing resonate internationally. In one survey of Christians in Kenya, respondents were asked to name the authors, Christian or not, that they read most frequently: Joyce Meyer was sixth and T.D. Jakes was eighth.[24] American evangelicals have an outsized influence on the global media landscape, and gendered narratives are among their most popular exports.

American evangelicalism did not develop in a religious vacuum. It always operated alongside the liberal Protestantism that dominated US culture through most of the twentieth century. From the founding of the National Association of Evangelicals in 1942, evangelicals made a sharp distinction between what they saw as their own brand of faith—theologically conservative, focused centrally on evangelism, and dubious about political involvement—and that of the ecumenical Protestant churches represented by the National Council of Churches and its world body, the World Council of Churches (WCC). They saw the ecumenical movement, with some accuracy, as heir to the Modernists who had squared off against Fundamentalists in the early twentieth century, committed to liberal ideas about Biblical authority and inerrancy, and oriented toward the social gospel.[25]

Starting in the 1950s, the National Council of Churches (like its precursor, the Federal Council of Churches) served as the voice of Protestant orthodoxy, the "moral establishment" whose leaders advised presidents and spoke authoritatively about scripture.[26] For evangelicals, this meant that their own approaches to theology and politics often had a pugnacious underdog quality—at least until the 1980s, when evangelicals began to construct their own establishment, their own sense of cultural ownership.[27]

On the global scene, the World Council of Churches was maligned and feared by evangelicals because it had successfully positioned itself as the voice of a united Christian community. The ideal of a worldwide church "united in Christ" was one that evangelicals, like other Christians, held dear—at least in the abstract. In the 1960s, the missionary thinker Arthur Glasser warned that evangelicals should be concerned about and even fearful of the World Council's "tendencies to become a power movement, a superchurch." This fear circulated not only among evangelical church leaders but also among those in the pews. The global reach of the WCC meant that the liberal churches in the United States had a serious claim to represent *the* voice of global Protestantism. To make matters worse, the WCC welcomed a broad range of churches, including Pentecostal and evangelical churches in the global South. American evangelicals criticized the WCC on theological grounds for minimizing doctrinal differences, and over time they would also oppose the WCC's broader interfaith activities.[28]

In the final analysis, however, neither of these issues—the ecumenical movement's institutional reach nor its liberalizing theology—were as galvanizing for evangelicals as the unabashedly liberal and worldly political positions the ecumenical movement took in the 1960s and 1970s. The National Council of Churches was a mainstay of opposition to the US war in Vietnam and a primary sponsor of Clergy and Laymen Concerned About Vietnam, an outspoken anti-war group that included a number of Protestant luminaries, including Martin Luther King Jr. From the late 1960s to the end of apartheid in the early 1990s, the WCC supported insurgent organizations in Southern Africa through its Program to Combat Racism. And in the 1990s, the WCC began to take a stronger pro-Palestinian stance, opposing the expansion of settlements and calling for a genuine Palestinian state.[29]

Evangelicals angrily denounced the theology and the actions of the WCC, but their ire toward what *Christianity Today* called the "worst incursion of churchmen into political affairs since the Middle Ages" was misleading. Evangelicals themselves were never as separate from politics as they liked to think. In the 1960s, they tended to see their own political commitments (to anti-communism, for example) as so obviously correct as to be invisible as "politics" per se.[30] With the rise of the religious Right in the 1980s, evangelical denunciations of those who mixed politics with religion diminished considerably. But the evangelical commitment to the idea that there was only one way to salvation did not change. Theologically, ecumenical Christianity was demarcated by a bright liberal line, beyond which only a few evangelicals dared, or cared, to venture.

Over the past fifty years, US evangelicals have been captured by two distinct (but linked) postures toward the rest of the world. The first of these I call "enchanted internationalism"—a longing for emotionally powerful forms of religious experience that American evangelicals have often identified with Christianity in the global South.[31] When Dick Robinson spoke blissfully of the opportunity to "luxuriate" in the "vibrant, healing worship of Africa," he knew that his audience would share the assumption that worship in the modern West was often stale and dry. American evangelicals believed themselves to live in a world that had become disenchanted.

The idea that the world was becoming disenchanted had emerged in Europe and the United States in the eighteenth century. As people in the scientific era began to think of themselves as distinctly "modern," they began to celebrate—but also to mourn—their commitment to rationality. Max Weber was not the first to describe this modernity, but he famously unpacked the transformations that occurred when people began to see themselves as inhabiting a "disenchanted" world, one freed of superstition but also stripped of the delights of a spirit-rich terrain.[32]

In reality, Europeans and Americans of the Enlightenment were never as rational as they claimed. Even as they busily narrated their own disenchantment, they remained immersed in religious language, sentimental practice, and passionate politics. The culture was saturated with promises of enchanted encounters, from artistic excursions into primitivism or Orientalism to the more populist pleasures of magic, occultism, and alternative sciences such as phrenology. And Europeans and Americans also looked outward: tourism was on the rise and images of exotic lands—in the form of stereoscope slides, travel narratives, and even items of home décor—were a staple of popular culture.[33]

Evangelicals were heir to the Enlightenment's ambivalence about enchantment—the sense that it described a way of being that "we" had outgrown but still deeply desired. As US evangelicals looked beyond their borders after 1960, they saw enchantment everywhere. With the Christian populations of Africa, Latin America, and Asia expanding dramatically, Americans no longer saw people in those regions only as heathens to be saved but also as models to be emulated—living embodiments of authenticity, passion, and zeal. In the charismatic worship styles of much of the evangelical community in Africa and Latin America—with their stories of miracles and faith healings, and their freedom, presumably, from the shackles of excessive wealth—American evangelicals saw an exemplary faith practiced by believers who were more intensely committed and more ideally Christian than most Europeans and Americans. Christians in the global South, they believed, inhabited a world and practiced a faith akin to that of the first Christians.

Enchanted internationalism is an orientation, a stance toward others, and an expectation for oneself. No matter which tradition American evangelicals came from—be it flinty Southern Baptists, self-consciously respectable AME churches, or the more expressive Assemblies of God—they increasingly sought to enliven and "re-enchant" their own religious experience. This longing manifested itself in many ways, including the rise of Pentecostalism and "spirit-filled" charismatic churches, the fascination with apocalypse and "end times" theology, a renewed focus on ritual, and a growing belief in faith healings.[34]

Enchantment works from the heart. Almost everywhere one looks in US evangelical culture today, people explain their commitments in this very specific language: "I have a heart for x or y." Since at least the mid-1990s, "having a heart" has been used to evoke a passion that goes beyond mere predilection: it suggests an unplanned moment of contact with an issue that leads the believer to an understanding of the particular walk God has in mind for her. Having a "heart for" something is simultaneously God-given and unusual in its intensity. It often, although not necessarily, involves crossing national borders.[35] The search for enchantment turned American evangelicals outward toward a world they imagined as more emotionally rich. But it also focused them inward, on the state of their being as much as the correctness of their doctrine.

The other lens through which evangelicals saw the world was "victim identification." Over the past fifty years, American evangelicals became galvanized by a vision of their own (global) persecution. They spoke of Christians being martyred all over the world, prevented from spreading the gospel and persecuted for their faith. These victims were sometimes American missionaries but more often were local Christian believers in Africa, Asia, or elsewhere who faced government oppression, conflict with other religious groups (often Muslims), or political marginalization. Evangelicals depicted these victims as facing persecution bravely, and consequently they became role models. Believers in the United States were invited to see themselves as part of the global Christian family, and thus to identify with the victimization they saw elsewhere.[36] By the turn of the twenty-first century, "persecution" had become a primary lens through which evangelicals viewed the world.

The attention to Christian persecution is far from new. As long as there have been Christians there have been martyrs, and the actual historical reality of martyrs' lives was far less important than the stories, images, statues, relics, and sermons that served to galvanize believers.[37] Early persecution stories were forms of Christian education, simultaneously engaging fear and bravery, spectacle and catechism. In the fifth century, St. Augustine told his readers that when they went to church and heard those stories, they were to engage them not in terms of their awfulness but in terms of the "completeness of faith" they represented:

A splendid spectacle offered to the eyes of the mind is a spirit whole and unbroken while the body is torn to pieces. That is what you people gaze on with pleasure when the accounts of such things are read in church. After all, if you didn't form some sort of picture of what happened, it would mean you weren't listening at all.[38]

The spectacle and display of the violated body was never simply informational. Instead, it engaged a complex Christian imaginary about the body—its centrality and its untrustworthiness.

The body, however, was also a metaphor for the church itself, understood to be the "body of Christ." Paul wrote to the Corinthians that "now you are the body of Christ, and each one of you is part of it" (1 Cor, 12:27, NIV). The belief that Christians everywhere should be "of one body" was endlessly affirmed among American evangelicals in the postwar period, even if in practice the church community was divided into a seemingly infinite number of denominational and national parts. The suffering of Christians was understood to be a wound to the body of the Church. Victim identification builds from the base of sanctified suffering, offering believers a sense of connection to Jesus's suffering on the cross.

The politics of suffering do not belong solely to the Left or the Right. Victim identification undergirded both liberal anti-apartheid activism and conservatives' shaping of the 1998 International Religious Freedom Act. It is less ideology than currency, and it circulates everywhere in evangelical life, in the United States and beyond.

Both enchanted internationalism and victim identification are double-edged. They allow American evangelicals to construct an image of themselves through a particular image of others. Those others are simultaneously glorified and abject; they are positioned as less powerful, but also as less encumbered by materialism. American believers' identification with idealized and suffering Christians elsewhere also allows them to see *themselves* as persecuted by a secular American public, making them fellow victims in a global assault on Christianity. This sense of identification can also mobilize an ethic of responsibility. Although American evangelicals often have exhibited a sense of benevolent self-satisfaction in their ability to help needy and presumably pliant sufferers, they also have identified with believers who were poor or persecuted, and have claimed them as Christian family. It is through an embrace of both enchantment and victimization—orientations that are religious, political, and emotional all at once—that American evangelicals have come to understand their place in the world.

The Kingdom of God Has No Borders is organized in three parts: Networks, Bodies, and Emotions. Each term points to a significant component of evangelical global reach.

Part I of the book highlights the networks that shaped the early postwar period—the spaces, institutions, and ideas that brought a broad range of evangelicals into conversation in the United States and globally. I start this story in the late 1950s with a number of people who saw themselves as part of a new generation of conservative Protestants. The neo-evangelicals who started the National Association of Evangelicals in 1942 and founded *Christianity Today* fourteen years later were self-consciously engaged in a process of making themselves into a community—defining boundaries, inviting participants, and choosing people who were worth disagreeing with.

The concept of "networks" tends to conjure clean graphics with stable nodes, but evangelical networks, like all others, are more unstable and mercurial than that.[39] In this book I discuss all sorts of networks—those forged at conferences, through television ministry, by denominations, or in organizations that cross denominations such as the InterVarsity Christian Fellowship. I also write about seminaries and Bible colleges. Many people fail to appreciate the importance of seminaries and their poorer cousins, the Bible colleges, but those institutions are key sites where evangelical identity is forged. Classrooms and coffee shops are community resources, where young evangelicals meet, talk, argue, and learn. The schools are also global hubs, having trained thousands of students from Africa, Asia, and Latin America in the past fifty years.

Part II examines the politics of the body. These chapters cover 1967 to 2001. There I analyze, among other things, evangelical responses to apartheid, as black bodies in South Africa were imprisoned, tortured, and shot. The chapters also explore how the religious freedom debates of the 1990s and activism in support of South Sudan in the 2000s were both built around notions of the persecuted body. An embrace of the church as the body of Christ and narratives of persecution were central to evangelical body politics. In this rich terrain, evangelicals have engaged suffering and martyrdom, highlighting bodies as symbols as well as embracing bodies as the most material sites of concern.[40]

Part III highlights the public circulation of emotion. Of course, emotions were present in each of the earlier periods, and I discuss them often, but in this part I highlight the ways that emotions are forms of public discourse. The philosopher Sara Ahmed argues that emotions orient us toward things in the world, directing our attention and sometimes capturing our bodily experience. "Emotions are not 'afterthoughts,'" she writes. They shape how we see the world, offering us sensibilities and helping to assemble our priorities.[41] Emotions are also never entirely private; they are part of our public life, shared and framed by others. Any of us might respond to events with our heart, but our hearts learn from the world of feeling around them.

For those of us who study international affairs, this approach takes us far away from rational actor theory by suggesting that our rationalities and our emotional attachments are deeply intertwined. In Part III, then, I show how the circulation of feeling is part of what constitutes the networks that connect evangelicals and part of what makes bodies so powerful as metaphors for that connection. I am interested in how evangelical hearts have enabled evangelical political commitments, especially internationally.

For fifty years, US evangelical life has been lived across borders, alive with passion and fraught with questions. Hope, anger, fear, and longing have shaped the ways that American believers operate on the global stage, as they have struggled to live in a world they understand to be God's kingdom. That kingdom is conceived as universal, borderless. And yet evangelicals, like everybody else, have lived in a world deeply divided by national borders, inhabited by refugees and migrants, riven by dramatically uneven distributions of wealth and power, and dominated by the United States as the most powerful state the world has ever known. The tension between what is posited as God's kingdom and what is lived as the world's reality is one that animates evangelical life, in the United States and beyond. It is the paradox at the heart of evangelical internationalism.

I

Networks

1

"The Fatherhood of God and the Brotherhood of Man"

RACISM AS A MISSIONARY PROBLEM

IN THE FALL of 1966, Sam Oni tried to go to church. As he approached the door of a Southern Baptist Church in Macon, Georgia, he was met by several deacons, dragged down the church steps, and pushed into a waiting police car. Oni was from Ghana, where he had converted to Christianity under the guidance of missionaries. One of those missionaries had encouraged him to confront injustice by applying to the Baptist-affiliated—and segregated—Mercer College. Oni's application to attend Mercer was no secret, and, even before he was admitted, his challenge to the status quo had been discussed excitedly in the Christian media. An editorial in the *Christian Index* had argued for admitting him precisely because he was the result of successful missions work. One letter to the editor agreed: "If one soul be lost of our missionaries by excluding this young man and I do not speak my heart, I have blood on my hands."[1] Oni arrived on Mercer's campus in 1963.

Three years later, Oni decided to attend a local church—or, at least, to show what would happen if he tried. He chose nearby Tattnall Square Baptist Church, where Rev. Thomas J. Holmes was pastor. Holmes was a racial liberal who had been advocating desegregation of the church for some time, but his congregation was deeply divided. Two of the deacons were Klansmen. In the summer of 1966, the church had voted down Holmes's proposal to allow black worshippers. A few weeks later, Oni arrived at Tattnall Square. Holmes was preaching, but he had no idea that Oni had come to the church, much less that he had been pushed down the front steps by angry worshippers. Those parishioners, unlike the admissions committee at Mercer, did not see Africans as an exception to their racial politics. Shortly thereafter, Holmes resigned after a vote of no confidence. In the aftermath, however, as condemnation of the church poured in from around the world, Holmes's supporters split from the church and formed a new congregation.[2]

American evangelical culture was fractured by the politics of race in the 1950s and 1960s. The civil rights movement was having a global impact, and the people whom missionaries were supposed to be evangelizing were acutely aware of racism within the borders of the United States. As they read the newspapers and listened to the radio, they learned about college students pushed off lunch counter stools and children facing down water hoses. They identified missionaries as representatives of the United States and often saw white missionaries in particular as exemplars of Americans' arrogance and presumptions of racial superiority. Why should they be interested in a faith that oppressed non-white people? For evangelicals, racism at home was beginning to impede their efforts to fulfill Jesus's command to "make disciples of all nations."

Additionally, missionaries on the ground sometimes acted in racist ways. As a number of observers pointed out, when missionaries were arrogant or condescending, or called the local people dim-witted or lazy, it weakened their arguments for the gospel. Africans and African Americans both commented on the ways in which the "missions crisis" around the world was an index of the larger structures of racism and imperialism.

Evangelical debates about that crisis happened in a number of places—in churches, on the radio, at seminaries and colleges, in the resolutions and political stances of evangelical denominations, and, especially, in print. Despite the reputation that evangelicals and fundamentalists had as being less educated than mainline Protestants, evangelicalism in the post-war era was a *reading* culture. Evangelical commentators operated in a broad array of genres—news reports, novels, missionary accounts, polemics, and theology—and through a range of sites, including books, magazines, and conferences. The feverish discussions about race and missionary work, and the increasingly hostile confrontations between those with opposing views, make clear that the story of evangelicalism in the United States cannot be told without thinking about race, and that race was not solely a domestic concern. Both white and black evangelicals understood that race was a global issue, that its meanings were changing rapidly on the ground, and that, as a result, evangelicalism would soon face a reckoning.

In 1957, the evangelist Howard Jones became the first black pastor on the staff of the Billy Graham Evangelistic Association (BGEA). At the time he joined Graham's ministry, Jones had served twelve years as a pastor in two churches associated with the theologically conservative, racially mixed Christian and Missionary Alliance. With his thick-rimmed glasses and high forehead, Jones looked a bit like the jazz musician he had planned to become back when he was studying clarinet and alto sax at his Ohio high school. As a pastor in New York and then back in Ohio, Jones already had developed international connections. Each week he sent tapes of his sermons to be broadcast as part of a radio ministry on station ELWA in Monrovia, Liberia. (ELWA, which stood for Eternal Love Winning Africa, was run by missionaries from the Sudan Interior Mission.) In 1957, Jones became the first African

American to hold large evangelistic rallies in West Africa, traveling to Liberia, Nigeria, and Ghana. Jones delighted in his experiences but was also sobered by the recognition that he was embraced so warmly in part because, even in the late 1950s, he was still an anomaly. There were strikingly few black missionaries in Africa. Most US missions agencies, Jones reported, explicitly or implicitly excluded African Americans with "racist application structures" that required theological or academic training that few African Americans would have been able to receive. It was a few months after his West African tour that Jones joined the BGEA. In that role, he returned with his wife to live in Liberia from 1959 to 1964.[3]

Jones later reported that during those years he was "plagued" by questions the local people were asking about civil rights. "[F]rom the modern cities to the underdeveloped bush sections of the country. . . They quizzed us about the Emmett Till lynching in Mississippi and other racial disturbances." They had heard the news, Jones said, through Radio Moscow and other communist outlets.[4]

Jones implied that it was quite reasonable for Africans to ask pointed questions about American racial hypocrisy, and long past time for Americans to ask questions about its global consequences. US policymakers were beginning to make the argument that, if the US wanted to replace Europe as the global hegemon, spectacles of racism were a dangerous impediment.[5] Jones and others argued that, similarly, when the United States looked like a racist power, Christianity's image suffered too. Mainline Protestants had been making this point for decades. *Time* magazine had reported in 1926 the remarks of a Methodist missionary who commented that "China, Japan, India wonder why we who would teach them have slaughtered each other in thousands, why we refuse to hold all races equal in our countries."[6]

By 1960, US evangelical foreign missions were fast becoming the dominant missions force in the world. The number of North American Protestants in the mission field in 1935 had been 12,000; within fifty years, the total would triple, as American missionaries came to replace Europeans as major players on the ground. Almost all of those gains would be made by evangelicals. In 1952, about half of US missionaries were evangelicals; by 1969, the number was 72 percent.

Non-denominational and theologically conservative organizations grew most quickly after World War II: Wycliffe Bible Translators, New Tribes Mission, The Evangelical Alliance Mission (TEAM), Africa Inland Mission—many of these doubled their forces within a few years after the end of the war. At the same time, many evangelical denominations also had rapidly expanding missions programs, including the Assemblies of God and the powerhouse Southern Baptist Convention (SBC). The Assemblies of God sponsored 230 overseas missionaries in 1936 and 626 in 1952 (and more than 2,500 in 2004). The SBC had four hundred missionaries in 1936 and one thousand in 1955.[7]

As these numbers grew, so did an awareness that missionaries themselves were part of the problem. In 1959, a missionary in South Africa castigated his fellow missionaries for their racist attitudes. Writing in *HIS* magazine, he pointed out that missionary racism was getting in the way of Christian witness: "[I]f I were an African," he wrote, "and some missionary came around fishing for my soul, but obviously didn't want to have anything to do with *me*, I'd soon tell him to go back where he came from." All missionaries had been forced out of China in 1953, and who could blame the Africans if they kicked the missionaries out as well? "It must seem like hypocrisy to the Africans," he wrote, "that you invited the believers to the Lord's table, but they can never expect to sit down to yours."[8]

By the late 1950s, then, some evangelicals had joined other Americans, Christian and secular, in recognizing the global impact of US racism. From *Christianity Today* to InterVarsity's *HIS* magazine, the mainstream of evangelical opinion converged on the problems of racism and racial violence. A young white female medical missionary to Nigeria, for example, raised many of the same concerns as Howard Jones. She reported to the Southern Baptist Convention's foreign missions magazine that she had been forced to explain the violence that accompanied the integration of the University of Georgia. She hardly knew how to reply. "Perhaps a native Georgian could have answered him more gracefully than I did, but I am asked similar things about Virginia, my home state, and I can't answer without embarrassment."[9] In 1955, the Nigerian Baptist Convention had passed a resolution stating that "Nigerians . . . identify themselves with the American Negro, and they consider racism in any form unjust."[10]

Debates about race intersected with a growing American ambivalence about missions. On the one hand, missionaries had long been celebrated as ideal Christians, icons of bravery and self-sacrifice. Accounts of missionaries' successes in heathen lands described beautiful landscapes, strange lifestyles, filth-ridden villages, and disgusting-but-fascinating non-Christian religious practices. These stories of unknown worlds provided a taste of "lurid fascination," coupled with the pleasures of a happy ending, in which the missionary arrives to save the people from their sin and their "backward" cultures.[11] The dramatic growth of missions in the late nineteenth century was accompanied by these success stories, with accounts of Bibles translated, remote peoples evangelized, and missionaries welcomed in villages in China or Brazil. It was missionary work that positioned evangelicals as global travelers—producers and recipients of emotionally and spiritually significant information about far-away places.

By the mid-twentieth century, Americans still expressed great respect for missionaries. The Catholic "jungle doctor" Thomas Dooley, for example, was widely commended for his work in Laos in the late 1950s. His books about his experiences—in which he represented himself as peacefully fighting communism with good works and a quiet faith— were bestsellers. In 1960 a Gallup poll found Dr. Dooley to be one of the most admired people in the country.[12]

At the same time, it was becoming more common for Americans to view missionaries as agents of imperialism—either directly, when they served as the advance guard of imperial power, or indirectly, as cultural imperialists who were certain of their own superiority. Protestant missionaries, particularly those from the mainline denominations, had themselves been raising questions about their own role in undermining local cultures and enabling the expansion of US or European power since the early part of the century. Novelist Pearl S. Buck, the daughter of missionaries to China, critiqued missionaries as ineffectual at best and imperialist at worst in her Pulitzer Prize-winning 1931 book, *The Good Earth*.[13] Historians in recent years have complicated this picture, portraying missionaries, including evangelicals, as both agents and critics of imperialism. In fact, often they were neither, operating at oblique angles to state power, with their own interests and agendas.

A year after *The Good Earth* was published, a group of northern liberal Protestant denominations underwrote a survey of missions across Asia. Conceived by John Mott and funded by John D. Rockefeller, *Re-Thinking Missions: A Laymen's Inquiry after 100 Years* was written by Harvard professor William Hocking. The "Hocking Report" shocked Protestant leaders by insisting that the time for traditional missions was over. The goal should not be conversion, the report said. Instead, Christians must be willing to provide services to those in need, "without any preaching" or condescension. Respect for the religions and diverse cultures of others should be paramount, even as Christians could rest assured that all religions would eventually lead to Christianity. Indeed, the greatest danger to Christianity was not other religions but lack of religion. All religions faced "the same menace, the rise of the secular spirit."[14] The idea that missions should no longer aim to convert people was exactly the kind of ecumenical vision that evangelicals found infuriating about liberal Protestantism. They saw themselves as stepping into the vacuum created by mainline Protestant abdication.

By the 1950s, however, the critique of missions had reached well beyond internal church reports. James Michener's bestselling *Hawaii* (1959) presented missionaries as vicious imperialists. In 1961 the film *The Sins of Rachel Cade*, based on a 1956 novel and starring Hollywood beauty Angie Dickinson, showed missionaries to Africa as passionate and good-hearted idealists who nonetheless embodied remnants of an imperialist past, and who must in the end leave Africa to the Africans.[15] Nigerian writer Chinua Achebe's remarkable dissection of the colonial encounter, the international bestseller *Things Fall Apart* (1958), included a riveting depiction of missionary blindness to local culture.[16]

For their part, most evangelical missionaries did not see themselves as colonialists. In fact, they felt that they were among the few Western individuals who were giving sacrificially to the people in Asia, Africa, the Middle East, and Latin America. Like their more liberal Protestant counterparts, many of whom had taken strong anti-colonial stances in China, Congo, and Latin America, they believed not only in their faith but also in their own moral compass as intermediaries between imperial power and local subjects.[17]

Unquestionably, missions work was difficult and demanded dedication. Middle-class or working-class Americans who served as missionaries would suffer privations that their friends and family members at home could hardly imagine. Even as they were criticized in some quarters, missionaries were idealized in much of evangelical culture precisely because of the hardships they endured and the dangers they faced.[18]

As the critique of missions grew more vocal, evangelicals became increasingly invested in stories of missionary suffering and success, which were recounted not just in Sunday school lessons or the annual visit of missionaries to a church's "missions week," but sometimes in mainstream media as well. Christians of all stripes were entranced by the dramatic story of the "Auca martyrs," a group of five male evangelical missionaries and two of their wives, mostly from Wheaton College, who in 1956 traveled to a remote jungle area in Ecuador to bring the gospel to the Waorani tribe (then known as the Auca Indians). The Auca were barely known in the United States, but when American journalists wrote about the group, they almost always described them as "warlike." When the missionaries arrived, they at first huddled in their camp, anxious and uncertain about meeting members of the tribe. They realized that the Waorani had been entirely cut off from contact with people from the outside.

Before long, however, the men began flying over the beach where the Waorani lived, dropping gifts from their small plane: machetes, cloth, and some cooking pots. After a few trips, the men took the next step, landing the plane on the beach. The initial contact seemed to go well. They met and gave gifts to local men and women, and even gave one of the Waorani a ride in their plane. But the next day, when the five men arrived on the beach, they were speared and hacked to death by a fearful group of Waorani warriors.

The story was national news. It unfolded over three articles published in *Life*, with hagiographic accounts of the missionaries' bravery and commitment.[19] Instead of being seen as naïfs who should have known better, they became icons of the new evangelicalism. The *Oregonian* described them as "strong young men [who] had left carpentry and law, the horrors of war and the arms of their wives to fly into a Latin-American jungle valley shadowed with death." These young men were presented as modern in their technological skill—they knew how to pilot planes and expertly repair radios—and yet committed to their faith in ways that modern "liberals" would not understand. This was what historian Kathryn Long has called the "classic evangelical missionary martyr narrative." It both recalled a history and set a standard.[20]

Within a year, two of the missionaries' wives returned to evangelize the Waorani, and most of them were eventually converted to Christianity. One of those women, Elizabeth Elliott, published *Through Gates of Splendor*, which recounted the men's commitment to reaching the unreached, and their expressed willingness to die, if necessary, in the process. The book was excerpted in *Reader's Digest* and by 1957 had sold more than 100,000 copies.[21]

The Auca story soon faded from the mainstream media, but it lived on among evangelicals, who were riveted by the account of these men and women, whose sacrifice seemed to transcend complicated debates about racial attitudes or colonialism. Over the course of the 1960s and 1970s, there were several films, a record-and-slide-show presentation (see figure 1.1), non-fiction books, and even a comic book about the "Auca martyrs." Looking back decades after the deaths, *Christianity Today* recalled: "The martyr's names—Nate Saint, Jim Elliot, Pete Fleming, Ed McCully, and Roger Youderian—and their sacrifice

FIGURE 1.1 *The Auca Story* phonograph album. Courtesy of the Billy Graham Center Archive.

galvanized a whole generation."[22] The missionaries had been martyred, and the Waoroni had become believers, who nonetheless remained living simple lives in their villages.

As it was told and retold in evangelical culture, the Auca story was infused with nostalgia. These young missionaries were engaged in the "real work" of saving souls—the work they were meant for, and which evangelicals saw as by definition apolitical. The Waoroni people were presented as exotic, illiterate, savage, and thus pure. When they converted en masse, they expressed gratitude for their salvation and for the missionaries' sacrifice. Both the joys of enchantment and the specter (and honor) of persecution infused this passionate missionary story. It provided some respite from debates over missions and racism.

Members of the Southern Baptist Convention were on the frontline of debates about missions, both in terms of racism at home and the behavior of missionaries abroad. With ten million members, the SBC was the second-largest Protestant denomination in the country in the 1950s. (It pulled ahead of the Methodist church in 1967.)[23] The SBC also supported an enormous missionary enterprise on five continents, the largest and most vibrant of any US Protestant denomination. The SBC membership held diverse views on race, even as it remained a highly conservative, almost entirely white, and largely

Southern church family.[24] Missionaries and their supporters played a key role in pushing the denomination slowly, often reluctantly, down the path toward desegregation.

Southern Baptists often said that they focused on individual salvation, not politics. This was misleading. In fact, the SBC had been born from a political conflict. In 1845 Southerners split from other Baptists, who had refused to appoint a slaveholder as a missionary. By the early twentieth century, the SBC was the all-but-official religion of the white South, and it easily operated as a cultural and political arbiter, openly supporting the racial power of whites while claiming a theological commitment to the equality of all souls before God. The SBC and its various state branches regularly offered social and political commentary of all sorts. Southern Baptists supported peace efforts in the post–World War I period and regularly issued statements supporting the right of labor to organize, although the convention's political statements were often couched in a haze of generalities, protected by a flurry of commentary that insisted that no real change could come about without the regeneration of man. But after World War II the SBC began to more openly embrace politics, offering policy statements on everything from the right of nations to self-government to the importance of ending trade restrictions.[25]

Southern Baptists also read the papers, and they well knew times were changing on issues of race. Starting with a 1939 resolution condemning lynching, and continuing for the next decade, the SBC passed a number of modestly moderate statements on race.[26] In 1947, they went further, issuing a Charter of Principles on Race Relations that was strikingly liberal in its rhetoric, especially given its white and largely Southern context. The charter, which was written by the new Committee on Race Relations, linked "Christian and Baptist principles" to moderate racial views. There was no call for desegregation; most of the document was carefully vague. For example, it stated only that Negros had a right to "receive equal service for equal payment" on buses and in stores. But the charter was given some teeth by the SBC's Social Service Commission, which followed up with statements that challenged the Ku Klux Klan and biblical justifications for segregation.[27]

The denomination's racial politics were also being shaped by its missionary thrust. The SBC had an impressive missionary bureaucracy, complete with a half dozen publications that were produced by the Home Missions Board, the Foreign Missions Board, and the Women's Missionary Union (WMU), with magazines aimed at women, men, young people, and students. Within this publishing empire, and within missionary work more generally, women were crucial. There they took leadership roles that were often denied to them in local churches, where women generally could not serve as pastors or deacons. Overseas, women served as missionaries in various capacities, often as medical missionaries and teachers. At home, they joined in missions study programs, where they learned about the challenge of reaching the unreached. And they took leadership in calling for changes in Southern Baptist racial politics.

The Women's Missionary Union was in fact one of the leading voices for racial liberalism in the denomination. The union took strong and sometimes controversial stances on race both domestically and abroad. By the mid-1940s, the WMU's magazine for women, *Royal Service,* already had published a number of articles that described racism as a problem, in terms that would become entirely familiar to a generation of readers. Racism was a crisis, the WMU said, one that was of particular concern to women, who would, after all, train the next generation. This was the classic argument for women who wanted to venture out of the "woman's sphere" in situations where such venturing was frowned upon: they needed to speak on behalf of the children. But the WMU also had its particular focus on missions, and it made arguments based on that global reach. As one female missionary to Hawaii put it in 1946, presaging arguments that would become commonplace: "We cannot expect the pagan peoples of the world, most of whom are dark-skinned, to have faith in our Gospel which teaches the fatherhood of God and the brotherhood of man, when our actions deny our professions."[28]

Only in the mid-1950s, however, did the SBC's position on race become a matter of great internal tumult. In 1954, when the Supreme Court issued its *Brown v. Board* decision mandating school desegregation, the denomination's Christian Life Commission (CLC) swung into action, calling on Southern Baptists to endorse the court's decision. The CLC, which was led by a series of activist Baptist leaders such as A.C. Miller and the indefatigable Foy Valentine, was the heart of the progressive wing of the convention. Valentine, who had written his 1949 doctoral thesis on Southern Baptists and race, became head of the CLC in 1960 and served for 27 years. From that platform, he wrote prodigiously on race and other issues. (In 1964, Valentine would publish a slim volume with perhaps the best and most succinct title of any book ever written by a Southern Baptist: *Believe and Behave.*[29])

Within the SBC, *Brown* was controversial and contested from the outset. The denomination had desegregated several of its seminaries earlier in the 1950s, but that decision was a pragmatic one. Africans and African Americans were needed as missionaries on the assumption that they might be able to better reach the lost in Africa, where the denomination's missionary force was weak. In 1945, there were only forty-five Southern Baptist missionaries in Africa, all of them in Nigeria. Ten years later, there were 248 stationed across several countries.[30]

Seminaries were one thing, perched on a hill and attended by the anointed few. Public school desegregation was another matter. The CLC was asking Southern Baptists to do something that cut much closer to the bone when it called on them to support the Supreme Court's decision. The CLC's report argued that America's leadership in the world was at stake, and so was the missionary imperative: "More and more . . . the sincerity of our interest in the colored peoples within their native lands will be judged by our treatment of the peoples of those lands in our own country." In addition, the CLC argued, segregation was simply wrong. It went against the Bible's teaching that every person was loved and valued by God.[31] The Women's Missionary Union supported the CLC's analysis, as did several leaders, including the SBC president and the head of the Foreign Missions Board.[32]

The CLC's report went before the denomination's annual convention, where such reports and their recommendations were usually accepted as a matter of course. ("Recommendations" were not official denominational resolutions, which were far fewer and carried more weight.) In this case, the CLC recommended only that the SBC "recognize" that the Supreme Court decision was constitutional, while expressing hope that all Christians "exercise patience and good will." Even this much was controversial, and there was a move on the convention floor to strike the recommendations, but the CLC's report was adopted overwhelmingly. Spontaneous applause rippled through the hall after the vote, followed by a chorus of the Baptist hymn "He Leadeth Me."[33]

Historians have argued about the significance of this moment. At one level, the SBC's resolution was a very limited statement, ambiguous enough to accommodate the broad support for segregation in the denomination's base. Still, some see this 1954 vote as an indication that Southern Baptists—or at least their denominational leaders—were far more liberal on race than has been previously acknowledged. (The largely northern- and midwestern-based National Association of Evangelicals did not even address the *Brown* decision at its 1955 national convention.)[34] The very fact of the vote was a powerful indication that there were deep fissures in white, Southern, evangelical culture's racial monolith. Still, it was no surprise that the denomination's decision to support the CLC's recommendations was immediately controversial among church members and was denounced in several state Baptist newspapers. In Mississippi, the *Baptist Record* was flooded with mail opposing the vote. The paper's editors concurred, pronouncing that "the lowest point in the whole Convention was when the Christian Life Commission went out of its field to dip its finger in politics."[35]

In the years immediately after *Brown*, the SBC's debate over segregation was often argued on the grounds of biblical theology, but it was lived in terms of concrete social and political investments. On the one hand, there were any number of white Southerners who believed they could assent to the theological proposition of racial equality before God while preserving their ordinary practices of segregation. On the other hand, there were an increasingly assertive set of racial liberals and missionary supporters who believed that Southern Baptists could do no such thing. The balance of power was constantly shifting. Certainly the pro-segregationist forces were strong, and, in the face of political and legal threats to white Southern power, they became increasingly defiant. Rev. Jerry Falwell of Thomas Road Baptist Church in Lynchburg, Virginia, preached in favor of segregation in the late 1950s, drawing on the old slaveholders' arguments that African peoples were the cursed descendants of Ham. Falwell was at this time merely the pastor of an independent Baptist church (not part of the Southern Baptist Convention) in a small Southern town. But his speech was indicative of what Paul Harvey describes as a "folk theology" of segregation.[36] God had made human beings into different races, the reasoning went, and, it would be ungodly to challenge His divine plan. An author in the *Arkansas Baptist Newsmagazine* urged his fellow believers not to follow "the leadership of this Devilish doctrine of destroying the handiwork of God in the creating of the races."[37] Such reasoning was rare in seminaries, and it was hard to find many Biblical verses that supported segregation, but it was the ordinary thinking of many people who had grown up with the Bible and were versed in it.

The historian David Chappell has argued that the most striking thing about most white Southern pastors during the civil rights movement is how *uninvolved* they were in actually supporting segregation from the pulpit. It is true, he says, that white opinion in the South was generally segregationist, and the churches were no different, but it was difficult for any minister to produce a serious argument that the Bible supported racial segregation. Most simply did not say much one way or the other.[38]

A number of local church pastors, however, were outspoken in *opposition* to segregation. They were a small minority, but they were unbowed. The Rev. Dale Cowling, for example, was a prominent Southern Baptist minister in Little Rock, Arkansas. As the crisis over desegregation at Little Rock High School was coming to a head in 1957, he preached at the church of Brooks Hays, a racial liberal who would become president of the SBC a year later. Rev. Cowling was polite. Those who preached that the Bible offered support for segregation, he opined, "are sincere beyond question." But any serious study of scripture would prove that "[t]hey are simply greatly mistaken in their efforts to prove God has marked the Negro race and relegated it to the role of a servant."[39]

For many Southerners—indeed, for many American Christians in general—the most powerful arguments against segregation and racism were built on the terrain of missions. Many missions supporters who avidly, almost desperately, embraced relatively liberal stances on race used a variety of biblical arguments, but the most frequently cited scripture was from Paul, who insisted in his letters to the Colossians and the Galatians that the church is one: "Where there is neither Greek nor Jew, circumcision nor uncircumcision, barbarian, Scythian, bond nor free: but Christ is all, and in all" (Col 3:11, KJV).[40] In 1945, a well-known missionary theorist from the Southern Baptist Theological Seminary, W.O. Carver, had made the point more bluntly when he commented that "Not for even one generation can all the power and force and ingenuity of the white races maintain a position of preferred tenants of God's earth which he has peopled with twice as many colored as white men."[41]

By the late 1950s, biblical arguments had fused with pragmatic concerns as word spread globally about racial politics in the United States. In 1958, less than a year after President Eisenhower had deployed the National Guard to protect nine black high school students in Little Rock, Arkansas, one pastor spoke to the issue at Florida's state Baptist Convention. He told a story about the children of Southern Baptist missionaries in Jordan. The children, he said, "were pelted with stones and the Arab children cried the only American words they knew, 'Little Rocks.'"[42] Such a story seems too beautifully metaphorical to be true. But there is no question that the sentiment behind it was widespread in Southern Baptist missionary circles, and among evangelical missions supporters generally. "Nothing reached my heart more than the pleas of our missionaries around the world," wrote one Florida minister in *Christianity Today* in 1962, in what was by then an entirely familiar (if far from universal) sentiment. "The eyes of the world were focused on our treatment of minority groups. Missionary after missionary warned that our attitudes were making their work less effective."[43]

Most evangelical leaders in the South through the 1960s also argued that, whatever their own views, Christians must obey established authority regarding desegregation and voting rights. The book of Romans had provided the basis for a longstanding stance of churchly acquiescence: "Let every soul be subject unto the higher powers. For there is no power but of God: the powers that be are ordained of God" (Romans 13:1, KJV). This often had been used as a cudgel to criticize civil rights movement activists for their civil disobedience. But Romans 13 cut both ways, and a number of Baptist leaders and even state conventions criticized those segregationists who had promised "massive resistance" to segregation.[44]

As the civil rights movement grew stronger, national civil rights legislation seemed likely to pass. In the larger evangelical movement, nationally known right-wing ministers girded themselves for a battle against the civil rights bill. Bob Jones Jr., the far-Right spokesman who headed Bob Jones University, made sure that segregationist minister Billy James Hargis and the right-wing idol Governor George Wallace both received honorary doctorates in the early 1960s. And it was no surprise to anyone when the ranting radical Carl McIntire, who had a thriving radio empire, wrote an open letter to Martin Luther King Jr. to complain about his lawlessness and communist sympathies.[45]

In 1964, with the proposed civil rights law being debated in Congress, the SBC General Convention was roiled by controversy. The SBC was mammoth, with more than ten million members and almost 33,000 churches under its umbrella. A few months before the convention's national meeting, President Lyndon Johnson had invited a group of 150 Baptist ministers from the South to the White House, where he lectured them on their responsibility to take a stance in favor of civil rights. Not surprisingly, many of the ministers were offended by what they saw as strong-arm tactics.[46]

Liberals in the SBC needed no such lectures. The Christian Life Commission's annual report for that year was unusually outspoken; it strongly condemned segregation, praised churches that opened their doors to all worshippers, and supported the civil rights bill. As usual, the CLC's report included several recommendations. But this time, perhaps remembering the CLC's controversial recommendation to support *Brown v. Board* ten years earlier, a group of Deep South messengers proposed an alternate, far milder set of recommendations as a substitute. These new statements said nothing about the civil rights bill and replaced a call for integrated worship with an avowal that such decisions should be left to local churches. After a heated two-hour debate, the replacement resolutions were passed.

This was not, however, the end of the story. Moderate and progressive members of the convention heaped scorn on those who had doctored the CLC's original proposals. Seminary professors told their former students how ashamed they were of them, and editors of Baptist papers in states such as North Carolina and Virginia castigated representatives ("messengers") at the meeting for their cowardly behavior. The convention, like the country, was deeply divided.[47]

While the SBC fought bitterly, evangelical leaders clustered around *Christianity Today* and the National Association of Evangelicals had moderately, and occasionally, supported civil rights. *CT* offered nothing like the intensive coverage of the civil rights movement provided by the mainstream media and other Protestant news outlets. The NAE had passed a relatively timid civil rights resolution at its 1964 meeting. But even this was too much for some evangelicals. One member of the Wesley Evangelical Methodist Church protested the NAE's resolution as an "unauthorized impertinence" and described the NAE as unpleasantly similar to the National Council of Churches.[48]

Still, by the mid-1960s, the tide was turning. This did not mean that most churches themselves desegregated. For the rest of the decade, racially mixed groups of worshippers showed up at segregated churches in the South for "kneel-ins" that challenged the de facto segregation of religious life.[49] Race remained a profound problem, including a missionary problem, for decades to come. But younger evangelicals were far more likely to support anti-racist action. When Ruth Lewis, an African American leader in InterVarsity Christian Fellowship, tried to desegregate the University of Alabama-Birmingham in 1963, InterVarsity's magazine *HIS* cheered her on. And when arch-conservative Republican presidential candidate Barry Goldwater held a campaign rally at the staunchly evangelical Wheaton College, located just outside of Chicago, in 1964, a group of fifty students protested his appearance, showing up with a group of black children from Chicago's South Side and holding up signs supporting Lyndon Johnson for president.[50]

While the debate about racism in the United States raged, evangelicals were also forced to face a different if closely related set of questions about their missions work, as people in the global South began making their own urgent demands. When the United Nations declared 1960 the "Year of Africa," it highlighted what would become a significant global transformation, as twenty nations shed their colonial yoke in a single year. As evangelicals looked outward, they faced urgent questions: where would they fit and how would missionaries fare—indeed would Christianity find a place at all—in a rapidly decolonizing world?

In this context, the behavior of missionaries, and their occasional role as exemplars of American power and arrogance, would become even more central to evangelicals' understandings of their own role in the world. In 1963, a white Southern Baptist missionary to Ghana, Harris Mosley, came to visit Mercer College. It was Mosley who had urged Sam Oni to apply to Mercer. On his furlough back to the United States, Mosley told his college audience that missionaries themselves were the cause of much of the hostility against missions. Missionaries were too separated from local people, he said, too invested in their own wealth and power, their own white privilege. "Let the missionary have his house full of servants, his 'boy-master relationship,'" Mosley fumed. "Let him mimic the colonial past. Let him have his big American car, horn blowing, dust flying . . . but let him also know that he is thereby destroying the Christian Gospel." For these comments, Mosley was chastised by the SBC's Foreign Missions Board for "exaggerations." He retired from missionary service the next year.[51]

2

"Peril and Persecution"

THE CONGO CRISIS

⌖ ———————————————————————————————

ON NOVEMBER 24, 1964, Dr. Paul Carlson, a white American missionary, was gunned down in the streets of Stanleyville, Congo, by antigovernment guerillas. Carlson, a member of the Evangelical Covenant Church, had been held hostage for several weeks by the Leftist Conseil National de Libération, the so-called Simba rebels. Congo had achieved independence from Belgium several years earlier, but the rebels saw the Congolese government as merely an extension of Belgian rule. The Simba, believing that Carlson was either a mercenary or a US military operative, had sentenced him to death, then reprieved him, then sentenced him again—several times over. The US State Department was alarmed, declaring "unequivocally" that Carlson was not a soldier, asking for support from the UN, and pressuring the Organization of African Unity to intervene.[1]

Carlson was taken prisoner while serving as a doctor in a remote region of Congo. By 1964, many missionaries had already been evacuated under threat of violence. In a country torn by civil war, Americans and Belgians were particularly at risk—remnants of colonialism in the rebels' eyes. Belgium was still extensively involved in Congolese politics, and the United States was supporting the Belgian-backed Congolese government with military equipment and advisors. The Simba had some ties to both the Soviet Union and China. In Stanleyville, rebels held scores of hostages—Europeans and Americans, missionaries, business people, and diplomats—scattered around the city. For weeks, the US government had been planning a rescue operation in conjunction with the Belgians. On the day of Carlson's death, Belgian paratroopers had parachuted into Stanleyville to extract the hostages. They arrived on planes supplied by the United States.[2] Because the rebels had singled out Carlson, he was already a figure of some notoriety when he was killed, along with fifty-nine others, in a spasm of violence as the paratroopers landed in the city. Carlson was one of only two Americans to die that day, and he immediately became a national martyr.

Carlson was featured on the covers of *Newsweek, Time,* and *Life.* Publishing magnate Henry Luce, himself a child of missionaries, was publisher of both *Time* and *Life,* and the two magazines treated the story as a national disaster. *Time* presented Carlson as a symbol of how "good whites" were being treated by "dazed, ignorant savages" who failed to appreciate the help they were being offered by Americans like Carlson. *Life* spoke in the language of faith and tragedy. It produced a wrenching story about Carlson's family that also featured shocking photos of the deaths in Stanleyville. A large close-up of Carlson's dead body was part of a sixteen-page spread that melodramatically recounted the hostages' hectic, fearful final moments. "The Radio Shrilled: Kill Them All," one headline read, next to a photo of a white man standing on the street, his shirt covered in blood. There were close-ups of Carlson's dead body, and of the body of a young girl, both with identification tags tied around their necks. The photographs invited fear, anger, and confused indignation.[3]

They contrasted with the cover image, a full-color picture of a smiling Carlson shaking hands with a large crowd of Congolese (figure 2.1). He was smiling; his outstretched hand met a group of outstretched hands—the symbolism could hardly be missed. Just as striking, though, was the young boy in the foreground, facing the camera and away from the adoring crowd around Carlson, his hand up in a greeting—or a fist. The gesture is ambiguous; was he protesting or just playing around? The boy would have no say, of course, in deciding how his image would be used, or what accounts of sacrifice or savagery it would be mobilized to support.[4]

White American evangelicals were particularly riveted by Carlson's story. Missionary martyrdom in Congo was widely covered in the dozens of denominational journals and missionary magazines that circulated in the 1960s. Just after Carlson's death, Billy Graham devoted two episodes of his weekly radio program, *The Hour of Decision,* to events in Congo. Graham, who saw nearly every international event as an example of communist subversion, interpreted the attacks in Congo as proof of the dangers of decolonization. What happened to Carlson "should arouse the people of the Western world," Graham urged; it "is a warning and a foretaste of things to come." The nations of Africa, he said, "have a lust for freedom."

> Right or wrong, wise or unwise, they long to be free: to chart their own course! To protect their own interests. And to plan their own future. Many of them, however, are failing miserably. Because they are not prepared to be free. Freedom imposes responsibility. And an irresponsible nation is not eligible to be free.[5]

Sounding like a parent chastising a teenager, Graham made clear that Africans had not yet proven their maturity. Lustful Africans, political longings, failures of "responsibility": race, sex, and danger were intertwined in this moment of Christian reflection on

FIGURE 2.1 Carlson on the cover of *Life*. LIFE logo and cover design © Time Inc. LIFE and the LIFE logo are registered trademarks of Time Inc. under license.

politics, as they would be consistently in evangelical thinking about the global South in the 1960s.

A few weeks later, college students who attended Urbana 64, InterVarsity Christian Fellowship's triennial conference on missions, gathered at a special memorial service for Carlson. Pastor Wilbert Norton read from Matthew 16, in which Jesus tells his disciples that they must take up their cross and follow him. Norton played a tape recording made by Carlson a few months before he died. In it, Carlson expressed hope that the Congolese church would be steadfast in the face of coming difficulties. He prayed that those listening would prove themselves worthy should their time come to be loyal to Jesus unto death. Norton exhorted the students: "Dr. Carlson's voice carries across the jungles of Congo as it speaks to us tonight on behalf of all the missionaries slain in recent times, of the charge unparalleled, the witness unashamed, and the triumph unquestioned."[6] In reality, the triumph *was* questioned, and the witness was not without shame. That was precisely the problem.

By the time of Carlson's death, Congolese Protestants had begun to raise very serious questions about missionary behavior. In a postcolonial state—albeit one still struggling to establish a secure central government—the old, imperialist style of missionary work was no longer tenable. Christians of all stripes, but particularly evangelical missionaries and their supporters, faced the crisis of race and racism with particular intensity in Congo. American evangelicals believed that every human had a soul and that God longed for the salvation of each person, without distinction. But they had lived in a culture saturated with colonialist views of Africa, in which most mission organizations sold an image of a benighted continent in order to raise support for their work. In that context, the ideal targets of missions should be desperate but not hopeless, eager but not competent. Even though missionaries had been and remained an important source of often nuanced and thoughtful accounts of life in their areas of service—they were sometimes sought out by US diplomats for insider knowledge—many also built lives and careers around assumptions of superiority.[7]

Decolonization made it seem that old-style missionary benevolence was on its way out. Political debates about power were often enacted through discussions of church issues: who would control education, who had the right to articulate the meaning of the Bible itself, or how missionaries used the money they received from overseas. In one case, profound tensions emerged from seemingly arcane debates over the formula for figuring out how Congolese pastors would be paid. This kind of everyday religion—not just ritual or theology, but committees and paychecks—was one of the battlegrounds on which decolonization was contested.[8] For Congolese, in this environment of struggle, the evacuation of a large number of missionaries in 1960, 1961, and 1964 sometimes appeared as abandonment.

For most white Americans, the suffering and martyrdom of Christian missionaries in Congo was a sign of their commitment—to Christianity and to Africa. African American Protestants, however, found that their support for global black liberation was sometimes in tension with their enthusiasm for missions and the reality of anti-Christian violence. White evangelicals had no such ambivalence. Instead, they saw Carlson and his fellow missionaries as the embodiment of how faithful Christians might expect to face suffering and persecution. They were well aware that Christians had faced hostility before, but now missionaries appeared to be under particular threat, attacked by citizens of assertive young nations who, it seemed, no longer wanted to be saved.

Since the arrival of missionaries in the nineteenth century, the vast majority of missionaries in Congo had been Catholic, but Protestant missionaries were present as well. They came from around Europe and the United States, joining together in a transnational project of evangelization, education, and "civilization." In 1960, there were more than 2,000 Protestant missionaries in the country, including between 1,000 and 1,500 Americans, operating under the auspices of more than forty-five mission organizations. More than half of these were identifiably evangelical.[9] The missionaries were largely white, but also included some African Americans who were serving in Congo with traditionally white denominations: Methodist, Presbyterian, and even Conservative Baptist.[10]

In Congo, as in the rest of Africa, missionaries were complex and compromised figures. It was through them that information about Africa got back to churches and political leaders in the west. They often depicted a savage continent, one captured by "witchcraft," and desperately in need of both preaching and funds for education or medical missions.[11]

At the turn of the twentieth century, it had been missionaries, particularly Protestants, who played a key role in challenging colonial policies in Congo. At the time, King Leopold II of Belgium ruled the area as his own personal fiefdom, and the collection of rubber was at the heart of the territory's vast wealth. As the "rubber frontier" rolled forward in the 1890s, Congolese were forced to harvest rubber and build roads, while living on the edge of starvation. Those who failed to harvest their assigned allotment of rubber were mutilated—their hands were cut off—or simply killed.

Soon a powerful social movement began to challenge these practices, with British and American missionaries at the forefront. William H. Sheppard was not only the first African American missionary to Africa, he was also one of the early and best-known advocates for native people in Congo. He soon became one of the most important figures in the burgeoning Congo Reform movement, embraced and idealized by activists on both sides of the Atlantic.[12]

British and American reformers aroused public opinion with the strategic use of photographs. Images of Congolese bodies in pain—starving people, children missing limbs, or people with their hands cut off—were circulated by missionaries on furlough or featured in secular media. In 1905, Mark Twain published a parody in which he had King Leopold complain about "the meddlesome missionaries" whose use of "the incorruptible *Kodak*" was destroying the harmony of his fine regime. Gradually, Europeans and Americans turned against Leopold's abuses. Although European observers almost never actually described the (still largely non-Christian) Congolese as martyrs, the images of wracked and damaged bodies were familiar to those steeped in the iconography of martyrdom.[13]

In 1908, King Leopold relinquished his personal control over Congo, and it was annexed by the Belgian parliament as a colony. As a result, the worst of the abuses ended and some limits were placed on the rubber companies. Forced labor did not end, however, nor did violent exploitation of the local population in the service of extractive industry—not just rubber but cobalt, copper, and diamonds. The Belgian state slowly began to institute its official policy of "paternalism," providing primary-level schooling and some basic health-care services but forbidding almost all political activity on the part of the Congolese.[14]

Missionaries' work continued apace under Belgian colonial rule, and, not surprisingly, the Congolese were of two minds about their "benevolence." The colonized people recognized the usefulness of educational and medical missions, but they were likely to see Catholic missionaries, in particular, as linked to often-brutal Belgian government behavior. Congolese were often attracted to the teachings of the Bible, but were quick to see the discrepancy between Catholic teaching and colonial practice. As one scholar sardonically put it: "Brotherhood, equality, and the other promised fruits of the new religion were not forthcoming."[15] Protestant missionaries were certainly not exempt from charges of hypocrisy, although many Protestants saw themselves as outsiders—untainted by colonial power—and as advocates for the Congolese.[16]

While Protestants did indeed have reserves of good will working in their favor, American missionaries often squandered those advantages through their presumptions of cultural superiority. Many of the white missionaries were from the South, and they saw no problem with demanding adherence to racial practices they brought from home. Methodists in Central Congo, for example, maintained and supported Belgian customs of segregation. Into the 1950s, "Africans were still . . . often received by some missionaries on the balcony of their homes. Very often the conversations took place through the doors' screen panels."[17]

In missionary churches, services often simply transplanted missionaries' home cultures: drinking and smoking were forbidden, the music was Western, the church benches were uncomfortable, and hymns were straight from the Baptist or Methodist hymnal (translated, at least, into the local language). Missionaries generally insisted that elements of African culture—from traditional forms of marriage (including polygyny) to the use of drums—were incompatible with Christianity. Starting in the late nineteenth century, some missionary advocates had already begun to argue for "indigenization" of the church—the adaptation of Christian faith to local cultures. The translation of the Bible into local languages was one component. There were also missionaries who argued for adapting worship to local customs, such as allowing the use of drums, and celebrating (or at least allowing) certain puberty rites. However this indigenization process was partial in Africa and much delayed in Congo. Some Congolese suspected, correctly, that many missionaries despised African culture on principle. Even some indigenization proponents made their case by saying that "civilization" was not necessary for Christianity.[18]

However fraught, the cultural interactions between missionaries and Congolese were never just morality plays in which Westerners tried to impose their cultures while locals resisted (or acquiesced). Historian Lamin Sanneh has argued that the very fact that missionaries translated the Bible into local languages set the stage for self-assertion by the people in mission fields. That is, whatever the missionaries themselves intended, the development of written languages (in some cases), the translation of the Bible into the language of ordinary life, and the expansion of literacy all empowered local populations to interpret the Bible for themselves and to shape the gospel—and ultimately the church itself—in their own image.[19]

Some of the most successful challenges to the Christian civilizing project came wrapped in its vestments. Starting in the 1920s and 1930s a number of alternative religious movements proliferated across Congo. These movements, several of which had truly mass followings, challenged missionary dominance, appropriated and revised Christian theology, and asserted African authority. Generally organized around charismatic leaders, these movements drew on key elements of missionary teachings and combined them with traditional African religious practices—and, sometimes, powerful anti-colonial rhetoric.[20]

At the national level, the most important of these movements was Kimbanguism. Simon Kimbagu, formerly a member of the Baptist missionary society in the lower Congo, began his ministry in the 1920s, and was arrested by the Belgians shortly thereafter. He died in prison thirty years later. During those three decades, Kimbangu's followers operated largely underground, but they developed into a significant force. As Adrian Hastings has argued, Kimbanguism was an extraordinary social movement, one in which Christian doctrine was combined with forms of traditional African religion and millennial hopes that carried a distinctly political edge. It flourished "in that intermediate moment when the old order was irretrievably slipping away but the new had not yet arrived."[21] As calls for independence increased in the late 1950s, Kimbanguism developed as a political force in its own right.[22] It also served as something of an object lesson for Protestant missionaries. On the one hand, a truly "contextualized" church had great appeal; on the other, missionaries saw in Kimbanguism the dangers of "too much" indigenization—an avowedly Christian movement that was well outside both the bounds of Protestant orthodoxy and the control of Western missionaries.

American missionaries in Congo might have seemed imperious, but they did not live in imperial luxury. Being a missionary was very hard work. All missionaries in Congo were required to train for one year in French (at least before 1960), and most learned one or two other African languages.[23] Some of them engaged in the difficult and complex task of translating the Bible, work that began in the nineteenth century and continued for many decades.

Those who served with non-denominational missions such as the African Inland Mission or the Unevangelized Fields Mission had to raise their own funds, both before they went to the field and again when they returned home on furlough. Those who served with denominations could generally count on some financial support, but during their year-long furloughs, which generally came every four to six years, they were required to travel to various churches to give reports and to encourage support for missions.[24]

The stories they told had to "sell" the savagery and poverty of Africa, much as the missionary reformers had fifty years before. In 1952, one Congolese Methodist leader, Wesley Shungu, traveled to the United States as the first Congolese delegate to the Methodist

General Conference. During his trip, he visited Asbury College in Kentucky, where a missionary on furlough reported on "African People and their Needs." Shungu was furious at what he heard, and he walked out of the meeting, protesting that missionaries always displayed unflattering pictures in order to raise money, and that the missionary's slides showed conditions in Africa in 1910 or 1914, not 1952.[25] For an ambitious and pious young man who saw himself as part of a continent on the cusp of transformation, it was no doubt humiliating to see how much Americans feasted on images of "benighted Africa."

The missionaries depended on their slide shows and lectures, however, to make it possible to do their work. And when they returned back to their mission stations, the labor was unrelenting. Whether pastors or their wives, doctors or nurses, teachers, or some combination of these, they spent long days at their assigned tasks, then evenings cooking, repairing equipment, or, when they could, reading or writing letters. They lived with heat and insects, exhaustion, and constant threats of disease.

Wheaton College graduate Vera Thiessen sailed to the Belgian Congo as a missionary nurse in 1946. She remained in Africa for three decades, and from the late 1940s until 1976, she described her hopes and difficulties in weekly letters home. Her days at the Africa Inland Mission (AIM) medical station at Oicha, in the Kivu province near the Ugandan border, were frustrating and often exhausting. But she was an intrepid believer in the power of encounter, and during the late 1950s and early 1960s she engaged in a sustained, complicated, and sometimes fraught navigation between her inherited views and the lives and politics of the people around her.

Vera, like most missionaries in Congo, lived with wealth and possessions unimaginable for local Christians. Often living on isolated compounds, in large homes that included shaded porches and nice windows, missionaries had little informal contact with any Congolese but the nurses in their hospitals or domestic workers in their residences (see figure 2.2). Vera's letters describe the strawberry jam, dumplings, and chicken salad that she and her colleagues ate, thanks to care packages from home. If missionary homes were lavish by local standards, however, they were hardly models of comfort, with no electricity and thatched roofs that allowed in the occasional snake. Missionaries were isolated from family and friends. Their letters often recounted their longing for mail, the pain of missed birthdays, and the sadness of spending holidays away from their families.

Vera worked at AIM's medical mission, which treated hundreds of Congolese each day, often saving lives or treating debilitating diseases. She did extensive work with the lepers who flocked to Oicha for treatment. She was often lonely and exhausted. When political crises intensified, the missionaries struggled to get basics such as flour and milk. They lived in fear of soldiers who set up roadblocks. They had to cope with the continuing, physically demanding routines of assisting in an operating room (with fewer and fewer supplies). And they shouldered the responsibility of hosting the remarkable number of guests who still came through the station. Vera also frequently complained about the inadequate work of the "medical boys" and the "house boy" and the "laundry girl" who were employed around the mission.

FIGURE 2.2 Missionary house in Congo, undated. GL Archive/Alamy Stock Photo.

From the late 1950s to the mid-1960s, Vera mentioned only one Congolese person by name, a young man named Benjamin whom she described as her "son"—the quotation marks are hers. He was a loyal Christian who trusted her, she wrote. In the fall of 1960, as political crises and evacuations happened all around her (Vera never left), she and her roommate, another missionary woman, invited Benjamin and his wife, along with another worker and his wife, to eat dinner with them. By that point, Thiessen might well have already read one of the many articles about missionaries and racism in the InterVarsity magazine *HIS*. She had recently received a gift subscription from her sister Lois, who sometimes wrote for the magazine.[26] Whatever the impetus for the dinner, Vera described it enthusiastically to her parents (in a letter that was also hand copied, probably by her mother, for distribution to others), explaining that she and her fellow missionary "had talked long ago about beginning to invite some Africans for occasional meals." The meal went well, she said, although Benjamin and his colleague had been nervous that "they might make mistakes." But "they comported themselves very well—even the wives." The conversation was a bit stiff, Vera reported, "but it was an interesting beginning."[27]

Thiessen wrote too about the task she took upon herself to train Benjamin's young wife in the rudiments of appropriate childcare and wifeliness—how to properly wash the baby and put clothes on the line.[28] The sources don't tell us what Benjamin or his wife thought, whether they were intimidated, impressed, indifferent, or hostile. What we can know is that Vera was engaging in what anthropologists Jean and John Comaroff describe as the heart of cultural imperialism: the power to shape everyday life.

This was not a matter of directly injecting local people with opinions. Africans were active agents who made their own decisions about how to respond to missionaries' overtures. Nor was it a matter of imposing overt political power. Many Protestant missionaries had a limited relationship with the Congolese state. But African people were required to engage in a "long conversation" with missionaries, whose most important influences were often on the structure of daily life: ideas about proper dress, the body, and the management of time, including the very notion that time was something to be "managed."[29]

It is not entirely clear whether Thiessen saw herself as part of a broad civilizing mission. It seems that she assumed that Benjamin's wife needed to learn how to hang laundry, not necessarily to become a good *Christian,* but simply to be cleaner and healthier in the American vein. It was through this kind of everyday interaction, this on-the-ground American "helpfulness," rather than through great modernizing projects like dam-building or the construction of fertilizer plants, that missionaries in Congo pushed Western ideas about economic and social development with quiet relentlessness.[30]

Commentators declared 1960 to be the Year of Africa, as seventeen independent nations were born. Even in the United States, where Africa had long been relegated to the margins of popular and diplomatic consciousness, the continent was finally getting sustained attention, as policymakers recognized the possibilities for creating alliances with newly decolonizing nations. American economic goals were minimal. What was really at stake was the Cold War.

In early 1960, Belgium announced that it would grant independence to its Congo colony in just six months, a remarkably rapid transition. An outspoken young nationalist, Patrice Lumumba, was soon elected prime minister. The move to independence was a tumultuous affair. It would lead to a five-year-long struggle for political control of the new state that was also a key battle in the African Cold War. The Congo Crisis provoked intensive US intervention, as Presidents Kennedy and then Johnson backed chosen allies with military aid and intelligence. Of the many conflicts in Africa in the 1960s, it was in Congo that "the stakes were by far the highest for both the United States and its rivals." Lumumba, who embodied the dream of a postcolonial Africa, had captured the imagination of liberals, Leftists, and black nationalists around the world. He soon ran afoul of the Belgians, however, as well as the United States, which had hoped for a leader who was friendlier to the West.[31]

When Congo became officially independent on June 30, 1960, the immediate response among the general Congolese population was delirious joy. Within two weeks, however, the army had mutinied and the large, mineral-rich province of Katanga had launched a war for secession. Shortly after, the United Nations dispatched troops to stabilize the country and limit Belgian interference in its former colony.

Starting in early September 1960, Lumumba faced what would become a deadly struggle for power in the new government. A young colonel named Joseph Mobutu launched a bloodless coup that ultimately favored Lumumba's rival Joseph Kasavubu, and Lumumba was placed under house arrest. The CIA issued an assassination order against Lumumba that was never carried out; instead, he escaped from house arrest in November of 1960, only to be arrested and held incommunicado by the Congolese leadership.[32]

In February 1961, Mobutu announced to the world that Lumumba had been caught and murdered by angry villagers. In fact, Lumumba had been secretly transferred to his arch enemies in the secessionist Katanga province, where he was murdered while Belgian military "advisors" looked on, although this would not be known with certainty for almost forty years.[33] Nonetheless, Mobutu's obvious charade outraged Lumumba's supporters, both in Congo and abroad. There were demonstrations in a dozen or more cities, from Accra to Amsterdam, including a dramatic protest at the UN Security Council, led by writers Maya Angelou and LeRoi Jones (Amiri Baraka) along with jazz singer Abbey Lincoln. The protest ended in a melee, and the UN building was closed to the public for two days.[34]

During the post-independence crisis of the early 1960s, US missionaries were evacuated from Congo several times. The first evacuation came a few weeks after Lumumba's election in June 1960, following a revolt by the military and the secessionist movement in Kantaga. With tensions rising, the US consulate in Kampala, Uganda, recommended that all missionaries in Eastern Congo evacuate. The order applied to more than 1,000 missionaries, perhaps as many as 1,700.[35] Most missionaries left, heading out to nearby countries or in some cases back to the United States. A few people stayed behind in Congo. In at least one case, a group of Congolese tried to prevent missionaries from leaving. The crowds were not hostile, the *Chicago Tribune* reported, they "simply wanted to head off the departure of men who served as doctors and teachers."[36]

Missionaries who had left Congo became sources of information for the people back home. In general, the almost entirely white missionary force was quite dubious about nationalist sentiment in Congo. They argued, as many secular commentators did, that the Congolese were not "ready" for independence. Missionaries, however, had the authority that came from intimacy, from time spent on the ground. Their views about self-rule also carried the weight of their presumed righteousness. One Baptist missionary told a reporter at the *Washington Post* that the Congolese "had no real conception of freedom. They thought it meant money and all the things they wanted."[37] Many missionary reports exempted "true" Congolese Christians, who, they insisted, were not interested in political independence.

The more immediate issue in summer 1960 was the violence that accompanied the early days of independence. Missionaries were understandably anxious and fearful, operating in a swirl of rumor. The *Evangelical Beacon*, magazine of the Evangelical Free Church, published a tense day-by-day account with a blaring headline: "Missionaries Leave Congo: 39 Missionaries, 36 Children All Safe in Major Evacuation" (figure 2.3).

One Conservative Baptist missionary couple wrote a private letter to their family after leaving Congo. "The black soldiers are no respecter of person nor religion," they reported. "This business of raping white women has spread all over Congo." A week later they wrote to insist that, while some people were saying that reports of rape had been exaggerated, the threat was everywhere.

FIGURE 2.3 Courtesy of the Evangelical Free Church of America.

Some people who were leaving Congo up North in AIM territory were stopped by natives with poisonous spears and had all their belongings taken away, even their rings and shoes and they tried to take the dresses off the women. We heard this report and when the refuge[e]s filed into Kampala, Uganda, one of the AIM missionaries went to talk to them and confirmed the reports.[38]

This was not an account of rape, but the missionaries treated it as such. The Congo crisis made the missionaries' racial and sexual panic dramatically visible.

Vera Thiessen summed up the ways that Americans, never unaware of race, nonetheless longed to wish it away. In December 1960, Vera wrote home, reporting that one of the other missionaries who had complained about the anti-white sentiment expressed in the days after independence had told her, "I don't mind suffering for Christ's sake, but I don't think I need to suffer because my skin is white." Vera expressed some sympathy with the view, but she also examined the question with more self-awareness than most of her colleagues. After all, she commented, "I'm sure there are plenty of American negroes who would probably say the same thing about the color of their skin. But it hurts just the same."[39]

Other reports from the evacuations, quite different in tone than the ones about rape, emphasized the loyalty of Congolese Christians who had risked themselves, either by helping missionaries to escape or by guarding the mission stations.[40] Indeed, the "loyal Christians" were the proof that Christianity was *working*, that there were Congolese who put their religious faith before their fears for their own safety. Soon, a number of Congolese would wonder aloud why Americans had not done the same.

As the largely white US missionary force evacuated en masse in the summer of 1960, African American denominations promised to step into the breach. At the time, there were probably fewer than twenty African American missionaries in Congo, almost all of them serving with the mainline churches, Methodist or Presbyterian.[41] The Belgian government had discouraged white-led denominations from sending African Americans as missionaries—probably to shield Congolese from the "bad example" of black people in positions of authority.[42] Independence offered an opportunity for African American churches to make their presence felt. The AME board declared the "present situation in Africa" to be "the greatest challenge" the denomination had ever faced and voted to expand support for missionary work in the area. Bishop John Bright, an American who had just been elected bishop for Central Africa, announced that he was leaving immediately to visit Congo on his way to take up his post. The Board of Directors of the National Baptist Convention, the largest African American denomination, voted unanimously to send missionaries to replace those who had evacuated.[43]

African American churches were deeply invested in the state of the church in Africa; they were equally committed to the political success of young African states. The AME *Voice of Missions* carried a number of stories about Lumumba in the fall of 1960. As he struggled to get back into power, *VOM* enthusiastically recounted that his following was increasing.[44] Once Lumumba's death became known in early 1961, *VOM* angrily followed the national and international response.[45] Other African American church leaders also spoke out. Rev. Smallwood Williams, the head of the Bible Way Church, an assembly of African American Pentecostal churches with a characteristically conservative theology, wrote a letter to the *Pittsburgh Courier* several weeks after the UN protests. The US government had seemed unable to distinguish nationalism from communism, Rev. Williams wrote, and anti-communist rhetoric that had been used against Lumumba was the same kind of smear used against civil rights activists at home.[46]

Both before and after independence, evangelicals in Congo were increasingly vocal about the issues of independence *within* the churches, and it was in the urgent and concrete struggles over resources that many of the most emotionally powerful debates about race, nation, and religious identity played out. Missionaries and their supporters had imagined that local churches would become more independent over time. Most evangelical missionary organizations saw their role, at least ideally, as converting an initial set of believers, training pastors, and then ceding control of the churches to indigenous believers.[47] In Congo, by and large, this had *not* happened, and missionaries retained positions of power as pastors, directors of medical clinics, and administrators of church-based schools. In the early 1960s, Congolese Christians began to insist on more control of these institutions. Conflicts over school fees or pastoral ordination were also debates about decolonization.

Those debates centered on three related issues. First was control over education—a topic so emotionally fraught and contentious that it badly fractured the Protestant community in parts of Congo. Second was syncretism, the threat that Congolese were falling away from true Christianity. The third was ecumenism: how much would different Protestant groups work as one great church in Congo (and the rest of Africa)? And, if they did so, would evangelical churches remain identifiably evangelical?

It is hard to overstate the importance of education to Congolese Protestants. Mission schools were horribly inadequate, which so deeply angered Congolese Christians that fights over control of the schools became a kind of proxy for larger questions of autonomy. Moreover, as independence neared, it was clear that the good jobs opening up in the government bureaucracy would be filled almost entirely by graduates of the Catholic schools. An education from the evangelical missions schools was almost useless.[48]

The reasons were complicated. By 1960, according to one estimate, Protestant missions had provided at least some primary school education to approximately one million Congolese.[49] Valuable as it was, this education was a mixed bag. Organizations such as AIM and the Conservative Baptist Foreign Missions Society (CBFMS), both of which were strong in Kivu (eastern Congo), had refused to accept state subsidies or teach the government-approved curriculum, which they believed was tainted by Catholicism.[50] As a result of that refusal, when Congolese finished their elementary education at these mission schools, they did not have certifications that would allow them to attend public high school and college.[51]

In fact, this was something of the point. These more fundamentalist missionaries did not necessarily *want* their graduates to get secular jobs and achieve worldly success. Excessive education, they believed, led to misdirected ambition, a focus on material prosperity rather than dependence on God. As pressure mounted on the conservative missions to accept government supervision, Paul Hurlburt Sr., the head of the Conservative Baptist mission station at Katwa (in Kivu), argued that he might be willing to accept changes that would allow students to receive certificates, but he would never accept subsidies from the government. This seemingly odd position was the result of the missionary's belief that subsidies would mean higher salaries for Congolese teachers, which would mean that teachers made more than pastors, which would further discourage believers from becoming pastors or doing other directly church-related work.[52]

Making matters worse, missionaries' views of the dangers of education seemed to apply only to *some* Congolese. In addition to the mission school, the Conservative Baptist mission at Kivu ran a nicely appointed boarding school for "orphans," mostly the abandoned mixed-race children of Western men (such as missionaries and mining company employees) and Congolese women. Those children got a much better education than was provided at the regular mission schools, including classes taught in English.

For a time, the person who ran this school was Deighton Douglin, an African American missionary serving with the Conservative Baptists. Douglin had attended Providence (RI) Bible Institute, where he met and married a biracial Congolese woman, Annie. Many years after leaving Congo, Douglin explained that he had been surprised that the orphanage school had caused anger among the local believers:

> I mean the mission had schools for nationals all along, and this [the orphanage] was new, a new investment and a new effort . . . . But somehow or other they felt that these children were getting better treatment than they were getting in the local, their own local schools. And so they wanted to send their children there.[53]

The controversy raged for several years; in 1959, the CBFMS voted to close the orphans' school rather than allow local Congolese to attend.[54]

Congolese believers were infuriated by the sense that they were being deliberately held back. In the summer of 1959, a group of Congolese associated with the Conservative Baptists invited missionaries to come discuss the problem. More than one hundred African Christians showed up, but no missionaries. In response, those who did attend drew up the Burungu Resolutions, which insisted that schools should not open that fall without subsidies. But they did not stop there. The resolutions also said that local churches would no longer submit statistical reports to the missionaries and that African believers would determine the needs of African pastors. Over the next several weeks there were school strikes. Police were called in to forcibly open the schools, and employees were fired from the mission hospital for sympathizing with the strikers. The conflict was ugly, and although it was resolved within a few months, with the missionaries agreeing to accept subsidies, the battle over the schools would fundamentally shape the relationships between Congolese and missionaries during the post-independence political struggles that wracked the country.[55]

The Conservative Baptist missionaries were evacuated shortly after independence. After a few weeks they returned to Kivu to find that things had changed dramatically. Two groups, one sympathetic to missionaries and the other more closely allied to nationalist (and pro-Lumumba) sentiments, battled for control over the churches and schools. Both sides appealed to the Congolese government for recognition, and as different local and national leaders came into power, conditions shifted on the ground. At her mission station many hundreds of miles away, Vera Theissen heard news of the literal battles over control of the pulpits and schools. In a letter home, she wrote that the Conservative Baptist church "has been divided for some time but Sunday those who have allied themselves with the missionaries were refused admission to the church." Soldiers stepped in and now both groups were supposed to appear at a hearing. "What shame such an episode brings to the Lord's name," Vera lamented.[56]

Religious conflicts sometimes outlasted political ones. One Congolese official wrote in the early 1960s that "the affairs of the [Kivu] area seem to be quiet except the war that is going on inside the protestant church!"[57] At one point, when Congo's President Kasavubu had been convinced to weigh in on the side of the missionaries and their supporters, some of the insurgents decided to try to appeal to a higher power: they wrote a letter to President John F. Kennedy. Complaining that "your compatriots at the Baptist Mission of the Kivu" had repudiated democratic proceedings in the church, the Congolese explained that the missionaries had fled the country and abandoned their missionary service, only to return and "proceed by armed force against our pastors and our churches." They were shocked at such aggression. "Is it the Baptist mission of rifles and cudgels?"[58]

The schools were a central node in the larger nexus of political and religious power that marked the evangelical missions. Without an awareness of how political debates about power and colonial mentalities were often funneled through discussions about education—or, in other cases, seemingly arcane debates over how, and how much, Congolese pastors would be paid—it is easy to miss the multiple ways that decolonization happened in Congo and the terms under which Americans were forced to rethink their benevolence.

The second issue that strained relations between Congolese and missionaries was syncretism—the sense that local Christians were not as theologically pure as the Americans believed themselves to be. One missionary for the Africa Inland Mission wrote to his New York office: "Religious wise, as you perhaps already know, in Congo there has been a great resurgence of native cults. This has made inroads into our church."[59] Missionaries and their allies did not hesitate to link political support for independence with what they saw as dangerous cultist tendencies. The Christian and Missionary Alliance magazine told its readers that some Africans, even those believed themselves to be Christian, might well allow their enthusiasm for independence to lure them into apostasy and witchcraft: "While seeking complete freedom from white-imposed restraint, some mistakenly turn to this horrible slavery where every death is attributed to a witch who has eaten the soul of the deceased."[60]

In fact, the political problem for many Congolese Christians, Protestant and Catholic, was the opposite: rather than being allied with local "cults," they were instead very much separated from traditional African religious practices and rituals. Congolese evangelical leaders were generally just as strict as missionaries in condemning signs of "backsliding" into traditional practices.[61] One church's rules for membership included no drinking, smoking, cursing, or stealing; no involvement in a polygamous marriage; and no partici-pation in any form of "cult" or use of any sort of "fetish." Theologian Kwame Bediako argues that members of missionary-derived churches were consistently unable to relate to their traditional culture "in terms other than enunciation of separateness."[62] Mission churches faced a particular crisis in the first years of independence, when Congolese "cults" like Kimbanguism were being mobilized as symbolic resources in the struggle against colonialism, leaving Congolese Christians subject to charges of imperialism by association. At the same time, Congolese Christians were sometimes seen as suspect by missionaries as well, always potentially at risk of sliding into "cultism."

Ultimately, however, it was the power of ecumenical Christianity, not traditional reli-gion, that most missionaries saw as the most urgent issue facing Protestantism in Congo. The ecumenical impulse was a push toward closer relationships among different churches, with the ultimate goal—or at least the implication—that all churches would eventually become one. There was obvious scriptural justification for ecumenism in several New Testament verses, including Paul's injunction that "there is one body and one Spirit . . . one Lord, one faith, one baptism" (Ephesians 4:4-5, KJV). But evangelicals were nothing if not clear on the importance of correct doctrine, and ecumenism, it seemed to many, would inevitably lead to a watered-down theology.

There was a specific concern that the World Council of Churches, led largely by mainline denominations, was emerging as a seemingly unstoppable force for bringing together Protestants from around the world. This created a crisis for evangelicals, who feared being marginalized by what they saw as a liberal juggernaut. More so than the fraught politics of education, or the anxieties about syncretism and rebellion, the dan-gers of liberalism captivated American evangelicals in Congo. Their razor-sharp focus on the problems with church unity was also a source of tension between missionaries and Congolese Christians, who were often dubious about the supposed danger posed by the ecumenical movement.

To an outsider, the internal debates about the structure of church organizations and the politics of ecumenism can seem petty at best, paranoid at worst. But there were real issues at stake. Theologically, many white evangelicals were worried that WCC churches were soft on matters of salvation. Politically, they correctly saw the WCC as quite liberal in its orientation. And institutionally, they were deeply torn. Evangelicals supported, in theory, the idea of a unified global church. But they feared that their specific organiza-tions and churches were going to be marginalized by the WCC's attempt to establish itself as an umbrella for Protestantism. Indeed, in many parts of Africa and some parts of Asia, the Protestant churches within a country eventually joined together into some sort of unified national body, often affiliated with the WCC.[63]

By the early 1960s, most US evangelicals working in Africa were balancing their fear of the ecumenical movement with the reality that many indigenous Christians were far less interested in denominational divides than Americans were. In 1960, the Congo Protestant Council (CPC), long dominated by missionaries, elected Pierre Shaumba as its first Congolese president. Shaumba was seen by some evangelicals as overly aligned with the World Council of Churches. This reputation was reinforced by the fact that, immediately upon assuming office, Shaumba called for a new kind of transparency between missionaries and African church members.[64] He insisted on more support for higher education (rather than only primary schools); he also demanded more openness about finances on the part of the missions, at a time when many Congolese felt that the missionaries were perhaps hoarding donations from the United States rather than making those donations available to Congolese-run churches.

At the same time, Shaumba also reassured conservative missionaries that he was in community with them. Writing in *Congo Mission News*, the official magazine of the CPC that was distributed to both Protestants in Congo and missionary supporters in the United States, Shaumba told his readers that "as we become independent as a nation, we become even more dependent on our Mother Churches of Europe and America who gave us birth."[65] Just a few years earlier, as a leader in the Methodist church, Shaumba had once walked out on a group of missionaries who dismissed the idea of Congolese independence.[66] But as leader of the CPC, he worked to persuade the conservative bloc of his political and religious trustworthiness: "I have but one passport to heaven, and that is my faith in Jesus Christ, not my affiliation with the WCC," he said at a meeting with AIM missionaries. "My faith in Him unites me with you Christians of the AIM, and it's that spiritual unity I want to guard."[67] In the fractured world of Protestant Congo, however, no one person could hold together consensus. Shaumba would have had a difficult time negotiating questions about ecumenism and power-sharing in any situation. But this was not any situation.

In 1963, a number of national churches across Africa formed the All Africa Council of Churches (AACC), affiliated with the WCC. Surveying plans for the new organization, Donald M'Timkulu of Northern Rhodesia (now Zambia) remarked that "the most powerful divisive force" for African Christians was "an extreme form of denominationalism which emphasized confessional difference and rivalries." Those divisions might have had some meaning in Europe, he said, but they had no place in Africa.[68]

In the face of such powerful sentiments, American evangelicals struggled. As one missionary reported, rather wearily, "It is difficult to find any objections to the spiritual language and tone of any of the communications sent out by the AACC." That was a problem, since it made it very hard for "our African brethren" to understand the dangerous agenda of the World Council of Churches. The Africans, he said, were "not able to discern the subtlety of this movement."[69]

Sometimes, the movement was not so subtle. At the ecumenical All Africa Christian Youth Assembly in Nairobi, which ran from December 28, 1962, to January 7, 1963, speakers took to the stage to call for African churches' independence from missionary organizations. They did not bother with the delicate language that some African Christians like Shaumba used in order to spare Western sensibilities. Kenyan James Ngugi, for example, told the approving audience that it was time to unlearn some of the lessons the missionaries had taught—lessons such as "blessedness in poverty and obedience to the master class."[70]

The reverberations of the Youth Congress were apparent in Congo. Kenneth Downing of the Evangelical Foreign Missions Association reported that during the 1963 meeting of the Congo Protestant Council, some who had attended the youth congress were now "outspoken against the missionaries." Peter Brashler of AIM sounded a similar alarm, warning that "the ecumenicals," who had previously been acting behind the scenes with "intrigue and propaganda," were now moving boldly to take leadership.[71]

Now that independence was a reality, evangelicals were afraid of losing their moral leadership among Congolese Protestants. If the World Council of Churches was proving to be a friendlier terrain for young radicals, then evangelicals would need to forge a power bloc of their own.

Between Lumumba's assassination in 1961 and Paul Carlson's murder in 1964, Congo was wracked by rebellion and internal power struggles. In addition to the on-and-off clashes in secessionist Katanga province in the south, the capital of Leopoldville saw a series of rebellions by those who allied themselves in some way with Lumumba's memory. By 1964, the Simba rebels, under the leadership of left-wing nationalist Christophe Gbenye, were the only major rebel force still operating. The Simba (Swahili for "lion") had organized with only moderate success for several years, but, starting in late 1963, they began to expand rapidly, leading US and UN officials to involve themselves more deeply in Congo, supplying planes and other equipment to the pro-Western government.[72] With rebels approaching, missionaries evacuated in droves, and scores of mission stations were soon in rebel-controlled territory (see figure 2.4). Paul Carlson did not leave, although his wife and children had departed earlier in the year. In October of 1964 he was captured and taken hostage along with a number of others. The Simba rebels initially identified the missionary doctor as a military officer. For Gbenye, Carlson was among those he routinely referred to the "impérialistes américains."[73]

Carlson was far from the only American evangelical missionary to die in the violence of the 1964 rebellion, as the Simba moved across territory controlled by dozens of different missions organizations on their way to Stanleyville. After Carlson's death made news, a number of US evangelical groups began to publish their own accounts of missionary sacrifice and martyrdom in church magazines or in pamphlets or Sunday bulletin inserts.[74] The World Evangelical Commission, for example, published a pamphlet that was structured by the Christian ideal of giving one's life for others, as Jesus had done: "Love's summit reached!" announced the cover, describing the death of six missionaries in Congo.[75]

The Unevangelized Fields Mission (UFM) sustained some of the heaviest losses, with nineteen people killed in the violence of the late fall of 1964. UFM was a British evangelical mission, born out of a missions push into Congo at the turn of the century. Its personnel were a mixed contingent of British, Irish, Americans, Canadians, and Australians. In many ways, the group exemplified the capacious meaning of "evangelical"

FIGURE 2.4 Missionaries evacuating Congo. USIS photo.

in this period: they were all white and committed to a conservative theology, but within that, there was real variety—one young woman had trained at the staunchly fundamentalist Moody Bible Institute in the United States, while one of the men was influenced by the Holiness-oriented British-based Keswick convention, with its focus on the possibility of living a nearly sinless life through the work of the Holy Spirit.[76]

Several UFM missionaries were among the hostages held at Stanleyville; others were held outside the city or in other stations around northeastern Congo. The organization's *Crusade* magazine reported on the rebellion and the killings of missionaries in great detail. It described the executions on the streets of Stanleyville, where three UFM missionaries escaped certain death by leaping over a nearby wall. Others of the UFM delegation, including children and wives, had been held under house arrest outside the city and were released shortly after the paratroopers took Stanleyville. In one particularly detailed and emotionally powerful account, *Crusade* told of how a group of Belgian mercenaries had launched an exhaustive search of the area of Banalia, in Orientale province, for a missing group of seven UFM missionaries and five of their children, only to have the trail end at a river, where they found only blood-soaked clothes and a Bible.[77] A few months after the missionaries' deaths, the organization published an eighteen-page pamphlet that described the lives of each of the missionaries, and, where possible, told the story of how they died. A twenty-eight-year-old missionary named Bill, for example, was taken to prison on Sept. 13, where he died a few days later. He had been tormented mentally and physically by the [rebels]. On one occasion . . . they fired five bullets past his head. He had been ill with filaria, malaria, and dysentery. When he was mistreated in jail by the [rebels], his body could take no more, and the Lord graciously took Bill home.[78]

The long history of the iconography of Christian martyrdom saturated the account, where heartbreak mixed with promise: for believers, readers were reminded, death is just going home.

There is an obvious political valence to this particular story, since the Belgian mercenaries are the heroes who rescued those who survived. But there is another, less obvious point. A theme that runs through almost every account is that of "ransom." Just as Jesus's death on the cross is the ransom for human sin, the reports tell us, these missionaries' lives were a ransom for the Congolese they loved. The stories also resonated with accounts of the persecution and self-sacrifice of believers in the early church. Missionary deaths, these narratives suggest, might best be understood as the same kind of martyrdom. To die at the hands of unbelievers was to embody Christian virtue and fearlessness.

Carlson was an icon for *Time* and *Life*, and for white American Christians from a variety of backgrounds. African American observers also expressed their concern and sadness over Carlson's death. Churchgoers were presumed to be a significant portion of the readership of the major black papers, and the black press reported Carlson's death as a tragedy of inherent concern to their audiences. The *Chicago Daily Defender*, for example, carried frequent, sympathetic reports on Carlson's captivity and then murder (generally drawn from the news service UPI). But the *Defender* also published opinion pieces that, while deploring the deaths of missionaries, highlighted the larger political dimensions of the violence and decried the "white arrogance" that had increased tensions and violence in Congo.[79]

In January 1965, the AME's *Voice of Missions* made a similar argument. The magazine insisted that US foreign policy was partly responsible for the events that led to Carlson's death, pointing out that many African nations had seen the parachuting of Belgian troops into Stanleyville as a threat to the idea of African independence, as just one more example of "Western intrigues." After the "tragic failures" of US foreign policy in Congo, the only hope was for the United States to disengage from the internal affairs of Congo altogether. Only then might the United States "emerge from this crisis with honor and continue to act as an influence for progress and development in Africa."[80]

The call for the United States to "continue" to act as a force for progress was typical of the AME's relatively mainstream politics; there would be no overt questioning of the benevolence of US power. Still, there were ironies that African American Protestants clearly noticed. After all, by the time Carlson died, the civil rights movement had already had its share of martyrs at home. When, in late February of 1965, Rev. Martin Luther King Jr. announced his plan to march from Selma to Birmingham, many people were fearful for his life. A group of black churches responded to King's announcement with a prayer meeting: on a specific Sunday in February, churchgoers around the country would offer concentrated prayer for missionaries and other Christians who were under threat of violence—in Africa *and* in Alabama.

In spring of 1965, a striking article appeared in *Congo Mission News*, the magazine published by the Congo Protestant Council. Entitled "An Author Makes a Comparison," it was written by Homer Dowdy, who had chronicled the attacks on Stanleyville in *Out of the Jaws of the Lion* and had written several other books about the church in Vietnam and China. The article was a classic piece of evangelical Cold War rhetoric, in which Dowdy offered a detailed political analysis while disavowing the very idea of a "political" church. It was obvious, Dowdy claimed, that Communist China was supplying the Simba rebels. It now seemed that a long guerilla war might be in the making. Almost certainly, Dowdy argued, the church in Congo would find itself pressured to choose sides between communist rebels and the government. In the "midst of peril and persecution," Congolese Christians should try to focus on what really mattered: the gospel. Merely by standing for their faith they would be at the front lines of the fight against communism.

The relevant "comparison" of the article's title was made via a large cartoon (figure 2.5). A figure in the shape of Congo stands in front of a mirror. The mirror, however, reflects

FIGURE 2.5 *Congo Mission News*, March 1965.

back the elongated shape of Vietnam, with tears streaming down its face. "Do I REALLY look like that?" Congo asks in the caption. The image was partly political, reflecting concerns expressed by US government officials and other observers that US involvement in Congo might escalate. It was also a religious image, indicating that Congolese Christians, like Vietnamese before them, would be asked to suffer for the gospel in a place where communists might well dominate.[81]

In the early 1960s, questions about race, faith, suffering, and politics played out in Congo. Paul Carlson was killed at a time when missionaries were facing profound criticism for having evacuated their mission stations. The basic facts were undeniable: most Protestant missionaries had abandoned their fellow Christians, not once but several times, rather than risk *actually* becoming martyrs. Carlson had not left and so lived out the missionary ideal—a sacrifice as rare as it was meaningful.

Most of the Protestants who lived in or looked toward Congo, including Congolese evangelicals, embraced the righteousness of suffering and sacrifice. What was up for debate was *whose* suffering mattered and how it would be made visible. Old-style missionary relationships were under assault, as "young churches" insisted on their rights to dignity, self-government, and eventually to ownership of the schools and hospitals that missionaries had once controlled.

For the many different groups of Americans who were invested in Congo, events there hit remarkably close to home. Africa might be far away, but missions were close to the heart. Evangelical internationalism certainly did not begin in Congo, but its global vision and racial politics were very much in evidence there. Yet American Christians, black or white, did not operate in a vacuum. Powerful as their fantasies of Africa might be, they also were forced to engage with the agency and assertiveness of the people of Congo— from Christian believers to government leaders to Simba rebels—who fundamentally shaped the terrain that missionaries and their supporters navigated. Congolese evangelicals were on the front lines of a struggle for authority within the global evangelical church. Their determination to decolonize the church as well as their nation would be echoed in countries around the world and would fundamentally reshape global evangelicalism in the decades to come.

3

"Have you Read the Communist Manifesto?"

CHRISTIAN REVOLUTIONS

IN MANY RESPECTS 1966 was the turning point, the moment when a cohort of mostly younger evangelicals came into their own.

It was in 1966 that an African American minister named Bill Pannell traveled to Berlin to participate in the World Congress on Evangelization organized by Billy Graham. Pannell saw the upheaval sweeping the globe and wanted to talk about how to preach the gospel to a world in turmoil. He was disappointed. Participants were focusing on the gospel, but, he recalled, "they weren't dealing with the world."[1]

Pannell did hear one speech that caught his attention. A young white evangelist from South Africa named Michael Cassidy gave an impassioned address denouncing apartheid and declaring that "powerful race feelings" among both white and black South Africans were an impediment to evangelism."[2] Cassidy was no radical. He condemned "militant" black nationalism as strongly as he did "white nationalism." Looking back at events in Congo just a few years earlier, he bemoaned what he saw as the "bestialities" perpetuated by rebels in the name of nationalism. As Christians, he said, we can never support anyone who puts "the so-called liberation struggle" ahead of a universal ethics.[3] But such ethics must include a commitment to racial equality.

Cassidy's equation of black and white race consciousness outraged his fellow South Africans. As soon as he finished speaking, one Afrikaaner delegate "furiously grabbed the mike and insisted that [Cassidy] withdraw [his speech]....They threatened to have Mike excluded from the country and to shut doors for him all over South Africa."[4] The official publication of the conference described the debate as characterized by "tense, frank, and open disagreement."[5]

Cassidy and Pannell were two relatively young men, both under 40 years old, who found common cause in their willingness to take racial politics seriously and to see those issues globally. Over the next decade Cassidy would be established as perhaps the most influential evangelical leader in South Africa. Pannell was on the cusp of becoming an evangelical star in the United States. Within two years his book-length meditation on evangelicals and race, *My Friend, The Enemy*, would catapult him to national prominence.[6] The two men were harbingers of momentous change.

By the mid-1960s, evangelicalism was one of the most dynamic religious movements in the United States, exceeded only by the black churches that were at the heart of the civil rights movement. Evangelicalism, however, was hardly a unified enterprise. Those who marched under the evangelical banner had such diverse theological and social views that the movement sometimes seemed to resemble the trading floor of an old-style stock exchange, where people shouted their opinions as if they were bids. At the same time, a new generation was emerging, one that was more committed to political and social issues, and was deeply aware of the realities of racism, decolonization, war, and humanitarian disaster. They were not all liberals, certainly—anticommunist conservatives remained a potent force—but over the course of the decade there developed both a liberal wing and a moderate core ready to take on the great political issues of the day without hiding behind the fig leaf of political neutrality, as their forbears had done. Members of the sixties generation were about to forge a new kind of network of believers. Like the larger evangelical movement, this network was theologically diverse—it included everyone from Pentecostals to Plymouth Brethren. And like the sixties generation in general, its members were determined to be authentic, relevant, and unafraid.

In 1966 traditional denominations remained the backbones of the day-to-day religious lives of evangelicals. They provided the worship services and Sunday school literature, the church choirs and vacation Bible schools. Non-denominational organizations, however, furnished a different kind of space, where people could think of themselves as part of something larger than their own home church. The flowering of those parachurch (literally "alongside the church") organizations was an anchor for the changing evangelical culture and politics of the sixties.

Organizations that worked beyond denominations had been around for many decades, particularly in the form of missions programs like China Inland Mission (founded in 1888), Africa Inland Mission (1895), the Unevangelized Fields Mission (1931), and Wycliffe Bible Translators (1942). For much of the twentieth century their impact had been to strengthen conservative trends rather than to nurture more liberal ones.[7] Yet other parts of the parachurch movement were more innovative. The Student Volunteer Movement at the turn of the twentieth century had engaged hundreds of thousands of young people as missionaries and supporters.[8] Parachurch groups like the Full Gospel Businessmen's Fellowship and InterVarsity Christian Fellowship flourished. By the 1960s, many theologically conservative Protestants were participating in these fluid and improvisational parachurch organizations even as they remained deeply committed to their home churches—to their identities as Baptists or Mennonites or Methodists.

The most influential parachurch organization was the National Association of Evangelicals. The NAE and likeminded institutions such as *Christianity Today* and Fuller Theological Seminary aimed to define themselves as "mainstream" evangelicalism. By the mid-sixties, they were well on their way to dominating the terrain. The NAE had incorporated a diverse array of denominations and individuals into the organization. The group's most influential leaders were committed to the Reformed theology that had emerged from John Calvin and his heirs, which emphasized the sovereignty and power of God. But there was also an energetic strain of Methodist (Wesleyan) beliefs, which emphasized free will, the importance of personal faith, and the authority of individual experience. Even Pentecostal churches, long greeted skeptically by most "traditional" evangelicals, were able to join. The Pentecostals believed that the expression of the Holy Spirit's work in a believer's life was evidenced by signs, such as speaking in tongues or miraculous healing.[9]

From the beginning, the neo-evangelicals who dominated the NAE and *Christianity Today* aimed for a more "worldly" orientation than their forebears. They wanted to reach outward and to live within the larger culture even while standing apart from its failings. Arthur Glasser was a former missionary to China and a neo-evangelical stalwart who would go on to become dean of the School of World Mission at Fuller Theological Seminary. Speaking at InterVarsity's Urbana convention in 1961 (see figure 3.1), Glasser made clear that he believed that evangelical students in the crowd were too isolated from the world around them, unsophisticated about politics and culture. He advised them to "read a weekly news periodical from cover to cover, including the sections on the theater and the arts. Our playwrights and other artists are trying to communicate to us a sense of the mood of our day." Read a religious magazine that makes you think, he continued. Read books. "But don't stop there. Have you read the Communist Manifesto? Have you read anything on nationalism?"[10] If not, he felt, it was time they did.

A number of African American evangelicals were also involved with neo-evangelical institutions, although often uneasily. In 1963, a group of African Americans founded the National Black Evangelical Association (originally the National Negro Evangelical Association). The founders emerged largely from institutions associated with "white" evangelicalism and fundamentalism. They included Howard Jones of the Billy Graham Evangelistic Association; Bill Pannell of Youth for Christ; Tom Skinner, who had founded the Harlem Evangelistic Association; Ruth Lewis Bentley, the InterVarsity staffer who would try to integrate the University of Alabama; and William Bentley, her husband, a minister with the United Pentecostal Council of the Assemblies of God, an African American denomination that had separated from the largely white Assemblies of God in 1919.

These black evangelicals were deeply influenced by their histories with white evangelicalism, shaped by the Scofield Reference Bible and the long arms of Moody Bible College

FIGURE 3.1 The stage at Urbana in 1961. © Urbana 61, InterVarsity's 7th Student Missions Conference.

and Dallas Theological Seminary. Not surprisingly, African Americans occupied complicated positions within those institutions. Mary McLeod Bethune, who would become one of the most important advocates for African American women in the early twentieth century, attended Moody as its only African American student in 1894. Moody later had more African American students, but from 1910 to 1938 the school required them to live off campus rather than with white students in dormitories.[11] The more common route for black students was to train at segregated Bible colleges or correspondence courses run by old style white-dominated fundamentalist institutions. For decades, these Bible colleges provided education to black students who were raised in Baptist, Pentecostal, or AME churches, brought together by the otherwise limited opportunities for theological study. These institutes were originally built by white patrons and staffed mostly from white seminaries. Carver Bible Institute in Atlanta, for example, was founded by two former missionaries to China who had been educated at Moody Bible College. When African Americans attended Carver, they learned classical fundamentalist doctrines.[12]

According to William Bentley, who would serve as president of the NBEA in the 1970s, this education meant that the early members of the NBEA were as critical of mainline black denominations as white evangelicals were of the mainline white ones. Bentley would come to see this critical stance as a mistake.[13] Still, he believed that black "Bible-believing" Christians shared much with their white evangelical brethren. The term "evangelical" was rarely used in black churches, he admitted. But while black denominations like the

AME and the National Baptist Convention were institutionally affiliated with mainline Protestantism, they held theologies that were "indistinguishable" from orthodox, conservative white Protestantism.[14] Black Pentecostal and Holiness churches (such as the Church of God in Christ) were "entirely evangelical," Bentley insisted.[15] And those churches had sustained African Americans through slavery and oppression. Thus, Bentley argued, those "mainline" churches were both evangelical, and historically important to the black community. Why shouldn't black evangelicals embrace them? As the sixties progressed, leaders in the NBEA began to invest in relationships with mainline black churches.

Important as neo-evangelicalism was, its institutions were only a small part of non-denominational evangelical life in the 1960s. College students were at the heart of the changes that were beginning to transform the evangelical subculture. Christian colleges were becoming sites where denominations mattered less than the shared experience of living a passionate faith in the light of youthful questioning. In the early part of the sixties, evangelical students, like their non-evangelical counterparts, were deeply concerned about the materialism and shallowness of modern life. As with the members of Students for a Democratic Society who wrote the Port Huron Statement in 1962, these young evangelicals were housed in universities, "bred in at least modest comfort," and "looking uncomfortably" at the world they would inherit. They also worried about excessive materialism, racism, and the dangers of the atomic bomb.[16] By the mid-1960s, students on evangelical campuses were asking hard questions about the assumptions that the neo-evangelicals themselves carried, including their definitions of Christian orthodoxy. At Wheaton College, the conservative evangelical institution that had nurtured several generations of fundamentalists, the student newspaper was by mid-decade regularly printing editorials and articles extolling the virtues of inquiry, criticism, "real community," and "authenticity."[17] This was not yet radical politics, but it was a cultural politics of dissent and a self-consciously questioning posture.

For younger evangelicals, no one raised big questions more resolutely than Francis Schaeffer, who aggressively challenged the cultural isolation of evangelical culture. Schaeffer had begun his career as a fundamentalist allied with the resolutely separatist Carl McIntire. After several years as pastor in the conservative Bible Presbyterian Church, Schaeffer and his wife, Edith, had made their way to Switzerland as missionaries. In 1955, they founded L'Abri, a retreat center in the Swiss Alps designed to attract students and other searchers. Schaeffer soon became known among evangelicals for his interest in art, literature, and music. He welcomed all sorts of people to L'Abri—European backpackers, earnest American college students, dropouts, believers, and seekers. Schaeffer didn't care if his visitors had long hair or declared themselves atheists. In fact, he seemed to relish both. More and more, evangelicals and others from Europe and the United States made L'Abri a destination, and it developed a cult-like status as a place of transnational conversation.

It was only when Schaeffer lectured at US college campuses, however, that he cemented his reputation as a daring challenger of evangelical cultural norms. Appearing for a brief tour in 1963, and a longer visit in 1965, he surprised and often thrilled audiences. Schaeffer was already more than fifty years old by the time he made his first trip, but he showed up dressed in Swiss lederhosen, with long hair and a beard—a striking figure made all the more so by his high-pitched voice and occasionally odd pronunciation.[18] Schaeffer used his lectures to make orthodox points about the dangers of relativism and humanism, but he did so by citing and then critiquing the work of artists such as Michelangelo and Picasso, and writers such as Henry Miller and Sartre. He discussed the films of Fellini, the poetry of Dylan Thomas, and the music of John Cage. His close associate Os Guinness described Schaeffer as "a door opener." He showed that "it was not only okay but right and proper and responsible, as a Christian, to understand the whole of life."[19]

Schaeffer was no liberal, either theologically or culturally. His goal was to engage secular Western culture in order to show its profound limits and failures. Only Christianity, he insisted, could provide a coherent and consistent worldview that could be lived without contradiction. But it was the engagement with culture as much as the orthodoxy of his teachings that enraptured his followers. As his son Frank would later describe his appeal (with some exaggeration): "In evangelical circles, if you wanted to know what Bob Dylan's songs meant, Francis Schaeffer was the man to ask. In the early 60s, he was probably the only fundamentalist who had heard of Bob Dylan."[20]

Schaeffer played fast and loose with his history and sometimes showed quite shallow understandings of the philosophies he critiqued. Years later, after Schaeffer had become a household name among evangelicals, one professor at Wheaton declared, "We . . . use Schaeffer as an example how *not* to do philosophy." His work, however, was both accessible and serious. In 1968, Schaeffer would publish two books that became blockbusters, *The God Who is There* and *Escape from Reason*.[21]

Schaeffer combined intellectualism with emotional intensity and cultural savoir faire. He embodied a culturally expansive and anti-technocratic spirituality, "a faith for all seasons that allowed for the supernatural in the quotidian and in all aspects of human experience."[22] Admittedly, there was little in any of his early books that spoke to politics. For the most part, his interest in international issues was limited to commentary on European museums. Still, many who became deeply interested in global politics in the sixties took from Schaeffer the message, as Guiness said, that Christians needed to "understand the whole of life."

Schaeffer thrilled students at Wheaton, but the vast majority of Christian young people were educated at secular institutions. And it was on those campuses that two of the most important post-war evangelical institutions emerged. InterVarsity Christian Fellowship and Campus Crusade were organized both to evangelize students and to serve those who were already believers. The two organizations were competitors, with distinctly different politics and cultural styles. Campus Crusade marked out the terrain on the Right of the political spectrum, while InterVarsity was more politically and culturally moderate. Crusade made anti-communism its calling card in the 1960s, along with a pared-down form of evangelism that was built on a little booklet, "Have You Heard of the Four

Spiritual Laws?" The pamphlet, which offered a very simple explanation of what was required to accept Jesus, soon became one of the most widely distributed evangelistic tools of all time. By 1970, Crusade had printed 25 million copies.[23]

Campus Crusade was part of a broader expansion of strongly conservative Christian institutions in the early 1960s. The right wing of white Protestantism was rapidly settling into a kind of respectability that had previously eluded it. White fundamentalists and evangelicals had "surged confidently into the mainstream comforts, suburban mores, and McCarthyite red scares of the 1950s," and with that came growth. Carl McIntire's radio network had grown from one to five hundred stations over the course of six years. The Christian Anti-Communist Crusade organized rallies around the country, with featured speakers that included Pat Boone, John Wayne, and Ronald Reagan. The *Christian Crusade*, published by the far-Right Billy James Hargis, doubled its circulation.[24]

InterVarsity was larger and had a broader base than Campus Crusade. The group had begun in the United States in 1939 (it had been founded in Britain). It endorsed a theologically conservative statement of faith that asserted the usual tenets of evangelical belief: the authority of the Bible, the necessity of the death of Jesus to bring about salvation, the literal resurrection, and the promise of the Second Coming. The organization was focused on converting and then strengthening the faith of college students, as well as encouraging them to consider becoming missionaries. InterVarsity had grown significantly in the 1950s and early 1960s, despite various internal crises and staff turnover. There were chapters of IVCF on hundreds of campuses. The group began publishing *HIS* magazine in 1941, and by the 1950s the magazine had become a sounding board for emerging concerns about racism, missionary colonialism, war, and gender. In 1947, IVCF started its own publishing company, which grew slowly. *HIS* magazine, however, blossomed. It had a circulation of ninety thousand by the early 1970s. As time went on, InterVarsity Press tried to polish its image to compete with secular publishers, developing better cover designs and more outlets for sales. In the late 1960s, it even developed a hippie-styled "underground" paper to advertise its books, *The (Lit) Pusher*. In 1967 and 1968, the press really took off when it published Francis Schaeffer's first two books. Over the coming years, InterVarsity Press would publish fourteen of Schaeffer's twenty-two books. With Schaeffer's sales, and those of Paul Little's *How to Give Away Your Faith*, InterVarsity Press quickly became a major player in the nation's blossoming evangelical publishing industry.[25]

InterVarsity was a touchstone, a decentralized organization that brought college students together to live their faith. The organization remained almost entirely white, although there were chapters at a number of historically black colleges, and a few African American and Asian American staff. Students in IVCF read the Bible, but they also read Albert Camus or perhaps Richard Wright in their college classes. They might watch staid movies about Paul Carlson's Congo martyrdom at a Sunday night youth group meeting, but some of them also watched *The Graduate* and *Who's Afraid of Virginia Woolf?* The majority of evangelical students were distinctly more conservative than the average college student in terms of style or sexual mores, and unquestionably opposed to any form of moral or religious relativism, but they were no less interested than their secular counterparts in the problem of relevance and the possibility of transformation.

The intellectual foment among young people was shot through with emotion as well: a longing for intensity, and the intense longing to *matter*. By the late 1960s, InterVarsity was also feeling the effects of the charismatic renewal that was sweeping the country. In 1960, an Episcopal priest in Southern California had begun talking about the "baptism in the Holy Spirit" that was happening in his church, even though Episcopalians were as far from the Pentecostal tradition, theologically and sociologically, as one could get. Over the next few years, both Protestant and Catholic churches felt the impact of such spirit-filled worship, which usually involved ecstatic and conspicuous expressions of religious experience. People who identified with the renewal movement were "not doing anything crazy," one wry commentator told *Christianity Today*. "They just glowed like little light bulbs."[26]

In 1963 *Time* magazine reported the emergence of speaking in tongues (glossolalia) among a group of students at Yale, mostly members of InterVarsity. They came from several denominations, including one Catholic student. *Time* called it a "spontaneous outpouring of syllables that sound like utter babble to most listeners." It sounded sometimes like Hebrew and sometimes like "unkempt Swedish."[27]

The national InterVarsity leadership was not particularly happy when those Yale students made the news in 1963. Most of the staff and board members came out of a Reformed tradition that was suspicious of excessive displays of emotion, but InterVarsity's interdenominational spirit required openness to multiple faith traditions. Just after the *Time* article, Charles Troutman, InterVarsity's general director, wrote a memo to IVCF staff that admitted the obvious: "increasingly and inevitably Inter-Varsity is being drawn into one of the modern expressions of a healing-tongue-prophecy movement." This was putting it mildly. By 1967, a number of InterVarsity chapters had split over the question of just how the Holy Spirit should be manifest.[28]

The charismatic movement was especially attractive to the younger generation, which felt their religious upbringing had been "dead" or legalistic. Building on the traditions of Pentecostal churches such as the Assemblies of God and Church of God in Christ, it reached into mainstream churches to touch all ages. Even Southern Baptists were affected. The denomination staunchly held to the view that miracles and indwellings of the Holy Spirit had ended with the original apostles, but many of its members were deeply influenced by the passionate forms of worship, if not the specific act of speaking in tongues.[29]

By the middle of the 1960s, InterVarsity's triennial Urbana convention had become something of a barometer for the changes taking place in evangelical cultural and political life. Those changes were conspicuous at the 1967 convention. InterVarsity's members showed up and acted like the *young* Christians they were: they questioned authority, debated the problems with "traditional" missionary attitudes, and called attention to racism and sexism. The 9,200 delegates seemed caught between deference to the older guard of evangelical leaders and their own, off-stage political consciousness. Concerns about American arrogance and the history of racism were pervasive, and global political upheaval was on everyone's minds. It had been just a few years since Arthur Glasser had encouraged students to "read a weekly newsmagazine," but now the Urbana participants showed up knowledgeable and ready to talk about the world. They were anxious to learn from the missionary and evangelical luminaries who spoke from the platform, but they also had their own ideas.

HIS reported that "little escaped criticism at the convention." The students challenged the speakers with questions about Vietnam, race, and civil disobedience. "They focused their most scathing indictment on their home churches," arguing that "the church [they know] is rigid, stereotyped, impervious to new ideas, resistant to change, without freedom and experimentation . . . It does not call God's people to face responsibility for the harsh realities of today's world."[30] A young man named Evan Adams, who had just joined InterVarsity's staff a few years before, told a story that was emblematic of the mood at the convention, the hostility toward church-as-usual:

I was [at a church] visiting a friend. The topic assigned for the speaker was 'Viet Nam in Prophecy.' Viet Nam in prophecy? How about Viet Nam in history? Aren't we facing Viet Nam today? In the balcony behind the speaker were about fifty college and high school students. Here were students who wanted to know about Viet Nam, students who might have to register with the Draft Board next week. And the speaker was speaking about Viet Nam in prophecy. He was having quite a job finding Viet Nam in the Old Testament.[31]

IVCF was not immune from these critiques, which began with the conference theme: "God's Men—From All Nations to All Nations." Women delegates protested the obvious sexism and the complete absence of any female speakers from the stage. It was a glaring omission at an event that supported missionary work. Evangelical women had enlisted in striking numbers as missionaries and were the backbones of missionary support organizations.[32] Now they were also calling for a seat on the dais. The men who dominated InterVarsity and the evangelical movement overall had not seemed the least bit interested in such demands. The quiet—and sometimes not so quiet—sexism of their assumptions about leadership, bravery, and pastoral calling meant that women would not easily be acknowledged beyond their roles as supporters.

African American students and staff also protested the lack of attention to domestic racism. One statement read from the floor pointed out that there were "no black men in leadership positions on the national staff."[33] There were *African* speakers at Urbana, as had been the case since the early days, but no African American speakers, male or female. After an all-night prayer meeting, the two hundred black students in attendance presented a list of demands for major changes in how IVCF reached out to African

Americans. With political tensions running high, InterVarsity staff regularly guarded the steps to the speakers' platform, to keep students from running onstage to give their own messages to the crowd.[34]

With all this energy, there was still little direct discussion of the two international issues that were much in the news: Vietnam and the Arab-Israeli war of the previous June. In fact, the speaker who perhaps had the most to say about international and political issues at Urbana 67 never mentioned them directly. John Stott, a British Anglican priest with evangelical sympathies, gave a series of four talks on the Apostle Paul's second letter to Timothy. Just as Paul, writing from a prison cell, exhorted Timothy to be strong for the gospel, Stott told the students that they must expect to suffer for the sake of their faith, and that their suffering—their willingness to endure hardship and toil, and their full commitment to the gospel at whatever price—was Jesus's command.

Stott's analysis echoed the writings of Dietrich Bonhoeffer, the German Lutheran theologian who had been executed in 1945 for plotting to kill Hitler. Bonhoeffer's *Cost of Discipleship*, published in the United States in 1959, was influential at seminaries across the Protestant spectrum. Bonhoeffer had argued against what he called "cheap grace." He believed that Christian faith required giving up all that had come before and practicing "single-minded obedience" to the radical demands of Jesus. Bonhoeffer had sacrificed his own life when he gave up the chance to escape Germany because it would have put others in danger. He was executed not long after. His martyrdom sanctified his theological argument about the radical relevance of faith for the world. By the 1960s, US Christians from a broad range of denominations were likely to know at least the basics of Bonhoeffer's story. The "cost of discipleship" had almost become a catchphrase, and "costly grace" a motto. Stott knew, then, that at least some of the participants at Urbana were likely to understand his implicit reference to Bonhoeffer. "Never expect your Christian service to cost you nothing," he told the students. "Christian service is a costly thing."[35]

The students were riveted by Stott's argument. It was as if, commented *HIS*, they realized that in their churches they had been given "a simplistic picture" of the Christian life as always a happy one.[36] The fact that "relevance" seemed so intimately tied to persecution was indicative of the multiple registers of suffering. A sense of persecution had operated as part of the idealization of missionaries in Congo. Here, the invocation of suffering was a gesture toward relevance for ordinary young Christians and a critique of the simplistic pieties of the well-to-do.

The two hundred African American attendees at Urbana 67 had pushed InterVarsity to support a more substantive discussion of black issues at the next conference, as well as a significant increase in African American participants. One of the students, Elward Ellis, helped to develop a recruitment film titled *What Went Down at Urbana 67*. Featuring the voices of black students speaking to other students about why Urbana 70 would be the place to address hard questions, the twenty-one-minute film was part political commentary, part hipster conclave, and part earnest pitch for missions.[37]

What Went Down begins with a close-up of a man playing a conga drum, then cuts to quick images of news photos: a black man facing a white mob; a soldier; a poster that says "Remember Brother Malcolm." Other images follow: students—black and white—protesting; a button reading "Free Huey"; another, "Help Biafra Now." The drum sounds continue. Images flash of the Vietnam War, with peasants crying as their houses burn and a young soldier being brought in, injured, on a gurney. The drums pick up pace, and the images slow down: there are poor children, shots of Ho Chi Minh, hippie protestors, and a globe, broken in half. The photos come fast, some in color, many in black and white. They include newspaper stories, political cartoons, photos from protests—iconic images of the moment. Scrolling through, backed by the beat of the drum, with the opening credits interspersed, these pictures tell one story: relevance.

The drumming ends, and a young man's voice asks: "Interested in Solutions? Come to Urbana 70." Anticipating skepticism, the camera cuts to a young man in an Afro and a jean jacket. "Can you be serious?" he asks. Elward Ellis comes on screen, in a loose dashiki, and says, yes, he is serious. It's time for Christians to understand God's program for the 1970s.

What Went Down sets the terms of black Christian engagement. To be a black Christian in the current moment, it says, is to address the social and political problems of the world. The longing to learn about God's plan for the world is linked to the need for missions— and to criticism of them. The film includes conversations with white students, international attendees at Urbana, and speakers of various backgrounds, but at its heart is a set of staged discussions among black students, representing a variety of opinions about politics and black Christianity and missions. The tone is set early on when one young man says to the camera: "Dig it: Mission isn't nothing but Christian racism." Subsequent scenes and conversations challenge that view.

Ellis introduces the audience to a group he describes as "some very hip black students" who are talking in a campus lounge. One person says that Christian missionaries have aligned themselves with neocolonial attitudes. A young man agrees, but thinks there is more to the story. Dressed in a fashionable combination of turtleneck and leather jacket, this quietly authoritative student says that black people need to understand their own role; there are places where others might not be heard, but black missionaries would be. "We should do it," another woman says, "We are black . . . We accept them and we accept ourselves." A young man in a Van Dyke beard puts it more bluntly: "A black man should go out and preach the gospel the way it *should* be and not with this honkified way of preaching the gospel."

The film goes on but the point has been made. Young black Christians care about the world. They care about politics. They do not care about a "honkified" gospel, but they do care about Jesus's commands. Urbana was a place to talk about all of those things.

In 1970, the Urbana conference—as spectacle, performance, and conflict zone— reached a fever pitch (figure 3.2). A year before the convention, *HIS* magazine had

FIGURE 3.2 Urbana 70 with Soul Liberation, © Urbana 70, InterVarsity's 9th Student Missions Conference.

published a near-despairing complaint that evangelical churches were once again failing to speak to real-world problems.

> The average churchgoer would not know, from what he hears in church, that we're engaged in a war in Vietnam, that peace talks are underway in Paris, that people are starving by the thousands in Biafra, that the Middle East is a ticking time bomb that could destroy the world, that students have been rioting in numerous colleges and universities, that the problems of our cities are not being solved, that local elections are taking place that may deeply affect his community, or that a new administration is discovering the complexities of making a government work.[38]

Urbana made sure that students knew.

Participation increased by more than a third, to twelve thousand, in 1970. Under the theme of "Christ the Liberator," a series of speakers denounced racism, colonialism, and the generally self-satisfied attitude of the North American church. Perhaps the most potent symbol of change involved who was *not* there: for the first time in Urbana's history, Billy Graham was not invited to speak. Younger evangelicals had made clear how disturbed they were by Graham's close associations with Richard Nixon, as well as his frequent "honor America" homilies. As the liberal *Christian Century* commented, with some satisfaction, many at Urbana believed that "Graham has sold his soul for a mess of prestige."[39]

No part of the event, from the hippie-style typeface of the program book to the selection of music, seemed untouched by the determination to render evangelicalism relevant. Speakers insisted that American evangelicals needed to think about structural inequality, stop trying to tell people in the rest of the world how to define their faith, and instead examine their own privilege in a system of oppression. The rhetoric of liberation—from sin, oppression, racism—was everywhere. Samuel Escobar, one of the leading evangelical thinkers in Latin America, gave an impassioned and often angry speech that called for evangelicals to develop a new concept of "sin," one that took political issues seriously. Escobar was on the staff of the International Fellowship of Evangelical Students, a group associated with InterVarsity. He had begun a sustained move to the Left at the Berlin Congress on World Evangelism in 1966. "When I came to Berlin, I heard Mike Cassidy from South Africa talking about obstacles to evangelism, and he mentioned apartheid as one of the obstacles." This inspired Escobar as he struggled in the increasingly radicalized environment in Latin America. In fact, just weeks before Urbana 70, Escobar had helped to found the Fraternidad Teológica Latinoamericana (FTL), the Latin American Theological Fraternity, in opposition to what Latin American evangelicals saw as the continuing paternalism of the North American church. Once again, the global networks of evangelicalism made intellectual and theological connections across national borders: A speech by South Africa's Michael Cassidy at a conference in Berlin, where Cassidy had met a key African American leader, had inspired a Peruvian, who would go on to castigate young Americans at Urbana.[40]

Escobar told his audience that most evangelicals were in "middle-class captivity" and so couldn't see outside their own comforts to the needs of others. Escobar argued that racism, greed, and oppression of the poor were as serious and damning as personal sin. To make his point, he turned to two theorists who in all likelihood had never been invoked positively at Urbana—or any other evangelical conference:

> Marx and Marcuse describe adequately the way in which money, power or lust have spoiled our Western societies. They wouldn't call it sin. We know what it is. But they have detected the depths of injustice with far more realism and acuteness than the average preacher who should know more about it.[41]

Clearly, what Americans were hearing—what they wanted to hear—was changing, at least for some. Escobar's workshop on "Social Concern and the Gospel" was one of the most popular at the conference, drawing 1,050 students.[42]

The fight against racism, both domestic and international, was arguably the emotional heart of Urbana 70. Speaker after speaker pronounced that no one could live a committed Christian life without opposing racial injustice. This time there were more than six hundred African American students at the meeting, two African American speakers on the platform, and an African American band (cleverly named Soul Liberation) replacing the "reverent" folk singers of three years before.

The second night of the program featured Tom Skinner, a youthful African American evangelical fast on his way to becoming a leading voice of theologically conservative, politically radical black Protestantism (figure 3.3). Animated, provocative, and funny, Skinner enthralled the audience with his survey of the sins of white evangelicalism. Skinner was a former member of a gang called the Harlem Lords, and he gave his personal witness in classic evangelical style, describing a move from a harsh life of violence to new life in Jesus. But Skinner also insisted that the church had failed him, indeed had failed black people in general. In the black community, he said, it had *not* been evangelicals who came to the cities and taught that "black is beautiful."

Like many others who were looking to "take back" the evangelical church, Skinner saw empowered masculinity as a cure for the sins of racism. He explained that the church had pushed away young men like him by offering up an effete Jesus—white and middle-class—who could not have survived a day in Skinner's neighborhood. But Skinner thought this was wrong. Jesus was "nobody's sissy": "he was a gutsy, contemporary, radical revolutionary, with hair on his chest and dirt under his fingernails."[43]

Skinner argued that following such a "radical revolutionary" meant giving up any claim to nationalism, any commitment to the status quo. Being a Christian meant not

FIGURE. 3.3 Tom Skinner. © Urbana 70, Intervarsity's 9th Student Missions Conference.

just challenging the racism of slavery or the problems of black neighborhoods, he said, but recognizing the global system of oppression and one's own place in it. "I disassociate myself from any argument, which says that God sends troops to Asia, that God is a capitalist, that God is a militarist, that God is the worker behind our system."[44]

Skinner was far from alone. In 1964, the black nationalist poet and playwright Amiri Baraka had written: "These are the last days of the American empire." For African Americans to love America, Baraka had insisted, was to become "equally culpable for the evil done to the rest of the world."[45] In fact, Skinner was speaking in a language of black radicalism that had emerged from secular thinkers and activists, even from people identified with the Nation of Islam, as Baraka was. Skinner was tossing his audience into an intellectual stream that was all but alien to evangelical pieties. At the end of his thirty-minute speech, the InterVarsity audience jumped to its feet, applauding wildly.[46]

The political and spiritual visions expressed at Urbana were indicative of changes in the evangelical movement overall. InterVarsity was one site where those changes were lived with particular self-consciousness and urgency: there were more interdenominational ties; more attention to social issues; the rise of an evangelical Left, albeit a small one, with a focus on racism and neo-colonialism; and, yet still, a near absence of attention to gender. But the organization stood on the liberal side of a conservative spectrum, and its changes did not go unnoticed. Shortly after Urbana, Tom Skinner's radio program was dropped from Moody Bible Institute's radio station. His messages were "too political."[47]

Indeed, although they were influential and visible, it is important to recognize that evangelical Leftists or even liberals were a minority voice. Even students were often supportive of the US role in Vietnam, as would become apparent in 1972, when 85,000 students, most in high school, gathered for Campus Crusade's "Explo '72." There, they listened to sermons and exhortations about evangelizing, but organizers also read to the participants a friendly telegraph from Richard Nixon. During a procession of international flags, they gave a standing ovation to the flag of South Vietnam.[48]

Over the next few years, however, evangelical critiques of race, missions, domestic poverty, and stultifying materialism would proliferate. These often accompanied an internal critique of the faith itself, as evangelicals—not all of them young—criticized its whiteness, emotional deadness, and irrelevance.

A self-identified evangelical Left became more visible and organized in the early 1970s. Most of those activists focused on anti-racism, poverty, and the Vietnam War. In 1971, a group of young radicals led by Jim Wallis started the slyly titled magazine, the *Post-American*. The shocking cover of its first issue was a picture of Jesus on a cross; the cross was covered in an American flag. Unlike much of the evangelical Left, the *Post-American* was deeply invested in foreign policy issues, particularly Vietnam. And Wallis did not pull punches. "A vote for Richard Nixon," he warned, "is a vote for the spread of Americanism as a missionary religion." Such a vote would ratify a national self-righteousness defined by aggression, arrogance, and imperialism.[49]

The National Black Evangelical Association became more radical after 1969. The young theologian James Cone published *Black Theology and Black Power* in 1970, and soon "black theology" became one of the most influential theological movements of the late twentieth century. It influenced the thinking of mainline Protestant theologians, black and white, in the United States and abroad. In the mid-1970s, the AME church would issue a position paper that strongly supported the idea of a black theology, arguing that "our quest for the liberation ethic and strategy can be realized only through radical identification with the dispossessed Black masses." Those masses would include people suffering everywhere, but "especially in Africa, South America, and the Caribbean."[50]

The Jesus movement emerged as another form of countercultural Christianity in the late 1960s and early 1970s. Innovative pastors founded churches that didn't police hair, beards, or clothing and that worshipped with contemporary music and accessible sermons. Chuck Smith's Calvary Chapel in Costa Mesa, California, for example, welcomed all comers and conducted baptisms in the Pacific Ocean. The church developed an inventive music program that eventually led to the founding of Maranatha Music, the iconic company that launched scores of contemporary Christian rock stars. The Jesus movement embraced an experiential faith, gathering for music and conversation in the new Christian coffeehouses that dotted the landscape. Jesus himself was viewed as both a friend and as "the true guide for a complete, authentic, and fulfilling life."[51] The movement was, as the *New York Times* put it, "youth culture at prayer."[52]

Theologically, however, Jesus people were usually conservative. Leaders were Biblical literalists. Smith himself was an ordained minister in the Church of the Foursquare Gospel, the Pentecostal denomination founded by Aimee Semple McPherson.[53] Participants held to a typical evangelical personal moral code—no drinking, drugs, or extramarital sex. But they maintained their countercultural ties in personal style. In fact, they were the front line of what would ultimately become one of the most profound transformations in American evangelical life in the late twentieth century: the move toward a more charismatic and expressive form of religious practice.

The Jesus people had passion and urgency, which was evident in demands to end the war in Vietnam, the fearful immediacy of end-times prophecy, and the quotidian imperative of saving souls.[54] Yet despite those statements opposing Vietnam, which by the late 1960s were no longer the province of radicals, the Jesus movement was surprisingly apolitical. These churches mostly saw the answer to social problems as a "real revolution" through acceptance of Jesus. The *Hollywood Free Paper*, steeped in the countercultural aesthetic, presented Jesus-first messages in a combination of New Leftist, Black Power, and psychedelic styles. One poster mimicked the Black Panther slogan "All power to the people," adding that "all power" would come "thru Jesus," who was the "one way" to third world liberation.[55]

By the early 1970s, political issues, both domestic and international, were straining the evangelical community. The war in Vietnam, US imperial reach more broadly, as well as racism, sexism, global poverty, American wealth, and evangelical complacency, all became points of contention. These issues didn't "break up" evangelicalism, which had always been a network-in-motion. But they changed the connections and the nature of dissent among evangelicals globally. Before long, American evangelicals would find themselves more deeply connected to evangelicals from Latin America, Africa, and Asia. But, first, significant numbers of evangelicals would find themselves galvanized by events in the Middle East.

4

"I Walked Today Where Jesus Walked"

CHRISTIANS AND THE FUTURE OF ISRAEL

IT WAS JUNE of 1967. Four days after the outbreak of war between Israel and three Arab states—four days into what was to be a war only six days long—the radio station run by the Moody Bible Institute hosted a discussion on "Bible prophecy and the Mid-East Crisis." Three Moody professors joined the panel to ponder what the war might signal. Was this the beginning of the end times?

One panelist, Alan Johnson, spoke of how relevant Bible prophecy felt. "Watching the Security Council meetings," he said, "I had opened before me chapters 38 and 39 of Ezekiel. It was quite an experience to read through these chapters as I listened to the various representatives of the concerned nations—including Israel and the surrounding Arab states. Many of these nations are mentioned in the Scriptures—if we understand the modern-day equivalents."[1] All the Moody professors agreed that, of course, it would be a mistake to think that believers could be sure about the prophetic significance of any given event. True, Israel now controlled Jerusalem, but it was impossible to know whether this control would be permanent. (It would be.)

Still, Jews were at the Wailing Wall for the first time since the founding of Israel. That was momentous. Was this the gathering of Israel back into its land, the return that was described in scripture with such ecstatic expectation? Was the "time of the Gentiles" now coming to an end? Nelson Bell thought it was certainly possible. The executive editor of *Christianity Today* wrote in July 1967 that the Israeli takeover of Jerusalem "gives a student of the Bible a thrill and a renewed faith in the accuracy and validity of the Bible. . . . If we say, as the Arabs do, that Israel has no right to exist, we may prove blind to her destiny under the providence of God."[2]

For most evangelicals (and many other Americans) interest in events in the Middle East quickened considerably with the 1967 war, although that interest neither started nor ended there. For some, the war was the culmination of two decades of thinking about Israel in biblical prophecy, beginning before its founding in 1948 and continuing right up to the short and shocking victory in 1967. But it was not the case that every evangelical viewed Israel in terms of biblical prophecy. In fact, there were many theologically conservative Protestants who made it to 1967 without thinking too much about Israel at all. For others, Israel was of interest primarily as a place to be visited, a tourist mecca, a historical site where the Bible came alive.

Whatever the 1967 war said about prophecy, it did bring one clear on-the-ground change for Americans. Holy Land tours would now include all of Jerusalem and Bethlehem, facilitated by Israel's rapidly expanding tourist infrastructure. Traveling to the Holy Land was a common practice even before 1967. It was an intensive, tactile form of encountering the "places where Jesus walked." After 1967, that travel would become easier, and it would take on a more specifically political character.

Prophecy-watching and Holy Land travels were central to American evangelicals' relationship to Israel. For prophecy watchers, Jerusalem and the Holy Land were deeply important as the center of a promised, redemptive future, where the terrible war of Armageddon would bring about the Second Coming of Jesus. For them, Israel mattered because of the way it closed the circle, from God's initial covenant with the Israelites in the Old Testament to His future return to His chosen people in the end times. For Christian travelers, on the other hand, it was the past that mattered: Israel and the Holy Land were physical embodiments of biblical history—the places where Abraham was buried, where Jesus had walked.

For evangelicals in the 1960s and 1970s, then, Israel was both a place and a time. They might encounter it as a biblical homeland and a living past or as a vacation destination; as a regional ally or as a future site for prophecy's fulfillment. After the 1967 war these multiple investments led to the emergence of an enthusiastic evangelical bloc with an activist pro-Israel politics. That bloc was not populated exclusively by conservatives. Within a decade of the war, love of Israel would transcend many of evangelicalism's political divides.

For most of the twentieth century, discussions of Bible prophecy were largely associated with dispensational premillennialism. First introduced by the Irish evangelist John Darby in the nineteenth century, this approach offered a dark view of the present and an anxious-yet-anticipatory belief that Armageddon was impending. Darby's model was "premillennial" in that it argued Christ must return to earth before the thousand-year reign of peace predicted in the Bible could begin. It was "dispensational" in that it postulated that world history was divided into "dispensations"—periods under which God worked in history through specific groups of people. Each of these groups had a covenant with God for the period of their dispensation. Different interpreters held differing views about the number and character of the dispensations; their estimates ranged from as few as three to as many as seven. Most agreed, however, that God had acted in history first through the Jews, then through the Church ("the Church Age"); and in the future, during the "end times," God would work through the Jewish people again.

Darby's most influential American convert was Dwight Moody. Moody founded the Moody Bible Institute in 1889 and established the school as a lodestar for prophecy-oriented fundamentalists. (The school was also a recruiting hub for evangelical missionaries, "the self-proclaimed West Point of Christian Service."[3]) The school's publication, *Moody Monthly,* was a popular source for biblical commentary and prophecy interpretation. Moody himself was well known for holding the view that the current dispensation, the "church age," was rapidly coming to an end. "I look on this world as a wrecked vessel," he famously said. "God has given me a life boat and said to me, 'Moody, save all you can.'"[4]

The most important text for prophecy interpreters was the *Scofield Reference Bible.* Published in 1909, it combined the text of the King James Bible with annotations by C.I. Scofield that highlighted prophetic passages, offering specific explanations for them. According to Scofield, the Bible's mention of a place called "Gog, the land of MaGog," referred to a specific location on a map, and Revelation's mention of seven plagues described real events that were to come. For believers, this meant that while the world might be a "wrecked vessel," you couldn't just write it off in the expectation of heavenly peace. The political machinations of worldly powers, the "wars and rumors of wars," were key to understanding just how God's plan would unfold at the end of days.

Although there were (and are) many disagreements—schools within schools of prophecy interpretation—most dispensationalists concurred that a specific series of events would occur before the Second Coming. A key signal would be the return of Jews to Jerusalem. As the end times approached, an Antichrist would arise, claiming to bring peace. At some point, Christians would be lifted into heaven in an event called the Rapture. After the Rapture (or perhaps before), the Antichrist would oversee seven years of "tribulation"—economic crisis, natural disasters, and suffering. Sometime during this period, Jews would rebuild the Jewish Temple in Jerusalem. Almost everyone agreed that when God showed His hand and the truth of the Christian Bible's prophecies were revealed, there would be mass conversion of Jews, who would recognize Jesus as their Messiah. At the end of the tribulation, Israel, threatened by a confederacy of most of the nations of the world, would face down her enemies in the final, terrible battle of Armageddon, during which Christ himself would return to fight for Israel. Afterward, the millennial reign of one thousand years of peace would begin.[5]

In this worldview, Israel was a time as much as a place. Place did matter: The battle of Armageddon would happen in the area of Har Megiddo (meaning Mount Megiddo, known as Tel Megiddo in modern Israel); Christ would certainly return to Jerusalem. But Israel mattered because it marked the future. It was the place where God would come full circle, returning to the holy city of the people He had chosen at the dawn of time.

For much of the twentieth century, this view of the end times was taught primarily at a number of fundamentalist institutions that were part of the Bible College movement. There was Moody, as well as the Bible Institute of Los Angeles (BIOLA), founded in 1908 with the backing of a wealthy oilman. The most important was Dallas Theological Seminary (DTS), founded in 1924. DTS would become a powerhouse of dispensationalism, attracting important fundamentalist theologians and producing generations of students shaped by them. The school ultimately became something of a headquarters for those who resisted the neo-evangelical accommodations of the 1950s and 1960s.[6]

Many international students attended DTS. They came on scholarship from all over the world and took the DTS theology back home with them. In this way, DTS eventually became one of the most important transnational institutions of conservative evangelical life. Byang Kato, a Nigerian intellectual who had spoken out for a conservative vision at Urbana 70, received his doctorate at DTS. Upon his return to Nigeria from Dallas, Kato was elected the first African president of the Association of Evangelicals in Africa and Madagascar. Kato's dissertation, published as *Theological Pitfalls in Africa*, was extremely influential. In that book and elsewhere, Kato supported a fundamentalist theology in the context of arguing for stronger theological training for Africans that would include adapting the gospel to local conditions.[7]

Tokunboh Adeyemo, who also got his doctorate from DTS, would become one of the most influential African evangelicals of his generation. Adeyemo was the author of more than ten books and editor of the massive *Africa Bible Commentary*, for which he also wrote an analysis of the end times prophecies in the book of Daniel. Adeyemo also served as general secretary of the Association of Evangelicals in Africa for more than twenty-five years, as well as chancellor of the Nairobi Evangelical Graduate School of Theology (now Africa International University)—a training ground for conservative Christians throughout Africa.[8]

Premillennialism was also an important tenet of the Pentecostal movement. Although Pentecostals were less likely than some others to codify their interpretations, the Azuza Street movement of the early twentieth century included a conviction that Jesus was coming soon and that the indwellings of the spirit they were experiencing were also signs of the end times. Pentecostals founded their own Bible institutes, including Aimee Semple McPherson's LIFE Bible College in Los Angeles (1923) and the Assembly of God's Central Bible College in Missouri (1922).[9]

One important exception to this dispensationalist tsunami in fundamentalist education was Wheaton College, which did not teach dispensationalism as a core principle. Similarly, the prestigious and conservative Princeton Theological Seminary was non-dispensationalist, although it united with dispensationalists in their critiques of modernist theology.[10]

As dispensationalists gained authority, they developed their own web of supporting institutions, not just Bible institutes but also conferences, publications, evangelistic agencies, and even missions programs. Dispensationalists remained present in many denominations and their seminaries, especially in the South; they were quite powerful in the Southern Baptist Convention. Over time, they developed what historian George

Marsden has called "an informal dispensationalist denomination" that was superimposed on other denominations, missions programs, and parachurch structures.[11]

Starting in the 1930s, American evangelicals began to pay close attention to what was happening to Jews in Europe and in the British territory of Palestine. No less a luminary than Harold Ockenga had looked at events in Europe in the early 1930s and described the rising persecution of the Jews as part of God's plan. Ockenga (who was still a pastor in Pittsburgh, on the cusp of joining the staff of Park Street Church in Boston, where he would become a renowned pastor and author) had toured Europe and returned to preach about the prophetic implications of what he saw. "Hitler does not know it, but he is an instrument in the hand of God for the driving of the Jews back to Palestine."[12] Ockenga's belief in the basics of the premillennialist timeline led him (and many others) toward political commentary, not away from it.

The founding of Israel only fueled the enthusiasm for prophecy interpretation.[13] This was surely the ingathering of Jews that marked the beginning of the end times. For a few prophecy interpreters, however, Israel's creation was initially a stumbling block. Many prophecy analysts had expected that Jews would take control of the Holy Land again only after they had come to believe in Jesus as the Messiah. The fact that they were returning instead "in unbelief" gave pause. But most simply embraced the new state. "A million Jews are on the move," the *Pentecostal Evangel* proclaimed with delight. "They are coming from Moslem lands, and from Holland, France, and Belgium, as well as from Eastern Europe. The world is witnessing the fulfillment of the ancient promise in Jeremiah 31:10: 'He that scattereth Israel will regather him.'"[14] William Culberson of the Moody Bible Institute later wrote that Israel's rebirth was "the most striking of all the signs" of an imminent Rapture.[15]

Evangelicals were not the only American Christians to welcome Israel enthusiastically. Mainline Protestants were divided. Missionaries to the Arab world often expressed a great deal of sympathy for Arab refugees and worried that US support for Israel would damage missions. Other Protestants were concerned about human rights violations and about what they perceived as the militarism of the new state. The liberal *Christian Century* wondered: "How long will Judaism, with its message of peace, continue to find satisfaction in believing that Israel is feared?"[16] But other Protestant leaders strongly supported Israel. Several of those supporters worked with Israel's Ministry of Religious Affairs to organize a 1949 trip for a number of prominent pastors, who saw the sights and met with Israeli leaders. The assumption, which turned out to be correct, was that pastors who received a warm welcome would return home to speak positively about Israel.[17]

Whether or not they believed the end was near, Americans were deeply interested in seeing the places where Jesus had walked and to which he would return—a place they believed to be the site of both Christian histories and Christian futures. After 1948, travel to the Holy Land carried a new kind of excitement and political energy.

Holy Land tourism was not new, of course. A fascination with the Holy Land had been a significant force in Protestant life since the nineteenth century, when church sermons and Bible studies were packed with information about the places in the Bible. By the 1850s hundreds of travelers were publishing accounts of their trips. The missionary William Thomason's *The Land and the Book* (1858) became a bestseller, as American Christians learned to think of the Holy Land as their heritage. By the late nineteenth century, "Holy Land mania" was widespread. Illustrated Bibles offered beautifully wrought images of Bible stories. Stereoscopes offered up three-dimensional photos viewed from a handheld viewfinder. In Chautauqua, New York, enthusiasts created a small-scale, walk-through model of the Holy Land.[18]

By the mid-twentieth century, travel to the Holy Land was much easier and cheaper than it had been a century earlier, although it was still a challenge. With jet airplanes, it was faster; travelers could enjoy trips that took only two weeks instead of five. And travel was cheaper: in 1925, a typical tour to the Holy Land cost 69 percent of the average income for an American family; by 1965, that had dropped to 11 percent.[19] Religious entrepreneurs, usually small local travel coordinators, played a central role in the rise in tourism to the region after 1948. These tourism companies were not major players individually, but they made a significant difference because they worked within "overlapping local networks" that funneled tourists into package trips. These small companies were not all evangelical—some of the innovators were Catholic—but evangelical tour companies acted as gateways, attracting pilgrims and then working with tour wholesalers to set up hotels, buses, and access to holy sites. Sometimes well-known church leaders from the United States served as guides—the tour operators called them "Pied Pipers" because they presumably brought their own stream of followers. More often, it was a lesser-known local minister who brought a group over and explained the biblical meanings of the places they visited, sometimes getting a free trip if he brought enough of his flock.[20]

However well organized the tours were, the political realities on the ground meant that even the simplest trips required visiting several countries. In 1959, the *Chicago Tribune's* foreign affairs correspondent offered a detailed account of the easiest way to enjoy the Holy Land on one's own. It was best to start in Beirut, he said, the "Middle East's San Francisco." Then take a car to Damascus, where you might enjoy the scenic markets. From there, get one of the flights that left from Damascus to Jerusalem each day—a "quick hop." On arriving at the Jordanian-controlled Old City of Jerusalem, one could visit the most important Christian sites—Bethlehem as well as the Mount of Olives and the Garden of Gethsemane (see figure 4.1). Then, the correspondent promised, an American tourist could get to the Israeli-occupied parts of the Old City fairly easily: "[he] can walk, carrying his baggage, thru Mandelbaum gate into Israel." The gate was not in fact a gate but a small road; "tall, concrete, anti-sniper screens line the gate, and troops guard both ends."[21]

The anti-sniper screens were exactly the kind of thing that most Holy Land tourists didn't want to think about as they enjoyed their nostalgic walk through the lands they had learned about in Sunday School. But, for some more intrepid travelers, part of the excitement of Holy Land trips before 1967 was the fact that they took place on contested terrain. The average evangelical tourist might not seem like

VISIT JORDAN

THE HOLY LAND

World travelers long since have learned that in Jordan they may expect to find Christianity's most revered shrines in old Jerusalem (below), in Bethlehem and Samaria, Jericho and Hebron. For here, indeed, are the pilgrim paths.

And others — as knowledgeable about antiquities — have found Jordan to be virtually an open-air museum, with famed sites like Jerash and Petra, Qumran and Karak. Arab, Greek, Roman and Crusader — all have left their mark to see.

Yet, as the International Tourist Year approaches, others are planning their Jordan holiday. They will relax on Red Sea and Dead Sea beaches, hunt for coral in the Aqaba Gulf, picnic in the Ajlun Forest, enjoy the cool delights of Ramallah and sightsee big city and charming village alike.

Jordan welcomes them all in 1967

Or any year!

▲

PETRA — The Siq and the Treasury
This immensely high and narrow gorge is the only entrance to Petra, and kept the Nabataean city safe against attacks for over a century, falling finally to Rome in 106 AD. The Treasury, glimpsed ahead through the dark slit of rock, is the most fabulously detailed and the best preserved of Petra's monuments . . . the statues, and carved detail have been defaced by man, not weather, as with most of the monuments. In sunlight the rock colour, as noted by Burckhardt who discovered Petra in 1812, " glows with a rosy dazzle ".

▶ General View of Jerusalem the old city from Mount o Olives, with the Dome of the Rock in the centre is surrounded by its beautiful crenellated stone walls.

FIGURE 4.1 Ad for Holy Land tourism, 1967. Courtesy of UN World Tourism Organization.

an adventurer: 70 percent were women older than fifty-five.[22] But one should not underestimate the church ladies. When a local Sunday school teacher returned from her visit to the Holy Land in 1956, the *Los Angeles Times* reported that her first trip abroad was "everything she hoped it would be, complete with storms on the ocean, seasickness . . . and enough international tension to give spice to her travels."[23] Certainly the border crossings, multiple modes of transportation, and "spicy" international tensions made such trips something quite different than, say, a bus tour through Scotland. The aura of danger, however slight, resonated with the broader Christian idealization of those who suffered for their faith.

Tourism mattered a great deal to both Israel and Jordan. It was the main source of foreign currency for Jordan and the second most important source for Israel, after citrus exports. In the 1950s, Israel averaged 47,000 tourists a year.[24] By 1966, it was more than 320,000. Jordan actually received significantly more visitors for general tourism, but many of them came from the Arab world and tended to spend less money during their trips.[25] In the early 1960s, Israel had begun to make a more concerted effort to attract Christian tourists from the United States and Europe, producing attractive ads, training local guides, and developing partnerships with airlines. It opened three tourism offices in the United States and five in other countries, and began to invite foreign journalists and travel agents for complimentary tours. The Ministry of Tourism organized public lectures, study seminars, window displays for travel agents, and film screenings.[26]

By the middle 1960s, "Pied Piper" tours had become more common as evangelical nonprofits got on board. World Vision, for example, hosted a number of Bible Lands tours led by theology professors. Ads for the tours promised a "life changing" experience.[27] And in 1966, a group of black Baptist pastors in New York state joined together to create Concreta Tour Service, designed to facilitate the travel of African American Christians to Rome, Israel, and divided Jerusalem. African American newspapers had long reported on the trips to the region taken by black Christians: a bishop of the Christian Methodist Episcopal church in Baltimore in 1966; a group of AME ministers from Chicago in 1958; an elderly woman from the Church of God in Chicago in 1960. There was every reason to believe that the African American Protestant market had yet to be fully tapped.[28]

In the early 1960s, a number of prominent evangelicals made their own excursions to the Holy Land—or, at least, to those holy sites controlled by Israel. In 1960, Billy Graham traveled to Israel at the invitation of the United Protestant Christian Council. Although the Israelis were officially welcoming, Graham's visit was a source of real concern. Just before his arrival, the *Jerusalem Post* remarked that Israeli Jews would not welcome any overt proselytizing. "Preaching Christianity to Jews has remained a sensitive area," the newspaper explained, "because over the centuries conversion was rarely a matter for individual feeling, but of yielding to intolerable social pressures." This was a rather understated explanation of the history of forced conversion in Europe, but the paper's comments made clear that Graham was facing some serious opposition. Government officials refused to allow the churches who sponsored his visit to rent a large hall in Tel Aviv, saying there might be violence if Graham tried to get "decisions for Christ" from the audience. Graham, making a quick appraisal of the situation, promised that he was in Israel to see the holy sites and to speak to Christian audiences, not to proselytize. Ultimately, Graham preached his unapologetically evangelistic message to an overflowing church in Tel Aviv, for an audience that *Time* estimated to be 70 percent Jewish, with no repercussions. Returning home, Graham, like many tourists before and after him, declared the visit to be one of "the most wonderful experiences of my life."[29]

That same year, Bill Bright, founder of Campus Crusade, had a rather different response to his tour. Complaining about commercialism and unfriendliness, Bright described his trip with unapologetic anti-Semitism: "[A]ll my old problems with Jews welled up again. I was so glad when the airplane flew out of Tel Aviv to Zürich." Later, Bright wrote: "I was so offended by the vendors, the peddlers, the people hawking their wares, the commercialism, that I determined that I would never return to Jerusalem."[30] Bright's views were perhaps not surprising. He was the head of a conservative evangelical organization funded in part by the founder of the John Birch Society, a group known for its anti-Semitism. But in complaining about commercialism, Bright was speaking to a broad concern among evangelicals, most of whom hoped to find a Holy Land that was familiar from childhood Bible studies. Israel's modernity was part of its appeal, but it would also be a consistent problem for evangelical tourists.

Then, in 1961, *Christianity Today* editor Carl Henry took his own ten-day tour of Israel. In a long six-part series on his trip, he meditated on the country and its meanings for evangelicals. He briefly discussed the prophetic relevance of Israel but turned quickly to events on the ground and the status of Christianity in Israel. Henry complained that the Israelis welcomed Christians, but only in certain capacities—as tourists, archaeological patrons, or missionaries to provide hospitals and schools.[31] Israel had, in his view, failed to adhere to proper (American) standards of religious freedom. According to Henry, one Israeli official had told him in no uncertain terms that "we don't believe in missionaries .... Let the Jews alone! Take your missionaries out! They threaten the stability of the nation and breed resentment!"[32] This, Henry implied, amounted to persecution of Christians, since evangelizing was a necessary part of their religious practice.

Henry's views of Israel were typical of a number of moderately conservative evangelicals in the early and mid-1960s, who were beginning to put aside the dispensationalist orientations of their fundamentalist past. Henry described himself as "broadly" premillennial, but he was determined that prophecy should take a back seat to thinking about the political, social, and theological questions that confronted evangelicals in daily life. Indeed, by the early 1960s, prophecy talk had been thoroughly marginalized by neo-evangelicals at places like Fuller Theological Seminary.[33] The project of unpacking prophecy had become something of a backwater for all but the most ardent enthusiasts, relegated to Dallas Theological Seminary classrooms and a few books of popularized prophecy interpretations.[34]

Then came the 1967 Arab-Israeli war. In May, longstanding tensions between Nasser's Egypt and Israel erupted into a full-blown crisis. Nasser asked for the removal of UN forces stationed at the border with Israel, a demand that some saw as paving the way for an Egyptian invasion. On June 5, Israel launched an attack that took out most of Egypt's air force in the first few hours. Syria and Jordan joined the battle, but in six days, the war was over, and Israel had gained territory from each of its adversaries: the Golan Heights (Syria), Sinai and Gaza (Egypt), and the West Bank and East Jerusalem (Jordan).

On the ground, Palestinian lives were once again transformed. People who had lived under Jordanian or Egyptian rule were now ruled by Israel. There were just under a million Arabs in the West Bank and Gaza in 1967. Many of them were still living in the refugee camps where they had moved after 1948. For the Israelis, the 1967 war was a victory. For the Palestinians, it was a disaster. They would live its consequences in a way that few American commentators, evangelical or otherwise, were inclined to acknowledge.[35]

For the first time, all of Jerusalem was under Jewish control. So was the rest of the West Bank, including the cities of Bethlehem and Jericho. The US evangelical press was aglow with enthusiasm. *Moody Monthly* had front-page coverage, devoting much of its October 1967 issue to the war. *Christianity Today* also celebrated the victory, and its readers joined in. One reader praised the magazine's coverage, saying that "[t]he prophetic clock of God is ticking while history moves inexorably toward the final climax. And as that clock ticks, the Christian believer lifts his head high, for he knows that a glorious redemption draws near."[36] Carl Henry mused that perhaps Israel's victory would open up more freedom for evangelization. Jerry Falwell, then a young minister in Lynchburg, Virginia, took the first of his many trips to the Holy Land shortly thereafter.[37]

Israel's victory fueled a wave of dispensational enthusiasm that soon swept up even the skeptical neo-evangelicals. After all, the folks at *Christianity Today* and the National Association of Evangelicals had never really been *against* prophecy; most of them were premillennialists, just not necessarily dispensationally-oriented or particularly zealous on the topic. In 1971 a remarkably diverse group of evangelicals gathered for the Jerusalem Conference on Biblical Prophecy. Spearheaded by none other than Carl Henry, the conference proved an impressive success, drawing 1,500 delegates from thirty-two nations. Attendees represented a broad range of denominations: there were Baptists and conservative Presbyterians and Seventh-day Adventists. Pentecostals were prominently included, symbolized in part by the performance of the Azuza College Choir.[38]

The event was welcomed by the Israeli government, which even provided the hall, an early example of what would become its long courtship of conservative evangelicals. As historian Paul Boyer points out, the Israeli leadership was not impressed by the intellectual content of evangelical prophecy talk, and privately "ridicule[d] the premillennialist readings of prophecy as those of a six-year-old child." But the Labor governments of the 1970s recognized the value of evangelicals as a political bloc and dealt with them accordingly. Israeli prime minister David Ben-Gurion greeted the guests. After his speech, the conservative Christian activist and actress Anita Bryant sang "I Walked Today Where Jesus Walked." Later, the attendees were entertained by the Jerusalem Symphony, as well as groups of Arab and Israeli schoolchildren.[39]

Looking back years later, some observers remembered the conference as an event that consolidated prophecy-oriented pro-Israel enthusiasm in the larger evangelical community. As one Seventh-day Adventist newsletter enthused, the gathering made clear that "the Protestant churches have come a long way since anyone . . . who preached prophecy was considered simplistic, speculative, and a theological non-person."[40] But the group gathered in Jerusalem was not at all in agreement about whether Israel's victory provided specific signs of the imminence of the Second Coming. Carl Henry managed to affirm how "awesome" it was to be part of the countdown to the final days, while offering up only the vague, tautological assurance that every passing day meant that the end was nearer than it had been the day before.[41]

John Stott, who had impressed students at Urbana 67 with his discussion of the centrality of suffering to the faith, expressed little interest in Israel's role in the Second Coming. He argued that it was the expansion of global missions, not the violence of global wars, that signaled the end times. Stott saw prophecy being fulfilled in the fact that the gospel was being spread to every nation. In Matthew, Jesus says that the gospel "will be preached in all the world and then the end will come" (Matt 24:14, KJV). "So what fills 'the last days,'" Stott told the audience, "is the mission of the church going out into the whole world in the power of the outpoured Spirit."[42] It was Christians going out to make converts, not Jews returning to make a nation, that would herald the Second Coming.

The war of 1967 transformed US tourism to the Middle East. Although there would be an overall decline in tourism in 1967 itself, tourists were surprisingly resilient, arriving as soon as Israel allowed, just a few weeks after the war. Israel's tourist companies had quickly realized what a boon the occupation of the West Bank would be. Within a month of the war's end, Israeli guides were venturing into the new territories. They "took the wrong roads, wandered mistakenly into strange quarters, and spent part of their time asking directions as they moved through Bethlehem and Jerusalem."[43] The control of those unfamiliar places would turn out to be quite lucrative as an avalanche of tourists and dollars began to flow into the region. The number of tourists increased from an average of 269,000 arrivals a year in the 1960s to 772,000 a year in the 1970s.[44]

The Israeli government moved quickly to encourage a sense that travel to Christian holy sites would now be protected by an umbrella of Jewish-Christian solidarity. The Israeli Government Tourist Office advertised in *Christianity Today,* promising evangelicals that "You won't need to buy a guidebook because you've already got the best one ever written."[45]

Eternity magazine, the organ of the Billy Graham Evangelistic Association, organized a Holy Land tour in 1969 led by the magazine's editor, Dr. Russell T. Hitt. The travel package was clearly a money-making proposition for the magazine (similar to the "Castles of Europe" tour the same year), but *Eternity* promised the trip of a lifetime. "No one who joins such a tour ever forgets the thrill of walking along the shores of Galilee or meditating at the Garden Tomb in old Jerusalem. Israel is the land of the Book with all its heroes and villains."[46] All of the holy sites could be offered in one package, with no borders to navigate, thanks to Israel's victory in the war. In *Christianity Today, World Vision, Moody Monthly,* and *Eternity,* and to a lesser degree the AME's *Voice of Missions* magazine, tour operators advertised trips that implicitly embraced Israeli control of holy sites as part of what made the visit luxurious and special. Already by the early 1970s, one reader of

Moody Monthly complained that "going to the Holy Land has become an obsession and a status symbol."[47]

When the right-wing Likud party came to power in 1977, Prime Minister Menachem Begin encouraged evangelicals of all stripes to travel to Israel and its occupied territories. The Ministry of Tourism increased its recruitment of evangelical leaders with "familiarization" tours that would encourage them to bring their flocks. Such church trips did indeed materialize, led by ministers from the Assemblies of God, the Southern Baptist Convention, and uncountable numbers of independent megachurches. One regular tour leader was Rev. Chuck Smith, pastor of Calvary Chapel in California. In the 1960s, Smith had been a hip pastor to the Jesus People, ordained in the Pentecostal Church of the Foursquare Gospel. He had developed a welcoming style and a following of young people who saw Jesus as a cultural radical. By the 1980s, Rev. Smith was teaching dispensationalist theology on frequent trips to Israel, where he was famous for mass baptisms. The Israelis allowed Smith to set up pedestrian barriers to mark the long lines of people waiting for him to baptize them in the River Jordan.[48]

Over time, the political value of Israel tours was increasingly apparent to both American evangelicals and the Israeli government. Those who traveled to the Holy Land often returned home feeling much more affection for the Israeli state as the keeper of the holy places. Organized tours were encouraged to use only Israeli ground transportation companies, and, after 1981, any group that used commercial transport (like a bus) was required to have a licensed tour guide. Prior to that, Palestinian tour guides had done fairly well; they had long experience working in East Jerusalem and Bethlehem when those areas were under Jordanian control, and they tended to have a good sense of the needs and sensibilities of US and European tourists. After the change in policy, the official guides were mostly Israeli Jews, though some were Palestinians with Israeli citizenship.[49]

Tourists were introduced to a nationalist Israeli perspective through the guides, whose training encouraged them to make strong ties between biblical history and the modern state of Israel. One guide in the mid-1980s led his group to the Temple Mount (Haram al-Sharif) and there read to them from the Bible about King Solomon's building of the first temple. The guide asked the group to lay their hands on the stones at the site and told them, "If anyone ever tells you the Jews don't have a right to this land, you tell them you touched these stones."[50]

The political power of tourism was made vividly apparent in 1980 when Bailey Smith, then president of the Southern Baptist Convention, made remarks that many Israelis and American Jews found deeply offensive. Smith was speaking before a gathering of ministers in Dallas when he commented disparagingly on the ecumenical trends of the major political parties: "It is interesting at great political rallies how you have a Protestant to pray, a Catholic to pray, and then you have a Jew to pray. With all due respect to those dear people, my friends, God Almighty does not hear the prayer of a Jew." That assertion set off a storm of criticism.[51] As Smith was being excoriated in the US media, Israeli officials and American Jews worked together to craft a response. Smith was immediately invited to come to Israel as a guest of the Israeli government, where he met with Israeli officials and saw the holy sites with Israeli guides. After his trip, Smith announced, "The bottom line is that you're going to read my name many times in the future in activities supporting the Jewish people and Israel."[52]

For some travelers, however, Holy Land tourism could be a let-down. The tours were designed to be emotionally rich experiences of reverence, but two issues consistently got in the way. The first was commercialism. The second was the highly visible Catholic and Orthodox occupation of religious sites. Both threatened the fine weave of Israel-Bible-America that most evangelical tours aimed to create.

After 1967, tourists were often offended and distracted by the commercialism of the places they visited. It wasn't that the tourists were surprised; Bill Bright was just one of many who had been complaining about the "hawking" of trinkets and the crowded religious sites. Still, evangelical tourists were frequently overwhelmed. Many people in Israel and the West Bank made their living off tourism: they sold souvenirs, proffered their service as guides, and garrulously greeted visitors as they walked by. The insistent sale of mementos at every venue, the expectation of tipping, the very fact of so many tourists like themselves crowding the spaces they imagined to be sites for religious experience—all of this was a source of frustration. "The Jordan River was like Disney World," one group of tourists complained. "As soon as you approach it you go through the gift shop, *of course*."[53]

This frustration was not unique to Israel. Tourist experiences are often shaped by the tensions between longings for authenticity and expectations of comfort and familiarity. A person who wants to buy souvenirs for family at home will nonetheless comment on the excessive selling of such souvenirs. A traveler who insists on a "decent hotel" will still search out a properly winding street that reflects their expectations of "Arabness." When the tourism is religious, the tensions are exacerbated. The search is for the timeless sacred, but the world is inhabited by humans and insistently changeable, and religious travelers view that with ambivalence. In the case of Israel, the sophistication of Israel's hotels and the often-touted capacities of its industry can be part of what charms visitors, as long as those things come along with views of olive groves and delicious tastes of hummus—a traditional Arab dish now imagined as an authentic Israeli one.[54]

Commercialism was a problem, but the more fundamental issue for many evangelicals was the fact that most of the Christian sites were run by Orthodox and Catholic churches that had long held primacy in Palestine. In 1963, Normal Vincent Peale found himself shocked by the ornateness and distinctly non-Protestant feel of the Church of the Nativity in Bethlehem. His group was so taken aback that they began to sing "O Little Town of Bethlehem" to "counteract the unsatisfying character of the place."[55] Indeed, sites run by Catholic and Orthodox churches were highly decorated and ritualized, in a style that was foreign to many evangelicals and which they found excessive. The Church of the Holy Sepulchre, built on what was said to be the site of Jesus's crucifixion and burial, was divided into six sections, each run by a different denomination. The interior was dark, rich in incense, the walls covered by images of Mary and Jesus that were often painted in distinctive styles. (The section of the church run by the Ethiopian Orthodox, for example, had very different images of Jesus than the section run by the Roman Catholic Church.) One nineteenth-century visitor had dismissed the church as one of the "puerile inventions of monkly credulity."[56] Late-twentieth-century evangelicals were more polite, but they often found the church uninspiring at best, more a matter of "selling religion" in one's own part of the church than of providing an uplifting religious space.

This dismissal was easier because most Protestants did not believe that the Church of the Holy Sepulchre was actually on the site of Jesus's crucifixion and burial. Skull Hill and the nearby Garden Tomb, which some nineteenth-century archaeologists had said were the likely places for Jesus's death, burial, and resurrection, fit more with evangelicals' idea of what an authentic biblical landscape should look like.[57]

> When you enter its gates, you are not ushered into a sacred shrine. There are no candles, no incense. Instead, you enter a mini paradise of majestic trees, luxuriant plants and beautiful flowers. If you glance to your left and below a small crag, you see a tomb carved by hand into large, smooth rock. There is no adornment to mark the spot and no fanfare to herald it.[58]

The possibility that this was the actual site of Jesus's crucifixion and/or burial was never strongly supported by archaeological evidence, but the location was accepted as authentic by many Anglo-American scholars until the mid-twentieth century. After that, scholars also began to reconsider the evidence, but such rethinking had virtually no influence on evangelical tourists.[59]

Archaeology mattered less than the inner sense of authenticity that places like the Garden Tomb provided. The landscape itself furnished the basis for Protestant experiences of reverence. Many tourists acknowledged that, after two thousand years of human occupation, the landscape would surely have changed since Jesus's time. But there was, and remains, a belief that the places of the Bible can be seen and experienced authentically through the modern landscape.

The anthropologist Jackie Feldman, who worked as a tour guide in Israel for more than a decade, describes the work of guides as a matter of facilitating this connection for Protestant tourists. The political and cultural ramifications are not primarily achieved through explicit ideological statements made by Israeli guides, Feldman writes, but through engagement with the landscape itself. Joking with tourists about how well they know their Bible and then promising to help that Bible come alive, providing an orientation to the landscape from the minute the bus leaves Ben Gurion Airport, standing in quiet reverence with the group as they look over Jerusalem from the Mount of Olives—tour guides help create meaningful experiences that wed tourists to the land.[60]

I saw an example of this on a Holy Land tour I took in 2007. Our British-Israeli tour guide, Malcolm Cartier, began the tour by driving out to the Judean hills. He pointed out the places that Jesus went during his forty days in the desert. We got a powerful sense of how desolate the place was. Showing us St. George's monastery, Malcolm talked about what a shepherd does; he showed us what he said might have been David's "valley of the shadow of death." We saw the importance of water. Malcolm encouraged us to look carefully at the land that he was sure would speak to us. "See, when you're here," he said, "this is what you begin to understand."[61] What we were to understand was obvious if unsaid: this place is the land of the Jewish people, as authorized in the Bible.

For evangelical tourists, that tie to the land remains a key part of how sites in Israel and the Palestinian territories become meaningful. In the face of commercialism and control by non-Protestants, the landscape serves as their cathedral. Music and worship cement the ties they feel. These days, for example, most American tourists take boat tours in the Sea of Galilee, where Jesus began his ministry. "Worship boats" bring tourists out onto the water where they often pray and sing. The boats then drop the pilgrims off for brief visits to a museum that houses a first-century fishing vessel that was discovered by two fishermen in 1986—the so-called "Jesus boat." One tourist who went on such a tour was particularly moved when her group sang the familiar hymn "I Walked Today Where Jesus Walked" while on a worship boat. At the end of the song she burst into tears. "I've sung that so many times," she explained, "but this was the first time it truly hit me, we're where he was!"[62]

When Jerry Falwell rose to prominence in the 1980s, he pushed evangelicals to involve themselves in electoral politics. As he did so, Falwell explicitly linked his American nationalism to an evangelical form of nationalism-for-Israel. During a Holy Land trip in 1978, funded by the Israeli government, Falwell told a group of reporters: "I believe that if we fail to protect Israel, we will cease to be important to God. . . . We can and must be involved in guiding America towards a biblical position regarding her stand on Israel."[63] What constituted a "biblical position" on Israel was never something that evangelicals all agreed upon, and the views among different subsets of the community would diverge significantly by the turn of the twenty-first century. But from 1967 onward, no other place in the world would have the same transformative emotional impact, the religious and sentimental power, that Israel had for evangelicals. They cherished the *land* of Israel, as it was visited and reconstructed and loved by Holy Land travelers; and they embraced the land *of Israel*, the place of God's people, with a biblical past and prophesied future that positioned it at the heart of much evangelical theology.

5

"Reaching the Unreached"

THE BATTLE OF LAUSANNE

EVERYONE KNEW WHAT to expect when René Padilla took the stage at the International Congress on World Evangelization in Lausanne, Switzerland, during the summer of 1974. The Lausanne Congress, sponsored by the Billy Graham Evangelistic Association, drew 2,700 people from around the globe—at the time the largest-ever gathering of evangelical Christian leaders. The assembled believers—ministers and lay people, racially diverse, the vast majority of them men—would be part of a singular moment in postwar evangelicalism.

Like all of the major presenters, Padilla had pre-circulated a paper, a rather scholarly treatise on the centrality of repentance to Christian ethics. The audience was not surprised, then, to hear Padilla lecture his fellow participants at Lausanne on the sins of the evangelical church, and on its failure—their own failure—to take seriously Jesus's call to social action. What *was* remarkable was the controlled fury emanating from the stage. Padilla (see figure 5.1) challenged the room to remember that Jesus had demanded that his followers confront the "darkness of the world." But evangelicals, he pronounced, had focused so long on individual sin that they had forgotten that darkness included materialism, racism, class division, political abuses, and, quoting Reinhold Niebuhr, "collective egotism."[1]

Padilla's jeremiad directly attacked the American church. Like so many other evangelical leaders from the global South, Padilla had attended Wheaton College. He had graduated in 1959 with both a BA in philosophy and an MA in theology. He had studied the typical conservative evangelical curriculum: Biblical interpretation, New and Old Testament studies, and languages, both Greek and Hebrew. Social issues were not on the agenda.[2] Now, fifteen years after leaving Wheaton, Padilla insisted that the "culture

FIGURE 5.1 Padilla speaking at the International Congress on World Evangelization. Courtesy of the Billy Graham Evangelistic Association.

Christianity" coming out of the United States had confused the American way of life with Christianity itself, and that it had replaced the demands of a full Christian discipleship with a ridiculous and triumphalist process of counting converts. The rigid equation of social conservatism with evangelism in the United States was a form of conformity to the world, rather than a way of speaking prophetically about the needs of that world. American evangelicals saw themselves as competing in a marketplace of religions, at home and abroad, and had stooped to "selling" Christianity as something simple, a brand that required only "accepting Christ" and not much else. This, he said, was what Dietrich Bonhoeffer had called "cheap grace."[3]

This selling of cheap grace, Padilla went on, "can only be the basis for unfaithful churches, for strongholds of racial and class discrimination, for religious clubs with a message that has no relevance to practical life in the social, the economic, and the political spheres."[4] Padilla allowed that perhaps he was being overly harsh: Americans were not the only ones to indulge in a faith that was more decorative than demanding. But because the United States played an outsized role in both world affairs and the spread of the gospel, "this particular form of Christianity, as no other today, has a powerful influence far beyond the borders of the nation."[5] There was a passionate response from other delegates. Years later, Padilla commented: "I found that unwittingly I had been voicing something that an awful lot of Third World people wanted to say themselves."[6]

Padilla was already a leader among a group of evangelicals who had arrived at Lausanne determined to raise "social concern" to an evangelical mantra. They had come to an event organized by Billy Graham's people to challenge Graham's model of Americanized mass evangelism. Several of these Young Turks, including Samuel Escobar, came out of the Latin American Theological Fraternity. FTL was a Protestant, theologically conservative but socially conscious alternative to both Catholic liberation theology and liberal Protestantism.[7] Padilla and his allies were challenging the evangelism-first orientation of the largely American contingent that dominated the congress. Both factions were creative and energized. One sign of the richness and complexity of global evangelicalism is that both groups—evangelism-first and social concern—would come to see Lausanne as their moment of triumph.

Lausanne showed off, by design, emerging forms of evangelical internationalism. Participation was by invitation only, and delegates represented 150 countries. Although organizers touted that most participants were younger than forty-five years old, one observer pointed out that there were "few young people and fewer women."[8] The number of participants from the West was limited: North Americans and Europeans were 25 percent each, and Asians, Africans, and Latin Americans were the other 50 percent.

But those numbers were hardly proportional. By the early 1970s, the demographics of global evangelicalism were changing rapidly, as millions of people in Latin America, Africa, and Asia converted to some form of Protestantism.[9] These new believers were not content to sit quietly on the sidelines while Americans and Europeans continued to presume that they were the moral center of Christendom.[10] Evangelicals were already well aware of the changing demographics of Christianity. During his first speech at the conference, Billy Graham would cheer the visibility and energy of "younger churches," as he stood before a multinational (see figure 5.2) and racially diverse crowd of delegates—who themselves spoke forcefully at the meeting as equals, not as missionary objects.[11]

Time magazine ran a long, largely friendly story that described the event as "possibly the widest ranging gathering of Christians ever held."[12] *Time* recognized that the event was a clear-cut challenge to the visibility and social power of the liberal-minded World Council of Churches. The very choice of Lausanne, located just thirty miles from the WCC headquarters in Geneva, was symbolic muscle-flexing for the global evangelical movement. As evangelical leaders had prepared for Lausanne, Billy Graham had made the point plain: "there is a vacuum developing in the world church. Radical theology has had its heyday." Evangelicals believed it was their moment to step up.[13]

Almost every news account noted the internal tensions at Lausanne. *Christianity Today* described the division as one between the "data-oriented church growth school and the discipleship-demanding compassion and justice group."[14] The two groups at the congress did not emerge fully formed from the waters of Lake Geneva. Each had already developed their own loose network. They had been writing books and in magazines, had their own intellectual spokespeople, and had struggled for power within the institutions of transnational evangelical life, including student groups, pastors' committees, missionary agencies, and aid organizations such as World Vision. Evangelism-minded thinkers Ralph Winter and Donald McGavran had both become well-known missions theorists and stalwarts of

FIGURE 5.2 Translation booths at Lausanne. Courtesy of the Billy Graham Evangelistic Association.

the influential Fuller Theological Seminary.[15] The discipleship group had not only Padilla and Escobar, but also the Mennonite theologian and pacifist John Howard Yoder, who had recently shaken up evangelical thinking with *The Politics of Jesus*, published two years before the congress. And several major African American evangelicals such as Tom Skinner had already published their own commentaries on the politics of race.[16]

The division between the two groups at Lausanne was real, but however diverse their political views and theologies, Lausanne attendees agreed on one thing: while some of them might believe social action was essential, they were not about to compromise genuine evangelical identity. Almost all of the delegates at Lausanne were biblical literalists and Christian exclusivists, deeply wary about ecumenism, theological liberalism, and secularism. The debates played out on those terms.

The evangelism-first faction certainly had tradition on its side. A long history of evangelism conferences, dating back to Edinburgh in 1910, had highlighted the importance of reaching the world for Jesus "in this generation." Its proponents argued that there was only one major task, evangelism, and only a few basic requirements for salvation. For these leaders, Lausanne was designed to set participants aflame with passion for "reaching the unreached." Donald McGavran, founding dean of the School of World Mission at Fuller Theological Seminary, was one of the chief proponents of this view. At the time of the congress, he was seventy-six years old, balding, with a gray goatee and an infectious grin. McGavran (see figure 5.3) was famous in evangelical circles for his long and enthusiastic prayers at public events, for his extensive correspondence filled with commentaries on books and journal articles, and for his ability to lecture for hours without notes.

FIGURE 5.3 Leaders of the church growth movement: Ralph Winter, Vergil Gerber, Donald McGavran, and C. Peter Wagner. Courtesy of Fuller Theological Seminary.

He was best known for his theories of "church growth," forged while he was a missionary in India. The idea was simple but fierce: churches in every locale should be growing, and rapidly. The missionary focus needed to be on places where the society was "receptive," and thus where large numbers of conversions were possible.[17] McGavran, like many participants at the Lausanne meeting, had been asked to fill out an advance questionnaire about what he hoped for from the event. McGavran responded that he wanted the congress to produce a clear statement of "the biblical foundations on which all Gospel-proclaiming, sinner-converting, and church-multiplying evangelism stands."[18]

By the time the evangelism-first evangelicals arrived at Lausanne, however, they were already on the defensive. For years, Protestants of all stripes had been launching critiques of Billy Graham's stadium-filling style of crusade evangelism. Graham would swoop into a country for only a few days, speak to the crowd the same way in Nairobi as he would in Nashville, and then depart. When Graham traveled on one of his crusades to a new city, masses of people usually came forward, declaring their acceptance of Jesus. They were counseled and encouraged to go to a local church, while Graham went on his way, off to the next city, the next outsized event. Many saw this approach as simplistic and shallow. And it was now coming under fire.

For those who disagreed with him, it was also easy to take Graham to task for being out of touch with the urgent realities of the world. The left-wing *Post-American*, for example, commented sardonically on Graham's evocation of the argument that Christians should be "in the world but not of it": "Having remained silent throughout two of America's gravest moral crises (Vietnam and Watergate), what else could Graham say?"[19] In fact, Graham had not been silent about Vietnam—he had often expressed support for the troops and was publicly in favor of the war, although he harbored private doubts. Graham also had been a dependable if moderate advocate of civil rights, and for more than a decade had insisted that his crusades should be integrated, both in the United States and, more recently, in South Africa. He had been a friend and advocate for both Presidents Johnson and Nixon, and had become fairly intoxicated by power, by his reputation as "pastor to the presidents." While evangelicals gathered in Lausanne, Graham's friend Richard Nixon was just days away from resigning the presidency.[20]

Addressing the gathering, Graham quietly admitted his own seduction, telling the audience that excessive identification with his own nation had been one of the "dangers" of his ministry. Clearly repentant, he remarked that "to tie the Gospel to any political system, secular program, or society is dangerous." Graham promised that he would move beyond nationalism: "When I go to preach the Gospel, I go as an ambassador of the kingdom of God—not America."[21] Following the classic evangelical model of sin and redemption, Graham claimed his own brush with political power caused him now to return to evangelism as the core of the Church. That he could do so at precisely the moment when he was still so closely identified with the president of the United States was a remarkable political feat in and of itself.

It wasn't just Graham-style mass-evangelism that was under siege. A debate was also raging over the very notion of missionary work. By the late 1960s, European and American missions to what was then known as the Third World had been challenged by calls for more equity and respect. This had intensified with movements for decolonization. Still, by the time of the congress, there remained vast numbers of European and American missionaries working throughout the world, and the majority were evangelicals. By 1974, evangelicals provided 66.5 percent of the funding—and 85 percent of the personnel—for US missions programs.[22] In almost all cases, those missionaries now officially served under the leadership of the national churches wherever they were stationed. However, the structural issues that had torn apart the Congo churches, over ownership of resources and control over missions activities, were far from resolved.

For some in the global South, the problem was not specific missionaries, but the entire First World missionary enterprise. John Gatu, general secretary of the Presbyterian church of East Africa, was a delegate to Lausanne, representing an evangelical strain of what in the United States was a mainline denomination. He had been deeply influenced by the East African revival, an evangelical movement that had swept across a number of countries starting in the 1930s.[23] For several years Gatu had led the call for a missionary moratorium, saying that missionaries from North America should stay out of Africa until Africans could fully decolonize their own churches. In theory, most missions worked at the invitation and under the direction of the people they served. In practice, however, this was still far from true.

Indeed, there were a number of reasons to question the missionary enterprise. By the late 1960s, American students in mainline seminaries, studying in the shadow of the Vietnam War, had become dubious about the benevolence of US missionary expansion. In 1968, one professor of missions at the University of Chicago Divinity School complained that "students are now cold, even hostile, to overseas missions."[24] By the time of the Lausanne Congress, little had changed on the mission field overall; in fact, the number of missionaries increased slightly in the early 1970s. But liberal Protestant groups in the United States, such as the United Methodists and United Presbyterians, were in the process of reducing their missionary forces. As historian Adrian Hastings writes, they were "Africanizing hard."[25] The call for a moratorium had recently been affirmed by the 1974 assembly of the WCC's African affiliate, the All Africa Conference of Churches, and Gatu had been embraced in ecumenical circles.

Some evangelicals accused the ecumenical churches of using the missionary moratorium as a "smoke screen" for their own decline. Writing in *Christianity Today*, one missions staffer argued that the moratorium had proven "very attractive" to churches whose missions programs were already in trouble because their membership was in "revolt against their radical political adventures." Noting the strong stances taken by the World Council of Churches on behalf of Third World liberation, evangelical observers insisted that the ecumenical churches were losing the capacity to send missionaries because ordinary members disagreed with their leaders' political radicalism. The WCC call for a moratorium was cynical, evangelicals argued—a necessity dressed up as justice.[26]

Lausanne brought the issue front and center for evangelicals. Some delegates were surprisingly receptive to a call that had been associated with ecumenical churches. One of the discussion groups at the congress, for example, listed problems related to missionary work: control over finances, "suspicion because of political differences," missionary distrust of local leaders, and missionaries' relatively high standards of living.[27]

Many delegates from the global South supported the moratorium or something like it, although there were also a number of doubters, including the rising evangelical star Byang Kato of Nigeria, who had spoken as a missions advocate at Urbana 70 and was vehemently opposed to any limitation on missionaries. In contrast to more Leftist African colleagues, Kato described the missionary moratorium as "blasphemous" and "unscriptural." Kato had recently received his doctorate from Dallas Theological Seminary, and, until his untimely death in 1975, he was a leading voice of conservative theology in Africa.[28]

In the end, the Lausanne Covenant, which emerged from the meeting, did suggest that perhaps it was time for a "reduction" in the number of missionaries in places where the local church was strong. This was not enough for Gatu, who felt that both "sending" countries and "receiving" countries were overly invested in the idea that the Third World churches were poor.[29]

Over the course of the next decade, the number of missionaries overall did decline in some specific countries, but largely as an effect of the Cold War and anti-American sentiment in the wake of Vietnam. Those countries with more pro-Western foreign policies—South Africa, Kenya, Rhodesia, Botswana—welcomed missionaries. Other postcolonial governments, including those in Ethiopia, Zaire, Uganda, and Nigeria, curtailed missionary activity. Most evangelical denominations added missionaries where they could. The Southern Baptists remained a lodestar, along with non-denominational groups like Wycliffe Bible Translators, New Tribes Mission, and Youth with a Mission. By the 1980s, the SBC and these non-denominational groups accounted for three-fifths of the US missionaries in the field and more than half of the money spent on missions. For American evangelicals, the limits that existed were external and political, not theological.[30]

Some missions enthusiasts made a different argument about the (somewhat mythical) decline in Western missions. US and European dominance of missions was ending, they insisted, and global South Christians would pick up the baton. Evangelical demographics made it seem inevitable that missionaries would be coming from the global South. The AME's *Voice of Missions*, for example, reported the determination of Africans to reach beyond their borders.[31] These still small movements of missionaries "from everyone to everywhere" would eventually come to shape the structure and theology of post-imperial evangelical life.[32] Some observers also believed that missionaries from "younger churches" would be more socially minded than Europeans and Americans. Lausanne seemed to provide strong evidence for that idea. In other words, it often seemed that demographics were destiny, and that destiny was headed Leftward.

Even as evangelism-first was on the defensive, its proponents were hardly inclined to obligingly demote themselves. They argued forcefully that Lausanne was about saving the unreached, the 2.7 billion people who had never even heard the gospel. The word "hell" was very rarely used at Lausanne, but it hung over the debate: why focus on ending earthly poverty, when the real issue was eternal life?

In fact, Lausanne provided an opportunity for some of the most well-known leaders of the church growth movement to cultivate their own constituency. They ran a large number of workshops, which promised participants that they would be exposed to the latest thinking about missions, thus becoming more sophisticated in their planning. Some of these sessions had their own in-group code words. For example, there were trainings on E-1, E-2, and E-3 evangelism (meaning, respectively, evangelism in one's own community, evangelism in similar communities, and cross-cultural evangelism). Presenters also offered specific evangelistic methods: personal evangelism, evangelicalism via mass communication, use of drama and art, open-air evangelism, and evangelism in high-rise apartment buildings. Some of the social justice faction made clear they were not giving ground, and offered their own panel on evangelism through social action and community development.[33]

For the evangelical community in the United States, nothing that came out of Lausanne would have as much impact as the concept of "Unreached Peoples." Just before the meeting, the Missions Advanced Research Center (MARC) released its first, rough list of the Unreached Peoples of the world, which was distributed to all conference participants and sent out with advance registration materials. The idea of evangelizing "peoples"—as opposed to "people"—ingeniously described the task ahead. It was a way of marking, and marketing, the idea that specific groups of people had not yet been adequately exposed to the gospel.

MARC was initially a joint project of Fuller Theological Seminary's School of World Mission and the evangelical aid organization World Vision. The MARC team drew on a hodgepodge of sources. They asked for information from missionaries and incoming international students at Fuller; they pulled from material gathered for other books on missions; and they distributed a bare-bones questionnaire to evangelical leaders and organizations, simply asking respondents to list "specific unreached peoples" they could think of, with only minimal instruction as to what the term might mean.[34]

Several organizations were interested in similar concepts, so there was competition to get the Unreached Peoples directory out, and in the rush to be ready for Lausanne, compromises were inevitable. Thus the *Unevangelized Peoples Directory* that arrived at Lausanne was a 120-page "non-book," a patchwork of uneven information drawn from incommensurate sources, which nonetheless had the appearance of comprehensive, up-to-the-minute data derived from sophisticated methods.[35]

The innovation of the Unreached Peoples concept was two-fold. First, the term "people groups" was designed to move beyond ideas about nationality as a key category for mapping missions. Instead, it proposed that within one nation there were often many different "groups," defined by language or culture or location. Second, the term "unreached" referred specifically to unevangelized *communities*, not individuals. Perhaps, for example, there were individual Mexicans in Mexico City who had *not* been "reached," but at least they had had their chance—there were evangelical churches and materials in Spanish aplenty. On the other hand, Indian communities in the interior of Mexico might have never really learned about Jesus. Those groups should be the priority.

The concept of Unreached Peoples also privileged so-called E-3 evangelism, highlighting missions to more exotic and potentially dangerous locations. As *Mission Frontiers* magazine explained in 1984: "These Hidden Peoples are found mainly among the Muslim, Chinese, Hindu, Buddhist, and tribal peoples of the world. These thousands of bypassed people groups, whether in cities or jungles, are the final frontiers of the gospel."[36] The idea of unreached peoples also increased the urgency of missions. True, evangelical missionaries had gone to virtually every nation in the world, but they had missed thousands of people groups.

After Lausanne, MARC began producing computer-assisted and highly quantitative annual lists of unreached groups. They were soon joined by other groups such as the World Evangelical Fellowship. Missionary theorist Ralph Winter threw his considerable weight behind the concept, founding the US Center for World Missions in Pasadena, California. Missions began to take on a distinctly social scientific tone. The classification schemes and computer-aided quantifications of gospel-impoverishment led to lists, tasks, strategies, carefully parsed targets of opportunity, and increasingly sophisticated charts, graphs, and pictures of the "types" of people to be reached. As one sardonic evangelical observer opined, those tools nicely met the "can-do spirit of [American] Baby Boomers looking for a cause."[37] The concept, or at least its promotional literature, reached broadly: the AME's *Voice of Missions* sometimes reproduced MARC's updates, for example. One 1978 article in *Voice of Missions* asked, with some frustration, "Why are we still so unconcerned" about the 2.4 billion unreached people?[38]

The Unreached Peoples contingent was also offering its own critique of Graham-type evangelism. In their view, there was little point in holding massive revivals in the major cities of Nigeria or Brazil, because few people in the cities were members of Unreached People groups. In fact, perhaps almost all urban missions, or missions to Europe for that matter, were a waste of precious resources, a showering of riches upon the spiritually wealthy. One observer reported that the "people groups movement . . . has shaken the missions community to its core."[39]

For many evangelical intellectuals, however, the idea of a "people group" was controversial from the start. The first and perhaps most daunting problem was defining the term, which conjured fantasies of organically homogenous cultures, neatly bounded in space, where everyone identified clearly with the same identity. A person could be slotted into the "Yoruba Muslim" people group, but what if she saw herself instead as a Nigerian nationalist or a pan-African socialist—or as all three?[40]

Compounding that issue, the Unreached Peoples teams sometimes identified groups so narrowly as to seem ridiculous—were "Urdu-speaking Muslim farmers" of the Punjab really their own group? What about "high-rise residents in Singapore"? Did it make sense to argue, as one 1979 survey did, that there were clear differences between "the Kau Nuba" in Kenya and their near neighbors, the "Mesakin Nuba"? The missions theorist C. Peter Wagner thought so: the Kau Nuba, he explained, were "described as wild and passionate," but the Mesakina Nauba were "gentle."[41] As some evangelical critics pointed out, this was not particularly useful either as a way of organizing missions work or understanding the world.[42]

Instead, proponents of the concept were turning unsorted masses of people into "populations," to make them more comprehensible, and thus more manageable, by various evangelical authorities. After all, Urdu-speaking Muslim farmers in the Punjab were not people groups in their own minds, and they did not produce themselves as obedient objects to be evangelized. Yet, drawing on such oddly precise definitions, Winter and others came up with a number: 16,750 unreached people groups.[43]

There were theorists of missionary work who used the concept of culture more subtly. Paul Hiebert of the School of World Missions (where C. Peter Wagner and others taught) insisted that missionaries and their supporters must take cultural difference seriously and analyze it carefully. He argued that missionaries needed to engage the tools of "postmodern" anthropology, which analyzed cultures as mobile, contested, and internally diverse. With that complexity in mind, Hiebert said, Western missionaries could support theologies and strategies that emerged from the churches of the global South, since the gospel is made meaningful in specific cultural contexts.[44]

Critiques aside, believers in the pews seemed to love the idea of Unreached Peoples. By the late 1970s, there was an *Unreached Peoples* magazine, a set of books that listed and illustrated the various groups of the unreached, and dozens of videos to be used in church education programs. Some organizations encouraged churches to "adopt a people" as a prayer target; others offered calendars with a daily prayer focus.[45] Every year the Lausanne Committee published an update.

Just as the concept of Unreached Peoples had produced a certain kind of population to be observed, it also helped to construct a certain kind of Christian, one who consumed its associated products, and who would understand herself as part of a transnational community. The "World Christian"—there were scores of conferences and meetings, books and articles, and even one magazine with this title—was caring and sophisticated. She took the time and trouble to learn about conditions in the rest of the world. This often involved finding a group of people to learn about and support through prayer and missionary work.[46] As one 1986 MA thesis from Jerry Falwell's Liberty University enthusiastically described, the focus on people groups implied a recognition of cultural difference and an ability to see the diversity within a nation, thus avoiding "people blindness."[47] It was one thing for Southern Baptist churchgoers to gather up tissues and pencils to send to the Lottie Moon Christmas offering, where the objects of evangelism were traditionally depicted as generically exotic Others. It was another for an evangelical believer to commit to learning something about one or more people groups in order to strategically pray for them. Focused, passionate, knowledgeable prayer—the kind of prayer that required both intellect and emotion—was at the heart of the Unreached Peoples strategy.

For all its data-driven list-making, reaching the unreached was no dry intellectual exercise. In a global church that increasingly highlighted the importance of emotionally resonant worship and the ongoing presence of "gifts of the spirit," the arduous work of evangelism was made rich with the promise of God's presence among communities that were hearing of Jesus (theoretically) for the first time. The *National Geographic*-style images of people groups, the careful study of their lifeways, the reports of outpouring of the Holy Spirit in previously unreached areas, and tales of great moments of spiritual warfare invited believers to both identify with and exoticize the unreached at the same time. Nothing else in the evangelical churches so beautifully combined metrics and mysticism.

Even as this new way of categorizing people took hold, the old forms of categorization were never far from view. Racism and race were painfully resonant issues at the Lausanne Congress. By the 1970s, evangelical pieties were anti-racist; evangelical realities were another matter. Clarence Hilliard was one of only twenty-five African American delegates to the congress (out of about six hundred Americans). In 1974, Hilliard was a pastor for Chicago's Circle Evangelical Free Church, a largely white denomination in which he ministered to a racially diverse congregation. He had marched with Martin Luther King Jr. and would later become a leader in the National Black Evangelical Association. He was also one of the few delegates who refused to sign the Lausanne Covenant.[48]

Writing in the left-wing evangelical journal *Post-American*, Hilliard disagreed strongly with the view that Lausanne marked a new era in evangelical social concern. As he explained, the final document had not gone nearly far enough in calling for social justice, or in accepting evangelicals' own responsibility for oppression. It was fine, Hilliard said, for the Covenant to insist that all human beings were made in the image of God, but the document failed to say the next, obvious thing: that every church, parachurch organization, and Christian should work to ensure that all people are respected. Similarly, while the document decried that evangelicals had "neglected" social and political issues, Hilliard thought it needed to go much further. It wasn't enough to say that political liberation was not salvation, Hilliard wrote, since the opposite point was equally important: salvation places "political responsibilities" on those who are saved.[49]

Another major concern was the profound underrepresentation of African Americans at the congress. Hilliard challenged—although "challenged" might be too gentle a word—the criteria by which African Americans were invited. First, he offered a short but rather shocking list of prominent black evangelicals who had been bypassed: evangelist Tom Skinner; William Bentley of the National Black Evangelical Association; and John Perkins, the groundbreaking social justice activist from Mississippi. Among those African Americans who were present, Hilliard said, most were strong supporters of the Billy Graham Evangelical Association, which did not represent African American evangelicals more broadly. Hilliard bluntly concluded, "The control over the selection of black participants would undoubtedly be considered by most blacks to be a classic example of plantation politics."[50] Critiques like Hilliard's make clear that racism was still very much an issue in the white-dominated world of American evangelical Christianity. Because of that, those African Americans who had been willing to identify as evangelical in the 1960s and 1970s were becoming increasingly disillusioned with the term.[51]

Despite, or because of, what he saw as the racism of the congress organizers, Hilliard joined the meetings of the social justice faction. That group included people from around the world, including a substantial faction of Europeans and Americans (both black and white). Its most important leaders, however, were from Latin America. Members of the Latin American Theological Fraternity felt called upon to respond to Catholic commitments to social justice in a region that was riven by civil war, impoverished, and oppressed both by global capitalist corporations and corrupt right-wing governments.

But evangelicals were not just following along behind Catholics. The members of the FTL had worked extensively with college students who were flocking to the universities, but who still faced meager job prospects after graduation. Those students were increasingly radicalized. And their Christian mentors soon discovered, as Escobar put it, that "[e]very question regarding violence and subversion touched, in one way or another, the field of theology and the teaching of the Bible." Padilla later made a similar point, saying that evangelicals in general had been too wary of Catholics, too dismissive of the points they had made. Evangelicals had not "done their homework" on key issues.[52]

The loose network of social action supporters at Lausanne formed their own ad hoc group on "Theology and Implications of Radical Discipleship." As every evangelical at the congress would have understood, "discipleship" was a kind of Christian shorthand: disciples are believers who give fully, who live the requirements of faith, who don't just believe in Jesus but who follow his example. Five hundred people attended the first meeting of the radical discipleship group.

At the end of the congress, this group issued its own alternative statement. It affirmed a commitment to evangelism, but insisted that "we must repudiate as demonic the attempt to drive a wedge between evangelism and social action." It was time for evangelicals to confess their sins, the group declared, and the list was long and political: We have frequently denied the rights of the underprivileged; we have distorted the gospel and offered simplistic answers to complex problems; we have been partisan in condemning totalitarianism but ignoring racism.[53]

Despite sometimes-heated rhetoric, and perhaps precisely because so much was at stake, the social concern and evangelism-first factions were not entirely distinct. The social concern group had its powerful supporters from Europe and the United States, notably John Stott, who was chair of the drafting committee for the official Covenant but who also threw his weight behind the ad hoc group, announcing at the end of the meeting that he would sign both the radicals' statement and the "consensus document."

Still, there was an immediate backlash to the alternative statement. "I felt the hostility of many Americans," Padilla said, "very much so. And afterwards, of course, many people were very critical of what we had said, and of the radical discipleship group, and of John Stott, who had given us his support, publicly." Nor did that hostility come only from Americans. Sasumu Uda of Japan argued that Lausanne must avoid the "humanistic and socialistic" message of the WCC. Churches were in decline, he said, wherever they were weakened by "relativism, diversity, dialogue, and leniency."[54]

At the same time, the more conservative Lausanne leaders attempted to accommodate the increasing calls for social concern. The congress's final document represented the "Lausanne consensus," and it tried to make both groups happy. The left wing successfully fought for the addition of more political language: direct reference to alienation, oppression, and discrimination, for example. The covenant also included another reference to Bonhoeffer: "in issuing the gospel invitation we have no liberty to conceal the cost of discipleship."[55] Discipleship was not just a matter of accepting grace; it was the arduous, sometimes exhausting labor of creating justice in God's kingdom on earth. (Later, evangelicals would invent a shorthand for this approach: "Kingdom work.")

Still, the strong hand of the traditionalists showed in the strained language of the compromise: "Although reconciliation with other people is not reconciliation with God, nor is social action evangelism, nor is political liberation salvation, nevertheless we affirm that evangelism and socio-political involvement are both part of our Christian duty."[56]

For most of the 1970s, the leaders of the left-wing group believed that they had "won" at Lausanne and that international evangelicalism had irrevocably committed itself to at least some version of social radicalism. Looking back at the meeting a year later, Padilla pronounced that the Lausanne Covenant had been a "death blow" to attempts to "reduce mission to the multiplication of Christians and churches through evangelism."[57] At some level, the social concern faction *had* won: In the Philippines, India, and Latin America, activist groups promoted a worldly faith. In the United States, a determined cohort pushed for discussions of how wealthy First-World Christians could commit themselves to a simple lifestyle and even commit to "resistance to unjust established orders."[58]

But church growth leaders were equally certain they had triumphed. On the one-year anniversary of the congress, missionary strategist C. Peter Wagner decried what he called the "diversionary tactics" of the social justice cohort. As a former missionary to Latin America, Wagner was quite familiar with the leaders of the radical discipleship group. And, although at times he had expressed support for taking seriously the calls for social justice, Wagner was seen by evangelicals like Escobar and Padilla as a rather imperious missionary who wanted to control the agenda. Had the radicals gotten their way, Wagner said, they would have "destroyed the central evangelistic nature of the congress." Fortunately, he explained, the follow-on meeting of the Lausanne Continuation Committee, held six months after the congress, had sidelined such efforts. Instead, the committee declared that "evangelism is primary." The committee would go on to launch the Lausanne Movement, and it successfully argued that the movement's focus should be on the "2.7 billion unreached peoples" of the world.[59]

Others simply revised the history of Lausanne, insisting that the social concern faction had never been that important. *Christianity Today* editor Harold Lindsell saw the congress as a triumph of the evangelical movement over ecumenical Christianity, one made possible by the congress's decision to define the saving of souls as primary.[60]

The ability of both sides to claim victory had to do in part with the dispersed nature of the movement. Global evangelicalism was nothing if not a constantly evolving network: as one cohort enthusiastically took up the issues of economic development, or dangers to the environment, others just as eagerly set up programs that established ever more inventive ways to evangelize. One group, for example, focused on the covenant's call for believers in affluent circumstances to adopt "a simple lifestyle" and to give more money away. Ron Sider, who would go on to write *Rich Christians in an Age of Hunger* (1977), headed up the Consultation on Simple Living, which held two years of small-group and regional meetings, then an international gathering in England in 1980. The document they produced insisted that Christians needed to ask hard questions about macroeconomic issues, development and growth, and the environment. Excess consumption, they said, was "choking the West with a surfeit of goods, services and waste."[61] Indeed, for almost a decade, there were so many consultations coming out of Lausanne that they produced twenty-nine different "Lausanne Occasional Papers," many (though not all) focused on social justice. In retrospect, it began to look very much like the radical social and political agenda had been neatly relegated to committee. As Padilla himself put it, "The Lausanne Movement, on the whole, ultimately sidestepped the whole issue of social concern."[62]

The Lausanne Movement, however, was just one coalition, and it was not the only keeper of the flame. Indeed, the ideal of social concern found its most enduring legacy in the turn to various forms of humanitarianism among evangelicals. In the 1970s and 1980s, evangelical aid organizations like World Vision, World Relief, Compassion International, Samaritan's Purse, and others grew dramatically, and they became one outlet for a particular, if limited, form of social concern. Historian David King's analysis of World Vision, for example, finds that it was perhaps the perfect embodiment of both legacies of Lausanne. On the one hand, World Vision had been one of two founding sponsors of MARC's Unreached Peoples surveys, but, on the other hand, the organization would become less focused on evangelism over time. By the 1990s, World Vision was the largest privately funded development organization in the world, and by 2008, it had a budget of $2.6 billion. During the 1980s and 1990s, World Vision's leaders increasingly talked about inequality and structural injustice, but in relatively gentle terms that allowed the group's supporters to do simple things such as skip a meal and donate the money they had saved. In this way the organization managed to walk the line that divided delegates at Lausanne. The genuinely radical origins of the "holistic" gospel were quietly ignored, but World Vision did emerge as a powerful force in evangelicalism that was willing to critique global inequality.[63]

At the same time, a different group of evangelicals also had begun to articulate their notion of a "worldly faith." The Moral Majority was founded just five years after Lausanne, and it brought American evangelicalism firmly into the realm of politics, highlighting a quite distinct set of social concerns. There is no reason to think the congress directly influenced the outsized televangelists who became some of the best-known figures of the religious Right—Jerry Falwell, Pat Robertson, Jimmy Swaggart, Jim Bakker, and so on. None of them had been invited to Lausanne and most were conspicuously spurned by the neo-evangelicals who had organized the congress. Not to be outscorned, members of the religious Right returned the favor. Some from the fundamentalist wing of the evangelical movement had criticized anyone who had attended the Lausanne Congress, with its suspicious breadth of theological views. John Walvrood, for example, one of the few from the prophecy wing of the movement to have even been invited to Lausanne, faced chastisement from others who thought he was giving in to theological compromise.[64]

Still, as Ron Sider pointed out, it did sometimes seem as if the lessons of the congress about the importance of speaking to "the gospel in its wholeness" had been picked up primarily by those on the Right, so that a new generation of conservative leaders were openly willing to make politics a central part of their pastoral mission. As Sider put it, "Theirs was just a very different politics."[65]

Perhaps nothing indicates this shift more clearly than the transformation of Francis Schaeffer. When he arrived at Lausanne, Schaeffer was the highly admired author of *The God Who is There* (1968) and *Escape from Reason* (1968). For years he had been receiving young people from around the world at his home-cum-retreat center in L'Abri, Switzerland. When he took his place at the pulpit at Lausanne, Schaeffer was no longer the *lederhosen*-clad lecturer who had toured the United States in the early 1960s, but he still cut a distinctive figure, with a beard and long, now graying hair. At Lausanne, he argued that material needs were no less "spiritual" than missions work, and that evangelicalism must be more than a series of "preaching points and activity generators." Instead, it must encompass every aspect of life, building a true beauty of community that would be visible to the world.[66]

It might seem surprising, then, that by the late 1970s, Schaeffer would move dramatically to the Right. After 1974, Schaeffer's long-standing brief against the Enlightenment became more thoroughly conservative and overtly political. In his 1976 book (and 1977 film), *How Should We Then Live?*, Schaeffer reiterated his attacks on those who promoted a rudderless moral universe. He expanded his critique of humanism, which now was represented not only by Michelangelo or the Beatles but by a Western, consumerist mentality that led to political passivity. Schaeffer thus drew on a liberal/Left tradition of critiquing the dangers of consumerism and selfishness. But he took the argument in a different direction. Without a Christian moral foundation, Schaeffer argued, Americans had no independent basis for judging right from wrong. Attending only on their own possessions and comfort, they simply accepted the rule of secular elites. In this, Americans were very much like those under communist rule who had learned to be obedient to the party's demands.

It was from this vantage point that Schaeffer first approached the issue of abortion, which had been legalized in 1973. For him, abortion was just another example of elites imposing rules and expecting acquiescence. In this instance, the elites of the Supreme Court had pronounced on the nature of human life, arbitrarily declaring that a third-trimester fetus was a person but a first-trimester fetus was not. Schaeffer argued that this made no sense medically and that it had no moral claim other than pragmatism. A population that cared primarily about its own comfort, he argued, would accept the irrational judgements of its elites while agreeing to value a woman's convenience over the life of a powerless person. [67]

Schaeffer thus wove together three of the most important strands of what was fast becoming the New Right: anti-communism, anti-elitism, and anti-abortion. He and his son, Frank, toured the United States and later Europe showing excerpts from *How Should We Then Live?* The tour was a success, with thousands of people showing up for screenings around the US and Europe (6,600 in Los Angeles alone). The book quickly sold hundreds of thousands of copies, and continued to sell well for the rest of the decade. Schaeffer's next book and film combination, the 1979 anti-abortion brief *Whatever Happened to the Human Race?* (co-written with C. Everett Koop, a Philadelphia surgeon who under President Reagan would become the US Surgeon General), catapulted him to stardom, but *How Should We Then Live?* set the terms of the debate, bringing the logic of social concern to the politics of abortion. Schaeffer became, as *Der Spiegel* aptly phrased it, the "philosopher of the Moral Majority."⁶⁸

Thanks largely to the work of Schaeffer and Koop, evangelicals, who had heretofore largely ignored abortion, began to pay attention. (In the 1970s, the Southern Baptist Convention had even supported legal abortion in certain circumstances.)⁶⁹ For those influenced by Schaeffer—and there were many who, without having read his work, were exposed to his ideas as they filtered through evangelical networks—opposition to abortion was understood as resistance to a larger "culture of death." It was tied to arguments against consumerism, selfishness, and otherworldliness that were quite powerful among evangelicals in the late 1960s and early 1970s.

Schaeffer encouraged the emergent Christian Right to join in coalition with Catholics, secular conservatives, and others to fight abortion and "secular humanism." Although the Catholic concept of a "seamless garment" of pro-life commitments got relatively little traction, and only a few left-wing evangelicals took up the entire array of issues that were linked in liberal Catholic social teaching (opposition to abortion, euthanasia, and capital punishment; protest against nuclear weapons; and concerns over poverty), anti-abortion activity brought a new willingness to step outside denominational lines. Jerry Falwell explained that it was Schaeffer who encouraged him to get over his fundamentalist, separatist tendencies and build a movement. "He was the one who pushed me into the arena and told me to put on the gloves."⁷⁰

Conservative evangelicals and conservative Catholics joined together in support of the "traditional family." They tied "abortion on demand" to "pornography, homosexuality, and godless humanism" and set aside the preoccupation with materialism and political passivity that social concern evangelicals had articulated at Lausanne.⁷¹ Eventually, abortion would be the central focus of moral outrage among American evangelicals, including many progressives. Lausanne had seeded the logic of social concern, from which anti-abortion politics and many other flowers bloomed.

The globalizing faith of evangelicals in the 1970s, and the short-lived triumph of a particular form of social concern, emerged from a rich intersection of postcolonial assertiveness by people from the global South and anti-racism within the United States. The legacy of that triumph was multifaceted, forging links between domestic and international politics, and creating shared frameworks between opponents of the suffering caused by the structures of global poverty and opponents of the structures of secular liberalism. Evangelicals from the Left and the Right, even when they disagreed vehemently, shared a language and a general theological orientation. This bond was meaningful enough, and the lines of concern intersected frequently enough, that leaders from all sides left the 1974 congress believing that there was a thing called global evangelicalism, and that the people at Lausanne were its exemplars and defenders. With the rise of the religious Right to power in the early 1980s, however, new battle lines were drawn, and new warriors were recruited. The evangelical Right would find its cause in the evils of the Soviet Union, while liberals (and some conservatives) would cast their eyes on apartheid South Africa.

II

Body Politics

6

"These Marks on My Body Are My Credentials"

JESUS TO THE COMMUNIST WORLD

IN 1966, the Romanian pastor Richard Wurmbrand testified before the Senate Judiciary Committee's Internal Security subcommittee. A Jewish convert and Lutheran minister, Wurmbrand had been imprisoned twice by the Romanian government for his activities as an "underground" minister before he finally escaped to the West in 1964. Standing before the committee (figure 6.1), he stripped to the waist and turned to display his deeply scarred back. According to the *New York Times*, Wurmbrand testified, "My body represents Romania, my country, which has been tortured to a point that it can no longer weep. These marks on my body are my credentials."[1]

During the Cold War, the bodies of suffering believers became contested terrain. Wurmbrand would go on to publish more than a dozen books on his experiences in Romania and the threat posed by communism. The best-known, *Tortured for Christ*, first published in 1967, became a global bestseller. In this short autobiographical account, Wurmbrand described in detail how he and his fellow prisoners in Romania were beaten, forced to stand in one position, and placed in refrigerated cells. The images were vivid: their bodies were wracked, fractured, and perforated. Yet Wurmbrand also insisted that "other things simply cannot be told .... They are too terrible and obscene to be put into writing."[2]

A year after his Senate testimony, Wurmbrand reprised his famous shirt removal in the film, *Tortured for Christ*.[3] Shaking his finger at the camera, Wurmbrand told the viewers that he knew they didn't always believe what they were told, because there was "much communist propaganda" in the United States.

"Look here," he said, over and over again, pointing to his scars, haranguing his audience for their presumed apathy. With a street preacher's angry cadence he declared that

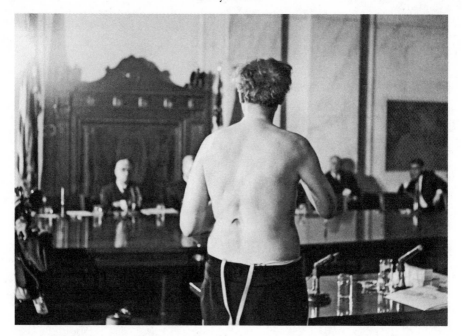

FIGURE 6.1 Richard Wurmbrand in the *New York Times*, May 7, 1966. Henry Griffin/Associated Press.

"you" are like Thomas, who needed to see the wounds of Christ before he believed that Jesus had risen from the dead. Christians behind the Iron Curtain were "happy to suffer," Wurmbrand pronounced, "but it is *your* duty to fight to stop these sufferings and to sustain with love your brothers behind the Iron Curtain, who suffer for the faith which you yourself have." American evangelicals would soon embrace the politics of suffering, acknowledging their own relative privilege while forging, through the bodies of others, a powerful transnational identity. As part of the global body of Christ, they would vicariously embrace the suffering of others, seeing themselves as both persecuted victim and compassionate rescuer.

Starting in the 1950s, but intensifying in the 1970s and 1980s, evangelical popular culture and political activism focused heavily on Eastern Europe and, more broadly, the communist world. Communist persecution of Christians became a primary lens through which American evangelicals thought about global politics, even if that narrative was challenged by evangelicals who supported the larger "social concern" agenda proposed at Lausanne. Christians living under communism were the dramatis personae of late Cold War evangelical internationalism. Theirs would be the bodies that suffered, and the violation of their human rights would be the issue that most broadly mobilized evangelical believers in the United States and Europe.

Evangelical, anti-communist activism in the Cold War is a story of embodiment, of representing and making bodies into icons of Christianity. Augustine had described the agony of the martyrs as a "splendid spectacle," a form of Christian education. He reminded his readers that, when they heard stories of the martyrs read in church, they would necessarily form "some sort of picture of what happened." If you did not, he said, "it would mean you weren't listening at all."[4] In Susan Sontag's study of the photography of war, *Regarding the Pain of Others*, she highlights the ways that people are drawn to images of violated bodies: paintings of Christian martyrs in torment; photographs of the war dead; or famine victims, eyes large and flat, who look straight into the camera or stare out into space. Such images ask the observer to *do something*.[5]

Early Christians who were persecuted for their faith, however, were never seen as passive victims. Martyrs struggled to be brave because they wanted to be models of Christian piety. They needed to make their pain *meaningful*, to shape their suffering bodies into testimony.[6] Similarly, the pain of Christians living under communism would be pictured and described in detail, drawing connections between Cold-War Protestants and Catholic martyrs. In both cases, representing the body in pain was a necessary condition of the politics of suffering.

For Cold Warriors, opposition to communism and support for religious freedom were foundational. The language of human rights, however, was relatively new. And yet it was that language, centered around the integrity of the human body, that would come to dominate evangelical internationalism in the 1970s and beyond.

Of course, evangelicals, and others, had long responded to political crises and atrocities abroad. And humanitarian responses to such crises depended upon, and helped to construct, a sense of obligation across borders.[7] In 1948, the United Nations had proclaimed its Declaration of Universal Human Rights, which led to a moment of hopeful activity. In fact, starting in the 1930s, a whole range of activists, many from outside the United States, had been developing visions of human dignity and of a world built on international collaboration and recognition of shared humanity. At the conference that founded the United Nations in 1945, mainline Protestants in the Federal Council of Churches were a key force behind a plank in support of human rights.[8] Their goal was not only to support the idea of human rights, but to affirm their own role as the moral voice of the country. At a time when mainline Protestants were a remarkably powerful social force—when presidents and professors and business leaders were statistically likely to be members of a few key denominations—support for human rights was at once utopian universalism and a reliably middle-of-the-road Americanism.[9]

The National Association of Evangelicals, on the other hand, was openly dubious. The NAE's members favored "basic freedoms for all mankind," but the UN declaration's failure to mention God as the source for human rights was a fatal flaw.[10] As one Rev. William Blessing colorfully described it, true Christians should denounce both the UN and the "God-denying, Christ-rejecting, Holy Ghost-blaspheming, Bible-hating, atheistic Federal Council of Churches." Such views were not uncommon among evangelicals in the 1940s.[11]

There was a more general problem with the human rights plank in the declaration. How could the UN guarantee the rights of individual people, which were held to be universal and transnational, if individual states were the organization's building blocks? As a matter of principle, states would rarely vote to give the UN power to violate national sovereignty. The system was built on a contradiction. As historian Mark Bradley has shown, for human rights to become truly relevant politically, it would take not only the work of the UN and professional diplomats, but also the enthusiastic practices of a whole coterie of "human rights amateurs." Those activists, artists, and writers would bring a deeply felt "human rights vernacular" into the sphere of politics.[12]

In the 1970s, human rights movements really began to make their mark. Amnesty International had been founded in England in 1961, but it began to take off in the early 1970s.[13] One of the signal events in the rise of human rights awareness was the December 1973 publication of Alexander Solzhenitsyn's extraordinary *Gulag Archipelago*, a four-volume, 1,800-page study that vividly described the oppression faced by dissidents in the Soviet Union. Solzhenitsyn combined a memoir of his own time in Soviet prison camps with personal testimony from other prisoners and a multipronged examination of Soviet history and culture. *Gulag Archipelago* spoke in the intense, first-person language of much testimony and witness, from Augustine to Amnesty International. It described a country that had, in essence, become entirely a gulag. Immediately after the book was released, Soviet President Leonid Brezhnev had Solzhenitsyn arrested and then expelled from the country. He soon settled in the United States. The book was embraced widely and sold extremely well, with more than three million copies purchased in the United States over the next decade.[14]

Evangelicals welcomed Solzhenitsyn as well, because they saw his book as an argument for the pervasiveness of sin. As *Eternity* magazine's review put it, the book warned that any soul has the capacity for the same "hardness of heart" that affected the Soviet prison guards and secret police.[15] From an evangelical perspective, this essential depravity was why human beings were so desperately in need of God's grace, as opposed to being "deserving" of rights. Francis Schaeffer argued that *Gulag Archipelago* had exposed modernity's crisis of moral relativism. Unsurprisingly, Schaeffer described the book as showing how Marxist-Leninism had no intellectual basis from which to respect the individual person; only Christianity provided that foundation.[16]

Schaeffer's was an early salvo in what would become a long discussion about the relationship between Christianity, specifically Protestantism, and a seemingly secular notion of human rights. Indeed, evangelical narratives of rights were fraught from the beginning with an essential tension. On the one hand, believers wanted to see human rights as essentially godly, based on the virtues and values of Christian faith. In Schaeffer's often-repeated logic, human rights made no sense if they were separated from God, who gave humans the inherent dignity that was the basis for "rights." Yet for many of its advocates, the very concept of "human rights" was based on a humanist presumption that individuals provided the authorization of their own rights—they did not need God. Schaeffer and others felt that secular human rights activists were essentially stealing a Christian belief about the dignity of the soul and trying to make it their own.

Despite these reservations about the human rights project, it was easy for Christian Cold Warriors to take up the cause of the "suffering church," and to subordinate whatever theological doubts they might have had to their certainty about the communist threat. All Christians were part of the body of Christ, they said, and the body of Christ was suffering under communism.

The most visible suffering religious community in the Soviet Union, however, was not Christians, but Jews. Starting in the early 1970s, a group of American Jews led a campaign—in conjunction with Catholics, evangelicals, and secular Cold Warriors—seeking US Congressional action to demand that the Soviets allow Jews to emigrate. Soviet persecution of Jews had recently intensified. Jewish activists in the USSR who spoke out were handed harsh prison sentences, and in 1972, the Soviet Union had added an overtly anti-Semitic "exit tax" for all who sought to emigrate, provoking outrage in the United States.

In 1974 Congress passed the Jackson-Vanik amendment, which instituted trade sanctions against "non-market countries" that restricted emigration—that is, the Soviet Union. The Nixon White House had opposed the bill; Henry Kissinger in particular thought Jackson-Vanik was the kind of public posturing that made it far more difficult to exert pressure via "quiet diplomacy." But Cold Warriors, liberal human rights activists, Jewish organizations, and Christians of all stripes agreed on the importance of protecting the rights of Jews in the Soviet Union, where human rights, religious freedom, racial persecution, and the Cold War intersected powerfully.[17]

In 1975, the Conference on Security and Cooperation in Europe passed the Helsinki Accords, designed to improve East-West cooperation. The Helsinki Final Act, which asserted both individual rights to freedom of belief and the collective right of peoples to self-determination, was to become the legal grounds for the Eastern European liberation movements of the late 1970s and 1980s.[18]

Then Jimmy Carter joined the conversation. During the 1976 election campaign, Carter had criticized President Gerald Ford for ignoring human rights, propping up dictators, and going too easy on the Soviet Union. Carter said that the United States needed to be a "beacon" for peace and freedom, for individual liberty and human rights. When Carter became president, he placed human rights at the center of his foreign policy.[19]

Many activists were enthusiastic about Carter's stance, but groups such as Amnesty International tried to keep human rights above politics, or political reproach. Indeed, for many people, the moral imagination of human rights was appealing because they saw it as apolitical: it was possible to be against suffering, no matter who inflicted it or who the victims were. Yet the reality of international politics meant that the appeal of human rights often seemed to be less their universality than their flexibility. Liberals generally focused on the violations by colonial powers or Latin American dictators; conservatives focused on the oppression in the Soviet Union and its satellites. Senator Daniel Patrick Moynihan (D-NY) described the détente between the liberal and conservative wings of the Democratic party in the mid-1970s: "We'll be against the dictator you don't like the most . . . if you'll be against the dictators we don't like the most."[20]

In the 1970s, several evangelical organizations undertook bold action against dictators they disliked. The group Open Doors, for example, was founded by "Brother Andrew" Vanderbiljl, a Dutch pastor who made his name smuggling Bibles into the Soviet Union and Eastern Europe, staging brilliant political theater in the process. Brother Andrew argued that what Christians behind the Iron Curtain really needed was Bibles—a perfectly evangelical view that true faith was only possible if individuals could read and understand the Bible for themselves. When stories circulated about churches being shut down or Christians arrested, Brother Andrew and his group made secret, cross-border forays into forbidden territory, delivering Bibles for believers, and recounting their daring escapes on their return.[21]

The practice was strongly criticized by both liberal Christians and other evangelicals. The provocative smuggling operations, said one leading figure in the Southern Baptist Convention, were "creating problems for the whole Christian witness" in communist areas. Working quietly with governments, however, was not likely to get a lot of fanfare or to raise money for an organization—which, critics implied, were the real goals behind practices like Bible smuggling.[22]

Richard Wurmbrand's organization, Jesus to the Communist World, also engaged in a good bit of attention-grabbing, intentionally reckless behavior. In May 1979, for example, two thirty-two-year-old men associated with the group flew their small plane over the Cuban coast, dropping six thousand copies of a pamphlet written by Wurmbrand. After the "Bible bombing," they lost their way in a storm and were forced to land in Cuba, where they were arrested and sentenced to twenty-four years in jail. They served seventeen months before being released in a general pardon of Americans. When they returned home, they described their horrific time in Cuban prisons in solitary confinement. One of the men reported that he had been repeatedly asked to confess to being a CIA agent. "All I would confess to was being a Christian."[23] The combination of masculine adventurism and steadfastness in the face of danger positioned the men as martyrs themselves—those who were, like the Christians behind the Iron Curtain whom they claimed to represent, perfect symbols of the need to bring Jesus to the Communist world.

Throughout the 1970s, there was an intense, sometimes quite nasty competition between organizations that were engaged in these kinds of activities. Their work, and their fundraising, often depended on promoting the exploits of charismatic leaders. Brother Andrew took out ads describing his dangerous trip across an East European border with a truckload of Bibles. Another organization planned a series of television specials that would "tell the unbelievable James Bond accounts" of their leader's activities abroad. Critics hammered these groups for their sensationalistic approaches and hardball fundraising, but one Christian activist, speaking anonymously to a reporter, admitted that the groups' mix of faith and politics was hard to beat: "The combined appeal of doing something to stamp out communism and sending Bibles into atheistic lands where believers are persecuted for Christ's sake draws big bucks."[24]

In the late 1970s, Jesus to the Communist World was the second-largest such organization in the country, but it was soon badly damaged by a particularly fractious and labyrinthine legal battle. The country's largest group was Underground Evangelism, run by former missionary and Pentecostal minister Joe Bass. Wurmbrand had worked briefly for Bass before founding his own organization, and now the two confronted each other over charges and countercharges of defamation. The claims were bizarre. In 1979, a young woman accused leaders in Underground Evangelism of having an affair (or two). She may or may not have been in alliance with Wurmbrand, but he made her charges public. Underground Evangelism sued Wurmbrand for defamation; he sued them for calling him a liar. The claims were settled out of court, but then some members of the leadership in Jesus to the Communist World renounced the settlement.[25] The organization eventually changed its name to Voice of the Martyrs and later became a leading player in the movement in support of the International Religious Freedom Act, painting a dark portrait of a global war on religion, with Christians the primary victims.

In the early 1980s, evangelicals found what would become a major cause célèbre, the case of the Siberian Seven. In June 1978, five members of the Vashchenko family and two of their neighbors had pushed their way into the US embassy in Moscow. The families were Pentecostals who said they faced discrimination and harassment for their religion. The group demanded that the US embassy protect them until the Soviet Union agreed to allow them out of the country. Remarkably, the embassy did just that. For the next five years, US and Soviet diplomats and politicians sparred over their fate.

The members of the group were savvy and stubborn political actors. They understood that, having sought asylum, their safety required sustaining the attention of the media and the support of Christians globally. By the time they entered the embassy, it had become increasingly clear that evangelicals in the Soviet Union, particularly Pentecostals, did face severe repression. While there was an officially recognized Baptist church, a range of underground Protestant churches refused to cooperate with the Soviet state. Pentecostals, who along with Baptists were one of the largest Protestant groups in the Soviet Union, were not recognized at all. One unnamed official speculated that Pentecostals were now being targeted because they were becoming too vocal about wanting to emigrate. The Soviets "don't want another Jewish movement."[26]

Indeed, Soviet Jews were still suffering. The Jackson-Vanik amendment seemed to have led to a backlash in the Soviet Union, and there had been a decline in the number of Jews being allowed to emigrate.[27] Now evangelicals joined their camp. In the spring of 1979, the US Commission on Security and Cooperation in Europe, charged with monitoring the implementation of the Helsinki Final Act, issued a list of ten thousand evangelicals who wanted to leave the Soviet Union. A year later, on June 12, 1980, a joint resolution of Congress criticizing Soviet treatment of Christians stated that the number was now at least fifty thousand. At the Madrid Conference on Security and Cooperation in Europe

(CSCE) in December 1980, some Western countries welcomed representatives from the Soviet evangelical community and then published their own figures, numbering the "persecuted Soviet Christians" at thirty thousand.[28]

It was in this context that the Siberian Seven became a sensation in the US media. *Time,* the *New York Times, Los Angeles Times,* and *Christian Science Monitor* all ran regular stories updating their situation—marking anniversaries, reporting on potential agreements, and, eventually, documenting the dramatic physical decline of Lidiya Vashchenko after she launched a hunger strike in late 1981. The "Vashchenko Affair" was broadly discussed even beyond the major urban media, as local newspapers also covered the story, updating their audience with accounts from the wire services.[29]

After Ronald Reagan became president in January 1981, the National Interreligious Task Force on Soviet Jewry told the president that it was "most anxious about the safety of the Pentecostal Seven."[30] People in the pews were attentive as well. The earliest and biggest response was in Europe. In summer of 1981, a group of activists in the United Kingdom founded the "Free the Siberian Seven" campaign, which organized street protests and demonstrations. The group Christian Solidarity International, which had been formed in Zürich in 1977, mobilized to support the Pentecostal families, producing materials in French, German, and Swedish, and organizing individuals to write letters to the Seven.[31]

In the United States, the story circulated but concrete action was at first minimal. The Northwest Baptist Convention approved a resolution demanding that the Siberian Seven be allowed to emigrate to the United States.[32] In 1980 Jonathan Pollack published an inspirational book called *The Siberian Seven*; the Christian Anti-Communist Crusade encouraged its members to buy it.[33] The sense of urgency increased over time, as the Seven spent year after year in the embassy. (Lidiya Vashchenko was evacuated to a Moscow hospital before the fourth anniversary, after her hunger strike left her near death.) In September 1981, a *Christianity Today* article complained about the lack of activity among US Christians, with "church organizations . . . remarkably unwilling to take official positions." The author speculated, probably correctly, that this was because major organizations, even Pentecostal ones, feared jeopardizing the ability of people in registered Soviet churches to travel and participate in international Christian organizations.[34]

Christianity Today treated the Pentecostals as fellow evangelicals in trouble, but the editors were not sure others were doing the same. While it might be hard for some traditional evangelicals to identify with Pentecostals, the magazine said, this was only because Americans had become too fond of highlighting small theological differences. What Pentecostals and, for example, Baptists had in common was a great deal more important than what divided them. It was time for readers to get on board with an expanded definition of "evangelical," *CT* argued, one that included Pentecostals, the fastest growing category of conservative Christians in the world.[35] Less than a year after *CT* complained about the church's silence, the magazine noted that things were changing, that several more organizations had taken up the case. The Siberian Seven had been "the preoccupation of some Western Christians for months and even years"; now US groups like the Christian Legal Aid Society were working with Congress, while students at Wheaton College and Seattle Pacific University had sent a petition to President Reagan.[36]

In late 1982 President Reagan took a personal interest in the Siberian Seven. He asked for a private meeting with the Soviet ambassador—the first time the two men had met, nearly two years into Reagan's first term. In that meeting, Reagan suggested that the two countries should make a "fresh start." The release of the Siberian Seven, he said, would be a good place to begin.[37]

Both Ronald Reagan and Billy Graham would later lay claim to having eventually secured the deal that allowed the family to emigrate. Graham and his team actually harbored some doubts about the group, intitally viewing them as opportunists who simply wanted to leave the country and were using religion as a fig leaf. But when Graham went to the Soviet Union in 1982, he felt he would be remiss (and highly criticized) if he did not visit them. The visit itself was tense. The Pentecostals wanted Graham to take a strong position in favor of their right to emigrate and were furious when he insisted that the visit was only pastoral. Graham, in keeping with the agreement that had allowed him to do his preaching tour, refused to criticize the Soviets publicly. Graham faced a barrage of criticism back home for ignoring the larger plight of Soviet Christians. *Newsweek* described the visit with the sarcastic summary: "Billy Renders to Caesar." Still, Graham's side claimed that they had quietly pushed for the Soviets to promise that they would allow the group to emigrate if they left the US embassy and applied for visas.[38]

President Reagan asked US negotiators at the CSCE meetings in Madrid to push for the freedom of the Pentecostals. When two of the Seven began a hunger strike in 1982, Reagan appealed to Brezhnev personally. Reagan also sought the release of Jewish prisoners, and there continued to be an active public campaign on their behalf. A few Christians began to make comparisons. One letter to the *New York Times* complained that "Christian victims" were being forgotten. While 150,000 Jews had fled the USSR, Christians were not so lucky—"not a single one" of the 30,000 Soviet evangelicals had been allowed to leave. Evangelicals' feelings toward Jews were warming overall, but remained a mix of solidarity, admiration, jealousy, and sometimes anger.[39]

In February of 1982, Lidiya Vashchenko left the embassy to get hospital treatment after her hunger strike. A year later, she received a visa to leave the country, and visas for the other six and their families followed shortly thereafter. Altogether, the group had spent five years inside the embassy. Of the almost thirty people who were eventually allowed to leave, most went to Israel. Two of the Vashchenko daughters settled in the United States.[40] It is difficult to calculate the Siberian Seven's role in the eventual Cold War thaw, but the "quiet diplomacy" carried out by members of the Reagan administration and Soviet diplomats may have helped create trust.[41]

Evangelicals were relieved for the Siberian Seven, but they weren't optimistic about the future. They—both activists and ordinary believers—continued to argue passionately that Christians behind the Iron Curtain were persecuted and must be defended.

In 1979, conservatives would mount a takeover of the Southern Baptist Convention that began with the election of Adrian Rogers as president. Just one year earlier, the denomination had been extolling the importance of universal human rights:

> We believe that every human being has basic human rights which may not rightly be relinquished, abridged, or denied. Moreover, we believe that Jesus Christ revealed His own support for human rights when He declared: "The Spirit of the Lord is upon me . . . He has sent me to proclaim release to the captives and recovering of sight to the blind, to set at liberty those who are oppressed, to proclaim the acceptable year of the Lord" (Luke 4:18–19, RSV).[42]

This resonated with the language of social concern from Lausanne. But, like human rights language more generally, it was fluid. Conservatives in the evangelical movement did not renounce human rights, they simply focused the human rights agenda on the lives and bodies of Christians.

Sara Killian Cooke, a pastor's wife in Richmond, Virginia, showed how images of faraway suffering could move a local church community. Cooke was part of a women's prayer group that gathered each week to pray for "Christ's suffering church." "We pool information" about the world, she said, from evangelical periodicals, news releases, and letters from missionaries and pastors, and then pray for those who need help: pastors in registered churches and those in unregistered churches, for those declared unstable and placed in psychiatric wards, for those who are brainwashed, and for those "children taken from believing parents and placed in communes." The list was a perfectly calibrated testament to the impact of the evangelical focus on communism in China, Russia, and Eastern Europe.

Cooke's prayer summed up the evangelical view of the persecuted church in need of strength:

> Father, for your servants about to be martyred, we ask a Christ-glorifying witness like Stephen's. For those undergoing torture, we ask power not to deny your name . . . Knowing our weakness, we pray for those who have fallen, those who mourn false confessions . . . For those alone in prison, we ask you to send the Holy Comforter . . . Savior, send to your suffering body divine intervention.

This rather extraordinary prayer continues, quivering with sentiment, "*May holy angels minister*" . . . may God "*heal their broken hearts.*"[43]

Cooke's prayer, indicative as it is of the focus on the communist world in this period, also marks a subtle change in how believers saw persecution. Throughout the 1960s and 1970s, attacks on Christians were most often represented as something that specific reprehensible regimes *did*, for their own (atheistic) reasons. Beginning in the 1980s, there emerged a sense that persecution of Christians was something that *was*; it existed wherever there were believers because suffering was a significant part of what it meant to be a Christian. In the Bible, followers of Jesus are repeatedly assured that they must suffer for his sake.[44] If that was less true for Americans than for others, they began to believe that such might not always be the case: "We have been insulated" from the suffering of persecuted Christians, Cooke wrote, but "someday we might also be forced to share their trial."[45]

Many causes fed into the rise of the religious Right in the late 1970s, and anti-communism was just one among them. Other concerns were equally important, including issues such as school prayer, public education, abortion, and feminism. The power of a conservative Christian business class also gave the movement clout.[46] But evangelical anti-communism was more than a Cold War stance; it was an expression of anxiety about the fate of Christians in the world, and that gave it great emotional power.

From the beginning, Jerry Falwell's Moral Majority made anti-communism (along with support for Israel) one of the central planks of its platform. One of the men who worked closely with Falwell in the early days of the Moral Majority, Elmer Towns, said that people believed that "the threat of communism was great," and that this was understood as both a domestic and an international threat. "[W]hether it was seen as a 'hot' war or an undermining action to take over this country by giving away our freedom and our rights, including the freedom to preach and the freedom to have a church and be separate and be different. . . . We felt a threat. . . . we [were] losing ground every day to society, to the world, to bureaucracy, to the federal government.'"[47] Nobody was trying to take away anybody's right to preach or have a church in the United States, but American evangelicals' strong identification with global Christianity made that threat seem more real. It could happen here, they thought, if they failed to turn back liberalism.

The power of televangelism played a role in the popularization of anti-communism. Although its influence has been sometimes overstated, televangelism's reach was significant. Several of the most popular TV preachers of the early 1980s—Oral Roberts, Robert Schuller, Rex Humbard, and Jimmy Swaggart—rarely addressed politics. But Jerry Falwell talked about political minutiae with the enthusiasm of a conspiracy-minded amateur historian, and his *Old Time Gospel Hour* had an audience of 1.4 million each week.[48] Pat Robertson's *700 Club* had been on the air since 1966, starting out on a handful of stations in the nascent Christian Broadcasting Network. His audience swelled in the late 1970s, as the *700 Club* went into national syndication. By 1985 it aired on 190 broadcast stations in addition to the CBN cable network; 27 million viewers watched the show at least once a month.[49] Robertson used his show to advocate for a broad range of conservative causes, including aid to the Nicaraguan Contras who were trying to overthrow the Marxist Sandinista government, support for the right-wing Likud government in Israel, and support for the white governments of South Africa and Rhodesia. In all cases, the threat was not just communism, but communism bent on persecuting its enemies. Christians believed they must be willing to face persecution and to watch their fellow believers suffer, but with Robertson suggesting anger and activism, they would not have to turn the other cheek.[50]

Nearly two decades after the passage of the 1974 Jackson-Vanik amendment, Christian activists pushing for a bill on international religious freedom would return to it as a model. That second generation of anti-persecution activists would also point to Jackson-Vanik as proof that they were justified in focusing on *Christian* persecution, because Jackson-Vanik was clearly designed to protect Jews.[51] From this would follow two debates that would engage evangelical activists for the next thirty years. The first was whether they should focus on championing "Christian rights" or "human rights." The second was whether the compromises of "quiet diplomacy" could provide a better route to change than visible, morally sanctified public action. What evangelical activists never doubted, however, was that global Christian suffering was profound, and that Christians in the United States would need to respond with more than Bible smuggling.

7

"The Suffering Church"

APARTHEID SOUTH AFRICA

IN OCTOBER OF 1985, a white American evangelical named David Howard was arrested in South Africa. Howard was the director of the World Evangelical Fellowship, a large and conservative global network of evangelical denominations and parachurch groups. He had come to South Africa to be the keynote speaker at the South African Conference of Evangelical Leaders; he expected to talk about winning souls. Instead he met a black South African named Caesar Molebatsi, just thirty-six years old, who was the dynamic director of an evangelical outreach program called Youth Alive Ministries. As a result, Howard would soon learn—quickly and directly—about the realities of apartheid.

Molebatsi and Howard made a strong connection almost immediately. Racial tensions had erupted early in the conference, and Howard had supported Molebatsi in a conflict with a representative of the Frontline Fellowship, a radical right-wing organization that grew out of the South African Defence Forces (SADF). Before one session, members of the group had asked Molebatsi to use his talk to denounce "black theology" as unbiblical. He had refused.[1]

The day after the conference ended, Molebatsi invited Howard to his house in the black township of Soweto for lunch. As the two men and another friend of Molebatsi's sat talking, the SADF came sweeping into the house. They were looking for the suspicious white American who dared to have lunch in a black township. The soldiers asked Howard to come to the local police station for questioning. Molebatsi then stepped up and told the soldiers that, if they were going to take his guest, he would have to come too. The soldiers obliged. Molebatsi's move was brave, even reckless. The SADF, he knew, had been looking for him because of his anti-apartheid activities.[2]

At the police station, the officer in charge questioned them closely. After threatening to keep both men in jail for the weekend, the officer released them. By South African standards, this was not much more than an inconvenience, but it made quite an impression on Howard. A few months after he returned home, he wrote about his experience in a special South Africa issue of *Transformation*, an evangelical journal that functioned as the voice of socially concerned evangelicals. Howard told of how he had been changed by the experience. Molebatsi was "a brilliant, godly man" who was doing God's work in South Africa. Meeting him had convinced Howard that it was time to speak out against apartheid.

In praising Molebatsi, Howard felt it necessary to stress that Molebatsi was a moderate; while he did not acquiesce to apartheid, he was also not one of the "black radicals" who engaged in violence. This was a fair-enough description of Molebatsi, but the South African made clear where the real dangers were. "I am not afraid of the black radicals," he told Howard. "But I greatly fear what my evangelical brethren will do to me."[3]

The mid-1980s was a time of upheaval over apartheid. In South Africa, townships were in revolt, with battles in the streets between black residents and the SADF. Meanwhile liberal Protestants and some Catholics were leading non-violent resistance. US campuses were afire with calls for divestment, cities and states were moving toward major divestment decisions, and violent anti-apartheid protests occurred in Europe. At the same time, President Ronald Reagan's administration was promoting its model of "constructive engagement" with South Africa, refusing to support a sanctions bill introduced by Democrats in the Senate.

Facing increasingly energized opposition to the apartheid regime, policymakers in both the United States and South Africa pointed out South Africa's impeccable anticommunist credentials as a stalwart ally in a regional field of Marxist governments (in Angola and Mozambique) and left-wing rebel movements (in Rhodesia and Namibia). In South Africa, the government lurched between promises of reform and spectacular acts of violence. When Pretoria declared a state of emergency in 1985 it was the beginning of the end of apartheid.

In this heated climate, evangelicals were inspired to speak up—on both sides of the struggle. After decades on the sidelines, evangelical churches in South Africa, almost always divided by race, began to issue proclamations and organize. For years, even decades, Americans had been coming to South Africa to preach or to attend conferences or to meet with politicians. Less frequently—but consequentially—South African evangelicals had traveled to the United States, to study and sometimes to teach at one of the major evangelical institutions. These networks were equally important to conservatives and to liberals, and to the many people who operated across those political categories. And when members of those networks met at conferences or prayer meetings, racial and national differences were unavoidable, and the realities of apartheid were palpable.

Apartheid was arguably the greatest moral crisis yet faced by the global evangelical movement. The fact that there were avowed and enthusiastic Christians who stood on both sides of this conflict made it particularly compelling and confusing.

Notably, advocates on both sides used the language of suffering and martyrdom to describe their own position and/or that of their allies in South Africa, although the language was most salient for apartheid's opponents. It was unconscionable, activists said, to stand by while the church, the body of Christ, was being wounded in South Africa. "The suffering church has a moral claim on the body of Christ," the staff at the liberal *Sojourners* would write in 1989. Unlike the cases of Congo or the USSR, no one would argue that Christians in South Africa were suffering merely for their religious beliefs. Instead, what mattered was the Christians' political stance: how they lived out the tenets that their faith affirmed.

The violence that accompanied apartheid had first garnered significant international attention a generation earlier, in March of 1960, when a group of five thousand black South Africans gathered at a police station in the township of Sharpeville, near Johannesburg, to protest the "pass laws" that required all black South Africans to carry passbooks that limited their travel and work opportunities. As people assembled in the yard outside the station, the police opened fire, killing 69 people.[4]

South Africa faced an international outcry. American Christians were among those shaken by the events. A week after the Sharpeville massacre, Reverend A. Chester Clark, secretary-treasurer of the Board of Missions of the AME Church, helped to organize a petition to demand that the UN expel South Africa. There were scores of AME churches in South Africa, born of a missionary movement in the early twentieth century, that were fully integrated in the US-based denomination. The Board of Missions petition called on all members of the church to protest, "employing every means at our command."[5]

A few days later, a large and interdenominational group of black ministers—a group that included Pastor Smallwood Williams of the Bible Way Church of Washington, DC, a Pentecostal denomination—silently picketed the South African consulate in New York wearing signs that asked, "What Color is Christ? Would Jesus Need a Pass in South Africa?"[6] At the national meeting of the AME Council of Bishops in Memphis later that spring, the church expressed shock and outrage in specifically religious terms: "[T]he fact that these crimes are perpetrated by a so-called Christian nation fills us with a sense of shame and horror."[7]

In South Africa, protests against the killings escalated, as did the brutal government response. The government banned the two largest black political organizations, the African National Congress (ANC) and the Pan-Africanist Congress, and arrested more than 18,000 people. Quickly, many leaders of both groups went underground, but in 1963 there was a roundup and arrest of almost all of the ANC leadership. Nelson Mandela and seven others were tried and convicted of sabotage, beginning what would be decades in prison.

In 1960, the ANC had managed to smuggle its president, Oliver Tambo, out of the country, so that someone could lead the movement from afar. From 1964 to 1991, he was the only major ANC leader not in jail. Shuttling around the world, Tambo, an Anglican who had been educated by missionaries, made links to religious communities very effectively. He worked with religious activists and with secular organizations to push for an arms embargo on South Africa as well as boycotts of South African goods, sporting teams, artists, and academics.[8]

Church activism was central to the global anti-apartheid movement. In 1968, the World Council of Churches held its meeting in Uppsala, Sweden. There, the WCC declared that combatting racism—which WCC leaders saw as egregiously dividing the body of Christ—was one of its most urgent goals. The Uppsala Assembly set the parameters for what would become the Program to Combat Racism, which would give grants to support anti-racist work around the world. The *Guardian* (United Kingdom) described the first meeting of the program's executive committee in 1969 as "part teach-in, part penitence, part act of redemption, and part morality play with unscripted episodes from Black Power." In 1970, the WCC made its first grants to several organizations engaged in struggles against the white governments in South Africa and Rhodesia, including the ANC. The grants were relatively small monetarily but very significant symbolically, and they provoked a firestorm of protest and outrage. One commentator described this as a key moment in the evolution of the ecumenical movement's social conscience. "The grants to liberation movements were a step across the line which has been drawn between charity, traditionally regarded as Christian, and solidarity, which has seldom been risked by the churches."[9]

In 1971, the Episcopal Church USA presented a shareholder resolution at the General Motors annual meeting that urged the company to withdraw from South Africa. The resolution did not pass; in fact, it received less than 5 percent of the votes.[10] Still it was a sign of what was to come, as, in the 1970s, the ecumenical movement made opposition to apartheid into a signature issue.

South Africa was officially a Christian country. The Dutch Reformed Church supported apartheid and was closely linked to the ruling National Party. (The DRC had separate branches, or "daughter churches," for black South Africans and for those people designated as "coloured," a distinct group with mixed ancestry.) The DRC was theologically conservative and often was considered to be an evangelical church, although it stood apart from most national evangelical bodies. The South African Council of Churches (SACC) was home to most of the other Protestant denominations in South Africa. It was a center of anti-apartheid activism, but its leadership would remain almost entirely white until Bishop Desmond Tutu became general secretary in 1978. The Catholic Church had made forceful statements condemning apartheid in 1957, 1960, and 1962, well before most Protestant churches. But while Archbishop Denis Hurley of Durban was an anti-apartheid leader, the Catholic churches themselves—even the black and Indian churches—were largely quiescent.[11]

By the 1960s, some Christians were taking more radical stances. Rev. Beyers Naudé, an Afrikaner who had been a priest in the Dutch Reformed Church, had founded the left-wing Christian Institute in 1963. The institute was a relentless critic of apartheid and racism, but went beyond that to call for a theology of liberation, a commitment to the poor, and a determined move toward black leadership.[12]

Evangelicals were less organized. There were denominations that ran the gamut from Baptist to Assemblies of God. There were independent African Initiated Churches (AICs), the term often used for churches that were started by Africans rather than by missionaries. And there were churches associated with specific, often American, missionary organizations. Evangelical churches were almost entirely segregated, and most of them, whether white or nonwhite, exhibited a strong strain of pietism—a fundamental anxiety about an "overly political" church.[13] By the early 1970s, however, exceptions were beginning to emerge.

In March of 1973, representatives of many of the evangelical churches came together to support Billy Graham's first—highly successful—crusade in South Africa. Graham's crusade was also timed to coincide with the South African Congress on Mission and Evangelism, a groundbreaking interracial gathering of church leaders. Both events were organized by evangelist Michael Cassidy (figure 7.1). In 1973, Cassidy was thirty-seven years old but looked younger, with an intensity and self-confidence that would shape his role as an evangelist and anti-apartheid leader. Cassidy had felt the call to ministry at a Graham crusade in New York in 1957 and had begun studies at Fuller Theological Seminary in 1959. In 1962, when he was still a seminary student, he founded African Enterprise, an evangelistic organization. He had held interracial "crusades" in South Africa since the mid-1960s, and had inspired both Bill Pannell and Samuel Escobar with his controversial 1966 speech in Berlin.[14]

FIGURE 7.1 Michael Cassidy and Billy Graham, 1973, by kind permission of African Enterprise.

Michael Cassidy was no radical, even by the standards of white South Africans. An Anglican who identified as evangelical, he had published a relatively long article in *Christianity Today* in 1971 explaining why, as a Christian, he was opposed to apartheid. But he peppered his argument with many caveats about why white South Africans felt so threatened by the idea of black rule. He argued for the value of small steps toward "reconciliation." He also praised the work of the left-wing Christian Institute and celebrated the increasing opposition to apartheid among the young.[15] This made Cassidy the perfect spokesperson for a still-rare form of liberal interracial evangelicalism in South Africa. And Graham was the ideal figure to bring respectability to Cassidy's cause.

The 1973 crusade was in many ways a triumph. Graham had declined many invitations to preach to segregated audiences in South Africa. It was Cassidy who arranged for the interracial gatherings that both men wanted.

Graham attracted huge crowds: forty thousand in Durban, more than sixty thousand in Johannesburg.[16] He appeared on a simple stage in front of the throngs of people, preaching in his signature style—straightforward, vibrant, and repetitive. He highlighted God's love for all people, "the black world, the white world, the yellow world, the rich world, the poor world." He went on to make the point that Jesus was *not* a white man, but was probably brown, "not unlike some of the Indian people here today." In the South African context, Graham was signaling a sociopolitical position. But he did not, and would not, directly condemn apartheid.

During his trip, Graham was repeatedly asked to comment on current events in South Africa, including the more than sixty strikes, involving more than sixty thousand workers, that had occurred in the first three months of the year. Pushed by a rather relentless group of reporters about what he thought a Christian position on sanctions against South Africa should be, Graham said that good Christian people could disagree on the issue, although he reported that he had recently met with three black churchmen in Durban who told him that change would be accomplished more quickly "if there were more inter-relationship . . . not isolationism."[17]

That was something of a misstatement. In addition to his public events, Graham had been a keynote speaker at Cassidy's South African Congress on Mission and Evangelism, where hundreds of ministers, black and white, had gathered. Cassidy and his allies had organized the congress in conjunction with Graham's visit, hoping to use it as a showcase for interracial Christian brotherhood. Instead, the congress nearly imploded over racial divisions. And the heart of the issue was how to respond to apartheid.

The nearly seven hundred conference participants had come from twenty-seven denominations. The congress was unusually broad, and was co-sponsored by the South African Council of Churches. The SACC had joined in with some trepidation, fearful that the evangelical contingent would dominate, but their church leaders showed up en masse.[18] Unsurprisingly, the Dutch Reformed Church had not sent representatives, although a few people came on their own. Also underrepresented were the African Initiated Churches, whose members were approximately 18 percent of the black population.[19] Still, the experience was memorable for most of the delegates, who had never encountered such a cross section of Christians in one place, from conservative white evangelicals to black Pentecostals to liberal Anglicans. Delegates quipped that the crowd covered everyone: "Sacramental, Fundamental, and Sentimental!"[20]

The initial excitement, however, centered on the simple fact that people of different races were living and working together. This was a remarkable experience, given that such intermixing was illegal in South Africa. After some tense negotiations—at some point, things were so difficult that the organizers considered chartering a boat as the meeting site—the conference had been granted an exception. "Every delegate became acutely aware of the excitement and joy at the breaking of one of South Africa's sacred cow traditions," commented one participant. The president of the Baptist Union of South Africa admitted that crossing racial barriers was a bit daunting at first, but he welcomed the experiment. "At this Congress we were able to stay together at the same hotel, eat from the same tables, and travel in the same buses—and the wonderful thing about it was that it seemed the most natural thing in the world to do." Of course, in South Africa this was *not* the most natural thing in the world; that was precisely what made the initial reports of the congress so heady.[21]

On the first night, John Gatu of Kenya offered the opening prayer. Gatu, who had proposed a moratorium on Western missionaries in 1971, was controversial among evangelicals in the United States and Europe. In Africa, however, he was almost universally admired. After the prayer, Gatu asked the participants (almost all male) to greet a member of another racial group by embracing him.[22] It was an emblematic moment—a performance of solidarity—a dream of what the congress hoped to be.

There were two Americans at the conference, Leighton Ford (who was white) and Howard Jones (who was black), both from the Billy Graham Evangelistic Association. Both men recognized the value of the interracial gathering itself, but they were less than enthused about the environment they faced outside the hotel walls. Twice during the congress they left the hotel to try to get a meal elsewhere. The first time, they went with two others to get hamburgers at the Wimpy chain, knowing—or expecting—that their racially mixed group couldn't eat inside the restaurant. Two of the white men ordered takeout, and the four found a quiet parking spot and ate in the car. The following night they found the hotel dining room closed and were sent to a drive-in down by the ocean. This time, to Ford's amusement, the restaurant was for "coloureds" only. Jones and Ford both went to stand in line. "Most of the people there looked at me in a rather surprised way!" Ford reported, but they were polite. Jones told the story slightly differently—the second event happened several days later, and not in Durban, as he recalled. More strikingly, he did not find any of it amusing in the least. Both Ford and Jones agreed that an important lesson had been learned. Ford reported that "[i]t was particularly good for me, a white man, to be traveling with a black brother. We felt the sting and restrictions of apartheid as neither one of us would have, and particularly me, in traveling alone."[23]

The conference overall was fractured. There were those who wanted to handle apartheid with "love and Christian community"—they were more likely to use the language of racial "reconciliation." And there were those who wanted to challenge apartheid directly, confronting it as an issue of racial power. These divisions did not align neatly with participants' theologies. Missions theorist David Bosch, for example, was a theological conservative, a professor at the University of South Africa at Pretoria, and a member of the Dutch Reformed Church. Bosch came as an individual since the DRC did not send any official representatives and was one of several speakers who pushed white delegates to challenge their own complacency. It was not enough to "put up a sign" on the church door "saying 'All are Welcome,'" Bosch told the delegates. "If we practice charity without solidarity, or passion without taking sides, or alms-giving without action, we are betraying the essence of the gospel." Grace is free yet costly, Bosch told his audience, in one of the meetings' many implicit and explicit references to Bonhoeffer.[24]

Some of the more conservative white delegates complained that they were talking too much about racism and not enough about evangelism. So did a few black leaders. Nicholas Bhengu, a leading evangelist and Assemblies of God minister, warned against "polluting the pure Gospel" by getting swept away with "current and sporadic trends and policies." The reverend was concerned that pastors were being judged by how closely they identified with the anti-apartheid struggle, and not by the content of their gospel message. Among the black participants, however, his views were in the minority.[25]

Nearly a week into the ten-day event, a dramatic development made the racial lines clear. A large group of nonwhite participants held a separate meeting to discuss grievances about whites dominating the conference. This decision left white delegates to meet on *their* own, feeling "discriminated against." It was definitely the end of the "honeymoon and hallelujah mood."[26]

The black and coloured group reported back to the white delegates that they had decided to stay at the meeting, but not until they had made clear what they saw as the limits of the event. The theologian Manas Buthelezi of the Evangelical Lutheran Church of Southern Africa spoke for many in the nonwhite group. Buthelezi had been deeply influenced by black liberation theology, and he shocked some members of the audience when he argued that, since Christianity in South Africa was predominantly black, the gospel needed to be relevant to the problems of black people if it were to matter at all. Talk of "reconciliation" was misplaced, Buthelezi argued. "Love can never be said to exist where normal fellowship is banned." Another black delegate spoke against "the white paternalism in the church." Some white delegates responded to any such critiques by retreating to an insistence that the focus should be on evangelism. "As long as we can get on with that," one summarized, "everything will be all right."[27]

What had begun so hopefully ended in disappointment. Many of the participants in the congress would go on to become major anti-apartheid activists. But the logic of reconciliation and brotherhood that was at the heart of Cassidy's vision would, for many of the people in the struggle, prove woefully inadequate to the realities of apartheid. Liberalism would show itself to be even more wanting later in the decade, when ordinary people in the townships wrested leadership from an older generation.

In 1976, the township of Soweto was desperately poor and overcrowded. Each small house had an average of fourteen occupants. Only one in three houses had electricity. No residents were allowed to own their homes, and rents were periodically raised when the local (white) administration needed money. In the midst of such poverty, crime was rampant. The quality of the education system would have been shocking in any other context—only 12 percent of teachers had completed high school themselves. More than half of the population was younger than twenty-five.[28]

Not surprisingly, young people in the townships were strongly attracted to the Black Consciousness movement, led by a young intellectual and activist named Steven Biko. Biko sought a new, black-centered way of thinking, one that was free of the sense of inferiority and passivity that he believed had been instilled by apartheid. Early on in his short career, Biko had been involved with South Africa's multiracial University Christian Movement. Frustrated by the behavior of white students in the group, he left to form the South African Students Organization, a group for black students built on the precepts of black autonomy and self-respect. Like Buthelezi, Biko was strongly influenced by the black theology of American James Cone—one of many examples of the intellectual ties between the black liberation movements in the United States and South Africa.[29]

Biko quickly became the radical voice of a younger generation of black activists who no longer found liberal multiracialism credible. It was time for black South Africans—and in this Biko included colored and any Asian South Africans who did not claim "almost-white" privilege—to find their own voices, create their own groups, and decolonize their minds.[30]

Biko was "banned" by the South African government in 1973, which meant that he could not gather in groups and could not speak in public. This did not dim his influence. By the mid-1970s, the Black Consciousness movement had unrivaled political momentum among black South Africans. One teacher in Soweto told a reporter that "Black Consciousness is germinating. It is spreading among youth and young adults, and has filtered through to their younger brothers and sisters."[31]

On June 16, 1976, as many as 15,000 young people took to the streets of Soweto to peacefully protest new government rules that mandated that they be educated in Afrikaans rather than English. The police responded with tear gas and gunfire. Soon the students were joined by angry crowds of residents who attacked and burned down government buildings. The police responded with more shooting. By the end of the day, fifteen people had been killed, and images of the violence had been broadcast around the world. Soon the uprising was replicated in other townships, where protests included a combination of targeted boycotts, general strikes, and attacks on administrative buildings and police stations. The apartheid state fully unleashed its military and police forces; over the following year, at least 575 people were killed and more than 21,000 people were prosecuted.[32]

Soweto radicalized a new generation. It emerged as the epicenter of a revitalized anti-apartheid movement in which high school and college students were central. That movement would shock South African society and shape the anti-apartheid movement for many years to come.

Shortly after Soweto, in 1977, Biko was arrested for sedition and killed while in police custody. At the time of his death, he had severe brain injuries and bruises all over his body; he had been shackled naked in an interrogation room for two days before finally being transported to a prison hospital 750 miles away. After Biko's death became known, photos of his bruised and bloody body were plastered on posters and signs as anti-apartheid activists around the world responded with outrage. The images of his tortured body were paired with images of his face, youthful and handsome, and quotes from his writings: "The most potent weapon in the hand of the oppressor is the mind of the oppressed."[33]

Among those radicalized by Soweto and Biko's death was Caesar Molebatsi. As a young man, Molebatsi, like Biko, had been involved with the multiracial University Christian Movement, which allowed for fellowship between black, white, coloured, and Asian students. But the organization was dominated by white students, and Molebatsi was disturbed, as Biko had been, by their paternalism.

The year before Biko was killed, Molebatsi had returned to South Africa from his time at Wheaton College, just outside Chicago. The college was then a hothouse for an emerging transnational evangelical Left. Important alumni included John Gatu, who had proposed the missionary moratorium; Pius Wakatama from Rhodesia, author of *Independence for the African Church* (1976); and Latin American theologian René Padilla, who had galvanized delegates at the Lausanne Congress. During his student days at Wheaton, Molebatsi engaged in many long discussions with other young African Christians, usually about the role of First World churches in the Third World. He began to believe that missionaries in South Africa had "stayed beyond their usefulness, accepting the reigning political philosophy of apartheid without challenging its inherent evil."[34]

Molebatsi returned to South Africa just a few days after the Soweto uprisings began. He soon became the executive director of Youth Alive, the American missionary organization that had led him to the faith. This was never an entirely comfortable position for him, given his critique of missionaries. Eventually, he also became minister of his own church, Ebenezer Evangelical Church.

Molebatsi had an ambivalent relationship to the anti-apartheid movement. He saw himself as standing between the various factions, religious and political, that shaped black life in South Africa. He had been converted in a white denomination, but he knew that white missionaries and the (white and black) evangelical churches in South Africa had been quiescent, or worse. He saw that theologically liberal churches were taking the lead in opposing apartheid, yet he remained resolutely evangelical, uncomfortable with liberal theology. "I had serious questions about much ecumenical theology that was blatantly un-biblical," he wrote, "yet the same ecumenicals stood for justice and righteousness in a way that evangelicals did not."[35] Molebatsi, like many black evangelicals, was also hesitant to engage directly in political activism. He had been influenced by Biko and the Black Consciousness movement, but he saw himself, first of all, as a soul winner.

Before long, Molebatsi's approach began to change as political realities became more urgent. After Soweto, Molebatsi's brother George had begun working with the ANC. In December 1979, George was arrested. Shortly thereafter, the police came for Caesar too. He was held in solitary confinement for two weeks as the police tried to get him to provide evidence against George. Molebatsi later described sleeping on a few thin and filthy blankets on a concrete floor, not knowing when or whether he would be released. He expected that he might be tortured.

Two interventions saved him. First was quick action by David Bosch, the anti-apartheid missionary thinker who had attended the conference in Durban, who demanded that Molebatsi have access to a lawyer and a doctor. Second was a barrage of telegrams sent to the South African government by Wheaton alumni. These not only helped get Molebatsi released, but also pulled Wheaton students into contact with political realities quite far from home. Soon, Molebatsi would find himself playing a key role in fostering anti-apartheid activism among black South African evangelicals.[36]

Meanwhile, events in Soweto had revealed the weakness of the ANC's hand and the organization's dependence on assistance from outside South Africa. Forced underground since mass arrests in the early 1960s, the ANC had very limited military or guerilla capabilities. But in 1974, the postcolonial Marxist governments of Mozambique and Angola offered the ANC moral and military support. The ANC developed particularly strong ties in Angola, where the left-wing government had beaten back a rebellion supported by both South Africa and the United States. Angola became the ANC's military base of operations. After 1976, the ANC also gained a flow of volunteers who, radicalized by Soweto, headed over the border for training. In addition, Soweto taught the ANC that it needed to strengthen its ties to the townships, which it began to do.[37]

These developments only clarified how much the fight against apartheid was caught up in the Cold War. This was the context in which American and global responses to events in Southern Africa would be shaped. However liberal they seemed, churches both inside and outside South Africa generally viewed communism with suspicion, often seeing it as a deep threat to religious expression. Staying silent about apartheid was no longer an option for many churches, but taking sides with the liberation struggle meant potentially being seen as aiding communism, and thus siding with those who were believed to persecute Christians and other religious people.

Nonetheless, after Soweto, Protestant churches in the United States and Europe became more deeply involved in anti-apartheid activism, joining a burgeoning group of activists, both religious and secular. They were inspired by, and helped to shape, the larger surge in human rights activism in the 1970s. Through a broad variety of human rights campaigns in the early 1970s, from Amnesty International's Campaign Against Torture to the fight for Soviet Jewry in the early and mid-1970s, Westerners had begun putting human rights language to work. Human rights activists claimed to be fighting for universal, basic truths, even when their activism was implicated—as it often was—in Cold War politics. Human rights activism was grassroots, creative, energizing—and sometimes deeply problematic in its assumptions about the universality of its claims about what "rights" were the most important, and what violence most horrific.[38]

In 1977, the UN established its mandatory arms embargo against South Africa, and some businesses in the United States began to change their practices. Polaroid, where employees had long advocated for an end to doing business in South Africa, announced that it was pulling out completely. That same year, the University of Massachusetts at Amherst, responding to pressure from student activists, divested fully from South Africa.[39]

Some business-minded observers worried that such activism would derail US corporate activity in South Africa altogether. In response, the Rev. Leon Sullivan, pastor emeritus of Philadelphia's Zion Baptist Church and the only African American member of the General Motors Board of Directors, proposed what became known as "The Sullivan Principles." Rev. Sullivan had long been a pragmatic and energetic supporter of civil rights. In 1971, he was the sole board member to vote in favor of the Episcopal Church's resolution to have GM withdraw from South Africa. But by the mid-1970s, Sullivan had come to believe that investor activism that focused on getting corporations to leave South Africa was not working. The Sullivan Principles, developed in conjunction with corporate leaders and the Carter administration, called on corporations operating in South Africa to end segregation in the workplace, offer equal pay for equal work, increase training to help nonwhite employees move into management, and enact other reforms.[40]

Critics of the Sullivan Principles argued that they allowed corporations to look virtuous, while, in practice, their presence just shored up white rule. But Sullivan's approach appealed to moderate religious people, including many in the mainline Protestant denominations, who wanted to do *something* without moving very fast or very far.[41]

Nothing so galvanized the anti-apartheid movement, however, as the 1980 election of Ronald Reagan. Reagan was strongly inclined to support South Africa's white majority as a bulwark against communism. His policy of "constructive engagement" involved expressing sympathy with white South African fears while officially (but feebly) opposing apartheid. The administration reasoned that white South Africans would be open to change if they were less worried about their borders. To that end, the United States needed to support a number of efforts: quieting the regional conflicts in Angola and Mozambique; peacefully ending white rule in Rhodesia (and so forestalling the influence of the USSR among the black majority); and seeking a resolution to the struggle over Namibia, which South Africa claimed as a buffer zone. Only after these remarkably ambitious changes had occurred could the United States pressure South Africa to dismantle apartheid.[42]

Not surprisingly, "constructive engagement" was widely criticized for its singular focus on the Cold War at the expense of human rights. The activist group TransAfrica was key to this opposition. TransAfrica had been founded in 1978 as an African American lobbying organization. A key constituency was African American churches. TransAfrica recruited leading African American pastors to support its efforts and worked with black churches on campaigns like Freedom Sundays. TransAfrica offered posters and educational materials to participating churches, which then displayed the "detailed signs describing the ravages of apartheid" in order to "educate their membership about South Africa and how events there affect us here." The money the churches paid for the posters went to fund TransAfrica's lobbying efforts. Ultimately TransAfrica also received significant support from mainline Protestant groups, including the World Council of Churches and the Episcopal Church.[43]

Through all of this, white US evangelical churches were almost entirely silent. *Christianity Today* covered South Africa only intermittently between 1976 and the mid-1980s. The magazine did publish one long, rather strange set of feature stories in July 1978 aimed at "Understanding the Afrikaaner." Despite the "understanding" framework, the articles were uniformly anti-apartheid. "What is going on in South Africa?" asked one. "What accounts for these gross travesties of justice inflicted by a government that calls itself Christian?"[44] Still, it was clear that some evangelicals were so impressed by the existence of an unabashedly Christian government in South Africa that they wanted to correct the Afrikaaners' "mistake" of having implemented a racially oppressive regime.

Stuart Briscoe wrote one of the essays after traveling to South Africa to preach and meet with Christians. Briscoe was a British church leader who had moved to the United States to serve as pastor of Elmbrook Church, just outside of Milwaukee, which in 1978 was well on its way to becoming one of the nation's largest churches. Briscoe insisted that, during his trip, he had met with a cross-section of South African evangelicals. He presented the Afrikaaners as understandably frustrated. They were fighting against communism, they insisted. So why were Americans criticizing them all the time?[45]

Briscoe was sympathetic, but he could not accept that Cold War logic as the entire story. Evangelicals were part of a global community of believers; they could not ignore what was happening to black Christians and anti-apartheid white Christians. "Have you read about the crackdown in Soweto? . . . And did you read how many churches and Christian organizations were raided at dawn?"[46] *CT*'s special issue did not make a distinction among the affected churches and did not emphasize that the raids had been focused on the Christian Institute and theologically liberal churches. What mattered was that the church in South Africa was persecuted. "We are witnessing Christ's body engaged in internal strife, torn and bleeding."[47] Here, as in so much of evangelical internationalism, it was the image of the body of Christ, broken and suffering, that undergirded the call to feeling, the cry to identify—and identify *with*—the victims. When a new round of uprisings began in South Africa in the 1980s, articles like those in *CT* had already begun to open the door for white American evangelicals to see themselves as part of the internally divided "body of Christ" in South Africa—as being both sympathetic with the Afrikaaner's presumed anti-communism and yet also in solidarity with the suffering black bodies that were under attack.

In the global evangelical community, Americans were not alone in their ambivalence and relative quietude about apartheid. Indeed, at the 1980 Lausanne follow-on meeting, a group of two hundred participants (about a third of those attending) issued a statement complaining that the international Lausanne movement was no longer sufficiently concerned about social and political issues. The statement cited a number of instances of evangelical support for oppression, particularly apartheid. "[T]here are Christians in and outside of South Africa who claim to be Bible-believing Christians and give implicit or explicit support to apartheid." There had been evangelical opposition, they noted, but *any* backing for the South African practice was a "great scandal." The Lausanne Committee, they argued, should help those evangelicals who had failed to speak out to begin to "repent and work for justice."[48]

In the early 1980s, South African Prime Minister P.W. Botha began to institute limited reforms that were designed to defang the growing anti-apartheid movement. The United Democratic Front (UDF), a broad coalition of liberal reform groups in South Africa, was founded in part to respond to these moves. The UDF was led by Allan Boesak, a coloured Reform minister who had recently been elected head of the World Alliance of Reformed Churches.[49]

During one protest march in 1984, police violently broke up the crowd, killing fourteen people. Shortly after, protests swept across the country, with rent strikes, marches, and "stayaways" from schools, as well as attacks on symbols of the apartheid state: school buildings, police stations, and the offices of black councilors. In what became a familiar pattern, the police and South African Defence Forces swept into townships to break up demonstrations, attacking and killing protestors, who often fought back. A funeral for the dead would follow, with more protests, and usually more violence.[50] Then, in November 1984, Bishop Desmond Tutu, the outspoken anti-apartheid leader and general secretary of the South African Council of Churches, was awarded the Nobel Peace Prize, demonstrating the high level of international attention focused on South Africa.

In July 1985, Botha declared a state of emergency in two of the most restive regions; a year later, it was extended nationwide. In the ensuing months, twenty thousand people were detained. Internal violence in the townships also took a toll, with activists determined to punish those they saw as collaborators or informers.[51] By mid-1985, both the ANC and non-violent UDF were moving quickly to organize the urban areas and turn an uprising into a sustainable political movement. The liberal churches were deeply involved in activism, as they had been for the previous decade. Now, black evangelicals were ready to make a stand.

A small group first met in September 1985. They called themselves the "Concerned Evangelicals." Among the leaders was Caesar Molebatsi. The goal of the group was to analyze "our role as evangelical Christians in the light of the crisis situation in our country and how this affects our mission to the world." They planned to "seek the Lord's mind" as to how to proceed amid township riots and the state of emergency crackdown.[52]

During their second meeting, the group watched as the South African Defence Forces descended upon two schools near the church where they had convened. At one, children broke windows to try to escape. At another, some of the students were arrested. The gathered evangelical leaders watched helplessly. The security forces were heavily armed, after all, and they knew that the military was "entitled to do whatever without question from anybody . . . on the basis of the emergency regulations."[53]

Shaken but determined, the group set several objectives for themselves. The first was simply to research what other anti-apartheid organizations were doing. They were not even sure what evangelical groups existed in Soweto, or what work those groups might be involved in, much less what was happening in the rest of the country. These leaders did feel confident of one thing: however much they valued their evangelical heritage, they had to accept "that our theology is inadequate as regards our social responsibility."[54]

The evangelicals knew that a group of black and white theologians and ministers was about to release the *Kairos Document*, an extensive critique of the role of Christians in supporting, or in failing to adequately oppose, apartheid. The document was signed by scores of people from the liberal Protestant churches, including Methodists, Presbyterians, and Anglicans, as well as some Catholics. Many members of the evangelical group admired the document. Indeed, a couple of them, including Molebatsi, had signed it. Over the next few years, *Kairos* would become the most widely circulated church statement about apartheid. Its influence abroad would be less, perhaps, than the statements and sermons of a global figure like Bishop Tutu, but the World Council of Churches and a number of global church bodies circulated thousands of copies around the world.[55]

Although these evangelicals supported the goals of *Kairos*, they wanted to be clear about their own distinctiveness. "The call to be 'born again' still holds," they wrote. "The call to new life, new creation, where the old has passed away, is still valid."[56] Here, more than ten years after Lausanne, it was still necessary to insist that social concern did not mean a turn away from evangelical theology.

It did, however, imply a transformation in evangelical practice. As Moss Ntlha, one of the core members of Concerned Evangelicals, later described it, black evangelicalism in South Africa had generally been "isolationist" and pietistic. In fact, it was pastors in particular who *could* avoid political issues; they were not in trade unions, or students in the university, not part of youth groups or working in white homes as domestics. Church members were, by necessity, "in the struggle," but their pastors need not be, and as a consequence church membership was in steep decline. Thus, the Concerned Evangelicals straddled two arguments: an insistence on justice for its own sake, and a more instrumental statement about the need to keep pace politically if the church was to grow.[57]

Within a month of their first meeting, a larger group of Concerned Evangelicals gathered for an all-day session. It was still only about thirty people, but many of them were pastors and leaders in the community. Molebatsi was appointed to the Steering Committee. A former pastor named Frank Chikane was there as well (figure 7.2). Chikane had been

FIGURE 7.2 Rev. Frank Chikane in 1986, speaking at a meeting of the United Democratic Front. Selwyn Tait/Getty Images.

briefly ordained in the Apostolic Faith Mission, a Pentecostal denomination that was perhaps the largest of the evangelical churches in South Africa. But Chikane had been suspended from the church five years earlier as a result of his anti-apartheid activity, and had began working for a religious think tank. Chikane had been central to the drafting of the *Kairos Document*. Now he joined the Concerned Evangelicals as a central player, along with Molebatsi, Moses Ntala, and a few others. At the October 1985 meeting, Chikane articulated the group's basic goals: to critique evangelical theology, to organize others, to work for justice and peace. Shortly thereafter the group would add another goal: "To expose white control/manipulation of black Evangelical Theology, Black clergy, and black theological training."[58]

All this took place amid great tumult among evangelicals in South Africa. There were three other important gatherings in the fall of 1985, and the radical agenda of Concerned Evangelicals would be both a complement and a challenge to each of them. First was the Evangelical Fellowship of South Africa's conference, where Molebatsi had met David Howard. At the end of the Evangelical Fellowship meeting, the group had issued a mild anti-apartheid statement, one that also made a call for "law and order." The statement was framed by the missionaries and white evangelicals who dominated the conference, while the black evangelicals were silenced. One concerned Evangelicals member commented that conservative groups like the Evangelical Fellowship had their own agenda, but "it is not God's agenda, it is an agenda of those people who are unconsciously dictated to by their self-interests."[59]

A more exciting development came out of South Africa's Baptist Union. When 250 delegates gathered for the Union's annual assembly in the Western Cape, the most urgent question in front of them was how to respond to the deteriorating situation in their country. The multiracial Union was largely white, with some Asian and coloured members as well as a few black pastors. One of the latter, Rev. Lukhele of the Lamontville Baptist Church, stood up during the assembly's debate to read a statement. Lukhele explained that his parishioners were asking him why the South African Baptist church was racially divided. And why, his parishioners asked, was the church not responding to their dire need? The pastor expressed his own despair:

> As a Black Baptist Believer, I sometimes feel like standing on top of the manse roof and crying, "CALL ME NOT A PASTOR." I feel so helpless.
>
> CALL ME NOT A PASTOR if I cannot do something about the crucial and heart-breaking experiences for the people whom God entrusted me to shepherd.

In a vote of 156 to 51, the union supported an open letter that called for an immediate end to apartheid. A number of the nonwhite delegates were delighted and surprised: "This wasn't the Baptist Union but a brand-new Union with a totally new approach to our country's problems," one coloured pastor told a reporter.[60]

The third important, and highly visible, event in the fall of 1985 was a National Day of Reconciliation organized by Michael Cassidy's African Enterprise. Desmond Tutu attended, as did a number of representatives from the Dutch Reformed Church, which was beginning to back away from its overt support for apartheid. The Day of Reconciliation provided an outlet for moderate-to-liberal Protestant Christians who were willing to openly oppose apartheid but unwilling to be radical about it. "God has called us here . . . to be a third race and a third force," the closing statement read, "operating between a lethally dangerous and embattled white conservatism and an equally dangerous black revolutionary violence which could irreparably tear our social fabric to pieces." At day's end, attendees presented a set of "requests" to President Botha, asking for an end to the state of emergency, the release of political prisoners, and talks with "authentic leaders" of the South African population.[61]

In this heated atmosphere, Concerned Evangelicals met to carve out a distinctly black, radical form of evangelical witness. It took nine months of meetings, consultations, drafts, and revisions, but in June 1986 the group issued *Evangelical Witness in South Africa.* The statement was a withering self-critique of South African evangelical politics and an angry denunciation of the role of white evangelicals, particularly Americans, in shaping South African evangelical life.

The statement's initial focus was, typically, on how the climate of racism in South Africa was hurting the preaching of the gospel. Recognizing the realities in townships and beyond, it had become "impossible to hold conventional evangelistic campaigns in this war situation." *Witness* complained, as the liberal churches' *Kairos* had done, that

Christian theology in South Africa had become hostage to the status quo, enamored of power and complacent in its assumptions. It also grappled with the question of how Romans 13, which called for Christians to obey governing authority, had been used to counsel acquiescence to oppressive government. Jesus turned the world upside down on behalf of the poor and the powerless, they declared. "The problem is that Jesus was a radical and we are moderates."[62]

Witness reserved special opprobrium for white American Christians who had come to South Africa to offer up their gospel of complacency. The televangelist Jimmy Swaggart, for example, was exceptionally popular with South Africans. Swaggart, who was a minister in the Assemblies of God church, had the second-largest television ministry in the United States after Oral Roberts. He was an influential figure on the religious Right. In South Africa, Swaggart's books and tapes sold very well among both black and white Christians. [63]

During his 1985 tour through the country, Swaggart had preached to integrated audiences and proudly proclaimed that his multiracial crowds were proof that "apartheid is dead." Swaggart's revivals were broadcast on South African state television, and many local Christians were furious. How could a "foreigner," the *Witness* writers asked, announce "that apartheid is dead when we know that it is alive and well, and that it kills."

> For us who are brutalized by white Christians in South Africa, with the western tradition of oppression and exploitation, for us who are oppressed and exploited by white Christians who are supported by the so-called Christian West, for us who have been called "communists" because we resisted apartheid, for some of us who have been detained in solitary confinement under the so-called "Terrorism" Act just for raising our voices against apartheid, for us this motive [for declaring apartheid dead] can only be seen to be coming from the devil.[64]

Couched as a confession, the document was a full-out assault.

In June of 1986, Concerned Evangelicals circulated *Evangelical Witness in South Africa* for signature. Within a few months, 132 people had signed. Clearly, there were limits to the appeal of its radicalism even among black evangelicals, but the numbers were not insignificant. After all, only 150 people had signed the *Kairos Document*, and that was already a classic of Christian social justice statements.[65]

Many conservative churches in South Africa apparently decided to ignore the document. Other evangelicals, both black and white, urged the Concerned Evangelicals to stick to what the Bible said. One white missionary working with the Evangelical Fellowship of South Africa reacted rather sympathetically, but with firm limits. "Surely," he said in an interview, "we mustn't let things pull us so that our primary identity is with a political cause, however good, however right that political cause is." The first loyalty must be to "Christ and his Gospel."[66] Socially concerned evangelicals had heard that before.

Internationally, response to *Witness* was mixed. There were a number of complaints about its rushed production, seemingly superficial theology, and polemical tone. But it circulated across Europe, the United States, and Africa. The international journal *Transformation*, a platform for the social concern wing of evangelicalism, published the entire document with commentaries in early 1987. Translations were widely circulated and debated in Germany and Holland, where the Dutch recognized their unique ties to the Afrikaner population. *Witness* also seemed to have an immediate effect on evangelicals in the rest of Africa. In 1987, the journal of the Association of Evangelicals in Africa and Madagascar published the document in full, and the group "acknowledged with anguish" that it had not been "as conspicuously vocal and active" as it should have been in the face of apartheid.[67]

The response in the United States was surprisingly muted. The evangelical publisher Eerdmans printed the statement as a small book, with a long preface by J. Deotis Roberts, an African American professor from Eastern Baptist Theological Seminary. One brief review in *Christianity and Crisis* by a white South African welcomed the book, but *Christianity Today* never mentioned it. Given the visibility of the anti-apartheid struggle by 1986, including debates in US churches, the omission seems willful: radical black evangelicals' critique of the self-satisfied evangelical status quo may well have hit too close to home for the keepers of moderately conservative evangelicalism in the United States.[68]

In 1985, Jerry Falwell also entered the maelstrom of South African politics. His words would be used as weapons by both sides. But they were felt most profoundly back in the United States, where the changing political climate—the expansion and intensification of anti-apartheid sentiment—made Falwell an embarrassment to a number of evangelical leaders.

Falwell had made his name in the 1970s as a popular television preacher and pastor of Thomas Road Baptist Church in Lynchburg, Virginia. In 1979, he founded the Moral Majority, which brought self-described fundamentalists into coalition with secular conservatives as well as Catholics. The Moral Majority was the most visible and successful manifestation of the ways in which the rhetoric of political engagement, borrowed from the social concern faction at Lausanne, became reformatted into the mantra of the religious Right. In 1985, Falwell was at the peak of his political power and media visibility. His many ministries—including Liberty University, the Lynchburg Academy for K-12 students, *The Old Time Gospel Hour*, and smaller programs such as a home for unwed mothers—employed one thousand people. Falwell traveled thousands of miles each year, giving sermons, attending rallies, and meeting with political and religious leaders around the world. In 1983, *US News and World Report* named him the second most-admired man in the country, after President Reagan.[69]

In August 1985, Falwell visited South Africa for a five-day "fact-finding" tour, which he took as an opportunity to tout the virtues of the South African government (figure 7.3). The divestment and sanctions movement was gaining traction in the United States. The first Congressional vote on the Comprehensive Anti-Apartheid Act was scheduled for September, and Falwell intended to lend his considerable public visibility to help defeat the bill. In the three-part television special he filmed while in South Africa, he insisted

FIGURE 7.3 Falwell on his return from South Africa, August 20, 1985. Keystone Pictures USA/ Alamy Stock Photo.

that he "vehemently oppose[d]" apartheid." He said the real question was how to end apartheid without allowing South Africa to fall under Soviet influence. The correct approach, he argued, was to "cut out the cancer without killing the patient."[70]

During his visit, Falwell conferred with South Africa President P.W. Botha, as well as a few elected municipal leaders from Soweto and elsewhere, most of whom had been put into office by the miniscule minority of black South Africans who voted in blacks-only local elections.[71] Those elections were widely considered shams, but Falwell took them at face value, reporting that these black leaders were uniformly opposed to sanctions. Indeed, he said, all the nonwhites he met had spoken out "in unison" against punitive measures, saying they would hurt poor blacks.[72]

Falwell's team also met Bishop Lekhanyane of the Zion Christian Church (ZCC), one of the largest churches in South Africa, with more than two million members.[73] Falwell reported that the bishop supported his position on the danger of sanctions. Church members also told him that it was frustrating for them that the international media focused on pastors like Desmond Tutu and Allan Boesak, who didn't speak for them. Just months before, the ZCC had invited President Botha to address a mass meeting of its members. Botha addressed the crowd on the need to obey governing authority, citing Romans 13.[74]

The story of the ZCC is more complicated than the visits by Falwell or Botha would suggest. It was far and away the largest of the African Initiated Churches, which were—and are—important South African institutions. The AICs, versions of which stretched across all of Africa, included everything from relatively orthodox Protestant churches that were simply not affiliated with a transnational denomination to churches built on charismatic authority, often with syncretic theologies and a black nationalist bent.[75] The ZCC had not been an explicitly political group. Some observers have described the invitation to Botha as a miscalculation on the part of the ZCC's leadership, one that they soon regretted. But Bishop Legkanyane seemed to insist on a pro-government stance, claiming that the famous black clergy who were being courted by the media did not represent *these* Christians.[76] It was a claim Falwell was all too happy to repeat. After his meeting with Bishop Legkanyane, Falwell felt emboldened enough to denounce Desmond Tutu to the media as a "phoney."[77] The Falwell incident tarnished the ZCC's reputation among anti-apartheid South Africans for many years.

When Falwell returned to the United States, he not only denounced sanctions and divestment, he also called for a "reverse campaign" that would *increase* investment in South Africa, urging Christians to buy Kruggerrands.[78] Most other conservative evangelicals were more careful, but a few were willing to at least tentatively support Falwell. Rep. Paul Henry, a Republican from Michigan (and son of long-time *Christianity Today* editor Carl Henry), said that Falwell should refrain from criticizing leaders such as Tutu and Boesak, but that his critics on the Left had failed to consider "the difficulty of change in a country that views itself as being surrounded by a sea of political instability and tribal authoritarian regimes throughout black Africa."[79]

Evangelical moderates and liberals, on the other hand, could barely contain their scorn. Two African American evangelical leaders were quick to respond. William Bentley, the past-president of the National Black Evangelical Association and president of the United Pentecostal Council (Assemblies of God), said that Falwell was a gradualist, but that gradualism was a painfully familiar stance to black Americans. "People who control the segregation process always say 'wait' . . . South Africans may not have the luxury of time unlimited to open the doors of policies of equality and justice." Clarence Hilliard, the Chicago pastor who had been a critic of Lausanne, said that Falwell was a bellwether; white evangelicals must now declare themselves against Falwell's stances or be identified with his views.[80]

In fact, a number of white evangelicals were beginning to disassociate themselves from Falwell—keeping pace with public opinion in the United States, which had swung dramatically in favor of sanctions. The head of the National Association of Evangelicals said that Falwell's campaign had likely diminished his influence for years to come. And the president of Asbury Seminary in Wilmore, Kentucky, commented angrily, "Rev. Mr. Falwell has the right to speak, but not as my spokesman. In my opinion, Mr. Falwell is over his head in international affairs, out of bounds when he presumes to speak for evangelical Christians, and far from the pulpit which he claims to be his primary calling."[81]

A small group of evangelicals went further. While Falwell was in South Africa, Left-leaning evangelicals led an anti-apartheid demonstration in Washington, calling for sanctions. The group included Jim Wallis of *Sojourners,* Ron Sider of Evangelicals for Social Action, and Southern Baptist James Dunn of the Baptist Joint Committee on Public

Affairs (BJCPA). Falwell was furious. These people were leading what was "supposedly an evangelical demonstration," but they were liberals, pacifists (in Sider's case), and agitators.[82]

Falwell was still an independent Baptist, but his trip was one of the reasons the Southern Baptist Convention began feeling pressure regarding South Africa. In the mid-1980s the SBC was changing rapidly. The denomination was moving decisively to the Right, both politically and theologically, but it was doing so amid demographic changes. The SBC was no longer isolated to the South; migrants from southern states had seeded congregations all over the country. As a result, the convention's self-image was increasingly national, and SBC churches were increasingly urban, its members more educated and wealthier than they had ever been.[83] These demographics had contributed to the strength of a moderate faction that had dominated the SBC in the 1960s and early 1970s, shaping the denomination where Jimmy Carter had taught Sunday School and Al Gore had developed his faith.

In the 1970s, however, a group of self-identified fundamentalists decided to unseat the moderates. In 1979, the SBC elected conservative Adrian Rogers to the presidency; he had run on a platform of biblical inerrancy. By the mid-1980s, the SBC was deeply divided, but the right wing was unquestionably ascendant, electing their candidate for president every year for the next two decades.

It was in this context that Southern Baptists addressed apartheid. After Falwell's trip, the *Baptist Press*, which had rarely reported on South Africa, began offering frequent updates. *Commission,* the organization's missions magazine, did the same. In a series of articles in the mid-1980s, the two SBC media outlets produced an inconsistent view of South Africa. Sometimes, they enthused over Baptist-affiliated groups in South Africa that denounced apartheid; more often, they emphasized the groups' deep opposition to violent township protests.[84]

At the same time, James Dunn, the combative head of the Baptist Joint Committee on Public Affairs, began to use the committee's monthly digest, *Report from the Capital,* to protest apartheid unabashedly. The joint committee was a coalition of eight Baptist denominations, two of which were traditionally African American. The Southern Baptist Convention was by far the largest of these denominations and the largest financial contributor, which made the SBC leadership sensitive to the positions the BJCPA took. In 1980, Dunn had become the group's executive director. Dunn, who liked to declare himself a "Texas-bred, Spirit-led, Bible-teaching, revival-preaching" Southern Baptist, came out of the theologically conservative traditions of small-town Texas, although he had studied with the great liberal Southern Baptist ethicist T.B. Maston at Southwestern Baptist Theological Seminary.[85]

Dunn came to the joint committee after twelve years as head of the Christian Life Commission of the Texas Baptist Convention, where he campaigned against the alcohol industry and against racism with equal fervor. Dunn was also a passionate advocate of the time-honored Baptist doctrine of "soul freedom" or "soul competency." Baptists traditionally brooked no denominational hierarchy, no strong creedal requirements, because of the denomination's standard position on the "priesthood of the believer": each individual Christian is responsible for interpreting the will of God for themselves. Dunn held soul freedom as one of his most cherished values.[86] He saw his job at the joint committee as focusing on religious liberty and church-state separation (which, at that time, Baptists could be counted on to support). But apartheid became an issue of increasing concern to him, and he used the bully pulpit that the joint committee offered him.

The April 1985 cover of *Report from the Capital*, for example, showed a group of people marching with anti-apartheid signs; by that point, the daily protests run by TransAfrica at the South African embassy were already all over the news. Two men were in the foreground of the cover photo; one was black, one white, both carrying signs that said "American Baptists" supported justice in South Africa. The accompanying story, "Churches Act to Thwart Apartheid," was a paean to the US divestment campaign. It declared—with some exaggeration—that religious groups were leading the anti-apartheid movement. The report explained that both the SBC and the United Methodists opposed divestment, but the Presbyterians had already shed holdings in Mobil, Texaco, and a few other corporations. It ended by reminding readers that the South African Council of Churches had recently taken the risky and illegal move of asking churches in other countries to divest, saying that the pressure was needed to help bring about fundamental change. The implication was quiet but clear: If the South African churches were taking such risks to ask for divestment, could Baptists in the United States do anything other than agree?[87]

Dunn was joined in his opposition to apartheid by a small but determined liberal Southern Baptist contingent. On December 12, 1985, just a few months after Falwell's trip to South Africa, a group of twenty Southern Baptists met in Nashville to discuss their denomination's response to apartheid. The meeting was called by the Christian Life Commission, a committee of the Southern Baptist Convention long known for its liberal stances, particularly on racial politics.[88] The group was hand-picked and racially mixed—mostly white Americans but also one white South African and several important African American ministers.

Participants received their schedule for the day with a well-known quote from Desmond Tutu printed across the top: "If you are neutral in a situation of injustice, you have chosen the side of the oppressor. If an elephant has his foot on the tail of a mouse, and you say you are neutral, the mouse will not appreciate your neutrality."[89] This group was not neutral. Their gathering was designed to push the SBC pension fund to divest from companies doing business in South Africa.

The main presentation of the day was by John Jonsson, a white South African Baptist minister who now taught at Southern Baptist Theological Seminary in Kentucky. Jonsson had been active against apartheid both before and after he left South Africa in 1982, and later worked in South Africa to help found the group Concerned Baptists, an ally and counterpart of Concerned Evangelicals. Jonsson was one of those traveling evangelicals, like Michael Cassidy, who used his transnational ties to further an internationalist network of evangelicalism and a political vision of anti-racist solidarity.

He was also a missiologist and leading Baptist thinker. In one of his essays, Jonsson sur-veyed the meaning of liberation in Baptist thought by evoking "three of our prominent world Baptists," Orlando Costa, Samuel Escobar, and René Padilla. It was no coincidence that Jonsson named three of the key leaders of the radical faction at Lausanne, remind-ing his readers of the political legacy of Baptist life beyond the United States. Jonsson argued that it was time for Southern Baptists to recognize that, in the face of apartheid, "benevolent neutrality" was not enough. For Jonsson, as for almost every late twentieth-century radical and liberal thinker in the Protestant tradition, Bonhoeffer set the terms. "For me . . . the finished work of our salvation had become a 'costly grace.' "[90]

Jonsson's lecture at the Nashville meeting was one long denunciation of the South African government's refusal to recognize the rights of the black and coloured popula-tions. Although he offered largely secular arguments, Jonsson analyzed the vexed ques-tion of violent resistance in distinctively religious terms. Quoting Psalm 137, he spoke of the Bible's affirmation of the Israelites' righteous anger against their oppressors. In a context where many Christians piously insisted that they opposed apartheid but could not support anything but non-violent resistance, Jonsson argued differently:

> We cannot be against violence unless we are also violently opposed to human sys-tems, structures and behavioral patterns which contribute towards the natural anger and indignation at the heart of human violence. And when the authorities use violence to stifle the frustrations of a voiceless and dispossessed people, then they are opening themselves up as a legitimate target for violence. The Word of the Lord declares it.[91]

That position was not what most people expected from one of the most conservative denominations in the United States. Indeed, it was probably not what most Southern Baptists expected either.

Attendees at the Christian Life Commission meeting were a "moral minority," in David Swartz's wry phrase, but nonetheless a significant constituency. Their presence in the SBC meant that the conversation about apartheid was more intricate and urgent than Falwell's positions would have led observers to expect. For a time, apartheid galvanized the anti-racist wing of the convention, the heirs of those who had declared racism a sin in the 1950s and 1960s.

Those gathered in Nashville failed, however, to convince the SBC to divest. The pension fund established some guidelines, saying that it would "consider" the extent to which com-panies were in line with the Sullivan Principles.[92] This was an altogether retrograde position in 1985, one that demonstrated the rapidly declining influence of the liberal and moder-ate wing. Indeed, within three years, the Christian Life Commission would be disbanded, reformed as the Ethics and Religious Liberty Commission under the conservative culture warrior Richard Land. He also would take up race as a central issue in the early years of his tenure, but, like so many conservatives before him, he would see opposition to racism as a matter of changing hearts and minds. Land's transnational solidarities soon would focus on Christians, particularly those "persecuted" by Muslims.

In January of 1986, a large group of US Protestant Churches banded together to form the Churches' Emergency Committee on South Africa; the group included most members of the National Council of Churches, including the AME and AME Zion churches, as well as a few others. Up until that point, even many of the liberal churches had been hesitant to divest, but the tide was beginning to turn. In October, Congress passed, and Reagan signed, the Comprehensive Anti-Apartheid Act. The legislative victory was the result of extraordinary mobilization: the determination of liberal and left-wing media to tell the story of what was happening in South Africa; the work of independent groups like TransAfrica; and pressure on Congress from a wide variety of Americans who believed it was time to act. Of course, the struggle was far from over. Once the sanctions were enacted, many complained that the Reagan administration was not really implementing the law it had claimed to support.[93]

The liberal evangelical magazine *Sojourners* reported in May 1987 that South Africa was still in crisis. The government's state of emergency had been in place for twenty months; seventeen more anti-apartheid organizations had just been banned. Protesters were marching, facing down water canons. The magazine's editor, Jim Wallis, described it as a moment of truth for the global church. The church in South Africa might be able to mobilize a large-scale, actively non-violent movement, but believers there might also face increasing state violence; indeed, martyrdom. If so, the rest of God's people would have to respond. A suffering church had a moral claim on the rest of the body of Christ.[94] Embracing the moral power of suffering that would animate almost every evangelical social movement, on the Right or the Left, in the late twentieth century, Wallis posited South African Christians as potentially persecuted—not for their faith per se, but for their faithfulness to the cause of justice.

South African church leaders such as Desmond Tutu, Allan Boesak, and Frank Chikane were touring the United States asking for support, for more pressure on the Reagan administration to enforce sanctions and for more divestment. In 1987, Boesak called specifically on US black churches to mobilize. A year later, Moses Ntala, one of the leaders of Concerned Evangelicals, traveled to Washington, DC, urging evangelicals to get involved.[95] In January of 1989, a number of black leaders attended a summit at which they denounced the recalcitrance of the South African government. There was some disagreement among the ministers who spoke. Bishop Ruben Speaks of the AME Zion Church said he had some doubts about whether Christians should support the ANC. Still, the leaders of the major black denominations, including the AME, AME Zion, the Church of God in Christ, and all three black Baptist denominations, issued a statement:

[T]he intensifying brutality of the Pretoria regime—death and detention of children, attacks against churches and church leaders—and the war against South

Africa's neighbors compel us to speak out as one united voice for an end to the pain being inflicted upon our sisters and brothers.[96]

As activism in some evangelical segments increased, the Washington-based Institute for Religion and Democracy (IRD) countered. The group was a center of the movement to support persecuted Christians and also a bastion of conservative thinking on US foreign policy.[97] IRD launched a "Building a New South Africa" program that invested in "empowering" South African black communities economically. This was a direct call for US corporations to stay in South Africa, "setting a corporate example" by adhering to the Sullivan Principles. (In 1987, Leon Sullivan denounced the principles as inadequate and called for an economic embargo on South Africa.) IRD imagined itself as occupying a different, far more respectable terrain than Falwell, but it similarly argued that "economic growth and the business community's role in attacking apartheid remains one of the most effective methods of precipitating genuine reform." The group called for more support for Michael Cassidy's National Initiative for Reconciliation, which by the mid-1980s had positioned itself on this same tenuous middle ground.[98]

In South Africa, as the end of apartheid neared, violence was often fierce. South African evangelicals, black and white, were divided on how to respond. Frank Chikane, who had been so central to both the *Evangelical Witness* statement and to the *Kairos Document*, had thrown his lot more fully in with the liberal camp. From 1987 to 1994, he was general secretary of the South African Council of Churches. In that role, he traveled to the United States in 1989 on a trip with Desmond Tutu and other South African church leaders to meet with Congress and President George H.W. Bush. In a strange turn of events, Chikane collapsed several times during the trip and nearly died. After Chikane was hospitalized in Madison, Wisconsin, doctors found evidence of neurotoxin poisoning. Chikane said at the time that he believed his clothes for the trip had been laced with poison. Years later, he was proven correct when the details of the plot were revealed, and five members of the Police Ministry received suspended sentences for their role in the plot to assassinate him.[99] After the end of apartheid, Chikane became a member of the ANC's Executive Committee, and ultimately served as director general in the office of President Thabo Mbeki. He was returned to his evangelical home when he was reinstated by the Apostolic Faith Mission in 1990. By then, it was the church that had changed.

Starting in the 1970s, there emerged among evangelicals in the United States and South Africa a genuine, if halting and sometimes compromised, anti-apartheid constituency. The emergence of that constituency—the transnational networks that undergirded it and the organized global forces that opposed it—was at the heart of what happened to US and global evangelical culture and politics in the 1980s. In the early part of the decade, US evangelical conservatism was in ascendance, indeed seemingly unstoppable, even if there were a few cracks in the edifice. But events in South Africa raised serious questions about the moral authority of those evangelicals, like Falwell, who were allying themselves with the apartheid government. The debate over South Africa did not undermine the conservative movement of the 1980s, but it exemplified many of the issues that cleaved evangelical culture. South Africa helped to clarify just how much race, anti-communism, and transnational solidarities of varying sorts were central to evangelicals.

The struggle over apartheid was also a struggle over the body. Over the decades, South African government forces attacked black South Africans with pronounced viciousness. For many people, Christian and otherwise, that violence demanded action. But the imagery of the suffering body resonated powerfully with Christians, for whom the tortured body of Jesus on the cross was the first instantiation of a church that must suffer in his name. There was also the image of the global church as the living body of Christ, and almost every Christian would aver that there *should, ideally,* be one church, one body. The photos and stories of attacks by a Christian-identified government on the largely Christian nonwhite population were, for a significant number of evangelicals in the United States and South Africa, a visible image of the church body in crisis.

When American evangelicals spoke out in opposition to apartheid, they often evoked this crisis and quoted the words of South African Christians as proof. But the body of Christ was a resource for all sides, so when Falwell or the Southern Baptist press insisted on limited measures, they too evoked the words of South African Christians, who they said would suffer from sanctions. Apartheid South Africa gave evidence of the multiple levels on which evangelical internationalism functioned; it was also one of the most profound examples of how capacious, how contradictory, and how potent the politics of suffering could be.

8

"The 10/40 Window"

THE STRUGGLE WITH ISLAM

IN THE 1990S, the map of the "10/40 Window" was one of the most widely recognized images in the evangelical community. The map had various incarnations, but all of them illustrated the same basic concept: there was a region of the world that stretched from Africa to Asia, from 10 degrees to 40 degrees north of the equator—a belt that included India, Pakistan, China, the Middle East, and parts of Africa—that desperately needed Jesus.

Argentine evangelist Luis Bush introduced the 10/40 Window on the opening night of the second International Congress on World Evangelization in 1989. This was the second "Lausanne" meeting, the official follow-up to the 1974 congress. But this time the location was Manila, a stark reminder that Christianity's center of gravity had shifted decisively to the global South. Standing before 3,600 evangelicals from 173 countries, Bush defined post-Cold War evangelical geography. He called on his fellow believers to focus their considerable energies on the task of evangelizing the "least evangelized" part of the world. The "Muslim block, the Hindu block, the Buddhist block" dominated the 10/40 Window. And now was the time, Bush insisted, to "redeploy our missionaries" to concentrate on this vast area of "unreached peoples," and especially those living in "Muslim contexts in the Third World."[1]

The audience was well aware that the world was on the verge of dramatic changes. The Cold War was winding down, which would improve the condition of Christians in Eastern Europe and the soon-to-be-former USSR. When the Manila meeting began, the destruction of the Berlin Wall was still a few months away, but Mikhail Gorbachev had introduced perestroika (restructuring) and glasnost (openness) to the USSR several years earlier. There was a strong sense of urgent, imminent change.

On the other hand, just a few months before the congress, China had violently suppressed the Tiananmen Square protests, indicating the profound limits of any political loosening in that country. American evangelicals were already deeply concerned about the fate of the "underground church" in China—those believers who worshipped in churches that refused to register with the government or to comply with its limitations on religious practice. On the first night, the Lausanne leadership announced that one hundred participants from China had been forbidden to come to Manila.[2] Both China's crackdown and the end of the Cold War breathed new life into the struggling religious Right in the United States. Jerry Falwell had announced just one month earlier that the Moral Majority was disbanding. But soon after, his chief rival, Pat Robertson, fresh off his loss in the 1988 Republican presidential primaries, founded the Christian Coalition, which would become a major player.[3]

The Middle East was on the agenda with renewed intensity. The Iranian revolution ten years earlier had awakened political Islam across the Middle East and elsewhere. In addition, Palestinians had recently embarked on the first intifada (uprising) (1987–1991), a series of highly visible street-level protests that strategically challenged Israeli rule in the Occupied Territories. A year after Manila, Iraq would invade Kuwait. The 1990–91 US-led response would be framed by the rhetoric of global transformation, what President George H.W. Bush would call the "new world order," in which the United States was the only superpower left on the international scene. As Cold War maps were about to be redrawn, evangelical Christians began to see Islam as a major global threat.

In this context, Luis Bush's speech hit with the force of a hurricane. Images of the 10/40 Window came in hundreds of versions (figure 8.1). Some maps showed national borders and some did not. Some featured sidebars showing images of unevangelized "people groups," others showed charts featuring the megacities where evangelism was particularly urgent. They circulated as wall maps, coffee mugs, screen savers, and calendars; they were the organizing concept for prayer books, DVDs, and online PowerPoints.

The effort was global. In 1992, the 13,000 delegates at a church-growth conference in Nigeria declared that they would hold a month of prayer for "the raising up of workers for all the countries, people groups, and cities in the 10/40 Window." Korean evangelicals promised to send two thousand missionaries and two thousand short-term mission

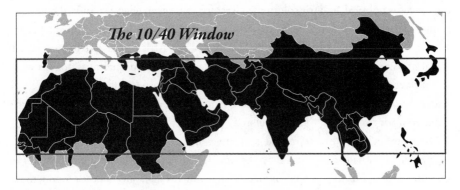

FIGURE 8.1 The 10/40 Window. Courtesy of the Joshua Project.

teams to target peoples in the 10/40 Window. Similarly, Brazilians reported that they had published 11,000 copies of a "Praying through the Window" prayer calendar.[4]

The seemingly unimaginable task of evangelizing the world by the year 2000 suddenly seemed more imaginable. Global South churches would join in the arduous work of evangelism, using business school-style strategies, while also highlighting the importance of emotionally resonant worship experience, a world made rich with the promise of God's immanent and manifest presence. As the church reached out, believers from all over the world would report remarkable mass conversions, outpourings of the Holy Spirit, and dramatic victories against the forces of darkness.

In 1989, evangelicals, like many other people across the globe, were about to face the challenge of the post-Cold War world. Officially, the 10/40 Window was a map of (missionary) opportunity; in practice, it was also a work of political and moral geography. It claimed to show the "enslaved" and unreached nations of the world, many of which would also be marked as persecutors of Christians. Since the 1979 Iranian revolution, "political Islam" had been a subject of increasing discussion in the secular news media. Now it was also a target for evangelicals, who promised to reach into its heart.

The 10/40 Window strategy drew heavily upon the Unreached Peoples movement. By 1989, a few organizations had already turned people groups into something akin to military targets. The Joshua Project, which started in 1987, organized (mostly young) evangelicals to visit "blockaded" countries and categorize the people groups there. The biblical Joshua's "mission" had been "to spy out the promised land and its people." Similarly, the modern Joshua Project would send out data gatherers, sometimes under the cover of other work.[5]

The project developed an elaborate database, along with precise criteria for deciding which people groups should be prioritized, based on the size of their population and lack of knowledge of the gospel. The Joshua Project was not the most intellectually serious organization of its kind, but it had the advantage of simplicity and the emotional edge that came from being an activist, adventurous, and youthful organization.

Sometimes unreached peoples were hard to reach because they were remote. But often the issue was political, and the solution, at least for some evangelicals, required boldness, cunning, and commitment. In many parts of the Muslim world, Christian missionaries were banned. In most of the Middle East and North Africa, proselytizing was either illegal or severely limited. In some countries, like Egypt, traditional missionaries were still allowed, but their activities were restricted and their prospects uncertain. Evangelical leaders, with characteristic enthusiasm for quantification and target lists, began categorizing countries as "closed," "partially closed," or "restricted."

Some evangelicals also developed a creative, and controversial, strategy for reaching people in "closed" countries: they obfuscated. Missionaries would apply for visas as English teachers, business people, or medical personnel. Then, once on the ground, these nontraditional missionaries would work in their jobs but their primary vocation would be evangelism. The strategy was known as "bi-vocational missions strategy" or, more colloquially, "tentmaking."

The term referred to the Apostle Paul, who often worked as a tentmaker while spreading the gospel. Tentmakers could have any occupation. They might be teachers, students, business people, nurses—or scientists. As one 1979 book on tentmaking put it: "[S]ince there are Christians who are self-supporting scientists even in Antarctica, tentmakers today can be lights in all seven continents."[6] The strategy could be controversial even among missions theorists—tentmakers were non-professional, perhaps utterly untrained in missionary work or strategies of cross-cultural encounter.

For those committed to missions, however, tentmaking had many advantages. The primary one, of course, was the ability to evangelize where traditional missionaries were unwelcome.[7] The tentmakers also supported themselves. Traditional missions agencies might give them some financial backing, but, mostly, they were self-sufficient. In missions programs that were perennially strapped for cash, this was no small advantage. But the disadvantages were also considerable. Agencies feared that lone-wolf missionaries, without training or accountability, were headed into some of the most sensitive regions of the world. If they acted recklessly or precipitously, they might put traditional missionaries or local Christians in danger. Still, at a working consultation on tentmaking in 1987, a group of missions leaders pronounced their newfound acceptance of the strategy.[8]

The number of tentmakers was probably never very large; by definition, statistics are almost impossible to get. But the concept fit beautifully with the emerging evangelical ethos of adventurism. Facing a world that was both dangerous and rapidly shrinking, US Christians became geographers, ethnographers, spies, tentmakers, and, ultimately, spiritual warriors.

The intensity of feeling surrounding the 10/40 Window emerged in part from the realities on the ground. In parts of Africa, South Asia, and the Middle East, Islam and Christianity were locked in ongoing conflict over adherents and access to resources. In places like Sudan, Nigeria, Egypt, Iraq, Ethiopia, India, Indonesia, the Philippines, and Lebanon, there were attacks on Christians, or riots that pitted Christian and Muslim communities against each other. In every case, the conflicts were not primarily theological; religious differences mattered, but so did factors such as social and political power, access to economic resources, and anger about international relations.[9]

Conservative Christians were particularly focused on Africa, where competition for adherents was fierce. In sub-Saharan Africa, Christians outnumbered Muslims (57 percent to 29 percent in 2010), but both groups had grown dramatically over the course of the twentieth century, as communities that once practiced traditional and local religions converted to one of the monotheistic faiths. Both Christians and Muslims significantly expanded their evangelization and aid work in the late 1980s. These missions involved not only proselytizing, but also building hospitals and orphanages and providing food aid. Nurturing bodies could serve as the route to conversion, with medical and food assistance as the entrée into the spirit. In turn, the bodies of adherents would be eagerly tallied. By the end of the twentieth century, there were very few people in Africa—fewer than 10 percent—who were not committed either to Islam or Christianity. To gain converts, each faith would have to target the other.[10]

The dynamism and numerical dominance of Christianity in sub-Saharan Africa had several sources, which were also linked to the changing dynamics between Muslims and Christians, both inside and outside of Africa.

First, African Christians had energy and self-confidence. They saw themselves, correctly, as the up-and-coming center of the faith. The historian Lamin Sanneh has argued that Islam and Christianity had historically constructed their communities very differently. The Arab Muslims who brought Islam to Africa encouraged locals to learn Arabic and to see themselves as part of a periphery to a Middle Eastern metropole. Christian missionaries, on the other hand, translated the Bible, which promoted local identities while also encouraging a sense that any community could have direct access to God. This, Sanneh argues, supported a more self-confident and assertive role for Africans in global Christianity than in Islam. Sanneh's theory has no small element of Christian self-aggrandizement, in that it associates Christianity with racial liberalism and a kind of democratic populism, while presenting Islam as restrictive and imperial. But Sanneh does highlight the ways in which Bible translation, the heart-blood of imperial missions, laid the groundwork for an authentic, self-assured, and expanding Christianity in Africa.[11]

Second, Pentecostalism had emerged as the quintessential form of African Christianity—combining transnational reach with localized and improvised practices. The body was crucial to Pentecostal experience, as the site of spiritual expression (raising hands, speaking in tongues, shedding tears, falling to one's knees) and the proof of God's power, in the form of healing and release from spiritual possession. Starting in the 1980s, Pentecostalism had become the fastest growing form of Christianity in the world, with Africa and Latin America as its strongholds. The transformations at first seemed more significant in Latin America. In Africa, however, economic crisis, political corruption, and the near collapse of many government services, along with the relative weakness of mainline Protestant churches, opened a vacuum for the expansion and growth of Pentecostalism.

Some scholars, such as historian Paul Gifford, have argued that African Pentecostal churches were being "globalized" by aggressive US-based evangelists armed with money, satellite networks, and a distinctively American brand of charismatic faith. The Americans emphasized televangelism, the prosperity gospel, and crusade-style preaching. In his study of Ghana, Gifford found that the impact of literature and videos by charismatic Americans such as Kenneth Hagin and Kenneth Copeland was so profound that "certain practices, expressions, even mannerisms can be traced to their origins outside the country."[12]

The Nigerian theologian Ogbu Kalu, on the other hand, argued vehemently against de-emphasizing the agency and creativity of African believers. The appeal of Pentecostalism in Africa, he insisted, came from how it built its practices on indigenous roots.[13]

This suggests an additional factor: flexibility. In Kalu's view, Pentecostalism in Africa created an innovative religious culture that wove together two distinct worldviews, Western Christianity and traditional African religion, to construct a powerfully local faith. The "local" might be as simple as using African musical styles in churches, or as serious as the development of a theology of an "Africanized" Jesus. In addition, since the colonial period there also had been a robust tradition of African Initiated Churches, which were independent of any US or European denomination but which had generally combined traditional evangelical doctrine with indigenous cultural practices.[14] Pentecostalism was also able to validate traditional beliefs, including witchcraft, sorcery, and a sense of ancestors' power, but it taught that Christianity would free believers from the grip of those forces. Pentecostalism displaced the more rationalistic forms of Christianity propagated in the older mission churches. "The spread of Pentecostalism," Kalu writes, "constitutes a challenge to the western world view which banished and demythologized the spiritual."[15] Indeed, the ecstatic forms of worship and healing that had always characterized Pentecostalism in the United States were ratcheted up in many African Pentecostal churches, which often featured healings and promised prosperity.

Christianity certainly was not unique in adapting to local conditions. Both Christians and Muslims shaped religious practices to their own life situations, as people have always done. By the 1990s, explicitly syncretic movements were rare, but the creative use of tradition was not. A 2008 poll found that most Christians and Muslims in Africa believed in "witchcraft, evil spirits, sacrifices to ancestors, traditional religious healers, reincarnation and other elements of traditional African religions."[16] In this linking of monotheistic religions such as Islam and Christianity with other beliefs and practices, Africans were not so very different from some Americans. It would not be unusual for a Methodist in the United States to read horoscopes, believe in ghosts, or buy Ayurvedic medicine. Such forms of localization are not unusual, and they did not mean that followers were not committed to or passionately identified with their faith.[17]

The situation for Christians in the Middle East was very different. The predominance of Islam meant that Christians were a minority community in every country, even in Lebanon, where they had significant political power. Christians might quietly evangelize in Egypt, but conversion from Islam to another faith was illegal there, as in most countries in the region. Many countries such as Lebanon, Iraq, and Syria had seen a significant outflow of Christians, although overall there was a much larger inflow of Christians—usually labor migrants—into the area. Filipinos, for example, often moved to the United Arab Emirates in search of work.[18] In any case, while there were evangelical and other Christians throughout the Middle East, there were few conversions and no real contest for believers. Africa was the battleground.

As the century waned, global Christian evangelism met newly missionary-minded forms of Islam in Africa, as several Muslim groups began to expand their understandings of how to propagate the faith. The theological concept of *da'wa* is extremely flexible, potentially encompassing everything from simple preaching to building a social welfare state.[19] It is connected to but distinct from the Islamic injunction to charity; charity may be, and often is, aimed at fellow believers, while *da'wa* is a matter of outward reach.[20] The *da'wa* movements of the late twentieth century supported not only the propagation of the faith through teaching or publishing, but also hospitals and clinics, basic poverty relief, schools, and mosque building, with programs all over the world, but particularly in Africa and parts of Asia. The practices of Christians clearly had an impact, as Muslims in places such as Tanzania and South Africa began to hand out tracts, put stickers on cars, distribute cassettes, and invite foreign "revivalists" to preach.[21]

American and European evangelicals played an undeniable role in shaping the struggle for believers. In 1991, for example, the faith-healing German evangelist Reinhard Bonnke traveled to preach in the northern Nigerian state of Kano. Bonnke was already a major player on the continent. In 1984, he had organized the Fire Convention in Harare, Zimbabwe, which brought together four thousand evangelists from forty-four African countries to listen to an array of keynote speakers from all over the world. (Only one of the keynote speakers was African: the Nigerian Benson Idahosa.)[22] In Nigeria, Bonnke was a familiar figure. He had visited Kano previously, in 1990, when he had preached to crowds that were, he claimed, one million people strong—each night. But when Bonnke tried to return in 1991, his arrival set off a riot. As many as eight thousand young Muslims gathered to meet his plane, their anger sparked by rumors of a negative comment that Bonnke was said to have made about Islam. A number of people died in the riot; accounts vary from "several" to "hundreds." Evangelists, including Bonnke, Benny Hinn, and others, may have seen themselves as simply spreading the message, but there was no question that they did so in a tense and competitive environment.[23]

Heightened competition led to a certain amount of hyperbole. One 2004 document from the Lausanne Committee, for example, anxiously reported that "the movement of Christians into Islam, long familiar to churches living under Shariah conditions, is becoming a significant challenge for the whole church."[24] In reality, there was relatively little conversion from one faith to another at the time, although recent projections suggest that, overall, the percentage of Muslims in sub-Saharan Africa will increase somewhat by 2050 because of religious switching, either from traditional religions or Christianity.[25]

These changes, and the larger political environment, led Christians in particular to feel threatened. A 2010 poll found that, while most people in sub-Saharan Africa found religious tension to be a less pressing concern than unemployment, corruption, or crime, they nonetheless saw religious conflict as a "very big problem." The anxiety was particularly high in Nigeria, Rwanda, Congo, and Djibouti. The two religious communities often had negative views of each other. Although both sides had some positive images—seeing each other as devout, honest, and respectful of women—Christians in particular thought of Muslims as violent. And in some countries, a third or more of Christians reported that they believed that many or most Muslims were hostile toward Christians. Muslims felt the reverse in only a few places.[26] Islam was viewed as a local threat by Christians in some other parts of the world as well, but Africa was a key site of conflict, where local realities were shaped by a larger discourse—prevalent both in and beyond evangelical communities—that presented Islam as a global danger.

As Luis Bush spoke in Manila in 1989, he understood that if he was going to set the agenda for the next stage of global outreach, he had to negotiate among three specific—and energized—evangelical constituencies: the church growth and Unreached Peoples movements; the spirit-filled charismatics and Pentecostals; and the social justice forces that, although pushed aside by church growth forces, had not gone away.[27] Indeed, by 1989, several, sometimes conflicting, developments were already shaping each of these segments of the global community of believers. There was the mainstreaming of certain forms of social concern, such as activism against global hunger or apartheid, combined with its seeming opposite, the rise of the religious Right in the United States. There was the increasing power of the global South leadership, which was concerned about poverty and other social issues but theologically conservative. And there was the enormous energy behind the Unreached Peoples movement, which combined with and augmented the millennialist and apocalyptic visions of both missions advocates and prophecy thinkers. In this environment, it was no longer possible to construct a game-changing argument without speaking simultaneously to church growth and social concern factions, while accounting for both apocalyptic urgency and global South insurgency. This is precisely what Luis Bush did.

On the platform at Manila, and later in myriad publications, Bush explained that the task of evangelizing in the 10/40 Window was critical because it was in these areas that Islam, Hinduism, and Buddhism "enslaved" the majority of their inhabitants and destroyed the lives of "billions of spiritually impoverished souls." Islam in particular was a challenge. From its center in the 10/40 Window, Islam was "reaching out energetically to all parts of the globe." Using a similar strategy, Bush said, "we must penetrate the heart of Islam with the liberating truth of the gospel."[28]

The 10/40 movement was no less interested in defining populations than the Unreached Peoples movement had been, although now the task was somewhat simpler. If you lived in this zone and were not yet a Christian, you were in the missionary crosshairs.[29] Exotic photographs and anthropological dissections of the "peoples of the 10/40 Window" were crucial to the project, as they had been to earlier endeavors. In the 1990s, for example, a group associated with the 10/40 Window project started to produce an annual booklet, "Thirty Days of Muslim Prayer," which encouraged Christians to pray for Muslims during the month of Ramadan. The prayer suggestions for each day described a specific issue or group to pray for: the Marsh Arabs of Iraq, the "people of Cairo," and Assamese Muslims (India). The booklet offered a list of "cultural bridges" that could help Christians connect to Muslims: one could emphasize respect for family, hospitality, and prayer.[30]

Churches used the banner of the 10/40 Window to organize prayer walks and vigils, to encourage donations, and to educate their members in Sunday school. Medical missionaries, humanitarian teams, short-term student groups, along with thousands of regular missionaries, operated in the Window. An interlocking network of people, including missions theorists, Unreached People activists, well-known preachers, and ordinary churchgoers transformed the Window from a debatable concept into evangelical common sense. Existing programs were rebranded to highlight their connection to the Window, while others were "scrutinized, even dropped, if they had the misfortune of being outside the Window."[31]

Americans played an outsized role in promoting the 10/40 Window. This is not surprising, given the size of the evangelical community in the United States and its remarkable wealth. Still, this new missions movement highlighted its own transnational credentials at every turn. Bush was perhaps exaggerating when he breathlessly described his earlier "AD2000" project—a missions push for reaching the whole world by the turn of the millennium—as having been fed by "the stream of life-giving water of regional movements from the two-thirds world." But his careful word choice, which described what used to be called the Third World as the "two-thirds world," was an indication of the importance that evangelicals placed on their own globalization.[32] And even assuming a fair amount of puffery in Bush's reports, it was clear that the 10/40 Window concept was taken up in many parts of the world. In 1994, a group of Brazilian "prayer warriors" focused on the 10/40 Window, and five years later twenty thousand Latin Americans turned out for a world missions conference that promised to send new missionaries to the Window.[33] In 1995, the second "Praying through the Window" campaign claimed to involve thirty million Christians in one hundred countries in a one-month program of prayer.[34]

Activists enthusiastically described the role of technology—satellite TV, radio, and even fax machines—in making such programs possible. "The net effect," *Christianity Today* explained, "was to minimize the boundaries of time, geography, and culture, generating a global and public prayer event."[35]

The very success of the movement was, for some evangelicals, precisely the problem. In fact, the 10/40 project was criticized for many of the same reasons the Unreached Peoples movement had been, and also for which the church growth school had been criticized at Lausanne. It swept away virtually everything else in its wake, ignoring or dismissing other forms of service and discipleship, such as building clinics, supporting churches, or training pastors. And, of course, it marginalized anything that happened outside that powerful, narrow, imaginary band.[36]

The evangelicals who opposed these models were not necessarily part of the social concern faction. Often the debates were between advocates of traditional missions and these newer activists, many of whom were enthusiastic about methods that didn't require the long-term commitments to language-learning and relationship-building that traditional missions did. Instead, they tended to support broadcast evangelism, short-term missions, or prayer walks through Muslim cities. Some establishment evangelicals decried these amateur approaches (or intense, democratic methods, depending on your perspective). The head of World Vision, Bryant Myers, told a conference on Missions to Muslims that "we American believers want to stay in our local congregations and reach the world, but that's too big a leap. What we need is a relational link, where you work together as two parts of the family of God over a long period of time." Others, more cynical or perhaps just more direct, dismissed the enthusiasm for the Window as "flavor of the month evangelism."[37] (The "month," however, lasted close to twenty years.) But supporters argued that the Window highlighted areas of great missionary need. There was something indulgent, they said, in the typical, non-strategic practice that sent yet more missionaries to areas where the gospel had already been proclaimed when those people had refused its message: "No one deserves to hear the gospel twice until everyone has heard it once," went one slogan.[38]

There was also the problem of shallowness. In the mid-1990s, one commentator in *Evangelical Missions Quarterly* argued that the AD2000 movement was overly centralized, and that it was perceived by many people as being a Western imposition, even as it aimed to present itself as global and grassroots-driven. Even worse was the movement's "hurry up!" millennialism, which replaced careful training of evangelists with the hectic energy of a deadline. Evangelicals should beware of any program, this writer said, that would ignore God's fundamental sovereignty by implying that Christians had to save everyone before a given date.[39]

The most urgent critique came from Christians and missionaries living in the 10/40 Window, many of whom said that some of the militant rhetoric coming from these campaigns was endangering Christians. When the campaign or its supporters produced material that was then made readily available on the internet—about people being "enslaved" by non-Christian religions; about Hinduism or Islam being "demonic"—word got out. The chair of the All India Christian Council said some Indian Christians were being negatively influenced by AD2000. He criticized the organization's "bombastic slogans, militant language, and a general demeaning of Indian culture." Other Indian Christian groups asked evangelical agencies to remove inflammatory material from their websites. All of this, they said, was fueling a "propaganda war" against Christians in India.[40]

The critiques had limited effect. In the 1990s, even the Southern Baptist Convention reorganized its venerable missions program to focus on the "frontiers" of the unreached in the 10/40 Window.[41] Stan Guthrie, a well-known evangelical author and an editor-at-large of *Christianity Today,* wrote in 2002 that it was probably time to "close the Window." But, he sighed, "[L]ike death and taxes, we will probably always have the Window with us."[42]

During the 1990s, Luis Bush worked closely with C. Peter Wagner, a leader in the spiritual warfare movement. Wagner had also been a key figure in the Unreached Peoples movement in the 1970s and 1980s, the chair of the Strategy Working Group of the Lausanne Committee, and a harsh critic of the social justice faction at Lausanne. Both Bush and Wagner were outspoken in their conviction that the 10/40 Window was more than just an area where peoples were "unreached"; it marked a region of great "spiritual darkness" and demonic power.

In the mid-1980s, Wagner and John Wimber had introduced a controversial course at Fuller Theological Seminary called "Signs, Wonders, and Church Growth." Wimber was the founder of the charismatic Vineyard Church, which had evolved into something like a nationwide denomination with scores of associated churches. The Fuller course not only taught about the rise in signs and wonders—miracles and manifestations of the Holy Spirit—in charismatic churches around the world, but also included in-class demonstrations of such signs, including healings. The course was popular among students, but it divided faculty, albeit unpredictably. Some liberals found the course appealing because it seemed anti-racist in that it highlighted practices of the non-Western church. Others on the liberal end of Fuller's spectrum found the theology of the course to be disturbingly lacking in rigor. Conservatives were also divided. Some appreciated the fact that the conservative theology of most global South churches was getting a forum. Other conservatives found the theology to be plain wrong. Classic fundamentalism held that the miracles described in the Bible had ended with the New Testament era. This was a tender spot, as the charismatic renewal had already affected most of the home denominations of Fuller faculty.[43]

Wagner was perfectly positioned to push signs and wonders, along with spiritual warfare, into the evangelical mainstream. As a missionary in Latin America, an influential member of the Lausanne Committee in the 1970s, and then a professor at Fuller, Wagner crossed the boundaries that sometimes separated Pentecostals and charismatics from other evangelicals. But Wagner was also operating in the context of a much larger embrace of spiritual warfare by conservative Christians. Increasingly, it made sense to American believers that the forces arrayed against them were not of this world.

Frank Peretti's novel *This Present Darkness,* published in 1986, presented itself as an unpacking of those forces. The book quoted Ephesians 6:12 on its cover, citing the struggle "against the powers of this dark world and against the spiritual forces of evil in the heavenly realms." Peretti's book and other popular works helped shape believers' ordinary theology. The plot centers on an occult conspiracy in the college town of Ashton, a community that was "small, innocent, and harmless, like the background for every Norman Rockwell painting."[44] One of the book's heroes is Marshall Hogan, a newspaper editor who attends a somewhat liberal church. That will change as he faces the forces of darkness and turns toward a more conservative Christianity. Marshall is assisted by a conservative evangelical pastor and a female reporter for Marshall's paper. Together they unveil the machinations of a female psychology professor and a New Age consciousness guru who plan to take over the town. The villains are aided by demons, whom Peretti describes in great detail—their various powers, their hierarchies, their investments in thwarting all human goodness. The heroes are backed by God's muscular, sword-bearing angels, who remain invisible but active (figure 8.2).

The book's sales were at first modest, but then fans began to spread the word. Pastors began to recommend it to their congregations, and the popular Christian musician Amy Grant promoted it at her concerts. The novel sold more than 1.5 million copies in its

FIGURE 8.2 Fan art of Angel Scion, a character in *This Present Darkness*. Courtesy of Keja Blank, www.kejablank.net.

first five years. One review suggested that Christians "were reading it more fervently and enthusiastically than the Bible."[45] Another lamented that the book had become "an interpretive paradigm by which an increasing number of Christians perceive reality."[46]

Like so many conservative Christian cultural products, Peretti's wildly popular books were all but invisible outside the evangelical community. Almost all of the sales of *This Present Darkness* were in Christian bookstores, which did not report to the *New York Times* or other bestseller lists at the time. Peretti's sequel, *Piercing the Darkness*, also sold well, as did many of the nearly dozen books of spiritual warfare fiction he wrote over the next twenty years.[47]

Conservative Christian commentators offered mixed reviews of *This Present Darkness*. One theologian commented dryly that "it celebrates a contemporary domination of feelings and intuition over biblical reasoning."[48] The *Reformed Review* argued that the book was theologically suspect—in fact, not Christian—on a number of levels, including its view of the power of angels, who seemed to be more relevant to human life than God himself. The *Review*, which represented that segment of evangelicalism most removed from charismatic and Pentecostal practices, also criticized the elevation of human "spiritual warriors," who have the power to destroy the demons through their prayers, even when God seems not to be able to. *Christianity Today* was more enthusiastic, saying that the novel might be a bit simplistic, but it was "opening thousands of minds to the reality of techniques of spiritual warfare."[49]

But this was precisely what upset many conservative Christian critics. Robert Guelich, a professor of the New Testament at Fuller Theological Seminary, reviewed the book for *Pnuema*, a journal of Pentecostal studies that was sympathetic to belief in the supernatural inhabitation of the Holy Spirit. Nonetheless, Guelich was frankly scornful of Peretti's theology. He singled out the book's presentation of demons as unbiblical. And he was disturbed by the fact that the main activity for all Christians in the book was spiritual warfare. There seemed to be little else in the way of Christian life, no other forms of prayer or worship to speak of. "Peretti's accent on spiritual warfare as the fundamental description of the Christian life," Guelich wrote, "risks turning the 'Prince of Peace' into the 'Commander-in-chief.'"[50]

But Peretti's success came from the fact that he took a general cultural fascination with the occult and paranormal in the United States in the 1970s and 1980s and combined it with the evangelical interest in distinctive forms of supernaturalism derived from Pentecostalism and the world of prophecy. Peretti welded these to a form of democratic spirituality, in which ordinary people could sense the truth about the supernatural world. The heroes of Peretti's books see and acknowledge the spiritual war they are in; they recognize the powers of darkness and are saved by angels of righteousness.

From their more respectable intellectual perch at Fuller, Wagner and Wimber also helped to foster among mainstream evangelicals the rather exotic practice of naming and exorcizing demons. And like Peretti, Wagner argued that evangelicals needed to understand that evil spirits were not only literal, they were also territorial, with responsibility for doing

Satan's works in specific places. In an article published in *Evangelical Missions Quarterly* in the summer of 1989, Wagner quoted a Nigerian Assemblies of God minister, Rev. Ajah, a convert who had previously practiced "occultism." Ajah explained that before his conversion, he had been assigned by Satan to control twelve spirits, each of whom controlled six hundred demons. These spirits and demons were appointed to specific areas in Nigeria. Understanding this territorial tethering of spirits was crucial, Wagner argued, because if demonic forces held control over specific places, then Christians could challenge that control through focused prayer and exorcism. To illustrate, Wagner had traveled to the ancient town of Ephesus to challenge the rule of a demon known as the "Queen of Heaven."[51]

For some evangelicals, this was simply too much: people like Wagner, they said, "have unwittingly internalized and are propagating animistic and magical notions of spirit power which are at odds with biblical teaching."[52] Evangelicals who identified with the Reformed tradition, which focused on the utter sovereignty of God (this would include Presbyterians, some Anglicans, and some Baptists) were less likely to see themselves as waging such literal, wide-ranging battles with Satan, although the lines were often blurry.[53]

Spiritual warfare eventually became common in many parts of the world, including Africa, Latin America, and Asia.[54] In Africa, spiritual warriors believed they confronted particularly dangerous enemies: Islam, certainly, but also the persistent power of traditional religion and its spirit worship. For some, the poverty and physical suffering of the people in the Window could be explained by the spiritual darkness there—a darkness that both Bush and Wagner specifically linked to the influence of Islam and traditional African religions. For example, *The Move of the Holy Spirit in the 10/40 Window* (1999), written by Bush and Beverly Pegues, told stories of the Holy Spirit at work. In North Africa, "many Muslims" were seeing visions of Jesus in their dreams and were converted; a young Christian in India had healed a woman of her headaches by praying for her release from a demon; in Ethiopia, the sister of a believer was raised from the dead. But the reverse was also true: in areas of Satan's reign, people "live in misery," Bush and Pegues said. These countries were under the spiritual control of Satan; the fruit of that demonic power included wars, disease, extreme poverty, famine, and drought.[55]

This focus on spiritual warfare by the leaders of the 10/40 Window movement was controversial from the beginning. One theologian, echoing complaints about Peretti's novels, complained to *Christianity Today* that "territorial demon" was "not a theological term."[56] But spiritual warriors from the United States gained traction in part because their innovations meshed with the views of many African evangelicals, including Pentecostals. And that lent moral authority to US-based spiritual warriors, who were implicitly allied with the rising force of global South Christianity.

The uncountable organizations and churches that took up the cause of the 10/40 Window were hardly under centralized command, and they often disagreed with the leadership's specific claims—if they even knew of them. The 10/40 Window was a sprawling, capacious, viral concept. Its meanings were not contained in a speech or a single organization. It lived in a pastor's PowerPoint presentation, a youth group's sale of 10/40 Window mugs to raise money for a retreat, in the fundraising strategies of countless missions organizations, both in the United States and abroad. No one regulated it. By the turn of the century, the Window had become part of the ordinary lives of a new generation of believers in the United States.

As of 2005, there were 16,300 Christian missionaries in the Muslim-majority world, plus an additional 41,000 in countries with large Muslim populations, such as India, Russia, and Nigeria.[57] The 10/40 Window mapped the passions of an evangelizing church, reaching outward from Latin America and Africa as well as Europe and the United States. But it also mapped its fears. For some, the 10/40 Window was a jubilant and energizing icon, an opportunity to become a "World Christian" through prayer, missions trips, or just attention to the people of an unfamiliar region. But the window also marked a zone of crisis, where, they believed, billions of people were bound by false beliefs. For some, it was also a place of darkness, where Satan's territorial ambitions were made manifest, and people were enslaved body and soul—souls entrapped by darkness and bodies suffering under poverty and oppression. Belief in the literal, imminent, and immediate activities of demons, and the similarly immediate possibilities of miraculous prayer, meant that the 10/40 Window was desperately in need of prayerful warriors for its cause.

For almost everyone who engaged with it, the 10/40 Window was, at the very least, a visible scar on the body of Christ. There were other areas where Christians might be under threat, evangelicals argued, but few places where they faced such opposition. All of this in turn facilitated the increasingly hostile attitudes toward Islam that would characterize evangelicalism at the turn of the twenty-first century, when opposition to Christian persecution would become a hallmark of evangelical activism. The Christians of the 10/40 Window were the most visible symbols of modern, suffering faith. Belief in their suffering would lead an energized group of US-based activists to take their cause to the streets—and to the halls of Washington.

9

"The Persecuted Body"

THE RELIGIOUS FREEDOM AGENDA

THE VIDEO OPENS with images of a young Sudanese boy sitting in front of a hut. "They wanted me to become a Muslim," he says through a translator. "But I told them I wouldn't. I am a Christian." He looks away as he lifts his shirt to reveal horrific scars from burns over one side of his thin body. "It was then," a deep male voiceover intones, "that he was thrown on a burning fire." Later, the narrator explains that in Sudan, "a government set on jihad" is persecuting Christians. There is footage of soldiers, then images of women lying on the ground, their mutilated limbs and open wounds viscerally on view. Bodies are displayed—violated and damaged.

Other scenes in the video tell similar stories of threats, punishment, and stalwart behavior. A Chinese pastor tells of being imprisoned, and he almost lifts up his shirt to show a scar. A young Indonesian girl, shown close up and weeping, tells of having a knife held to her throat. "They tried to get me to deny Christ," the girl says. "But," the narrator explains, "she refused to deny her savior."

Each tale is a melodrama of steadfastness: "All around the world," the narrator says, "Christians are dying for their faith. They could save themselves by denying Christ. But they didn't—and they won't." A graphic of a revolving globe spins out the names of nations that persecute Christians: Sudan, Indonesia, Saudi Arabia. "These people are not heroes or statistics; they are family."

The video was made in the early 2000s by the US-based Christian evangelical group Voice of the Martyrs (VOM), the organization founded in the late 1960s by Richard Wurmbrand, author of *Tortured for Christ*. The video was simultaneously a documentary and a fundraising tool, circulated in churches and at conferences, and available for purchase on the VOM website, where one could also read the latest news about Christian persecution or sign up for a monthly newsletter or a weekly email update. Frequently, VOM materials quoted the church father Tertullian: "The blood of the martyrs is the seed of the church."[1]

In the last decades of the twentieth century, a passionate concern with the persecution of Christians united conservative, liberal, and moderate evangelicals. Christians were being martyred all over the world, they argued, prevented from spreading the gospel and targeted for their faith. Persecution was chronicled in magazines ranging from deeply conservative venues such as *World* magazine to the moderately conservative *Christianity Today* to the Left-leaning *Sojourners*, described in books and on websites, and pictured in the fundraising newsletters and DVDs sold in church basements. The issue was embraced by Catholics as well. Pope John Paul II endorsed the issue with his apostolic letter in 1994: "At the end of the second millennium, the Church has once again become a church of martyrs . . . The witness of Christ borne even to the shedding of blood has become a common inheritance of Catholics, Orthodox, Anglicans, and Protestants."[2] The persecuted body—the body, or church, of Christ, and the literal bodies of believers—became an icon of faith and a potent political symbol.

Persecution narratives took on new forms and enhanced social-emotional power starting in the early 1990s. The impact was profound. Most obviously, it led American evangelicals to join with others in pushing for the International Religious Freedom Act of 1998 (IRFA), which institutionalized attention to religious freedom in the US foreign policy apparatus. The coalition that fought for IRFA was led by evangelicals, but it included Jews, Catholics, and Tibetan Buddhists. The bill required that the United States produce every year a list of "countries of concern" that were guilty of violating religious freedoms. The president was—and is—then required to choose from a a range of sanctions to impose, from expressing concern to cutting off trade, although sanctions can be waived for reasons of national security.[3]

The signing of IRFA was a high point for US evangelical activists who wanted to make global issues central to their community. Their success was due to good organizing, certainly, but it was undergirded by the enthusiasms of the global evangelical movement. Energized by the 10/40 Window campaign, and increasingly focused on Islam as a competitor, evangelicals in the United States, Europe, Asia, Africa, and Latin America were all outspoken about the dangers that Christians faced. Poverty remained a rallying cry, and soon other issues would also become important—HIV/AIDS in particular. But by the early 2000s, a focus on persecution had all but eclipsed social concern as the language of evangelical compassion. Attention to the suffering of "persecuted Christians" inherited much of the crusading spirit, global social awareness, and affective power that had animated the social concern movement at Lausanne and anti-apartheid activists in the 1980s. International religious freedom campaigns were the product of a new kind of "common sense" about human rights that emerged in the transnational evangelical public sphere, where, since the 1960s, religious persecution had been the stuff of novels, memoirs, movies, magazine articles, web pages, and public lectures. IRFA became a signature example of how evangelicals might influence international affairs in ways that built upon their own passions but which spoke the language of the secular political world.

Evangelicals' work for the Jackson-Vanik amendment in the 1970s and the Siberian Seven in the 1980s set the stage for how they would navigate Christian persecution in the early 1990s, when the discourse of human rights had a near universal political currency in the United States. Evangelicals had certainly thought a great deal about the persecution of Christians in the rest of the world, as we have seen in the case of Congo and of Christians under communism. But many evangelicals found the notion of human rights per se to be rather dubious—at once empowering and deeply problematic. They debated whether it was best—theologically and politically—to focus on championing Christian rights specifically or human rights generally. Jackson-Vanik had been a human rights amendment, true, but it had focused on the situation of Jews in the Soviet Union, and its fundamental premise seemed to support a believers-first logic. However, in the early 1990s, a broad range of evangelical intellectuals and activists pushed their community to take up the mantle of human rights writ large.

In 1992, *Christianity Today* produced a special issue on "Freedoms Under Fire." The editors acknowledged that human rights doctrine placed the self, rather than God, at the center of moral discourse. Even so, they said, the time had come to embrace human rights, to recognize that caring about human rights was "a Christian duty, with an inescapable foundation in the Bible."[4] *CT*'s headlines were visceral: "How to Keep a Prisoner Alive" and "They Shoot Christians, Don't They?" And so were the images: a parade of bodies—some shown in photographs, some in black and white sketches—kneeling, handcuffed, and damaged. The resonance with the visual culture of secular human rights activism was surely as intentional as it was unavoidable.[5]

Carl Henry, the magazine's former editor, insisted that Christians had been too narrowly focused on their own rights, giving off the impression that "evangelicals are interested only in defending their issues, not in a broad-based commitment to liberties for all."[6] One personal account exemplified the magazine's careful, sometimes awkward embrace of human rights. In "They Tortured My Friend," Tim Stafford, a Christian worker in Kenya, described the persecution of several Kenyan evangelicals. One was a member of parliament who had been in prison for a year, during which time he lost seventy pounds. Another was an Anglican bishop who spoke out against political corruption and was killed under suspicious circumstances. Stafford had become convinced of the importance of working for human rights. He argued that, in the face of oppression and evil, "the strongest weapon most people have is this thin tissue of language—'rights' language, which asserts a moral consensus."[7]

For some evangelicals, however, what was most important was the changing nature of the threat to religious rights. Marxism, "the twentieth century's scourge on religion," was being rooted out of Europe, Diane Knippers of the Institute on Religion and Democracy wrote. But there was a new threat "looming on the religious-freedom horizon": Islam.

"Islam is inextricably bound with the political realm," she wrote, and the heart of Islam is sharia law. Under sharia, state-sponsored religious persecution is likely, and not infrequently this leads to terrorism and "talk of Islamic *jihad*" (a term that in 1992 still required italics and a definition). Knippers was careful to note that there were "exceptions" to her generalizations about Islam, but she nonetheless posited that Muslims had failed to accept the church-state separation that American Christians claimed as a mark of their own commitment to freedom.[8]

Knippers' argument had more than a whiff of disingenuousness, since, from her post at the Institute for Religion and Democracy, she had spent much of the 1980s arguing for conservative evangelicals to become more involved in politics and to make more claims on the state. Her focus on the dangers of Islam was less about Islam's politics than her own. It was the sign of a pivot in orientation, a remapping of the world that built on the logic of the 10/40 Window: the great divisions of the Cold War had ended, but there would still be parts of the world that must be mapped in red. The Muslim world would be understood not only as a place of "spiritual darkness," as Luis Bush would have it, but also as a space where human rights were inevitably threatened by a "politicized" religion.[9]

Several years later, Max Stackhouse, the internationally regarded, theologically conservative professor at Princeton Theological Seminary, would argue that a capacious understanding of human rights was part of what made Christianity superior to Islam and to secularism. Stackhouse argued that belief in God, and specifically in a Christian view of God, required a commitment to human rights. God required respect for the dignity of human beings. But Stackhouse claimed that this also worked in the reverse: a commitment to human rights could not survive without a religious foundation. "[W]ithout the impetus of theological insight, human rights concepts would not have come to their current widespread recognition, and . . . they are likely to fade over time if they are not anchored in a universal, context-transcending, metaphysical reality."[10]

Here, Stackhouse was making a familiar argument posited most notably by Francis Schaeffer. Like Schaeffer, but with considerably more intellectual rigor, Stackhouse argued that Enlightenment thinkers only *thought* they had done away with the necessity of a belief in God; in practice, no coherent vision of human equality could be truly secular. A person could only believe that all humans were inherently equal if s/he also believed that they were made so as part of God's plan.[11] Stackhouse also insisted that religions were not all equal on this point. He argued that history showed that Christianity was more likely than other forms of belief to encourage religious freedom, that it alone was the basis for a state secularism that protected other religions. Those parts of the world where Christianity had been most influential were "the safest havens for non-established and non-majoritarian religions."[12] Stackhouse expressed confidence in Christian secularism, but his argument also exhibited the anxiety that lay just under the surface of almost every evangelical discussion of human rights: if human rights were secular and liberal, they were arrogant and dangerous; if human rights were God-given and universal, they were inspired and best protected by Christianity.

In 1995, Michael Horowitz galvanized the attention of evangelical elites with an editorial in the *Wall Street Journal* that took aim at Islamic countries for persecuting their Christian minorities. He listed atrocities committed by Muslims against Christians in Ethiopia, Pakistan, Sudan, Egypt, and Iran. Some of the horrific stories were widely known: three Iranian pastors killed in 1994; the routine abduction of children in South Sudan. Other examples seemed pulled from the less-documented folklore of the emerging anti-persecution movement: a pastor in Ethiopia whose eyes were put out by local Muslim officials; Christian students in Egypt "routinely" beaten and called "devils" by their classmates. The overall argument was that Christians had too long stood by, while "in a growing number of other countries, the rise of Islamic fundamentalism has effectively criminalized the practice of Christianity."[13]

That Horowitz was Jewish rather than Christian only strengthened his credibility, because he was presumably not speaking from self-interest. Both Christians and Jews were morally obligated to respond to persecution, Horowitz said, by challenging immigration and asylum policies within the United States and calling for changes in US foreign policy toward guilty governments. Over the course of the late 1990s, Horowitz was celebrated by leading evangelicals such as Charles Colson and Michael Cromartie and profiled in several national papers for his role in galvanizing a "sleeping church."[14] Horowitz felt, and others agreed, that the time had come to push for some kind of legislation that would force the United States to take specific actions to respond to Christian persecution.

Starting in the 1980s and mushrooming in the 1990s, a newly confident and well-connected generation of activist intellectuals had worked to raise awareness, legitimize religious concerns in policymaking, and increase funding for faith-based organizations in general. These intellectuals did not always constitute a coherent or even congenial group; they spanned the political spectrum, from the deeply conservative to Left-liberal. They included Christians and Jews as well as people of other faiths. But they shared in common a desire to have religious people taken seriously as thinkers and as policy-shapers, not only as activists. As Richard John Neuhaus had suggested in *The Naked Public Square,* they wanted a seat at the table—not just a place on the streets.[15]

These intellectual leaders were fully aware of the political force that evangelicals in particular had begun to wield in the 1980s. But rising power for the religious Right had meant that the long-established representatives of American evangelicalism, such as the National Association of Evangelicals and the editors at *Christianity Today*, were no longer able to convince the media that they represented the whole. Evangelical scholar Larry Eskridge argues that the religious Right in the 1980s pushed aside other, more moderate conservatives. "With the onset of the 'culture wars' as Falwell, Dobson, and the rest emerged, the whole ballgame changed, and the ambiguous role of the NAE as being some overarching evangelical spokes-organization began to unravel."[16] In the 1990s, new coalitions and other organizations would become preeminent. Think tanks such as the Ethics and Public Policy Center, the Institute for Religion and Democracy, and the Institute for Global Engagement developed research agendas that supported Christian activism, particularly on foreign policy.[17]

Looking around at the intellectual field in 1995, Horowitz found an impressive conservative Christian output on topics relating to religious freedom. Books such as *A Fragrance of Oppression* and *How to Prepare for the Coming Persecution*, as well as Wurmbrand's many books about Christians in the communist world, fanned the flames. Even the sixteenth-century classic *Foxe's Book of Martyrs* was reprinted and then updated—in 1981, 1990, 1997, and 1998.[18]

Within what Horowitz called the "exciting little explosion of books and articles" on the topic of Christian persecution, two were particularly important: Nina Shea's *In the Lion's Den: Persecuted Christians and what the Western Church Can Do About It* and Paul Marshall's *Their Blood Cries Out*. The sensationalist titles were part of the point, and in the late 1990s, these two books became for the anti-persecution movement what Frantz Fanon's *Wretched of the Earth* had been to a different group of activists in the 1960s—angry, righteous documents of oppression that were carried around from meeting to meeting.[19]

Both Shea and Marshall had ties to the conservative human rights organization Freedom House, but their books served slightly different audiences. Marshall's more academic book was long, detailed, and expansive. Like most evangelical commentators, he focused quite extensively on the dangers of Islam, but he also discussed everything from the status of evangelicals in Russia to the "forgotten outcasts" in India, Burma, and elsewhere. Shea's more activist manifesto was short, lurid, and lightly documented, essentially a compilation of photos and prisoner stories gathered from groups such as Voice of the Martyrs and Christian Solidarity International.[20] Shea was a Catholic who had started out in the secular human rights movement, but who had moved to the Right when she began to feel that human rights activists were not willing to address the persecution of Christians. *In the Lion's Den* repeated the now standard script of the anti-persecution movement, arguing that for Christians, there were two zones of global concern: places where Islam was dominant and countries of the still extant communist world (frequently called "the communist remnant").

The most significant part of Shea's book was its construction of a particular kind of image: a Christian, probably living in the global South, whose body was damaged or under threat by anti-Christian fanatics. The many photos in the book were grainy, and often dark, but they made the point that the Christian body was being violated, and the church—including Catholics, Orthodox, and Protestants—was under assault. Shea's relentless displays of suffering nonetheless involved a certain circumspection about women. They might be scarred, missing limbs, or disfigured by acid thrown on their faces, but they would not partially disrobe. Perhaps activists were conscious of the danger of visual display sliding into pornography. Perhaps it just seemed natural that Christian women, of whatever race or nationality, would not be asked for that particular kind of exposure.

In an editorial titled "Christians Without A Prayer," published on Christmas Eve 1996, the *Wall Street Journal* embraced Shea's book. Citing her analysis and examples, the *Journal's* editors opined that religious persecution around the world was common, but that "when the victims are Christians, too little attention is often paid to their plight." Christians were victimized twice—once when they were persecuted and again when people in the West cared less about them than other victims.[21]

One marker of the early success of the anti-persecution movement was the creation of the International Day of Prayer for the Persecuted Church (figure 9.1). Started in 1996, with the support of activists such as Horowitz as well as organizations such as the NAE (which issued its own statement about persecution that year), the International Day of Prayer became an extraordinarily successful annual event. The first year, five thousand churches participated. In 1997, organizers claimed that seventy thousand churches had received materials. The International Day of Prayer was not keyed specifically to the

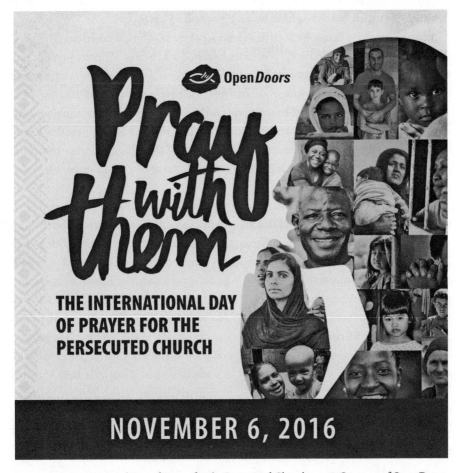

FIGURE 9.1 International Day of Prayer for the Persecuted Church, 2016. Courtesy of Open Doors.

nascent legislative battle over religious freedom, but it did a great deal to raise awareness and to help create a "common sense" about the ubiquity of persecution.[22]

Still, some advocates were frustrated that not enough was being done. Marshall strongly criticized evangelicals for their complacency, relative ignorance about the rest of the world, excessive nationalism, and overinvestment in end-times prophecy. It was hard to imagine, Marshall wrote, that such believers could "get their noses out of their navels long enough to consider whether their peace should be tied to the fate of suffering sisters and brothers around the world."[23]

In fact, a cohort of activists did bring concern about their "suffering sisters and brothers" into the mainstream of US politics. Starting in 1995, Congress, primarily the House of Representatives, held multiple and sometimes competing hearings on religious persecution. The series had begun when Chris Smith (R-NJ), chair of the Subcommittee on International Operations and Human Rights of the House International Relations Committee, called witnesses to discuss "Religious Freedom and the Persecution of Christians." Like many congressional hearings, these were designed as a performance—to display the suffering of Christians, to justify the focus on that suffering, and to bring the stories of Christians from the global South into the US Capitol.[24]

In 1997, Sen. Sam Brownback (R-KS) held separate hearings, focused on "Religious Persecution in the Middle East." Witnesses included a Lebanese Christian colonel, an Iranian exile, and an "Anonymous Witness from Pakistan." Whether the victims were Catholics or Protestants, Egyptians or Iranians, their reports almost all had the same structure: here is my country of concern; this is the general situation there; here is a list of the names of specific people and particular villages; this is what happened to them. Statements reprised the ritualized, apolitical quality of most human rights reporting, which often minimizes the specific political context in favor of a broad appeal to sympathy for anyone who is oppressed.

An uncomfortable moment came during the testimony of Father Keith Roderick, of the Coalition for the Defense of Human Rights in Macomb, Illinois. Father Roderick, an American Catholic, described the suffering of Christians in Muslim countries. But when Roderick was asked by Senator Brownback to estimate how many Christians around the world had been murdered in the past year, he replied that it was hard to know, but probably about one thousand. Brownback replied, uncomprehendingly, "What was that number you used? One hundred thousand?" No, Roderick replied, one thousand. At this point, the savvier Michael Horowitz, who was also giving testimony that day, jumped in to answer the question. Insisting that figures such as Roderick's were soft, Horowitz assured senators that *some* numbers could be trusted, such as those that Paul Marshall had provided in his book on persecution: 400 million Christians who lived with intense discrimination and 225 million who faced serious persecution. He did not include a number of deaths. Father Roderick hurried to agree that, indeed, Mr. Horowitz made a good point.[25]

Activists and policymakers circled uncomfortably around the question of how to represent Islam. On the one hand, Senator Brownback insisted that he would "not tolerate any religion being made a scapegoat in these hearings." Rep. Frank Wolf (R-VA) concurred that Islam per se was not the issue. "There are many good, overwhelmingly decent Muslims . . . What I am condemning are the governments or the radical Muslims who persecute and oppress people."[26] But the focus of the hearings was the Middle East, and the persecutors were consistently described as Muslim, and everyone knew that Islam was going to be invoked repeatedly, and almost always negatively.

In 1997 and 1998, two religious freedom bills were introduced to Congress, each with rather different views of the issue and the most appropriate US government response. The first was a bill co-sponsored by Wolf and Sen. Arlen Specter (R-PA), which made its way successfully through the House. But in the Senate, support for the bill was weak, and in summer 1998, Senators Don Nickles (R-OK) and Joseph Lieberman (D-CT) introduced an alternative bill, which differed in some particulars and was more flexible. Both bills included mechanisms to monitor other countries' levels of religious freedom and for the president to impose sanctions on non-compliant countries.

There was a fairly broad consensus that the issue of religious persecution was quite real and that Christians were frequently victims. "To suggest that the persecution of Christians is not a serious problem is nonsense," William F. Schulz, the executive director of Amnesty International USA told a reporter.[27] And because no one in Washington or elsewhere was interested in declaring themselves to be *in favor* of religious persecution, there was a strong push to pass some sort of legislation.

Notwithstanding sometimes sharp divisions between those who supported the Wolf-Specter version of the bill and those who supported the Senate alternative, the move for a religious freedom law had multiple constituencies. The primary backers were, of course, anti-persecution activists. The core operatives were themselves from several different religious communities (Protestant, Catholic, and Jewish), but they often focused on organizing evangelicals to support the cause. As Jeffrey Goldberg reported in the *New York Times Magazine*, this was "hardly a movement that arose by spontaneous combustion in some church basement." Rather, it had been "midwifed by a handful of veteran organizers," who saw not only a moral imperative, but also a "wedge issue" that would allow them to challenge the policies of the Clinton administration.[28]

In addition to strong evangelical support for the bill, several important Jewish leaders also signed on, including A.M. Rosenthal, editor of the *New York Times*. He, and others, saw frightening parallels with the persecution of Jews in Europe.[29] Other Jewish supporters argued that they were simply "repaying a favor." Since evangelicals had helped pass Jackson-Vanik, it was time to support them when they wanted to fight for their own community.[30] Finally, some saw the bill as a way of supporting Israel. Religious persecution was an issue that could highlight how much Israel and America had in common against the largely Muslim nations being targeted by the legislation.[31]

Although there was a broad range of support for the bill, a number of constituencies were distinctly worried, particularly about the House's Wolf-Specter bill. The Clinton administration opposed it as an unnecessary limit on the president's discretion and the work of the State Department. The free trade lobby fought it hard, opposing any imposition of sanctions.

Other opponents included traditional human rights groups such as Human Rights Watch and Amnesty International, as well as some liberal mainline Protestant denominations. As several observers pointed out, what was often seen as *religious* persecution was in fact motivated by a range of causes—racial, ethnic, political, or economic. The focus on religion might, in fact, miss the causes and thus the potential solutions for any given problem.[32] Wolf-Specter was, in the words of the former chair of the Congressional Black Caucus, Mervyn Dymally, "a diplomatic sledgehammer" that would "harm the very people we are trying to help."[33] Some Christians from outside the United States implicitly made the point that the bill could backfire in their home countries. One Orthodox priest from Jerusalem, speaking to a gathering in Washington, pointed to copies of several anti-persecution books and exclaimed, "These titles are *not* helpful."[34]

Human Rights Watch and others also worried that the participants in the anti-persecution movement cared only about Christians. Some groups suspected a right-wing agenda behind the bill. Why focus on religious persecution separately from other kinds of human rights violations? Would this push attention toward one specific set of problems—Christians in China or the Middle East—and diminish attention to persecution elsewhere? Several major Jewish organizations agreed with this objection. The Anti-Defamation League eventually signed on, but to the Senate's version of the bill, not Wolf-Specter.[35]

Sojourners supported the bill, but voiced concerns. Columnist Ron Dart argued that liberals should not ignore persecution just because it was the darling issue on the Right. Still, Dart wondered, why is it that some oppressed Christians were put front-and-center, while others were all but ignored? For example, what about Christians in Latin America—did their Left-leaning tendencies make them unworthy?[36]

Finally, there was well-funded opposition to the international religious freedom bill from economic conservatives within the Republican Party. The National Foreign Trade Council, the National Association of Manufacturers, USA Engage, and trade unionists all worked hard against IRFA. Free-trade senators, particularly Rod Grams (R-MN), blocked an initial vote on the Senate version of the bill.[37] *Christianity Today* responded angrily, commenting that evangelical forces "felt abandoned by otherwise supportive business leaders who put profits ahead of morality."[38]

There were even evangelical opponents of some versions of the bill. Interestingly, they emerged from the most zealous of the anti-persecution activists. Early drafts of the bill had included proposals to ease asylum provisions for people facing religious persecution. That left some Christian leaders worried about the effect on churches in the global South if getting into the United States was too easy. In Middle Eastern countries, in particular, churches might be "emptied out." That, they argued, would undo "the labor of Christian missionaries and martyrs over centuries."[39] A related issue was more directly theological: if "the blood of the Christians is the seed of the church," then the suffering of believers could lead to conversions and greater faith. Persecution might be part of God's plan.

The clear backdrop to the religious freedom legislation as everyone understood, was the US relationship with three countries in particular. First was Sudan, where for two decades a civil war had pitted the Islamist government in Khartoum against the people of the south, a significant number of whom were Christian. To what degree Sudan's civil war could be described as a religious war was a matter of great debate, but, for at least some of the activists, Sudan's government was a paradigmatic example of the threat Islamists posed to Christians. The second was China. There, the official Christian church was large and growing, but many believers worshipped at illegal "underground" churches, and they were vulnerable to harassment and arrest. In addition, China occupied Tibet and was systematically oppressing Tibetan Buddhists. Both conservative evangelicals and some Hollywood liberals were interested in China. Third was Saudi Arabia, which was surely guilty of religious persecution and which, just as surely, was not about to be placed under US sanctions. The anti-persecution movement was strong, but it was not going to trump the politics of oil or the US Central Command.

IRFA became law in 1998. It established two competing centers of gravity. The first was in the State Department, where the position of Ambassador for Religious Freedom was created. The law also required the State Department to complete annual country reports on religious freedom. The reports are exhaustive, often hundreds of pages long, and examine the state of religious freedom in every country in the world (except the United States). But they are also deeply political.[40] For the first few years, for example, the State Department did not include Saudi Arabia on its list of Countries of Particular Concern.[41] "To the extent the government contrives ways to keep American allies off its list," the *Washington Post* complained in 2003, "the designation process is a political joke."[42] Saudi Arabia was listed as a country of particular concern in 2004 and for the next twelve years, but Presidents Bush and Obama waived sanctions every year.[43] Similarly, Pakistan was not listed as a Country of Concern at any time after 2002, almost surely because it was a partner in the US "war on terror."

The second center of gravity was the quasi-governmental US Commission on International Religious Freedom (USCIRF). The commission was designed to play a watchdog role. Its members would write their own separate reports and keep an eye on the State Department's presumed tendency to whitewash information about the behavior of close allies. As Nina Shea later reported, the commission was a "saving grace" for those who had advocated for a law with stronger sanctions built in. Over the next decade, the commission would provide a space for multiple hearings, press conferences, trips abroad, and other kinds of public performances of concern.[44]

The commission consistently pushed back against the State Department, issuing its own commentaries on the annual reports, offering its own alternative reports and lists of egregious violators, and demanding more aggressive action on sanctions.[45] Over the years, the members of the commission have been relatively diverse, with Muslim, Jewish, and sometimes secular members, as well as Catholics and Protestants. The group has been largely white, but has included African Americans, Arab Americans, and Asian Americans. The push for activism on the commission, however, came in large part from an initial core of Christian conservatives, who, from the beginning, were criticized for focusing too much on the suffering of Christians and for being biased against Muslims.[46] Khaled Abou el Fadl, a commissioner from 2003 to 2007, told a reporter that "It was predetermined who the bad guys are and who the good guys are . . . There is a very pronounced view of the world, and it is that victims of religious discrimination are invariably Christian. It was rather suffocating."[47]

This agenda did not always endear the commission to religious freedom advocates elsewhere. In 2002, a USCIRF delegation went to Egypt, where they received a "frosty reception" even from Coptic religious freedom advocates, who saw any identification with the commission's hardline stance as a hindrance to their cause. Partly, they worried that the very idea of religious freedom would be identified with US foreign policy.[48]

In 1999, Clinton appointed Robert Seiple as the first Ambassador-at-Large for International Religious Freedom. Seiple had most recently served for eleven years as the president of the evangelical aid organization World Vision—then the largest privately funded relief and development organization in the world. At the time of his appointment, Seiple seemed like the perfect candidate. He was a Vietnam veteran with an Ivy League degree who had also served as president of Eastern College and Eastern Theological Seminary, an evangelical school with a reputation for "social concern." Seiple was also a highly respected Washington insider, a political conservative who had cultivated both sides of the aisle during his many years at World Vision.

Once appointed, however, he found himself at odds with the commission. These independent "watchdogs," he insisted, were too focused on producing their expansive lists of Countries of Particular Concern and issuing frequent calls for punishment for violators. The group's "misguided agenda," Seiple said, was not really about promoting religious freedom so much as indulging in the moral satisfaction of denouncing religious persecution. As a diplomat, Seiple thought that these displays made the commission something of a joke, staffed by self-righteous activists whose antics got in the way of the behind-the-scenes advocacy by the State Department. Two years after he left his post as ambassador, Seiple wrote a bitter commentary in *Christianity Today*. "That which was conceived in error and delivered in chaos," he asserted, "has now been consigned to irrelevancy."[49]

Seiple was perhaps correct about the decidedly non-diplomatic agenda of the commission, but he was wrong about its relevance. Largely because of the work of think tanks, policy analysts, and Christian activist organizations, USCIRF's righteous anger helped make religious persecution a key intellectual and cultural concern among policymakers as well as among many ordinary Christians and Jews. Diplomatic historians often debate the role of culture in shaping policy, but they have far less frequently examined the reverse. In the case of IRFA, however, a policy decision gave renewed impetus to the cultural movement on behalf of persecuted Christians.

In the years after IFRA, the persecuted Christians movement became increasingly active, institutionalized, and visible. Materials available to ordinary believers expanded dramatically in quantity and quality. There were hundreds of true life stories in print and DVDs—from Brother Yun's *Heavenly Man* to *A Cry from Iran*, a film by Joseph and Andre Hovsepian about their father, an Iranian pastor killed in the 1990s. The popular evangelical writer Randy Alcorn published the bestselling novel *Safely Home*, the story of an American businessman who learns, firsthand, about the sufferings of the Chinese church through the experiences of his old college roommate. Voice of the Martyrs (the group founded by Wurmbrand) reached new audiences through its somewhat surprising partnership with the Christian hip-hop group DC Talk.[50]

After 9/11, while US- and UK-based organizations still dominated the evangelical movement against religious persecution, European, Asian, and African activists began taking on leadership roles, just as they had after the Lausanne conference. Their activism was undergirded by a strong set of international institutions, which worked in multiple languages and convened church leaders from around the world.

Starting in the 1990s, for example, the World Evangelical Alliance (WEA), a network of evangelical organizations from more than one hundred countries, began to promote religious freedom as a key area of concern. The organization's Religious Liberty Commission, founded in 1992, began sending out weekly email updates, telling the stories of Christians who were being persecuted.[51] The Lausanne Committee, larger and more formal, was slower to take up the issue, but in 2004, it produced *The Persecuted Church*, a long and substantial report. The primary author of the report was Patrick Sookhdeo, a British evangelical Anglican priest of South Asian background, known for his activism and his dire warnings about Islam.[52] In 2009, WEA formed its own think tank, the International Institute for Religious Freedom, which had offices in in Bonn, Cape Town, and Colombo. It was clearly deliberate that none of these centers were in the United States. With their money and prodigious powers of cultural production, Americans could potentially overwhelm any movement, but anti-persecution politics was global.

US organizations across the spectrum, such as the International Center for Religion and Diplomacy, the Ethics and Public Policy Center, the Institute on Religion and Democracy, and the Institute for Global Engagement (opened in 2000), played major roles in promoting awareness of persecution. They hosted conferences, issued reports, and conducted workshops for church leaders or journalists. This intellectual world was augmented by other non-evangelical institutions, such as Georgetown's Berkley Center for Religion, Peace, and World Affairs, and the Pew Research Center for Religion and

Public Life, the country's largest and most important think tank on religious and public policy issues. Both the Berkley Center and Pew developed research programs that made religious freedom a key part of their intellectual agendas.[53] Although there were significant differences among advocates over how to respond to persecution, the conversation crossed political lines and traversed religious communities.

Among US evangelicals in particular, the Institute for Global Engagement (IGE) was a crucial player, speaking out for a moderate vision of Christian-Muslim encounter. IGE had been organized by Seiple after he left his position as US Ambassador for Religious Freedom in 2001. The group published a serious journal (*The Journal of Faith and International Affairs*) and organized conferences. In 2009 and 2010, the annual conference theme was "Evangelicals and Muslims: Conversations on Respect, Reconciliation, and Religious Freedom." IGE sent delegations to Pakistan, Laos, and elsewhere in what the organization straightforwardly described as "top-down engagement." Seiple argued for respectful interaction as a way of "fighting extremism" among Muslims. For Seiple, this meant an NGO version of the behind-the-scenes diplomacy he valued.

Seiple was also distinctive in arguing that evangelicals themselves were part of the problem. Christians were persecuted, he said, but sometimes that was in response to their aggressive proselytism. Seiple told one audience in Washington, DC, that he had seen remarkably reckless behavior when he was on the US embassy staff in Saudi Arabia in the 1990s. A diplomatic crisis had developed after a group of Filipino believers who were working in Saudi Arabia devised a plan to smuggle twenty thousand Bibles into the country by the year 2000. In 1998, inspired by apocalyptic fervor, they walked through Riyadh throwing Bibles over courtyard walls.

It seemed to Seiple that these evangelicals were less interested in actually reaching people with the Christian message than in provoking a conflict with the government. The Saudis obliged by throwing fourteen Filipinos and one Dutch citizen in jail, then deporting them. This crisis, Seiple said, was due to the utter lack of religious freedom in Saudi Arabia, but it was also a problem of working from "evangelistic Cliff Notes": a narrow theology and shorthand understanding of Christian discipleship. Seiple liked to say that evangelicals should be "wary as serpents and innocent as doves" (Matt 10:16). Posturing had no place in the equation. When persecution comes, Seiple told his American audience, "let's make sure it's for righteousness sake."[54]

In the early twenty-first century, evangelical activism moved online. Actually, evangelical organizations had been making use of the internet for some time, sending out email alerts and developing simple but effective sites for telling the "stories of the persecuted." Groups like Open Doors, the Barabus Fund, Voice of the Martyrs, Christian Freedom International, Compass Direct, and a host of others raised money and solicited prayers for Christian sufferers in Africa, the Middle East, China, and elsewhere. All of them trafficked in detailed stories of suffering; many made use of equally dramatic photos.

Open Doors was founded by Bible smuggler Brother Andrew. The organization's budget was not particularly large—$25 million in 2009—but it made a commitment to web-based activism that gave it an impressive media footprint.[55] The website was a multi-layered document that, with every page, provided new paths into knowledge about persecution (figure 9.2). Beautiful photos scrolled across the top of the page, each linked to a specific campaign on behalf of "the persecuted." One photo showed two dark-skinned boys holding goats; the next image showed two white men standing in front of the UN building, with flags of the world arrayed behind them. Most of the pictures faded to a sepia hue, the yellow-brown tones suggesting the earth, and also warmth and connection. This opening page reproduced romanticized images of abject-yet-lovely people in need of Westerners to save them. It was enchanting, condescending, and shallow in equal measure.

These types of sentimental and depoliticized images have been long familiar in the Western humanitarian imagination.[56] And here, as with other humanitarian images, viewers were invited to act. In the early 2000s, they could click on one of several options, choosing, for example, the "Campaign in Support of Iraqi Christians." There a visitor could listen to a lecture about the "religious-cide" in Iraq and the dangers of an Islamist upsurge. Or perhaps send money for a care package that included "basic necessities and a Bible." The page linked to a letter from "a Christian in Baghdad," which recounted an attack on a church in which fifty-eight people were killed. Underneath the letter were links to two relevant BBC stories about the fearful situation faced by Iraqi Christians.[57]

The Open Doors site was more than a fundraising tool. It was also a space to perform an authenticating ritual that connected the presumably comfortable American Christian with the realities of their oppressed fellow believers. The requests were not only material. Viewers were invited, over and over again, to pray. The sample prayers—offered in PowerPoint presentations or by email subscription—asked God to give courage to the persecuted, to strengthen and comfort them. Open Doors suggested that believers tell God that "our hearts ache" when we hear stories of women raped and children kidnapped. Ask God to encourage those who suffer. The call was there, asking European and American Christians to see the beauty and the pain embodied in the suffering bodies of global South believers. The Open Doors website was the persecuted Christians movement in miniature.

Sometimes, however, the sample prayers were oddly concrete. One suggestion, for example, was that the reader should pray that God would grant persecuted pastors a

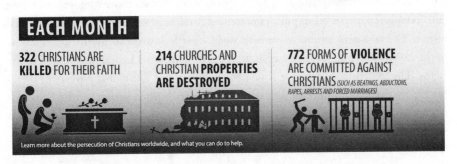

FIGURE 9.2 OpenDoorsUSA.org

chance to have Bible training. Another was that God help people in congregations to start businesses. Both were services that Open Doors just happened to provide. Prayers and fundraising were none-too-subtly linked.

By 2014 or so, it seemed as if the international religious freedom network was losing steam. The Obama administration had shown little interest in the office of International Religious Freedom in its first two years. Obama eventually appointed Suzan Johnson Cook, an African American Baptist minister, as international ambassador for religious freedom, but the Senate took many months to approve her appointment. She resigned less than two years into her term, replaced by the highly regarded Reform rabbi, David Sapperstein.[58] Some people speculated that the institutions arrayed around the issue of international religious freedom were being overshadowed by the new Office of Religion and Global Affairs, which was designed as something like the carrot to IRFA's stick. The office was set up to support the State Department in increasing its outreach to religious groups around the world. The intellectual problems that accompanied the work on religious freedom did not entirely go away, in that deciding to "engage" religious groups and leaders was also a matter of selecting and authenticating which religious groups in other countries the United States would decide to enlist.[59] There was no question that US engagement with some groups rather than others would shape the political and religious terrain in any country where the United States worked. But the conversation was shifting, and the ability of conservatives to define the issues had diminished.

From the mid-1990s and through the early 2000s, the persecuted Christians movement showed the border-spanning power of visions of the body in pain. Through concrete details and powerful emotions, using both the colors of connection and the black and white of news, testimonies from persecuted Christians followed a script of gratitude and fortitude. Attention to persecution was a form of transnational solidarity. By highlighting the righteous suffering of Christians in Africa, Asia, Latin America, and the Middle East, hailing them as stalwarts of a faith that was everywhere under fire, evangelicals built a movement on images of bodies—wracked and damaged, or perhaps just praying and tearful.

In defining Islam as a threat, the persecuted Christians movement positioned Christians as simultaneously victims and warriors. Focused on those who were suffering and endangered, persecution politics presented itself as a matter of international social justice. The anti-persecution movement was a clear follow-on to the 10/40 Window of the early 1990s, but in many ways it was equally heir to the Lausanne moment of the 1970s. The structural violence at issue now, however, was not global poverty or dictatorship, but religious oppression. It was a profoundly limited version of the Lausanne consciousness, but it harnessed those energies. It had one goal: to make persecution into what social concern had been three decades earlier—the defining issue of a generation.

10

"Leave the Nuances for the Diplomats"

REDEEMING SUDAN

IN THE SUMMER of 2001, Gloria White-Hammond set off for Sudan to redeem slaves. A pediatrician in Boston's racially and economically mixed Jamaica Plain neighborhood, White-Hammond's warm and expressive face was featured on billboards advertising the South End Community Health Center where she worked. She was a local celebrity, known for her humanitarian work in Africa as well as her commitment to her patients at home.

White-Hammond was also co-pastor of Jamaica Plain's Bethel AME church. She traveled to Sudan along with several other African American leaders from Boston, including Ray Hammond, her husband and co-pastor; Gerald Bell, pastor of the Southern Baptist Church in the largely African American neighborhood of Roxbury; and Liz Walker, the long-time anchor of CBS-4 news in Boston and a member of the Hammonds' congregation who was also an ordained AME minister attending Harvard Divinity School.

By 2001, Sudan's long civil war had left hundreds of thousands of civilians dead, and famine had exacerbated the death toll. Militias allied with the government had been raiding villages and taking captives in parts of the south of Sudan, where many people were at least nominally Christian. The captors often forced women and children to work in their homes, tending cattle or doing housework, sometimes in horrific conditions. In some cases, they demanded that their captives convert to Islam.

Gloria and her group saw this as a modern form of slavery, a mirror of African Americans' own devastating history. And as Christians they saw the attacks on non-Muslims as a threat to religious freedom. They knew that complex forces had led to the war. They knew, too, that the southern rebels were hardly saints, that they could be vicious and brutal. Except for the civilians caught in the crossfire, "there were no real good guys in this," White-Hammond said. Yet the systematic oppression they saw outweighed everything else. As Ray Hammond put it: "At some point, you leave the nuances for the diplomats."[1]

White-Hammond and her group were organized by Christian Solidarity International (CSI), a Swiss-based organization that had pioneered the practice of "slave redemptions"—paying traders from the north of Sudan to purchase captives and return them to their homes in the south. For the Boston pastors, the trip was more difficult than they had ever imagined, although their route was one that CSI had followed many times before. By the late 1990s, CSI's slave redemption trips had settled into a fairly standardized routine. When the American (or sometimes European) groups arrived at the designated site, they would find a number of southern Sudanese, mostly women and children, sitting under a tree. A representative from CSI, working with members of the Southern People's Liberation Army (SPLA), would meet with the Sudanese traders from the north who had brought abductees back to the village. A bundle of cash was then demonstratively handed over, and the captives were officially free. The redemption ceremony itself was informal. Some members of the Sudanese group were generally called upon to tell their stories, describing the violence they had undergone and their joy at returning home. The Sudanese were then usually addressed by the Christians who had redeemed them. Often, there was singing.

After her 2001 trip, White-Hammond became a major national figure as an advocate for southern Sudan. (South Sudan would become an independent country in 2011.) "It was one of those really transformative kinds of experiences for me," White-Hammond recalled of her first journey. She hadn't realized that most of the people they redeemed would be women and children. White-Hammond frequently described her horror at the accounts she heard that day. "I wasn't prepared for the stories of unconscionable abuse," she told an audience at Wellesley College. She remembered particularly a young woman who was taken captive along with her two small children when her village was raided. The raiders demanded that she carry supplies on the trip north, but the woman said she was worried that her children might get away from her if she couldn't hold onto them. "They [the raiders] solved the dilemma for her," White-Hammond told her audience. "They quite simply shot her children to death."[2]

The slave redemptions were designed to bring those stories home, to make clear, in a deeply personal way, the violence of the conflict in Sudan. Viewing the abductions as a modern form of slavery, White-Hammond and her group perceived slave redemption as a way for them, as African American Christians, to respond to the amalgam of burdens they carried regarding Africa and slavery. During the 2001 trip, Sudanese captives were told by CSI that they were freed because there were people in America—Christians, African Americans—who were moved by their plight. "That was the key to this whole thing," Rev. Gerald Bell later said. "Because they were so proud that the African Americans were coming."[3]

Starting in the 1990s, Sudan entered US evangelical consciousness as a site of Christian persecution and a space of solidarity, religious and racial. By the end of the decade, it had become the "abiding international preoccupation" of American evangelical activists, black and white, perhaps second only to Israel in the amount of attention it received.[4] And, just a decade after the divisions over anti-apartheid activism had highlighted racial and political divides among theologically conservative believers, the moral claims of Southern Sudanese brought black and white US evangelicals together as little else had.

In fact, the Sudan campaign would ultimately move well beyond evangelicals, becoming one of the most successful and broad-based political coalitions on international issues since the fall of apartheid. Secular activists ran the gamut from the *National Review* to Amnesty International. Ecumenical churches played a role, as did members of the Congressional Black Caucus. They were joined by conservative pro-Israel groups, who were making Sudan exhibit C—behind Osama bin Laden and Hamas—in their campaign against the "threat of militant Islam." But evangelicals, black and white, were crucial to the movement, and a changing politics of race was central to their work. American believers were deeply moved by a situation in which southern Sudanese, whom they understood to be black as well as Christian, were oppressed by northern Sudanese, who were understood to be Arab as well as Muslim. In this context, Arab stood for white. Sudan was one space in which the American evangelical community forged new coalitions across the bounds of race.

Support for African Christians was a key point of solidarity. It made the fact of a globalizing faith the basis for a refashioning of the domestic religious community. The ritualized performance of slave redemptions resonated profoundly with the history of slavery in the United States. Participation in slave redemptions registered participants—Americans and Sudanese—as freedom practitioners. This time, though, all of the Americans were on the anti-slavery side of the enterprise.

Once again, the political power of suffering was paramount. And, once again, evangelicals focused their energies on the "persecuted body"—the body or church of Christ, and the literal bodies of believers. US evangelicals asked that their government both recognize their grievances and represent their ideals. Sudanese Christians were both victims and allies.

Before Sudanese independence in 1956, Britain had been the colonial power in Sudan, although it generally operated in collaboration with Egyptian representatives of the Ottoman empire. To maintain its power, the British administration in Sudan used the time-honored tactic of cultivating differences within the population, using region and religion as the divides. The war between north and south that would wrack Sudan for decades in the twentieth century had its origins, at least in part, in the British policy of divide and rule. Small numbers of Coptic Christians had lived in Sudan for hundreds of years, and the British also heavily promoted Christian missions in the south as a bulwark against Islam in the north.[5] "The British did not create the differences between North and South," argues one historian, "but in almost sixty years did little deliberately to moderate them and much to sharpen them."[6]

A strong anti-colonial nationalist movement in Sudan emerged in the 1920s and 1930s, based largely in Khartoum. Nationalist leaders promoted their Islamic and Arab identity. This Arab-Muslim identity would challenge British power, lay claim to a distinctive Sudanese nation, and call for sympathy and support from the Arab world.[7] The multiple non-Arab cultures of the south were a challenge to the Sudanese-ness emerging in the north. The more the north asserted its dominance, the more allegiances became polarized as Muslim versus Christian or Arab versus African.[8]

When in 1956 Sudan declared its independence, the new government in Khartoum quickly began aggressive attempts at "Sudanization" of the south, with the promotion of Arabic as a national language and insistence on Islam as the state religion. Christian mission schools were nationalized, Arabic replaced English as the language of instruction, and the building of new churches was prohibited. In 1964, all foreign missionaries were expelled.[9]

Starting in the 1970s, with Sudan wracked by internal conflict, Khartoum began to emerge as a close US ally, dependably anti-communist in a region where Marxism had some traction. Relations were up and down, but by the mid-1980s, Sudan had received more US economic aid than any other country in sub-Saharan Africa.[10] Still, it largely remained off the radar of most Americans, including conservative evangelicals.

Then, in 1989, Omar al-Bashir staged a military coup in the name of Islam, and relations with the United States deteriorated rapidly. (Sudan would harbor Osama bin Laden from 1991 to 1996.) Soon, political battles for control of Sudan led al-Bashir's government to crack down on any dissent; al-Bashir's dictatorial regime was violent and oppressive even in the core areas of his rule. Not surprisingly, he also increasingly discriminated against Christians and other religious minorities. Al-Bashir declared the war in the south a jihad and pursued it with ferocity, attacking civilians indiscriminately.[11]

During the 1980s, several rebel groups emerged in the south. The largest and most effective was the Southern People's Liberation Movement, with its military wing, the Southern People's Liberation Army. The various rebel groups battled each other for military and ideological control, and the SPLA itself fractured into opposing factions. Battles between the various rebel groups were often vicious, and each of them was guilty of attacking civilians in "hostile" areas. In 1999, the Washington Office on Africa reported that more southern Sudanese had been killed by the factions of the SPLA or in interethnic violence than in the north-south war.[12]

Religion remained a factor throughout these years, but in complex ways. The religious composition of the south was not entirely clear. Well into the 1990s some policymakers argued that most southern Sudanese were still followers of African traditional religions. Other observers, including the Catholic Church, estimated that Christians were a majority of the southern population. It was clear, however, that southern Sudanese Christians often combined Christianity with traditional beliefs and practices, including magic and ancestor veneration.[13] In addition, the government in Khartoum began aggressively promoting Arab identity and linking it to Islam. As a result, Christianity increasingly functioned as one marker of oppositional African-ness. Christianity, according to one scholar of southern Sudan, provided one means of articulating a vision of "political equality, community development, and self-enhancement in the context of an increasingly coercive and stratified nation-state inspired by Islamist ideals."[14]

Modern slavery in Sudan was first reported in US and British papers in the late 1980s, when semi-independent groups of raiders from Sudan's north began to attack villages in the south. Historically, slavery—or perhaps more accurately, the transaction of people as war captives, gifts, or compensation—was an institution in many African societies, including several of those in the region that became Sudan. When Muslim Arab groups came to eastern Africa as early as the eighth century, they added a religious justification to the trade in peoples, arguing that it was immoral to enslave another believer, but it was permissible to enslave heathens. In the eighteenth century, however, slavery became a very different kind of institution, as European, Sudanese, and Turko-Egyptian traders set up shop. They encouraged local tribes to attack each other and sell the prisoners into their markets, where the captives were bought by Europeans, Americans, and some elite Egyptians. Officially, the Atlantic slave trade had been abolished in the nineteenth century, but the practice of taking captives in local wars had not entirely disappeared. In the 1980s, the government in Khartoum backed some militias in their raids on southern villages, during which they stole cattle and other goods. They also abducted people, who were then sold as slaves to northern Sudanese households.[15]

Details were sketchy at first. A 1987 report authored by a Sudanese professor described the arming of some northern tribes who had taken slaves in Dinka territory. (The professor was soon arrested in Khartoum.) The London-based Anti-Slavery Society reported in 1988 that some desperate southerners were selling their children into various kinds of servitude as they tried to escape from their war-ravaged villages. Another report told of more than four hundred Dinka abducted.[16]

Reports increased throughout the 1980s and early 1990s. Then, in October of 1995, the UN Commission on Human Rights published a detailed study of slavery and slave markets in Sudan. For those who wanted to deny the existence of slavery, as Khartoum repeatedly did, the UN report was a damning indictment, linking abductions to deliberate government policy. The report made clear that the attacks were more than just random raids by "autonomous" northern tribes: "The abduction of southern civilians, men, women and children, whether Muslims, Christians or of traditional African beliefs, regardless of their social status or ethnic belonging, became a way of conducting the war."[17]

By 1996, the existence of slavery in Sudan was widely reported in the US media, from investigative reports in the *Baltimore Sun* to a special edition of *Dateline NBC*.[18] Nat Hentoff of the *Washington Post* wrote regular columns on Sudan and slavery, attacking those who refused to admit its existence and extolling activists and journalists who reported on it.[19] Starting in the mid-1990s, the evangelical press also began to consistently

cover events in Sudan. *Christianity Today* took up the issue; one report simplisti-
cally described the conflict there as one driven by "[t]heology and a clash of religious
values between fundamentalist Muslims, Christians, and animist groups."[20]

The stories of abductees, like those told to Gloria White-Hammond, were horrific tales
of abuse. Many of the women who returned to their villages in the south described how
they had been raped by their masters; others watched family members die—children, parents, and siblings. Others said that their captors had demanded that they take Muslim
names and follow Islamic customs.[21] Although the number of reported abductions varied
to an extraordinary degree—from eleven thousand to several hundred thousand—taking
captives was clearly an important wartime tactic.[22] But slavery was one among many horrific realities of the war: disease, famine, and the bombing of villages threatened far more
people.

Gloria White-Hammond (or, Pastor Gloria, as she preferred to be called) didn't want to
go to Sudan. She was a soft-spoken woman who dressed with a casual elegance (figure
10.1). She was *not* the kind of person, she explained with wry humor, who went camping.
She was also not the kind of person who went to ravaged villages in Sudan.

> We got a message from Liz Walker, who had been invited to go to Sudan and
> wanted us to go. My husband, Ray, was excited about it; I was *not* excited about it.
> We would have to leave about a week after my daughter's birthday, and her gradu-
> ation celebration. [She was graduating from Stanford]. It was so topsy-turvy. I had
> no idea where the passports were . . . And I didn't feel like we had the time to take
> up another cause.[23]

Indeed, the Hammonds had charitable and political investments across the spectrum.
Gloria was interested in women's issues and did her work as a physician in a low-income,
community-based health service. At the same time, Ray was one of the founders of the
Alliance for Marriage, which was pushing for a constitutional amendment banning gay
marriage.[24] Their commitments differed, but together they represented a certain kind of
African American politics, invested in improving the economic, physical, and spiritual
health of their community, while generally conservative on social issues such as gay rights
and abortion. In 2001, Ray also had just been made Chair of the Boston Foundation, a
well-heeled grant-making organization that funded programs that advocated for such
causes as support for charter schools or an increase in low-income housing. The Boston
Foundation attracted the involvement of many of the most powerful people in the city.
Ray Hammond was one of those people.

After some consideration, Pastor Gloria changed her mind about Sudan. "So I met
with my prayer partners, and we prayed week after week that Ray would come to his
senses. And we still don't even know where our passports are! Obviously this is a sign
from God," she said laughing. Still, in the end, she didn't want Ray to go alone. "I didn't

FIGURE 10.1 Rev. Gloria White-Hammond in 2003. Rick Friedman/Getty Images.

want him to go and die without my being able to say that I was with him up to his last gasping breath, and that I had held him in my arms, and so, for those reasons, I ended up packing up and heading out with him."

Pastor Gerald Bell also never thought he would go to Sudan. But Bell was a very different person than White-Hammond. An energetic, voluble, and strongly built man, when I met him he wore fashionable dark sunglasses and a slightly rumpled three-piece suit. His church, in a low-income neighborhood that abutted Boston's gentrified South End, was small but lovely, with a recently remodeled sanctuary containing stained glass windows depicting biblical stories. And he himself was a remarkable storyteller—a mid-level bank employee turned preacher, whose eye for the telling detail was joined to a self-conscious, down-home directness. "I'm just a street kid at heart," he told me. "My family is not preachers; they're moonshiners, pimps, players. You know, I'm just street. Period."[25] His story of that 2001 trip was primarily an adventure story with a political bent.

Like White-Hammond, Bell initially had real doubts about whether he had the energy or the resources to go to Sudan. His church barely had enough money to pay his salary. His work in a low-income community was exhausting. Bell said that when he was first approached about going to Sudan, he was incredulous. "I'm not going to Sudan!" he thought. "I can't even get across town! What do you want me to do about it? I'm not going to Africa. I'm from a small church, and I'm just trying to figure my way." Bell knew that the trip would be grueling. Everything about the plan was secretive. They weren't supposed to tell people when they were going, or even that they were going. He was given a budget for purchasing gear. "I went straight to Eastern Mountain Sports," he said, "and I got *everything* they had! I'm an old survivalist from the way back."[26]

These Boston church leaders were not alone in their turn to Sudan. A number of other important African American leaders were involved in slave redemptions because they too saw a profound resonance with the history of US slavery. African American communities in the 1990s were already moving toward the construction of Arabs as white—a vision that was very different from that of the 1960s, when many African Americans embraced the idea of an African-Arab global alliance.[27] Civil rights activist Joe Madison, a Washington, DC, talk show host and NAACP board member, went with CSI on a slave redemption trip in 2000. Madison was not a pastor but, along with White-Hammond, he became one of the most important African Americans in the Sudan movement. After he returned, he told a reporter that watching former slaves being returned home "felt like someone put me in a time machine, like I was in a scene from *Roots*. I was literally just torn apart."[28]

Black pastors had a particular role to play because they could speak to both race and religion. Activist ministers such as Rev. Walter Fauntroy and Rev. Al Sharpton also went to southern Sudan.[29] Like others, they gave interviews to the media and spoke at rallies and at their churches. One group of African American pastors wrote to the Congressional Black Caucus to demand more leadership on the issue of slavery in Sudan.[30] In the spring of 2001, Fauntroy and Madison, along with Michael Horowitz (who had been central to the campaign for the International Religious Freedom Act in the mid-1990s), were arrested after they handcuffed themselves to the doors of the Sudanese embassy. The protests was designed to resonate with the scenes of people getting arrested in the anti-apartheid protests outside the South African embassy in the 1980s. The goal, Sudan activists said, was to launch a national grassroots movement.[31]

Slave redemption was only one aspect of the movement, but it was its emotional center. Slave redemptions in Sudan were religious and political rituals (figure 10.2). For participants, they were emotionally evocative, morally uncomplicated—and difficult. But most of the people who became passionate about Sudan did so not because they went to Sudan themselves, but because they heard stories of slavery and redemption, and adopted those stories as their own. As the mainstream media took up the issue, and more people heard about what was happening on the ground, slave redemption also moved into the

FIGURE 10.2 Slaves returning to a village to be redeemed by a CSI team. Courtesy of Didier Ruef.

realm of genuine grassroots activism. As *Newsweek* reported, "Freeing Sudan's slaves may be one of the world's most compelling human-rights crusades."[32]

In 1998, a Colorado public school teacher, Barbara Vogel, read a newspaper account of Christian Solidarity International's work to her fifth-grade students. "They sat at my feet and tears streamed down their faces," she told a reporter. The class had just studied the US Civil War and had thought slavery was a thing of the past. Vogel encouraged her students to raise money for CSI's redemption project. The children brought in lunch money and set up lemonade stands, sold T-shirts, and wrote their elected officials. Soon the news of their actions made the national press, and other donations, some from corporations and wealthy individuals, started pouring in. Every time they raised $50—they had been told this was the price needed to buy back a slave—they cut out an image of a person from brown paper and displayed it on the classroom wall.[33]

With the help of their many donors, the class raised $50,000, enough to redeem one thousand people. In the process, they became symbols of average Americans who were willing to act, to make a difference. Vogel and her students inspired others around the country. Grade school students performed a play about slavery to raise money for slave redemptions. In 2001, the National Association of Basketball Coaches presented CSI with a $100,000 check during halftime of the NCAA basketball finals.[34] Activists in President Bush's hometown of Midland, Texas, organized a series of concerts and performances. Sudanese exiles had built a "real" Sudanese village as part of a vigil; later, the exiles and local activists reenacted a raid, in which parts of the village were burned down and some of its inhabitants "fled" into the surrounding desert.[35]

The ritual of raising money for slave redemption in Sudan operated at several levels. First, the act of purchasing freedom resonated uncomfortably with the American history of slavery: however much buying freedom was a legitimate practice when other options were off the table, it also meant participating in the fact of African peoples being sold, once again.[36] Slave "redemption" also spoke unquestionably in the register of a specifically Christian worldview. Its rhetoric, and the emotions it elicited, allied perfectly with an understanding of Jesus as first and foremost the redeemer of humanity. An old hymn hauntingly evokes the emotional power of the biblical account: "Sing, oh sing, of my Redeemer. With His blood, He purchased me."[37] If Jesus purchased believers with his blood, then believers were obligated to redeem others. All the more so if the enslaved were also Christians, whose heavenly redemption was assured but whose worldly suffering was a matter of ongoing evangelical concern. In slave redemptions, religious freedom became racial freedom; black slaves became modern Christian martyrs; black bodies became global Christian icons. The logic of religious suffering was melded onto a politics of racial liberation.

In 1993, Charles Jacobs, a management consultant, heard a news report about slavery in Sudan and was appalled. As a Jew and a former civil rights activist, he felt that he could not stand idly by in the face of this kind of atrocity. The next year, he quit his job and started the American Anti-Slavery Group (AASG). Headquartered in Boston, AASG played a major role in funneling Americans, particularly African Americans, into CSI's slave redemption trips.

Jacobs' story was far more complicated, however, than this simple morality tale of a man moved by his civil rights past to respond to current injustice. The political investments he brought to his anti-slavery work included a strong commitment to the most conservative wing of the US pro-Israel movement, and would evolve into an activist agenda on the dangers of "Islamic extremism" that eventually pitted him against most of the liberal and progressive Jewish community in Boston. In the 1980s, Jacobs had been deputy director of the Boston chapter of the conservative watchdog Committee for Accuracy in Middle East Reporting in America. After founding AASG in the 1990s, Jacobs also began working with another organization he had founded to produce a movie that described the Middle East studies program at Columbia University as anti-Israel and hostile to Jews. There and elsewhere, Jacobs created a storm of controversy as he argued that almost any criticism of Israel was tantamount to anti-Semitism.[38] In 2008, Jacobs would go on to found Americans for Peace and Tolerance, which organized against the building of a Boston-area Islamic center. Jacobs depicted the center as the beachhead for a dangerous agenda. "The goal of radical Islam in America is to radicalize the historically moderate Muslim population here and conduct a long march through our institutions and become legitimized," Jacobs said. He blamed progressive Jewish leaders in particular for being too willing to engage in dialogue, thus giving "radical Muslim leaders a good housekeeping seal of approval . . . effectively, they have given radicals a key to the city."[39]

Jacobs saw his Sudan work as related to his pro-Israel activism. After White-Hammond and her colleagues went to Sudan on their first trip, which Jacobs had helped arrange, he invited all of them to travel to Israel, where they toured religious sites and met Israelis who told their side of the Israeli-Palestinian conflict. White-Hammond later told me that she would have liked to meet Palestinians on that trip, but it was not on the agenda.

In relation to Sudan, Jacobs focused on building coalitions across political, religious, and racial lines, organized around an unarguable premise: slavery was wrong. AASG's promotional material claimed that the group had support across the spectrum: "From Congressman Barney Frank (D-MA) to former Senator Jesse Helms (R-NC), the late Johnnie Cochrane to Kenneth Starr, and Al Sharpton to Pat Robertson." Within a few years, Jacobs built AASG into the single most important force in the emerging anti-slavery movement.[40]

Several Sudanese who lived in the United States worked closely with AASG. One key player was Simon Deng. Deng often spoke of how his village was raided when he was eight. During the attack, he saw one of his friends shot, but he was spared. A year later, in 1968, during the first civil war, he was lured away from home by a family friend and forced to work for a Muslim family in northern Sudan. Eventually, Deng obtained his freedom and traveled to the United States, receiving political asylum in 1990. In 1998, he read an article about contemporary slavery in Sudan and decided to become active. While working as a lifeguard at Coney Island, Deng quickly became a leading spokesperson on the issue of slavery, giving interviews and organizing events. In 2006, he organized the Sudan Freedom Walk, a three-hundred-mile trek from New York to Washington. That walk ended with a rally attended by Sen. Hillary Clinton (D-NY) and Sen. Sam Brownback (R-KS), followed by a meeting with President Bush.[41]

Deng was outspoken in his view that the suffering of the southern Sudanese was due to "radical Islam" in the north. In 2005, representing AASG, he spoke to the Victims of Jihad Conference in Geneva. After the Holocaust, he said, nations had gathered to say "Never Again." After Pol Pot's genocide in Cambodia, the world said the same. But clearly, the world was standing by while his people were massacred. "I have begun to think that the right question to ask the so-called civilized world," he said, is whether they should just "stop saying 'Never Again,' since those words carry no meaning." Deng was no less outspoken in his condemnation of a "jihadist Islam" that was responsible for the attacks in the south. "No religious authority or system of justice holds the perpetrators responsible because their crimes are a matter of government policy and are sanctioned by the state religion, a religion that pretends to be universal but that slaughters the 'other' without mercy."[42]

Over the next several years, Deng railed against Islam while treating the Sudan conflict as part of a larger war in which Israel was a key protagonist. In 2011, Deng gave a speech at a "counter conference" to a UN meeting commemorating the tenth anniversary of the UN's World Conference on Racism in Durban, South Africa. At the original UN meeting in 2001, controversy had erupted over language in a draft statement that linked

Zionism to racism. Now, Deng argued that the United Nations and the world community were guilty of excessively criticizing Israel while ignoring what Khartoum was doing to the southern Sudanese, whose horrific situation had been "driven off the front pages by exaggerations of Palestinian suffering."[43] For Deng and Jacobs, Sudan activism was part of a broader agenda of challenging "radical Islam" and uncritically supporting Israel.[44]

Many supporters of AASG's work probably saw it as a straightforward fight against slavery and in favor of human rights. They had little idea that the group was linked to any larger agenda. Gloria White-Hammond, for example, spoke of her Sudan activism in terms of God's work in her heart: "I've been to other countries where I did missions work, and I could go back or I could not go back." Sudan, however, had captured her spirit. Using a phrase that had become common among evangelicals in the 1990s, she summarized: "It was a God thing."

White-Hammond felt a similar sense of calling on the trip to Israel that Jacobs had organized. While in Tel Aviv, the group had visited Yad Vashem, the Holocaust museum. While Gloria was aware of the bias of the trip in ignoring contemporary Palestinian suffering, she was nonetheless deeply moved by what she learned about Christians who had worked to save Jews during the Holocaust. Her group had toured the Garden of the Righteous Gentiles. Looking back, Gloria likened those European Gentiles who had risked themselves for Jews to worshippers in African American "storefront churches." In the cities of the United States in the early twentieth century, some African American preachers gathered congregations in small spaces that had once been stores or shops. These storefront churches were cramped, their congregants were often poor, and they were known for their passionate, Pentecostal-style outpourings of emotion.[45] Gloria explained to me that the Righteous Gentiles in Europe were like those worshippers; they were not people who had attended big, anonymous churches. They must have instead worshipped in smaller congregations, storefront equivalents, "where people knew each other and had a real commitment to one another," where they were accountable. Writing European history in an African American register, Gloria considered her own calling. "I want to be a storefront kind of Christian, who can worship when there is no stained glass, and no oak pews. Just to worship God authentically," she said. "I would have wanted to be a righteous Gentile."

It is perhaps not surprising that as slave redemptions became more visible, and as more people from the United States and Europe participated, criticism of the practice also became more pronounced. Already in the summer of 1999, UNICEF's branch of Operation Lifeline Sudan (a coalition of more than sixty groups that provided aid in south Sudan) and the London-based Anti-Slavery International had both criticized slave redemption as likely to raise the price on slaves and encourage more slave trading.[46] Journalists and academics alike argued that the arrival of groups like Christian Solidarity International had made it more profitable to take and sell slaves. CSI countered that the price of slaves had *not* gone up since they had been operating and clarified that they would not pay more than the standard rate of US$50.[47]

Another issue was the role of the main rebel group, the Southern People's Liberation Army, in the redemption process (figure 10.3). The SPLA controlled the redemptions in that they made the deals with the traders from the north, arranged the time and place of the redemption ceremonies, and handled the transactions that changed US dollars into Sudanese pounds. By taking a cut of the price or manipulating the currency exchange, the SPLA could make money for itself in the process.[48] Some SPLA officials were straight-forward about the role of redemption money in supporting their cause. As a result of the exchanges, they had been able to buy uniforms, fuel, and vehicles to support the war effort.[49]

For some of the Americans and Europeans involved in slave redemption, it was abhorrent to think that the high-minded practice of saving people from slavery was also funding weapons used in the war. Other pro-South activists were more comfortable with the deal, believing that only a well-armed SPLA could ultimately help bring Khartoum to the negotiating table. Still, by the early 2000s it was clear even to the staunchest SPLA supporters that the organization was not simply a united front of brave Christians fighting for their faith. It was a strategic military and political organization, a collection of insurgent fighters of varying religious and ethnic allegiances—and, crucially, an armed force that had also committed atrocities.

A third major concern was the possibility of outright deception. In the early 2000s, a number of people in southern Sudan, including SPLA officials, aid workers, and others, argued that some, perhaps many, of the people who were supposedly being redeemed were just local women and children who had been recruited to play the part of slaves for

FIGURE 10.3 CSI slave redemption. Courtesy of Didier Ruef.

the sake of getting money from the redeemers. As one former senior SPLA official put it, "The more children, the more money." Another aid worker said that she had seen "slave" children who were clearly already living in the area, wearing bracelets that allowed them to get food at local feeding centers.[50]

Commentators argued that CSI and other organizations had an interest in ignoring such possible scams because they made headlines with their numbers. In 2004, CSI claimed to have freed 48,000 slaves, which certainly sounded very impressive for a small NGO.[51] Upon investigation, these numbers appeared impossibly high. The Nairobi-based Rift Valley Institute compiled a database of 11,000 Dinka people who had been abducted from 1994 to 2004. The report made clear that this was probably an undercount, owing to the limits of sources, but even so, the numbers were starkly different. Could CSI have freed almost five times as many people as the Rift Valley Institute counted as having ever been taken?[52]

Christian leaders in Sudan and the United States had mixed feelings. Several important Sudanese Christians, such as Catholic Bishop Marcram Gassis and Bishop Henry Cuir Riak of the Episcopal Church of Sudan, were enthusiastic about the redemptions.[53] Others were opposed or at least cautious. The US president of World Relief, the humanitarian arm of the National Association of Evangelicals, argued that Southern Sudanese were more concerned about the dangers of the war—the starvation and bombings that killed masses of southerners—than the far smaller number of people who were under threat by slave abductions. "We jump up and down about the forcible Islamization of a child who has been kidnapped and taken into slavery, while we sit by and watch as half a dozen children starve to death."[54]

The issue of slavery was emotionally wrenching, and the promise of freeing slaves was powerfully affecting, but there were two additional sets of activists on the issue of Sudan's civil war, each with a significant evangelical component. First were the humanitarian organizations that aimed to bring in food and supplies to the war zone. Second were anti-corporate activists, who fought to stop Khartoum from benefiting from the sale of oil.

In 1989, when al-Bashir came to power, Sudan was facing famine for the second time in a decade. The first famine, in 1984–85, had also affected Ethiopia, and had created a humanitarian crisis that had inspired a massive European and American response.[55] When the specter of famine returned, al-Bashir faced immediate pressure from the United States and Europe to respond to the threat of starvation in the south. The ruler signed an accord with the UN and the SPLA that allowed for a significant amount of food to be delivered by international NGOs. The resulting aid caravan, Operation Lifeline Sudan (OLS), would endure for more than fifteen years. The US government was one of the effort's largest supporters, donating more than $700 million between 1989 and 1998.[56]

In its successes and its sometimes spectacular failures, OLS embodied the processes that made humanitarianism so politically and morally fraught. Michael Barnett has argued that humanitarian organizations often struggle with the question of how to respond to "emergencies" that stem, not infrequently, from larger structural problems. This was clearly the case in Sudan, where the famine could not be separated from the war.[57] Most of the agencies that participated in Operation Lifeline Sudan were dedicated to neutrality. In fact, neutrality was at the heart of how organizations like Oxfam or CARE perceived themselves. But the government of Sudan (and sometimes the SPLA) controlled when and whether the aid agencies could do their work. Rebel factions in the south fought over access to relief supplies, and they regularly "taxed" incoming aid in order to feed their soldiers. For its part, the Sudanese government routinely denied travel permits and landing rights to aid agencies working in the south. All sides saw aid as a weapon in the war. And they were right.[58]

For many smaller evangelical organizations that came to operate in Sudan, OLS would become the symbol of all that was wrong with official humanitarianism. The secular humanitarian ruling class had sold out, some evangelicals argued. Larger organizations were so committed to neutrality and safety that they refused to deliver aid in dangerous circumstances, or when the government of Sudan decided to forbid it. Groups such as CSI and Christian Solidarity Worldwide, major players in the slave redemption programs, were aid agencies as well. They made it clear that they would continue to fly no matter what the official agreements said or the conditions on the ground were, ignoring OLS guidelines.[59]

For its part, the government in Khartoum seemed to make a point of alienating evangelical humanitarian agencies. It quite unwisely appeared to concentrate its fire on one of the best-known evangelists in the United States at the time, Franklin Graham, son of Billy. Franklin had made his reputation as the head of an international aid organization, Samaritan's Purse. By the early 2000s, Graham's group had been deeply involved in providing humanitarian aid—and proselytizing—in some of the most devastated parts of the globe, arriving early and staying late on the ground in Rwanda, Somalia, and elsewhere.

Samaritan's Purse ran an eighty-bed hospital in the southern Sudanese town of Lui. In the winter of 2000, the hospital was bombed by Sudanese government planes four times in a single month. One patient and several people who lived near the hospital were killed in the attacks. Voice of the Martyrs, the anti-persecution group that had been founded by Richard Wurmbrand in the 1960s, ran another nearby hospital. The Sudanese government also dropped as many as a dozen bombs in its vicinity.[60]

Graham soon became an important voice on behalf of southern Sudanese, and it didn't hurt that he was able to speak from his position as one who had served basic human needs while standing up against both Khartoum and what he saw as the weak-kneed humanitarian mainstream. In the spring of 2000, for example, Graham published an editorial in the *Wall Street Journal* demanding that policymakers pay attention to events in Sudan, where, he said, the "Muslim government is waging a brutal war against Christians." How was it, he wondered, that while the international community had (rightly) responded to the plight of Muslims in Yugoslavia, it had not tried to help the southern Sudanese? Maybe the hesitation was due to racism: "[A]re the lives of Europeans more valuable than those of Africans?" Graham asked. Or perhaps Christians were being ignored while

Muslims had been heard.[61] Here Graham's framing of the conflict as a religious one misrepresented what was in fact a far more complex weave of politics, economics, and ethnic conflict in Sudan.

Starting in the late 1990s, another group of activists, evangelical and otherwise, decided on a different approach to Sudan's crisis: they went after oil companies. The goal was simple, and seemingly impossible. Activists sought to pressure oil companies that did business in Sudan to pull out. US oil companies were not operating in Sudan at the time: in 1993, the Clinton administration had named Sudan as a state sponsor of terrorism and imposed limited sanctions. In 1997, the United States accused Sudan of serving as a "refuge, nexus, and training hub" for terrorist groups and imposed comprehensive sanctions, outlawing any trade or financial transactions with Sudan by US companies. (In 1998, Clinton authorized a cruise missile strike against a pharmaceutical plant in retaliation for attacks on US embassies in Kenya and Tanzania.)[62]

Despite US sanctions, oil was fueling the conflict, and several major, non-US oil companies—PetroChina; Petronas, Malaysia's national oil company; and Canada's Talisman Energy—had large operations there. Most of the major oil fields in Sudan straddled the border between north and south. The south contained most of the oil reserves—70 percent by most estimates—but Khartoum controlled the pipeline. From the perspective of the southern Sudanese rebels, prodigious oil reserves were fueling the attacks against them. The SPLA declared that Talisman Energy had essentially taken a side in the war; as punishment, the group abducted some Canadian oil workers in the spring of 1999.[63] The oil pipeline was also sabotaged multiple times in 1999 and 2000. The government of Khartoum began to try to destabilize the SPLA's access to the pipeline by attacking the villages that surrounded the oil fields.[64]

In this context, oil became a major issue for American (and Canadian) activists, who focused primarily on two strategies. The first was to encourage individuals and funds to refuse to invest in either PetroChina or Talisman. Second, and more radically, they wanted to prevent *any* company that was doing business in Sudan from trading on US stock exchanges. A set of conservative activists insisted that, while they were fully in favor of the free market, it could not run unfettered in every case. Just as business should not have opposed sanctions against violators of religious freedom, oil companies and others should not be making money off the oppression of people in south Sudan.[65] International capitalism, they argued, simply could not operate as a morality-free zone.

This lesson was not lost in March of 2001, when members of Congress introduced the Sudan Peace Act for the second time. The initial bill, put forth in 1999, had died in committee. This time around, Rep. Spencer Bachus (R-AL) proposed an amendment to the House version that would have disallowed any companies involved in oil or gas operations in Sudan from being traded on the New York Stock Exchange or NASDAQ. To the profound surprise of many observers, the Bachus amendment was included in the House version of the bill, which passed by a 422-to-2 vote. "When you have to make a choice between dollars and lives," Bachus later explained, "you choose lives."[66]

Wall Street was outraged and soon launched a campaign to make sure that the provision wouldn't make it into any final version of the bill. The Bush administration quietly sided with Wall Street while trying to maintain an image of being very tough on Sudan.[67] Advocates for the Bachus amendment kept fighting, however. A few weeks after her first trip to Sudan, Gloria White-Hammond and Charles Jacobs went to Capitol Hill to push for the strongest possible version of the bill. They were set to hold a press conference on the morning of September 11, 2001. Just before the event started, the participants were ordered to evacuate.[68]

The attacks on New York and Washington pushed everything else off the table. Congress was convinced to pull the Sudan Peace Act from consideration as the Bush administration worked hard to enlist Sudan to help in the "war on terrorism."[69] Despite this, the US Committee on International Religious Freedom kept the pressure up, as did evangelical media like *Christianity Today,* which published a furious analysis of the failure to pass the Sudan Peace Act.[70] John Danforth, President Bush's special envoy to Sudan, put forth a series of confidence-building measures designed to shore up tentative moves toward peace on the ground in Sudan. Some evangelicals were dubious. The international director of Samaritan's Purse argued that any negotiations with Khartoum were based on a "fantasy—that the government of Sudan will be an honest broker."[71] Representative Bachus put it rather more strongly when he told the National Association of Evangelicals that al-Bashir's government was "a Hitler-style government. Any deal you make with them is a deal with the devil."[72]

In October 2002, the Sudan Peace Act finally passed resoundingly in both houses and was signed by President Bush. The bill provided for as much as $100 million in humanitarian aid to areas outside government control, meaning the south. It called for Khartoum to negotiate in "good faith" with the SPLA or face sanctions.[73] *Christianity Today* hastened to assure its readers that the act "has teeth," even though international oil companies were free and clear, and other sanctions would come only at the discretion of the president.[74]

From there it was a long and difficult road to Sudan's Comprehensive Peace Act, signed in January 2005. Rather remarkably, the act included the provision that southern Sudan would be able to have a referendum on independence in six years. Many American evangelicals were delighted at what they believed to be a validation of their work and the beginning of real hope for the south. "This is truly an answer to the fervent and frequent prayers of Christians around the globe," said Carl Moeller, president of Open Doors USA.[75] Ninety-eight percent of the south voted for independence in the January 2011 referendum, and South Sudan became an independent nation in 2012.

After independence, South Sudanese Christians, long lionized by Americans, began working through the unglamorous process of nation-building, and doing so in conjunction with Muslims and followers of African traditional religions.[76] The messy reality of power politics meant that many evangelicals (and most other Americans) paid less attention. South Sudan suddenly became less interesting when its people were no longer oppressed by Muslims. Still the legacy of US activism was crucial to the formation of this new nation. The country's founding was filled with hope, but South Sudan would soon find itself embroiled in its own horrifically costly civil war between different factions of what had been the SPLA. It remains one of the most undeveloped and war-torn countries in the world.

The issue of slavery and conflict in Sudan provided the basis for a profound example of evangelical internationalism at its most politically effective and, for many, its most emotionally profound. It was and is an emblem of how American evangelicals positioned themselves as political actors, working on behalf of what they saw as a global church whose ties were built in part on a narrative of suffering. Their passions made them politically salient, but their hearts made them problematic actors. Just as humanitarians had in previous crises—from the starvation in Biafra in the late 1960s to the crises in Somalia in the 1990s—people in the United States had acted with generosity and moral certainty, only to find that their American helpfulness was inadequate to the situation on the ground. The suffering faced by the people in South Sudan after the country's founding had complex origins and no easy answers. One thing was certain, however: religion was neither the cause of, nor the solution to, South Sudan's pain.

III

Emotions

11

"I'll Go Where You Send Me"

SHORT-TERM MISSIONS

IN 2000, the Christian rock group Audio Adrenaline produced what was essentially a three-minute ad for short-term missionary work in the form of a video for their hit song "Your Hands, Your Feet."[1] The song, an upbeat rock anthem, is a call or a promise to God that "I'll go where you send me." There is a close-up of Mark Stuart, the bandana-wearing lead singer, as he sings of his desire to serve God: "I wanna be your hands; I wanna be your feet; to go where you send me." The band is soon in a canoe, traveling down a river surrounded by jungle. They arrive in a remote village, where beautiful children are filmed in poor-but-photogenic settings. The band plays with the children, throwing them into the water from an overhang. At times the video cuts to images of the children, and some of the band members, holding up signs: "Go." "Serve." "Abandon self." The band members pray with the villagers. There are close-ups of the damaged or diseased hands and feet of the local people. The prayer service seems to be one of a Pentecostal-style healing—a laying on of hands.

The video engages a historically entrenched fantasy of the "benevolent imperialist," as well as a more traditional missionary narrative. The band members pour their hearts out to the children, who presumably do not mind that the visitors don't speak the language or know their history. At the same time, the video is influenced by secular music and a good bit of postmodern ironic style. The band self-represents as influenced by grunge, 60s rock, and pop. It is the rock-radical, anti-bourgeois stance of a great deal of popular music; but for young evangelicals in the 1990s it represented something distinct—an implied refusal of what many saw as the smug certainties of the televangelist generation. It was their own version of what every generation of postwar US evangelicals had insisted upon: their parents' evangelicalism had been too domesticated, too focused on piety, not worldly or engaged enough to challenge conventions and reimagine the faith.

By the time this video was released, the short-term missions movement had become a major phenomenon, particularly among evangelicals. Short-term missions (STMs) had spread slowly and fitfully starting in the 1960s. By the 1990s, the missions trips, usually one to four weeks long (most went for two weeks or less), had become perhaps the paradigmatic activity of socially concerned evangelicals, especially but not only young people. The count of total participants is almost impossible to glean, but observers estimate that by the early 2000s about 1.6 million American Christians a year were going on some sort of short-term service trip abroad. The Southern Baptist Convention alone sends thirty thousand people annually. Most go to Latin America or the Caribbean, but they have increasingly begun to travel to Africa, Asia, and the Middle East as well. It is assumed that participants pay their own way, but some people, especially students, gather sponsors to support their trip. The average short-term mission costs between $2500 and $3000; multiplied by well over a million people a year, the total financial commitment by American Christians is staggering.[2]

During their short visits, groups sometimes help build a clinic or paint a school. They perhaps work in an orphanage—holding babies or playing with the kids. Older participants might run a Vacation Bible School or teach English. If a mission includes the pastor of a church or an experienced layperson, the goals could be different: a series of sermons or an extended Bible study, or perhaps a training session on some aspect of church leadership. For many participants, the goal of personal transformation is central. Young people in particular go on trips with the idea that they can and should change, that the experience will involve emotional intensities and spiritual development. There are other, non-religious versions of these kinds of trips—"alternative spring breaks" for college students, or summer service programs. Even study abroad, which has expanded dramatically in the past twenty-five years, carries many of the same connotations, not necessarily of service, but of human-to-human connection and possible transformation.[3]

Short-term missions are controversial, however, even—or especially—among evangelicals themselves. Their legions of promoters claim that short-term missions are a "God-commanded" opportunity to take parochial Americans and make them into "World Christians." Detractors—fewer in number, but vocal—describe short-term missions as being little more that tourism with the veneer of spiritual justification. Although STMs were controversial from their beginnings in the 1960s, the debate changed and intensified in the early 1990s, when, after the end of the Cold War and the rise of the United States as the global hyper-power, American Christians began to travel more, and farther, and sometimes to more dangerous areas. In particular, they went to Muslim-majority countries, or to Muslim areas of places like India. The trips also became shorter, more decentralized, and increasingly targeted to the young. Professional travel facilitators and evangelical organizers in the tourism industry sometimes became fierce competitors for the market of summer travelers.

Starting in the 1990s, then, theologically conservative Protestants were crossing national borders in the hope of making, or perhaps just tasting, a form of evangelical internationalism that they hoped would alter and enhance their perspective, offering a sanctified kind of travel that they believed would change, if not the lives of others, then at least their own hearts and minds.

In 1966, Dorothy Birkhoff applied to Short Terms Abroad (STA) for placement as a volunteer missionary. Dorothy was a widow in her fifties and an intrepid traveler. According to her application essay, she was already an experienced evangelist. She had taught summer Bible school for a number of years, but, she wrote, "I've had a desire to teach or work abroad, as I have prayed God has increased my love & desire to go."[4]

She was far from alone in her desire to apply her talents through short-term missions. By the mid-1960s, a broad range of Christian groups, including evangelicals, had begun to experiment with ways of "energizing" missionary work by shortening the time it required. At its start, the short-term missions movement was relatively small, disorganized, provisional, and controversial. In the immediate aftermath of World War II, Youth for Christ, the organization that launched Billy Graham, had established "invasion teams" that spent three to six months evangelizing, mostly in Europe. Unlike most career missionaries, the teams brought their American-style mass evangelism with them. Each visit was heavily promoted; the events featured up-tempo music, Christian celebrities, and revival-style preaching.[5] At the time, this was an unusual type of short-term trip. In fact, throughout the 1950s and for most of the 1960s, most "short-term missionaries" were those who served in the field not for weeks or months, but for one or two years, doing specialized work such as nursing or agricultural training.

Still, shorter short-term missions were the wave of the future. In 1961, one evangelical entrepreneur, George Vesser, started actively recruiting high school and college students for what he called "Operation Mobilization." He argued that older adults were too settled in their ways to get out and do the necessary evangelizing. At about the same time, Loren Cunningham founded what would later become one of the largest mission organizations, Youth with a Mission (YWAM). Both groups focused on students, albeit with rather different visions of how long and in what capacities those students would work. And both grew to become very large and powerful proponents of short-term missions. By 2005, YWAM claimed to be sending out 25,000 people a year.[6]

The vision of short-term service expanded dramatically with the founding of the Peace Corps in 1961. Within months after President Kennedy announced the program, the Peace Corps had received thousands of applications, and, within five years, 15,000 Americans were living and working as volunteers abroad.[7] Christian agencies took notice, and commentators applauded the young people who were willing to commit themselves to service. In fact, the Peace Corps itself had been influenced by Operation Crossroads Africa, a short-term service organization founded by Rev. James Robinson of Harlem's Morningside Presbyterian Church, which specialized in sending multiracial groups of students to Africa.[8]

The Peace Corps was wildly successful and highly popular. Its model was built on the larger ideology of "modernization" that shaped US foreign policy in the 1950s and 1960s. The premise was that the United States could extend its Cold War influence over decolonizing nations by offering concrete support. Modernization theory was built around two sometimes contradictory assumptions. First was a belief in the unequivocal good of large-scale projects such as dams and highways, which would establish the base from which a largely agricultural economy might become a more complex industrializing one. The second was that economic change was fundamentally individual: societies would be transformed by teaching "backward" people not only about modern technology but also, just as crucially, modern attitudes.[9] This was the scaffolding of the Peace Corps' faith in the ability of young, usually untrained Americans to show up in a village in Latin America or Asia, ready to fight global structural inequalities by helping to build a well, even if the volunteer had no personal experience in building wells. Despite its obvious flaws, the idea was too seductive to resist: young Americans sacrificing their comforts to join in the struggle for hearts and minds, not on the battlefield but in the corn field.[10]

Evangelical organizations set out to beat the Peace Corps at its own game by establishing—or beefing up—Christian counterparts. Over the 1960s a hodgepodge of ventures arose, many of which offered both two-year Peace Corps-style projects and the more popular option of the summer service trip. Like the Peace Corps, Christian organizations presented their work as relevant to the Cold War. One fundraising letter from 1965, for example, argued that: "Latin America seethes with unrest because of spiritual darkness and Satanic power, providing the fertile ground for the growth of atheistic Communism."[11]

Traditionally, missionary service was supposed to be a response to God's call, a life's work. The notion that some missionaries would commit only a small number of months or years to service was contested from the beginning, and would remain so over the coming decades. One early organization, Laymen's Overseas Service (LAOS), addressed doubts head on, presenting itself as a pioneer movement that was training a *new* kind of missionary: "the physician or teacher willing to share a month's time . . . the retired person with time on his hands."[12] The organization was Christian but not specifically evangelical. Its acronym, LAOS, was the Greek word for "people" or "tribe," and the leadership stressed that the organization was for the "whole church," including Catholics. Early advocates who heralded the biblical validity of short-term missionaries drew upon the evangelical call to spread God's word to the nations. There was more need than there were missionaries, so the pull seemed obvious. As one promotional booklet put it: "Christ's command was to 'go everywhere,' but he did not say how long we should stay."[13]

For some people, however, short-term missions were more than an idea about spreading the gospel or doing good. They represented a new kind of democratic possibility for Protestants of various stripes—a social movement, essentially, that would challenge smug church hierarchies and empower lay people. These STM advocates called upon the theological doctrine of the "priesthood of all believers." What else did the priesthood of all believers mean, after all, but that every person had a responsibility to respond to God's call as s/he saw fit? LAOS, for example, saw itself as countering a straightforward kind of discrimination: "One of the grave shortcomings of the institutional church is that its ministers pay only lip service to the doctrine of the priesthood of all believers, that they act as if they do not believe laymen have a specific witness to give and thus do not challenge them to offer their services."[14]

The multiplicity and notorious independence of various Protestant denominations meant that short-term missions were strewn like wildflowers across the evangelical field; there were obviously a great many of them, but they were hard to catalog. At Wheaton College, where students had been involved in summer service programs since the late 1950s, one group of enthusiasts tried to bring some sort of organization to the proliferation of programs by founding Short Terms Abroad as a clearinghouse that took applications from Christians who wanted to go abroad and matched them with requests for volunteers from missions programs. For the first seven years of its existence, from 1965 to 1972, STA received hundreds of applications from people young and old, whose application essays poured out stories of their religious beliefs, motivations for missionary work, and attitudes toward "racial and cultural difference."[15]

The personnel files of 186 candidates show that the motivations for applying were often fairly straightforward: applicants mentioned their belief in missionary work in general, their desire to "serve," and, sometimes, a wish to travel. One young woman who applied in 1968, at the age of twenty-nine, articulated a fairly typical combination of religious sensibility and worldly investments: "I wish to make a direct contribution to the most important and most noble task assigned to mankind: that of winning souls to the Lord Jesus Christ. At the same time, I wish to be a good representative of the United States and of the democratic way of life."[16] Another applicant, a sixty-two-year-old man who applied with his wife, wrote: "I would like to combine my desire to travel and work with people and things. I would like to feel that I am doing something worthwhile in trying to improve the material as well as the spiritual life of others less fortunate than I, thus making the world a better place to live in."[17]

There were many opportunities. Volunteers might apply to STA, as many did, or apply directly to organizations like TEAM (The Evangelical Alliance Mission) or Operation Mobilization. (For examples of how STA tried to convince people to volunteer, see figure 11.1.) Denominations also joined in, with mainline Methodists and Presbyterians, as well as evangelical churches like Southern Baptists and Assemblies of God, establishing programs to send short-termers. By 1967, at least six thousand people were in the field on trips ranging from two months to two years.[18]

Short-term missions opened up travel and adventure to a broad range of people, and ads for the programs often made that explicit, even if the fun aspect was sometimes seen as slightly shameful, at least at first. A lay Christian could see the world, meet new people, and move far beyond the confines of her local church or community, but in a way that was safe, even sanctified. One brochure offering an opportunity for "Evangelism

FIGURE 11.1 Short Terms Abroad Bulletin, 1968.

in Bolivia" in 1969 described what evangelists could expect during their sixteen-day trip: "You will actually be living with missionaries!" "Witness for Jesus Christ!" But there was more: "See Aymara Indians with their colorful dress and take a trip through the jungle . . . [to] visit with a tribe of Indians who most recently have accepted Jesus Christ."[19]

Then, as now, what participants actually did during those trips varied considerably. Those who had special technical skills (nurses or electricians) made use of them. One man with a math degree spent a year helping Wycliffe Bible Translators in Mexico work out the bugs in their computer system; a recent grad spent several months as a medical technologist in Kathmandu.[20] In 1967, one radio announcer went to Aruba for four weeks, giving the American manager of the local Christian station a chance to take a vacation.[21]

Often, given that they were on location only a few weeks or months, the volunteers did work that helped missionaries take care of their regular duties, doing everything from babysitting their children to teaching their Sunday School classes. The volunteers might also do much-needed but tedious paperwork for the local mission as clerical volunteers. They occasionally did evangelism, as when a youth team from the Assemblies of God paired with local Christians in British Honduras and Jamaica to distribute the *Pentecostal Evangel* to homes in each country.[22]

The middle-aged Dorothy Birkhoff was never placed by Short Terms Abroad. When STA tried to place her with a summer program in the Midwest run by Pioneer Girls, she responded by pointing out that, if she had wanted a job teaching Bible at a summer camp in the United States, she could have arranged it herself. "Maybe I was misinformed about Short Terms Abroad," she wrote in one rather tart letter to the organization's headquarters. "I thought the name meant <u>work abroad</u>. Which I am interested in." Two years later, Dorothy wrote STA that she would not need their efforts to find her a match that year. In fact, she explained cheerfully, yet pointedly, that although STA had not found her a position, she had been able to work in a different foreign country each of the previous three summers—in Guatemala, Japan, and Taiwan, working with World Vision and Overseas Radio and Television. "God is working in great ways today through Short Term Missionaries," she commented. "It is more refreshing to missionaries on the field for a new person to be sent for a short time." In 1969, Dorothy wrote to STA again, explaining that she had just been to India and Taiwan, this time with the ventriloquist puppet that she used for her entrepreneurial evangelism. She had performed with the puppet on TV in Taiwan, and she wished she could have stayed much longer in India. There was so much to do. And, she added, without undue modesty, "they begged and begged me to stay." Over the course of five years, Dorothy went overseas many times.[23]

David Bryant, InterVarsity Christian Fellowship's missions specialist from 1978 to 1988, believed that Christians had a duty to support missions. But he also promised to show evangelicals that missions mindedness was not duty alone; it could be energizing and renewing for those who might feel desultory in their faith. In 1979, he put forth these ideas in a book called *In the Gap*. Revised and rereleased numerous times since then, the book is an evangelical classic.

Bryant defined "standing in the gap" as being committed to "discipleship without limits," a willingness to do whatever God wanted of you, wherever he sent you. The boredoms and frustrations of "pea-sized Christianity" and Christian life could be overcome once people looked outward. The cross-cultural mission was "absolutely vital" for three main reasons: it was God's commandment, it was morally right, and it was empowering. [24]

In the Gap also argued that readers needed to begin to see themselves as "World Christians"—people committed to a global vision of their faith. As such, they should put themselves to doing "Kingdom work." Here, Bryant was deploying a kind of evangelical code. Jesus had said that "my kingdom is not of this world" (John 18:36, NIV). But many believers felt it was important to stress that God also is sovereign everywhere, fully present in the created order. "Kingdom work" meant something very specific: to invest here and now in Jesus's calls for a redeemed world, not just focus on redemption in heaven.[25] In that model, the real goal of short-term trips was to create, in the words of *World Christian* magazine, "compassionate, committed people who want their whole lives to count for the world that doesn't know Jesus' love."[26] Bryant recommended that Christians form Action Teams, small groups that could do anything from deciding to learn about and pray for a particular "hidden people group" to raising the money to send one of their own as a short-term missionary. But in 1979, he still imagined short-term missions as one option among many, not a prerequisite for understanding the world's needs.[27]

When Bryant first published *In the Gap*, short-term missions were still far from routine. Within a few years, they would become a primary vector for young Christians to express their longing to connect with the world. Evangelical denominations were increasingly getting into the act, signing up participants with new or revitalized programs for lay people. The Southern Baptist Convention had lumbered onto the short-term missions scene in the late 1970s when it formed the Mission Service Corps, built on the two-year Peace Corps model that was already being outflanked by shorter programs. In 1983, the SBC launched a summer program aimed specifically at young people, "Acteens." SBC reported that more than six thousand members of the convention had volunteered for overseas trips in 1984—a 30 percent increase over 1983.[28]

National organizations were only partly in control. Increasingly, smaller groups such as local churches or branches of national organizations or just informal Christian networks were making short-term trips using whatever connections they had—more or less on their own, without national coordination. Members of one InterVarsity chapter in California, for example, helpfully wrote to the national office in 1983 to report that they had sent out two hundred STMers. That kind of entrepreneurial effort would be repeated countless times over the coming decades.[29]

Evangelical media were also crucial to short-term mission outreach. At 1987's Urbana conference, InterVarsity showed *The Wait of the World*, a fictional film about a group of journalists who were covering the work of missionaries in Africa, only to find themselves personally drawn into the human suffering and deeply impressed by the missionaries and their work. Already, as supporting quotes for the film suggested, one of the selling points of STMs was the "experience."[30] On this model, students were not just serving, they also were participating and engaging in ways that were pleasurable and life-changing.

Short-term missions really exploded in the 1990s. The internet and cell phones contributed to this, since they allowed short-term travelers to communicate with their families back home. But trips became the defining aspect of young evangelical life only after they became a product—marketed and sold as an evangelical experience, an augmentation of faith that also brought adventure and emotional satisfaction.

The real entrepreneurs of short-term missions—the engines for expansion and the source of much innovation—were scores of private groups that began to operate as missions "outfitters" in the 1990s. With names such as Mission Outfitter, Real Impact Missions, STEM (Short-Term Evangelical Missions), and Adventures in Missions, these operated as essentially not-for-profit businesses. Some required adherence to a particular set of doctrines; others took pretty much anyone who wanted to go. Individuals or groups paid a fee and the outfitter made logistical arrangements and usually organized on-site activities.

The problem with such outfitters was not necessarily that they were making money from organizing missions (some were, some were non-profits); it was that they worked by selling specific experiences. As one evangelical commentator pointed out, "mission organizations have had to adapt to a competitive market."[31] Soon a number of more traditional organizations began to prepare for these more consumer-driven models: redesigning logos, dispensing free wall calendars and CDs, and selling T-shirts and tea towels.

The Christian popular culture industry helped advertise the short-term experience. Evangelicals were enthusiastic readers, and in the late 1990s books about missionaries— an old genre—made an explosive comeback. These books were not usually about short-term missionaries, but they transmitted the missionary ideal to a new generation. There were DVDs and maps of opportunity—the 10/40 Window was, in some contexts, also a window onto potential STM trips.

Service was certainly part of the story; adventure and a muscular Christianity were important as well. For example, in the early 2000s, Wycliffe Bible Translators, known for its specialized scholarly work, began to advertise short-term opportunities on its website with a photo of an all-terrain vehicle traveling through the early morning light in an exotic-looking landscape. The tag line—"Get Outta Town . . . with short-term missions"—appealed with Wild-West language, a faux-aggressive message, and the association of Jeeps with adventure. Groups like TEAM offered a gentler model of affectionate transnational relationships in an outdoor setting (figure 11.2).

For a time, one of the more successful missions outfitters was Global Frontier Missions. The group ran courses that brought together individuals or small groups in pre-packaged programs, including one to Oaxaca, Mexico, in the early 2000s. That trip was evangelism-oriented, so its participants went through a three-day orientation, then headed to Oaxaca for four days of "relationship evangelism." A promotional brochure promised "a fun, high-energy, camp-like atmosphere" where participants could "focus on spiritual growth" and "be challenged in your faith!" The goal was for participants to work under the leadership of local churches when possible, to do whatever was needed—labor-intensive projects such as painting or construction, or perhaps something more sedate such as teaching English. Mostly, the brochure explained, the idea was to build trust with local people. This would open doors for long-term missionaries to do their work. That this

FIGURE 11.2 Promoting short-term missions. Courtesy of The Evangelical Alliance Mission.

was more fantasy than any kind of authentic evangelistic work was made inadvertently clear by the fact that no language skills were required.[32]

Perhaps nothing was as important as Christian popular music to developing the vision of the short-term traveler. The genre "Contemporary Christian Music" emerged in the early 1980s, built from the foundations of the Jesus Movement and the Christian coffeehouse culture of the 1960s. In its earliest manifestations, Contemporary Christian music had a folk-rock sound (Amy Grant and Keith Green were singer-songwriter stars), with some gospel influence. As time went on, the music evolved to include subgenres like Christian metal and punk (Stryper, Petra, and Relient K) and hip-hop (DC Talk and Lecrae). Until the late 1990s, Christian music had been largely apolitical, a jumble of "worship" music, love songs to Jesus, and/or stories of struggle to find or keep faith. At times, bands took up issues like abortion, gay rights, and even evolution. This was uncommon, however, and the political gestures were almost never international.[33] That began to change as short-term missions gained momentum.

Perhaps the most sustained musical engagement with the short-term missions movement was produced by folk-rock band Caedmon's Call in 2004. In the early 2000s, the group was a mainstay of the contemporary Christian music scene, with more than ten albums and several EPs. The band had an evolving membership over the years. It was built primarily around a married couple, Danielle and Cliff Young, and included, intermittently, Derek Webb and Andy Osenga, both well-regarded singer-songwriters.[34]

In 2004, the band released *Share the Well*.[35] At the time, Caedmon's Call was not the biggest act in Christian rock, but the group was highly acclaimed and had an enthusiastic fan base. To make the album, the band traveled to Ecuador, Brazil, and India, playing with local musicians and recording some of the tracks in local studios. When *Share the Well* was released, the group described it as their "missions" album—that is, a set of tracks built around the modern evangelical understanding of "missions," which combines a commitment to traditional missionary work with more open-ended involvement in humanitarian aid and development projects. The songs addressed global poverty, world Christianity, and social justice. Critically acclaimed for its use of world music and its rich sound—reviewers compared it to Paul Simon's *Graceland*—the album nonetheless foundered commercially. In retrospect, however, it has come to be understood as a signature moment in the budding global awareness expressed in Christian music.

"Share the Well" is the album's title track and biggest hit. With a peppy, energetic beat backed by drums, it opens with the intonation of "Je Ra Ji Ra, De Ji Ra"—a set of soundings that are not uncommon in Indian music and which are utilized here to signal authenticity. Like other songs on the album, this one speaks of the Dalit people of India, once known as the "untouchables." The reference to sharing the well refers to the fact that Dalit were traditionally not allowed to share wells with members of the castes. The resonances are also specific for a Christian audience, who surely would think of Jesus's meeting at the well with the despised Samaritan woman to whom he offered "living water" (John 4: 4-13).

In general, fans have seen *Share the Well* as a cry for global social justice, within a genre that has often been limited by its solipsism. Fans use songs from the album as background to scores of YouTube videos about short-term mission trips (figures 11.3 and 11.4). The album is understood as a call to awareness and a plea to participate in the ongoing struggle to define and to live (youthful) Christian social engagement. As one fan, with the intriguing web name "Third World Symphony," wrote:

30 million orphans who desperately need the love of Christ!

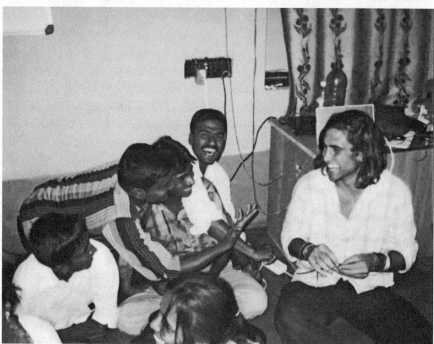

FIGURES 11.3 AND 11.4 Two images from YouTube videos posted by participants in short-term missions, featuring Caedmon's Call music as background. Sources: Crossroads Worldwide India trip https://www.youtube.com/watch?v=IZSNxTIBg30&t=1s and Sarala, My India Experience https://www.youtube.com/watch?v=vpXItP5mVt8&t=46s

I've long despised the Contemporary Christian Music industry, with its narrow-minded ideas about Christianity, music, and social issues. This CD might not right all those wrongs, but it is clearly a collection of music from a bunch of Christians who actually got it right. Christianity isn't just some pie-in-the-sky philosophy, Jesus was concerned with helping those in need and showing compassion to all. This album delivers just that by showing us the stories of the "least of these" in remote corners of the world and the people who went there to meet them and returned changed forever.

The fan goes on to state angrily that the rest of the Contemporary Christian world can stay in "their safe isolated community" and make "crappy art all they want to, I won't give them a dime of my money." But this album "blazes new ground" and "anyone with a heart for humanitarian work and great music from all over the world" should buy it, "ASAP!"[36] On the one hand, the album is important because it speaks to authentic Christians with a "heart" for humanitarian work. On the other hand, the fan implies, the music is important precisely because the level of evangelical self-awareness is so low.

One of the most powerful songs on *Share the Well* is a strange and quite beautiful piece that invited the audience to a passionate form of enchantment. "Mother India" is an elegiac ballad, drawing on soaring instrumentation and the fine, expressive voice of Dawn Young to express a particular kind of alliance with "Indian-ness." In its outsized emotionality, it invites a fusion of religious longing and evocative identification.

The complexity of the song begins with its title. For those familiar with the history of British and US imperialism, it immediately calls to mind *Mother India*, the 1927 pro-imperialist text by American Katherine Mayo that became a controversial international sensation. In the declining years of British power in India, Mayo's book set itself up as an exposé of the dangerous and degenerate practices of Hinduism, which, she argued, led to the oppression of women and the weakness of men. Mayo also criticized a range of other behaviors, such as cruelty to animals and the treatment of the untouchables. All of this made clear, she insisted, that Indians were not capable of self-government. The transnational impact of Mayo's text was not exactly what she intended. The book so angered many Indians that it actually energized Indian nationalism, while also leading some American imperialists to criticize the British model of colonialism for not doing enough to reform Hindu society. The book nonetheless remained in circulation for decades as an exposé of "facts." Even into the 1950s it was republished as a treatise on the realities of life in India, and in the 1970s a few US feminists tried to recuperate it as an early example of international feminism.[37]

Caedmon's Call's "Mother India" fuses exoticism and spiritual longing with an implicit political critique that reaches toward genuine solidarity. Like many other pieces on the album, "Mother India" explicitly evokes the Dalit, here in a paraphrase of the beatitudes from the book of Matthew: "how blessed are the poor, the sick, the weak." The music expresses desire, repentance, and pleasurable swept-up-ness. But as the lyrics continue, they suggest a very different kind of alliance than the self-satisfied "sharing" demanded by the album's title track. In "Mother India," the singer calls on "Father" to forgive her, because she has failed to believe. She has, like India itself, "groaned and grieved"—whether in doubt or sorrow is left unsaid. The grieving and suffering (are they a result of the failure to believe? or a cause of it?) are healed only when God-the-father reaches out to India:

> Your Spirit falls on India,
> and captured me in Your embrace.

The American singer does not bring God's grace to India; God's reach begins there and brings her in. It is a quiet plea for connection—a vision of how people might live, in globalized intimacy, in public.

Short-term missions were designed in part to give lay people the chance to see the realities of poverty, to have their consciousness changed, perhaps to evangelize, and to return newly committed to both missions and to helping change the lives of the poor. Robert Priest, professor of missions at Trinity Evangelical Divinity School, likened the trips to pilgrimages, "rituals of intensification" where participants leave their ordinary lives "for an extraordinary, voluntary sacred experience 'away from home' in a liminal space where sacred goals are pursued, physical and spiritual tests are faced, normal structures are dissolved, *communitas* is experienced, and personal transformation occurs."[38]

As STMs grew exponentially in the 1990s, however, so did the level and intensity of criticism among believers themselves. Evangelical intellectuals were often apoplectic at the ignorance and "neo-colonial" attitudes displayed by short-term missions participants. One objection was simply that Americans exhibited condescending or merely ignorant behavior. One commentator argued that believers had begun to see trips as "spiritual tourism," something closer to a package holiday in which "no real engagement occurs nor are emotional ties forged." Rather than giving the participants new ways of thinking, "the exercise simply reinforces worn stereotypes and old power relations."[39] Young participants often noted the poverty and desperate circumstances of people they visited, for example, but also interpreted the smiles and kindness of the local people as proof that they were happy even without wealth and resources. One educator described how one high school-aged group saw their Ecuadoran hosts as "living with enviable vitality." Instead of unpacking the inequalities that left their hosts in poverty, the Americans took the lesson to be that they themselves should learn to be less materialistic so that they could have that kind of authentic life.[40] Often there was a kind of willful determination to be enchanted rather than disturbed by the poverty of the people they met.

Other objections to short-term missions had to do with resources. Hundreds of millions of dollars every year were going to support these trips, and many times the work was of relatively little significance. American visitors often liked to do specific and concrete things during their trips—they wanted to paint walls or build houses. This was fine when the work was needed, but sometimes it was simply a way of making sure short-termers felt good about themselves. "It isn't that they didn't work hard," one Zimbabwean Christian said of the Americans who built a clinic in his community. "But they must remember that we built buildings before they came, and we will build buildings after they leave. Unfortunately, while they were here, they acted like they were the only ones who knew how to build buildings."[41]

One evangelical writer described his conversation with a friend who coordinated STMs to Mexico. "I've got this wall," the friend explained. "When a group comes that can't handle what's required to build relationships with Mexican kids, or insists on completing a task so they can 'accomplish' something, I put them to work on The Wall. They feel like they're a big help, and it keeps them out of everyone's hair so the ministry isn't compromised." When the team left, the locals would tear down the wall.[42] Needless to say, these were not the kind of stories that led observers to feel good about the financial and human resources being appropriated by short-term trips.

Still others objected to American expectations of gratitude. One short-term missions enthusiast had to explain to potential participants that they should expect to work as collaborators and partners, not as Lady Bountifuls who arrived with goods and wisdom in hand. "Our financial wealth, and all the amenities that accompany that, easily inclines us to think we know what these people need." The people of the global South are not there for you to use, he warned. He added an injunction that made the point about American attitudes with biting clarity: "Don't pet the poor." These are your equals; they are not to be treated as feel-good companions.[43]

Some proponents retorted that these critiques missed the point. In the end, the primary goal of such trips was to help Americans change their understandings of the world. If they arrived in the global South being ignorant or insensitive, they might leave less so.[44] And if the point was to help American Christians deepen their own spiritual lives and expand their political awareness, and if that deepening then made a difference in churches back home, then the efficacy of donating resources to short-term missions could not simply be calculated by the usefulness of building a wall. Evangelical young people and their families were like almost everyone else in the United States, within or beyond the churches, in that their donations toward global justice causes were miniscule—when they were made at all. So, given that the money for the trips was probably *not* going to be redirected to other global or even just churchly causes, the question for evangelical observers then became whether short-term missions provided a useful way to help people see the world differently. Did believers come to understand their place in the world and their own faith in new, more activist ways? Were they changed?

Many evangelicals believed that short-term missions did just that. Participants who were interviewed shortly after their return almost uniformly expressed their sense that they had been educated and were newly committed to global justice and to missions. In fact, one study found that the *less* qualified participants were, in terms of skills or background, the *more* they said they experienced "significant life changes" as a result of their trip.[45] This did not reflect well on their usefulness, but it did highlight the trips' possible spiritual and political impact. For those who most needed to learn, perhaps these hands-on experiences were the most direct route to transformation.

Others disagreed. "We justify our efforts by saying [youth] will come back and make a difference in their own communities, but the research has demonstrated it's not happening," one leading missionary thinker told the *Christian Science Monitor*. "Kids are going down and 'loving on' Mexican kids for a week and then coming home and being the same racist white kids they were toward their Latino classmates before they went on the trip."[46]

Sometimes the very claim that short-term trips were enriching primarily for participants sent commentators into near despair. One deeply ambivalent professor at Azusa Pacific University, who supported STMs but wanted them improved, described many missions trips as "staged tourist spaces" where each side engaged in a performance. The eager "missioners" pulled out their guidebooks, and local Christians prepared their smiles, each side hoping to get something they needed out of the encounter. If this was a long way from a genuinely meaningful engagement, a real part of the problem lay in the insistence by Americans that their trips be intense and "life-changing." "While we may cite the example of Jesus as the basis for our short-term projects," the professor commented, "his sending was expressly not about providing the messengers an unforgettable experience."[47]

In this longing for connection, evangelicals were far from unique. The cultural theorist Lauren Berlant has argued that human beings often engage in projects of trying to find our place in the world through attachments to something beyond ourselves. These attachments are often both optimistic and "cruel." The optimism is easy to comprehend, Berlant says, "if we describe optimism as the force that moves you out of yourself and into the world in order to bring closer the satisfying *something* that you cannot generate on your own."[48] The cruelty comes when our attachments actually get in the way of making a better world possible, for ourselves or others. For Berlant, the cruelty we experience is often from the world itself, which can easily disappoint, turning our hopes back against us. But optimism can lead people to inflict cruelty as well. When evangelicals or other travelers engage in border-crossing travel with the expectation of experiencing global community, they often work from the hope, or demand, that the world will be made available and accessible—the impossible dream of frictionless and yet educational encounter.[49] Evangelicals' attachments, including their attachment to the enchanted otherness of their fellow Christians, can inflict cruelty, as they abandon children they have spent a week hugging and loving, or leave behind a lingering sense among locals that they saw themselves as superior.

With this level of critique, even outrage, from evangelicals themselves, it might seem surprising that short-term missions continued at all, but they had become embedded in evangelical life. In 2002, a number of organizations with short-term missions programs, among them InterVarsity, Campus Crusade, and the Southern Baptist Convention, announced a set of "Standards of Excellence" for short-term missions. The standards, which were designed specifically to respond to earlier critiques, stated that short-term trips should be "God-Centered" and use "culturally appropriate methods." Groups that signed the standards would agree to "truthfulness in promotion, finances, and reporting results," and would offer "Biblical" and "timely" training to participants, along with comprehensive follow-up. The standards were vague but clearly designed to make a statement: There should be no more fly-by-night, culturally insensitive mission trips.[50]

Groups such as InterVarsity did take these standards seriously. They designed programs that lasted longer and provided more intensive training to students—demanding more from them in terms of engagement with the host culture. At the same time, some groups decided that truth in advertising meant that they should stop calling the trips missions, if they resulted in neither meaningful evangelism nor effective aid. InterVarsity, for example, had long called its summer program "Urban Trek," and others began to use terms like "experience" or "vision trips."

Short-term trips continued to grow rapidly after 2001, despite anxieties over the increasingly unsettled global political environment. The events of 9/11 certainly made some participants (and their parents) more wary, but the terrorist attacks also increased a sense of urgency. Short-term missions reached their height in the early 2000s, as both adults and students raced abroad, including to the Middle East, with the idea of increasing positive contact and/or reaching Muslims with the gospel. After 2008, however, some groups reported that their STM numbers were dramatically down, largely because of the economic crisis. With less money to spend, fewer people were willing or able to find the funds for $3,000 trips. Mission Data International reported in 2010 that overseas trips had decreased by 15 percent in the previous two years.[51]

Trips within the United States apparently increased, however. One missions-planning company, Adventures in Mission, said that international trips in 2009 were just 26 percent of all its trips, compared with 57 percent just four years before. Global Frontier Missions, which had focused on Mexico, India, and Thailand in 2006, shifted its focus for 2012 and 2013 entirely to domestic trips, some devoted to service and others focused on getting to know people of other religions in parts of the United States.[52]

No matter how they were organized, short-term trips made the global stage a site of particularly powerful cultural work. Enchanted internationalism was a stance toward the world as well as a kind of self-making. It depended on an expectation that Christians abroad had a spiritual wealth that was lacking in the United States, and in that sense it exoticized people in the global South. Yet short-term missions also laid the groundwork for young evangelicals to begin accepting non-Americans as spiritual equals, and even as spiritual role models. The conversations that church leaders were having about racism, neo-colonialism, and spiritual arrogance were finding their way into missions manuals, news articles, and study guides for short-term missionaries. It is striking to imagine how much more training in examining their racial/cultural assumptions some evangelical high school students would get than most college students would ever receive before their semester abroad.

And yet the enchantment that infused so much of evangelical culture's representation of the global South implied a feeling of intensity that shaped what participants saw, what they wanted to believe about the happiness and spiritual authenticity of the people they met. Enchantment even colored the leaves on the trees and the light in the sky, if Audio Adrenaline were to be believed. Young evangelicals wanted to go where God sent them, but they expected God to choose someplace extraordinary.

12

"The Greatest Failing of Our Christian Obedience"

THE WAR IN IRAQ

IN THE WAKE of the September 11 attacks, evangelicals were deeply divided over how to explain what had happened. Shortly after the attacks, several conservative evangelicals had made headlines with rhetoric attacking Islam. Franklin Graham called Islam "an evil and wicked religion," while Jerry Falwell used an appearance on *The 700 Club* to comment on domestic threats, saying "I really believe that the pagans, and the abortionists, and the feminists, and the gays and the lesbians who are actively trying to make that an alternative lifestyle, the ACLU, People for the American Way, all of them who have tried to secularize America—I point the finger in their face and say, 'you helped this to happen.'"[1]

The comments were widely reported in both the US media and in the Arab and Muslim world, and many Americans, including evangelicals, found them offensive. Shortly thereafter, a group of moderate evangelicals within the National Association of Evangelicals called a meeting to discuss "dialogue" with Muslims, to which Falwell was not invited. These moderate leaders were consciously trying to fashion a more positive engagement with Muslims. At the same time, they remained convinced that Christianity was the only truth, and criticized "naïve" mainline Protestants for minimizing the differences between Muslims and Christians.[2]

These leaders, like the vast majority of evangelicals in the United States, were interested in evangelizing Muslims, in the Middle East and elsewhere. And while September 11 was the starting point for an evangelical conversation about the nature of US power in twenty-first century, it was the Iraq War that would bring that conversation to a head.

In the immediate aftermath of the attacks of September 11, President Bush reached out to American Muslims, describing them as "true Americans." He made clear that he believed that Islam was a "religion of peace." The president visited a mosque, and a Muslim cleric participated in the National Day of Prayer on September 14, 2001. As Bush launched the war in Afghanistan, and soon the larger war on terrorism, the president declared repeatedly that his acts were not a "war against Islam," but a war against the "evildoers," fought on behalf of civilization.[3]

Still, among American evangelicals and in the general public, anti-Muslim rhetoric intensified. The assertion that Islam was a danger to civilization, to human rights, and to Christians was hardly new. But the question emerged with new intensity: how should Christians understand the Muslim world and the nature of Islam? This was a frequent topic in evangelical magazines, on radio talk shows, and in books with titles such as *Secrets of the Koran* and *Married to Muhammad*.[4] Conservative evangelicals in particular were inclined to believe in a "clash of civilizations," because it highlighted the importance of religious identity and the distinction between Islam and Christianity. That distinction already had been honed by the 10/40 Window movement and discussions of Christian persecution over the previous decades.

At the same time, there were evangelicals, both in the United States and elsewhere, who wanted to further a sense of respectful encounter. In the United States, Ambassador Robert Seiple, president of the Institute for Global Engagement and former Ambassador for Religious Freedom under President Bush, was a frequent voice of moderation. Seiple spoke from the rather unusual crossroads he inhabited, as an evangelical Christian, a political conservative, and a great believer in interreligious dialogue. At IGE, Seiple published articles and gave talks about the need for a respectful attitude toward Islam. Not just toward Muslims—not just a matter of being nice to individual people—but respectful toward Islam, as a faith. In 2004, speaking to a public event sponsored by the Pew Research Center on Religion and Public Life, Seiple told a story, one he repeated often, about a brave Christian woman in Lebanon who was shot by a fanatical Muslim and rendered quadriplegic, but who forgave him. Seiple used the story to explain the importance of speaking out for one's own faith while remaining respectful of others. He gestured at the familiar theme of "cheap grace":

We have a mantra at the Institute for Global Engagement that goes like this: Understand your own faith at its deepest and richest best . . .

And at the same time, understand your neighbors in such a way that you will respect how they feel. You'll respect how they believe. You'll respect the differences that they bring to the table. I did not use the word "tolerance." In my way of thinking, tolerance is nothing more than a cheap form of grace applied to people that I don't really care for . . . "Respect" speaks to what we have in common.[5]

However ecumenical his sensibility, Seiple's politics were entirely compatible with those of President Bush. In the aftermath of September 11, the Bush administration had wanted to set a tone that did not blame "Islam" for the attacks. In part, they hoped this would discourage hate crimes against Muslims in the United States. Just as surely, policymakers knew from the beginning that they would need to seek allies in the Arab and Muslim world, and that any rhetoric that positioned the United States as opposing Islam would severely hamper foreign policy. After all, the ideological backing for remaking the Middle East as "democratic" and "friendly" was offered up to Americans in the language of idealism: "When it comes to the common rights and needs of men and women," Bush said in one speech, "there is no clash of civilizations. The requirements of freedom apply fully to Africa and Latin America and the entire Islamic world."[6]

Yet Bush also offered another set of messages about the nature of the conflict at hand. In the early days after 9/11, he infamously referred to his administration's plans for fighting terrorism as a "crusade," inflaming anger in the Middle East and elsewhere among those who feared exactly that—that the United States would launch its own holy war to take control of the Middle East. Bush also consistently used religious language that went beyond vague pieties voiced by most presidents and politicians, hinting that the United States was a Christian nation. The president spoke frequently and generically of the importance of "faith" in resolving the nation's crises after 9/11, but he also peppered his talks with implicit references to evangelical Protestantism. For example, in the 2003 State of the Union, he evoked a well-loved hymn when he spoke of "the power, the wonder-working power" of the goodness and faith of the American people. Bush also spoke of "our calling as a blessed country," a distinctly Protestant conception of America as a city on a hill.[7]

Thus, the tension between embracing Muslim allies, on the one hand, and positioning the United States as a Christian nation with a mission, on the other, was an ongoing rhetorical and political problem in the Bush administration, one that emerged from conflicts among different constituencies and competing policy goals. Domestically, the idea of a clash with Islam mobilized support for US policy in some Christian and secular audiences. Internationally, however, it was an unworkable, fundamentally destabilizing posture. And for those in the Bush administration who were determined not only to fight terrorism but to remake the political landscape of the Middle East by overthrowing Saddam Hussein, it was crucial to argue not for cultural clash but for universal values: if given a chance, all nations could and would embrace American-style democracy. Bush launched the war in Iraq on this premise, although there were also other motivations and material interests, of course.[8] But democracy, and the righteousness of American power, was at the heart of the public debate about the war.

On March 11, 2003, on the eve of the Iraq invasion, Larry King hosted a live debate among a group of Christian pastors and authors, posing the question: "What Would Jesus Do in Iraq?" The group included a white Catholic priest and a racially and theologically diverse group of Protestants who were invited to spar with each other and the audience over the relationship between faith and politics. The question they were asked referenced a pop culture phenomenon among younger evangelicals, who had taken to wearing bracelets and T-shirts adorned with "WWJD?"

The WWJD movement was a particularly evangelical concept, invoking the presence of Jesus as so immediate, so accessible, that a believer could ask herself in any situation, "What would Jesus do?"—and then presumably do likewise. By 2003, the question had a new urgency, as religious people in the United States, leaders and ordinary lay people alike, spoke out about the coming war. Religious forces were one of the key components of the anti-war movement. But religious voices—particularly those of American evangelicals—were equally outspoken in favor of the invasion.

Certainly, the Larry King show made for a lively debate. First up among the panelists, the priest Michael Manning opposed the war as violating traditional Catholic Just War doctrine. The presiding bishop of the United Methodist Church, Melvin Talbert, also spoke strongly against the war. That was not surprising since Talbert, the African American leader of a mainline Protestant denomination, already had also been featured on a television ad sponsored by the National Council of Churches. The pending war, he said in that ad, "violates God's law and the teachings of Jesus Christ."[9]

The conservative white evangelicals, on the other hand (three out of six guests on the panel) all argued in support of the war. Pastor and author John MacArthur was the most outspoken. In a rather agitated exchange with King and the other panelists, he said that Jesus had spoken of the strategies of a king in battle, thus using war as a "noble illustration." When one of the other panelists scoffed, MacArthur insisted: "Jesus himself spoke out for the possibility of a just war. He said, 'He who has no sword,' to his disciples, 'let him sell his garment and buy one.' . . . He knew there would be persecution. . . . and told them, get a sword because you may have to protect yourself." King appeared taken aback: "So he endorsed war. He endorsed . . ." And MacArthur replied, "He endorsed the fact of protection and just war."[10]

Each side blended scripture with more worldly arguments. Viewers called in, demanding to know how the panel saw Islam, whether the war was imperialist, and why Christians around the world were condemning the war while American Christians were largely supporting it. Throughout, white evangelicals offered variations of the pro-war view, while Catholic and mainline Protestants spoke for liberal opposition. And therein lay the problem. While King's show highlighted the intensity of religious debate, it presented a vision of American evangelicals that simply reproduced a common, and erroneous, journalistic frame—one that constructed the definition of evangelicals as universally white and conservative. There were no black or Latino evangelicals on the panel, no liberals or even genuine moderates, and no women of any denomination.

In fact, although white evangelicals overall strongly supported the war, there was still a range of opinion among evangelicals, rooted in multiple and sometimes conflicting motivations and values. The pro-war views of American evangelicals undoubtedly helped to frame the popular debate in ways that enabled the Bush administration to go to war with relative impunity. But a few evangelicals raised questions from the outset. First, they debated the theological/political issue of whether or not Iraq was a "Just War." And second, they wondered how missionary work in the Middle East would be affected. In fact, nothing was as charged, religiously significant, or deeply contentious as the question of when and how to evangelize in Iraq. A great deal was at stake, because missionary work included not only evangelization, but also desperately needed social service and humanitarian work.

As the *Larry King Live* debate made clear, just before the invasion of Iraq, American churches were deeply divided. Liberal churches were outspoken, and the leadership of nearly every major mainline Protestant denomination took a position that opposed or seriously questioned the war. The Catholic Church did the same. These denominations joined with Jews, Muslims, and others to form the heart of the Win without War Coalition, which was the center of much of the activism against the war in 2002 and 2003. Internationally, Christian leaders from around the world denounced the war, or at least raised serious doubts. Among others, the head of the Middle East Council of Churches, Riad Jarjour, argued that the US-led invasion "lacks justification and has no discernible or constructive goal."[11] At home a group of religious leaders took out a full-page ad in the *New York Times* directed at President Bush. Referring to the president's public affirmations of his faith, the ad admonished: "President Bush, Jesus changed your heart. Now let him change your mind."[12]

But that sentiment didn't necessarily flow down to the people in the pews. When polled, mainline Protestant churchgoers said they had heard some things about the war from the pulpit, but that their ministers generally had not taken a clear position. Certainly, the strong anti-war stances of the various denominations' national leadership seemed to have relatively little effect. In March 2003, 62 percent of mainline Protestants supported the war, and the vast majority said that religion was a small part of how they reached their decision.

African American churchgoers were a different story. They heard more talk of the war from their ministers, and the sermons were far more frequently opposed to the war than in support of it. Thirty-eight percent of black Christians (Protestant and Catholic) said they had heard sermons opposing the war, in comparison with only 5 percent of white evangelical Protestants. In the months leading up to the war, African Americans generally were opposed, 56 percent to 37 percent, according to Gallup.[13]

In white evangelical churches, on the other hand, there was little ambiguity. National leaders, clergy, and churchgoers all lined up to support the war. In the spring of 2003, just before the start of the war, 77 percent of white evangelicals supported military action.[14] Among the most visible was the Southern Baptist Convention's Richard Land, whose comment was widely quoted. "Romans 13 makes it very clear," he argued, that "God ordained the civil magistrate to punish those who do evil and to reward those who do right."[15] (As had been the case during the civil rights movement in the United States and the anti-apartheid movement in South Africa, Romans 13 served as a tool in the hands of those who wanted to support the status quo.) Various other evangelical leaders also reliably offered up support for the war. In the fall of 2002, Charles Colson of Prison Fellowship, James Dobson of Focus on the Family, right-wing publisher Marvin Olasky, and evangelist Franklin Graham were among them. Richard Cizik of the NAE offered more tempered support for the president.[16]

Across the political spectrum, evangelical leaders drew heavily on the newly revitalized discourse of "Just War," even as they also weighed in on factual and tactical questions about weapons of mass destruction, UN resolutions, and funding for terrorism. Just War theory, originally developed by Augustine, Thomas Aquinas, and others, was an attempt to challenge the pacifism of some Christian traditions. "They who have waged war in obedience to the divine command," Augustine wrote, "or in conformity with His laws . . . have by no means violated the commandment, 'Thou shalt not kill.' "[17] A Just War must be both justified in its cause and just in the way it is carried out, deploying proportional force and avoiding civilian casualties.[18]

The question of whether Just War doctrine was meant to enable war or limit it was wide open, and some evangelicals saw that opening and drove right through it. Marvin Olasky, editor of *World* magazine, enthusiastically described the Just War tradition as enabling the invasion of Iraq: "Theologians such as Augustine, Aquinas, Luther, and Calvin all saw some form of war as inevitable, due to the depravity of human nature . . . [Thus] Christians developed codes of 'just war' that emphasized the use of necessary means of warfare but the avoidance of savagery."[19] It was a muscular interpretation of Just War doctrine, and it gave cover to Christians who might want to support a preemptive war in Iraq.

Early evangelical opposition to the Just War argument was rather defensive. The war's opponents knew they were in the minority, in the country and among evangelicals, and so frequently felt called to ward off charges that they were unpatriotic or did not, in the ubiquitous phrase, "support the troops." One Memphis newspaper ran a column by a local Christian who explained his opposition to the war in Just War terms, saying that he was not unpatriotic. "Christians who oppose the war," he complained, "should be respected instead of attacked." He was right to be worried. In the summer of 2003, one of the pastors at an evangelical church in Portland, Oregon, wrote a blog post about the excessive patriotism at his church's July 4 service. The essay was enthusiastically received and widely shared on social media, but, at home, the pastor soon found himself out of a job.[20]

The lead-up to the Iraq War also summoned a great deal of prophecy speculation. The fascination with the Middle East that had animated prophecy talk after the 1967 war had waxed and waned in previous decades, but never fully abated. And with the rise of the internet, the opportunities for theorizing about the relationship between current events and Biblical predictions were virtually unlimited.

In the winter and spring of 2003, debates about prophecy and politics got particularly heated. Almost by definition, the war triggered apocalyptic speculation. The 1990–91 war against Iraq had led to many predictions of a great final battle, but in 2003 the discussion was intense and anxiety-ridden. In the wake of September 11, with an ongoing war in Afghanistan and Osama bin Laden still at large, and the sense of risk that attended the US plans for a ground invasion, both worry and excitement were very much on display. "I have never had such a bad feeling about a war ever before," wrote Sha Twa in April 2003. This war, she said, "has given me such a 'heaviness' in my heart, knowing that it is only the beginning of more to come . . . I do believe we are living in the end times and that this war with Iraq is the precursor war to Armageddon . . . never have there been so many signs as now in history."[21]

As the United States prepared for and then launched the war, one central theme on the prophecy sites was a sense of betrayal and anger at President Bush for his "selling out" to the enemies of Israel. Many participants were angered by Bush's support for an Israeli-Palestinian peace plan (the Roadmap), which they viewed as asking too many concessions of Israel. More viscerally, writers expressed fury at the president's statements after September 11 in which he had asserted that Islam was a religion of peace.[22]

In fact, there was for a short time an active and entirely serious thread on the discussion board for the bestselling *Left Behind* book series with the title "Bush: Antichrist?" Under that heading, participants debated whether President Bush himself might be the Antichrist, given what some saw as his push for a false peace and his suspicious religious eclecticism.

When President Bush offered a rare criticism of Israeli policy in the spring of 2002, after Israeli Prime Minister Ariel Sharon had launched a major military offensive into Palestinian cities and towns, Jerry Falwell and others devised for nearly one hundred thousand emails to be sent to the White House to protest.[23] There was some opposition to this intensive evangelical support of the Israeli Right. As events escalated, moderates like Robert Seiple at the Institute of Global Engagement and Richard Mouw of Fuller Theological Seminary wrote President Bush to say that evangelicals were not a "monolithic bloc in full support of present Israeli policy." When word got out about that letter, however, a group of twenty-four conservative leaders wrote an opposing letter to Bush, saying that "even-handedness" regarding Israel was "morally reprehensible."[24] That was the dominant view. Indeed, one commentator in the *Jerusalem Post* summarized what had now become obvious: "The US is Israel's best friend largely because the American Christian community wills it to be so."[25]

Prophecy watchers might be critical of the president, but on the *Left Behind* discussion boards, most posters quickly jumped in to say that it simply was not and could not be the case that Bush was the Antichrist, for both political and theological reasons. Some posters strongly supported the president. Others said that although Bush had made mistakes, they believed he was still a Christian and a good leader. A few others warily agreed that the president was probably not the Antichrist, but still insisted that he needed to be carefully watched.

The debates about whether the Iraq war was justified positioned evangelical actors as liberal or conservative, nationalist or globalist, in fairly straightforward ways. But another major issue—a core one for evangelicals of all stripes—was the war's impact on missionaries and local Christians, in the Middle East and elsewhere. In the early phases of the war, no opportunity seemed more ripe for missionary work, but few dangers were more immediate. At one level, it might seem like a practical question: how would US military action enable or threaten evangelical proselytizing or social service work, and how should evangelicals respond to the situation on the ground? Individuals who agreed very closely on theology or politics might well part ways quickly on the topic of how to do missionary work in a war zone. For some, assertive evangelism was an obligation and the war might provide an opportunity. For others, the evangelism-at-any-price was a threat to Christians in the region, and perhaps around the world. And so, on this issue as much as any other facing evangelicals after September 11, pragmatic concerns and theological commitments were often strikingly at odds.

In pre-invasion Iraq, proselytizing of any kind was dangerous and both missionaries and Iraqi Christians lived in an uncertain and unstable situation. Many US evangelical organizations, especially those with workers on the ground in Muslim countries, were quite worried about how Christians might be affected by the war and the increasing climate of hostility. The outspoken white evangelical support for the war in the fall of 2002 became more muted. In January of 2003, a group of Southern Baptists sent an open letter to their own community, highlighting how negative comments about Islam endangered missionaries.[26] (There were obvious parallels to the problems of racism and missions in the 1960s.) Similarly, the NAE found itself unable to issue a statement about the war, despite significant pro-war sentiment in the organization, because of fears about the response in the Middle East. As the NAE's Richard Cizik told an interviewer: "[I]n many Middle Eastern countries, the word 'American' and 'Christian' are synonymous, and those angry with the United States might say, 'We can't do anything about the planes up there, but here's people [local Christians or missionaries] who are linked to Americans.' "[27] Ted Haggard of the charismatic New Life Church, who would soon be elected president of the NAE, was more blunt: "Missionaries will die; Christians will die."[28]

In the twenty-first century, evangelical missionary projects generally took one of three forms, focused on salvation (proselytism), incarnation (social services), or transformation (a total Christian remaking of society). All three were part of missions work in Iraq.

The first model, proselytizing or salvation-focused, put evangelism first and foremost. It focused on proclaiming the gospel and starting churches. This was the traditional missionary approach that had been so criticized at Lausanne. For missions groups working in this mode, there was little excuse for *not* prioritizing the saving of souls. Aid was important but clearly secondary; often it was used as a strategy to open the door to proclaiming the gospel. Southern Baptists, for example, sent thousands of boxes of dry food to Iraq in the early days of the war. Each box also contained a passage from the gospel of John translated into Arabic. Other organizations, like Franklin Graham's Samaritan's Purse, worked on an even bigger scale. Samaritan's Purse was "poised and ready" on Jordan's border with Iraq, stocked with fresh drinking water for twenty thousand people and medical kits for one hundred thousand. These supplies would serve all sorts of people, and not just those who came to hear a sermon. But many of the packages also included evangelical tracts (figure 12.1). "As we work," Graham said, "God will always give us opportunities to tell others about his Son."[29]

The second model, incarnation, was hotly debated. Liberal Catholics and many mainline Protestant churches argued that humanitarian assistance had a purpose all its own. "Incarnational mission" was the duty to embody the love of Jesus and follow his model. There was a Christian duty to show God's love to others, even if it never led to people being converted. In previous decades, evangelicals had tended to define incarnational mission differently than other Christians. For them, the idea of living God's love was key, but it could not be separated from proselytizing. "The most effective witness the church makes will always be in the lives of those who in Christ's name bury themselves in the lives and struggles of another people, missionaries who serve the people, learn to speak their language, develop the capacity to feel their hurt and hunger, and 'who learn to love them personally and individually.'"[30] Such missionaries practiced a kind of radical contextualization, living fully in the environment in which they were serving in order to better evangelize. But in the early 2000s, more evangelicals were using "incarnational" in ways that were closer to how mainline Protestants had used the term, or how those evangelicals who supported social concern (or "holistic mission") had done. Missions were a matter of obedience to Jesus's call to love one another.[31]

The "transformation" model was more explicit about the requirement for evangelism: missions organizations could and should provide assistance, but real social and economic change could occur only through a large-scale adoption of Christianity. At a 2007

FIGURE 12.1 Christian brochures that will be included in care packages donated by Samaritan's Purse in Iraq. Courtesy of Samaritan's Purse.

conference on global faith-based organizations, Deborah Dortzbach of World Relief argued that "faith fuels behavior change—bringing foundational principles and standards, common language, impersonal accountability, and [the ability] to impact change." She insisted, in other words, that the best aid recipients were Christians.[32]

The vast majority of evangelical missions organizations mixed the three models, combining evangelism with incarnational humanitarianism and some kind of commitment to social change (of varying definitions). World Vision, for example, the largest Christian aid organization in the world, sometimes provided humanitarian aid only, with no evangelical content. However, when it could—when funding and local conditions allowed—it combined humanitarian aid with evangelism. A hospital clinic, for example, might be attached to a chapel.[33]

Not surprisingly, however, some prominent evangelical groups—especially those committed to a proselytizing model—saw the invasion of Iraq less as a humanitarian emergency and more as an extraordinary opportunity to do missions work in a country that had been extremely difficult to access. Iraq, like most Muslim countries, had not allowed foreign missionaries into the country. That changed with the US-led invasion, and Iraq became the frontline, a kind of proving ground, for the larger project of reaching Muslims everywhere with the gospel.

In all of the debates about missionaries, the idea of a clash of civilizations loomed—either as a presumed reality or a fearful concern. DVDs, films, web pages, and books continued the long conversation among evangelicals about how to understand Islam. On the Right, Marvin Olasky at *World* magazine commented that the war was necessary because "Islam is a works-based religion that emphasizes winning: Muhammad and his successors spread the faith by wielding the sword."[34] The relatively liberal evangelicals at Fuller Theological Seminary, on the other hand, started a $1 million program to develop greater and more respectful understandings of Islam.[35] And the diplomacy-oriented moderates at the Institute for Global Engagement set up conferences, held workshops, and traveled to the Muslim world to try to create dialogue. "As evangelicals," one workshop leader said, "we need to hear from Islamic voices so that the 'CNN moments'—the flashes of something 'newsworthy' that enter our experience and then vanish—don't blind us to the diversity and vitality of the Muslim tradition."[36] These more moderate voices gained some influence, over time, but when the Iraq War began, the general climate was hostile. In one 2002 survey sponsored by Beliefnet and the Ethics and Public Policy Center, a Christian think tank, 77 percent of evangelicals said their overall view of Islam was "negative." And 97 percent thought it was "very important" or "somewhat important" to evangelize Muslims at home and abroad.[37]

In this context, many people in Iraq and elsewhere in the Middle East were quite suspicious of the motives of evangelical missionary and humanitarian organizations. Abdulaziz Sachedina, a scholar of Islam at the University of Virginia, argued that "On the one hand, they [Iraqis] want [aid organizations] to come in; at the same time . . . America does . . . stand out as a Christian nation, as a Christian nation that is anti-Islamic at the moment. Therefore there's a lot of suspicion of what exactly the missions are trying to accomplish."[38]

Those suspicions had real consequences. As it turned out, it was unclear whether the arrival of American evangelicals either helped Christians or increased conversions in Iraq. In 2004, news accounts reported a notable growth in Protestant Christianity. Nine evangelical churches had opened in Baghdad, where there were thirty full-time evangelical missionaries and scores of others arriving for short-term missions.[39] But over time, as the war dragged on, spaces for evangelism diminished. Liberal evangelical author and radio host Tony Campolo argued that the invasion had been bad for both Iraqi Christians and missionaries: "Sadly, one of the consequences of our support of our nation's foreign policies is that the doors for missionary work are being shut . . . In Iraq, Christians, who even during the evil days of the Hussein regime had the privilege of boldly worshipping and evangelizing, are now being threatened."[40]

Indeed, over the course of the five years between 2003 and March 2008, at least twenty US and other foreign missionaries were attacked in Iraq. In the spring of 2004 alone, eight American missionaries were killed in drive-by shootings and six South Koreans were abducted.[41] Uncountable numbers of Iraqi Christians also faced increased danger, including a series of attacks on churches that led to a dramatic exodus among the already small Christian population. By 2005, every major Christian foreign aid organization, and most other humanitarian organizations, had pulled out of Iraq.[42] After 2008, with the US military surge, some foreign aid organizations returned, especially to Kurdish areas. But things got much worse for Christians in Iraq after the emergence of the Islamic State in 2013. Of course, things got much worse for Muslims too, because Islamic State targeted certain Muslims in the Middle East, and "anyone and everyone" in Europe.[43]

As American evangelicals made statements, sent medical supplies, or worked with Christians in the Middle East to try to start churches in Iraq, they also located themselves in relationship to each other, creating a network of practitioners with varied but intersecting goals. For proselytizing evangelicals such as Franklin Graham, the opportunities opened up by the war were immediate and unproblematic, part of a global struggle for souls. Others, whether or not they had supported the war, saw the opportunity to provide services in Iraq as a way of incarnating their faith by serving those in need. But they could not separate themselves out by the nature of their intentions: the Iraq War structured every enterprise, and the idea of a clash between Islam and Christianity was made real by the fact that some people, Muslim and Christian, enacted it on the ground.[44]

When the atrocities at Abu Ghraib were revealed in May 2004, Americans were shocked and polarized. Dozens of photographs showed members of a US Army reserve unit brutalizing prisoners. One, which became the iconic symbol of Abu Ghraib, showed a man in a black hood standing on a cardboard box, his arms stretched out, with electrodes attached to his hands and apparently to his genitals. No one could help but notice that his posture paralleled that of Jesus on the cross.

In all of the photographs, the violence done to detainees, and the bodies naked and in pain, was made even more horrific by the smiling young Americans alongside them. The news unraveled a carefully constructed set of official narratives about the United States in Iraq, supposedly there to liberate those who had been tortured by Saddam Hussein, and surely not to engage in torture in turn.[45] For evangelicals, however, the revelations at Abu Ghraib raised very particular moral and theological questions. This wasn't just a political issue, or a question of American character. It was a question of sin.

The Vatican and mainline Protestant churches immediately spoke eloquently and angrily about the images. One group of religious leaders developed an ad to run on two Middle East satellite stations in which representatives of different faiths—Jewish, Catholic, Protestant, and Muslim—apologized for "the sinful and systemic abuses committed in our name, and pledge to work to right these wrongs."[46] Some evangelical groups also spoke out. *Sojourners* called for Defense Secretary Donald Rumsfeld's resignation, arguing that he had known for months about the treatment of prisoners at Abu Ghraib.[47]

But in the first weeks and even months after the revelations, most evangelicals had remarkably little to say. A community that had largely supported President Bush and the war seemed stunned into silence. When evangelicals did comment, they mostly echoed the sentiments of secular Americans, musing on the horror of what the guards at Abu Ghraib had done, noting the sexual lewdness, commenting on the specifically anti-Muslim tenor of the behavior.

Two concerns, however, were particular to evangelicals. The first was about self-scrutiny. Several of the perpetrators publicly identified as (Protestant) Christians. Specialist Charles Graner, the apparent ringleader of the group, had disturbingly evoked his faith when he described the sexual and physical abuse he and his colleagues perpetrated. "The Christian in me says it's wrong," he told another reservist, "but the corrections officer in me says, 'I love to make a grown man piss himself.'" Now, on display for the world, was an image of American Christians as persecutors and torturers—violators of fundamental human rights who also relished, and photographed, their abuses.[48]

The second distinct issue for evangelicals was theological. There was ready agreement among evangelicals that, whatever else it was, Abu Ghraib was a demonstration of the inherent sinfulness of human beings. Across the theological and political spectrum of American evangelicalism, commentators highlighted the essentially "fallen" nature of human beings. Southern Baptist Theological Seminary President Albert Mohler articulated a common sentiment, saying that "moral romanticists" might be befuddled by what had happened, but "Christians, on the other hand, are informed by the biblical teaching that human evil is written into the very warp and woof of humanity."[49]

Evangelicals differed widely, however, on the implications of this belief. Gary Bauer of the conservative Focus on the Family, for example, insisted, as many secular conservatives did, that the events at Abu Ghraib were "the perverse acts of a few," caused by "man's sinfulness multiplied by wartime pressures." In his view, Abu Ghraib said nothing about the war itself or the overall situation in Iraq. Individuals are responsible for their sin, Bauer argued, not history or context, and not political leaders.[50]

That was one approach, but it wasn't the only one, even among conservatives. Some did see the sins of Abu Ghraib as firmly rooted in historical context, although not necessarily that of the war. Instead, some evangelicals saw domestic culture as the problem. The Abu Ghraib photos were clearly pornographic, and so, some conservatives rushed to conclude, pornography had caused the problem. Americans had allowed pornography to flourish, and without a steady diet of those images, soldiers at Abu Ghraib would never have been able to *imagine* the things they did. (News outlets later reported that some of those treatments were actually suggested by senior officers in military intelligence.) "A good question for the public debate at the moment," Chuck Colson commented in 2004, "is whether we have brought all of this on ourselves by our addiction to or toleration for pornography."[51]

Colson's critique, however much it might have been a cynical move designed to turn the gaze away from the war, did resonate. Observers commented frequently on the combination of sexual explicitness and violence that accompanied the eerie expressions of glee on the reservists' faces. "The events are in part designed to be photographed," Susan Sontag wrote. "The grin is a grin for the camera. There would be something missing if, after stacking the naked men, you couldn't take a picture of them."[52] These were bodies on exhibit, abused and tortured. The display of injury was a familiar sight for evangelicals who had seen the videos and websites of persecuted Christians. Now, however, it was Muslims whose tortured bodies would tell a story about US power and religious hostility.

Whatever the specific position of these evangelical conservatives—whether they focused on pornography as the problem or insisted that there was no problem beyond a crime committed by a few bad apples—most managed to deftly extract the sins of Abu Ghraib from the Iraq War itself, which was, they insisted, neither their context nor cause.

Moderate and Left-liberal evangelicals responded with anger, not only at the images, but at the responses of the religious Right. Writing in *Christianity Today,* evangelical author and journalist Stephen Gertz roundly criticized Christian conservative leaders who had tried to push the scandal under the rug. Invoking the Apostle Paul, Gertz argued that the soldiers' actions were indeed a symptom of sin, "a disease we are all infected with." Gertz argued that a proper understanding of sin required not only an "accounting for the crimes committed" but recognizing one's own responsibility to act. Gertz had few specific recommendations for how other Christians should "counter the evil" of Abu Ghraib, but his overall vision was clear. Christians constitute a community that somehow must atone for the failures of any part of that community.[53]

There were also other histories, and other sins, to speak to. Major newspapers and magazines widely noted the particular history of race evoked by the soldiers' photos and their shocking similarity to early twentieth-century photographs of lynching.[54] While there are other examples of images of the dead taken as souvenirs, of soldiers taking photographs of dead bodies on battlefields, or otherwise collecting gruesome trophies of body parts, lynching photos were among the few cases where the killers place themselves in the frame, anxious to show their own participation in the suffering. In this, the Abu Ghraib photos linked US power with American racial oppression.

The nationally renowned African American pastor and author T.D. Jakes, who usually positioned himself as apolitical, told an interviewer that he was not surprised at the photos. He had seen similar things before.

> We grew up with stories of lynchings and beatings, and I've seen even as late as the 60s people beaten and left in cornfields in Mississippi. So it's very believable that somebody with too much power and privacy would pervert that power and abuse someone who had no control. Or strip them down and tar and feather them as they did our forefathers, or rape our women. This has always been amidst the singing of hymns on Sunday morning. It was very believable to me.[55]

Jakes offered a pointed reminder to white evangelicals: it wasn't the first time that Christians had been persecutors. Six months later, the leaders of the four black Baptist denominations met to develop a united stance on major political issues. At the end of the meeting, they issued a call for the withdrawal of US troops from Iraq.[56]

If what happened at Abu Ghraib had at first seemed singular in its grotesque horror, it soon became clear that this was just the first in a series of revelations of broad, systematic mistreatment of prisoners in US custody. Over the following year, the media reported accusations of torture at Guantanamo (soon borne out) and revealed the practice of "extraordinary rendition"—sending prisoners to be interrogated by nations that were known to practice torture.[57] Again, many major religious Right organizations defended the Bush administration, or remained strategically silent. Unlike Abu Ghraib, this torture was clearly not a matter of individual choices, but a question of US policy in the war on terror. With their history in support of the war, and their reluctance to criticize the president, these conservatives seemed to believe that human rights enforcement ended at the White House door. In this, of course, they were joined by secular conservatives as well.

Other evangelicals, however, countenanced no such limitations on their fundamental Christian conviction that each human life was sacred. A few months after the revelation of the "torture memos," *Christianity Today* ran a cover story: "5 Reasons Why Torture is Always Wrong; And Why There Should Be No Exceptions." Written by the widely respected evangelical author and ethicist David Gushee, the story opens with descriptions of three people being tortured: one electrocuted, one asphyxiated, and one humiliated in a bra and thong. "[W]e do not want to call torture what it is," Gushee said. "We deny that we are torturing ... We give every evidence of the kind of self-deception that is characteristic of a descent into sin."[58]

Liberal evangelical author Randall Balmer described his reaction in even harsher language. Balmer recounted that in 2005, he sent a query to eight religious Right organizations asking for their statements on torture. Only two responded, and both defended the Bush administration, even as they claimed to oppose torture in principle. Balmer was disgusted: "Surely no one who calls himself a child of God or who professes to hear a 'fetal scream' could possibly countenance the use of torture" in any circumstances.[59]

At about this time, a group of evangelical intellectuals and activists began the two-year process of drafting "An Evangelical Declaration against Torture," issued in March 2007. David Gushee was the primary author; others included evangelical liberals Brian McLaren and Ron Sider. Still others, however, were moderate conservatives such as David Neff, editor of *Christianity Today*; Rebecca Hestenes, the minister-at-large for World Vision; and professors at several evangelical theological seminaries. Basing its argument against torture on a human rights ethic and a commitment to the "sanctity of life," the declaration insisted that "human rights places a shield around people, even when (especially when) our hearts cry out for vengeance."[60]

The drafters insisted that the declaration was not an attack on the Christian Right, or on "the Republican president of the United States," and it repeatedly praised the US military for its stances against torture and rules about interrogation. Still, the document was clearly intended to make room for an expansive interpretation of evangelical moral principles. The declaration made links to Catholic theology, Reinhold Niebuhr's mainline Protestantism, and the global, secular human rights movement. It cited the Geneva Conventions in detail, honing to a strict view of what defined torture. The declaration also gestured repeatedly toward traditional evangelical moral concerns. It argued that human rights commitments were based on the Christian view of the "sanctity of life," mobilizing the hallmark language of the anti-abortion movement, and linking its anti-torture position to key tropes of conservative evangelical activism.

The overall thrust of the document was to open up the critique among evangelicals that had begun with Abu Ghraib. The issue was no longer just human sin, but also human responsibility to protect the dignity of others. For most evangelicals, that moral vision would not and could not be separated from opposition to abortion, but it was now commonplace to insist that life concerns must extend beyond the womb. Human rights were not just about protecting the unborn, or persecuted Christians. "We know we really care about human rights," Gushee wrote, "when we care about the rights of our enemies and those we fear, not just ourselves or our friends."[61] Shortly after it was issued, the declaration was endorsed by the generally conservative NAE.[62]

Right-wing reaction to the declaration was limited but fierce. Daniel Heimbach, who had been vocal in crafting a Just War theory to support the Iraq War, called the declaration a "moral travesty" intended to divide evangelicals. A more serious and sustained critique by Keith Pavlischek argued, correctly, that the declaration had failed to define "torture" with any precision. As Pavischek pointed out, the declaration aimed for broad agreement beyond simple opposition to torture, and it achieved that by remaining vague on the most serious areas of contention among evangelical liberals and moderates.[63] Indeed, the declaration was an act of position-taking, one designed to mark evangelicals (at least those who signed the statement) as expansive in their moral vision, global in their orientation, yet pragmatic and diplomatic in their political approaches.[64] It was the calling card of post-Moral Majority evangelical moderation, with all the possibilities and limits that such a position entailed.

By mid-2006, white evangelical support for the war had fallen sharply—down to 58 percent from 77 percent in 2003—and approval of President Bush had declined even more sharply, especially among younger evangelicals.[65] On both counts, evangelical support was still higher than in the population overall, which by large margins wanted the United States out of Iraq and increasingly saw the war as a mistake. By all accounts, those evangelicals in the pews who turned against the war did so for the same reasons the rest of the population did: higher numbers of US casualties (more than three thousand dead by mid-2006), and increasing sectarian violence in Iraq, with little in the way of real political solutions in sight. By and large, and with the exception of prophecy watchers, evangelicals did not raise specifically theological concerns about departing Iraq.

While the rising evangelical criticism of the war did not emerge for specifically religious reasons, the changing positions did have a significant political effect within the evangelical community. Those evangelicals who had questioned the war from the beginning became increasingly self-confident and assertive. No longer content to defensively insist on their own patriotism, some members of the evangelical Left called on evangelical conservatives to repent of their previous views.

Writing in the *New York Times* in early 2006, Charles Marsh, a professor of religion at the University of Virginia and a self-described evangelical, excoriated his fellow believers for falling into line behind the Bush administration. Marsh had re-read sermons by influential American evangelicals before the war, and found that "[t]he single common theme among the war sermons appeared to be this: our president is a real brother in Christ, and because he has discerned that God's will for our nation to be at war against Iraq, we shall gloriously comply." In their near-uniform support for the war, Marsh said, American evangelicals had been guilty of "mistaken loyalty," putting nationalism and love of power before the Christian call to be peacemakers. "The Hebrew prophets might call us to repentance," he concluded, "but repentance is a tough demand for a people utterly convinced of their righteousness."[66]

The calls to repent had particular relevance when calling out conservative evangelicals, who for many decades had been insisting that the nation should repent of its sins of sexual immorality, cultural relativism, and liberalism. Now, evangelical liberals were speaking broadly of the need for conservative evangelicals to repent—of support for the war, certainly, but also of a more general American arrogance. Jim Wallis, always a standard-bearer for anti-war evangelicals, titled the January 2008 cover story in *Sojourners* "A Call to Repentance."

Support for US wars and foreign policy is still the area where American Christians are most "conformed to the world" (Romans 12:2). This is our Achilles' heel, our biggest blind spot, our least questioned allegiance, the worst compromise of our Christian identity, and the greatest failing of our Christian obedience.[67]

To fully claim their membership in the global Christian community, Wallis said, Americans would need to join that community in its opposition to the war.

Similarly, Randall Balmer wrote that it was about time for the religious Right to face what they had done in supporting the war. "My Bible," he wrote, "teaches that those who refuse to act with justice or who neglect the plight of those less fortunate have some explaining to do." But with repentance, even the religious Right might be able to come into the fold: "My evangelical theology assures me that no one, not even Karl Rove or James Dobson, lies beyond the reach of redemption, and that even a people led astray can find their way home."[68]

The scorn that liberal evangelicals heaped on the logic of support for the war was striking, and although theirs was far from the majority view, it did indicate the changing contours of evangelical opinion. In 2003, evangelical opponents of the war had not marshalled quite the same kind of righteous anger. By 2007, however, this group was beginning to make stronger claims: that the "mistakes" of the pro-war camp were sins of an evangelical conservatism that was now on the wane. And so, Jim Wallis, who had something of a reputation for always being certain that the change he longed for was just around the corner, nonetheless spoke for a larger community when he posited the emergence of a "post-religious right America."[69]

Of course, most evangelical conservatives did not consider their movement to be in danger of imminent demise, and they did not back down from their support of the war. Richard Land of the Southern Baptist Convention continued to insist that the invasion of Iraq had been an act of liberation, although he was "extremely disappointed in many aspects of the prosecution of the war."[70] And Rick Scarborough, head of Vision America and a major standard bearer of the religious Right, organized a conference in October 2007 in which he, Gary Bauer, and a number of others defended the Iraq War as a necessary front in the larger battle against terrorism. Not about to cede any territory to the moderates who were talking about torture as a "sanctity of life" issue, Scarborough announced that the war on terror was "the ultimate life issue. If radical Islam succeeds in its ultimate goals, Christianity ceases to exist."[71]

But right-wing evangelicals could no longer count on the deference they once enjoyed. They were not about to go away, by any means, but by the 2008 elections they were in a genuine competition with moderates and liberals to define "common sense" evangelical politics. Among evangelicals, the term "prophetic" is often used very specifically, to mean a type of speech or action that speaks the truth in the face of a disbelieving world, regardless of the consequences. In that sense, the early opposition to the Iraq War by liberals and the evangelical Left was marginal, but it was prophetic precisely *because* it was marginal; the evangelical Left had been willing to speak truth to power. By 2008, opposition to the Iraq War had positioned evangelical liberals as prophetic in the more prosaic sense: they had correctly predicted that the war would be a disaster. The evangelical Left was stronger than it had been since the heyday of Lausanne's social concern contingent. Given the stranglehold of the Right on evangelicalism in the late twentieth century, it was a remarkable development. A war that had seemed to index perfectly evangelical anxieties about Islam ended as a challenge to a whole range of conservative pieties. At least, so it seemed at the dawn of the age of Obama.

13

"I Am Not a Big Checkbook"

CHURCHES AND MONEY IN SOUTH SUDAN

IN DECEMBER OF 2006, I was sitting in the open-air coffee shop of a small, ramshackle airport in Lokichogio, in Northern Kenya, waiting to fly with a group of American evangelicals into southern Sudan. We were five white Americans—me plus four members of Elmbrook Church, a non-denominational megachurch located in Brookfield, Wisconsin, a suburb of Milwaukee. The leader of our group was Elmbrook's Senior Associate Pastor, Dick Robinson. We were headed into southern Sudan for a week, during which time we would travel to several villages, meeting with Sudanese Christians. Beyond that, our plans were still something of a mystery to me.

Elmbrook Church was in many ways a typical suburban megachurch. Each week it brought in an average of six thousand worshippers to its modern, unadorned auditorium. The congregation was largely white, middle-class, and casually dressed. The services were very much like those of other, similar churches that dotted the US religious landscape: Rick Warren's Saddleback in California, McLean Bible Church outside of DC, or Willow Creek Community Church in Chicago. When the pastor or guests spoke, they were projected onto large screens near the stage. The music on Sunday mornings was upbeat and energetic; occasionally, professional musicians played live. There was usually a short video, celebrating some aspect of the church's work.

Elmbrook is a "seeker-friendly" church, which means it presents itself as accessible, open, a place where people do not obsess over fine theological distinctions or rail about hellfire and brimstone. The "Who We Are" section of its website opened with the simple declaration: "We love Jesus. We love people." Nonetheless Elmbrook was fully conservative in its theology: the Bible was "without error"; a person must receive Jesus Christ in order to be saved; Christ's return was "imminent." Only men could serve as elders or as a senior pastor, a fact that upset Dick, who believed, he told me, in "the full and absolute equality of women."[1]

The Elmbrook leadership was proud of its missions. Every year it sent dozens of teams on short-term trips to Asia, Latin America, and Africa. Our trip, however, was an unusual one. We were traveling to a remote area of southern Sudan, impoverished and ravaged by war, where there would be no cell phones or even electricity. This was hardly a typical short-term trip, given the fact that we were a very small group of mostly middle-aged people. I thought it unlikely that we would be painting a church or building a useless wall.

Before we left the States, I had asked Dick exactly what the group was going to do in Sudan. This was a "particularly American question," he responded, to which he had only "an African answer." The plan was to visit their Sudanese friends, he said, to be with other Christians and "encourage" them. We would go to one village where Dick knew the local evangelist. Perhaps we would go to another village and visit a school that Elmbrook Church supported. During our many conversations on the trip, Dick insisted to me that they were not traveling to Sudan as "missionaries." He didn't have a plan to try to fix other people's problems, and he wasn't there to try to evangelize non-Christians. They were there to be in fellowship with Sudanese believers, to learn from them, to see the work they were doing, and to pray with them. I was there to try to understand.

The members of the team had a number of different reasons for being on the trip. Randy, a former Hewlett-Packard sales executive, had retired early to take a far less lucrative position as Elmbrook's financial planner. In his mid-50s, handsome and fit, he was garrulous, funny, and a bit sarcastic. Randy was a practical-minded person, as befitted his past in business. "My wife is much more spiritual than me," he often said. He didn't like to talk about politics. But, quietly and behind the scenes, Randy was an agenda setter. Over the course of the trip, I began to suspect that he was a silent but substantial donor to the programs we were going to visit, and that we were there, at least in part, for him to see how things were going.

Mary, also in her fifties, was reserved and unassuming, but, like Randy, she too had made major life changes for the sake of her faith. She had worked for many years at the YMCA in Milwaukee but recently had also studied part-time at Trinity Divinity School, an evangelical seminary not far from Brookfield. She had recently left her job to focus on her degree. She didn't know what was coming next.

Jim was the youngest member of our group at thirty-six. He also felt himself at a crossroads. He had grown up in Elmbrook, and was now studying full-time at Fuller Theological Seminary. Jim was still "seeking God's will" for his life, he said. He was working part-time at a church, but not feeling particularly settled there. He was loosely considering the idea of returning to Sudan full-time as a missionary. (A few years after our trip, Jim would come out as gay and move to a liberal Episcopal church in California.)

When I first met Dick, at the Wheaton College missions conference six months earlier, he was giving a passionate speech about his vision of a globalized, multilingual congregation of people worshipping together. His job was to oversee the missions program at

Elmbrook, traveling constantly to China, Sudan, Congo, Peru, and a dozen other countries each year—preaching, or teaching, and sometimes, as I would learn, just hanging out. Dick, it seemed to me, lived for elsewhere.

Dick and his brother, Paul, had grown up in Congo, the children of missionaries. (Paul spent decades as professor in the Human Needs and Global Resources [HUNGR] Program at Wheaton College.) Dick moved to the United States for high school. In 1967, after trying college but feeling uninspired by it, he joined the Marines to avoid being drafted into the infantry. He married his girlfriend Peggy just before he shipped out to Vietnam. When Dick returned home, he and Peggy began going to church together. He also started reading Francis Schaeffer and was inspired by the idea that it was possible to be skeptical and critical about faith without being cynical. Before long, he rededicated himself to evangelical Christianity, returning, not exactly as a prodigal son, but as a wanderer who had found his way home. Later, Dick would go back to college, and then to get an MA in theology from Trinity Evangelical Divinity School.

I was surprised and delighted when Dick allowed me to join the group on the trip to Sudan, and wondered whether the invitation reflected his inability, or refusal, to conform entirely to the evangelical mold. I was a stranger to him, and I described myself, when asked, as a "secular person." During the course of my research, I had been turned away from missions trips or interviews on a number of occasions by people who were understandably wary of my intentions. But Dick liked to make unusual decisions. Besides, he was of that breed of evangelicals who believe their lives are *supposed* to represent faith well lived, and that it would be wrong to be fearful. The good heart speaks for itself, and they must be the best representatives of Jesus's love they can be. God handles the rest. That conviction on Dick's part had landed me as part of this evangelical group, drinking sodas in a small airport in northern Kenya.

When it was time to leave Lokichogio, the five members of our group walked over to an eight-seat Cessna. The pilot was an American who worked for Missionary Aviation Fellowship, an evangelical organization that provides transport for Christian groups headed to difficult-to-reach areas. We loaded ourselves and our considerable gear into the plane. Before we took off, the pilot asked us to bow our heads for a brief prayer, placing us in God's hands.

Soon we were soaring low over the beautiful country of northern Kenya. The rainy season had just ended, and the land was green and hilly. No long after, we saw the more arid areas of southern Sudan: flat, low grasslands, punctuated with lines of scrubby acacia trees and slow-moving muddy rivers. After a couple of hours, we arrived in Otallo, a remote village that was home to about five hundred people. The airstrip was much like others we would encounter on the trip—a small patch of cleared but unpaved land, situated right next to the village.

The long civil war had just ended. Independence was still almost five years away, but the Southern People's Liberation Army controlled all the territory we traveled in. The region was poor. In March 2011, the World Bank estimated that just over half the population lived below the global poverty line of $1.25 a day. Education rates were extraordinarily low; in three out of four families, the head of household had no formal education at all. The Americans from Wisconsin, on the other hand, represented a wealthy church in one of the sixty wealthiest counties in the United States.[2] Inevitably, money would be on the agenda.

The man who met us in Otallo was a scholarly-looking Anuak man named John Philip Omat. Forty-eight years old, with close-cropped hair graying slightly at the temples, John Philip was tall and thin, like many Anuak people. He had just returned to live in the village after almost thirty years away. He was dressed almost elegantly in pants and a scrupulously clean shirt, no small feat in a village where the dirt of the dry months gave way only to the mud of the rainy season.

The village itself was notable for its isolation and poverty, even in southern Sudan, where both are the norm. There was no electricity, even by generator; no running water; no health care; not even a market. The nearest place to buy even the simplest items—matches or tea—was in Pochala, two hours away by truck. John Philip took us to the compound where we would be staying, which consisted of a group of *tukuls* (cone-shaped huts) with thickly woven roofs set above the rest of the village. The sides were open, except for the beams that held up the structure. The dirt floors were covered in gazelle skins. Elmbrook members slept there, and ate the sorghum and (for us) peanut butter that John Philip had thoughtfully provided. The villagers also very generously killed a goat for us; they rarely got to eat meat.

Dick had visited southern Sudan many times, and his love for the place was obvious. From the time we arrived in Otallo, he softened a bit, as if he felt safer there. Dick was a fine photographer and took extraordinary photos of the people: colorful, striking close-ups of people's faces; images of groups dancing; and shots of people coming and going to church. As we walked through the village we saw women and children everywhere. Women were outside their huts, pounding sorghum grain into flour using giant poles, or walking to get water, or cooking. But there were almost no men younger than forty. John Philip explained that some of the younger men were away at a political meeting in Pochala, along with the leader of the Anuak, trying to resolve some political tensions. But most of the young men from the village were long gone. They had left home more or less permanently, looking for work or education elsewhere. Or they had joined the SPLA during the civil war, leaving wives and children behind. There was nothing in Otallo for these men, no way to feed their families except perhaps by raising a few cows or goats. It was as if, once they turned fourteen or fifteen, the boys disappeared, while the young women, apparently *ex nihilo*, began to give birth.

Dick and Randy knew John Philip from their previous trips to Kenya and Sudan, and for the past several years, Elmbrook Church had paid John Philip a stipend as he finished his Bible training. John Philip had grown up in this part of Sudan. His father had converted to Christianity during a sojourn in Ethiopia and had started Otallo's first church in 1969. Although John Philip was a native son, he was back in Otallo essentially as a missionary. When he was a teen, the civil war between northern and southern Sudan was ongoing, with periodic fighting. At that point, John Philip wanted to join the SPLA, the largest and most powerful of the rebel groups. "I was tempted," he said. "But because my younger brother was with me, I decided not to join. Because if I leave him, who will take care of him?" His plan was to finish high school, where he was studying accounting. *Then* he would join the rebels. But, as John Philip explained it, he went to Khartoum to work for a short time in the late 1980s to earn some money and ended up starting classes at a Bible College. "And then my whole way of thinking changed."

When he finished his studies in Khartoum, John Philip began leading an almost nomadic life, trying to find places where he was needed to preach or start churches, and not infrequently finding himself running up against local authorities. John Philip was unassuming, but, when asked, he told stories of dramatic confrontations, threats of death to him and other evangelists, and late-night travels to different, safer villages. The Islamist government in Khartoum had not wanted him to return to this area to preach and had forced him out at least once for not having the proper papers. When he did periodically make it back to Otallo to preach or teach, he often found himself opposing the local village leaders, many of whom, he said, wanted their cut of whatever resources he had gathered to build schools or clinics.

John Philip had left his wife and children back in Nairobi, where the family had lived while he finished his degree at Pan African Christian College. Because John Philip was educated, and had lived elsewhere—and also because of the small salary he received from Elmbrook—he stood out. Now that he was back in Otallo, he lived, by necessity, a border-crossing life. He would fly to Nairobi to visit his family when he could. News and messages would be sent via others who were navigating similarly dispersed lives.

John Philip's job now was to somehow get money and teachers for the barely functioning school in Otallo, while also bringing new energy to the local church. Elmbrook would continue to pay him a salary, but, beyond that, the Wisconsin church had no other clear commitments. "I'm not here as a big checkbook," Dick kept saying. Perhaps John Philip understood that. Others in the community, however, saw things differently.

The people of Otallo knew we had arrived, and they were aware of what the team from Elmbrook represented. Early on in our visit, we were summoned to meet with a group of village elders, about twenty men sitting under the shade of a large bamboo tree. Many looked quite old, and some of the younger ones sported the remnants of uniforms from their days with rebel forces.

The Elmbrook team was asked to greet the village leaders as John Philip translated. Each of us stood up in turn, saying how happy we were to be there and how honored we were to meet them. One or two people assured the gathered men that Americans cared about the Sudanese people and wanted what was best for them. This was not quite the truth. The long civil war had attracted the attention of many evangelicals, black and white, but most other people in the United States knew little about it. At the time of our visit, the violence in Darfur, in western Sudan, seemed to have captured Americans' limited allotment of attention to Africa. In reality, most Americans had certainly forgotten *these* Sudanese, if they had ever known of them. Even evangelicals had largely moved on. Elmbrook was unusual; its commitment had outlasted the fashion.

When the old men stood up to speak, they each delivered the same message: the village has many needs. We need medicines, they said; we need teachers. One man in a traditional long white robe had no time for niceties. "We need so many things," he said, sounding frustrated. "You can see this around you. You can *see* that we have nothing." For these men, the agenda was clear. Americans with money had arrived, and they needed to make their case for aid.

Dick responded by giving a talk that on the face of it sounded quite respectful. Using the rhythmic cadence and the repetitions that would always mark his presentations in Sudan, he praised the elders' ancestors. "You have been in this land for a long time," he said. "Your fathers and your grandfathers were here. And they were wise. They knew how to live in this land, with the floods and the droughts. They knew how to respond to the floods and the droughts. And you have the benefit of their wisdom. You have been in this land for a long time." The tone was one of praise, but it would have been hard to miss the underlying message: You have the resources to solve your problems. We aren't here to solve them for you.

Dick's unwillingness to be seen as the great white checkbook was understandable, given the problematic history of both missionary "benevolence" and US humanitarian aid. He knew well the history of colonialism. Too many times, Western missionaries or aid workers set off for Africa or Asia or Latin America with the salutary goal of educating the children, feeding the poor, or healing the sick only to discover—or fail to discover—the profound limits of colonial-style altruism. Southern Sudan had actually seen very few of the grand modernization schemes of the 1950s and 1960s. The government in Khartoum had deliberately underdeveloped this region. Still, the lessons were there. It no longer made sense to imagine that modernization projects would end poverty, or that "development" was a panacea.[3]

Nonetheless, it seemed to me that saying "your forefathers were wise" was hardly adequate to the situation. I had imagined that the Elmbrook team was going to be an example of compassion-in-action. Then again, compassion is admittedly quite complicated. It is only one of several possible responses to the recognition of others' suffering. We don't react identically to each bit off adversity we witness. Sometimes we react with apathy, or anger, or condescension, with solidarity, fear, or guilt. Some things rouse us to action, while others do not. What we are compelled by, and what we are compelled to do, varies a great deal. Compassion is powerful, contradictory, and historical. The compassion I had expected was not absent, but the question of how to enact it was very much unresolved.[4]

We arrived in Sudan at a moment in history in which humanitarian aid had become the dominant path for distributing Western compassion. Humanitarianism's rise in the late twentieth century was tied in part to the increased awareness, through media, of the world's suffering. Whether it was civil war and starvation in Biafra in the 1960s, famine in Ethiopia in the 1980s, the devastation in New Orleans after Katrina, or the meltdown of a nuclear reactor in Japan in 2011, we could now see images of disaster instantly and respond with a check or a click.

In the twenty-first century, "we have become used to the global spectacle of suffering and the global display of succor."[5] This means that good works of humanitarianism are also, inevitably, about power. Some people—"they"—are profoundly vulnerable in their need, and other people—"we"—give because we can, because we are generous. And yet compassion can also be more than that. If compassion leads to political awareness and solidarity with people who are in distress, then it can lead us to support not only their immediate needs, but also strategies for change. And these strategies would not necessarily be defined by officials in humanitarian organizations; they could be devised by the people on the ground. The change would not always be about economic improvement or development. It might also be about power: the power to vote and have it matter; the power to negotiate the end of a war; or the power to fight for a country of one's own.

The humanitarian agenda of the late twentieth- and early twenty-first century embodied these tensions—between compassion as a form of international solidarity and compassion as a form of self-gratifying performance. As both the goals and the implementation of humanitarian and development programs began to evolve from their Cold War versions, new questions had arisen. The paradigmatic humanitarian crises—refugees, famine, civilians under threat in a war zone—did not change, but humanitarians themselves began to ask why the humanitarian system was constantly responding to crises that could have been prevented with longer-term development and planning.[6]

Those questions led a number of organizations, including major funders such as the World Bank and the US government, toward supporting economic and social development rather than just relief. It was not a wholesale transformation; organizations such as Oxfam or Doctors without Borders still focused their work around traditional humanitarian goals of responding to crisis, providing food and binding wounds in urgent situations. One noticeable change, however, was that, starting in the 1990s, development and humanitarian assistance was increasingly handled by NGOs rather than directly by governments. The term NGO designated everything from a global organization to a local non-profit. But, whatever their size or mission, NGOs now did jobs that governments once had done. In 1990, for example, only 10 percent of the projects supported by the World Bank were run by NGOs. Most of the rest were run by governments. By 2001, NGOs received 40 percent of the World Bank's funds.[7]

The profusion of NGOs was nowhere more evident than in Christian humanitarian and development organizations. Samaritan's Purse, run by Franklin Graham, was a relatively small organization in the early 1990s. By 2015, it had a budget of $520 million, making it the twenty-fifth largest charity in the United States. It was almost impossible to tell what percentage of that money was used for missionary work and what purely for humanitarian purposes, given how much evangelism was woven into what the organization did, but its programs included emergency relief, community development, and medical services.[8]

Many smaller NGOs had an outsized profile. MegaCare, for example, was an independent charity associated with T.D. Jakes's church, Potter's House, in Dallas. Potter's House had thirty thousand members in 2015, and Jakes's television show, radio sermons, podcasts, and internet streaming garnered hundreds of thousands of listeners. Thus, when Jakes founded MegaCare (a name that resonated with his massive MegaFests each summer), it immediately had a high profile. Jakes's ministry had not been involved in international development work until the early 2000s, but it soon supported a series of wells in Kenya, hospitals in Kenya and Nairobi, and computer learning centers in Kenya, Zambia, and Mexico.[9] As part of his humanitarian work, Jakes traveled regularly to Kenya, where he became a well-known figure.

Among the top twenty-five organizations on *Forbes*'s 2015 list of the largest US charities were four evangelical groups that did significant international work: World Vision (#11), Compassion International (#14); Cru (formerly Campus Crusade, #24), and Samaritan's Purse (#25). Other Christian groups in the top twenty-five were Salvation Army (#2); Food for the Poor (#8); Habitat for Humanity (#13); Catholic Charities (#15), and Lutheran Services in America (#17).[10]

Of the evangelical groups, World Vision was by far the largest and most influential, and the most dramatically changed by the NGO surge. It had begun as a missionary organization and until the 1970s basically operated through "adopt-a-child" fundraising programs that largely supported missionary orphanages. Beginning in 1970, however, World Vision established a range of programs to draw attention to world hunger, and its income increased dramatically over the decade, from $4 million to $94 million. After the 1984 Ethiopian famine, donations poured into World Vision and other relief organizations. World Vision began to invest more in programs that offered not just temporary assistance but built local capacity—drilling wells and introducing new agricultural techniques, for example.[11] The organization did not stop doing relief or humanitarian aid, but it combined those programs with a larger development agenda.

In the first decades of the twenty-first century, World Vision expanded even more rapidly. In 2000, it was already an impressively large organization, with a budget of $886 million.[12] In 2014, the organization's expenditures were $2.8 billion, 48 percent of which was spent in Africa. It had offices in one hundred countries, with forty thousand employees. In addition, its new microfinance arm, Vision Fund, provided 1.5 million small loans totaling $900 million.[13] This made World Vision a behemoth in the world of international NGOs, an economic powerhouse whose projects and perspectives would shape both humanitarianism and development globally.

For decades, the debate about organizations such as World Vision was how they linked religious proselytization and development work. If they received US government funding, as they increasingly did, then that funding was not supposed to be used to evangelize, although the rules that prevented it were complicated and hard to enforce. (Traditionally, an organization that received US funds could not have religious services in the same location as its medical clinic, for example.) These rules were relaxed after President George W. Bush launched his program to support faith-based initiatives in 2004.[14] In practice, the rules were never much of an issue, since World Vision employees on the ground often saw the two components as inextricable. "Even when you are not necessarily buying a Bible for somebody but buying seeds, you are introducing God and saying how God can be involved in that situation," one employee explained.[15] By the twenty-first century, World Vision had evolved into a professionally led development organization. Although the group still required that all employees sign a statement of faith, most of its projects could not be distinguished from those of secular development programs.

As a major player in development work, World Vision also participated in what James Ferguson has described as the "anti-politics machine." Even as many NGOs had moved away from providing only crisis aid and toward funding longer-term development projects, they began to advance a common and sometimes problematic understanding of what "development" required. Development organizations, Ferguson argues, operate a global network that produces a particular set of understandings about what development should be, what the limits on it are, what expertise is needed to make it happen. This network seems to exist in similar ways all over Africa and beyond. These institutions and their staffs—Ferguson calls them the "development apparatus"; Alex de Waal calls them the "humanitarian international"—turn issues of development into a set of technical questions and push aside the reality that political choices are also being made. In other words, it is common for development organizations to ask themselves pragmatic questions about what seeds work best or whether it is better to charge people a nominal fee for mosquito nets or give them away free. But if those are the only questions, then they are failing to ask—and failing to encourage donors to ask—whether, for example, a famine is the result of a drought alone or the consequence of political decisions in the capital about what groups of people have land and tools for farming.[16] In this sense, development is an "anti-politics" machine because the development process "depoliticizes everything it touches, everywhere whisking political realities out of sight, all the while performing, almost unnoticed, its own pre-eminently political operation of expanding bureaucratic power."[17]

Some evangelical observers made similar arguments. The evangelical author and pastor Brian McLaren thought that many of the religious leaders who were interested in aid had not yet recognized the realities of structural injustice. Well-meaning people might set up programs, but they had failed to understand that development was a political issue. "Everybody knows the Micah passage," McLaren said. ("And what does the Lord require of you? To act justly and to love mercy and to walk humbly with your God." Micah 6:8, NIV)

> And, sure, walking humbly with God, that makes sense spiritually. . . . But eventually you realize that there are systemic causes that keep people poor . . . when people

start dealing with justice, that's when their lives get messy. . . . [For example,] if Rick Warren keeps going back to Rwanda and bringing other people to Rwanda, eventually he's going to have to realize that US trade policy [is an issue].

If you're not careful, McLaren said, "you're actually subsidizing US and European Union trade injustice."[18]

When the Elmbrook team went to Sudan, its members were asked to show compassion for the people they met. Lobbying for better trade policies or debt relief back home might be a good idea, but how would they respond in the moment, in the face of statements of need like those of the men gathered under that tree in Otallo?

If the Elmbrook team needed a reminder of how desperately money was needed in Otallo and yet how easy it was for Americans to fail in their attempts to help, they needed only to look just down the hill, where Otallo's half-finished schoolhouse sat, without chairs or doors, without schoolbooks, and largely without teachers. Dick and Randy explained to me that the school had originally been funded by World Relief, the nonprofit development group associated with the NAE. World Relief had poured money into the project, and Elmbrook had offered a special donation to support it. But either the money ran out, or the war came too close, or both. The local staff person for the project left, and World Relief had simply closed up shop.

In the face of that half-built schoolhouse, I would learn later, it turned out that the checkbook wasn't actually so far away; Elmbrook would sign on to help finish the schoolhouse and to fund its ongoing operation. While we were in Otallo, Randy, the practical-minded and energetic former business executive, immediately began to think about plans. They would find some money for the school. Maybe a health clinic. They needed to figure out how to get internet or radio access for John Philip, so that he could reach his family. The networks were kicking in, and back at Elmbrook, significant money would be raised for Otallo.

The Elmbrook team gave money and raised funds quietly, but they enthusiastically and openly offered "spiritual encouragement" through prayer and worship (figure 13.1). For Dick, one of the high points of the trip was the day we spent worshipping with Otallo's Christians at the village's small church. There were two services that Sunday. Both were long and revolved largely around music. The Sudanese sang and drummed before and after every sermon, every prayer, every greeting. John Philip preached in the morning. Dick preached in the afternoon.

Dick's sermon—the one about the beautiful crocodile eggs that he and his brother had brought home when they lived in Congo, which had then hatched into not-so-beautiful crocodiles—had to be translated by John Philip into Anuak, so every speech took a very long time. After Dick spoke, all of the other team members also stood up to say something. Jim, the seminary student, gave his own short sermon. Mary and I just said hello—women did not preach, for which, in that context, I was grateful. Throughout all of this, as John

FIGURE 13.1 John Philip Omat, Dick Robinson, and Ramadan Chan (l to r) baptizing a new believer in southern Sudan, 2006. Courtesy of Dick Robinson.

Philip translated for each person, I wondered what the Sudanese in the church thought of these messages, of these Americans who landed one day and were preaching to them the next. Later, Dick talked about the beauty and spiritual richness of the service. My own sense was that the energy of the music had something to do with the congregation being relieved that the long talking and translating were over with. But Dick saw it differently. It was amazing, he later told me, to see the expressions on the faces of the people there, to sense the marvelous power of God working in that room. "It was a holy experience."

Dick would not find it odd to hear himself described as "enchanted" by Africa. Indeed, in many ways he embodied the complex logic of enchanted internationalism. He idealized the Sudanese; he loved what he saw as their spiritual openness. Across the thicket of language, translation, and culture, such idealizations are both spiritually rich and politically dangerous. The richness comes when people allow themselves to be open to diversity, when they work to see people whose lives are different, not as a threat to their comfort or as a resource for their self-cultivation, but as sisters or brothers or comrades. This is the fundamental internationalist promise of many religions, including evangelical Christianity, and of many political movements as well. The danger comes when idealized, spiritualized people start making prosaic demands—when they get angry or hopeless, make pointed requests for money, or deliver barbed political commentary. What happens, in other words, when people refuse to be enchanting?

After the group left Otallo, John Philip came with us, and we traveled by Cessna to the market town of Yabus. There we met up with Ramadan Chan, a tall and imposing man who would be our host for this part of the trip. A Christian evangelist with a distinctively Muslim name, Ramadan was an impressive person: charismatic and energetic, with an easy laugh. He was on the staff of the local Intercultural Christian Council, which received some funding from Elmbrook and ran several local projects.

From his name, I assumed that Ramadan had converted to Christianity as an adult, but in fact his ancestry was more complicated. Both his parents were Christian, but his grandmother was a Muslim. His father was away when he was born, and by tradition his grandmother could give him a temporary name. If his father arrived back before the fortieth day, he could then name his child, but dad did not return in time, and the child kept the grandmother's choice of a name. I noted that the grandmother was certainly making a statement, giving her Christian grandson such a name. Ramadan just laughed and said that, well, sometimes it had been useful for an evangelist to be named after the Muslim holy month.

Ramadan had fought with the SPLA during the war and sometimes at night could be convinced to tell stories of his dramatic escapes from Sudanese government forces. In the little compound where we stayed in Yabus, he held court—people were in and out of the dirt courtyard area all day and evening, asking for help or advice, or just stopping by to pay respects. His various meetings did not seem to be primarily about church matters. Former SPLA soldiers came by the camp. The wife of an important SPLA leader arrived in the village on the back of a truck, and Ramadan seemed to be in charge of keeping her safe. "One day, Ramadan is going to be President of South Sudan," Dick said to me proudly. At the time, there was no such country.

The day after we arrived, we were scheduled to go to visit another village, Koma Ganza, which was two hours away on foot. When Ramadan showed up that morning to lead us to the village, he was wearing a large hat and carrying a walking stick, dressed like a nineteenth-century British imperialist. The area of southern Sudan where the Koma Ganza people live was very difficult to reach. Jeeps can sometimes get there, but not when the rainy season washes out the roads. The trek through the countryside was beautiful, though, with swaying acacia trees and tall grasses under a startling blue sky. The path was littered with signs of the civil war: an abandoned rebel outpost on one side of the path, old pieces of military equipment discarded nearby. Our group was accompanied by a few security people from the SPLA who said they were protecting us. But sometimes it can be difficult to tell the difference between being protected and being under surveillance.

The Koma Ganza people are not really one tribe, but a gathering of people who speak similar languages. As we approached our destination, we saw a dozen or more small, almost hidden, tukuls spread far apart. It was a very poor community, even more so than Otallo. Food, other than peanuts, was scarce, and there was no health care available nearby. The Elmbrook team was at Koma Ganza to visit the new village school, which had been built and staffed with funding from an anonymous Elmbrook parishioner.

Hope School comprised three fairly large tukuls around a dirt courtyard. Compared with much of what I had seen in Sudan, it was impressive: the courtyard was spacious, the tukuls seemed relatively airy, and the area was swept (perhaps for our visit). This was a proudly Christian school, with Ramadan serving as something like a program officer. The school was staffed by three Christian teachers from other parts of Sudan, who were, essentially, missionaries. Very few of the Koma Ganza people were actually Christian— most practiced traditional African religions. But the school taught Bible lessons along with English and math. The goals were clear: the school would hopefully make Christians of the children, and through them, reach their parents. Whatever the parents thought of this, they sent their children en masse. Many of the students walked two or three hours each way to the school; there were no others nearby. The school provided lunches and sometimes clothes.

Simon, one of the missionary teachers, was from another ethnic group from a different part of Sudan. He was the lead teacher at Hope, and he proudly showed us the teachers' office, a small hut, very dark and low, divided in the middle by a grass wall. On one side were a couple of small benches; on the other, some (empty) shelves. There seemed to be nothing else in the room: no papers, writing implements, or teaching materials. On the hut's grass wall, there were two or three UNICEF-issued posters. One showed the alphabet; the other was a brightly illustrated set of instructions on how to identify landmines.

School was out of session when we arrived, but teachers had nonetheless summoned students to appear. About fifty of them did, aged six to sixteen, wearing matching T-shirts that read "Hope School: Forward Ever, Backwards Never" (figure 13.2). They gathered in the courtyard, standing in neat rows. Ramadan and Dick each offered greetings and congratulations. Ramadan began by telling students and teachers who we were. "Let me introduce you," he said in Arabic. "Let me introduce you to these white people from America." I understood enough Arabic to realize what he had said, and later I asked him what he would have said if our group had included African American Christians. He smiled and replied: "I would have said, 'Let me introduce you to these white people from America.'" Race in southern Sudan was not a matter of color but of location. Southern Sudanese were black or African; the equally dark-skinned northern Sudanese were Arab; and Americans, apparently, are by definition white.[19]

The translation system for the opening greetings was quite complicated. When Dick offered his comments, Ramadan translated Dick's words into Arabic, and a local boy who happened to know some Arabic translated that into Ganza. "You are lucky to have these teachers and this school," Dick said. "You are doing important things." In his lilting African prayer-meeting style, he pointed to each of the groups of children in turn: "*you* are the hope of Sudan; *you* are the hope of Sudan; *you* are the hope of Sudan."

The school offered very rudimentary education. Since it had just opened, everyone was essentially in first grade. Several of the children had been assigned to show something

FIGURE 13.2 Boys at Koma Ganza's Hope School. Courtesy of Dick Robinson.

of what they had learned. One boy who stepped forward was about twelve. He stood in the center of the circle and offered examples of basic addition: "Two plus four equals six," he said, in English. "Five plus four equals nine."

Several elders from the village also made statements. The village leader thanked Dick and Ramadan, and made very clear how grateful they were. Part of the implicit contract between compassionate givers and fortunate receivers is that receivers must be ready— "sometimes to tell their story, frequently to mend their ways, and always to show their gratitude."[20] One elder, who was dressed in white and wearing a skull cap, spoke for some time. "We were marginalized before and we had nothing," he said. "Now we have this school. We need to keep the school going. We need to be able to feed the students in the school. We would like for some of the students to be able to stay in the school." The requests were gentler than they had been in Otallo, or maybe the translations just made them seem so. In either case, the point was the same.

Before we left Koma Ganza, we went into the tiny church just beside the school. I joined Dick and Randy there, as they listened to a young, blind man who was playing Christian songs on his one-stringed instrument, a *masenqo*. He didn't speak English, but he knew several American Sunday School songs: "I will sing, sing, sing for Jesus; I will jump, jump, jump for Jesus." He repeated the chorus over and over, sitting and playing, basked in shimmering light. The two men from Elmbrook looked on, rapturous at this vision of a Sudanese Christian man, who had been taught to sing about Jesus in English. Their sense of joy and connection was palpable. This, they believed, was Jesus without borders.

An outsider might see this moment differently, not as a moment of connection but as an example of neocolonialism. After all, we were in a village where Bible school and English were being taught, and Western-style clothes dispensed. Yet what was happening at Koma Ganza was not just a case of American Christians showing up to educate and Christianize "the natives." In the richly populated terrain of global development work, "partnership" was the watchword, and the many different partners in this village school each had their own investments. Ramadan and the school's teachers were neither missionary objects nor colonialist collaborators. They were *all* Christian missionaries, in a part of the world where Christianity had been part of the landscape for hundreds of years. These Sudanese believers were actors and agents whose Christianity and good luck linked them to the power and resources of an American church. In a region where decades of violent conflict had targeted civilians and devastated livelihoods for many people, they were also political players, where being a Christian might well mean having a history with the SPLA, and where walking from village to village meant passing through the haunting relics of a war whose legacy was still far from certain. Many of the people we met asked for charity, but the people that Dick and his group were closest to, Ramadan and John Philip, were allies. They expected, and received, a kind of solidarity.

A few years after that trip to Sudan, Dick Robinson met his second wife, Ruth Hidalgo de Robinson, a Peruvian teacher and missionary. (Peggy had died of cancer in the 1990s.) Ruth and Dick then formed Riverwind, which works with a team of indigenous people to carry out evangelism and humanitarian assistance in communities along the Ucayali River in Peru. Dick and Ruth plant churches, dig wells, and host short-term medical teams. It is an arduous ministry, involving dangerous eighteen-hour trips upriver in a canoe, visiting remote villages, living for weeks with relatively little in the way of food or amenities. But Dick has never minded anything arduous. Dick and Ruth are supported as full-time missionaries by the contributions of four churches, including Elmbrook.

Looking back on our trip to south Sudan, Dick wrote to me that "my thoughts were never to make them like us." The idea was "simply to be with them—Sudanese, Chinese, Indians, Peruvians—as fellow members of the Christian community." He found that his identity and political views were changing. "I also view America, or the United States, as simply the latest empire . . . I no longer view myself as an uncritical citizen of any particular country. I prefer to believe that I am a member of the Kingdom of God."

In 2008, Ramadan Chan Liol was elected secretary general of the Sudan Council of Churches. As the January 2011 referendum on South Sudan's independence neared, he traveled around the world to urge international institutions to make sure that the government in Khartoum did not interfere with the promised vote. At a meeting at the Council of Foreign Relations in New York in October 2010, religious leaders, including Ramadan, asked for vigilant monitoring and protection of the borders of what would soon become independent South Sudan. When the independence vote was complete in 2011, he advocated for peace among the South Sudanese.[21]

In the new country of South Sudan, the situation deteriorated quickly and disastrously. After an initial period of celebration, the political tensions between the leaders of South Sudan's two major factions began to split the country apart. Soon there was a new civil war, in which tens of thousands of people were killed and more than two million people were internally displaced in factional fighting that targeted civilians for rape and murder. Hundreds of thousands of people packed into UN-run refugee camps. In 2014, a massive humanitarian response averted a severe famine. Even so, one in four children below the age of five was acutely malnourished.[22]

The civil war and falling oil prices sent South Sudan's already weak economy into a tailspin. The country received billions of dollars in aid from 2011 to 2016, including more than $1 billion from the United States alone.[23] Most of the money went to NGOs, not to the government itself. South Sudan's Undersecretary for Humanitarian Affairs complained in 2015 that "we don't have information on the NGOs that are receiving the funding from the American government and how they are utilizing this funding in the country, for which type of project: is it food, health, water, education?"[24] In his frustration, this official was expressing a view that scholars of development have articulated in a different way—that in some sense the NGOs had become a force unto themselves, doing development or relief or medical care only where and when they saw fit.

Then again, transparency can sometimes seem like a technicality. By May of 2015, as gunmen torched towns, aid workers were abducted, and the killing of civilians escalated, World Vision, Doctors without Borders, and a number of other aid agencies suspended operations.[25] Facing intense pressure from Western governments, the two South Sudanese factions signed a peace agreement, but it soon fell apart. By the summer of 2016, there was fighting in the streets of Juba, the capital, as hundreds more people were killed. The US embassy evacuated all non-essential personnel, and a number of countries—Germany, the United Kingdom, India, and Uganda among them—evacuated all their citizens from Juba.

"You are the hope of Sudan," Dick had told the children in Koma Ganza. But hope for their future was rapidly being undermined, if not destroyed. Compassion for South Sudanese did not go far enough. Neither the international humanitarian system nor the networks of transnational Christian solidarity could heal the wounds that were ravaging the country. And now, just a few years after South Sudan had received its longed-for independence, the prospects for a peaceful and democratic society seemed as far away as ever.

14

"The Power of a Weeping Christian"

SEXUAL POLITICS AND HIV/AIDS IN AFRICA

IN DECEMBER OF 2009, Pastor Rick Warren released an unusual video, which he described as a "letter to Ugandan pastors." Warren is the pastor of Saddleback Church, a megachurch in Orange County, California, which is affiliated with the Southern Baptist Convention. He is also the author of the monumental bestseller, *A Purpose-Driven Life*, which has sold tens of millions of copies and been translated into at least eighty-five languages. Warren was deeply involved in both economic development programs and HIV/AIDS prevention and treatment in Africa, which is what had led him to this moment.

In his video letter, Warren was—uncomfortably and carefully—negotiating his response to a bill then pending in Uganda's Parliament. The Anti-Homosexuality Bill called for the death penalty for any Ugandan convicted of "aggravated homosexuality," meaning homosexuals who "recruited" young people or HIV-positive people who had homosexual sex. Lesser sentences, such as life imprisonment, could be meted out for merely engaging in homosexual activity. Warren had connections to a number of anti-homosexual activists in Uganda, but particularly to a minister named Martin Ssempa.

Sitting in a warmly lit office (figure 14.1), with an image of the globe to his right, Warren calmly began his message by saying that it was not his role to interfere in the politics of other nations.[1] But he needed to correct the "lies and errors and false reports" that had associated him with a law that "I had nothing to do with, I completely oppose, and that I vigorously condemn." A few days earlier Warren had issued a press release stating that "Martin Ssempa does not represent me; my wife, Kay; Saddleback Church; nor the Global PEACE Plan strategy."[2]

That Warren had to make this statement was itself remarkable. Warren was a pastor who, despite his clearly conservative views on homosexuality, had developed a reputation

FIGURE 14.1 Rick Warren's video letter to Ugandan pastors, December 9, 2009. Source: Available at https://www.youtube.com/watch?v=1jmGu9o4fDE&list=TL887eiospWPU

as a compassionate activist in the fight against HIV/AIDS. His church held a yearly HIV/AIDS Global Summit, which attracted thousands of participants from all over the world. And he did extensive work in Africa, not only on HIV/AIDS but also on issues of poverty and economic development, through his PEACE project. This had made him the darling of many commentators, both secular and religious. It is probably also what had motivated President Obama to invite him to offer a prayer at the president's inauguration eleven months earlier.[3] Yet now those connections had embroiled Warren in one of the most unsettling controversies of his career.

Warren advised Uganda's pastors to stand up against this "terrible" law. While it was not his role to be political, Warren said, "It *is* my role to speak out on moral issues. It is my role to shepherd other pastors who look to me for guidance." In reality, Ugandans had not particularly looked to him for guidance on this issue, and Warren pretended not to know that a number of important Ugandan pastors had supported the law. Instead Warren acted as though his allies just needed a little help in standing up for what they knew was right. He called the law "unchristian."

A few weeks after Warren posted his commentary, Ssempa, who pastored Makerere Community Church in Kampala, posted his own furious video response. Ssempa was one of Uganda's best known pastors and had for years fought to make support for sexual abstinence into the primary plank of HIV/AIDS education in Uganda. He had strong US ties, including a degree from Philadelphia Bible University. He ran abstinence programs funded by the US government, and dozens of US churches and pastors worked with or funded him.[4] Ssempa had attended the first two HIV/AIDS summits at Saddleback, preaching the virtues of abstinence.[5]

Now, he appeared in this video with the flag of Uganda behind him and a "Fight HIV/AIDS" button affixed to his shirt. He pronounced himself angry and confused by

Warren's betrayal. In his twenty-minute diatribe, Ssempa said that the bill's provisions had been greatly misrepresented, that the death penalty was only for "aggravated" homosexuality, which meant primarily those who had sex with underage boys. This was about protecting *children*, Ssempa said, visibly frustrated.

Ssempa (along with his allies who had also signed the letter) said that he had once believed that Warren had the courage to stand on the word of God, but apparently Warren had bowed to pressure from "homosexual champions." As a Christian and an African, Ssempa would not be so weak.

> Our fathers have handed down a rich heritage where they have taught us that homosexuality is against the laws of our fathers. How can we turn around and betray five thousand years of history because some pastor in America or Barack Obama is telling us to bend over to homosexuality? *We cannot.*[6]

For Ssempa the bill was a matter of African pride, God's word, and America's global power. It was also a grave threat to LGBTQ Ugandans. The bill divided evangelical Christians, most obviously separating moderate US evangelicals such as Warren from the conservative Ugandans who claimed to speak for African Christianity. At the same time, Ugandan Christians were also divided among themselves.

When the bill was introduced, many people detected the malign influence of right-wing American evangelicals. Certainly gay rights were very much on the agenda in the United States, and in 2008, the vice president of the NAE, Richard Cizik, had learned the limits of dissent. He was forced to resign after making comments in a radio interview that indicated his support for civil unions for gay couples as well as his commitment to fighting climate change. That put Cizik's views very much in line with many younger evangelicals, on both issues, but the mainstream of evangelicalism was firmly set against gay marriage. Dissent cost Cizik his job.[7]

Observers noted, correctly, that for years American evangelicals had been holding anti-gay workshops and conferences in Uganda, and many blamed the anti-gay environment there on US influence. Certainly there was some evidence for that. Lou Engle, the right-wing Pentecostal pastor of the International House of Prayer, preached a strong anti-gay message in Uganda. Engle was known for his promotion of spiritual warfare, including casting out demons that he believed caused homosexuality. (Engle was deeply influenced by the writings of missionary theorist C. Peter Wagner, who had begun the Signs and Wonders course at Fuller Theological Seminary.) In 2008 Engle had held a series of large rallies in California in support of Proposition 8, to outlaw gay marriage.[8]

Two years later, with the anti-homosexuality bill under consideration, Engle took his act to Uganda. Engle claimed that he had not known about the law before he scheduled a stadium rally and that he did not support Uganda's bill as written. But the rally itself—which organizers said was to focus on homosexuality, witchcraft, corruption, and violence—was far less circumspect about the law. A Ugandan pastor prayed for the bill to pass, and a government official claimed it would pass without debate. Engle was careful to avoid declaring his support, instead expressing his desire to "join with the church of Uganda to encourage you . . . who are showing courage to take a stand for righteousness in the earth."[9] In 2009 and 2010, Engle was only one of a number of American pastors who spoke enthusiastically to Ugandans about the importance of their righteous stance. Indeed, at first it can seem hard to argue with the summary offered by National Public Radio: "US Exports Cultural War to Uganda."[10]

But this analysis misses a great deal. Americans were indeed crossing borders and talking about the dangers of homosexuality, but no one injected religious ideas into Ugandans.[11] Americans' interventions were part of long-standing evangelical networks in which Ugandans were both influenced and influential. Globalizing evangelicalism enabled the transnational flow of people, money, and ideas in many directions.

Underlying the Anti-Homosexuality Bill was a major schism in the global Anglican Communion (which includes the Episcopal Church in the United States) over the ordination of LGBTQ people. The debate over the bill was also shaped by American evangelicals' support for a dramatic increase in US funding for HIV/AIDS prevention and treatment in Africa generally. Finally, HIV/AIDS prevention, treatment, and activism in Uganda were funded massively by the United States, the UN, and others, with money going to both conservative faith-based groups and more liberal secular ones. In the process, Ugandan and American evangelicals developed meaningful alliances. But the infusion of money also led to acute resentment of NGOs and the liberal and individualist values they were said to impart. Anger at NGOs was a driving force behind the Anti-Homosexuality Bill.

In 2014, Uganda's population was 85 percent Christian.[12] While most of those were Catholic or Anglican, one-third of the population claimed to have been "born again." New churches were everywhere in the early part of the twenty-first century, one journalist explained, "springing up in warehouses, shacks, school auditoriums, and village clearings." Two of the country's four TV stations were devoted solely to religious programming, and "quotations from scripture [had] become part of everyday speech."[13] Much of this television programming was Pentecostal, often broadcast from the United States but including preachers from around the world. Pentecostal churches drew increasing numbers of adherents, particularly young people.[14]

The Anglican Church, however, was the largest Protestant denomination in Uganda, the result of more than a century of missions. With Anglicanism—like the rest of Christianity—shifting ever southward, East African churches had become central to the global Anglican Communion.

The Anglican Church in Uganda operated at the intersection of two transformations. The first was the East African Revival, which had begun sweeping through the region in the 1930s. The second was the emergence, in the 1990s, of the Anglican Church of Uganda as a center of transnational Anglican conservatism. Ugandans and other African Christians would play an outsized role in one of the great religious dramas of the late twentieth and early twenty-first centuries, when the world's largest Protestant denomination began to unravel over divergent attitudes toward homosexuality.

The East African Revival had roiled Uganda, Rwanda, Kenya, Burundi, and Tanganyika, in one form or another, until the 1970s (figure 14.2). During the revival, hundreds of thousands of people converted to Christianity. At the same time, many Christians, including a number of missionaries and pastors, became convinced of their failure to be good, true Christians.[15] Although it had Western influences—American missionaries, British Anglican bishops, the Scofield Reference Bible, and the British-based transnational Keswick revival of the 1870s—the revival was a distinctly African phenomenon: "an unlikely blend of Wesleyan-Anglican theology, Pentecostal fervor, and African passion."[16]

From the 1930s on, the revival's advocates traveled far and wide, usually on bicycles, to testify and preach. They crossed borders as missionaries and as preachers, and they sent each other long, detailed letters recounting their life stories, which were often published in missionary newsletters or otherwise circulated in the United Kingdom and beyond. Many of the converts were Anglicans, or went on to join Anglican churches, but the revival crossed denominations as freely as it traversed borders.

The revivalists, or *balokole,* were radically enthusiastic about their salvation, and in its early days the movement was also intensely apocalyptic, as believers had dreams and visions of Jesus's imminent return. The revival also focused intensively on the need for

FIGURE 14.2 East African Revival meeting at Gahini, Rwanda, 1952. Courtesy of Cambridge Centre for Christianity Worldwide, JECP/A51.

personal repentance as a requisite for cleansing past sin. Once converted, revivalists danced and prayed in all-night meetings and testified before other believers about their sins. Wives started confessing their infidelities; workers began enumerating the items, large and small, they had stolen; and men began repenting of their drunkenness. Not surprisingly, those whose names were called out as partners in the sin—the lovers, the drinking buddies—were not inclined to appreciate such confessions.

Many African Christians and a good number of the region's missionaries found the balokole to be undisciplined in their behavior and their theology. The non-revivalists were offended, at least at first, by "the hysterical weeping, the all night-prayer and singing meetings, the closer black-white relations [among revivalists]."[17]

Women's behavior was a particular problem. In many of the diverse cultures of East Africa, decorum and respect for hierarchies were highly valued. Women in particular were expected to be modest, often veiled, generally quiet and respectful. Now women revivalists were taking off their veils or traditional clothing; they were speaking about their faith and confessing their sins in public.[18]

Tribal chiefs and colonial police officials also found themselves called out by revivalists for their abuses. Neither the upholders of colonial power, nor local chiefs, nor, ultimately, nationalist intellectuals responded positively to such denunciations. If these were shocking behaviors, however, the revivalists intended to shock. The balokole were all too willing to challenge or ignore state power.

The most disquieting of the revivalists' effusions were the public confessions of sexual misconduct. "'Confession is salvation' . . . is their theme," read one missionary's horrified 1944 report. "Things I have never known or heard of are being broadcast—appalling iniquity." One convert in Buganda wrote to several female missionaries saying that he had been tempted, before his conversion, to try to commit adultery with them. Indeed, one Anglican bishop angrily commented that the balokole spent so much time confessing adultery that they were giving other people ideas.[19] This fascination with the details of sexual sin would return to Ugandan churches decades later, in debates over homosexuality.

After Uganda's independence in 1962, the Anglicans began to appoint African bishops. By that point, the revival had become a broadly accepted part of Uganda's Anglican church, and people influenced by it would take up major positions in the Anglican Communion, including as bishops. In the early 1970s, a number of these bishops risked their lives to challenge the murderous behavior of Idi Amin, the dictator who had taken over Uganda's government after a military coup in 1971. One of those bishops was murdered by Amin in 1973; another, the intrepid evangelist Festo Kivengere, barely escaped with his life. Kivengere later became renowned for his testament to Christian forgiveness, *I Love Idi Amin.*[20]

By the time Kivengere escaped Uganda in 1973, he was already a well-known figure in the transnational evangelical circuit. He had translated for Billy Graham in his 1960 "Safari for Souls" in eastern Africa. The next year Kivengere was a featured speaker on the topic of "revival" at InterVarsity's 1961 Urbana conference, where there was at least a general awareness of the East African Revival.[21] East Africa was already beginning to stand as an idealized symbol of religious zeal for Americans. Kivengere went on to found the East African arm of African Enterprise, and he and South African Michael Cassidy—the liberal opponent of apartheid—often traveled together preaching in the United States, Egypt, other parts of Africa, and Europe (figure 14.3).[22]

Three years after Kivengere spoke at Urbana, the Catholic church brought attention to another aspect of Uganda's Christian history, when in 1964 it canonized the Uganda Martyrs. The martyrs were a group of Christian boys, pages for the Buganda king, who were burned alive on the king's orders in 1886. They were killed, according to accounts at the time, both for their secret conversions to Christianity and for refusing to submit to the king's sexual demands. Every year on June 3, Ugandans commemorate the boys on Martyrs' Day. One Ugandan newspaper estimated that in 2001 almost five hundred thousand pilgrims from across East Africa came to Uganda for the celebration of the martyrs' resoluteness. Africans who celebrated Martyrs' Day were compelled by both aspects of the story: Christians martyred for their faith and young boys refusing homosexuality. Martyrs' Day was part of Uganda's national narrative, integral to an embrace of the ideal of Christian bravery against sexual predation.[23]

A major conflict within the Anglican Community broke out at the 1998 Lambeth conference, the once-a-decade meeting of Anglican bishops, where a resolution was passed that, among other things, opposed the ordination of gay priests or bishops. Homosexuality had been a divisive issue in the US Episcopal Church for almost a decade. In the early

FIGURE 14.3 Festo Kivengere and Michael Cassidy, by kind permission of African Enterprise.

1990s, some American bishops had begun quietly ordaining openly gay men as priests, and some priests had begun to preside over services that blessed lesbian and gay relationships. In 1995, a group of conservative Episcopal bishops in the United States brought heresy charges against another bishop for ordaining a non-celibate gay man. After the case was dismissed, conservative Episcopalians began pushing the larger Anglican Communion to take a stance against the liberal practices of the US church.[24]

At the 1998 Lambeth meeting, the dissident Americans worked closely with Anglican bishops from the global South, many of them veterans of the decades-long revival in East Africa, to craft a strongly conservative statement about homosexuality in the church. A majority of the Lambeth attendees were from outside the United States and Europe, and African bishops would be a major force.[25] For well over a year before the meeting, a group of conservative Anglicans had been meeting regularly—in Dallas, Kuala Lumpur, and Kampala—to clarify doctrine and craft strategies.[26] Americans were the primary organizers, but they had strong support, particularly from parts of Africa and Asia. The sexuality resolution at Lambeth was only one of many resolutions on a broad range of topics that these gatherings produced, but it was one of the most anticipated.

Nine days before the meeting, one liberal American gave an interview to a journalist that previewed the confrontation. He announced that the Africans were "superstitious, fundamentalist Christians" who had just "moved out of animism . . . [and have] yet to face the intellectual revolution of Copernicus and Einstein that we've had to face in the developing world; that is just not on their radar screen."[27] This did not go over well. Or, rather, it went over quite well, in that the conservative bishops made sure the interview circulated widely. Not surprisingly, delegates from the global South were furious. One Ugandan bishop fumed that African bishops had the same training as Westerners, "[b]ut they are saying we have not gone very far, we are still primitive, untrained, because we supported orthodox teaching."[28]

The resolution put before the meeting was unequivocal. It defined marriage as "between a man and a woman in lifelong union," rejected "homosexual practice as incompatible with Scripture," and opposed the ordination of "those involved in same-gender unions" (that is, non-celibate LGBTQ people). One liberal glimmer was a call for Anglican clergy to offer pastoral care and to welcome persons of homosexual orientation into the church. The resolution passed by an overwhelming majority.[29]

Many opponents of the resolution tended to see the vote as one in which American conservatives mobilized, and in some sense manipulated, the Africans to sign on to an agenda that had not been of particular interest to them before. But this was far from the full story. It was clear, after all, that the African Anglicans were not beholden to their American colleagues. During that same meeting, Africans almost uniformly voted for Jubilee 2000, the liberal plank that called for complete debt forgiveness for nations in the global South, quietly ignoring the microfinance program proposed by the market-oriented neoliberals from the United States.[30]

Indeed, global South delegates were newly outspoken at Lambeth. And no one could miss the racial divide in the Communion. As one journalist described it, when the vote on the homosexuality resolution was called, those in favor of the conservative resolution displayed a "multiracial sea of hands": black, Asian, and white. Then, when the call came for the other side to vote, it became obvious who supported a liberal view of homosexuality. As one Ugandan bishop later put it—"all of them, we saw their white hands up!"[31]

In reality, the demographics were more complicated. There were, and are, black Anglicans in Africa who strongly support gay rights. Dr. Kapya Kaoma, for example, a Zambian cleric who has published widely on LGBTQ rights, was one of the first people to analyze the ties between conservative American evangelicals and conservative Christians in Uganda.[32] Still, the Lambeth vote was a visible sign of changing racial and sexual politics within global Christianity. It put liberals who supported LGBTQ rights and saw themselves as anti-colonial and anti-racist in a very uncomfortable position. Now conservatives could convincingly argue that *they* were on the cutting edge of Anglicanism's multiracial future. Conservative Episcopalians in the United States would garner even more credibility when a number of congregations, frustrated by the fact that the US church was not changing its liberal ways, began to withdraw from the Episcopal Church and place themselves under the umbrella of Anglican bishops in Rwanda and Uganda.[33]

In 2000, World Vision International wanted to begin supporting AIDS treatment in Africa, but was uncertain how its supporters would respond. So, the organization surveyed its donors. The results were "devastating." When asked if they would be willing to give to a Christian organization to help children who had lost both parents to AIDS, only 7 percent said they would definitely help, while more than 50 percent said they probably would not. "It was stark and clear," one staff member said, "that our donors felt that AIDS sufferers had somehow deserved their fate."[34]

Yet within two years everything would change. In February 2002, Franklin Graham organized a global conference on HIV/AIDS. Graham had staked out a highly conservative position on any number of political and cultural issues. But he was also the director of an aid agency, Samaritan's Purse. That organization was far smaller than World Vision, but it had evangelists and aid workers serving at missionary hospitals in Africa, and they had for years been reporting increasing numbers of patients with HIV/AIDS. In his memoir, Graham acknowledged that most evangelical Christians, himself included, had wanted nothing to do with AIDS. But now the disease was devastating the continent, and Christians had a moral obligation to respond.

Graham made clear that he believed that sex outside of "the parameters that God gave" was what caused HIV/AIDS.[35] But, he said, "I as a Christian have to ask: What would Jesus do? . . . If Jesus were on this Earth today—walking as he did 2,000 years ago—I think you would find him on the forefront of this issue."[36] This kind of argument had purchase among evangelicals, and Franklin Graham carried all the authority of his father's name, his well-known conservatism, and his humanitarian record.

Later that year, Graham joined rock singer Bono and right-wing Senator Jesse Helms (R-NC) in asking President Bush to increase HIV/AIDS funding for Africa.

The president's response came in his January 2003 State of the Union address, when he announced the President's Emergency Fund for AIDS Relief (PEPFAR).[37] PEPFAR committed $15 billion over five years for prevention and treatment of HIV/AIDS in Africa and the Caribbean. (The legislation also provided funds for malaria and tuberculosis.) On a trip to Uganda later that year, the president described it as a "great mission of rescue." Bush explained that he believed that "God has called us into action . . . We are a great nation, we're a wealthy nation. We have a responsibility to help a neighbor in need, a brother and sister in crisis."[38] Many health-care advocates and aid agencies cheered Bush's announcement.[39]

It was around this time that Rick Warren's wife, Kay, had an epiphany. As she and Rick tell the story, Ms. Warren was flipping through a magazine one day in 2002 when she saw an article about AIDS. She read it and learned that there were twelve million children in Africa who were orphaned because of the disease. She likened her revelation to the Apostle Paul's: "It was as if I fell off the donkey on the Damascus road because I had no clue. I didn't know one single orphan." This haunted her, she later said. "From there I began to learn and study. God just broke my heart. He just wiped me out. There is not a day that goes by that I don't cry over what I've learned and what I've seen."[40] Kay Warren's imagery speaks not only of a broken heart but of a heart broken intentionally by God, who wanted her to see and to feel. Without God's intervention, Ms. Warren believed, she might never have discovered her "heart" for orphans or found the courage to act on HIV/AIDS.

In 2004, Kay Warren founded Saddleback's "HIV & AIDS Initiative." Saddleback held its first global AIDS summit at the church the next year; 1,600 people attended. Rev. Martin Ssempa, still very much in the Warrens' good graces, delivered a keynote address on Uganda's fight against AIDS and also led a breakout session on abstinence-only education. The keynote "had the audience on the edge of its seats," according to Saddelback's public relations agency.[41]

The Saddleback HIV/AIDS summit became an annual tradition, as political leaders and advocates gathered on or around World AIDS Day (December 1). In 2006, Senators Sam Brownback and Barack Obama both spoke, followed by Franklin Graham.[42] Rev. Ssempa returned, and by this time he had become a warmly welcomed colleague and ally. Kay Warren spoke to him from the stage, saying "You are my brother, Martin, and I love you."[43] The Warrens were also joined by Bill and Lynne Hybels of the Willow Creek Community Church, one of the country's largest churches, which also has an extensive national network of loosely affiliated congregations. Like Kay Warren, Lynn Hybels would also make HIV/AIDS a signature issue.

Both women later described how they had responded with tears when they first learned about the devastation of AIDS. The two pastors' wives "know the power of a weeping Christian," wrote *Christianity Today*. Indeed. In evangelical culture, weeping can be sign of conviction and humanity. Evangelicals often point out that "Jesus wept" (John 11:35) is the shortest verse in the Bible but one of the most powerful. "We should weep over our inaction," *Christianity Today* intoned, "our inappropriately judgmental attitudes, and our reluctance to work with people who don't look or behave like we do."[44]

American evangelicals began to pay attention to HIV/AIDS just as the disease was reaching pandemic proportions in Africa. In 2004, there were 23.6 million people living with HIV in sub-Saharan Africa, and 1.9 million deaths due to AIDS.[45] Most transmissions were through heterosexual sex, although mother-to-child transmission was also significant. PEPFAR provided an infusion of funds at a crucial moment in the global fight. The increase in US support was dramatic. In fiscal year 2002, the US government spent $287 million on AIDS relief in Africa; by 2006, the budget was $1.3 billion.[46]

That part of the funding devoted to AIDS treatment was slow to get off the ground but it would eventually provide life-saving retroviral medications.[47] The more controversial part of PEPFAR was the limits it placed on HIV-prevention programs. The law mandated that at least one-third of all prevention funds had to be used to promote sexual abstinence. That seemed like a shockingly high percentage to many AIDS activists and educators. But the numbers were actually even more skewed. In 2006, only 50 percent of prevention funding was spent on stopping sexual transmission; other funds focused on things like encouraging the use of clean needles and protective masks in hospitals. This meant that in order to meet the requirement that one-third of *all* prevention funds be spent on abstinence education, PEPFAR had to ensure that 66 percent of programs that dealt with sexual transmission were centrally organized around abstinence.[48] In addition, PEPFAR included a provision against funding organizations that did not have a policy explicitly opposing prostitution and sex trafficking. That meant that groups that reached out to sex workers were unlikely to get funding.[49]

In setting this demand, Congress and the Bush administration had constructed their argument around the dramatic success of Uganda in lowering the rate of HIV/AIDS transmission, and around a particular misreading of that success. In the 1980s, Ugandan HIV rates had been the highest in the world, with 15 percent of the population affected. The government of President Yoweri Museveni launched a massive HIV/AIDS prevention program that was designed to educate people about the disease and encourage changes in behavior that would help limit the spread of HIV.[50] The program would later be described as "ABC"—Abstinence, Be Faithful, Use a Condom. Both of the first two components were controversial: urging men to limit or stop extramarital sex was difficult in a country where it was common, even expected, for men to have multiple sexual partners. These were usually long-term relationships, although short-term sexual encounters were not unusual.

Uganda's program was multifaceted and community-based. It recruited churches and mosques to provide information about HIV/AIDS, offered voluntary counseling and testing for HIV, campaigned to raise awareness and end the stigma of the disease, devised programs to empower young people and women to take greater control of their bodies and lives, and distributed condoms. One of the key components of the program was its focus on face-to-face education and counseling, in which young people, teachers, people with AIDS, and others were hired to engage in personal discussions with members of their community. Men began to have fewer partners; more people delayed the onset of sexual activity; and many more people used condoms.[51]

Uganda, then, had become the global success story for HIV/AIDS prevention, but it was not because of a strict focus on abstinence. In the late 1990s, however, Ugandan officials began to downplay this history—especially after First Lady Janet Museveni converted to evangelical Christianity in 1999. In 2002, Ms. Museveni flew to Washington to lobby Congress, saying that its funding for HIV/AIDS prevention should support a focus on abstinence-only education.[52] She found a welcoming audience.

Once PEPFAR funds were fully available, Uganda was awash in AIDS money, which increased the availability of testing, retroviral treatments, and general medical support. There had been money available for HIV/AIDS programs for a number of years, through the Global Fund to Fight AIDS, Tuberculosis, and Malaria, as well as other governments, foundations, and research institutes, but PEPFAR changed the scope dramatically. In the first five years of PEPFAR, Uganda received $285 million from the United States alone. That money rarely went to the government of Uganda directly; it mostly went to NGOs for specific projects.[53]

The money also prompted a surge of new NGOs, both local and international, whose work and perceived agendas reshaped local discourses on sex and power. By 2004, the Ugandan AIDS Commission estimated that there were approximately two thousand NGOs working on HIV/AIDS in Uganda. Many of these were transnational organizations that either launched or increased their work in Uganda after PEPFAR. The US-based group True Love Waits, for example, had been working on abstinence education in Uganda since the mid-1990s, but expanded its curriculum.[54] In other cases, national or local churches, mosques, or non-profit organizations launched new programs. One analyst calls these types of small groups "invisible NGOs": dispersed, hard to monitor, and understudied by scholars.[55]

Long before PEPFAR, "NGO" was a category well known to ordinary Ugandans, especially those in the cities. And people had complex feelings about the organizations, many of which had real economic and political power. The largest international groups often had seemingly unlimited access to funds. They offered services that people often desperately needed, and they could be a source of coveted jobs. They also often promoted distinctive ideologies: individualistic notions of personhood, demands for accountability, and promises that "entrepreneurship" or "micro-loans" or hard work would forge routes out of deepening poverty and insecurity.[56] But in an impoverished country run by an increasingly dictatorial leader, the path of "personal responsibility" failed to allieviate most people's dire circumstances. In that case, NGOs could seem a bit like snake oil salesmen. What they were selling, it appeared, was false hope.

Given PEPFAR's focus on abstinence, conservative Christian organizations took a leading part in the new NGO-fueled economy. First Lady Janet Museveni had an organization, Uganda Youth Forum; there was also the Glory of Virginity Movement and the Family Life Network. Martin Ssempa started the Campus Alliance to Wipe Out AIDS.[57] Many religious groups, especially conservative evangelical churches, expanded their work with young people.

Many of these programs taught similar lessons: young people need to make good choices. Pre-marital sex is a bad choice, both because it is sinful and because of the risks it poses. These messages might be transmitted via study guides or Christian pop music, sermons or individual counseling. Participants in a program might write and perform their own skits, in the time-honored way of church youth groups. They might wear T-shirts or hold signs for a pro-abstinence demonstration. Sometimes abstinence supporters bought ads on billboards. "Until recently, all HIV-related billboards were about condoms," Rev. Ssempa told the BBC in 2005. "Those of us calling for abstinence and faithfulness need billboards too."[58]

The anthropologist Lydia Boyd spent several years studying the HIV/AIDS prevention programs organized by the dynamic pastor of University Hill Church in Kampala. University Hill is an independent evangelical church attended by a number of students from nearby Makerere University. Boyd describes the complicated ways that students at the church negotiated abstinence messages. On the one hand, they often embraced the idea of abstinence for themselves and others as an ideal. They believed that sex outside of marriage was not what God wanted for them. At the same time, young people wanted to establish their sexuality as something that they could control, separate from the desires of their families about who or when they should marry. They saw abstinence as a way to negotiate competing demands around them—the push from families to get married early; their own desire to get an education; the moral dangers of a large and impersonal city, where sexual temptation was everywhere. Embracing sexual purity was not a matter of returning to "traditional" values. Instead, the self-discipline that young Christians cultivated through abstinence was "a rational, quite modern calculation through which time, energy, and money were conserved in pursuit of other life goals [like studying for a career]."[59]

For most of the youth at the church, like many young people in Uganda, the threat of dying from HIV/AIDS was not the primary motivation for abstinence. There were so many other dangers, from malaria to extreme poverty, that scare tactics about AIDS were not particularly compelling. Instead, abstinence was believed to cultivate focus and drive, to teach a kind of "intentionality" about life choices. "There are two pieces," one young man told Boyd. "When you give yourself away, you give something more than your body. You give your dreams."[60] The abstinence message was heard, but young people embraced it for a variety of reasons that were often pragmatic, economic, and organized around ideas of success, working alongside the religious injunctions.

PEPFAR had dramatically increased funding for abstinence education, but Christian conservatives in Uganda were not satisfied. In 2005, Ssempa testified as an expert on HIV/AIDS before the US House Committee on International Relations. Ssempa argued, as he often did, that HIV/AIDS was the result of sexual misbehavior: "I mince no words with you. The reasons why other Africans and Ugandans are dying is because of sexual promiscuity. That is what is killing us." The problem, he insisted, was that the US Agency for International Development (USAID) and the Centers for Disease Control were skeptical of abstinence-and-fidelity programs. "USAID's philosophy is condoms for everyone, even though many of us in Uganda feel that this approach actually encourages promiscuity, the very behavior that is killing us."[61] This revisionist account resonated perfectly with the image that Ssempa was cultivating of an anti-imperialist fighting off international bureauacries and their non-African values.

As HIV/AIDS programs were growing, the environment in Uganda had grown increasingly hostile toward LGBTQ people. In October 2004, for example, the Ugandan Broadcasting Council fined a radio station 1.8 million shillings (more than $1,000) for hosting a lesbian and two gay men on a talk show, where they protested against discrimination and called for repeal of sodomy laws. Two years later, the newspaper *Red Pepper* published the first names and professions of forty-five gay men. Later, it would sink to publishing last names and addresses.[62]

Rev. Ssempa began to focus more consistently on the issue of homosexuality. In 2007, he led hundreds of people through the streets in Kampala to demand arrest and punishment of homosexuals (or, as Ssempa described gay activists, "homosexual promoters").[63] Ssempa was already known for his controversial activities, including burning condoms. He was also infamous for showing pornography during his sermons in order to shock and appall his Christian audiences. In 2010, he held a press conference in which he showed a scatological scene from a gay porn movie, describing the scene with disgust and horror.[64]

Ssempa presented homosexuality as a foreign import, taught to Ugandans by outsiders and then promoted by gay people within. This fed a narrative about recruitment into homosexuality—frequently expressed as anxiety that young boys (and to a lesser degree, girls) might be subject to influence by older homosexuals or coercion by foreign forces. Urban legends circulated in which boys were recruited into homosexuality by wealthy foreigners, including NGO workers.[65] In 2002, there had been an outcry about a UNICEF educational document for teenagers that stated that homosexuality was "natural." Pastor Michael Kyazze spoke out, saying "The homos use UNICEF—this is true! To attempt to colonize Uganda." David Bahati, who was secretary of the Ugandan branch of the US-based evangelical network the Family, talked often about gay recruitment, claiming that homosexuals recruited children by giving them laptops and iPads. In 2009, Bahati, by then a legislator, introduced the Anti-Homosexuality Bill.[66]

The run-up to the 2008 Lambeth meeting and the 2009 Gay Agenda conference in Kampala together illustrated how Ugandan evangelicals' stances on homosexuality evolved in a transnational context, while also rebutting the common misperception that the 2009 Anti-Homosexuality Bill was almost entirely the result of foreign interference.

In spring of 2008, Anglican bishops began to prepare for the next Lambeth convention. Much had changed in the previous decade. A month before the meeting, a group of conservative bishops from around the world—a plurality of them from Africa—met in Jerusalem.[67] The meeting brought together two very different types of Anglican conservatives—the more liturgical and tradition-oriented "High Church" Anglo-Catholic wing and the Evangelical "Low Church" wing, both of whom wanted to affirm a vision of Anglican orthodoxy that asserted Biblical authority, particularly but not only on issues of gender and sexuality. At the end of the gathering, the group issued the Jerusalem Declaration, which included the statement that a "false gospel" was circulating in the church, one that "promotes a variety of sexual preferences and immoral behaviour as a universal human right."[68] The meeting created a new group, the Fellowship of Confessing Anglicans. This was not intended as an alternative to the Anglican Communion—the plan was to own the Communion, not give it away—but it provided a space for conservatives to connect.

The Church of Uganda had already announced that it would be joining Nigeria and Rwanda in boycotting the Lambeth meeting.[69] Rick Warren spoke out in favor of the boycott. Warren was a Southern Baptist, but he had developed a number of ties with conservative Anglican bishops in Uganda, Kenya, and Rwanda, and felt no compunction about opining on Anglican politics. Declaring homosexuality an unnatural way of life, he stated that "the Church of England is wrong, and I support the Church of Uganda."[70] Most Anglican leaders did go to Lambeth in 2008, but tensions ran high. Vinay Samuel—the widely admired head of the Oxford Centre for Mission Studies and a leading liberal on issues of poverty and respectful relations with Muslims—accused the leader of the communion, Rowan Williams, of a "colonial mindset."[71]

Then in 2009, American evangelist Scott Lively arrived in Uganda for the Gay Agenda conference. Lively was a far-Right activist, head of Abiding Truth ministries, and author of *The Pink Swastika,* which blamed the Holocaust on gay men. Lively had no significant following in the United States, but his trip to Uganda earned him international recognition. The conference was hosted by Ssempa and Stephen Langa of the Family Life Network. The three speakers were Lively and two evangelical advocates of "conversion therapy." The audience numbered in the thousands. For three days, they listened to presentations on the "homosexual agenda."[72] With Ssempa's support, Lively also managed to get an invitation to speak to Uganda's Parliament, where he held forth for several hours. Lively later described the visit as a "nuclear bomb against the gay agenda in Uganda."[73]

Scholars and journalists reported this conference as the quintessential example of the influence of the US Christian Right on Ugandan faith and politics. American evangelicals, observers explained, were "exploiting popular naivety in Africa" and manipulating Africans to sign onto a US-based agenda about homosexuality.[74] Certainly the influence was real and in some ways profound. It was not the case, however, that African church leaders were naïve. They had clear arguments for why their position was biblical as well as a long tradition, rooted in the East African Revival, of speaking openly about "sexual sin."

As several scholars have argued, sexuality had been contested terrain throughout much of the nineteenth and twentieth centuries, as Ugandans, like others in Africa, worked to mobilize and also construct various forms of "tradition" as a barrier against

colonialism and neocolonialism. The claim of conservatives like Ssempa that homosexuality was not part of African life was empirically wrong, but empiricism was hardly
the point. Rather, the idea was to define a Ugandan identity—specifically a Ugandan
Christian identity—that its proponents believed would be able to stand up to Western
culture and US and European state power.[75]

The 2009 Anti-Homosexuality Bill proposed a seven-year jail term for homosexual acts
and the death penalty for "aggravated homosexuality," which included having sex with
a minor or a person with disabilities if the offender was HIV-positive. Martin Ssempa
led marches in favor of the bill (figure 14.4), and Museveni's government immediately
embraced it. The Minister of State for Ethics and Integrity said that the government was
determined to pass the law "even if it meant withdrawing from international treaties and
conventions or losing donor funding."[76] Public homophobia worsened. That year and the
next, Ugandan newspapers ran stories that listed the "Top Homos" in Uganda; one headline cried out: "Hang them; They are after our kids!!" Gay rights activists were terrified.
"Now we really have to go undercover," one told a reporter.[77]

The international outcry against the law began immediately. The Swedish government threatened to withhold $50 million in aid. Human Rights Watch and the inter-
national news media produced one withering condemnation after another.[78] Even the
head of Exodus International, the US-based organization that claimed it was possible
to "recover" from homosexuality, wrote to President Museveni in opposition. President
Obama called the proposed law "odious" in his speech at the National Prayer Breakfast in
2010.[79] In Uganda, a group of civil rights activists organized to oppose the law. The Civil

FIGURE 14.4 Martin Ssempa leading a march in favor of the Anti-Homosexuality Bill, 2009. Photo
by Edward Echwalu.

Society Coalition on Human Rights and Constitutional Law combined its campaign against the legislation with activism designed to combat the danger and violence that LGBTQ people faced in ordinary life—the threat of "corrective rape" against lesbians, the beatings, the constant public harassment.[80]

It took Rick Warren almost two months to craft his video letter opposing the bill. Warren was roundly criticized in the US press for his delay, and liberal critics accused him of dissimulation. Kapya Kaoma, the Anglican priest who wrote a major report criticizing homophobia in Africa, commented, "In America Warren says; 'I love gays.' In Africa, he says it's not a natural way of life."[81] It was not surprising that Warren was confounded. He surely understood that any association with the Ugandan anti-homosexuality movement was harmful to his reputation as a moderate in the United States. But Warren also knew the history of debates between East African pastors and liberal American Episcopalians. He was fully aware of how conservative Ugandan clergy and their allies were likely to view people they believed to be condescending to them on matters of doctrine.

The external pressure against the bill in some ways only strengthened its support in the Ugandan Parliament, and the calls for cuts in funding or the denunciations by groups such as Human Rights Watch, although appropriate and necessary from a human rights perspective, provided another opportunity for supporters to show their independence. The sense among some Ugandans was that the West was launching an offensive, "with the tip of the spear being NGOs and human rights activists."[82]

Uganda's churches had a mixed view of the bill. Its supporters claimed to have the mass of Christians on their side, and there was evidence of that. A meeting of two hundred members of the Interreligious Council of Uganda, which included Catholic, Protestant, and Muslim representatives, came out in support of the bill, saying that the Ugandan Parliament should resist foreign pressure to abandon or moderate it.[83] Ssempa organized his Pastors' Task Force, which included Anglican, Pentecostal, Orthodox, Catholic, and Muslim leaders. Uganda's Catholic Church remained notably quiet. "They may not like the harsher elements of the bill," one observer commented, "but they also share the suspicion that Western forces are trying to cram a liberal social agenda down Africa's throat, and they don't want to discourage efforts to defend African values."[84]

The Anglican Church of Uganda issued a statement saying that it opposed the use of the death penalty and was also disturbed by the provision that required clergy, doctors, and teachers to report homosexuality. The church agreed, however, that homosexuality should not be a human right, and it commended the law's objective of defining marriage as between a man and woman. The church also wanted to strengthen the law by prohibiting "procurement of material and [the] promotion of homosexuality as normal or an alternative lifestyle." In other words, the Anglicans in Uganda suggested specific revisions that would keep the basic punitive goals of the law intact.[85]

Rt. Rev. Dr. David Zac Niringiye, assistant bishop of Kampala in the Church of Uganda, argued that Western reaction against the law was condescending—and an imposition of an unbiblical attitude toward homosexuality. "The international community is behaving like they can't trust Ugandans to come up with a law that is fair. No! No! That is not fair! . . . I simply say to Rick Warren or anybody, let's be biblical. God has called Christians in Uganda to be witnesses for Christ in Uganda. We need the support of brothers and sisters all over the world."[86] Ssempa, never one to mince words, accused Warren of cowardice. "Rick you are our friend, we have bought many of your books and have been blessed by them," he wrote. "Do not let the pressure of bloggers and popular media intimidate you into becoming a negotiator for homosexual pedophilia rights in Africa."[87]

Those who opposed the anti-homosexuality law often blamed the influence of a few right-wing American conservative Christians who managed to co-opt Ugandan ministers into their own agenda. Similar arguments had been made about the 1998 vote on homosexuality at Lambeth. At the same time, supporters of the law within Uganda also blamed outsiders—gay activists, international NGOs, and self-righteous US or European governments—for pressuring them to drop the bill. These outsiders should stop trying to set the political agenda, they argued, for Africans, who were perfectly capable of governing—and interpreting the Bible—for themselves.

In October 2010, with the bill still before Parliament, the Ugandan tabloid *Rolling Stone* published the full names, addresses, and photographs of one hundred allegedly gay men and lesbians. The headline read "Hang Them." A few months later, gay rights activist David Kato, whose picture had been on the front page of the story, was beaten to death with a hammer. Kato, in his mid-forties, had been an early and vocal gay rights activist, and had felt under threat for several years. Kato had first publicly acknowledged his homosexuality in a press conference in 1998; he was imprisoned immediately thereafter.[88] He had devoted the last year of his life to trying to defeat the Anti-Homosexuality Bill. At the funeral, the local Anglican priest, realizing belatedly that he was scheduled to give burial rites for a gay man, used the opportunity to ask those present to "repent and return to God." He refused to bury Kato. Among the attendees at the funeral was Christopher Senyonjo, an elderly Anglican bishop who had been excommunicated for supporting gay community. Senyonjo was asked to speak at the gravesite. "God showed me that Christ doesn't discriminate [against] anyone," he said. "I am free because I know the truth! And I will stand for that truth." He continued, "God loves you, Kato. He knows you. He brought you into the world. And you have done your work. So rest in peace."[89]

David Bahati withdrew the original Anti-Homosexuality Bill and introduced a revised version in February 2012. The new bill removed the death penalty, but added a clause that would prohibit any organization that supported gay rights from working in Uganda. That clause could potentially shut out the development arms of many foreign governments.[90] A revised bill was passed by Parliament and signed into law in February 2014. The next day, the tabloid *Red Pepper* again published a list of Uganda's "Top Gays."[91] In the months following, attacks on LGBTQ people once again increased. In June 2014, President Obama enacted largely symbolic sanctions, which banned individual Ugandans who had been involved in human rights abuses against the LGBTQ community from entering the United States. The sanctions also provided for discontinuing or redirecting funds for a few of the programs that had been planned with the Ministry of Health and other agencies. But administration officials made clear that Uganda was one of the most important military allies the United States had in Africa, and Uganda and the US would continue to work together to fight the Lord's Resistance Army, along with al-Shabab in Somalia, and in coordinating anti-terrorism strategies for East Africa in general. The sanctions did not prevent Sam Kutesa, Uganda's foreign minister, from traveling to the United States to take up his position as president of the UN General Assembly.[92]

In August 2014, the law was nullified by the Ugandan Supreme Court on procedural grounds. The ruling happened just as President Museveni was about to lead a delegation to the United States, and many observers thought the ruling was a political maneuver designed to keep him from embarrassment. Ssempa agreed with this assessment, telling a reporter that "unfortunately, it has everything to do with pressure from Barack Obama and the homosexuals of Europe."[93] On his return from the United States, Museveni promised to reintroduce the law yet again, but perhaps without penalties for consenting adults. This, he hoped, would be a law that would escape international outrage. "We agreed to come up with a new version," said one supporter, something that "protects" Ugandans but "that doesn't hurt our Western friends."[94] As of this writing, however, no new bill has been introduced.

What drove the debate over Uganda's Anti-Homosexuality Bill was a decades-long history of theological discussion, as well as a complex set of allegiances tied to the changing demographics of global Christianity. The movement in favor of the bill was made possible—thinkable—by the convergence of intra-Anglican and postcolonial politics. Anglican bishops from the global South were trying to hold the line on homosexuality. And in Uganda, the lives of LGBTQ people were threatened, as their bodies and desires became the terrain that some conservative evangelicals used to fashion themselves into anti-colonial actors. In doing so, the conservatives drew on public feelings of fear, anger, and resentment toward Western arrogance about the superiority of its cultural values. When religious leaders urged their Parliament not to back down on a single aspect of the bill, they saw themselves as participating in a larger struggle over autonomy and respect.

That resentment was not just based in the churches and was not focused solely on sexual politics. It emerged from a larger sense of threat in a country suffering from debt, corruption, poverty, and violence. Many Ugandans saw Western NGOs as purveyors of a liberal agenda that was not responsive to their values or their lives. To a degree, they were right. Many of the development programs, microfinance projects, and health centers did impart, implicitly or explicitly, ideas about individualism and entrepreneurial resourcefulness that offered little in the way of solutions to the large-scale problems that shaped life in Uganda.

But the fact that many Ugandans saw the NGOs as liberal on issues of sexuality was ironic, in that the HIV/AIDS funding that poured into Uganda after PEPFAR did as much to shore up conservative Christian ideas about sex and the body as it did to promote liberal secular ones. President Museveni had lobbied for US funding that focused heavily on abstinence, a position that won him allies both in the US Congress and among Ugandan pastors. Both US-based transnational NGOs and local Christian organizations that promoted abstinence were generously supported. The flow of treatment funds and basic prevention strategies did offer vital assistance for people living with HIV/AIDS, but the public conversation about prevention moved increasingly toward a conservative model of controlling sexuality. Openly gay Ugandans, liberal Christians, and those who supported homosexual rights in Uganda were easily branded as Westernized and potentially traitorous. At best, they were marginalized; at worst, they were murdered.

But the US state was also an ambivalent and contradictory actor in this scenario, its power over Uganda dressed in AIDS money, queer rights activism, and the sometimes strained relationship between the US state and the NGOs, including evangelical ones, that it funded lavishly. It was security state politics specifically that cemented the relationship—the need for cooperation against the Lord's Resistance Army or al-Shabab in Somalia. US money was used not only against external enemies, but against internal opponents. Museveni might play his part in courting evangelical activists, quietly watching as Parliament and politicians announced that they would stand up to the United States, but his government would not do anything to risk its US alliance. Nor would the United States forcefully sanction a Ugandan government that it needed for the "real work" of fighting terrorism and assuring the US position in the region.

American evangelicals also found themselves increasingly involved in the complex political and sexual terrain in Uganda. There were those, such as Scott Lively and Lou Engle, who cultivated an audience for their anti-gay agenda. There were others, such as Kay and Rick Warren, who focused on the issue of HIV/AIDS and the sexual politics of abstinence promotion. American evangelicals such as the Warrens responded to the situation in Uganda with great emotion: their hearts cried out; they were overwhelmed by tears; they were angry or shocked; or, at times, they were calculating and political. Rick Warren found himself in a painfully awkward position, caught between his own conservative but not murderous views on homosexuality and the alliances with Africans that had been so much a part of his public persona in the 2000s.

What Warren discovered was that his partnerships with African churches and his celebration of global South Christianity had been built, implicitly, on a certain kind of compliance by African Christians. The lessons here are many, but for evangelicals, a key reality is that the Biblical interpretations of global South Christians were not under US control. They would not necessarily shore up the respectable conservatism that people like Warren were trying to promote and project. Warren was quite willing to support transnational Anglican conservativism and its positions on homosexuality in the church. But when his allies took what seemed to them like an important next step, he was confounded by the reality of what a truly independent and globalized church might sometimes mean. When those disjunctures appeared, it became clear that humanitarianism, debates about church doctrine, sexuality, and concerns over neocolonialism within the church were fundamentally intertwined. Americans were divided, but none of them controlled the terms of debate in a global evangelical community of which they were, increasingly, only one small part.

In Uganda, global South Christians were not obligingly presenting themselves as enchanting or as victimized brothers and sisters in Christ who were in need of support. And their theology did not necessarily align with American-style respectable conservatism. Certainly people in Africa disagreed about the Bible and its politics as vociferously as Americans did, but as American evangelicals continued to navigate the terrain of a truly globalized faith, they began to face the genuine and sometimes uncomfortable limits of their power. In a way, the debate about sexual politics in Uganda mirrored what had happened at Lausanne. There Americans found that people from the global South were setting the terms, outflanking them on the Left and reshaping transnational evangelical politics. Now, the mainstream of US evangelicalism was also being taught a lesson, but this time from the Right. People like Rick and Kay Warren might embrace the passions that they found in themselves—their broken hearts, their brotherly love—but they did not and could not control the terms of the global evangelical debate about sexuality.

15

"Despair is an Unmerciful Tyrant"

YOUTH AND JUSTICE IN CAIRO

WHEN REEM TEACHES ENGLISH, she does it with her whole body.[1] A beautiful and confident young American woman of twenty, she is in Cairo, standing in front of a group of Sudanese refugee children, going over a lesson in opposites. "Tall!" she says enthusiastically, and pulls a Dinka boy of about twelve out of his seat to illustrate. "Short!" and she stands beside him, bending her knees to highlight the contrast with her petite frame. "Tall! Short!" she repeats. It is hard not to appreciate her enthusiasm, and the students clearly do. After class is over, Reem accompanies them to the playground of this Anglican-run school in the middle of Cairo, jumping rope or joining one of the seemingly constant games of soccer.

In fact, Reem's enthusiasm is the most important tool in her toolbox, since she never taught anything before she showed up in Cairo. She also doesn't speak Arabic, of either the Sudanese or Egyptian dialect, although her dark hair and olive skin leave many Egyptians convinced she is one of them. In fact, her Arab name comes from her Moroccan father, a "nominal Muslim," she says, whose marriage to her Mennonite mother shocked both families. Reem is in Cairo to live out her Christian faith—although, given her family background, this is a rather fraught decision.

I met Reem when I joined a group of sixteen college students and two staffers from InterVarsity Christian Fellowship who were spending five weeks in Cairo as part of the organization's annual short-term missions program, called the Global Urban Trek. Groups of fifteen to twenty students traveled to cities around the world (Dhaka, Manila, Kolkata, Bangkok, and Mexico City, among others), where they lived in slums and worked with local agencies or churches. In Kolkata, students might teach children or help develop microenterprises; in Bangkok, they would likely work with people afflicted with leprosy. Reem's group was helping teach English to Sudanese migrants in some of the poorest areas of Cairo. But their primary task was simply to live with the poor in their communities, to show solidarity and humility, "to raise up flesh and blood followers of Jesus to incarnate the gospel to the urban poor."[2] Founded in the early 2000s, the trek was a legacy of, as well as a critical reaction to, the short-term missions explosion of the 1990s.

The IV team had come from universities and colleges scattered across the United States. The members were mostly white but included two Arab Americans, three Asian Americans, and one Latino. There were two staffers, both women, one white and one African American. The students, whose average age was twenty, had decamped for a Muslim country (which terrified many of their parents), in what was for most of them an unprecedented adventure. Because proselytizing is illegal in Egypt, the group worked with a southern Sudanese population that largely identified as Christian.

Traveling to Cairo without much in the way of accouterments (no iPhones, no internet access, only one camera for the team) and very little cash, the students saw their mission as going to help the poor. They were not unaware of the potentially problematic nature of that mission; InterVarsity's preparation materials had warned against the dangers of a "colonialist mentality." The students were taught to avoid thinking that they had the answers to the problems they would see. Most members of the team embraced InterVarsity's central message, which was that urban treks existed to give North American college students "the privilege of living in solidarity with the poor." They were there to "build relationships," and, with their loving presence, to counter the "despair" of slum life. "Despair is an unmerciful tyrant," the Trek's vision statement explained, "and we are convinced that Jesus Christ is the only satisfying answer to the question of despair. The arrival of God's Kingdom is the good news."[3]

To evangelical insiders, InterVarsity was signaling several things. First, it was focused on "Kingdom work," that common way of describing one's commitment to social justice issues, affirming the idea that faith was not all about heaven. This world, too, was God's kingdom.[4] Second, the Trek was simultaneously insisting that it *was* evangelical. The organization placed the "good news"—the gospel—at the heart of that kingdom work. This good news "is conveyed through living creatures, people who take up residence alongside the despairing." Third, although it evoked social justice, InterVarsity's model for the Trek was one of witness, of attesting to suffering. All of this language is common among contemporary evangelicals. What made the Trek distinctive is that students were invited not only to give food to the poor, but also to ask why the poor are hungry.[5]

Urban Trek was not the largest of the many short-term programs in the United States in the 2000s, but it was one of the most interesting, precisely because InterVarsity was a theologically conservative organization, with a firm commitment of biblical literalism, that for decades had taken on issues of social and economic justice. The Cairo Trek was five weeks long, designed to give the students time to learn about the community where they were working and perhaps to do something rather more useful than was typical of short-term missions. Whether they *were* in fact "more useful" was an open question, including for the students themselves.

InterVarsity's descriptions of the Trek called for "solidarity," which meant that students were expected to live with, and like, the poor in some of the most difficult slum conditions in the world. The Egyptian team was rather shocked and embarrassed, then, by the fact that their team leader had found a living arrangement for them that was nowhere near a slum. Instead, the group had two decent apartments in a quiet, wealthy section of the city (Heliopolis). They had a kitchen, basic cooking utensils, and hot running water. The leader had gotten an excellent deal from the Seventh-day Adventist church that owned the apartments. Thus, the team members were told, and told themselves, that this living situation was a matter of stewarding resources. If they could live cheaper in a nice neighborhood, then there was more money for other necessary things. But the disappointment was palpable. They had imagined that solidarity required their removal from American comforts; living incarnationally meant, they believed, doing what Jesus had done in relinquishing privileges and power. It meant not only embodying God's love but also stepping forward to meet his children with a willingness—even a longing—to suffer with them. Tiff, an energetic linguistics major at the University of Maryland, expressed it this way:

> It's gonna be hot; it's gonna be icky; we might not have plumbing. You know, those kind of difficult things. And then it ended up being . . . a nice place . . . That was really difficult, even though it was easy, like our life was easy, our lifestyle was easy.

Even so, the group lived simply. The Trek expected that participants would learn to be critical of the habits of American travelers, and especially those of some short-term missionaries, who swooped into a locale, benevolently handing out goodies while drinking Cokes in front of people who could not afford them.

The Cairo students took the critiques of American self-indulgence to heart. They took public transportation or walked to the schools where they worked; on the buses, they were almost always the only foreigners. They dressed modestly—long skirts or loose pants for the women, long pants for the men, and long sleeves for everyone. Their modest style emerged as a cross between bohemian and sporty—very unlike either other Westerners or Europeans. The students' food and transportation costs were covered by the $3,400 they paid for the trip. Beyond that, they committed to bringing only $30 in spending money for the five-week journey.

The group of students was politically as well as culturally diverse, although most of them (with the clear exception of Reem) would describe themselves as "conservative" in some fashion. Dan, a young white man who grew up on the West Coast, was in many ways the kind of person one might expect to find at InterVarsity. He had considered attending West Point, but had instead enrolled in a school in Oregon and had interned at the aggressively right-wing Institute for Religion and Democracy. Kanesha, on the other hand, was an African American woman from Baltimore in her late twenties. The associate staff person for the group, she had attended York College, a small college in Pennsylvania, which is where she got involved with InterVarsity. Like other InterVarsity staff, she was responsible for raising her own salary. Other students inhabited a range of political positions and social backgrounds.

The members of the group were intensely conscious of the fact that they had arrived in a Muslim country, in a city that many of them found intimidating as well as potentially exciting and exotic. Most said that their parents were very anxious about the trip, worried about terrorism, foreignness, and distance. And, unlike most young travelers, the members of this group would not be allowed to call home or email friends or family.

The InterVarsity group would not get to know many Egyptian Muslims very well; their primary experience would be with Sudanese Christians. But they did learn a good bit about the realities of everyday life for the poor in Egypt because they would travel on buses, meet people in the street, and talk to veiled women and, less often, devoutly Muslim men. These encounters happened often enough to make an impression. Dan had his eyes opened:

> I certainly have had my images of Islam and Arabs changed. Those stereotypes that we all have. I know that among my working-class family, they have two things they are worried about, or that they see as threats. One is liberals and the liberal media; the other is Muslims. And these are the big things for them.

While in Cairo, students also hoped to engage profoundly with the people and the place, to learn about the world and expand their religious horizons. Like other short-term missions participants, they longed for an experience of numinous intensity.[6] Being twenty-first-century Americans, they also expected to document this experience online. Tracy, a white woman who was a rising junior at Reed College, was the group scribe, the only person allowed to access the internet during the trip. A tomboy, unassuming and thoughtful, Tracy was a self-described science geek, who aimed to one day write a book of "math poetry." She had come from a small town in Wisconsin and had decided when she was only twelve that she had no interest in the "lukewarm" Christianity of her parents. Over time, she became more faithful, read her Bible at home, and started asking questions at church. She described herself as a political conservative—"fairly supportive," she said, of President Bush.

Tracy posted updates on the Trek website every week. Her blog posts were quietly ironic documents of a young woman very well aware of her own position as a she-who-speaks-about-the-transformation-of-us. In one of her first posts, Tracy faced up to a question that would bedevil the students: was what they did in Cairo *meaningful,* and, if so, exactly how?

> So you might be thinking, This has all been very nice Tracy, but what are you DOING in Cairo?

This took us a while to figure out, too.

Physically, we were helping teach at schools, playing with kids, making friends on the metro, and getting out to see Cairo once in a while. This has been very frustrating to all of us. I can't speak for everyone at once, but the general trend seemed to be that we all felt that God wanted us here, but nobody knew what He wanted us for.[7]

Tracy wrote with a sense of wry irony, with the voice of a young woman who was used to being a bit out of place. One question she was asked a lot, she said, is why a committed Christian like her would choose to go to Reed, which "everybody knows" is the most non-Christian school in the country. She thought about that often, but was still not sure of the answer. She just knew she wanted to go there. I was not surprised by her choice. However much she was in the minority at Reed, she was surrounded by other highly intellectual kids who could care less about "fitting in" to a normal middle-class life—at least for their college years. Tracy had "expected to be the only Christian." She was not, of course, but she did have to search to find the small community of evangelicals. Eventually she found her way to InterVarsity.

On the blog, Tracy provided enthusiastic descriptions of the group's adventures and their dogged insistence on playing soccer with pretty much everyone they met. She also offered descriptions of the city and her own emotions during the trip. Here, for example, is how she described Cairo in one of her early blog postings:

One of the things I love about Cairo is that everything looks like it's made of chalk pastels . . . I think the soft lighting effect is probably aided by pollution, but the end result is that whenever I look at building scenery for the first time, I feel like if I breathe too hard, the chalk pastel dust will blow away. Even now, the colors all seem so soft and powdery that if I hold up my hand too carelessly, I might smudge the architecture.[8]

For five weeks, Tracy would provide a sensitive and self-conscious narration of the adventure that brought conservative Christians to a conservative Muslim country to work with Sudanese Christian refugees.

The InterVarsity short-termers were divided up among five schools scattered around the city. By working with Christians, they avoided the impression of proselytizing. Proselytizing was illegal in Egypt, as in many Muslim countries, but helping Christians with services and education was not.

One group worked at Centrale school, in an area called Arba'a wu-Nuss, which means "four and a half" in Arabic. The area is just four and a half miles from Cairo city center, but it seemed worlds apart. To arrive for the start of the school day, the team had to leave very early to catch their bus. I got on with Tracy and two other students at seven one morning and rode for about half an hour. "The buses are crazy," Tracy wrote in one of her updates. "You know the Knight (sic) Bus in Harry Potter? Sometimes it feels like they're driving around kind of like that, but there's no magic."

The two other team members teaching at Arba'a wu-Nuss were Tiffany (everybody called her Tiff) and Brian. Brian was a large guy, tall and broad, a bit shy. Tiff was blond, petite, and intense. A linguistics major at the University of Maryland, she described herself as a "follower of Jesus," and told me that she was in Cairo because she had "a heart for the lost nations." She "just was so moved by the idea that there are so many people who haven't had the chance to have a personal relationship with Jesus, to feel his love." Tiff was also delighted to meet so many Sudanese Christians. "What I've learned," she said, "is that heaven is gonna be packed!"

Arba'a wu-Nuss is an informal settlement on the outskirts of Cairo, where land was first appropriated by a lone entrepreneur who built and then rented houses. Most had gained electricity only recently; it was not uncommon to have no running water. The population was made up mostly of migrants from the south of Egypt plus some thousands of Sudanese.[9] The streets in the area were thick with dust and trash. Most of the buildings were half-finished, but they were also many stories tall—apartment complexes that promised clean interiors and modern amenities if they ever were completed, which seemed unlikely.

The Centrale school was small and distinctly less well-appointed than some of the other schools where the InterVarsity group was volunteering. It ran on fees the Sudanese parents paid. The whole compound was just a group of dark classrooms surrounding a dirt courtyard. Inside, though, the place was clean and organized. George Hakim, the administrator, presided over the program from a small, neat office. "This is a Christian school," he explained, when asked about the school's mission. "We are here to teach the students not only English, but also to support their faith."

At Centrale, the school day began with songs. All the kids lined up in the small, dusty courtyard, arranged by height. Most students seemed to be having a great time—but one girl in the middle row, about fourteen or fifteen years old, slumped and hunched her shoulders, refusing to sing. The girl exuded adolescent disdain. She also had her hair loosely covered—a Muslim girl, as one of the teachers later confirmed.

While Centrale was open to Muslim students (many of whom were arriving from Darfur), they had to accept the school's Christian mission. They did not have to convert, which was important. Most services for Sudanese in Egypt were provided by churches and church-affiliated groups, and there was a potent rumor that the churches were pressuring Muslim Sudanese families to convert and were offering generous financial incentives to do so.[10]

Tracy, Tiff, and their fellow Americans were certainly helping out, but the truth was that the Sudanese teachers and staff had no urgent need for Americans to come to teach English. After all, the InterVarsity team worked for only a few weeks in the summer, assisting in schools that were in session year-round. The schools already had English teachers, and those teachers were present. So the InterVarsity group helped where they could. They assisted the teachers by handing out papers to the students or offering individual assistance. Sometimes they filled in when a teacher needed a break.

Tracy and Tiff, like Reem at the Anglican school, tried to make up in enthusiasm what they lacked in experience or skill. In one class, they found themselves standing in front of a small group of seven- or eight-year-olds. Their assignment was to help them learn the English words for weather. "The weather is hot today," Tiff or Tracy would say to the students, several of whom were barely fending off a nap. The students would then repeat, in the style of Sudanese schools, whatever the "teachers" said. But the kids seemingly understood very little, and while Tiff and Tracy tried everything short of a Broadway musical to get their attention, everyone was, at some level, just waiting for class to be over. Lunch would be next, and they could all play outside, and Tracy and Tiff could do what they felt most comfortable doing—playing with kids in the school yard, throwing a ball around, and hugging the girls who would gather around them at the end of every recess.

Most of the InterVarsity participants recognized these limitations. They were aware of intense debates about the costs and impact of short-term missions, and they worried openly and frequently about whether they were aiding the Sudanese in any substantive way. Dan told me:

Sometimes I really want to feel like we are getting things *done,* but it doesn't work like that here. I feel very obligated to my donors . . . but in the long term [I am obligated] to God, to make something of my time here. To have it be a good investment.

Several InterVarsity students struggled likewise with the question of what their investment—of time and money and prayer—had meant.

Some Sudanese did in fact tell students that they were "doing" enough just by being there. Emmanuel, a teacher at Centrale, once sat with two members of the team and told them his story of growing up in a Christian home in Juba, Sudan, then making his way north, through Khartoum, before coming to Cairo. He repeatedly told the group at Centrale how happy he was that they were there and what a blessing they were. He invited some of the students to his home the last night they were in town, and they shared food and stories. Emmanuel insisted that, just by coming, the students had "encouraged" the Sudanese who met them. The group desperately wanted it to be true.

Not all the Sudanese felt the same way. Peter, a teacher at the Anglican school where Reem and others on the team worked, told me that he was none too impressed. It was nothing personal, he said, and it was fine if the Americans wanted to fill out their résumés. But they shouldn't pretend that they were there to help *him.* In any case, there was little they could do to help with the real issues facing Sudanese refugees.

Peter was one of the many Sudanese in Egypt who were waiting for the UN to certify their refugee status. The Egyptian government had refused to take up the task, so it was left to the UN High Commission for Refugees (UNHCR). In 2006, the number of Sudanese living in Cairo was estimated at between two hundred thousand (UNHCR) and four million (the Egyptian government).[11] Being declared a refugee allowed you to receive a "blue card," which made you eligible either for more formal status in Egypt or, most desirably, the small resettlement program (three thousand people a year) that allowed Sudanese to go to Canada, Australia, the United States, or elsewhere.[12]

Sudanese migrants were often unhappy in Cairo. The Sudanese generally lived in extreme poverty, sharing space and competing for resources with other marginalized people—internal migrants, the unemployed, the homeless, squatters, and street children. And Egyptians often treated them with hostility that included everything from racist slurs to denial of jobs.[13]

While many Sudanese were able to find or create housing in Cairo, it was often in informal settlements like Arba'a wu-Nuss. If they found work, it was often temporary. And they struggled to find—or appropriate—water, electricity, and other basic services.

The UNHCR's procedures, on which hope for escaping these conditions depended, were at best Byzantine and at worst cursory and unfair. Most Sudanese never even applied, and those who did were often deeply frustrated. The perception was that the UN rejected the vast majority of applicants anyway. (From 1994 to 2005, only 29 percent of applicants were given refugee status and resettled in third countries.)[14]

In January 2005, the UNHRC suspended its process for designating refugees, citing the ceasefire that had been declared between the government of Sudan and the Southern People's Liberation Army. Sudanese were encouraged to leave Cairo and return to southern Sudan.[15] Most did not. Then, in September 2005, a group of Sudanese refugees began a sit-in at the square located just across from the offices of the UNHCR in Cairo, asking for more attention to their claims for third-party resettlement. Ultimately, 2,500 to 3,000 Sudanese joined the protests. "Life in Egypt has become impossible," one protestor said, "and life in Sudan was, and remains, impossible . . . We just want to move to a third country where we can be treated as humans."[16] On December 30, the Egyptian government sent police and security forces to forcibly remove the protestors, which led to at least twenty-eight deaths, scores of injuries, and hundreds of arrests.[17]

Sudanese in Egypt often believed that being a Christian was helpful to the process of getting refugee status. Peter, for example, identified himself to me as Christian, although he also still practiced the religious traditions of his parents and grandparents. Officially, though, Peter was Christian, period; he felt it was a good strategy for someone in his position. The church groups that provided many of the basic services to Sudanese refugees—including Caritas, Catholic Relief Services, the Anglican Church, and World Vision—were resolute in providing services to Sudanese regardless of their religion. But their resources were stretched and many Sudanese received no services. In such a tense and fraught context, it was not surprising that people should be working to assess every possible angle to increase their chances for both getting services and gaining refugee status. Peter was angry about his seemingly hopeless situation in Cairo. When he looked at the InterVarsity team working in the school where he worked, he didn't think these energetic American students had anything to offer him.

For the Urban Trek students, oppression and economic injustice were central concerns. InterVarsity had established a curriculum on the topic: a training guide, a reading list, and a Bible study program. Many nights, the Cairo team sat together to read the Old Testament book of Amos, which had been chosen as one of the scripture texts for the Trek that year.

The prophet Amos pronounces a violent sentence on the people of Israel, who, he explains, "trample on the heads of the poor as on the dust of the ground, and deny justice to the oppressed" (Amos 2:7, NIV). As a result, their homes and lands will be plundered. "I will tear down the winter house along with the summer house," the Lord tells Amos, and "the mansions will be demolished" (3:15). The Lord tells the people of Israel, through Amos, that he has no interest in their religious festivals or their offerings.

> Away with the noise of your songs!
> I will not listen to the music of your harps.
> But let justice roll on like a river,
> righteousness like a never-falling stream! (5:24)

The message is that God is not interested in the outward trappings of faith. Although the book ends with a promise of the people's return to their land, it also makes clear that God will deal harshly with those who are corrupt or who oppress others.

Students grappled with this message. A few weeks after the trip, Jennifer, a quiet young woman from Portland, wrote a letter to her supporters, describing what she felt she had learned from that conversation.

> Once a week, we studied the book of Amos . . . [The] nation was in a high point of their history economically. The people went through the motions of worshipping their God, but every action was revolting to Him. To put it simply, they oppressed the poor . . . Our bible study focused on how we could change our lives so that we will not become people "who turn justice into bitterness and cast righteousness to the ground" (Amos 5:8).

Jennifer felt that she had learned that "God does not want me to focus solely on my own life," but she was far from certain what that might mean in practice.

Reem, too, often talked about oppression, wealth, and responsibility. Even in high school she had been intensely conscious of the problem of hyper-consumption. She had purchased most of her clothes at used clothing stores and had lived what she called "a very Takoma Park life," referring to the DC suburb once known for its Left radicalism. But Reem put a political spin on her understanding of what the Bible required. She believed every word in the Bible to be literally true, including all injunctions to care for the poor. "And that," she said, "is exactly why I'm a socialist."

Reem's self-conscious, left-wing politics were hardly typical of the group, and in fact Reem herself seemed to use "socialism" to describe any intense willingness to respond to injustice. But Reem's broad sense of social concern was not unusual, and harkened back to many permutations of radicalism since the Lausanne meeting in 1974—a meeting that none of the InterVarsity students had heard of, but to which they were all heirs.

Tracy, for example, had taken to heart the InterVarsity injunction to attend to social justice and saw it as entirely compatible with her conservative politics. She believed in working for what Bryant Myers, whose book *Walking with the Poor* was assigned to Trek participants, described as "a whole gospel for all of life."[18] Before coming to Cairo, Tracy had participated in an InterVarsity training program on international issues. Students were divided into groups, each assigned to a region of the world, and each group was allotted resources proportional to their region's real-world resources. Tracy was in the African group, which of course had little in the way of food or water resources. She loved telling the story of how the Latin American group had tried to break the rules to sneak goods over to her African group. That seemed right to her, that willingness to challenge norms for the sake of justice. These were the final words on Tracy's post of July 12, a couple of weeks into the Trek:

I hear Christians telling people that to follow Jesus, you have to be born again, because Jesus said that once in the New Testament. So I think I can tell them to sell everything they have and give to the poor. Jesus said that once, too.
                              —paraphrase of a comment by Rich Mullins[19]

For Tracy, this didn't conflict with her political conservatism. She wanted a world where both individualism and conservative morality were valued, but she also felt obligated to think hard about that injunction to sell all you have, to give everything to the world's poor. How that would play out when she returned to her college life was still hazy.

For many members of the team, and maybe for any adventurous group of twenty-year-olds, being in Egypt meant lowering their guards and making connections with local people in whatever ways they could. Doing what might seem risky or perhaps just rude in another context came to seem like an opportunity for "native" contact, and perhaps a chance to gain the sense of authenticity and enchantment that they so longed for. Tracy's blog described a visit with an Egyptian family living near Mount Sinai, where the group went for a weekend.

[We] got ourselves invited over to the house of Nura's family. Nura is a little girl, 8 years old and an accomplished beggar. She met us on the road and asked us for money going to and from St. Catherine's [a monastery in the Sinai]. On the way back, we went to visit her house. None of them spoke any English and we quickly ran out of Arabic phrases. Nevertheless, their hospitality was outstanding. The women, Fatma and Lila, invited us in to sit on cushions on the floor of what was perhaps a 2- or 3-room house. They served us the best tea I've had here yet and we all stared at each other and smiled because we were out of conversational Arabic.[20]

Tracy was happy to be invited to Nura's home, and she also felt there was something powerful in the experience of just trying to live—in evangelical terms—incarnationally, being present and building relationships with Egyptian people. Then again, Tracy also knew that sitting politely and with uncomprehending smiles was not exactly the solidarity with the poor she had imagined.

Between the study of Amos and their own anomalous position in Cairo, the students were deeply concerned about finances. What does it mean to be wealthy, they asked, while living in the middle of poverty? One night the Bible study consisted mostly of a long discussion about money. Like most foreigners in Egypt, the students had realized very quickly that they were being asked to pay more than Egyptians did for food or a cab ride, which did not seem fair to most of them. After all, they were not "ugly Americans." They were not living in fancy hotels, or buying gadgets from the tourist markets. They were cooking their own meals and buying food for those meals from local stores. They were riding on buses and the subway. They did not see themselves as average tourists, and in many ways they were not. This, several of them said, meant they should not be expected to pay the "tourist rate" for things.

"It's not fair to be charged extra just because we're foreign," one student argued. But Charles, who was Arab American, asked, "What does it mean to be sitting there arguing with a guy over what is, in effect, 40 cents? Isn't that a bit ridiculous?" Wasn't it possible, he said, that paying the foreigners' price was in fact a kind of fairness? "Maybe you're right," another student said, but "it isn't always the right thing just to act like the big spender." Putting on a display of "'I can *totally* afford this,' and 'Let ME pay, it means nothing to me,'" she pointed out, was also not appealing as a model of a Christian life.

The team's grappling with questions about how to deal with their own privilege and respond to poverty and injustice animated much of their time that summer, as many of them struggled over what, exactly, constituted justice. They seemed to agree that, given the larger structures of global inequality, their own relationships with poor Egyptians they met would necessarily be fraught. They wondered how to distinguish between magnanimity and condescension.

Although they were working with Sudanese Christians, students enthusiastically embraced the opportunity to meet Egyptians whenever they could. They worked on Friday nights at one of the local Egyptian churches, for example. InterVarsity staff wanted to make sure they met some Egyptians and saw that they could be very nice people. Otherwise, it might have been possible for them to leave Egypt having seen Egyptians only through Sudanese eyes. In practice, this was not much of an issue, because the students took particular pleasure in meeting and talking to Muslims. Making friends with Egyptians was one of the primary leisure activities of the Trek.

Reem spent a good bit of time with Fatna, one of the women who sat beside the Heliopolis metro with a blanket spread on the ground from which she sold trinkets, packages of tissues, and other inexpensive items. After meeting Fatna during her walk to the metro one day, Reem made it a point to go down regularly to meet up with her and the other women and children there. As Reem put it, she wanted to spend time with her "Muslim sisters." Fatna was a poverty-stricken, fully veiled Muslim woman with whom Reem could not communicate except through her very few words of Arabic. Still, Reem made a consistent effort, and after a few weeks, she was well known in the area; people called out in greeting when she walked past. Reem especially liked spending time with young girls there, playing games and communicating through gestures and smiles.

Reem wanted to be generous with her new friends; for example, she purchased all of her gifts for people at home from Fatna. But it was also a source of pride that she believed they saw her as a friend too—that she was not treated just as a source of funds. Looking back on those relationships later, she said:

> I really want to trust the scripture, like Jesus in the parables, that these passing encounters mean something. Never turn any away . . . Because unintentionally you may have been entertaining angels.
>
> Not to sound too cheesy . . . [but] those [girls at the metro] are my angels. My little girl Ladona – [one time] another girl came up and asked for money, and Ladona hit her hand and said no, that's not what she's here for. You do *not* ask Reem for money.

Actually, Reem could not have understood exactly what Ladona said. Reem did not speak Arabic; the little girl did not speak English. In this sense, Reem was engaging in just the kind of drive-by analysis that was a chronic feature of short-term missions.[21] Reem engaged in compulsive interpretative work, making meanings where meanings were uncertain. But she had also done something notable, in that she had shown up, consistently, and attempted to understand. She perhaps trusted too much in her reading of the situation and in the relationships that felt so real to her. It would have been hard for her to understand the ways in which poor Egyptians might see her hesitance to hand out money as unkindness. It was here, as much as anywhere, that students benefitted from InterVarsity's rule about cash: in truth, Reem had almost no money to give.

Reem's relationship with local Muslims was complicated further by the politics of race. Reem and Kanesha, the African American female staffer, had their differences on this topic. The two of them had known each other before the Trek, having met at the York College chapter when Reem was a student and Kanesha was on staff. That meant, in InterVarsity terms, that Kanesha was Reem's staffer—her supporter, but also her superior. Kanesha was also older. And her Egypt experience was very different from Reem's.

In fact, Kanesha's overall relationship with InterVarsity was distinctive and somewhat burdened. At home in Pennsylvania, Kanesha had her frustrations with the organization. As a staff member, she, like other IV staff, had the responsibility to raise her own salary through donations, but Kanesha, a working-class young woman, simply did not have the resources that some of the wealthier, largely white InterVarsity staff did. Middle-class or upper-middle-class staffers could ask family or friends to donate thousands of dollars a year toward their support. Kanesha had no such well-heeled friends or family. Some of her white friends in InterVarsity did support her financially; that is, some other staff took money that they had raised for their own support and shared it with Kanesha. She told me how appreciative she was that she had such great friends in the organization. But, still, she thought that something wasn't quite right about how hard it was for her to raise money.

InterVarsity was not unaware of the issue. Starting in the early 1980s, IV staff had agreed to tax themselves half a percent of the money that each of them raised to be donated to "Multi-Ethnic Ministries." That amount was matched by the national office, so that there was a fund equal to 1 percent of the total budget that was dedicated to work in black and other campus ministries. There were other programs too, including a $1.1 million donation given in the early 2000s that offered grants to staff of color. It was unclear to me how much Kanesha knew about these programs, all of which were part of InterVarsity's commitment to supporting diversity.

Still, a staffer like Kanesha might well have to struggle to make a living wage. According to InterVarsity's Executive Vice President of People and Cultures, it was likely to be especially hard if Kanesha was raised in a traditional black church, because many of those churches had little familiarity with parachurch groups like InterVarsity. They might also not have a tradition of supporting missionaries directly, as many white evangelical churches did. Black staff were not alone in the difficulties they faced—people from rural communities or Latinos might also have particular challenges in fundraising. But Kanesha's story was representative of a larger problem—one InterVarsity was accurately aware of—with recruiting and keeping black staff in the organization.[22]

In Egypt, Kanesha, who was dark-skinned and taller than average, faced very overt and personal racism. Many Egyptians, she thought, assumed she was Sudanese, and she got the same kind of treatment the Sudanese complained about: hostility, stares, and angry words that she couldn't understand. Once she was blocked from getting out of the subway car at her stop. She was sure the Egyptian women were doing it intentionally as a way of hassling her. Kanesha loved the Sudanese, but not the Egyptians.

The problem was not Islam. Instead, Kanesha saw Egyptians as fundamentally racist people. Without much context for understanding the history of colonialism in Egypt or the complex relations between Egypt and Sudan, Kanesha experienced something of the lived resonance of those historical tensions. In contrast, Reem felt more connected to Egyptians than did Kanesha or almost any of the other students. She hung out, attempted conversation, and drank tea. She wanted to return to Egypt to be a nurse to work with the "Muslim sisters" she felt she already loved.

While they were in Cairo, Reem and Kanesha had some tough conversations about the fact that, in essence, they were on two different trips, forging very different sets of experiences and connections. Reem said later that Kanesha had "called me OUT" on not being sensitive enough to Egyptian racism. Essentially, Kanesha accused Reem of being enchanted, of wanting an exotic experience with Muslims and refusing to face what was happening to Kanesha, her sister in Christ, as an African American woman. And Reem accepted the criticism, agreed that maybe she didn't want to see Egyptians in that way, as racist and aggressive—although Reem also felt great sympathy toward the Sudanese. At the same time, Reem also pushed back with Kanesha. "It's easy, isn't it, to love the Sudanese?" she said. "They speak English and dress in beautiful, bright colors and don't have so many rules about men and women's behavior. Maybe Egyptians are harder; and maybe this stuff we're doing is *supposed* to be hard."

The InterVarsity team struggled, too, with the complicated and sometimes contradictory messages they were getting from Sudanese teachers they worked with. While some people told them that their "ministry of presence" was just what was needed, others wanted more from the team. InterVarsity had given the students a great deal of reading material on poverty and social justice, but they had learned almost nothing about the specific situation facing the Sudanese. Despite having worked for several weeks at Sudanese schools, most of the Americans knew very little about the history of Sudan, the politics of the civil war there, or even how the Sudanese had ended up in Cairo. Some had heard a great deal about Sudan from the teachers, but mostly how beautiful and wonderful southern Sudan was. "I would love to go there," one of the students said, sighing slightly. "I think it must be the most beautiful place on earth." It is unsurprising that the Sudanese longed for their homeland; what is stiking, however, is the student's naïve acceptance of the homesick descriptions of what was then one of the poorest and most war-torn places in the world.

The lack of political context was particularly notable because evangelicals had had such a long and intensive history of involvement in Sudan. Because of this ignorance, few of the students saw the conflict in Sudan as a Muslim-Christian conflict, despite the fact that the evangelical community in the United States had spent the better part of a decade crafting just that narrative.[23] The InterVarsity team was in Cairo in summer 2006, eighteen months after the Comprehensive Peace Treaty had been signed that ended the twenty-year civil war. Many of the Sudanese were talking delightedly and hopefully about returning home, although they were also fearful that the treaty would not hold and peace would be fleeting.

One Friday during their trip, two Sudanese teachers came to speak to the group about the experiences of Sudanese living in Cairo and their larger needs. Sudanese teachers spoke to the group at their apartments in Heliopolis. The presentation was unlike anything the students had heard all summer. A teacher named Zacharia told the students that it was not enough for them to just come to Cairo and then go home. The students needed to commit to working politically on behalf of southern Sudan, to do *something* in this situation of crisis. Zacharia was fearful and angry, and now that he had a group of Americans to speak to, he had no intention of patting them on the head for their generosity, for their mere appearance in Cairo.

Reem found the presentation enormously challenging. "I felt kind of stunned," she said. As a pacifist and a self-proclaimed socialist, someone who had opposed the war in Iraq, Reem saw herself as an activist. But she realized that she had never had *this* kind of encounter, with someone who had lived in the middle of war and was now telling her what he wanted and needed from her. So she pushed herself to listen to Zacharia: "I wanted to know more about these issues. Because here is Zach, giving me such a different perspective. Zach was HOPELESS. . . . He's saying: what are you going to *do*?" There had been many visitors and reporters, he told the group, those who claim to want to help, but they ended up doing nothing. The students needed to go home and use their capacities to support the people of South Sudan. Reem found herself taken aback. She described how she had talked to herself about what happened:

And you know, [Reem], you've spent your life being pissed off about war, and now you have the blessing of being around people who can teach you SO much. So you'd better open both ears and your heart WIDE.

As she later put it: "I had to get a smack down." She described trying to wrap her mind around Zacharia's anger:

There have been so many people who are so gracious, who are "thank you for being here, you are a blessing." And he's just, like, not there right now. "I don't want to talk to you if you're not going to do something." And you know, Zacharia, that is 100% OK.

How should she respond? "He is definitely [asking for] something concrete. Not just presence. And that's great: I like concrete."

This was hard for Reem and others in part because what she and her fellow students might have seen as the alternative—the "concrete" experience of many short-term missions, the activities of building or painting something, or teaching a vacation Bible school—was not on the table in Cairo. In the face of that limit, they had convinced themselves of the value of presence, of being a kind of witness and, in evangelical language, "providing encouragement." The very fact that students were on the trip for more than a few weeks, however, provided the possibility that they might gain a more detailed understanding of what their hosts faced, and thus recognize that the Sudanese they met neither needed a building painted nor necessarily basked in their presence. Zacharia, at least, wanted other kinds of concrete action: political work, engagement, and some recognition by the Americans of the power they held.

A month after the students returned to the United States, I interviewed Reem at her family's home in Takoma Park. We had dinner with her family, her two sisters and a brother, along with her quiet Mennonite mother and her garrulous, edgy Moroccan father.

A good bit of our conversation focused on the social justice issues that so animated her. "I found that, when I was in that whole high school process of deciding what my faith meant," she said, "a huge overwhelming part of that was this *guilt* over being an American, living as an American, being a *consumer*." She had tried to live out her beliefs. "And that's when I became a vegetarian. Started buying my clothes from used clothing stores . . . because I didn't want to support sweatshops. And I'm just sick of people sweeping it under the rug, saying that's just how it is."

Still, it didn't seem enough, this buying from the food co-op and the used clothing stores, this alternative lifestyle. Was it ever possible to live the life that a committed faith seemed to require? Being at Urban Trek made the question real for most of the students. The answers, however, were not easy to find or to forge, especially when they returned home.

Reem determined that, when she went back to school in the fall, she would prioritize helping the Sudanese. She was deeply invested in "taking on" the Sudan issue and was planning on becoming politically motivated and knowledgeable. Then again, she also realized that in just a few weeks she was going back to college for her junior year, and she was a student who sometimes struggled with her studies. She knew that she had spent too much time in previous years in social pursuits: being a friend, going on dates, grappling with issues of identity, sexuality, and faith. She noted that the political identity she had held so strongly as a high school student in Takoma Park had waned since she had started college, at a school where her friends were mostly conservative.

After dinner, as we drank coffee and listened to folk music in a Takoma Park coffee house, Reem said that, in truth, she was exhausted. She also knew that her college experience had not encouraged her social justice politics. In her first two years, she had been focused on her relationships with family and friends: "At the end of the day, it is probably more important that I began to heal with my dad. Or to walk with females— my friends, people who are attempting suicide, or who are struggling with eating disorders." She embraced that fact: "that's what was most important; totally relational. And heart stuff too." She went on to explain the ways in which she felt torn, using a paraphrase of Micah 6:8:

> So [there is] the cycle of feeling like, so, *true religion is this: look after the widows and orphans and walk humbly with your God.* But then that can become almost like a false religion, something you are trying to do void of God. . . . I don't want to become that kind of person, who says [she switches to a harsh, rigid voice]: "*I* am *trying* to write a letter to my senator about Darfur! Don't get in my way!"

It was a wonderful image of the young woman she did not want to be, one who self-righteously held up her political commitments like a badge when someone in her immediate vicinity was asking something personal of her. She could also see the danger of giving herself over to "heart stuff," only to be left devoid of political integrity. But she worried about pursuing a false religion of righteous politics, of commitments without real compassion.

Reem told me that she wasn't sure what her junior year would look like. In order to get admitted to nursing school, she needed to "get this struggling brain of mine to work right." Schoolwork and friends loomed large. If she wanted to go to the Muslim world eventually, to actually serve the people she believed she wanted to serve, she thought she might need to get her grades up—which meant not getting too entangled in either politics or personal dynamics. Her experience in Cairo remained vivid and emotionally powerful, but she was unsure where it would lead her. She believed that her faith required both her heart and her political commitment, but at times she felt overwhelmed by the needs she saw, including her own.

In the early twenty-first century, InterVarsity was just one of a number of evangelical organizations that self-consciously struggled with issues of race, cultural imperialism, and global poverty. World Vision was working on microfinance, a church in Wisconsin was traveling to Sudan to support schools and pastoral training, and young people were flocking to the global South on short-term missions. All of these endeavors were problematic in their own way, but all of them also highlighted how some American evangelicals were seeking to change—to become more worldly and committed to justice, often in concert with the educational and political work being done by their fellow believers in Africa, Asia, and Latin America. "What is your heart for?" was a question that, at the turn of the century, implied an answer that might well focus on social problems, on people in need.

As evangelicals looked to Egypt and Sudan and beyond, the forms of justice they imagined were in many ways quite different than the liberal or left-wing social justice visions of secular activists. Yet there were connections as well, both in their dreams of solidarity and their analysis of power. InterVarsity sent young people to cities all over the world and dared them to open their hearts to the poor. Those young people did, and asked serious questions about their own privilege in the process. Those questions were not very different from what young Americans of all backgrounds tended to ask themselves if, during their college years, they became aware of the world's fundamental inequalities. If these questions were to prove to be short-lived or limited, that, too, was not uncommon for college students.

These InterVarsity students did not just go to a poor part of the world, however; they went to Egypt. The fact that they were in a Muslim country was central to the experience. Even if they met relatively few Muslims, they were intensely conscious of being in a place where Islam was a dominant force. This was what had made their parents nervous and part of what had made their trip an adventure. Being in Egypt was an opportunity, if not for evangelism, then at least for encounter. Tiff went to Cairo because she had "a heart for the lost nations"; Dan came with questions about the stereotypes of Muslims he knew he carried; Reem dreamed of helping her "Muslim sisters." In each case, they arrived in Cairo knowing that they lived in a world in which Islam and Christianity were mapped as opposites and potentially as enemies.

In the end, however, most of them had very few of the kind of meaningful interactions with Muslims that they might have imagined or hoped for. There was little in the experience that taught them about Islam, or about the ways in which Egyptian Muslims lived their faith. InterVarsity's educational program in Cairo was richly interested in teaching students about "the poor," but it was silent on the poverty of these young Christians' understanding of Islam.

In the Sudanese, however, the InterVarsity students discovered fellow believers from half a world away, and they came away from their trip with a joyous sense that heaven would be "packed" with people who were both like and not like them. This world of faith was far more expansive than what many of them had grown up with—different, for example, than the fear of liberals and Muslims that Dan's parents had bequeathed to him. In addition, the south Sudanese they met were people whose suffering (as southerners and Christians in Sudan, as Sudanese in Egypt) was both real and compelling. The InterVarsity students felt connected to them as believers, which meant that they felt not only sympathy for the plight of the Sudanese but also a sense of themselves as part of a community of believers who were persecuted. They recognized their privilege as wealthy Americans, but they felt a certain shared vulnerability as believers. In other words, they were both culprits and victims. And that itself was enchanting.

Epilogue

THE STORY I have told here is central to the history of evangelicalism, both in the United States and globally. While it's true that most American evangelicals don't live and breathe international affairs, they are increasingly conscious of events outside US borders, especially those affecting what they see as the worldwide body of Christ. When we look at the history of American evangelicalism through a global lens, then, the picture changes significantly. Evangelical politics are not only about abortion and same-sex marriage, but also colonialism and neocolonialism, war and global poverty, religious freedom and Islam. The profound political differences that exist among evangelicals are easier to see if your vision encompasses both Kinshasa and Kansas.

This reality means that we have to pay attention to different, or at least additional, lead actors. We still have Franklin Graham, and the leaders of the religious Right in the 1980s, and the valiant but small evangelical Left, but an international frame pushes us to add the African American staff of the Billy Graham Evangelistic Association, the leaders of major NGOs like World Vision, and the people who went to Sudan to redeem slaves. People outside the United States also become important to the story of American evangelicalism, from the Romanian who took off his shirt in the US Congress to the South Africans, black and white, who brought their country's crisis to America's churches. This frame invites us to bring in Congolese Christians who challenged missionaries in the 1960s, and Ugandan Anglicans who argued a conservative position on homosexuality in the 2010s. In fact, the boundaries between American evangelicals and believers in Europe or the global South get blurry, as people travel across borders for college or seminary, new jobs, or missionary work. When a white South African teaching at a Southern Baptist seminary in Kentucky tries to convince the SBC to divest from South Africa, he is operating at the messy intersections that show how much evangelicalism is a truly global phenomenon.

Just because borders are indistinct, however, doesn't mean they are erased. When American evangelicals have been able to harness the power of the US state, they have used it to shape religious communities and global politics alike. We saw that when the United States went to war in Iraq, and when the International Religious Freedom Act shaped US policy in Sudan.

The complexity of the history I've traced here is real, but it might seem irrelevant in the face of one fact: in November 2016, 81 percent of white self-identified evangelicals voted for Donald Trump in the US presidential election.[1] They did so in the face of a candidate whose personal behavior and stated values were very different from those proclaimed by evangelicals. In fact, in the Republican primaries in the winter and spring of 2016, most US evangelical leaders—from James Dobson of Focus on the Family to Russell Moore of the SBC—had encouraged evangelicals to support someone else in the primaries: Ted Cruz, or perhaps Marco Rubio, or even, for a while, Ben Carson, all three of whom represented the non-Anglo future of evangelicalism. But people in the pews ignored that advice, as a plurality voted for Trump even with those avowedly conservative Christians in the race.[2]

Trump soon had his team of well-known evangelical supporters, with Jerry Falwell Jr. an early endorser, and by the time he was the presumptive Republican nominee, he had an evangelical "advisory board" that included not only Falwell but also Bishop Harry Jackson, the African American author and pastor of a megachurch outside of Washington, DC; Pentecostal televangelist Paula White; James Dobson, who found his way over to Trump once Cruz was defeated; and a dozen other televangelists, authors, and megachurch pastors from New York to Dallas to California.[3]

In the general election, Trump won the white evangelical vote hands down. Once again, however, the polls that asked how "evangelicals" voted repeated the same category mistake, in that few non-white people were slotted into the evangelical camp.[4] Many leading evangelicals of color were outspoken supporters of Clinton, or at least opponents of Trump. The day after the vote, T.D. Jakes, no liberal, described African Americans as "traumatized" by Trump's election.[5] Others said that the election had opened a racial wound among US evangelicals that would not be easily healed. Yolanda Pierce, the dean of Howard University's Divinity School, wrote that "something had broken" for her after the election. She had been working on teaching about issues of race and gender in the church for years, but now:

> I watched as 81 percent of white evangelicals and born-again Christians dismissed his affairs, adultery, multiple marriages, participation in porn subculture, refusals to release his tax returns, failure to donate to charities to which he promised money, mockery of his own supporters (including their wives and parents), participation in racist lies about President Obama, stereotyping of African Americans, Mexican Americans and Muslims—and still voted for him.[6]

Right after the election, Jenny Yang of World Relief, the aid organization sponsored by the NAE, told *Christianity Today*: "Many people of color are feeling incredibly vulnerable at the prospect of a Trump presidency while trying to heal from the trauma of this past year. It is not easy to overlook such barbed attacks on your identity as immigrants, minorities, or the disabled." But Yang wanted to find the missionary opportunity in what she saw as a crisis. "This difficult time," she said, "means there is an incredible opportunity for the church to stand in the gap and live out what we believe about the gospel to reach those who are hurting and on the margins."[7] Others were less hopeful. On an international conference call, a group of global evangelical leaders expressed great frustration with Trump's victory, saying that it would hurt Christian witness, because people outside the United States saw that American (white) evangelicals had chosen such an amoral person as their leader.[8]

Most evangelicals who voted for Trump cited the Supreme Court as a primary motivator. It is likely that the president will make multiple appointments to the court in his term, and Trump's evangelical supporters claimed religious freedom as a central concern. Many of the religious freedom issues that might be brought before the court will be domestic, such as whether conservative evangelicals, or others, have the right to discriminate against LGBTQ people in providing services or in hiring. Federal contractors, including defense contractors, have asked to be released from the requirement that they not discriminate. In his first year, Trump also moved to free religious employers of the requirement that they provide certain kinds of birth control as part of their mandate under the Affordable Care Act, even as he and the Republicans in Congress failed to gut the ACA altogether.[9] Trump frequently positioned himself as a protector of an interpretation of the first amendment that allowed religious groups greater freedom to call on the power of the state. In his acceptance speech at the Republican National Convention, Trump called for overturning the 1954 law that prohibits tax-exempt organizations from participating in political activities. In fall of 2016, the Trump Department of Justice filed a legal brief on behalf of the cake store owners who asserted their right to refuse LGBTQ customers in *Materpiece Cakeshop v. Colorado Civil Rights Commission*.[10]

It is one of the ironies of Trump's presidency that religious freedom will likely be a signature issue for both liberals and conservatives. Liberals are worried because they believe that a Trump presidency will challenge the separations that prevent, or at least limit, government support of religion, such as prayers before public meetings or allowing religiously inflected teachings in public schools.[11] But perhaps the most important issue for liberals, including evangelical liberals, is the status of Muslims. The Trump campaign unleashed a tsunami of racist, anti-immigrant, and anti-Muslim rhetoric, and Muslims faced a dramatic increase in violence; in 2015, assaults on Muslims reached levels that had not been seen since the immediate post- 9/11 period.[12] As of this writing, the president has tried repeatedly to ban immigrants from Muslim-majority countries, or to reinvigorate a national Muslims registry, or both. Muslims in the United States face threats to their safety as well as a broadly hostile political climate. And yet 57 percent of white evangelicals told pollsters that they believe Christians face a great deal of discrimination in the US today, while only 44 percent said the same was true of Muslims. In other words, the discourse of "persecuted Christians" that emerged on the international stage profoundly shapes how many American evangelicals see the domestic realities around them.[13]

The question of whether and how the United States protects the Muslims within its borders has international relevance. As President Obama left office, the United States remained at war in Iraq and Afghanistan, was fighting ISIS in Syria, backing Saudi attacks on Yemen, and launching drone attacks around the world. Yet, with a few exceptions (such as Egypt), most Muslim countries held more positive views of the United States in 2015 than they did when Obama took office in 2009.[14] This could easily be reversed, of course, should the Trump administration be seen as launching an attack on Muslim civil rights.

Globally, the evangelical movement continues to organize against what it sees as the persecution of Christians. The Center for the Study of Global Christianity recently released a report estimating that ninety thousand Christians had been martyred from 2005–2015. The team used a broad definition, which included any Christian who died in communal violence or genocide, whether or not they were killed specifically for their faith. That kind of capacious approach was designed to show "Christian Martyrdom as a pervasive phenomenon."[15] But it did little to explain the long and complex histories that placed Christians, Muslims, and others in situations of violent conflict, of terrorism and war.

I have argued here that Christian persecution, however real in certain times and places, also became a symbol that resonated far beyond what might be expected from the facts on the ground. Persecution became the logic through which some evangelicals envisioned a global conflict with Islam. This was never uncontested, but it was politically and religiously powerful. From the time Richard Wurmbrand stood up and showed his scarred back on the Senate floor in 1966 to the time that Sudanese Christians displayed their own scars in a video about persecution, the persecuted body has been a rich resource for evangelicals' self-fashioning. In some instances, as in South Africa, the act of victim identification has created forms of community and solidarity that reached for liberation. Too often, however, the discourse of persecution has tended to read political conflict as religious conflict; intentionally or not, it augmented the sense of anxiety, anger, and religious aggression that dominated far too much of the world's politics in the twenty-first century.

Increasingly, some traditional conservative Christians have begun to have doubts about the ways that religious Right leaders continue to embrace Trump. Michael Gerson, an avowed evangelical who had been a speechwriter for President George W. Bush, bemoaned the close ties between white evangelical leaders and the president's former advisor Steve Bannon. "Evidently," Gerson commented unhappily, "the Christian approach to social justice is miraculously identical to 1930s Republican protectionism, isolationism and nativism."[16]

Over the past fifty years, American evangelicals have operated in many registers, crossing borders as they created networks, constructing their sense of a multiracial faith community that is always embodied, often imperiled, and frequently enchanted. In the process, US evangelical life has become intricately linked to the experiences and values of believers around the world. Those links were not always liberalizing, but they have been transformative.

White American evangelicals helped put Donald Trump in the White House, and they did so in a global climate of increasing hostility toward Muslims, Christian fears of persecution, and ongoing tensions around sexuality and gender. But the transnational evangelical community is also racially and politically diverse, and the America-first vision of a leader like Trump is deeply offensive to many believers, within and beyond US shores. The American evangelicals who support this worldview must now face hard questions about their values from the global community they have claimed as their own. The kingdom of God may have no borders, but American evangelicals have yet to craft a politics made to the measure of the world.

ACKNOWLEDGMENTS

Writing this book has been an exciting, surprising, and sometimes exhausting process. I owe a tremendous debt of gratitude to the family, friends, and colleagues who made this book possible with their support, good humor, and good ideas. I began this project more than ten years ago, as I was finishing the second edition of *Epic Encounters*, and it has gone through several iterations during that time. I first want to thank my colleagues and students at George Washington University, which has been my intellectual home for the past twenty years. From my graduate students, I have learned more than it is probably wise to admit, and I feel very grateful for that. My colleagues in American Studies are wonderful intellectuals and friends, and just very decent humans, which has been a gift. I am sad to say that we lost three beloved colleagues in the last few years. I miss Phyllis Palmer, James O. Horton, and my dear friend James A. Miller.

I received research help from a number of students at GW and beyond, including some who have gone on to become faculty themselves. Thank you to Ashley Brown, Ahana Das, Meghan Drury, Julie Elman, Sandra Heard, Joe Kye (Yale), David Kieran, Zoe Jenkins, Laurie Lahey, Daniel Landsman, Laura Smith-Gary (Princeton), Tovah Liebowitz, Kim Pendleton, Katie Russell (University of Arkansas), Kevin Strait, Alyson Thomas (Fuller Theological Seminary), Andrew Warne (Northwestern), and Natalie Zelt. I owe a special thanks to Shannon Mancus, who has worked with me over several years, and to Abigail Pioch, who made a huge difference at the last minute.

I have presented parts of this work at conferences, workshops, and public lectures over the past decade, and have learned a great deal from the conversations and interactions there. I want to thank the people who came, listened, and asked hard questions.

Several friends have read large segments of the book and/or have talked through its ideas with me in great detail over the years. I owe particular thanks to Mona Atia, Michael Barnett, Brooke Blower, Nemata Blyden, Mark Bradley, Marie Griffith, David Hollinger, Amy Kaplan, Andrew Preston, Penny von Eschen, and an anonymous reader for Oxford University Press for reading large segments of the manuscript, and for their comments and detailed suggestions at key points in this project. Pamela Haag edited the entire manuscript as it neared the end. Several members of a missions theology reading group were also kind enough to read the whole manuscript and offer their comments; my thanks to Ned Hale, the late Vernon Visick, and Kristine Whitnable. I am also delighted to have been part of a European and US working group on American evangelicalism in a global context, helmed by Uta Balbier, Kendrick Oliver, Axel Schäfer, and Hans Krabbendam.

I received important advice and counsel on specific issues or chapters from Libby Anker, Mona Azadi, Uta Balbier, Stephanie Batiste, Megan Black, Jennifer Brinkerhoff, Anthea Butler, Julie Chamberlain, Krista Comer, Jonathan Ebel, Julie Elman, David Engerman, Ramzi Fawaz, Ruth Feldstein, Max Friedman, Paula Fuller, Jane Gerhard, Faye Ginsberg, Inderpal Grewal, Zareena Grewal, Richard Grinker, Tom Guglielmo, Michael Horka, Elizabeth Shakman Hurd, Gordon Hutner, Laura Cook Kenna, Kip Kosek, Eid Mohamed, Bethany Moreton, Hilton Obenzinger, Kendrick Oliver, Kim Pendleton, Uta Poiger, Saba Mahmood, Daniel Rodgers, Doug Rossinow, David Ryan, Noah Salomon, Barbara Savage, Alex Schäfer, Malini Schueller, Stephanie Schulte, Winnifred Sullivan, Chris Toesing, Robert Vitalis, Gayle Wald, Priscilla Wald, Barbie Zelizer, and Angela Zito.

A number of archives and archivists went out of their way to help me with research for this project. I owe particular thanks to the staff at the Billy Graham Center Archives in Wheaton, Illinois, where I spent many weeks over a number of years. Thank you in particular to Bob Schuster and Paul Ericksen, who have been generous with their time and expertise. I owe thanks as well to Adam Gossman at the DuPlessis Archives at Fuller Theological Seminary, Michelle Crites at the Flowers Pentecostal Heritage Center, and all of the staff at the other archives I consulted. I also want to thank the many people who agreed to be interviewed for this project, not all of whom are listed in the notes. Thank you for taking the time to share your stories.

I am very grateful for the financial support and time off that have made this project possible. I received time off and intellectual community from Princeton University's Davis Center for Historical Studies and the University of Pennsylvania's Annenberg School of Communication, as well as GW's Columbian College of Arts and Sciences Dean's Research Chair. I received research travel and research assistance support via an Asian, Black, Hispanic, and Native American United Methodist History Research Grant; a Larry E. May Study Grant, Southern Baptist Historical Library and Archive; and GW's University Facilitating Fund and Columbian College Facilitating Fund.

Theo Calderara at Oxford University Press is a remarkable editor, who worked closely and patiently with me over many years. His close reading of the near final draft was detailed and insightful, and I am grateful to him for shepherding and supporting this book through its many stages. Thank you also to Drew Anderla, Damian Penfold, and Derek Gottlieb for their work on production.

People perhaps use the word "amazing" too easily these days, but I can't think of anything else that quite captures the experience of reading political theory and talking about politics and life with my reading group, who have been both intellectual allies and among my dearest friends. Thank you to Mona Atia, Johanna Bockman, Elliott Colla, Ilana Feldman, Despina Kakoudaki, Dina Khoury, Kevin Martin, Shira Robinson, and Andrew Zimmerman.

Other friends and my family have lived with this book for a long time, and I am grateful for every moment of laughter and love. For listening, talking, and just being there, my heartfelt thanks to David Brown, Debra Budiani, David Hawkins, Jeff Covington, Jennifer James, Amy Kaplan, Carla Lillvik, my sister Julie McAlister, Ann Munson, Richard Ogden, Tony Palomba, Kelly Pemberton, Uta Poiger, Gary Simoneau, and Gayle Wald. I am also grateful to my friend Wendy Eudy and her family, who have taken care of me and my family in more ways than I can count.

I owe a particular debt to Dick Robinson, who has been more central to this project than he knows. From our first meeting in 2006, he impressed me with his energy, open-mindedness, and loving stance toward the world. He opened several doors for me, took me to Sudan with his church group, and answered many hours of questions. Dick has trusted me with his story; and that story helped me understand the larger history I tell in this book. I am very grateful for his generosity.

This book is dedicated to my parents. My father, Gene McAlister, has put up with delayed visits and a distracted daughter but has remained patient and caring throughout. I am very lucky to have him in my life. My mother, Katie Slater McAlister, died while I was completing this book after she had lived a number of years with Alzheimer's. During the last part of her life, she didn't understand much about my work or this book, but she understood how much I loved her. And that was all that mattered.

And—first and last and always—are the thanks I owe to my life partner, Carl Conetta, who has lived with this project as my brilliant interlocutor and constant support. He asked hard questions and brought home cupcakes. He read chapters with remarkable clarity of insight and then insisted we go for a walk. Carl has put up with a research and writing process that has shaped our lives for more than a decade. This book could never have happened without him. More importantly, our life together is the foundation of my world.

NOTES

‹շ_____

Abbreviations

PERIODICALS

CT	Christianity Today
CSM	Christian Science Monitor
EMQ	Evangelical Missions Quarterly
LAT	Los Angeles Times
NYT	New York Times
VM	Voice of Missions
WP	Washington Post (Washington Post & Times Herald, 1959-1973)

ARCHIVES CONSULTED

APC	Alan Paton Centre archives, Pietermaritzburg, South Africa
	PC130: Michael Cassidy Papers
BGCA	Billy Graham Center Archives, Wheaton, Illinois
	CN 46: Lausanne Committee on World Evangelization
	CN 81: Africa Inland Mission
	CN 84: Vera Edna Thiessen Papers

CN 141: Oral Histories and Manuscripts Project
CN 165: Evangelical Foreign Missions Association
CN 179: Short Terms Abroad
CN 191: BGEA Hour of Decision Radio Program
CN 214: BGEA Worldwide Pictures
CN 300: Intervarsity Christian Fellowship
CN 352: International Foreign Missions Association
CN 459: Fellowship Foundation
CN 498: Bill Pannell Interview
CN 599: Ephemera of "Auca" Incident
CN 629: Harold Ockenga

BHP   University of Arkansas, Billy Hargis Papers
DuP   David DuPlessis Archives, Fuller Theological Seminary, Pasadena, California
Coll 38: Arthur Glasser Papers
Coll 66: Duane Pederson, Jesus People International, and Hollywood Free Paper Collection
EGP   Easter Gordon Papers, University of the Western Cape, Capetown, South Africa
FPHC   Flowers Pentecostal Heritage Center, Springfield, Missouri
SAHA   South Africa Historical Archive, Johannesburg, South Africa
AL2457: Original SAHA Collection
AL3066: Faith Hearings Collection
SBHLA   Southern Baptist Historical Library and Archives, Nashville, Tennessee
AR138-1 and AR138-2: Christian Life Commission Resource Files
AR140: Christian Life Commission/ Ethics and Religious Liberty Commission Publications
AR550: Baptist World Alliance Collection
AR551: International Mission Board
AR905: Emmanuel Lemuel McCall papers
SCRBC   Schomburg Center for Research in Black Culture, New York Public Library
Alexander and Shirlene Stewart Pentecostal Collection
AME *Voice of Missions* magazine
South African Black Consciousness Movement Collection
WITS   Historical Papers, Witwaterswand University, Johannesburg, South Africa
AB1064: South Africa Congress on Mission and Evangelism
AB1291: World Council of Churches
AB3214: Michael Worship papers
AG2613: Justice and Peace Records
AG2843: Institute for Contextual Theology
AG2918: Kairos Collection
WSC   Wheaton College Special Collections, Wheaton, Illinois
SC113: National Association of Evangelicals Publications

INTRODUCTION

1. Robinson, "A Case Study in Partnership," June 4, 2006, from the conference handout.

2. Tyrrell, *Reforming the World*.

3. The scholarship on the Religious Right is too vast to list here, but particularly useful examples include: Heineman, *God Is a Conservative*; Carpenter, *Revive Us Again*; Martin, *With God On Our Side*; Miller, *Billy Graham*; Goldberg, *Kingdom Coming*. On the US evangelical Left, see Swartz, *Moral Minority*; Gasaway, *Progressive Evangelicals*.

4. The *Journal of American Studies* special issue on US global evangelicalism (November 2017) includes a number of contributors who are doing important work on evangelical internationalism, including Uta Balbier, Heather Curtis, Hans Krabbendam, Kendrick Oliver, Axel Schäfer, and David Swartz. See also King, "The New Internationalists," and Turek, "To Bring Good News to All Nations." An important argument for the existence, and importance, of the evangelical center is Gushee, *Future of Faith*.

5. Wuthnow, *Boundless Faith*, 94. In the massive literature on Americanization and the debates around it, see Poiger, *Jazz, Rock, and Rebels*; Rosenberg, *Spreading the American Dream*. For important critiques that focus specifically on religion and cultural imperialism, see Landau, *Realm of the Word*; Dunch, "Beyond Cultural Imperialism."

6. Hackett and Grim, "Global Christianity"; Pew Research Center, "Future of World Religions."

7. Hackett and Grim, "Global Christianity," 64.

8. Lugo and Copperman, "Tolerance and Tension," 154.

9. On debates over biblical authority among evangelicals, see Worthen, *Apostles of Reason*.

10. Bebbington, *Evangelicalism in Modern Britain*, 1–19. George Marsden adds to this definition "the importance of a spiritually transformed life." Marsden, *Understanding Fundamentalism and Evangelicalism*, 5.

11. Harold J. Ockenga, "Resurgent Evangelical Leadership," *CT*, October 10, 1960, 11–15. Ockenga seems to have been quoting from the definition of "evangel" in the *Desk Standard Dictionary of the English Language* (Funk and Wagnalls, 1919). The rich literature that critiques the theological focus of some religious history and turns toward lived religion as a category of analysis includes Hall, *Lived Religion in America*; Bell, *Ritual Theory, Ritual Practice*; Asad, *Genealogies of Religion*.

12. Watt makes a similar point about the evangelical focus on living a Christian life as more important than strict orthodoxy in *A Transforming Faith*, 23–28. George Marsden's description of early-20th-century holiness traditions describes the "personal piety, optimism, and activism that . . . might well have been taken for the overwhelmingly dominant traits of conservative American Protestantism overall." Marsden, *Fundamentalism and American Culture*, 101.

13. The low number is from Ed Stetzer, "Barna: How Many Have a Biblical Worldview?" *CT* (web only), March 9, 2009, http://www.christianitytoday.com/edstetzer/2009/march/barna-how-many-have-biblical-worldview.html. The largest percentages are from the Baylor Religion Survey, "American Piety in the 21st Century." Pew Research also finds this: when pollsters ask if a person is evangelical or "born again," 35 percent of people say yes, including 22 percent of American Catholics. Ed Stetzer, "In a Dramatic Shift, the American Church Is More Evangelical than Ever," *WP*, May 14, 2015, https://www.washingtonpost.com/news/acts-of-faith/wp/2015/05/14/in-a-dramatic-shift-the-american-church-is-more-evangelical-than-ever. The NAE statement of faith

is here: http://nae.net/statement-of-faith/. The NAE's own research, conducted with LifeWay, uses a simpler but similar definition, as explained here: http://nae.net/evangelical-beliefs-research-definition/. However, as the NAE explains, just 59 percent of Protestants who identify themselves as evangelicals strongly agree with all four statements. An important critique of religious polling is Wuthnow, *Inventing American Religion.*

Sometimes a pollster simply decides which denominations are evangelical and then counts their membership. A leading example of this methodology is the standard-setting Pew Religious Landscape survey, completed most recently in May 2015. Pew places the number of people attending evangelical churches at 25.4 percent. It does not include traditionally black churches in this formulation; the survey places the number in those churches at 6.5 percent (http://www.pewforum. org/files/2015/05/RLS-08-26-full-report.pdf). Pew's survey finds that of those people defined as evangelical, 11 percent are Latino, 6 percent black, 2 percent Asian, and 5 percent other. Of course, the African American percentage would be much higher if Pew included historically black churches.

14. The Pew Research Center does a large and comprehensive report on global Christianity that uses two methods simultaneously. To determine whether a person in Norway or Nigeria is a Christian or another religion, Pew goes by self-identification on the census. If 50 percent of people in Nigeria say they are Christian (and they do), then that is the number Pew uses. But censuses rarely ask about more specific identifications such as evangelical or Pentecostal. To estimate the number of evangelicals in the world, Pew identified a set of denominations that it considers evangelical and counts all of those members. It then draws on survey data to estimate what percentage of the members of *other* denominations are evangelical. It is not that this method is wrong; it is just that it necessarily depends on a great deal of estimation. And it is fundamentally different than most surveys of people in the United States, which generally depend on how a person self-identifies. Hackett and Grim, "Global Christianity," 89–97.

15. Bentley, "Bible Believers"; "NAE, LifeWay Research Publish Evangelical Beliefs Research Definition," November 19, 2015, http://nae.net/evangelical-beliefs-research-definition/.

16. Frank Newport and Joseph Carroll, "Another Look at Evangelicals in America Today," *Gallup.com*, December 2, 2005, http://www.gallup.com/poll/20242/Another-Look-Evangelicals-America-Today.aspx; Pew Research Center, "A Religious Portrait of African-Americans." African Americans are almost certainly undercounted as members of primarily white churches, especially if they gave a "vague" definition of their denomination. In the Pew Research Center's standard-bearing survey, between 35 and 53 percent of respondents gave only a general denominational affiliation—for example, "I'm just a Methodist." If the person who gave that general denominational identity was black, and if their denomination was one that had a sizeable representation of historically black churches, then that person was coded as part of the historically black church. So, for example, if an African American person said, "I'm just a Baptist," she would have been coded as part of the historically black church because there are important black churches that are Baptist, including the National Baptist Convention. But if a white person said, "I'm just a Baptist," she would have been coded either as an evangelical or a mainline Protestant, depending on how she answered a follow-up question about whether she identified as born again/evangelical. Pew Research Center, "America's Changing Religious Landscape," 24.

17. Pew Research Center, "Shifting Religious Identity of Latinos" and Pew Research Center, "Asian Americans," 7, 37. On this diversity, see also Balmer, *Mine Eyes Have Seen the Glory.*

18. Two groundbreaking works on gender and Christianity in general, among many others, are Daly, *The Church and the Second Sex*; Pagels, *The Gnostic Gospels.*

19. Prothero, *American Jesus*, 94. See also Fox, *Jesus in America.*

20. Sutton, *Aimee Semple McPherson*. On Pentecostals in the early twentieth century, see Wacker, *Heaven Below*.

21. Savage, *Your Spirits Walk Beside Us*, 132. Savage is quoting Bethune, "The Progress of Negro Women," an address given at the Chicago Women's Federation, June 1933.

22. Griffith, *God's Daughters*.

23. Jakes, *Woman, Thou Art Loosed*; Winner, "T.D. Jakes Feels Your Pain: Though Critics Question His Theology, This Fiery Preacher Packs Arenas with a Message of Emotional Healing," *CT*, February 7, 2000, 52-59. On masculinity and celebrity pastors in an earlier era, see Lofton, "The Preacher Paradigm."

24. Frederick, *Colored Television*, 87–114. Frederick is citing an unpublished paper by anthropologist and missionary theorist Robert Priest. See also Walton, *Watch This!*

25. On the debate about Biblical criticism and modernist theology, see Kuklick, *Puritans in Babylon*.

26. On "moral establishment," see Sehat, *Myth of American Religious Freedom*. On the cultural dominance of the mainline Protestantism, see Hedstrom, *Liberal Religion*; Preston, *Sword of the Spirit*; Hollinger, *After Cloven Tongues of Fire*; Coffman, *Christian Century*.

27. Numerous studies cover the history of modern evangelicalism; those that pay close attention to the relationship with mainline Protestantism include Ammerman, *Bible Believers*; Carpenter, *Revive Us Again*; FitzGerald, *The Evangelicals*; Marsden, *Reforming Fundamentalism*.

28. Glasser, "The Mission Board and the Church." On ecumenical-evangelical relations, see Hollinger, *After Cloven Tongues of Fire*, 18–55; Preston, *Sword of the Spirit*, 477–95; Inboden, *Religion and American Foreign Policy*. On the theological debates, see Bassham, *Mission Theology*, 61. For the interwar period, see Kosek, *Acts of Conscience*.

29. Bassham, *Mission Theology*, 60–73; Preston, "Tempered by the Fires of War," 191–200; Lefever, *Amsterdam to Nairobi*, 35; Welch, "Mobilizing Morality"; "WCC Endorses Divestment from Israel," *Christian Century*, March 22, 2005, 16.

30. *CT* quoted in Lefever, *Amsterdam to Nairobi*, 25; Preston, "Tempered by the Fires of War," and "Evangelical Internationalism."

31. McAlister, "What Is Your Heart For?"

32. Weber, *Protestant Ethic,* and "Science as a Vocation."

33. Within the large literature on primitivism and orientalism, see Torgovnick, *Gone Primitive*; Lockman, *Contending Visions*; Marr, *Cultural Roots of American Islamicism*; Edwards, *Morocco Bound*; Hoganson, *Consumers' Imperium*; Tweed, *American Encounter with Buddhism*. Also see Latour, *We Have Never Been Modern*.

34. Jones, *The New Christians*; McAlister, "Left Behind and the Politics of Prophecy Talk."

35. I discuss this in detail in McAlister, "What Is Your Heart For?"

36. This speaks to the larger discourse that is identified in Brown, *States of Injury*.

37. Castelli, *Martyrdom and Memory*, 173.

38. Augustine, *Sermons* 51:2, quoted in ibid., 105.

39. Latour, *Reassembling the Social*, 31.

40. On the many meanings and uses of the body in Christianity, see Asad, *Genealogies of Religion*, 83–170; Griffith, *Born Again Bodies*.

41. Ahmed, *Promise of Happiness*, 230. Much recent work in affect theory has focused on cognitive or perhaps pre-cognitive approaches, seeing the concept of affect as a way of talking about the neuroscience of emotion, its biochemical baseline. See Massumi, *Parables for the Virtual*. For a clear and hard-hitting debate on affect theory, see Leys, "The Turn to Affect"; Connolly,

"The Complexity of Intention." In this framing of emotion, I am drawing on Berlant, "Compassion (and Withholding)."

CHAPTER I

1. Newman, *Getting Right with God*, 142. For a discussion of Oni's admission, see also Willis, *All According to God's Plan*, 170–72.

2. A media report with Oni and Holmes on September 26, 1966, after the church's decision to split, can be found at http://crdl.usg.edu/. See also "Minister is Ousted Over Racial Issue," *NYT*, September 26, 1966; "150 Tattnall Baptist Quit Church, Form Integrated Body," *Afro-American*, October 29, 1966. For a discussion of Oni's actions, see Willis, *All According to God's Plan*, 180–81; Mays, *Born to Rebel*, 246–49; Newman, *Getting Right with God*, 140–45; Harvey, *Freedom's Coming*, 244–45. Harvey mistakenly refers to Oni as Omi and places the date earlier, in 1964.

3. Jones and Gilbreath, *Gospel Trailblazer*, 123–26, 150–58. (Liberia had more black missionaries than most countries, because the Church of God in Christ had a missionary presence there, as did the AME church.)

4. Swartz, *Moral Minority*, 131.

5. On racism as a US foreign policy issue, see Dudziak, *Cold War Civil Rights*; Borstelmann, *Cold War and Color Line*. On racism and missions for mainline Protestants, see Sharkey, "American Presbyterians." A more general discussion of the issue is Hollinger, *After Cloven Tongues of Fire*. On race and empire, in the United States and beyond, see Johnson, *African American Religions*.

6. "Man to be Heard," *Time*, November 8, 1926, 32.

7. Carpenter, *Revive Us Again*, 184–85; Wuthnow, *Boundless Faith*, 125–26; Anderson, "In Pursuit of Mission," 108–10; Carpenter, "Propagating the Faith."

8. Letchford, "Dialog on Racial Prejudice," *HIS,* October 1959, 10.

9. Willis, *All According to God's Plan*, 82–83.

10. Ibid., 80. Also in 1957, the Southern Baptist missionaries in Nigeria adopted a resolution that states, "Racism is inconsistent with, and a hindrance to, the world mission task to which Southern Baptists have committed themselves." Newman, *Getting Right with God*, 137.

11. Kent, *Converting Women*, 53.

12. Klein, *Cold War Orientalism*, 87–99.

13. Wacker, "The Waning of the Missionary Impulse"; Lian, *Conversion of Missionaries*; Buck, *The Good Earth*. On missionaries and the state more generally, see Balbier et al., "Introduction: Exploring the Global History of American Evangelicalism."

14. Hollinger, *Protestants Abroad*, 70. The book is Hocking, *Re-Thinking Missions*. See also Hutchison, *Errand to the World*, 146–75; Boger, "American Protestantism in the Asian Crucible, 1919–1939."

15. The film was based on the novel. Mercer, *Rachel Cade*; Michener, *Hawaii*. On Michener's book and its impact, Klein, *Cold War Orientalism*, 223–64. On images of missionaries more broadly, see Ruble, *Gospel of Freedom*.

16. Achebe, *Things Fall Apart*.

17. Preston, *Sword of the Spirit*, 182–86.

18. Ruble, *Gospel of Freedom*.

19. "'Go Ye and Preach the Gospel': Five Do and Die," *Life*, January 30, 1956, 10-19; Elisabeth Elliot, "Through Gates of Splendor," *Reader's Digest*, August 1956, 56ff.

20. Long, "In the Modern World But Not of It," 229. See also Cook, "Five Lives for the Aucas," *Moody Monthly*, March 1956, 38-42; Lois Thiessen, "A Song in Aucaland," *HIS*, May 1960, 20; "Death in the Jungle," *WP*, January 14, 1956; "Ecuador: Mission to the Aucas," *Time*, January 22, 1956, 24.

21. "Martyr's Widows Return to Teach in Jungle," *Life*, May 20, 1957, 24–31; Ellisabeth Elliot, "Child Among Her Father's Killers: Missionaries Live with Aucas," *Life*, November 24, 1958, 349. Elisabeth Elliott went on to become a well-known author of evangelical books on sexual morality, including the (in)famous 1984 advice manual for young women, *Passion and Purity: Bringing your Love Life under God's Control*.

22. Lisa Ann Cockrel, "Reviews: End of the Spear," *CT Movies*, January 20, 2006, http://www.christianitytoday.com/ct/2006/januaryweb-only/endofthespear.html.

23. On ten million, see Ammerman, *Baptist Battles*, 52. Comparison to Methodist Church: Kelley, *Why Conservative Churches Are Growing*, 27–28. The Methodist Church was formed from the unification of its northern and southern branches in 1939. The United Methodist Church was formed in 1968 by a unification of the Methodist Church and the Evangelical United Brethren Church.

24. By the 1940s, Southern evangelicals, including some of the SBC, were moving westward, establishing outposts in California particularly. But the SBC remained a largely Southern denomination into the 1980s. Ammerman, *Baptist Battles*, 50–63. Also Dochuk, *From Bible Belt to Sunbelt*.

25. Leonard, *Baptists in America*, 28–30; Eighmy, *Churches in Cultural Captivity*, 109–23, 144–47.

26. Newman, *Getting Right with God*, 1–19.

27. "Race Relations: A Charter of Principles," Southern Baptist Convention, May 1947, Folder 6-6, AR140, SBHLA; Newman, *Getting Right With God*, 72–74.

28. McCormick, "Saviour for the Negro in Africa and in America," *Royal Service,* September 1948, 25, cited in Maxwell, "This Only Christian Women Can Supply," 258.

29. Valentine, *Believe and Behave*. Valentine wrote his dissertation under the direction of T.B. Maston, one of the most important liberal theologians in the SBC.

30. Willis, *All According to God's Plan*, 68. The number for 1956 is from Newman, *Getting Right with God*, 137.

31. *Annual Report of the Southern Baptist Convention, 1954*, 403–04, at http://www.sbhla.org/sbc_annuals/. The report is quoting a conversation with Baptist leader M.T. Rankin.

32. Newman, *Getting Right with God*, 23–25, 87–109.

33. *Annual Report of the Southern Baptist Convention, 1954,* 55–56. The convention was asked to accept the report and its recommendations, but only the recommendations were discussed on the floor. The full report was, however, submitted as part of the convention's "Annual Report," on pages 400–09. On the singing, see Dupont, *Mississippi Praying*, 63.

34. Stephens, "It Has to Come From the Hearts of the People," 11.

35. Goodrich, "The SBC Convention," *Baptist Record*, June 10, 1954, 3, quoted in Roach, "The Southern Baptist Convention and Civil Rights, 1954-1995," 26.

36. Williams, "Jerry Falwell's Sunbelt Politics"; Harding, *Book of Jerry Falwell*, 14–29; Heineman, *God Is a Conservative*, 14–24; Harvey, *Freedom's Coming*, 231; Stephens, "It Has to Come From the Hearts of the People," 3.

37. McCorthy letter to the *Arkansas Baptist Newsmagazine*, September 10, 1964, quoted in Newman, *Getting Right with God*, 52.

38. The literature on evangelicalism, civil rights, and race (particularly white and African American racial tensions) is extensive and growing. In addition to Chappell, *A Stone of Hope*,

and other books specifically cited in this chapter, see also Thompson, *Richmond's Priests and Prophets*; Mathews, *Doctrine and Race*; Wadsworth, *Ambivalent Miracles*; Billingsley, *It's a New Day*; Leonard, *God's Last and Only Hope*; Manis, *Southern Civil Religions in Conflict*; Noll, *God and Race in American Politics*.

39. Chappell, *A Stone of Hope*, 116.

40. There is a detailed discussion of this verse by Thomas Buford Maston, "Biblical Teachings and Race Relations," *Review & Expositor*, July 1959, 233–42.

41. Carver was writing in *Commission*. Quoted by Willis, *All According to God's Plan*, 42.

42. Newman, *Getting Right with God*, 137–38.

43. James L. Monroe, "The White Man's Dilemma," *CT*, October 26, 1962, 15–16.

44. Newman, *Getting Right with God*, 28.

45. Stephens, "It Has to Come From the Hearts of the People," 14.

46. Ibid., 14–15.

47. Dupont, *Mississippi Praying*, 173–77; Roach, "The Southern Baptist Convention and Civil Rights, 1954–1995," 80–84.

48. Elton Crowson, "Letter to the Editor," *CT*, June 19, 1964, 17. See also Stephens, "It Has to Come From the Hearts of the People," 16–18.

49. Haynes, *The Last Segregated Hour*.

50. Swartz, *Moral Minority*, 27–28.

51. Harris Mobley, quoted in Willis, *All According to God's Plan*, 81.

CHAPTER 2

1. Various documents from the State Department, its memos to the OAU, UN, and rebel leader Christopher Gbenye are recorded in "United States Cooperates with Belgium in Rescue of Hostages from the Congo," *Department of State Bulletin*, December 14, 1964, 838–46.

2. In fact, US officials held the key to the rescue, and the Belgians could only move forward with US approval to send its planes and pilots. The pivotal role of the United States is made clear in a number of government memos, including "Telephone Conversation Between President Johnson and Secretary of State Rusk," Document 352 in *Foreign Relations of the United States, 1964–68*, edited by Howland, Humphrey, and Schwar.

On the US role in the rescue, see also Namikas, *Battleground Africa*, 109–209; Weissman, *Foreign Policy in the Congo*, 238–47.

3. "Congo Martyr: Dr. Paul Carlson," *Life*, December 4, 1964, 38–42; "The Congo Massacre," *Time*, December 4, 1964, 54ff.

4. On reading images as documents of encounter, see Azoulay, *Civil Contract*.

5. Graham, "Tragedy of the Congo," *Hour of Decision*, December 13, 1964, Tape 778, CN 91, BGCA. On Graham in this period, see Martin, *Prophet with Honor*, especially chapters 9 and 10; Kruse, *One Nation Under God*, chapter 2.

6. Wilbert Norton, "Memorial Service—God's Word," *Urbana.org*, December 1964, http://www.urbana.org/articles/memorial-service. See also UPI, "Dr. Carlson, 31 Others, Honored at Convention," *Chicago Daily Defender*, December 31, 1964.

7. On missionaries as a source of information, see Dow, "Missionary Factor."

8. The term "ordinary religion" is used by Albanese to describe religion that is so enmeshed in the culture of a society that it is almost invisible—separated from "extraordinary" religious

experience. See Albanese, *America*. Here I mean something slightly different. I refer to religious activities that hover across analytic categories, being at once "lived religion," theology, and church history or institutions.

9. The number 2,600 Protestant missionaries (with no separation of Americans) is given by Elmer Neufield, "The Unfinished Revolution: Congo History and Missionary-African Relations Today," *MCC Report,* Spring 1963, 1–29. Francis Hendrickson did a survey of Protestant missionaries in Congo in 1964 for his doctoral dissertation; he lists 1,039 total, with approximately 600 of those serving with the National Council of Churches foreign missions program (and thus, generally speaking, not evangelical), and 438 in one of the evangelically-oriented missions programs (the EFMA, IFMA, or independent boards). Hendrickson, "Study of Reactions of Congo Missionaries," 30. *Time* claimed 2,000 total, of whom 1,200 were Americans. "Christianity & the Congo," *Time*, August 1, 1960, 44.

10. It is often difficult to assess the race of particular missionaries, particularly within denominations that sent both white and black missionaries. African American newspapers covered missionary doings in general, but reported specifically on marriages and funerals of, or interviews with, African Americans. Thus we can gain some sense of the presence of African Americans serving in Congo: "Methodist Missionaries Returning to Congo," *New Journal and Guide*, November 19, 1960; "Congo Missionaries Evacuated 2nd Time," *Afro-American*, February 18, 1961; "Congo Missionary Marries Chicago Methodist Minister," *Atlanta Daily World*, July 21, 1961; "Congo Missionary Funeral Held in PA," *Afro-American*, September 22, 1962; "Southern Couple Answers Need of Church and Congo," *Chicago Daily Defender*, December 1, 1965.

African American denominations had active missionary programs in Africa in this period, but largely in Liberia, Southern Africa, and Nigeria. Exact information about the missionaries deployed by AME or COGIC churches in this period is hard to come by. Irvine lists a few AME congregations meeting in house churches in Congo, started by workers who had been converted by AME missionaries in Rhodesia. But churches could not own property or buildings, and had to remain under the care of a pastor in Northern Rhodesia until the church was officially recognized in 1977. Irvine, *Church of Christ in Zaire*.

11. See Landau, "An Amazing Distance."

12. Grant, *A Civilised Savagery*, 39–78; Lagergren, *Mission and State in Congo*, 295–310. A comprehensive history of the Congo reform movement is Hochschild, *King Leopold's Ghost*, 185–308. On African Americans and Congo more broadly, see Dworkin, "American Congo."

13. Grant, *A Civilised Savagery*, 61–68. Twain, *King Leopold's Soliloquy,* 7, 40. On the other hand, for an analysis of the photograph as part of the work of colonial rule, see Schildkrout, "Though the Lens of Herbert Lang."

14. Nzongola-Ntalaja, *The Congo*; Gondola, *History of Congo*.

15. Markowitz, *Cross and Sword*, 135.

16. Ibid., 109. On the history of Protestant missions across Congo in the early twentieth century, see Braekman, *Histoire Du Protestantisme Au Congo*.

17. Kasongo, *Methodist Church*, 89. On Baptist missionaries, see Nelson, *Christian Missionizing*, 75.

18. Hendrickson, "Study of Reactions of Congo Missionaries," 146–49. On indigenization more broadly, see Chang et al., "Paul G. Hiebert and Critical Contextualization"; Priest, "Anthropology and Missiology."

19. Sanneh, *Translating the Message*.

20. Markowitz, *Cross and Sword*, 135–43; Hastings, *African Christianity*, 84. See also Comhaire, "Sociétés Secrètes." Some scholars have argued that various forms of syncretism continue as a vital practice in Congo and elsewhere in Africa today, and that mixed practices are not necessarily understood as unorthodox. Hastings, *African Christianity*, 149.

21. Hastings, *African Christianity*, 130.

22. Ibid., 149.

23. Philip Dow quotes interviews with several missionaries to this effect in Dow, "Missionary Factor." Also Brashler, *Change*. Almost every missionary source points to the requirement for French training in Belgium. See, for example, Deal and Randall, *Out of the Mouth of the Lion*, 24–25; Petersen, *Another Hand on Mine*, 13.

24. Irvine, *Church of Christ in Zaire*. This remarkable little book lists every Protestant mission in Congo over a one-hundred-year period, with a brief history and a comprehensive map of mission stations.

25. Kasongo, *Methodist Church*, 91.

26. Thiessen to Sis, June 30, 1960, Folder 1-13; CN 84, BGCA.

27. Thiessen to Parents, September 29, 1960, Folder 1-13, CN 84, BGCA.

28. Thiessen to Parents, November 3, 1960. Folder 1-13, CN 84, BGCA.

29. Comaroff and Comaroff, *Of Revelation and Revolution*, vol. 2, 1–32.

30. On missionaries and domesticity, see Hill, *The World Their Household*; Robert, *Gospel Bearers*. On development knowledge, see Engerman et al., *Staging Growth*; Engerman, "The Anti-Politics of Inequality."

31. Westad, *Global Cold War*, 136–57, q. 136; Namikas, *Battleground Africa*, 33–98. US enmity against Lumumba was such that even a year after he was killed, a major US policymaker reported in some detail on the history of US policy in Congo without once mentioning his name. Ball, "American Policy."

32. Gerard and Kuklick, *Death in the Congo*, 150–55.

33. de Witte, *Assassination of Lumumba*; Kalb, *Congo Cables*, 101–2. See also the report from the UN commission that investigated the death in late 1961, "Excerpts From Report by U.N. Commission on Inquiry Into Lumumba's Death," *NYT*, November 15, 1961. De Witte's *Assassination of Lumumba* was written before a number of clarifying documents were released. More detailed accounts of his escape, arrest, and murder are in Gerard and Kuklick, *Death in the Congo*, 177–214; Namikas, *Battleground Africa*, 118–26.

34. "Rioters Protest Lumumba Death," *NYT*, February 15, 1961; "Riot in Gallery Halts UN Debate: American Negroes Ejected After Invading Session," *NYT*, February 16, 1961; "Embassies Attacked in Cairo," *NYT*, February 16, 1961; "Protests in Several Nations," *NYT*, February 17, 1961; "Congo Issue Stirs Rioting in London; Police Halt Mob's Attempt to Rush Belgian Embassy," *NYT*, February 20, 1961; Joseph, *Waiting 'Til the Midnight Hour*, 39–42; Nesbitt, *Race for Sanctions*, 41–42. On Cairo and China, Namikas, *Battleground Africa*, 133.

35. The *Chicago Tribune*, quoting US government sources, claimed 1,700 US missionaries were ordered evacuated in July 1960: "Congo Troops Beat, Trample Missionaries," *Chicago Tribune*, July 17, 1960. One missions executive listed dozens of US Protestant organizations by name and the number of their missionaries in 1960, with a total of 980, although this number would not have included Americans who worked with non-US-based missionary organizations. Nelson, *Congo Crisis and Christian Mission*.

36. "Africans Halt Flight of Missionaries," *Chicago Tribune*, July 18, 1960. The report quoted the US embassy as saying that about one-half of approximately two thousand Americans had

been evacuated, and most others were out of danger. See also "400 Yanks Quit Congo; 100 Others Decide to Stay," *Chicago Tribune*, July 14, 1960; "D.C. Couple's Daughter Evacuated from Congo," *WP*, July 16, 1960; Milton Viorst, "Congo Rescues Related by Missionary Here," *WP*, July 20, 1960.

37. Phil Casey, "Congo Families Land in Capital," *WP*, July 22, 1960.

38. William and Flossie Battishill, "Report from Congo," July 22, 1960, Folder 101-5, CN 165, BGCA; William and Flossie Battishill, "Report from Congo," July 30, 1960, Folder 101-5, CN 165, BGCA. Both letters are attachments to J. Albert Kee to Clyde Taylor, August 4, 1960, Folder 101-5, CN165, BGCA.

39. Thiessen to Sis, December 29, 1960, Folder 1-13, CN 84, BGCA.

40. The more upbeat letter is Sidney Langford, "To the Relatives, Churches and Friends of Our Congo Missionaries," July 26, 1960, Folder 101-5, CN165, BGCA.

41. For some sense of the denominations that were sponsoring African American missionaries in Congo, we can see the reports in African American newspapers in this period. "Congo Missionary Marries Chicago Methodist Minister," *Atlanta Daily World*, July 21, 1961; "Southern Couple Answers Need of Church and Congo," *Chicago Daily Defender*, December 1, 1965. See also Mahaniah, "Presence of Black Americans in Lower Congo."

42. On Belgians discouraging African Americans as missionaries, see Kasongo, *Methodist Church*, 46. Weissman makes a similar argument about the State Department banning African American diplomats from Congo. Weissman, *Foreign Policy in the Congo*, 44. James Campbell points out that white denominations, which had initially sent African American missionaries to Africa with some enthusiasm, began to retreat from the policy in the early 1900s, largely under pressure from colonial officials. Campbell, *Middle Passages*, 143.

43. "AME Church to Meet Challenge of Congo Crisis," *Afro-American*, July 30, 1960; "Baptist Sending Negros to Congo," *New York Amsterdam News*, September 10, 1960. John D. Bright was one of the AME leaders most involved in the black liberation movement. In 1966, he signed a controversial document by the National Council of Negro Churchmen that supported black power. National Council of Negro Churchmen, "A Challenge to White Power," *Negro Digest*, December 1966, 16-24.

44. "Pro-Lumumba Pressures Mounting in Congo," *Voice of Missions*, February 19, 1961, 14.

45. "UN Assembly Back at Work: President Nkrumah Speaks," *Voice of Missions*, April 1961, 8–9.

46. Meriwether, *Proudly We Can Be Africans*, 232. Quoting Williams, "Letter to the Editor," *Pittsburgh Courier*, March 19, 1961.

47. This is one version of the "three selfs" model of nineteenth-century missionary theorists such as Rufus Anderson. Hutchison, *Errand to the World*; Van Engen, "A Broadening Vision."

48. Nelson, *Christian Missionizing*, 67–73, 76–78. On the issue of mission schools and educational policy more broadly, see Markowitz, *Cross and Sword*.

49. This is Philip Dow's estimate, extrapolating from the number of missionary-run schools in 1951 (based on a report from the Council of Protestant Missions in Congo), and the expected amount of annual turnover in each school. Dow argues that this is a conservative estimate, and I believe he is right in that. Dow, "Missionary Factor."

50. Petersen, *Another Hand on Mine*, 165.

51. The Conservative Baptist Foreign Missions Society was formed in 1943 by fundamentalists in the Northern Baptist Convention as a more conservative alternative to the convention's official missions board. Marsden, *Reforming Fundamentalism*, 46.

52. Nelson, *Christian Missionizing*, 77.

53. Deighton Douglin and Alice Douglin, University of Massachusetts Lowell, Center for Lowell History, Lowell Historical Society Leaders II Oral History Project.

54. Nelson describes some of the conflict over the school at Ndoluma and the decision to close it, although he doesn't identify Douglin as the headmaster of the school. Nelson, *Christian Missionizing*, 68.

55. Ibid., 77–82. See also Hendrickson, "Study of Reactions of Congo Missionaries," 70–71. On the larger issue of how African Christians in general viewed the Protestant mission schools, see All Africa Church Conference, *Christian Education in Africa*.

56. Thiessen to Family, November 24, 1960, Folder 1-13; CN 84, BGCA.

57. Nelson, *Christian Missionizing*, 113.

58. Ibid., 118. Nelson is citing a letter from Lawy Bakulu and Luc Mangolopa, May 28, 1962, from the CBFMS archives.

59. George Klein to Sidney Langford, August 12, 1963, Folder 38-1, CN 81, BGCA. Klein refers to the "Ngunza" movement. Ngunza means prophet in Swahili. Klein may have been referring to Kimbanguism, which did have a resurgence in this area. See MacGaffey, "Cultural Roots of Kongo Prophetism."

60. "Ministry of Prayer: Congo," *Alliance Witness*, April 28, 1965, https://www.cmalliance.org/resources/archives/alifepdf/AW-1965-04-28.pdf.

61. Phillipe Decorvet, "Des Missionaires Nouvelles," *Congo Mission News/Nouvelles Missionaires Du Congo*, October 1961, 20–21.

62. Bediako, *Christianity in Africa*, 68–69.

63. Hollinger, *Protestants Abroad*, 94-116; Hutchison, *Errand to the World*, 176–83.

64. Neufield, "Unfinished Revolution," 21.

65. Pierre Shaumba, "God's Transforming Power in Africa," *Congo Mission News/Nouvelles Missionaires Du Congo*, August 1960, 5.

66. Kasongo, *Methodist Church,* 105.

67. Shaumba is quoted in a "Dear Colleagues" letter from the field director of AIM's Congo mission: Peter Brashler to AIM Africa Committee, March 7, 1963, Folder 38-1, CN 81, BGCA. US missionaries mention Shaumba positively in a number of sources including Law, *Appointment Congo*; and Neufield, "Unfinished Revolution."

68. M'Timkulu, "The All Africa Church Conference," 109–10. The All Africa Council of Churches would later be renamed the All Africa Conference of Churches.

69. "Report of the IFMA Africa Committee," December 1962, Folder 37-9, CN 81, BGCA.

70. Roger East, "Africanized Christian Church Sought," *CSM*, January 26, 1963.

71. Kenneth Downing, "Report on Visit to Burundi and Congo," February 14–March 14, 1963, Folder 5-11, CN 165, BGCA. Jeunesse was also the name of an explicitly Lumumbist movement, but if Downing meant to refer to that, it was likely only by association, not with the idea that Lumumba supporters were actually coming to the CPC meeting. Peter Brashler to AIM Africa Committee, March 7, 1963, Folder 38-1, CN 81, BGCA.

72. Namikas, *Battleground Africa*, 194–209.

73. See Gbenye's telegram of October 24, 1964 and the document published in *Le Martyr,* October 30, 1964, both in C.R.I.S.P, *Congo 1964*, 384–85. On the AIM stations, see Petersen, *Another Hand on Mine*, 189–91. Paul Carlson's wife and children were evacuated from Northwest Congo in September. A timeline of Carlson's capture and the Belgian documents associated

with the events is found in C.R.I.S.P, *Congo 1964*, 383–88; the status of Carlson's family is in "Telégramme," October 24, 1964, 383.

74. Nettie Berg, "More Heroes in the Congo," *Christian Leader*, January 1965, 7; Angeline Tucker, "Crisis Days in the Congo," *Pentecostal Evangel*, February 14, 1965, 1ff; William A. Deans, "Flight from the Congo!," *Interlit*, fourth quarter 1964, all Folder 102-2, CN 165, BGCA.

75. Worldwide Evangelization Crusade, "Congo: Tragedy or Triumph?" *Worldwide Thrust: WEC's Monthly Communique*, January–February 1965, Folder 102-2, CN 165, BGCA.

76. On the history of the UFM, see McAllister, "Problems of Protestant Church Leadership."

77. D.W. Truby, "Congo: The Facts," *Crusade*, April 1965, 7–8, Folder 102-2, CN 165, BGCA. A full-length account of the drama in Stanleyville and beyond, which includes details of the captivity of a number of the missionaries, is in Dowdy, *Jaws of the Lion*.

78. Unevangelized Fields Mission, "Tragedy to Triumph," *Lifeline*, 1965, Folder 102-2, CN 165, BGCA. William Scholten's death is also described in Dowdy, *Jaws of a Lion*, 64–67.

79. Editorial, "The Massacre," *Chicago Daily Defender*, November 30, 1964; "Is Congo Missionary Living?," *Chicago Daily Defender*, November 18, 1964; "Kin May Follow in Footsteps of Congo Victim," *Chicago Daily Defender*, December 8, 1964.

80. "U.S. Policy and The Congo," *Voice of Missions*, January 1965, 13.

81. Homer Dowdy, "An Author Makes a Comparison," *Congo Mission News/Nouvelles Missionaires Du Congo*, March 1965, 4–5.

CHAPTER 3

1. Pannell, "Interviews 1995-2007," Tape 4, CN 498, BGCA. On the Congress, see Balbier, "The World Congress on Evangelism 1966 in Berlin."

2. Cassidy, "The Ethics of Political Nationalism," 314. Paul Little describes the opposition to Cassidy's speech in a letter to John Kidd, February 21, 1968, Folder 142–1, CN 300, BGCA.

3. Cassidy, "The Ethics of Political Nationalism," 315.

4. Paul Little to John Kidd, February 21, 1968, Folder 142–1, CN 300, BGCA.

5. Moffett, "Report of Group Discussion," 317.

6. Pannell, *My Friend, The Enemy*.

7. Carpenter, "Propagating the Faith."

8. Parker, *Kingdom of Character*; Robert, "The Origin of the Student Volunteer Watchword"; Showalter, *End of a Crusade*.

9. On the history of neo-evangelicalism and particularly the influence of Reformed theology, see Worthen, *Apostles of Reason*.

10. Glasser, "The Urgency of the Hour," 203–4.

11. Gloege, *Guaranteed Pure*, 93, 159–60. On Bethune, see Savage, *Your Spirits Walk Beside Us*, 121–62.

12. Miller, "Construction of a Black Fundamentalist Worldview," 722.

13. Bentley, *National Black Evangelical Association*, 14–15; Bentley, "Bible Believers," 111–13.

14. Bentley, *National Black Evangelical Association*, 17.

15. Bentley, "Bible Believers," 111–13.

16. Port Huron Statement, 1962, reprinted at http://coursesa.matrix.msu.edu/~hst306/documents/huron.html.

17. Swartz, "Left Behind," 62–63.

18. For descriptions of Schaeffer's series of lectures, see Hamilton, "The Dissatisfaction of Francis Schaeffer," *CT*, March 3, 1997, 22–30; Duriez, *Francis Schaeffer*, 160–65; Worthen, *Apostles of Reason*, 210–12; Swartz, *Moral Minority*, 98–100.

19. Martin, *With God On Our Side*, 159.

20. Schaeffer, *Crazy for God*, 118. See the useful discussion of Schaeffer's theology in Hankins, *Francis Schaeffer*; Worthen, *Apostles of Reason*, 209–16. For a good discussion of Schaeffer's life and political thought, Hartman, *War for the Soul of America*, 70–101. See also Swartz, *Moral Minority*, 96–102.

21. Kenneth Woodward, "Guru of Fundamentalism," *Newsweek*, November 1, 1982, 88 (italics mine). Schaeffer, *The God Who Is There*; Schaeffer and Moreland, *Escape from Reason*. The third book of Schaeffer's trilogy of apologetics is Schaeffer, *He Is There*.

22. Shires, *Hippies of the Religious Right*, 50.

23. Turner, *Bill Bright*, 101–3; Watt, *A Transforming Faith*, 15–32. The pamphlet is available for sale at the Campus Crusade website, but is also available for free, in scores of languages, via http://www.4laws.com/laws/languages.html.

24. Preston, *Sword of the Spirit*, 543.

25. Schaeffer's books had total sales of 2.5 million copies by 1975. Hankins, *Francis Schaeffer*, 79; Swartz, *Moral Minority*, 100. On InterVarsity Press, Peau and Doll, *Heart, Soul, Mind, Strength*, 33–53.

26. David Neff, "Ardor and Order: The Charismatic Renewal Has Disappeared like Yeast into Bread Dough," *CT*, May 2010, 53. On the renewal, see Synan, *The Holiness-Pentecostal Tradition*, 220–78.

27. "Blue Tongues," *Time*, March 29, 1963, 76.

28. Hunt, *For Christ and the University*, 225, 249–51.

29. Schenkel, "New Wine and Baptist Wineskins."

30. Ella Weldon, "What Is the Question?," *HIS*, June 1968, 8–10.

31. Adams, "Youth and Tradition," 145–46.

32. The literature on women in missions includes Butler, *Women in the Church of God in Christ*; Hill, *The World Their Household*; Hunter, *To Change the World*; Robert, *Gospel Bearers*.

33. Swartz, *Moral Minority*, 34.

34. Hunt, *For Christ and the University*, 252–53.

35. Stott, "The Charge to Suffer for the Gospel"; Bonhoeffer, *Cost of Discipleship*. On the importance of Bonhoeffer, see Quebedeaux, *Young Evangelicals*, 65–68; Marty, *Letters and Papers from Prison*. *Christianity Today* listed *Cost of Discipleship* as nineteenth among the top most influential books among American evangelicals: "The Top Books that have Shaped American Evangelicals," *CT*, October 6, 2006, 51–55.

36. Ella Weldon, "What is the Question?" *HIS*, June 1968, 8–10.

37. Ellis, *What Went Down*. Elward Ellis was no relation to Carl Ellis, who attended Hampton and later became a staff member for Tom Skinner and Associates. Elward joined the staff of InterVarsity in 1980 as its first director of Black Campus Ministries. http://intervarsity.org/news/remembrance-%E2%80%93-elward-ellis.

38. Frank Breisch, "Young Prophets," *HIS*, October 1, 1969, 28–30.

39. The reference is to Esau selling his birthright to Jacob for a mess of pottage (stew) in Gen 25:29–34. Wineke, "Evangelical Students at Urbana 70: Zeal and Social Passion," *Christian Century*, February 17, 1971, 226. See also Quebedeaux, *Young Evangelicals*, 83.

40. On the FTL, see Swartz, *Moral Minority,* 116-20. Escobar remembers Cassidy in an interview with him and René Padilla on stage at Cape Town in 2010, at the third Lausanne Congress. Available at https://www.youtube.com/watch?v=nqWsFL1pO0A.

41. Escobar, "Social Concern and World Evangelism," 107.

42. Swartz, *Moral Minority,* 122.

43. Skinner, "US Racial Crisis." Skinner was the author of *Black and Free.* On various images of a manly Jesus, see Prothero, *American Jesus,* 87–123. See also Fox, *Jesus in America.*

44. Skinner, "US Racial Crisis."

45. Baraka, "Last Days," 226. I discuss Baraka's critiques of racism and US policy in McAlister, *Epic Encounters,* 84–124. Skinner would go on to publish several important books on race and evangelism, including Skinner, *How Black Is the Gospel?*

46. See also Quebedeaux, *Young Evangelicals,* 92.

47. Potter, "The New Black Evangelicals," 304.

48. Turner, *Bill Bright,* 141–46.

49. Jim Wallis, "The Issue of 1972," *Post-American,* Fall 1972, 2–3, cited in Gasaway, "An Alternative Soul of Politics," 48. Also see Gasaway, *Progressive Evangelicals,* 33-43 and Swartz, *Moral Minority,* 47–67.

50. AME General Conference of 1976, "Liberation Movements," 294.

51. Shires, *Hippies of the Religious Right,* 97.

52. Edward B. Fiske, "In a Good Old American Tradition," *NYT,* July 4, 1971.

53. Barfoot, *McPherson and Modern Pentecostalism;* Sutton, *Aimee Semple McPherson.*

54. Scholarship that takes up at least some part of the Jesus movement has expanded dramatically in recent years. One contemporary account of the movement is Enroth, Ericson, Jr., and Peters, *The Jesus People.* Recent scholarly work includes Shires, *Hippies of the Religious Right;* Luhr, *Witnessing Suburbia;* Dochuk, *From Bible Belt to Sunbelt,* 293–325; Schäfer, *Countercultural Conservatives;* Swartz, *Moral Minority,* 86–112; Young, *Gray Sabbath.*

55. Luhr, "A Revolutionary Mission," 72–73.

CHAPTER 4

1. "Bible Prophecy and the Mid-East Crisis," *Moody Monthly,* August 1967, 22–24ff.

2. Nelson Bell, "Unfolding Destiny," *CT,* July 21, 1967, 28.

3. Carpenter, "Propagating the Faith," 105.

4. Marsden, *Understanding Fundamentalism and Evangelicalism,* 21. On Moody, see also Sutton, *American Apocalypse,* 71–78.

5. I discuss this theology in McAlister, *Epic Encounters,* 165–78. See also Boyer, *When Time Shall Be No More.*

6. On the history of Moody and (to a lesser degree) BIOLA, see Gloege, *Guaranteed Pure.* In this period, DTS was called Evangelical Theological College. For useful and detailed discussions of its early days, see Hannah, *An Uncommon Union* and Laats, *Fundamentalism and Education in the Scopes Era,* 181–82.

7. Kato, *Theological Pitfalls in Africa;* Ferdinando, "The Legacy of Byang Kato."

8. "Obituary: Tokunboh Adeyemo," *International Bulletin of Missionary Research,* July 2010, 167; Adeyemo, *Africa Bible Commentary,* 1015–38.

9. Blumhofer, *Restoring the Faith,* 11–42, 142–63.

10. Marsden, *Reforming Fundamentalism*, 35–36.

11. Ibid., 37.

12. Sutton, *American Apocalypse*, 220.

13. The literature on evangelical relationships with Israel is large and various. Key works include Ariel, *On Behalf of Israel*; Ariel, *An Unusual Relationship*; Carenen, *Fervent Embrace*; Clark, *Allies for Armageddon*; Goldman, *Zeal for Zion*; Kiracofe, *Dark Crusade*; Spector, *Evangelicals and Israel*; Weber, *On the Road to Armageddon*.

14. Carenen, *Fervent Embrace*, 79. Citing "Jews Demand Jerusalem," *Pentecostal Evangel*, April 1949, 9.

15. "Could the Rapture be Today?," *Moody Monthly,* May 1960, quoted in Boyer, 187.

16. Carenen, *Fervent Embrace*, 64. Citing "Do the World's Jews Want to be Feared?," *Christian Century*, June 16, 1948, 589.

17. Carenen, *Fervent Embrace*, 71–74. See also Mart, *Eye on Israel*, 85–108.

18. Davis, *The Landscape of Belief*, 73–74, 89–94.

19. Kaell, *Walking Where Jesus Walked*, 7.

20. Kaell, "Pilgrimage in the Jet Age," 27–30.

21. Arthur Veysey, "Age of Tourist for Holy Land Still to Come: Holy Land an Ideal Place for Holiday," *Chicago Daily Tribune*, May 3, 1959. In 1961, an article in the *NYT* implicitly suggested that tourists just skip Israel altogether, focusing instead on the pleasures of Beirut, Damascus, and Jerusalem. Richard P. Hunt, "Roundabout Road to Holy Land: Modern Pilgrims Find New Paths in Syria, Lebanon, Jordan," *NYT*, February 26, 1961.

22. Kaell, "Pilgrimage in the Jet Age," 28.

23. Dan L. Thrapp, "Church Leader Reports Holy Land Looks to U.S.: American Dollar Talisman Everywhere, Alhambra Woman Finds on Near East Trip," *LAT*, September 2, 1956.

24. *Israel in Statistics, 1948–2007* (Jerusalem: Central Bureau of Statistics, 2008), http://www.cbs.gov.il/statistical/statistical60_eng.pdf.

25. James Feron, "Tourists Crowd Jerusalem's Holy Places," *NYT*, July 9, 1967.

26. Kaell, "Pilgrimage in the Jet Age," 32.

27. Advertisement for Bible Lands and World Tours, *World Vision*, January 1967, 30.

28. "Urge Negroes Expand Travel Around World," *Voice of Missions*, February 1966, 11–12; "AME Clergymen Set For Tour Of Holy Land, Africa," *Chicago Daily Defender*, August 4, 1966; "Cleric Back From Holy Land Tour," *Chicago Daily Defender*, March 29, 1958; "Holy Land Trip To Spark Visit Abroad," *Chicago Daily Defender,* July 4, 1960.

29. The *Jerusalem Post* is quoted in "Visit by Graham Worrying Israel," *NYT*, March 17, 1960. See also "Religion: Mission's End," *Time,* March 28, 1960, 65. Graham quoted in "Billy Graham Headed Home," *LAT*, March 23, 1960. See also "Graham Acts to Head Off Israel Clash," *WP*, March 18, 1960. Martin briefly discusses the trip in Martin, *Prophet with Honor*, 264–65. There were different but related concerns about US evangelicals' attempts to convert American Jews. See Ariel, *Evangelizing the Chosen People*.

30. Turner, *Bill Bright*, 182.

31. Carl Henry, "Christian Witness in Israel, p1," *CT,* July 31, 1961, 22–23.

32. Carl Henry, "The Christian Witness in Israel, p2," *CT*, August 28, 1961, 17–21.

33. Watt, "Private Hopes," 162-64; Swartz, "Left Behind," 34–36.

34. The most important prophecy interpreter in this period was Walvoord; see *Israel in Prophecy*. Walvoord had been writing regularly on prophecy for *Biblioteca Sacra*, the DTS journal.

He was also a recognized theologian on other issues, such as the doctrine of the Holy Spirit and the personhood of Christ.

35. On Palestinian dispossession in 1948, see Davis, *Palestinian Village Histories*; Saʾdi and Abu-Lughod, *Nakba*; Said and Palestine Human Rights Campaign, *A Profile of the Palestinian People*. On Arabs as marginalized citizens in Israel, see Robinson, *Citizen Strangers*. On refugees and humanitarian practice re: Palestinians, see Cohen, "Elusive Neutrality"; Feldman, *Governing Gaza*.

36. Letters to the Editor, *CT*, July 21, 1967, 20, quoted in Lahr, *Millennial Dreams*, 157.

37. Carl Henry, "Casting Lots for Jerusalem," *CT*, August 18, 1967, 30. See Halsell, *Prophecy and Politics*, 72–73; Simon, *Jerry Falwell and the Jews*, 61–65.

38. Henry, *Prophecy in the Making*, 9. See my discussion in McAlister, *Epic Encounters*, 170–71.

39. Boyer, *When Time Shall Be No More*, 204. The conference is described in pages 181–88.

40. John Fowler, "O.W. Editor Attends Jerusalem Conference," *Southern Asia Tidings* 66, no. 8 (August 1971): 1ff, q.7, http://www.adventistarchives.org.

41. Henry, "Jesus Christ and the Last Days," 181.

42. Stott, "The Gospel and the Nations," 232.

43. David Feron, "Israel Opens Holy Sites in Jordan to Tourists: 160 Cruise Ship Passengers Visit Shrines in Bethlehem and Old City of Jerusalem," *NYT*, June 24, 1967. See also Larsen, "Israel's Tourist Trade Is Purring Right Along," *LAT*, September 14, 1967.

44. *Israel in Statistics, 1948-2007* (Jerusalem: Central Bureau of Statistics, 2008); Mansfeld, "Tourism to Israel."

45. Advertisement, "Let the Bible Be your Guide," *CT*, January 21, 1977, 4.

46. "Tour the Land of Our Lord," *Eternity*, February 1969, 7.

47. Kaell, *Walking Where Jesus Walked*, 55.

48. Weber, *On the Road to Armageddon*, 214; Halsell, *Prophecy and Politics*, 120–24.

49. Bowman, "Politics of Tour Guiding," 122–24. After 1994 and the Oslo peace accords, an arrangement between Israel and the Palestinian Authority meant that Palestinians on the West Bank were allowed to lead tours in the Old City of Jerusalem and Bethlehem.

50. Ibid., 127.

51. Martin, *With God On Our Side*, 215.

52. Halsell, *Prophecy and Politics*, 122; Blitzer, *Between Washington and Jerusalem*, 198.

53. Kaell, *Walking Where Jesus Walked*, 129–30.

54. Collins-Kreiner, Kliot, and Sagi, *Christian Tourism to the Holy Land*, 20. On the search for authenticity among Jewish Israelis touring Arab villages within Israel, see Stein, *Itineraries in Conflict*.

55. Kaell, *Walking Where Jesus Walked*, 92.

56. Ibid., 33. Kaell is citing Smith, "War and Tourism."

57. Kaell, *Walking Where Jesus Walked*, 78–79.

58. Hilsden, "Making a Case for the Garden Tomb," *Charisma Magazine*, May 13, 2013, http://www.charismamag.com/site-archives/1505-412-magazine-articles/features/15025-the-case-for-the-garden-tomb.

59. Taylor, "Golgotha."

60. Feldman, "Constructing a Shared Bible Land."

61. I went on an individualized tour with Malcolm Cartier, a highly respected tour guide among conservative evangelicals. The only members of the tour were Hilton Obenzinger (author

of *America's Palestine*) and myself. I told Cartier I was writing a book that included an examination of evangelicals and Israel. He was not the least bit concerned about this and seemed to give the same tour that he would have to an evangelical group.

62. Kaell, *Walking Where Jesus Walked*, 91.

63. Strober and Tomczak, *Jerry Falwell*, 167.

CHAPTER 5

1. Padilla, "Evangelism and the World: Pre-Circulated Paper," 121–22.

2. Kirkpatrick, "C. René Padilla and the Origins of Integral Mission," 360–62.

3. Bonhoeffer, *Cost of Discipleship*, 126.

4. Padilla, "Evangelism and the World: Paper as Presented," 138.

5. Ibid., 136.

6. René Padilla Interviewed by Paul Ericksen, March 12, 1987, Tape 3, CN 361, BGCA.

7. Heaney, *Contextual Theology*; Swartz, *Moral Minority*, 113–34.

8. Jim Parker, "Voices from Lausanne: A Report," *Post-American*, November 1974, 13–14.

9. Noll, *New Shape of World Christianity*; Jenkins, *Next Christendom*.

10. Padilla, *New Face of Evangelicalism*.

11. Graham, "Why Lausanne?"

12. "Religion: A Challenge from Evangelicals," *Time*, August 5, 1974. In addition to the other cited articles, see also: "Congress Due in Lausanne," *Los Angeles Sentinel*, July 18, 1974; Russell Chandler, "Evangelical Protestants Organize," *WP*, July 26, 1974; Russell Chandler, "Evangelical Leaders Offer 14-Point Statement of Faith, World Strategy," *LAT*, July 20, 1974.

13. Stanley, *Global Diffusion*, 156. Stanley is quoting Graham from a 1971 meeting, the World Evangelization Strategy Consultation, that was preparation for Lausanne.

14. "The Spirit of Lausanne," *CT*, August 30, 1974, 27.

15. McGavran had published *Understanding Church Growth* in 1970. Winter was known for his development of the idea of Theological Education by Extension while he was a missionary in Guatemala. Fockett, *Ralph D. Winter Story*; Winter, *Theological Education by Extension*.

16. Yoder, *The Politics of Jesus*; Skinner, *Black and Free*.

17. Hunter, "Legacy of McGavran"; McGavran, "My Pilgrimage in Mission." Also Kenneth Mulholland, "Donald McGavran's Legacy to Evangelical Missions," *EMQ*, January 1991, https://www.emqonline.com/node/525.

18. Donald McGavran, "Statement on Evangelism," July 11, 1972, Folder 09.1, Arthur Glasser papers, DuP.

19. Jim Parker, "Voices from Lausanne," *Post-American*, November 1974, 13–14.

20. Preston, *Sword of the Spirit*, 533–35. On Graham's relationships with presidents, see Wacker, *America's Pastor*, 204–20.

21. Graham, "Why Lausanne?," 30.

22. Anderson, "In Pursuit of Mission," 111.

23. On Gatu and the moratorium: Reese, "John Gatu and the Moratorium"; Stanley, " 'Lausanne 1974.' " On the revival, see Peterson, *East African Revival*. Even those who were friendlier to the concept of a moratorium had some doubts. In 1976, Pius Wakatama of Zimbabwe, a leader in the global South insurgence, called only for a "selective moratorium" that would allow for some

missionaries to provide educational or technical training. Wakatama, *Independence for the Third World Church.*

24. Anderson, "American Protestants," 112. See also Hollinger, *Protestants Abroad*, 252–65.

25. Hastings, *African Christianity*, 225.

26. Wade T. Coggins, "What's behind the Idea of a Missionary Moratorium," *CT*, November 22, 1974, 8. Also see Lefever, *Amsterdam to Nairobi.*

27. James W. Reapsome, "Lausanne 74: Strategy and Theological Groups," *EMQ*, October 1974, https://emqonline.com/node/1094. This is also discussed in "No Moratorium but Less Dependency," *Lausanne Congress Daily*, Issue 7, Monday 22 July, OS27, CN 53, BGCA.

28. Byang Kato, "Lausanne 74: An African Perspective," *EMQ*, October 1974, https://emqon-line.com/node/1096. Kato actually quotes "some participants" as describing the missionary moratorium in those terms, but his approval is clear. Also, Byang Kato, "Africa's Christian Future," *CT*, October 10, 1975, 14. For a biographical sketch of Kato, see Noll and Nystrom, *Clouds of Witnesses*, 80–96; Breman, "A Portrait of Dr Byang H Kato." For Kato's arguments about missions, black theology, and other issues, see Kato, *Biblical Christianity in Africa.*

29. Gatu, "The Urgency of the Evangelistic Task," 172–73.

30. Hastings, *African Christianity*, 225–27; Bays and Wacker, *Foreign Missionary Enterprise*, 188.

31. Arthur H. Matthews, "A Vision for World Evangelization," *Voice of Missions*, June 1974, 20.

32. Escobar, *New Global Mission.*

33. The workshops are described in news accounts: Paul E. Little, "Looking Ahead to Lausanne," *CT*, November 23, 1973, 4–6; Donald E. Hoke, "Lausanne May Be a Bomb," *CT*, March 15, 1974, 12–16. The slightly sardonic but accurate list of evangelistic methods is taken from Parker, "Voices from Lausanne."

34. A copy of "Unreached Peoples" is available in Folder 3-7, CN 53, BGCA. Also "Unreached Peoples Questionnaire," MARC, November 1972, Folder 9.01, Glasser papers, DuP; Edward Pentecost memo to Arthur Glasser et al., "Definitions of Unreached Peoples," January 30, 1973, Folder 9.01, Glasser papers, DuP.

35. On MARC, see Van Engen, "A Broadening Vision," 222. Other competing groups are discussed by Donald McGavran, memo October 20, 1972, Folder 9.01, Glasser papers, DuP. The term "non-book" is used positively, in "Unreached Peoples," *MARC Newsletter*, September 1974, Folder 10.14, Glasser papers, DuP. One School of World Missions professor described some of the work as "a bit shoddy" in a note to Arthur Glasser, July 1, 1974, Folder 10.14, Glasser papers, DuP.

36. Table of Contents sidebar, *Mission Frontiers* 6, no. 3, March 1984, 3.

37. David Dougherty, "What's Happening to Missions Mobilization?," *EMQ*, July 1998, https://emqonline.com/node/543.

38. "Guest Editorial: The MARC Newsletter—Reaching the Unreached, the 2.4 Billion: Why Are We Still So Unconcerned?" *Voice of Missions*, June 1978, 3–4.

39. Jim Reapsome, "People Groups: Beyond the Push to Reach Them Lie Some Contrary Opinions," *EMQ*, January 1984, https://emqonline.com/node/1271.

40. The evangelical objection is summarized in Wade Coggins, "COWE: An Assessment of Progress and Work Left Undone," *EMQ*, October 1980, https://emqonline.com/node/1235. On the problems with the "culture concept" in general, see Stocking, "Franz Boas and the Culture Concept."

41. Wagner, *Unreached Peoples '79*, 99. "High rise residents of Singapore" are mentioned in several places as an example of a people group, including a fundraising letter from the Lausanne Committee: Leighton Ford and Lausanne Committee for World Evangelization, "Fundraising Letter," April 1978, Folder 09.2, Glasser papers, DuP.

42. Reapsome, "People Groups."

43. On populations, see Foucault, *Security, Territory, Population*; Foucault, *Government of Self and Others*. My description of the key actors is drawn from Reapsome, "People Groups."

44. Hiebert, "Missions and the Understanding of Culture" and "Missions and Anthropology." On Hiebert, see Whiteman, "Anthropological Reflections." More generally, Priest, "Anthropology and Missiology." Ecumenical Protestant missionaries had been writing and thinking about similar issues since well before the groundbreaking international ecumenical congress at Madras, India, in 1938. See Hollinger, *Protestants Abroad*, 71–80.

45. Adopt-a-People Campaign Office, "Missions in a Suitcase," *Mission Frontiers*, July 1997, http://www.missionfrontiers.org/issue/article/missions-in-a-suitcase. Among the hundreds of book titles was the annual survey sponsored by MARC: *Unreached Peoples 79, 80, 81*, etc. Also, Assemblies of God, *Unreached People*; Johnstone, Hanna, and Smith, *Praying Through the Window III*; Caleb Project, *Life-Changing Encounters*; Schreck and Lausanne Committee, *Unreached Peoples*.

46. Borthwick, *How to Be a World-Class Christian*. "World Christian Handbooks" are the materials given out at regular IVCF World Christian Conferences. Copies in Folder 275–1, CN 300, BGCA. *World Christian* magazine was a "bimonthly magazine for compassionate, committed people who want their whole lives to count for the world that doesn't know Jesus' love." One example is found in Folder 236–16, CN 300, BGCA.

47. LeGrande, "Historical & Contemporary Reasons For the Existence of 17,000 Unreached People Groups."

48. "Rev. Clarence Hilliard, Champion of Justice," *Chicago Defender*, February 8, 2005.

49. Charles Hilliard, "Voices from Lausanne: A Dissent," *Post-American*, November 1, 1974, 15–16.

50. Ibid., 16.

51. Bentley, "Bible Believers," 110–11. See also Pannell, "The Religious Heritage of Blacks."

52. Kirkpatrick, "René Padilla and the Origins of Integral Mission," 363. Kirkpatrick is quoting Escobar, *La Chispa Y La Llama: Breve Historia de La Comunidad Internacional de Estudiantes Evangélicos En América Latina* (Buenos Aires: Ediciones Certeza, 1978), 86. Padilla Interview, March 12, 1987, Tape 3, CN 361, BGCA.

53. Ad Hoc working group, "Theology Implications of Radical Discipleship."

54. Padilla Interview, March 12, 1987, Tape 3, CN 361, BGCA; Uda, "Biblical Authority and Evangelism," 86.

55. "The Lausanne Covenant," July 25, 1974, sec 4, http://www.lausanne.org/content/covenant/lausanne-covenant. See also Gill, "Christian Social Responsibility."

56. "The Lausanne Covenant," sec. 5.

57. Padilla, "Introduction," 12, 14.

58. Tizon, *Transformation after Lausanne*, 50. See also Padilla, "Integral Mission and Its Historical Development."

59. Wagner, "Lausanne Twelve Months Later," *CT*, July 4, 1975, 7–9. See also Stanley, *Global Diffusion*, 172–75. On Wagner's role at the founding of the FTL in 1970, see Swartz, *Moral Minority*, 118–19. Wagner's critique of the early evangelical left in Latin America is his *Latin American Theology*.

60. "Lausanne 74: An Appraisal," *CT*, September 13, 1974, 21–22.

61. "LOP 20: An Evangelical Commitment to Simple Life-Style." The Lausanne Occasional Papers are all available at http://www.lausanne.org/lausanne-occasional-papers-lops.html.

62. Padilla Interview, March 12, 1987, Tape 3, CN 361, BGCA.

63. King, "The New Internationalists"; King, "Seeking a Global Vision."

64. Hannah, *An Uncommon Union*, 144–45.

65. Personal interview with Ronald Sider, Philadelphia, April 7, 2010.

66. Schaeffer made the points about orthodoxy of community in his pre-circulated paper: Schaeffer, "Form and Freedom in the Church: Pre-Circulated Paper." The quotes are from the talk he actually delivered at the conference: Schaeffer, "Form and Freedom in the Church: Paper as Delivered." Schaeffer's talk was quoted prominently as an example of social concern at Lausanne by Allan R. Brockway, "Christian Lifestyle: Reflections on Lausanne," *Engage/Social Action*, November 1, 1974, 47–54.

67. Schaeffer, *How Should We Then Live?* 222–25.

68. Schaeffer, *Whatever Happened?*; Duriez, *Francis Schaeffer*, 181–87. Book sales are from Philip Yancey, "Francis Schaeffer: Prophet of our Time?" *CT*, March 23, 1979, 15-18. The *Der Spiegel* quote is from Duriez, 191.

69. Dillon, "Religion and Culture in Tension"; Roach, "How Southern Baptists Became pro-Life," *Baptist Press*, January 16, 2015, at bpnews.net/44055/how-southern-baptists-became-prolife.

70. Williams, *God's Own Party*, 173. Also Byrnes, "How 'Seamless' a Garment?"

71. Ziegler, *After Roe*, 155.

CHAPTER 6

1. "Cleric Tells of Communist Torture," *NYT*, May 7, 1966. *Communist Exploitation of Religion, Hearing Before The Subcommittee to Investigate the Administration of the Internal Security Act, of the Committee on the Judiciary*, 89th Cong (1966) (statement of Rev. Richard Wurmbrand, evangelical minister).

2. Wurmbrand, *Tortured for Christ*, 37.

3. The film is available at http://www.archive.org/details/TorturedForChrist-CommunistPrisonFor14YearsAndTorturedForBeingA.

4. Augustine, *Sermons*, 51:2, quoted in Castelli, *Martyrdom and Memory*, 105.

5. Sontag, *Regarding the Pain of Others*, 41, 6.

6. Asad, *Formations of the Secular*, 67–99.

7. Hunt, *Inventing Human Rights*; Barnett, *Empire of Humanity*.

8. On the UN Declaration, Inboden, *Religion and American Foreign Policy*, 30–31. See also Nurser, *For All Peoples and All Nations*.

9. In Europe, as historian Samuel Moyn describes, human rights after World War II worked well in service of a conservative vision of restraint (from government), while also shoring up a vision of freedom (for the individual) that crossed liberal and conservative lines. Moyn, *Christian Human Rights*.

10. Inboden, *Religion and American Foreign Policy*, 58.

11. Preston, *Sword of the Spirit*, 398–409, q. 403. Blessing would go on to become a major supporter of the theory that the Bible included accounts of aliens landing on the earth. See Blessing et al., *Innner Earth People and Outer Space People*.

12. Bradley, *World Reimagined*, 6.

13. On the argument for the 1970s as foundational, see Moyn, *Last Utopia*. On the works of Amnesty International and human rights activism, see Keys, *Reclaiming American Virtue*, 178–213; Cmiel, "The Emergence of Human Rights Politics in the United States"; Baldwin, *Amnesty International and U.S. Foreign Policy*.

14. Bradley, *World Reimagined*, 164–82.

15. D. Bruce Lockerbie, "Gulag's 'Terrifying Reality' Points at Us All," *Eternity*, December 1974, 30–31.

16. Schaeffer, *How Should We Then Live?* 215.

17. There is an enormous literature in diplomatic history on Jackson-Vanik. The best overall summaries are Keys, *Reclaiming American Virtue*, 103–26; Sargent, *A Superpower Transformed*, 209–14; Preston, *Sword of the Spirit*, 562–73. Two useful arguments with differing perspectives are Korey, "Jackson-Vanik and Soviet Jewry"; Kovachi, "Insights Abandoned, Flexibility Lost." See also Peretz, "Nixon et Le Vote Juif."

18. Snyder, *Human Rights Activism*; Morgan, "The United States and the Making of the Helsinki Final Act"; Birnbaum, "Human Rights and East-West Relations."

19. Bradley, *World Reimagined*, 123–27; Keys, *Reclaiming American Virtue*, 178–268.

20. Daniel P. Moynihan, "The Politics of Human Rights," *Commentary*, August 1, 1977, 19–26. Cited in Sellars, *The Rise and Rise of Human Rights*, 117.

21. Brother Andrew, *God's Smuggler*. See also Gouverneur, "Underground Evangelism"; Boel, "Bible Smuggling and Human Rights"; Castelli, "Praying for the Persecuted Church."

22. "Bible Smuggling Controversy," *Christian Century*, December 3, 1980, 1184.

23. Art Harris, "30 Americans Return From Cuban Prison," *WP*, October 28, 1980. The news coverage was considerable, especially in Los Angeles (Jesus to the Communist World was then based in Glendale, CA) and in Washington (one of the men was from Newport News, VA, about two hours from DC). Among many examples: "A 17-Month Stay on 'The Planet of the Apes,'" *WP*, November 7, 1980; John Dart, "Man Gets 24 Years for Cuba Flyover," *LAT*, January 19, 1980.

24. Russell Chandler, "Iron Curtain: Smuggled Goods: The Good Book," *LAT*, April 23, 1978.

25. Religious News Service, "Bible Smuggling Groups Sue Each Others' Leaders," *WP*, May 12, 1978; "Two Bible-Smuggling Groups Battling in Court," *LAT*, April 23, 1978; John Dart, "Religion Notes: Feud Between Bible-Smuggling Groups Erupts Anew," *LAT*, November 3, 1979; "Bible-Smuggling Group Ends Dispute," *LAT*, July 7, 1979; Eric Malnic and Russell Changler, "L. Joe Bass—A Man on a Mission or a Power Trip?" *LAT*, April 8, 1985.

26. Dan Fisher, "Russ Apparently Pressing New Crackdown on Pentecostalists," *LAT*, February 7, 1978.

27. The Soviets did raise the number of emigrants when they were looking for support for the SALT II arms treaty in 1979. Keys, *Reclaiming American Virtue*, 124; David K. Willis, "Soviet Jews Exploit Madrid Talks to Dramatize Their Plight on Emigration," *CSM*, November 13, 1980.

28. Frank Church, *Expressing the Sense of the Congress with Respect to the Treatment of Christians by the Union of Soviet Socialist Republics*; Jane Monahan, "Plight of Persecuted Soviet Christians Finds Concerned Audience at Madrid Conference," *CSM*, December 17, 1980; Carol Franklin and Stan Hastey, "Vins: Pressure from West Resulted in His Release," *Baptist Press*, June 7, 1979, http://media.sbhla.org.s3.amazonaws.com/4859,07-Jun-1979.pdf.

29. A sampling of the hundreds of articles nationally: Kevin Klose, "Pentecostalists Still Hold Out at US Embassy in Moscow," *WP*, September 25, 1978; George W. Cornell, "'Dungeon' Conditions in Moscow: 7 Pentecostals Languish in U.S. Embassy," *LAT*, March 10, 1979;

David K. Willis, "Moscow's 'Siberian Seven': Two Years in US Embassy," *CSM*, June 11, 1980; "Religion: Deadly Game in a U.S. Embassy," *Time,* January 25, 1982, 48; Robert Gillette, "US Officials Take Fasting Protester to Soviet Hospital," *LAT,* January 31, 1982; *World News Tonight,* ABC, May 11, 1982.

30. Preston, *Sword of the Spirit*, 595.

31. David K. Willis, "Human Rights: British Put Heat on Soviets," *CSM*, January 18, 1983; David K. Willis, "New Hope for Six in Moscow Seeking Religious Freedom," *CSM*, April 7, 1983; Dan Wooding, "Meeting up Again with the Man Who Helped Change the Lives of the 'Siberian Seven,'" *Assist News Service*, December 13, 2006, http://www.oldassistnews.net/Stories/2006/s06120062.htm.

32. "Northwest Asks SBC to Accept Canadians," *Baptist Press*, November 16, 1981, http://media.sbhla.org.s3.amazonaws.com/5364,16-Nov-1981.pdf.

33. Pollock, *The Siberian Seven*; Fred Schwarz, "Christian Prisoners in Moscow," *CACC (Christian Anti-Communism Crusade) Newsletter*, November 18, 1981, http://www.schwarzreport.org/uploads/schwarz-report-pdf/schwarz-report-1981-11-01.pdf.

34. Kent Richmond Hill, "After Three Long Years: Glimmers of Movement in 'Siberian Seven' impasse," *CT*, September 18, 1981, 32–37.

35. "The 'Siberian seven' Completed Two Years of Refuge in the US Embassy in Moscow," *CT*, July 18, 1980, 59; Harry Genet, "Siberian 7: A Desperate Situation," *CT*, February 5, 1982, 76; Harry Genet, "The 'Siberian Seven' families Win a Round with the Soviet Monolith," *CT*, August 5, 1983, 42–43; Robert O'Brien, "Soviet Baptist Dilemma Surfaces in Indianapolis," *Baptist Press*, April 10, 1978, http://media.sbhla.org.s3.amazonaws.com/4608,10-Apr-1978.pdf.

36. Genet, "Siberian 7."

37. Preston, *Sword of the Spirit*, 595–97.

38. Kenneth Woodward, "Billy Renders Unto Caesar," *Newsweek*, May 24, 1982, 89; Martin, *Prophet with Honor*, 489–513.

39. Snyder, *Human Rights Activism*, 141–47; Frances E. Moyer, "Letter: Forgotten Christian Victims of Soviet Repression," *NYT*, February 10, 1982.

40. Sawatsky, *Soviet Evangelicals Since World War II*.

41. Preston, *Sword of the Spirit*, 597.

42. Christian Life Commission, "Declaration of Human Rights," Southern Baptist Convention, 1978. Folder 1.19, AR905, SBHLA.

43. Cooke, "Pray for Those 'Walking to Calvary.'" *CT*, July 16, 1982, 54–55. Italics in original.

44. Most well-known was Jesus' injunction in Luke 9:23, "Then he said to them all: 'If anyone would come after me, he must deny himself and take up his cross daily and follow me.'" Also 1 Peter 4:13, "But rejoice that you participate in the sufferings of Christ, so that you may be overjoyed when his glory is revealed." Both from the New International Version.

45. Cooke, "Pray for Those," 55.

46. On domestic issues see Martin, *With God On Our Side*; Williams, *God's Own Party*; Diamond, *Roads to Dominion*. On Israel see McAlister, *Epic Encounters*, 155–97. On economic factors and the religious Right, see Dochuk, *From Bible Belt to Sunbelt*; McGirr, *Suburban Warriors*; Kruse, *White Flight*.

47. Martin, *With God On Our Side*, 210.

48. Ibid., 213.

49. Williams, *God's Own Party*, 220.

50. Turek, "To Bring the Good News."

51. Daniel Kurtzman, "Focus on Issues: Recalling Soviet Jewry Campaign, Christians Seek to End Persecution," *Jewish Telegraphic Agency*, March 24, 1997, 9; "Jews' Experience Aiding Christians: Hill Hears of Persecution," *Forward*, May 2, 1997, 1.

CHAPTER 7

1. Howard, "The South African Conference on Evangelical Leadership"; Phiri, *Proclaiming Political Pluralism*, 108–9.

2. The arrest is recorded in three places, with slightly differing details. Howard, "Personal Encounter"; Howard, *What I Saw God Do*; Molebatsi, *A Flame for Justice*, 124–28.

3. Howard, "Personal Encounter," 22.

4. Lodge, *Sharpeville*. On the history of US–South African relations in the early apartheid period, see Borstelmann, *Apartheid's Reluctant Uncle*.

5. "Ministers Protest Africa Lynchings," *New York Amsterdam News*, March 26, 1960; Campbell, *Songs of Zion*.

6. "AME's Picket South African Consulate," *New York Amsterdam News*, April 9, 1960.

7. Thaddeaus Stokes, "AME Bishops Council asks African Aid," *Atlanta Daily World*, April 15, 1960. See also Meriwether, *Proudly We Can Be Africans*, 206, 232.

8. One of the best histories of the global anti-apartheid movement is Field, *Have You Heard?* On US government relations with South Africa and debates in the United Nations, see Massie, *Loosing the Bonds*; Edgar, *Sanctioning Apartheid*. Also see UN General Assembly, Resolution 2396, The Policies of Apartheid of the Government of South Africa, December 2, 1968.

9. Welch, "Mobilizing Morality," 867; Adler, *Small Beginning*, 16. See also Mbali, *The Churches and Racism*.

10. Nesbitt, *Race for Sanctions*, 90–96; Massie, *Loosing the Bonds*, 271–73.

11. De Gruchy, *Church Struggle*, 112–20; Jubber, "The Roman Catholic Church and Apartheid"; Walshe, *Church Versus State*, 76–79; Higgs, "Silence, Disobedience, and African Catholic Sisters." See also Kearney, *Guardian of the Light*.

12. On the Christian Institute, see Walshe, *Church Versus State*. On Naudé, see Masuku and Niemandt, "Ministry of Beyers Naudé."

13. Walker, "Evangelicals and Apartheid," 47.

14. Paul Myers, "Interview with Michael Cassidy," *African Enterprise Outlook*, August 1967, Folder 1/1/4, PC130, APC.

15. Michael Cassidy, "South African Christian Confronts Apartheid," *CT*, November 19, 1971, 3–6.

16. *South Africa Crusade*, Billy Graham Evangelistic Association film, 1973, Film 34, CN 214, BGCA.

17. Billy Graham's press conference in Johannesburg, March 21, 1973, Folder 3–21, CN 24, BGCA; Clark and Worger, *South Africa*, 77.

18. John Rees to Michael Cassidy, July 2, 1972, Folder 1/12/3, PC130, APC.

19. David Bosch, "Racism and Revolution: Response of the Churches in South Africa," *Occasional Bulletin of Missionary Research*, January 1979, 14.

20. Johanson, "South African Congress," 57.

21. "Durban Hotel Becomes 'Island of Hope,'" *Dimension*, April 8, 1973, Folder 1/1/10, PC130, APC; R.J. Voke, "Durban Congress: Presidential Point-of-View," *South African Baptist*, May

1973, Folder 1/1/10, PC130, APC. On the boat idea, see SACC Meeting notes, February 23, 1972, Folder 1972, AB1064, WITS.

22. Weber, "South African Travel Diary," 339.

23. Leighton Ford to Michael Cassidy, November 16, 1973, Folder 1/12/3, PC130, APC; Jones and Gilbreath, *Gospel Trailblazer*, 173–75.

24. "We Must Die to Ourselves," *Dimension*, April 1973, Folder 1/1/10, PC130, APC.

25. Rev. F. J. Buchler, "How Another Delegate Saw It," *South African Baptist*, May 1973, Folder 1/1/10, PC130 1/1/10, APC; "Church Told to Battle Injustices," *Witness*, March 16, 1973, Folder 1/1/10, PC130, APC; Bhengu, "My Search for the Fullness of God." See also Balcomb, "Nicholas Bhengu."

26. Weber, "Travel Diary," 339–40.

27. Hopkins, *Black Theology*, 98–102; Weber, "Travel Diary," 339. Also Rev. M.T. Chigwida, "The Need to Face Reality," *Christian Leader*, June 1973; "Racial Split at Mission Congress," *Natal Mercury*, March 21, 1973; "Church and Race—Blacks Hit Out," *Daily News*, March 19, 1973, all in Folder 1/1/10, PC130, APC.

28. Welsh, *Rise and Fall*, 151–55; Massie, *Loosing the Bonds*, 393–95.

29. Frederickson, *Black Liberation*. These transnational links in an earlier era are traced in detail in Von Eschen, *Race Against Empire*.

30. Biko, *I Write What I Like*, 21. A useful discussion of the position of black college students in Biko's era can be found in Louw, *Rise, Fall, and Legacy*, 124–29.

31. Welsh, *Rise and Fall*, 151–55; Massie, *Loosing the Bonds*, 373–403, q. 395.

32. Welsh, *Rise and Fall*, 142–71; Price, *Apartheid State*, 46–52.

33. Biko, *I Write What I Like*, 92.

34. Molebatsi, *A Flame for Justice*, 84. On Wheaton alums, see Swartz, *Moral Minority*, 121–22.

35. Molebatsi, *A Flame for Justice*, 119.

36. Ibid., 101–6.

37. On the regional struggle, see Gleijeses, *Conflicting Missions*; Gleijeses, *Visions of Freedom*.

38. Keys, *Reclaiming American Virtue*; Turek, "To Bring the Good News."

39. Morgan, "The World Is Watching"; Massie, *Loosing the Bonds*, 427–42; Field, *Have You Heard?*, episode 5.

40. Massie, *Loosing the Bonds*, 287–90; 406–11.

41. "New Conduct Code Asked for Firms in South Africa," *Afro-American*, May 5, 1979.

42. Thomson, *Incomplete Engagement*, 65–116; Baker, *The US and South Africa*.

43. Harold J. Logan, "A Black Political Group Set Up as Africa Lobby," *WP*, May 21, 1978; Gerald Horne, "South Africa: The Struggle Continues," *Afro-American,* May 15, 1982; Crisipin Campbell, "Group Seeks Denunciation Of Apartheid: Churches Asked to Buy, Post Signs Denouncing South Africa Apartheid," *WP*, November 24, 1982; Williams, "Adversarial Diplomacy and African American Politics," 177–78.

44. Nicholas Wolterstorff, "Can Violence Be Avoided?," *CT*, July 21, 1978, 20–25.

45. D. Stuart Briscoe, "It All Goes back to the Battle of Blood River," *CT*, July 21, 1978, 15. On Elmbrook, see Tom Heinen, "Faith Put Into Action: Stuart and Jill Briscoe Helped Shape Elmbrook Church," *Milwaukee Journal Sentinel*, March 2, 2008, http://www.jsonline.com/news/waukesha/29394014.html.

46. D. Stuart Briscoe, "It All Goes back to the Battle of Blood River," *CT*, July 21, 1978, 19.

47. Wolterstorff, "Can Violence Be Avoided?," 24

48. Padilla and Sugden, *Texts on Evangelical and Social Ethics, 1974-1983 (I)*, 22–24. Also quoted in Walker, "Evangelicals and Apartheid," 50–51.

49. Welsh, *Rise and Fall*, 208–30.

50. Ibid., 289–98; Price, *Apartheid State*, 182–84; Louw, *Rise, Fall, and Legacy*, 135, 140–45; Lodberg, "Desmond Tutu."

51. Louw, *Rise, Fall, and Legacy*, 101; Welsh, *Rise and Fall*, 288–311.

52. Concerned Evangelicals, "Memorandum of Association," November 1985, Folder Jc (Concerned Evangelicals), AG2843, WITS.

53. Concerned Evangelicals, *Evangelical Witness*, 17.

54. "Notes on the Follow-Up Meeting of Concerned Evangelicals in Soweto," September 13, 1985, Folder Jc (Concerned Evangelicals), AG2843, WITS.

55. Theologians, *The Kairos Document*. On the document's impact, see De Gruchy, "The Church and the Struggle for South Africa"; Goba, "Kairos Document and Its Implications"; Du Toit, "Theology, Kairos, and the Church."

56. Concerned Evangelicals, *Evangelical Witness*, 37.

57. Ntlha, "Evangelical Witness," 139–40.

58. "Minutes of the Meeting Held on October 10, 1985," Folder Jc (Concerned Evangelicals), AG2843, WITS; "Minutes of the Steering Committee of the 'Concerned Evangelicals,'" October 15, 1985, Folder Jc (Concerned Evangelicals), AG2843, WITS.

59. Balcomb, "Left, Right and Centre," 147–48; "Report on the Seminar of 'Concerned Evangelicals' Held on the 12th April 1986 at Funda Centre, Soweto," April 12, 1986, Folder Jc (Concerned Evangelicals), AG2843, WITS.

60. Rev. W. Lukhele, "Call Me Not a Pastor," October 1985, Folder 55.15, AR138-2, SBHLA; Baptist Union of South Africa, "Open Letter to Pres. Botha," October 21, 1985, Folder 164.18, AR 138-2, SBHLA; Robert O'Brien, "South African Baptists Urge End of 'Evil' Apartheid," *Baptist Press*, October 22, 1985, http://media.sbhla.org.s3.amazonaws.com/6017,22-Oct-1985. pdf. The Baptist Union's 1986 statement was more muted, probably in response to right-wing criticism. Walker, "Evangelicals and Apartheid," 49; Lund, "Critical Examination," 46.

61. "South Africa: Church Leaders Work for Racial Reconciliation," *CT*, November 8, 1985, 69; De Gruchy, *Church Struggle*, 196; Phiri, *Proclaiming Political Pluralism*, 111; Walshe, *Prophetic Christianity*, 40.

62. Concerned Evangelicals, *Evangelical Witness*, 20, 23.

63. Bowler, *Blessed*, 105.

64. Concerned Evangelicals, *Evangelical Witness*, 40, 39.

65. "Development Report," April 1987, Folder Jc (Concerned Evangelicals), AG2843, WITS. The report indicates that 250 copies were handed out in two weeks in February 1987. Other minutes do not indicate information about when and how copies were handed out, but the distribution began in the fall of 1986 and continued for almost a year.

66. Lund, "Critical Examination," 58.

67. Concerned Evangelicals, "Evangelical Witness in South Africa." Also discussed in Walker, "Evangelicals and Apartheid," 48.

68. Charles Villa-Vicencio, "Evangelical Witness in South Africa: A Critique of Evangelical Theology and Practice by South African Evangelicals," *Christianity and Crisis*, April 18, 1988, 14.

69. Harding, *Book of Jerry Falwell*, 13–15; Lichtman, *White Protestant Nation*, 387.

70. "Falwell Live: South Africa, The Untold Story," Part I (August 25, 1985), Part II (September 8, 1985), Part III (September 15, 1985), all available at the Center for Right-Wing Studies,

University of California–Berkeley. Falwell, "Why Did We Go to South Africa?," *Fundamentalist Journal*, October 1985, 1.

71. Gifford, *Religious Right*, 36–37; Worden, *The Making of Modern South Africa*, 134–36.

72. "The Call for Sanctions: What Do the People of South Africa Really Want?," *Fundamentalist Journal*, October 1985; Jonsson, "When You Put Your Body Where Your Mouth Is."

73. Deborah Huff, "Falwell and Jackson Debate South Africa," *Fundamentalist Journal*, October 1985, 16. A useful study of the Zion Christian church is Peagler, "Blow the Trumpet in Black Zion."

74. Freston, *Evangelicals and Politics*, 172–73; Kuperus, "Political Role and Democratic Contribution of Churches," 299–302.

75. Comaroff, *Body of Power, Spirit of Resistance*, 159–93.

76. Freston, *Evangelicals and Politics*, 173.

77. Robert Pear, "Falwell Denounces Tutu as a 'Phony,' " *NYT*, August 21, 1985; Falwell, "Interview."

78. Neil A. Lewis, "In the Middle: US Feels the Heat on South Africa," *NYT*, August 25, 1985.

79. Beth Spring, "Falwell Raises a Stir by Opposing Sanctions Against South Africa," *CT*, October 4, 1985, 52–56; q. 54.

80. Ibid, 53.

81. Ibid.

82. "Falwell Live: South Africa, The Untold Story, Part II."

83. Ammerman, *Baptist Battles*, 57.

84. "Baptist World Alliance Denounces Apartheid," *Baptist Press,* September 26, 1985, http://media.sbhla.org.s3.amazonaws.com/6005,26-Sep-1985.pdf; Robert O'Brien, "Apartheid Protest Breeds Intolerance in Reverse," *Baptist Press*, November 7, 1985, http://media.sbhla.org.s3.amazonaws.com/6097,07-Nov-1985.pdf; Kathy Palen, "Bishop Tutu Predicts End to Apartheid," *Baptist Press*, January 10, 1986, http://media.sbhla.org.s3.amazonaws.com/6121,10-Jan-1986.pdf; Marv Knox, "Author of Sullivan Principles Calls for Christian Involvement," *Baptist Press*, March 18, 1986, http://media.sbhla.org.s3.amazonaws.com/6155,18-Mar-1986.pdf; Robert O'Brien, "South Africa: No Easy Answer," *The Commission*, March 1987, 11ff, SBHLA.

85. Weaver, *James M. Dunn.*

86. Dunn and Cothen, *Soul Freedom*; Weaver, *James M. Dunn.*

87. James Owens, "Churches Act to Thwart Apartheid," *Report from the Capital*, February 1985, 11, SBHLA.

88. Willis, *All According to God's Plan.*

89. Agenda, December 12, 1985, Southern Baptists and Apartheid meeting, Folder 164.17, AR138-1 , SBHLA.

90. Jonsson, "Missions and the Liberation of Human Life," 677. See also Jonsson, "Baptists in Socio-Political Life in South Africa."

91. John Jonsson, "Contextual Trauma Within the Republic of South Africa," lecture at Southern Baptists and Apartheid meeting, December 12, 1985, Folder 164.16, AR132-2, SBHLA.

92. Owens, "Churches Act to Thwart Apartheid"; Ray Furr, "Annuity Trustees Establish South Africa Investment Policy," *Baptist Press,* November 4, 1985, http://media.sbhla.org.s3.amazonaws.com/6094,04-Nov-1985.pdf; Mike Land, "Divesture in South Africa Thorny Issue for US Churches," *Alabama Journal & Advertiser*, September 20, 1986, Folder 164.7, AR138-2, SBHLA.

93. "US Church Leaders Unite Against Apartheid," *Houston Chronicle*, January 14, 1986; MacDougall, "Implementation of the Anti-Apartheid Act."

94. Jim Wallis, "South Africa: The Church Steps Forward," *Sojourners*, May 1, 1988, 4–5.

95. "Apartheid and American Christians," *CT*, October 21, 1988, 44–45; Molebatsi, "The 'Relentless Grind,'" *CT*, October 21, 1988, 45–46.

96. Religious News Service, "Church Leaders Announce Anti-Apartheid Campaign," *LAT*, January 14, 1989. Also quoted in Nesbitt, *Race for Sanctions*, 152.

97. Winston, "Back to the Future"; Griffith and McAlister, "Is the Public Square Still Naked?"

98. Kansteiner, *South Africa, Revolution or Reconciliation?* 86.

99. Gina Kolata, "Poisoning of African Church Leader Charged," *NYT*, June 9, 1989; Chikane, *No Life of My Own*, chapter 21. On the bizarre spectacle of the police minister asking forgiveness of those he had wronged—and washing Frank Chikane's feet—see Eve Fairbanks, "I Have Sinned Against the Lord and Against You! Will You Forgive Me?" *New Republic*, June 30, 2014, 34–41.

CHAPTER 8

1. Bush, "The Challenge Before Us," 61. A good summary of the event is Coote, "Lausanne II."

2. Lambert, "Post-Tiananmen Chinese Communist Party Religious Policy." On the longstanding US evangelical opposition to China, see Inboden, *Religion and American Foreign Policy*, 63–104.

3. Peter Steinfels, "Moral Majority to Dissolve; Says Mission Accomplished," *NYT*, June 12, 1989; Heineman, *God Is a Conservative*, 167–68.

4. Peter Wagner, "13,000 Meet in Lagos Nigeria for AD2000," *Mission Frontiers*, December 1992, http://www.missionfrontiers.org/issue/article/13000-meet-in-lagos-nigeria-for-ad2000; Mary Robinson, "Joshua Project Step 2: Cooperating Church Leaders from Every Region of the World," *Mission Frontiers*, December 1995, http://www.missionfrontiers.org/issue/article/joshua-project-2000-step-2-cooperating-with-church-leaders-from-every-region; Luis Bush, "Brazil, A Sleeping Giant Awakens," *Mission Frontiers*, February 1994, http://www.missionfrontiers.org/issue/article/brazil-a-sleeping-giant-awakens.

5. The pamphlet is attached to a letter sent to David Bryant of IVCF from a Joshua Project leader: Joshua Project, "Joshua Project: Finding Ways to Finish the Task," 1987, and Gregory Fitz to David Bryant, September 25, 1987, both Folder 236-17, CN 300, BGCA.

6. Wilson, *Today's Tentmakers*, 18.

7. This argument is made in "Facing the Challenge of the Restricted Access World," *Strategic Times: News and Comments from ISSACHAR Frontier Missions Research*, January/February 1987, Folder 122-5, CN 165, BGCA.

8. "Report from The Christmas Consultation on Tentmaking and Mission Agencies," held at the Billy Graham Center, Wheaton, IL, December 16 and 17, 1987, Folder 122-5, CN 165, BGCA. Participating organizations included the Southern Baptist convention, Christian and Missionary Alliance, The Evangelical Alliance Mission (TEAM), and others.

9. One useful discussion is Cooper, *Evangelical Christians in the Muslim Sahel*.

10. Lugo and Copperman, "Tolerance and Tension."

11. See Sanneh, "Christian Experience of Islamic Da'wah"; Sanneh, *Piety and Power*.

12. Gifford, *Ghana's New Christianity*, 198. The literature on Pentecostalism in Africa is vast. Some important works include: Maxwell, *African Gifts of the Spirit*; Marshall, *Political*

Spiritualities; Burgess, *Nigeria's Christian Revolution*; Corten and Marshall-Fratani, *Between Babel and Pentecost*; Gifford, *Ghana's New Christianity*; Klaits, *Death in a Church of Life*. On Pentecostalism in Latin America, see O'Neill, *Secure the Soul*.

13. Kalu, "Global Pentecostal Discourse," 43.

14. Anderson, *African Reformation*.

15. Kalu, "Pentecostal and Charismatic Reshaping," 121. See also Anderson, *To the Ends of the Earth*, 37–60; Oha, "Yoruba Christian Video."

16. Lugo and Copperman, "Tolerance and Tension," 33–35. Drawing on questions about seven specific beliefs, the survey concluded that the percentage of people (Muslim and Christian) exhibiting "high levels of belief and practice" in traditional religion was 25 percent overall, which range from 3 percent in Rwanda to 62 percent in Tanzania.

17. On such mobile forms of faith in the United States, see Tweed, *Crossing and Dwelling*; Bender, *The New Metaphysicals*; Lofton, *Oprah*; Clark, *Angels to Aliens*.

18. Pew Research Center, "Future of World Religions," 51–54; Malit and Al Youha, "Labor Migration in the United Arab Emirates."

19. Johnson and Scoggins, "Christian Missions and Islamic Daʿwah"; Haron, "Daʾwah Movements and Sufi Tariqahs"; Janson, "Daʿwa"; Chesworth, "Fundamentalism and Outreach Strategies in East Africa." On *daʾwa*, see also Ahmad, *Everyday Conversions*.

20. On Islamic charity in the context of neoliberalism and changing roles of the state, see Atia, *Building a House in Heaven*.

21. Westerlund and Svanberg, *Islam Outside the Arab World*, 97–125.

22. Gifford, "Africa Shall Be Saved."

23. Kalu, *African Pentecostalism*, 240. Corrie Cutrer, "Looking for a Miracle," *CT* (web only), November 1, 2000, http://www.christianitytoday.com/ct/2000/novemberweb-only/23.0a.html; Birai, "Islamic Tajdid and the Political Process in Nigeria"; "At Least 8 Dead in Nigerian City As Muslim-Christian Riots Go On," *NYT*, October 17, 1991.

24. Lausanne Committee, "LOP 49: Understanding Muslims," 9. The report is utterly vague about specifics, so it is impossible to tell which areas or regions it is talking about specifically. But given that there are relatively few Christians in the Middle East, the most likely reference is sub-Saharan Africa.

25. Pew Research Center, "Future of World Religions," 11. Most of the projected increase in the Muslim population in sub-Saharan Africa is due to higher fertility rates among Muslims than Christians. This is true globally, where Muslims are expected to grow twice as fast as the overall population, and also in Africa, where the Muslim population was expected to increase from 30 percent to 35 percent by 2050.

26. Lugo and Copperman, "Tolerance and Tension," 7–8. Sudan was not included in the survey.

27. Jay Gary, "AD 2000 Call Sounded at Lausanne II," *AD 2000 Monitor*, August 18, 1989, reprinted at http://www.christianfutures.com/evlcwe/. For a discussion of the presence of social concern forces at Lausanne II: Vinay Samuel, "San Antonio and Lausanne II: 'Ecumenical', 'evangelical'," *One World*, October 1989, 9–11; Coote, "Lausanne II"; John Piper, "Thoughts from Lausanne II in Manila," *Desiring God*, July 21, 1989, http://www.desiringgod.org/articles/thoughts-from-lausanne-ii-in-manila; Wagner, *Wrestling with Alligators, Prophets and Theologians*.

28. The first elaboration of the concept is a 1990 paper that was published on the AD 2000 and Beyond website. This same essay is published in 1997 as "Reaching the Core of the Core," and is reprinted at *Renewal Journal* https://renewaljournal.wordpress.com/2011/07/22/

reaching-the-core-of-the-core-bylouis-bush/. In subsequent years, the essay was reproduced on scores of websites.

29. Coote, "AD 2000 and the 10/40 Window." Coote discusses Bush's explanation of the Window in his various publications.

30. World Christian Staff, *30 Days: Muslim Prayer Focus.* The 30 Days Prayer Network claims to distribute between 250,000 and 400,000 pamphlets each year, in 30 languages.

31. Guthrie, *Missions in the Third Millennium,* 70–71. Even before he arrived at Manila, Bush had helped to launch the AD 2000 and Beyond project, which focused on time (the millennium) rather than geography (the window), and developed its publications, CDs, and prayer guides. Wang, "By the Year 2000"; Rick Wood, "GCOWE Mission Executives Meeting: The Dream of William Carey Become Reality," *Mission Frontiers,* October 1997, http://www.missionfrontiers. org/issue/article/gcowe-mission-executives-meeting.

32. Luis Bush, "Brief Historical Overview of AD2000 & Beyond," http://www.ad2000.org/ histover.htm.

33. During the late 1980s and early 1990s, several articles in *Missions Frontiers,* an activist journal for missions supporters published by Ralph Winter's US Center for World Missions, promoted the activities of AD 2000 and Beyond. Among others, see Allen Finley, "Project 2000: Partnerships That Help Emerging Third World Missions Penetrate Unreached Peoples," *Mission Frontiers,* December 1988, http://www.missionfrontiers.org/oldsite/1988/1112/nd8812.htm; Ralph Winter, "The 'Rallying Cry' of the AD 2000 Movement Is 'A Church for Every People and the Gospel for Every Person by the Year 2000," *Mission Frontiers,* January–February 1992, http:// www.missionfrontiers.org/issue/article/the-rallying-cry-of-the-ad2000-movement-is. The Latin American conference is described in Guthrie, *Missions in the Third Millennium,* 69.

34. Edward Gilbreath, "Millions to Pray in Worldwide Rally," *CT,* October 2, 1995, 106-07.

35. Andres Tapia, "Is a Great Global Awakening Just Around the Corner?," *CT,* November 14, 1994, 85–86. Among historians there has been an extensive discussion of evangelicals and technology. See, for example, Sutton, *Aimee Semple McPherson.*

36. For one example of this critique, see David Nelson, "More Than a Window," *EMQ,* January 2003, https://www.emqonline.com/node/1539.

37. Both quotes in Steve Rabey, "Mission-Minded Design Strategy for Muslim World," *CT,* March 4, 1996, 76.

38. Guthrie, *Missions in the Third Millennium,* 67.

39. Robert Rasmussen, "Global Push or Grandiose Schemes?," *EMQ,* July 1996, https:// emqonline.com/node/691; Donald Neff, "The Future of Missions?," *CT (*web only*),* November 1999, http://www.christianitytoday.com/ct/1999/novemberweb-only/12.0.html.

40. Guthrie, *Missions in the Third Millennium,* 72.

41. "The Southern Baptists Restructure to Reach the Unreached Peoples," *Mission Frontiers,* July–August 1997, http://www.missionfrontiers.org/issue/article/the-southern-baptists-restructure-to-reach-the-unreached-peoples. One commentator claimed that the SBC was one of the few organizations to significantly change its practice in response to the Unreached Peoples movement. Stan Guthrie, "Global Report: Past Midnight," *EMQ,* January 2000, https://emqonline. com/node/470.

42. Guthrie, *Missions in the Third Millennium,* 73.

43. Marsden, *Reforming Fundamentalism,* 292–95. See also Wagner, *Signs & Wonders Today.*

44. Peretti, *This Present Darkness,* 11.

45. Sales info from Steve Rabney, "Spiritual Warfare, Supernatural Sales," *CT*, December 9, 1988, 69. Quote from Boogaart and Boogaart, "Review of *This Present Darkness*," 5.

46. Guelich, "Spiritual Warfare," 52.

47. Ibid., 34.

48. J. Lanier Burns, "This Present Darkness." *Bibliotheca Sacra*, April 1990, 240–42.

49. Boogaart and Boogaart, "Review of *This Present Darkness*"; Rabney, "Spiritual Warfare, Supernatural Sales."

50. Guelich, "Spiritual Warfare," 63.

51. Wagner, "Territorial Spirits."

52. Quoted in Guthrie, *Missions in the Third Millennium*, 96. See also Priest, Campbell, and Mullen, "Missiological Syncretism," 11–12.

53. For a detailed discussion of the importance of the Reformed tradition in evangelical theology, see Noll, *The Scandal of the Evangelical Mind*; Worthen, *Apostles of Reason*.

54. Holvast, *Spiritual Mapping*.

55. Bush and Pegues, *Move of the Holy Spirit*, 47–66, 37.

56. Gilbreath, "Millions to Pray."

57. Johnson and Scoggins, "Christian Missions and Islamic Da'wah."

CHAPTER 9

1. *Apologeticum*, chapter 50: 13. There are several translations of Tertullian's apologetics available, although I have not been able to find any others that translate his statement in precisely this formula. Bill Jordan in Princeton's history department kindly translated it for me as "the blood of the martyrs is the seed of Christians."

2. Apostolic Letter, "Tertio Millennio Adveniente," of His Holiness Pope John Paul II, November 10, 1994, http://w2.vatican.va/content/john-paul-ii/en/apost_letters/1994/documents/hf_jp-ii_apl_19941110_tertio-millennio-adveniente.html.

3. The text of the law is at https://www.state.gov/documents/organization/2297.pdf. See also Abrams, *The Influence of Faith*.

4. Timothy K. Jones, "Who's Afraid of Human Rights?," *CT*, July 20, 1992, 19.

5. On the visual culture and rhetoric of rights, see Bradley and Petro, "Introduction"; Balfour and Cadava, "The Claims of Human Rights."

6. Carl Henry, "A Summons to Justice," *CT*, July 20, 1992, 40.

7. Tim Stafford, "They Tortured My Friend," *CT*, July 20, 1992, 30–31. *CT* had begun to cover some human rights issues in the 1980s. See, for example, Thomas Niccolls, "Human Rights: A Concern of the Righteous," *CT*, May 25, 1979, 23–27; "US State Department Joins Religious Groups to Consider Human Rights Questions," *CT*, June 14, 1985, 64–66.

8. Dianne Knippers, "They Shoot Christians, Don't They?" *CT*, July 20, 1992, 33–36.

9. On how this representation of Islam plays out in the discourse of the US state, see Hurd, *Beyond Religious Freedom*.

10. Stackhouse, "Why Human Rights Needs God." Although the book is published in 2005, Stackhouse's essay is a revision of a 1998 article.

11. See my discussion of Schaeffer in chapter 5. See also Patterson, "Cultural Pessimism in Modern Evangelical Thought."

12. Stackhouse, "Why Human Rights Needs God," 39.

13. Michael Horowitz, "New Intolerance between Crescent and Cross," *Wall Street Journal*, July 5, 1995.

14. Susan Bergman, "Faith Unto Death, Part 1," *CT*, August 12, 1996, 18. See also Peter Waldman, "Diplomatic Mission: Evangelicals Give U.S. Foreign Policy An Activist Tinge," *Wall Street Journal*, May 26, 2004.

15. Neuhaus, *Naked Public Square*.

16. Sarah Pulliam, "Richard Cizik Resigns from the National Association of Evangelicals," *CT* (web only), December 11, 2008, http://www.christianitytoday.com/ct/2008/decemberweb-only/150-42.0.html. On the loss of the center, see Gushee, *Future of Faith*.

17. In 2005, on the occasion of a memorial for Knippers, Richard Neuhaus called on his fellow IRD members to focus more on the threat of Islam as being a parallel to the threat of communism. Neuhaus, "Reflections on IRD," *Institute for Religion and Democracy*, October 2005, https://theird.org/about/our-history/reflections-on-ird/.

18. Schlossberg, *A Fragrance of Oppression*; Poland, *How to Prepare for the Coming Persecution*. Wurmbrand's prodigious production included Wurmbrand, *The Church in Chains*; Wurmbrand, *If Prison Walls Could Speak*; and Wurmbrand, *From Suffering to Triumph*. On the rhetoric of the anti-persecution movement, see Castelli, "Praying for the Persecuted Church." Also Croft, "'Thy Will Be Done.'"

19. Of the many articles and public speeches that invoke Shea and Marshall, see, for example: Ralph Kinney Bennett, "The Global War on Christians," *Reader's Digest*, August 1997, 51–55; Diane Knippers, "Review of In the Lion's Den," *CT*, 1997, 58–59; Carroll Bogert, "Facing the Lions," *Newsweek*, August 25, 1997, 38. Horowitz made his comments at the Senate hearing. *Religious Persecution in the Middle East* (statement of Michael Horowitz, Senior Fellow, Hudson Institute).

20. Shea, *In the Lion's Den*.

21. "Christians Without a Prayer," *Wall Street Journal*, December 24, 1996.

22. "Groups Focus on Persecuted Church," *CT*, August 12, 1996, 62; "Churches Wrap Up Persecution Focus," *CT*, November 17, 1997, 74; "60,000 Churches Join Prayer Effort," *CT*, October 5, 1998, 17; Editorial, *Today's Christian Woman*, November 11, 2005. The NAE's statement is https://www.nae.net/worldwide-religious-persecution/. See also Haynes, *Religion, Politics and International Relations*.

23. Marshall, *Their Blood Cries Out*, 154.

24. On the hearings, see Castelli, "Praying for the Persecuted Church."

25. *Religious Persecution in the Middle East* (statement of Rev. Keith Roderick, Secretary General, Coalition for the Defense of Human Rights Under Islamization).

26. *Religious Persecution in the Middle East* (statement of Rep. Frank Wolf, R-VA).

27. Abernathy, "America's Evangelicals, Part II: Evangelicals and Politics," *PBS Religion & Ethics NewsWeekly*, April 23, 2004, http://www.pbs.org/wnet/religionandethics/week734/special.html.

28. Jeffrey Goldberg, "Washington Discovers Christian Persecution," *NYT Magazine*, December 21, 1997, 46–52ff.

29. A.M. Rosenthal, "On My Mind; The Double Crime." *NYT*, April 25, 1997. Rosenthal wrote many editorials on the issue in 1997.

30. Jerry Goodman, founding executive director of the National Conference on Soviet Jewry, made this point in his testimony in one hearing (as did several other commentators). *Freedom*

from Religious Persecution Act of 1997 (statement of Goodman). See also Larry Witham, "'Learn from Our Example,' They Urge," *Washington Times*, March 19, 1997.

31. "Jews' Experience Aiding Christians: Hill Hears of Persecution," *Forward*, May 2, 1997.

32. These and other criticisms of the bill are laid out in Winnifred F. Sullivan, "Exporting Religion," *Commonweal*, February 26, 1999, 10. See also Hurd, *Beyond Religious Freedom*.

33. "Black Clergy Task Force Joins Clinton State Department in Move to Defeat Religious Persecution Legislation," *Tennessee Tribune*, October 9, 1997.

34. Jeffrey Goldberg, "Washington Discovers Christian Persecution," *NYT Magazine*, December 21, 1997, 46.

35. Daniel Kurtzman, "Behind the Headlines: Religious Persecution Measure Poses Dilemma for Jewish Groups," *Jewish Telegraphic Agency*, September 17, 1997.

36. Ron Dart, "Beyond Clan Politics," *Sojourners*, February 1998, 14.

37. Steven Lee Meyers, "Converting the Dollar into a Bludgeon," *NYT*, April 20, 1997; Thomas Lippman, "Rethinking US Economic Sanctions; State Dept. Weights Costs, Impact of Trade Restrictions," *WP*, January 26, 1998.

38. Tony Carnes, "Religious Persecution Bill Encounters Stiff Resistance," *CT*, October 5, 1998, 26.

39. Mary Cagney, "Senators Champion Rival Bill on Religious Persecution," *CT,* May 18, 1998, 20–21. Hertzke describes the debates in *Freeing God's Children*, 183–236.

40. On the history of the State Department reports and their limits, see Moore, "Genres of Religious Freedom."

41. The designations are based upon, but separate from, the State Department reports. Reports before 2001 are archived, no longer available at the main page, www.state.gov. For 1999, the report is at https://1997-2001.state.gov/global/human_rights/irf/irf_rpt/index.html; the 2000 report is at https://www.gpo.gov/fdsys/pkg/CPRT-106JPRT66723/pdf/CPRT-106JPRT66723.pdf. Reports after 2001 can be accessed at https://www.state.gov/j/drl/irf/.

42. Editorial, "No Particular Concern," *WP,* March 17, 2003.

43. Obama did not technically waive sanctions on Saudi Arabia, since the waiver was in place for an indeterminate length of time, whereas most other waivers were for six months, renewable. So, in order to respond to violations in Saudi Arabia, a president first would have to "unwaive" the country.

44. Shea, "Origins and Legacy of the Movement," 29.

45. USCIRF annual reports and other publications are at http://www.uscirf.gov/reports-briefs.

46. Gunn, "American Exceptionalism," 139, 13n.

47. Michelle Boorstein, "Allegations of Religious Bias Against Complaint Monitors," *WP*, February 17, 2000.

48. Vickie Langohr, "Frosty Reception for US Religious Freedom Commission in Egypt," *Middle East Report,* March 29, 2001, http://www.merip.org/mero/mero032901. See also Mahmood, *Religious Difference in a Secular Age*, 94–97.

49. Robert Seiple, "Speaking Out: The USCIRF Is Only Cursing the Darkness," *CT* (web only), October 2002, http://www.christianitytoday.com/ct/2002/octoberweb-only/10-14-31.0.html.

50. The band, best known for its anthem, "Jesus Freaks," joined up with Voice of the Martyrs to produce a series of books for teenagers about martyrdom, including *Jesus Freaks: Martyrs* (1999) and *Jesus Freaks, Vol II* (2005).

51. The WEA Religious Liberty Commission News and Analysis email list. The website is http://www.worldevangelicalalliance.com/commissions/rlc/.

52. Sookhdeo, *LOP 32: The Persecuted Church*. Also Patrick Sookhdeo, "A Religion That Sanctions Violence: Glossing Over the Realities of Islam Will Help No One," *Daily Telegraph* (London), September 17, 2001; Sookhdeo, *A People Betrayed*; Sookhdeo, *Global Jihad*.

53. See, for example, the Berkley's Center's mini-conference, "Proselytism and Religious Freedom in the 21st Century," and its three-part lecture series on the tenth anniversary of IRFA, starting with "Why Religious Freedom?" Similarly, Pew hosted a number of forums in 2007 and 2008, including Hanford III, Shattuck, and Farr, "International Religious Freedom"; Shah et al., "Legislating International Religious Freedom."

54. Seiple's presentation at The Falls Church, in Falls Church, VA, on October 28, 2005.

55. Opendoorsusa.org. Financials available at https://projects.propublica.org/nonprofits/organizations/330523832.

56. On humanitarian images, see Fehrenbach and Rodogno, *Humanitarian Photography*; Cookman, "Gilles Caron's Coverage of the Crisis in Biafra."

57. Open Doors UK, http://www.opendoorsuk.org/resources/letter/iraq.php.

58. Cook's appointment originally stalled in the Senate, but she was eventually confirmed in April 2011. Ethan Cole, "Former NY Pastor Sworn In as Religious Freedom Ambassador," *Christian Post*, May 17, 2011. David Saperstein, a Reform rabbi who replaced Cook, had been chair of the UNCIRF in 1999.

59. Austin Dacey, "Why Is the State Department Opening an Office of 'Religious Engagement'?" *Religion Dispatches*, August 8, 2013, http://religiondispatches.org/why-is-the-state-department-opening-an-office-of-religious-engagement/; Melani McAlister, "Engaging Religion at the Department of State," *The Immanent Frame*, July 30, 2013, https://tif.ssrc.org/2013/07/30/engaging-religion-at-the-department-of-state/#McAlister.

CHAPTER 10

1. Personal interview with White-Hammond, Boston, June 30, 2005; personal interview with Ray Hammond, Boston, July 1, 2005.

2. Report on Gloria White-Hammond's lecture, "Standing on the Shoulders of Harriet Tubman: I Am My Sister's Keeper," cosponsored by the Boston Research Center for the 21st Century and the Wellesley Centers for Women, January 27, 2005, http://www.brc21.org/ht_summary.html. See also Jane Lampman, "Boston Pastors, Ex-Slave Tell Story." *CSM,* September 13, 2001.

3. Personal interview with Gerald Bell, Boston, July 1, 2005.

4. Will Higham, "The Evangelical Crusade," *New Statesman*, August 9, 2004, 14. On evangelicals and sex trafficking as anti-slavery work, see Pendleton, "The Other Sex Industry," and Bernstein, "Sexual Politics of the 'New Abolitionism.'"

5. Johnson, *Root Causes*, 11–17.

6. Daly, "Islam, Secularism and Ethnic Identity in the Sudan," 2.

7. Daly, *Imperial Sudan*, 47–83.

8. de Waal, "Sudan: What Kind of State?"

9. Collins, *A History of Modern Sudan*, 77–82; McClintock, "The Southern Sudan Problem"; Glickman, "When and How to Resolve Ethnic Conflicts."

10. Smith, "George Bush in Khartoum."

11. Lesch, "Sudan"; Phares, "The Sudanese Battle for American Opinion"; Erlich, *Islam and Christianity in the Horn of Africa*.

12. Johnson, *Root Causes*, 91–100; Washington Office on Africa, "Slavery, War and Peace in Sudan."

13. On the population numbers, see Lesch, *The Sudan*, 20.

14. Hutchinson, *Nuer Dilemmas*, 346.

15. Powell, *A Different Shade of Colonialism*; Sharkey, *Living with Colonialism*; Lobban, "Slavery in the Sudan since 1989." This was particularly true in Bahr al-Ghazal and the Nuba Mountains.

16. Robert Press, "Sudanese Teacher Arrested over Slave Report," *CSM*, December 31, 1987; Robert Press, "Sudanese Sell Children to Avert Starvation," *CSM*, July 27, 1988.

17. Bíró, "Interim Report."

18. Gilbert Lewthwaite and Gregory Kane, "Witness to Slavery," *Baltimore Sun*, June 16, 1996; Walter Goodman, "Television Review: Reports of Slavery in a Divided Land," *NYT*, December 10, 1996. Also: Ken Ringle, "Activists Call for Action on North African Slavery," *WP*, March 14, 1996.

19. Among his half-dozen articles, see Nat Hentoff, "Blind Eye to Slavery," *WP*, August 23, 1996, and "Fifth Grade Freedom Fighters," *WP*, August 1, 1998.

20. Bruce Brander, "Muslim-Christian Conflicts May Destabilize East Africa: Christians Raped, Forced into Slavery, and Killed," *CT*, April 29, 1996, 52-53. See also Caroline Cox, "How Apin Akot Redeemed his Daughter," *CT*, March 2, 1998, 56; Paul Liben, "Murder in the Sudan," *First Things*, August–September 1995, 44–46.

21. Eibner, "My Career Redeeming Slaves."

22. In 2002, the International Eminent Persons Group said it could not establish the scale of the abductions, because of lack of information, that both the government of Sudan and the SPLA had obstructed research. International Eminent Persons Group, "Slavery, Abduction and Forced Servitude in Sudan." From 2001 to 2004, the Rift Valley Institute carried out a project to register the names of all the people taken captive from northern Bahr el-Ghazal. (They did not study slave raiding in the Nuba Mountains and had limited or no access to some Dinka areas.) They developed a database of more than 11,000 abductees. Ryle, Jok, and Boyle, "The Sudan Abduction and Slavery Project"; Jok, "Slavery and Slave Redemption in Sudan," 152.

An SPLA leader told the *Atlantic* in 1999 that he very roughly estimated that 20,000 were captured. Miniter, "The False Promise of Slave Redemption." CSI estimated the total number of "chattel slaves" as 100,000. Eibner, "My Career Redeeming Slaves."

23. All of the following taken from an interview with Gloria White-Hammond on June 30, 2005. White-Hamond has also told her story in numerous magazine and television interviews.

24. Franklin Foer, "Marriage Counselor," *Atlantic,* March 2004, 39-40.

25. Gerald Bell, personal interview, July 1, 2005.

26. Ibid.

27. Aidi, "Slavery, Genocide and the Politics of Outrage." On the history of African American and Arab solidarity, see Lubin, *Geographies of Liberation*; Feldman, *A Shadow over Palestine*.

28. Steven Mufson, "Christians' Plight in Sudan Tests A Bush Stance; Evangelicals Urge Intervention," *WP*, March 24, 2001.

29. Charisse Jones, "A Once-Shunned Sharpton on a Comeback," *USA Today*, August 15, 2001.

30. Kimberly Davis, "The Truth about Slavery in Sudan," *Ebony*, August 2001, 37–38; Nat Hentoff, "Black Pastors Demand Justice," *Village Voice*, July 5, 2000, 38; Hertzke, *Freeing God's Children*, 254–55.

31. Steven Mufson, "3 Arrested in Protests at Sudanese Embassy," *WP*, April 14, 2001.

32. Marcus Mabry, "The Price Tag on Freedom," *Newsweek*, May 3, 1999, 50.

33. Quoted in Christine Gardner, "Slave Redemption," *CT*, August 9, 1999, 28-33. See also Nat Hentoff, "Fifth Grade Freedom Fighters," *WP*, August 1, 1998; Gail Russell Chaddock, "Slavery in Sudan Becomes a 'Cause' in US," *CSM*, October 5, 2000; Mindy Sink, "Schoolchildren Set out to Liberate Slaves in Sudan," *NYT*, December 2, 1998; Miniter, "The False Promise of Slave Redemption."

34. Christine Gardner, "Slave Redemption," *CT*, August 9, 1999, 28-33. Karl Vick, "Ripping Off Slave 'Redeemers'; Rebels Exploit Westerners' Efforts to Buy Emancipation for Sudanese," *WP*, February 26, 2002.

35. Hertzke, *Freeing God's Children*, 252, 266.

36. Slaves in the US who were able to gain some money by selling their skills would use that money to purchase their own freedom or that of their families. Whitman, *Price of Freedom*.

37. Philip P. Bliss, "I Will Sing of My Redeemer," 1876.

38. Sam Dillon, "Columbia to Check Reports of Anti-Jewish Harassment," *NYT*, October 29, 2004; N.R. Kleinfield, "Mideast Tensions Are Getting Personal on Campus at Columbia," *NYT*, January 18, 2005; Karen Arenson, "Panel's Report on Faculty at Columbia Spurs Debate," *NYT*, April 1, 2005.

39. Jerry Gordon, "Fighting Muslim Brotherhood Lawfare and Rabbinic Fatwas: An Interview with Dr. Charles Jacobs," *New English Review*, February 2011, http://www.newenglishreview.org/custpage.cfm/frm/81228/sec_id/81228.

40. This description was taken from AASG's website, Iabolish, in 2007. The website was then inactive for a number of years and has since been relaunched, with a new description of the organization, at http://www.iabolish.org/. A good description of AASG at the early stages of its Sudan work is Darren Garnick, "Buy Freedom," *Jerusalem Report*, August 30, 1999, 35ff.

41. Heather Robinson, "Sudan's Extermination of Christians: An Interview with Simon Deng," *Center for Security Policy*, August 27, 2009, http://www.centerforsecuritypolicy.org/2009/08/27/sudans-extermination-of-christians-an-interview-with-simon-deng-2/; Alex Magnet, "Former Sudanese Slave Tells His Story to Gather Support for Freedom Walk," *New York Sun*, March 6, 2006. On the rally and meeting with Bush, Jonathan LeMire, "Coney Lifeguard Is Lifeline to Bush," *Daily News*, July 16, 2006.

42. Transcript of the talk at Deng, "Remarks to 'Victims of Jihad' Symposium," originally available at the International Humanist and Ethical Union, archived at https://web.archive.org/web/20071027094709/http://www.iheu.org/node/1539.

43. Larry Derfner, "Voice for the Voiceless," *Jerusalem Post*, May 30, 2008.

44. Darren Garnick, "Buy Freedom," *Jerusalem Report*, August 30, 1999, 35; Charles Jacobs, "New Abolitionists Open Window on Middle East," *Forward*, May 23, 1997; "Social Educator," *Harvard Magazine*, June 2002, http://harvardmagazine.com/2002/05/social-educator.html.

45. On modern storefront churches, McRoberts, *Streets of Glory*.

46. Angelique Chrisafis, "The Lady and The Slave Trade: Baroness Cox Has Bought and Freed 1,500 People," *Observer*, January 28, 2001; Robin Lodge, "Buying Freedom for Sudanese Slaves Encourages Elicit Trade, UN Says," *Ottowa Citizen*, July 9, 1999.

47. Miniter, "The False Promise of Slave Redemption"; Rogers and Swinnerton, "Slave Redemption When It Takes Time."

48. Mostly, it seems, the SPLA made money by taking the hard currency and manipulating the currency exchange rate, although it is quite likely that the group also took a cut or a tax. Jok, "Slavery and Slave Redemption in Sudan."

49. Karl Vick, "Ripping off Slave Redeemers," *WP*, February 26, 2002. Similar stories were published elsewhere: Michael McMahon, "The Great Slave Scam," *Irish Times*, February 23, 2002; Declan Walsh, "Scam in Sudan: An Elaborate Hoax Involving Fake African Slaves and Less-Than-Honest Interpreters Is Duping Concerned Westerners," *Independent on Sunday*, February 24, 2002.

50. Karl Vick, "Ripping off Slave Redeemers," *WP*, February 26, 2002.

51. Will Higham, "The Evangelical Crusade," *New Statesman*, August 9, 2004, 14.

52. International Eminent Persons Group, "Slavery, Abduction and Forced Servitude in Sudan"; Ryle, Jok, and Boyle, "The Sudan Abduction and Slavery Project."

53. On Riak, see Lawrence Morahan, "CBS' Dan Rather 'Duped' in Report on Sudanese Slavery, Critics Say," *Baptist Press*, May 31, 2002, http://www.bpnews.net/issue-05/31/2002. The view of Bishop Gassis is reported in Miniter, "The False Promise of Slave Redemption."

54. Christine Gardner, "Slave Redemption," *CT*, August 9, 1999, 28–33.

55. de Waal, *Famine Crimes*, 122.

56. Washington Office on Africa, "Slavery, War and Peace in Sudan."

57. Barnett, *Empire of Humanity*, 19–48. See also Taylor-Robinson, "Operation Lifeline Sudan"; Van Voorhis, "Food as a Weapon for Peace"; Johnson, *Root Causes*, 143–55.

58. Van Voorhis, "Food as a Weapon for Peace"; Akol, "Operation Lifeline Sudan"; Barnett, *Empire of Humanity*, 161–219; Maxwell, Santschi, and Gordon, "Looking Back."

59. David Bar-Illan, "When War, Genocide, and Slavery Are Not a Story," *Jerusalem Post*, July 7, 1995; Rachelle Thackray, "5 Days in the Life of … Caroline Cox," *The Independent* (UK), May 31, 1998.

60. "Bombs Continue to Fall on Ministry Hospitals in Sudan," *CT* (web only), March 1, 2000, http://www.christianitytoday.com/ct/2000/marchweb-only/54.0b.html.

61. Franklin Graham, "Stand Up For Sudan's Christians," *Wall Street Journal*, March 16, 2000.

62. Davis, "The Clinton Model"; Huliaras, "Evangelists, Oil Companies, and Terrorists."

63. Gagnon, Maklin, and Simons, "Deconstructing Engagement."

64. Human Rights Watch, *Sudan, Oil, and Human Rights*, 143.

65. Diamond, "The PetroChina Syndrome," 39–40; Hertzke, *Freeing God's Children*, 276–89; Huliaras, "Evangelists, Oil Companies, and Terrorists"; Debra Fieguth, "Oil Exports Draw Protests: Christians Urge Divestment from Canadian Company," *CT*, November 15, 1999, 20.

66. Hertzke, *Freeing God's Children*, 282. Bachus was speaking to the National Association of Evangelicals' Summit on Religious Persecution, May 1, 2002.

67. Mike Allen and Steven Mufson, "US to Press Sudan to Halt War on Christians," *WP*, May 4, 2001.

68. Interview with Gloria-White Hammond, June 30, 2005.

69. Alan Sipress, "Sudan Gives US Intelligence Against Bin Laden," *WP*, September 29, 2001; Steven Mufson, "New Casualty: Sudan Peace Act; Activists Fear Crackdown on Khartoum May Be Sidelined," *WP*, October 5, 2001.

70. Art Moore, "Justice Delayed: Sudan Peace Act May Be a Casualty of the War on Terrorism," *CT*, November 12, 2001, 23–24.

71. Danforth, *The Outlook for Peace in Sudan*. Quote from the international director of Franklin Graham's Samaritan's Purse in Mindy Belz, "Misdirection Play?," *World,* September 20, 2003.

72. Sebastian Mallaby, "Saving Sudan," *WP*, May 27, 2002.

73. Sudan Peace Act, 2002, sec 6, paragraph 2, https://www.congress.gov/107/plaws/publ245/PLAW-107publ245.pdf.

74. Timothy Callahan, "Sudan Peace Act 'Has Teeth': but Sanctions Are at President's Discretion," *CT*, December 9, 2002, 17–22.

75. "Despite Sudanese Peace Plan, Humanitarian Crisis & Threat of Ethnic Genocide Loom," *Baptist Press*, May 28, 2004, http://bpnews.net/18369/despite-sudanese-peace-plan-humanitarian-crisis-and-threat-of-ethnic-genocide-loom.

76. Salomon, "The Ruse of Law"; Zahar, "A Journey of a Thousand Steps."

CHAPTER 11

1. Audio Adrenaline, "Your Hands, Your Feet," from *Underdog*, Forefront Records, 1999, video at https://www.youtube.com/watch?v=pFHyVdugFEM.

2. Wuthnow, *Boundless Faith*, 170, 126; Priest et al., "Researching the Short-Term Mission Movement."

3. Approximately 315,000 students went abroad in 2014–2015; this was well over three times what it had been in 1990. Institute of International Education, "Top 25 Destinations of US Study Abroad Students, 2013/14-2014/15," in *Open Doors Report on International Educational Exchange*, 2016, https://www.iie.org/Research-and-Insights/Open-Doors/Data/US-Study-Abroad/Leading-Destinations/2013-15.

4. All of the information about Dorothy Birkoff is from her file in the Short Terms Abroad papers, Folder 1-17, CN 179, BGCA.

5. King, "Heartbroken for God's World," 74.

6. Cunningham and Rogers, *Is That Really You, God?*

7. Hoffman, *All You Need is Love*, 189.

8. Sarkela and Mazzeo, "Freedom's Distant Shores"; Robinson, *Africa at the Crossroads*. On the link with the Peace Corps, see the CBS news report from 1961 on the Operation Crossroads Africa website: http://operationcrossroadsafrica.org/crossroaders-photos-and-videos/cbs-reports-video-operation-crossroads-africa-and-peace-corps-1961.

9. In the rich literature on theories and practices of development and modernization, see Engerman, *Modernization from the Other Shore*; Cullather, *The Hungry World*; Gilman, *Mandarins of the Future*; Milne, *America's Rasputin*; Black, "Interior's Exterior." The alternative focus on small-scale visions of development is traced by Immerwahr, *Thinking Small*.

10. Hoffman, *All You Need Is Love*, 53–58; Latham, *Modernization as Ideology*, 109–50.

11. The organization was Soldiers of Christ. A fundraising letter describes teams of young people from Moody Bible Institute going to Latin America for summer campaigns. Soldiers of Christ Fundraising Letter, March 17, 1965, Folder 11-57; CN 179, BGCA.

12. John C. Crosby, "LAOS: Laymen in Mission," *Christian Century*, July 27, 1966, 931–33, q. 931.

13. Barr, "Short Term Service," Folder 11-72, CN 179, BGCA; Richard Wolff, "The Call," *STA Bulletin*, February 1968, 1ff, Folder 11-76, CN 179, BGCA.

14. John C. Crosby, "LAOS: Laymen in Mission," *Christian Century*, July 27, 1966, 931–933, q. 932; R.B. Kochtitzky, "LAOS—Laymen's Overseas Service," *Occasional Bulletin, Missionary Research Library*, November 1965, Folder 204-10, CN 165, BGCA.

15. The basic history of STA is outlined in the archival notes for the Short Terms Abroad archives at BGCA. This introduction to the organization is found at: http://www.wheaton.edu/bgc/archives/GUIDES/179.htm#1.

16. Aubrey Berndt, Folder 1-14, Personnel files of Short Terms Abroad, CN 179, BGCA.

17. Mr. and Mrs. Edward Campbell, Folder 1-25, Personnel files of Short Terms Abroad, CN 179, BGCA.

18. Judy Barr cites "at least" 5,786 short-termers in the field, based on a survey done by Short Terms Abroad. Barr, "Short Term Service," Folder 11-72, CN 179, BGCA. Page 27 in the pamphlet "Opportunities 1973," distributed by Short Terms Abroad, reads: "The average short term is one year, but some have stayed for only a few weeks and others for two years or more." In fact, most of the listings were for commitments of two years, or "indefinite." This pamphlet was produced each year from 1972 to 1976; in 1974, STA distributed more than 24,000 copies. Folder 12-92, CN 179, BCGA.

19. World Missions Tours brochure, "Evangelism in Bolivia," 1969, Folder 15-10, CN 179, BGCA.

20. "International Mailbag," *STA Bulletin*, February 1969, 6, Folder 11-75; CN 179, BGCA.

21. "Radio Victoria PJA-6," *STA Bulletin*, September 1967, 1, Folder 11-17, CN 179, BGCA; Marlene Le Fever, "Longest Short-Termer," *STA Bulletin*, June 1968, 7, Folder 11-76, CN 179, BGCA.

22. "1966 Caribbean Youth Witness," *Pentecostal Evangel*, September 11, 1966, 16-17, FPHC.

23. Dorothy Birkhoff, Folder 1-17, CN 179, BGCA. The number of missions organizations that expressed a willingness to take on short-term volunteers increased from 126 in 1973 to 256 in 1979. Kane, *A Concise History of the Christian World Mission*, 189–91.

24. Bryant, *In the Gap*, 64–65.

25. Berry, Heltzel, and Benson, *Prophetic Evangelicals*.

26. Letter from David Bryant to Bonnie Coleman, dated May 1, 1986, Folder 236-16, CN 300, BGCA. The *World Christian* ad is from a flyer attached to the letter.

27. Bryant, *In the Gap*, 219–43.

28. *Annual Report of the Southern Baptist Convention, 1985*, 35, at http://media2.sbhla.org.s3.amazonaws.com/annuals/SBC_Annual_1985.pdf.

29. Presentation by Ted Elder at the Chicago "Perspectives" Coordinators Conference of January 23–24, 1986, as reported in *Network Newsletter*, 1:1, Folder 237-24, CN 300, BGCA; "US Center for World Mission," Folder 237-24, CN 300, BGCA.

30. David Bryant to John Schmidt, offering quotes for the film's promotion, October 27, 1987, Folder 236-10, CN 300, BGCA.

31. Maclure, "Wholly Available," i.

32. Global Frontier Missions Information 2006 brochure. The brochure is no longer available, but there is a brief description of the trip at www.missions-trip.com/mission-trip-detail/tid/283.htm, and a YouTube video promotion at http://www.youtube.com/watch?v=U8NwB8UBqnM.

33. Luhr, *Witnessing Suburbia*.

34. Webb left for a solo career in 2003 and returned for the 2007 album *Overdressed*; thus, Webb was not on board for *Share the Well*.

35. Caedmon's Call, *Share the Well,* Essential Records, 2004.

36. Third World Symphony, "Customer Reviews: Share the Well," Amazon.com, May 4, 2007, http://www.amazon.com/review/product/B00049QLZK/ref=cm_cr_dp_synop?%5Fencodin g=UTF8&sortBy=bySubmissionDateDescending#R1F6K5R.

37. Sinha, *Specters of Mother India.*

38. Priest et al., "Researching the Short-Term Mission Movement."

39. Maclure, "Wholly Available," ii.

40. Linhart, "They Were So Alive!"

41. Schwartz, "Two Awesome Problems," 28.

42. Becchetti, "Why Most Mission Trips Are a Waste of Time (And How to Make Sure Yours Isn't)," n.d., http://www.csm.org/articlewhymost.php.

43. Livermore, *Serving with Eyes Wide Open,* 94, 71.

44. Ver Beek, "Impact of Short-Term Mission."

45. Ibid.

46. Jeffrey MacDonald, "Rise of Sunshine Samaritans: On a Mission or Holiday?," *CSM,* May 25, 2006.

47. Richard Slimbach, "First, Do No Harm," *EMQ,* October 2000, https://emqonline.com/node/384.

48. Berlant, *Cruel Optimism,* 1–2.

49. Tsing, *Friction.*

50. For the complete list, see the Standards of Excellence (SOE) site: http://www.soe.org/explore/the-7-standards/; Ken Walker, "Agencies Announce Short-Term Mission Standards," *CT,* October 2003, 30.

51. Walker, "Homeward Bound? Short-Term Missions May Be Shifting Domestic," *CT,* June 2010, 15–22.

52. Ibid. A list of 2012 and 2013 programs for Global Frontier Missions was at https://www.globalfrontiermissions.org/go.html as of Aug. 1, 2012.

CHAPTER 12

1. Laurie Goodstein, "Falwell: Blame Abortionists, Feminists and Gays," *Guardian* (UK), September 19, 2001.

2. Alan Cooperman, "Ministers Asked to Curb Remarks About Islam," *WP,* May 08, 2003; Laurie Goodstein, "Top Evangelicals Critical of Colleagues over Islam," *NYT,* May 7, 2003.

3. Dana Milbank and Wax, "Bush Visits Mosque to Forestall Hate Crimes; President Condemns an Increase in Violence Aimed at Arab Americans," *WP,* September 18, 2001.

4. Cati, *Married to Muhammad*; Richardson, *Secrets of the Koran.* On Islamophobia in general in this period, see Kumar, *Islamophobia and the Politics of Empire*; Ali et al., "Fear, Inc."; Bayoumi, *This Muslim American Life*; Esposito and Kalin, *Islamophobia.*

5. Seiple and Borchini, "Religion and Security." See also Seiple and Hoover, *Religion and Security.*

6. George W. Bush, "President Bush Delivers Graduation Speech at West Point," White House Office of the Press Secretary, June 1, 2002, http://www.whitehouse.gov/news/releases/2002/06/20020601-3.html. I analyze Bush's policies in McAlister, "Rethinking the 'Clash of Civilizations.'"

7. George W. Bush, State of the Union speech, January 28, 2003, at http://www.whitehouse.gov/news/releases/2003/01/20030128-19.html; John Donnelly, "Fighting Terror/Theologians: Some Voice Concern over President's Religious Rhetoric," *Boston Globe*, February 13, 2003.

8. I discuss the motivations and the lead-up to the war in McAlister, *Epic Encounters*, 266–302.

9. Alan Cooperman, "Bishop in Bush's Church in New Antiwar Ad," *WP*, January 31, 2003.

10. "Panel of Christians Speaks Out on War with Iraq—Transcript," *CNN Larry King Live*, March 11, 2003, http://transcripts.cnn.com/TRANSCRIPTS/0303/11/lkl.00.html.

11. "Mideast Churches Warn against Iraq Invasion," *Christian Century*, September 28, 2002, 15. On the anti-war coalition generally, see Rebecca Phillips, "The Religious Left's Moment," *Beliefnet.com*, January 2003, http://www.beliefnet.com/story/121/story_12148_1.html.

12. "American, Canadian, British Church Leaders Call on U.S. to 'Stop the Rush to War,'" *National Council of Churches*, August 29, 2002, http://www.ncccusa.org/news/02news82.html; Religious Leaders for Sensible Priorities, "President Bush, Let Jesus Change Your Mind," *NYT*, December 4, 2002.

13. Pew Center for the People and the Press, "Different Faiths, Different Messages." The Gallup poll, conducted in December 2002 is cited by Jonathan Tilove, "Blacks' Opposition to Iraq War Rooted in History," *Newhouse News Service*, February 13, 2003. According to Zogby poll in March 2003, only 23 percent of African Americans supported the war. Quoted by Liz Marlantes, "From Alabama Pews, a Wary Look at War," *CSM*, March 10, 2003. Pew gave a more divided picture in a February 2003 poll, reporting that 47 percent of African Americans opposed and 44 percent were in favor of the invasion. Pew Center for the People and the Press, "U.S. Needs More International Backing."

14. Pew Center for the People and the Press, "Different Faiths, Different Messages."

15. "Evangelicals for War," NPR, February 26, 2003, http://www.npr.org/templates/story/story.php?storyId=1175601; Art Toalston and Dwayne Hastings, "Land: Military Action against Iraq Meets Ethical Standards for War," *Baptist Press News*, September 9, 2002, http://bpnews.net/14198/land-military-action-against-iraq-meets-ethical-standards-for-war.

16. Bill Broadway, "Religious Leaders' Voices Rise on Iraq," *WP*, September 28, 2002; Editors, "Bully Culprit," *CT* (web only), September 1, 2002, http://www.christianitytoday.com/ct/2002/septemberweb-only/9-30-11.0.html.

17. Augustine of Hippo, *The City of God*, 25.

18. The feminist social theorist Jean Elshtain created outrage when she published her theorization of Just War, which supported the war in Iraq. However controversial her conclusions, Elshtain's basic description of the requirements of the theory is useful. Elshtain, *Just War Against Terror*.

19. Marvin Olasky, "Make Love, Not War: But What If Making War Is the More Compassionate Response?," *World*, March 17, 2007.

20. Keith English, "War in Iraq Fails in Two Christian Traditions," *Commercial Appeal* (Memphis), October 23, 2005; Bob Hyatt, "Profoundly Disturbed on the Fourth of July: God, the Flag and the End of America," June 25, 2004, reposted at http://bobhyatt.me/2005/06/tis_the_season_/.

21. These sites are no longer online.

22. Julie Duin, "Summit Criticizes anti-Islam remarks; But Evangelicals Differ with Their Leaders," *Washington Times*, May 8, 2003; James Beverley, "Is Islam a Religion of Peace?," *CT*, January 7, 2002, 32ff. Poll by Beliefnet and the Ethics and Public Policy Center, "Evangelical

Views of Islam, Fall 2002, results released April 7, 2003, and posted at http://www.beliefnet.com/news/politics/2003/04/evangelical-views-of-islam.aspx.

23. Tatsha Robertson, "Evangelicals Flock to Israel's Banner; Christian Zionists see Jewish state bringing Messiah," *Boston Globe*, October 21, 2002.

24. Shriver, "Evangelicals and World Affairs," 54.

25. David Klinghoffer, "Just be Gracious," *Jerusalem Post*, August 16, 2002.

26. Todd Hertz, "Comments on Islam Endanger Missionaries, Letter Says," *CT* (web only), January 1, 2003,http://www.christianitytoday.com/ct/2003/januaryweb-only/1-13-53.0.html.

27. Cizik is quoted in "Evangelicals for War," NPR, February 26, 2003, http://www.npr.org/templates/story/story.php?storyId=1175601.

28. Bill Broadway, "Evangelicals' Voices Speak Softly About Iraq," *WP*, January 25, 2003.

29. Alexandra Alter, "News: Groups Weigh Risks, Morality of Evangelizing in Postwar Iraq," *Religion News Service*, June 5, 2003; Deborah Caldwell, "Why Iraq Beckons," *Beliefnet*, http://www.beliefnet.com/faiths/2003/04/why-iraq-beckons.aspx.

30. Alan Neely, "Incarnational Mission," in Moreau, *Evangelical Dictionary of World Missions*, 475. Neely is citing M. Theron Rankin of the Southern Baptist Convention.

31. Hirsch and Frost, *Shaping of Things to Come*. For a critique of the ways that most missions theorists use the term, see John Starke, "The Incarnation Is about a Person, Not a Mission," *TGC—The Gospel Coalition*, https://www.thegospelcoalition.org/article/the-incarnation-is-about-a-person-not-a-mission.

32. "A Discussion with Deborah Dortzbach," Berkley Center for Religion, Peace, and World Affairs, April 5, 2007, https://berkleycenter.georgetown.edu/interviews/a-discussion-with-deborah-dortzbach-international-director-for-hiv-aids-programs-world-relief.

33. King, "Seeking a Global Vision." More recently, World Vision has stated that it does not evangelize, http://www.wvi.org/faqs#7.

34. Marvin Olasky, "Refining Cruelty: An Army of Compassion Finds That War Is Hell," *World*, March 10, 2007.

35. Teresa Watanabe, "Seminary Is Reaching Out to Muslims; An Evangelical School Launches an Interfaith Effort to Allay Tensions Deriving from 9/11," *LAT*, December 6, 2003.

36. "Why We Should Listen to Muslim Voices" IGE Global Leadership Forum, Washington, D.C, September 22, 2007, https://globalengage.org/faith-international-affairs/articles/why-we-should-listen-to-muslim-voices.

37. "EPPC/Beliefnet Poll: Evangelical Views of Islam," *Beliefnet*, April 7, 2003, http://www.beliefnet.com/news/politics/2003/04/evangelical-views-of-islam.aspx.

38. Michael Lawrence et al., "Ministering to Those in Need: The Rights and Wrongs of Missions and Humanitarian Assistance in Iraq," Public Forum, Washington, DC, June 4, 2003, http://www.pewforum.org/2003/06/04/ministering-to-those-in-need-the-rights-and-wrongs-of-missions-and-humanitarian-assistance-in-iraq/.

39. Charles Duhigg, "Evangelicals Flock Into Iraq on a Mission of Faith," *LAT*, March 18, 2004.

40. Tony Campolo, "Is Christianity a Casualty of War?" *Huffington Post*, January 5, 2006, http://www.huffingtonpost.com/tony-campolo/is-christianity-a-casualt_b_13329.html.

41. Four American pastors were shot and killed in February 2004, and four Southern Baptists were killed in a car bomb in March 2004. Several South Korean missionaries were abducted and later released. Doug Bandow, "Christians in the Crossfire," *American Conservative*, October 23, 2006, 13–15; Arian Eujung Cha, "Christian Missionaries Battle For Hearts and Minds in

Iraq," *WP*, May 16, 2004; Willis Witter, "Christianity in a Crucible; In Iraq, Seeking Converts Dangerous for Evangelists," *Washington Times*, March 21, 2004; Edward Wong and James Glanz, "South Korean Is Killed in Iraq By His Captors," *NYT*, June 23, 2004.

42. Bill Broadway, "For Iraqi Christians, A Shadow of Insecurity," *WP*, July 17, 2004; Scheherezade Faramarzi, "Iraq Church Bombings Leave Empty Pews," *Associated Press*, October 16, 2004; David George, "Iraq's Besieged Christians Weigh Taking up Arms, Fleeing into Exile," *Knight Ridder*, December 14, 2004; Jeffrey Gettleman, "Gunmen Kidnap the Catholic Archbishop of Mosul as Pre-Election Violence Flares in Iraq," *NYT*, January 18, 2005; Martin Asser, "Arab Christians Squeezed by Conflict," *BBC News Online*, March 24, 2003, http://news.bbc.co.uk/2/hi/middle_east/2879853.stm.

43. Lizzie Dearden, "Death Toll from Isis Bombing in Baghdad Rises to 250," *Independent* (UK), July 6, 2016; Rukmini Callimachi, "ISIS Seems to Tailor Attacks for Different Audiences," *NYT*, July 2, 2016.

44. On the functional reality of concepts, see Bourdieu, *The Logic of Practice*, 52–65.

45. McAlister, *Epic Encounters*, 266–308.

46. Mark Glassman, "The Reach of War: Broadcast; U.S. Religious Figures Offer Abuse Apology on Arab TV," *NYT*, June 11, 2004.

47. Ted Olsen, "Weblog: Rounding Up the Few Christian Voices on the Iraq Prison Scandal," *CT* (web only), May 1, 2004, http://www.ctlibrary.com/ct/2004/mayweb-only/5-10-22.0.html.

48. Ted Olsen, "Weblog: The Religious Side of the Abu Ghraib Scandal," *CT* (web only), May 1, 2004, http://www.christianitytoday.com/ct/2004/mayweb-only/5-24-12.0.html.

49. Albert Mohler, "First Person: The Prison Abuse Scandal & the Human Heart," *Baptist Press*, May 24, 2004, http://bpnews.net/18342/firstperson-the-prison-abuse-scandal-and-the-human-heart.

50. Gary Bauer, "Frenzy," *Beliefnet*, May 10, 2004, at http://www.beliefnet.com/news/2004/05/frenzy.aspx.

51. Colson, "Problems Abroad, Problems at Home," *Prison Fellowship*, May 4, 2006, http://breakpoint.org/2006/05/problems-abroad-problems-home/

52. Susan Sontag, "Regarding the Torture of Others," *NYT Magazine*, May 23, 2004, 24–29ff.

53. Steven Gertz, "Torture Then and Now," *CT* (web only), May 1, 2004, http://www.ctlibrary.com/ct/2004/mayweb-only/5-24-53.0.html.

54. Carby, " 'On the Threshold of Woman's Era' "; Allen et al., *Without Sanctuary*.

55. Deborah Caldwell, "Serving His Generation," *Beliefnet*, June 2004, http://www.beliefnet.com/faiths/christianity/2004/06/serving-his-generation.aspx.

56. Neela Banerjee, "Black Churches Struggle Over Their Role in Politics," *NYT*, March 6, 2005.

57. Danner, *Torture and Truth*.

58. David Gushee, "5 Reasons Torture Is Always Wrong," *CT*, February 2006, 32–37.

59. Balmer, *Thy Kingdom Come*, 152.

60. Evangelicals for Human Rights, "Evangelical Declaration Against Torture," 46.

61. Gushee, "How to Read 'An Evangelical Declaration Against Torture.' " By 2007, it had been signed by 286 individuals.

62. Sarah Pulliam, "NAE Endorses Statement Against Torture," *CT* (web only), March 16, 2007, http://www.christianitytoday.com/ct/2007/marchweb-only/111-54.0.html.

63. Erin Roach, "Ethicist: NAE Torture Declaration 'Irrational,' " *Baptist Press*, March 15, 2007, http://www.sbcbaptistpress.org/BPnews.asp?ID=25190; Keith Pavlischek, "Human Rights and

Justice in an Age of Terror," *Books & Culture: A Christian Review*, October 2007. http://www. booksandculture.com/articles/webexclusives/2007/september/ept24a.html.

64. On "position-taking," see Bourdieu, *Field of Cultural Production*.

65. On Bush, see Scott Keeter, "Evangelicals and the GOP: An Update," October 18, 2006, at http://www.pewresearch.org/2006/10/18/evangelicals-and-the-gop-an-update/. A Pew Forum survey in September 2007 that showed younger evangelicals' support for President Bush had dropped from 87 percent approval in 2002 to 45 percent in 2007. Cox, "Pew Forum: Young White Evangelicals."

66. Charles Marsh, "Wayward Christian Soldiers," *NYT*, January 20, 2006. See also Marsh, *Wayward Christian Soldiers*.

67. Jim Wallis, "A Call to Repentance," *Sojourners*, January 2008, 12-17.

68. Balmer, *Thy Kingdom Come*, 191.

69. Wallis, *The Great Awakening*. On the argument that the religious Right was dead, see also Charles Marsh, "God and Country," *Boston Globe*, July 8, 2007.

70. "Evangelicalism: Richard Land and Randall Balmer Discuss the Politics of the Religious Right," *On Faith*, Spring 2007, archived at https://web.archive.org/web/20070519172137/http:// newsweek.washingtonpost.com/onfaith/evangelicalism.html.

71. Eric Gorski, " 'Radical Islam' Should Jolt Voters, Evangelicals Say," *USA Today*, November 2007.

CHAPTER 13

1. Personal Interview with Dick Robinson, December 8, 2006. The senior pastor at the time was Mel Lawrenz, who served from 2000 to 2010. This home page content was changed in 2015.

2. World Bank, "A Poverty Profile for the Southern States of Sudan"; "Top 100 Counties— Median Household Income, 2011," *WP*, September 20, 2012, http://www.washingtonpost.com/ wp-srv/special/local/highest-income-counties/.

3. On the history of development projects and the modernization theory that often accompanied them, see Cullather, *The Hungry World*; Engerman, *Modernization from the Other Shore*; Latham, *Modernization as Ideology*; Ferguson, *Global Shadows*; Gilman, *Mandarins of the Future*.

4. Berlant, "Compassion."

5. Fassin, *Humanitarian Reason*, ix. On the long history of such responses, see Barnett, *Empire of Humanity*.

6. Barnett and Weiss, *Humanitarianism in Question*; Feldman, *Governing Gaza*; Feldman and Ticktin, *In the Name of Humanity*; Biehl and Eskerod, *Vita*; Fassin, "Heart of Humanness"; Redfield, *Life in Crisis*; Bornstein, *Disquieting Gifts*.

7. Hofer, "Role of Evangelical NGOs," 384.

8. *Annual Report 2015* (Boone, NC, Samaritan's Purse, 2015), https://s3.amazonaws.com/ static.samaritanspurse.org/pdfs/2015-SP-Ministry-Report.pdf.

9. See MegaCareMissions.org. Also Anthony Karanja, "US Pastor TD Jakes apologizes over Kenya Comments," *Daily Nation* (Nairobi), October 18, 2003.

10. "The Largest U.S. Charities," *Forbes*, http://www.forbes.com/top-charities/list/. This list is updated yearly.

11. King, "The New Internationalists"; King, "Seeking a Global Vision."

12. *World Vision International Annual Review 2000* (Monrovia, CA: World Vision, 2001).

13. *World Vision International Annual Review 2014* (Monrovia, CA: World Vision, 2015). See also King, "World Vision."

14. Griffith and McAlister, "Is the Public Square Still Naked?"

15. Bornstein, "Developing Faith," 10. See also Bornstein, *The Spirit of Development*.

16. de Waal, *Famine Crimes*.

17. Ferguson, *The Anti-Politics Machine*, xv.

18. Personal Interview with Brian McLaren, July 10, 2007, Columbia, MD.

19. This way of coding African Americans was not unusual, but it was not always the norm. Many historians of African American relations to Africa have described their warm reception as being built on assumptions of shared blackness. Kevin Gaines, for example, describes how African American expatriates in Ghana found that they were accepted contributors to the cause of creating a new and democratic Africa. Gaines, *African Americans in Ghana*, 132. See also Singh, *Black Is a Country*; Gilroy, *The Black Atlantic*; Dworkin, "In the Country of My Forefathers."

20. Fassin, *Humanitarian Reason*, 3.

21. Eron Henry, "Sudan Church Unites," *EthicsDaily.com*, April 18, 2008, http://www.ethicsdaily.com/sudan-church-unites-cms-12534; Victoria Cavaliere, "Religious Leaders Urge Strong International Support Ahead of Sudan Referendum," *Voice of America*, October 27, 2010, http://www.voanews.com/content/southern-sudan-church-leaders-urge-strong-international-support-ahead-of-referendum-106015548/156501.html; Daniel Adwok Kur et al., "The Prospect for Peace in Sudan," Public panel at Council on Foreign Relations, New York, October 14, 2010. See also "Interview with Ramadan Chan of the Sudan Interior Church," *Baptist Times* (UK), no date, c. 2013, http://www.baptist.org.uk/Articles/370754/Interview_with_Ramadan.aspx.

22. "Crisis in South Sudan," *Oxfam International*, July 6, 2016, archived at https://web.archive.org/web/20161025025803/https://www.oxfam.org/en/emergencies/crisis-south-sudan. See also European Commission Civil Protection and Humanitarian Aid Operations, "Crise du Soudan du Sud," Février 2017, http://ec.europa.eu/echo/files/aid/countries/factsheets/south-sudan_fr.pdf.

23. The United States spent $1.6 billion as of June 2016, but that total included funding for South Sudanese who were refugees outside the country. U.S. Agency for International Development, "South Sudan Crisis Fact Sheet #9 FY2016," June 24, 2016, https://www.usaid.gov/sites/default/files/documents/1866/south_sudan_fs09_06-24-2016.pdf.

24. "US Aid to South Sudan Exceeds $1 Billion," *Voice of America*, April 23, 2015, http://www.voanews.com/content/south-sudan-us-aid-billion/2732632.html.

25. Frederick Nzwili, "World Vision Suspends Operations in Key South Sudan State over Escalating Violence," *WP*, May 13, 2015; de Waal, "No Money, No Peace."

CHAPTER 14

1. Rick Warren, "Letter to the Pastors of Uganda," December 2009, https://www.youtube.com/watch?v=1jmGu904fDE.

2. Lisa Miller, "Pastor Rick Warren Responds to Proposed Antigay Ugandan Legislation," *Newsweek*, November 29, 2009, 31; Kathleen Parker, "Uganda and Moral Colonialism," *WP*, February 18, 2010.

3. Max Blumenthal, "Kill Or Convert, Brought To You By the Pentagon," *Nation*, August 7, 2007.

4. For example, Canyon Ridge Christian Church in Las Vegas—a megachurch with some six thousand congregants each week—financially supported Ssempa. Barbara Bradley Hagerty, "US Church Lends Help to AntiGay Ugandan Pastor," NPR, July 13, 2010, http://www.npr.org/templates/story/story.php?storyId=128491183.

5. Sarah Pulliam Bailey, "Intercontinental Divide: Global Pressure Mounts for Uganda to Defeat Anti-Gay Bill," *CT*, February 1, 2010, 17–19.

6. Martin Ssempa, "Ugandan Pastors' Response Video Letter to Rick Warren, part I," 2009, https://www.youtube.com/watch?v=3YqEw6rq-V8. See also Martin Ssempa, "Uganda Pastors' Response Letter to Rick Warren, part II," 2009, https://www.youtube.com/watch?v=dRNyZsYI17Q.

7. Cizik, "My Journey."

8. On Lou Engle and the larger New Apostolic Movement of which he is a part, see Weaver, *New Apostolic Reformation*.

9. Michael Wilkerson, "Lou Engle's 'The Call Uganda' Rallies Support For Anti-Homosexuality Bill," *Religion Dispatches*, May 4, 2010, http://religiondispatches.org/american-supports-ugandan-anti-gay-bill/. See also Josh Kron, "In Uganda, Push to Curb Gays Draws U.S. Guest," *NYT*, May 2, 2010; Waymon Hudson, "The Call Uganda: Anti-Gay American Evangelical Going to Inflame Hate in Uganda," *Huffington Post*, June 30, 2010, http://www.huffingtonpost.com/waymon-hudson/thecall-uganda-anti-gay-a_b_558890.html. On the apostolic movement in Haiti, see Elizabeth McAlister, "Humanitarian Adhocracy."

10. Barbara Bradley Hagerty, "U.S. Exports Cultural War to Uganda," NPR, January 15, 2010, http://www.npr.org/templates/story/story.php?storyId=122572951.

11. On anti-homosexuality discourse in Haiti, for example, see Erin Durban-Albrecht, "Performing Postcolonial Homophobia."

12. Uganda Bureau of Statistics, *National Population and Housing Census 2014*, 19. Of the total population, 39 percent were Catholic; 32 percent were part of the Church of Uganda, which is Anglican; and 11 percent were Pentecostal. Muslims were almost 14 percent of the population. Less than one-tenth of 1 percent of Ugandans identified as practicing African traditional religion. The numbers in the previous census, in 2002, were similar, with the biggest change being that Pentecostals had more than doubled in twelve years. Uganda Bureau of Statistics, *Uganda Population and Housing Census 2002*, viii.

13. Epstein, "God and the Fight Against AIDS."

14. On changes in African Christianity in this period, see Jenkins, *The New Faces of Christianity*.

15. In this discussion I rely on Peterson, *East African Revival*. See also Ward and Wild-Wood, *East African Revival*.

16. Noll, *New Shape of World Christianity*, 186.

17. Coomes, *Festo Kivengere*, 74.

18. As historian Mark Noll notes, the revival "arose in a twentieth-century context where issues of sexuality were always crucial for Christian self-definition." Noll, *New Shape of World Christianity*, 186.

19. Peterson, *East African Revival*, 94, 99, 95.

20. Kivengere, *I Love Idi Amin*.

21. Kivengere, "Personal Revival."

22. Michael Cassidy, "Black and White Africans Preach in USA," *African Enterprise*, November 1973, Folder 3/6/11, PC130, APC; E. Russell Chandler, "Enterprising Africans," *CT*, November 9, 1973, 54–56.

23. Ward, "Same-Sex Relations in Africa"; Hassett, *Anglican Communion*, 82–83. Ghana's missionary history and the modern links between missions and nationalism figured quite differently. See Fancello, "Gagner les Nations à Jésus."

24. Hassett, *Anglican Communion*, 33–34.

25. Ibid., 54.

26. Ward, "Same-Sex Relations in Africa"; Sadgrove et al., "Constructing the Boundaries of Anglican Orthodoxy."

27. Hassett, *Anglican Communion*, 72.

28. Ibid., 73.

29. Anglican Consultative Council, *The Lambeth Conference: Resolutions Archive from 1998* (London: Anglican Communion Office, 2005), 9, http://www.anglicancommunion.org/media/76650/1998.pdf.

30. Hassett, *Anglican Communion*, 95–98.

31. Ibid., 79.

32. Kaoma, *Globalizing the Culture Wars*; Kaoma, "How US Clergy Brought Hate to Uganda."

33. Cantrell, "The Anglican Church of Rwanda"; Hassett, *Anglican Communion*, 131–49. Phillip Jenkins and Michael Cromartie, "Transcript: Global Schism: Is the Anglican Communion Rift the First Stage in a Wider Christian Split?," Pew Forum Faith Angle Conference, Key West, FL, May 14, 2007, http://www.pewforum.org/2007/05/14/global-schism-is-the-anglican-communion-rift-the-first-stage-in-a-wider-christian-split/.

34. Gardner, *Making Chastity Sexy*. She is quoting World Vision CEO Richard Stearns and Ken Casey, head of the Hope Initiative.

35. Graham, *The Name*, 169–82.

36. Franklin Graham, "AIDS Victims Need Churches' Help," *USA Today*, February 26, 2002.

37. Merson et al., "The President's Emergency Plan For AIDS Relief"; Donnelly, "How George W. Bush And Aides Came To 'Think Big' On Battling HIV."

38. "President Bush Promotes HIV Initiative & Tours Africa," *Foreign Policy Bulletin*, February 2005, 175–23; Geraldine Sealey, "An Epidemic Failure," *Rolling Stone*, June 16, 2005, 45–46, 48.

39. Geoff Dyer, "As the Pandemic Spreads, Developed Nations Must Respond to a New Challenge from the White House," *Financial Times*, June 2, 2003.

40. Kim A. Lawton, "Rick & Kay Warren Extended Interview," *Religion & Ethics NewsWeekly*, September 1, 2006, http://www.pbs.org/wnet/religionandethics/2006/09/01/september-1-2006-rick-kay-warren-extended-interview/3647; Michelle Vu, "Kay Warren on HIV/AIDS: God Broke My Heart, Wiped Me Out," *Christian Post*, December 1, 2010, http://www.christianpost.com/news/47890/.

41. Max Blumenthal, "Rick Warren's Africa Problem," *Daily Beast*, January 7, 2009, http://www.thedailybeast.com/blogs-and-stories/2009-01-07/the-truth-about-rick-warren-in-africa/.

42. Susana Enriquez, "Saddleback Makes AIDS a Mission," *LAT*, December 1, 2005; Timothy Morgan, "Warren, Hybels Urge Churches to Wage 'War on AIDS,'" *CT* (web only), December 5, 2005, http://www.christianitytoday.com/ct/2005/decemberweb-only/12.0.html; Kelli Cottrell, "Rick Warren Welcomes Obama, Brownback to Saddleback's AIDS Summit," *Baptist Press*, December 4, 2006, http://www.bpnews.net/24509/rick-warren-welcomes-obama--brownback-to-saddlebacks-aids-summit.

43. Max Blumenthal, "Rick Warren's Africa Problem," *Daily Beast*, January 7, 2009, http://www.thedailybeast.com/blogs-and-stories/2009-01-07/the-truth-about-rick-warren-in-africa/.

44. Editors, "Close Encounters with HIV," *CT*, February 2006, 30–31.

45. *AIDS Epidemic Update* (Geneva: Joint United Nations Programme on HIV/AIDS & World Health Organization, December 2006), 2–3.

46. Boyd, *Preaching Prevention*, 36–37.

47. "PEPFAR's Glowing Report Card, 10 Years Later," *WP*, February 25, 2013.

48. Government Accountability Office, *Global Health*; Dietrich, "Politics of PEPFAR."

49. *U.S. Response to Global AIDS Crisis* (statement by Randall Tobias, US Global AIDS Coordinator, Department of State), 17.

50. Trinitapoli and Weinreb, *Religion and AIDS in Africa*, 85–86.

51. Green et al., "Uganda's HIV Prevention Success"; Halperin and Epstein, "Concurrent Sexual Partnerships." See also Thornton, *Unimagined Community*.

52. Max Blumenthal, "Rick Warren's Africa Problem," *Daily Beast*, January 7, 2009, http://www.thedailybeast.com/blogs-and-stories/2009-01-07/the-truth-about-rick-warren-in-africa/.

53. Boyd, *Preaching Prevention*, 10.

54. Gardner, *Making Chastity Sexy*, 143.

55. Hearn, "The 'Invisible' NGO."

56. Crane, *Scrambling for Africa*; Boyd, *Preaching Prevention;* Keough, "Conquering Slim."

57. Epstein, "God and the Fight Against AIDS."

58. Ibid.

59. Boyd, *Preaching Prevention*, 94.

60. Ibid., 128.

61. *U.S. Response to Global AIDS Crisis* (statement of Rev. Martin Ssempa, Director, Makere Youth Ministry), 40.

62. Human Rights Watch, "Press Release—Uganda: Rising Homophobia Threatens HIV Prevention," October 11, 2007; "Top Homos in Uganda Named," *Red Pepper*, April 19, 2009, http://www.boxturtlebulletin.com/btb/wp-content/uploads/2009/04/redpepperretouched.png.

63. Waymon Hudson, "Uganda's 'Kill the Gays' Bill Goes XXX?," Bilerico Project, January 26, 2010, http://www.bilerico.com/2010/01/ugandas_kill_the_gays_bill_goes_xxx.php; Max Blumenthal, "Rick Warren's Africa Problem," *Daily Beast*, January 7, 2009, http://www.thedaily-beast.com/blogs-and-stories/2009-01-07/the-truth-about-rick-warren-in-africa/.

64. Epstein, "God and the Fight Against AIDS"; Xan Rice, "Gay Activists Attack Ugandan Preacher's Porn Slideshow," *Guardian* (UK), February 18, 2010; "Uganda Gay-Porn Stunt 'Twisted,'" *BBC*, February 18, 2010, http://news.bbc.co.uk/2/hi/africa/8522039.stm.

65. Boyd, *Preaching Prevention*, 167–72.

66. Sharlet, *C Street*, 130, 148–49.

67. The meeting was the Global Anglican Futures Conference, or GAFCON. Rubenstein, "Anglicans in the Postcolony"; Sadgrove et al., "Constructing the Boundaries of Anglican Orthodoxy."

68. Brittain and McKinnon, "Homosexuality and the Construction of 'Anglican Orthodoxy'"; "The Complete Jerusalem Statement," GAFCON, June 28, 2009, https://www.gafcon.org/resources/the-complete-jerusalem-statement.

69. On Lambeth boycott: "Uganda Boycotts Anglican Meeting," *BBC*, February 14, 2008, http://news.bbc.co.uk/2/hi/uk_news/7244196.stm; Razat Butt, "Lambeth Conference: The Absentees," *Guardian* (UK), July 15, 2008.

70. Evelyn Lirri, "Uganda: Gay Row – US Pastor Rick Warren Supports Country on Boycott," Virtue Online: The Voice for Global Orthodox Anglicanism, March 289, 2008,

http://www.virtueonline.org/uganda-gay-row-us-pastor-rick-warren-supports-country-boycott. See also Kaoma, "Globalizing the Culture Wars," 10.

71. Anderson, "Conservative Christianity," 1591–92.

72. Lively and Abrams, *Pink Swastika*; Ohlheiser, Abby, "Uganda's New Anti-Homosexuality Law Was Inspired by American Activists," *Atlantic*, December 20, 2013, https://www.theatlantic.com/international/archive/2013/12/uganda-passes-law-punishes-homosexuality-life-imprisonment/356365/; Jeffrey Gettleman, "After US Evangelicals Visit, Ugandan Considers Death for Gays," *NYT*, January 4, 2010.

73. Scott Lively, "Defend the Family—Pro-Family Resource Center—Resource Archives," *Pro-Family Resource Center*, March 17, 2009, http://www.defendthefamily.com/pfrc/archives.php?id=2345952.

74. Epprecht, *Sexuality and Social Justice in Africa*, 146; Jeffrey Gettleman, "After US Evangelicals Visit, Ugandan Considers Death for Gays," *NYT*, January 4, 2010.

75. Cheney, "Locating Neocolonialism."

76. Sadgrove et al., "Morality Plays and Money Matters," 104.

77. Xan Rice, "Ugandan Paper Calls for Gay People to Be Hanged," *Guardian* (UK), October 21, 2010; Jeffrey Gettleman, "After US Evangelicals Visit, Ugandan Considers Death for Gays," *NYT*, January 4, 2010.

78. Sarah Pulliam Bailey, "Intercontinental Divide: Global Pressure Mounts for Uganda to Defeat Anti-Gay Bill," *CT*, February 1, 2010, 17–19; Human Rights Watch, Press Statement, "Uganda: 'Anti-Homosexuality' Bill Threatens Liberties and Human Rights Defenders," http://www.hrw.org/news/2009/10/15/uganda-anti-homosexuality-bill-threatens-liberties-and-human-rights-defenders; Human Rights Watch, Press Statement, "UN: Landmark Meeting Denounces Rights Abuses Based on Sexual Orientation, Gender Identity," http://www.hrw.org/news/2009/12/11/un-landmark-meeting-denounces-rights-abuses-based-sexual-orientation-gender-identity.

79. Sarah Pulliam Bailey, "Intercontinental Divide: Global Pressure Mounts for Uganda to Defeat Anti-Gay Bill," *CT*, February 1, 2010, 17–19; "Remarks by the President at the National Prayer Breakfast," White House Office of the Press Secretary, February 4, 2010, https://obamawhitehouse.archives.gov/the-press-office/remarks-president-national-prayer-breakfast.

80. Sarah Posner, "The US Religious Right and the LGBT Crisis In Uganda," *Religion Dispatches*, October 21, 2010, http://religiondispatches.org/the-us-religious-right-and-the-lgbt-crisis-in-uganda/.

81. Kapya Kaoma, "The US Christian Right and the Attack on Gays in Africa," Political Research Associates, October 2009, http://www.publiceye.org/magazine/v24n4/us-christian-right-attack-on-gays-in-africa.html. See also Andrew Sullivan, "Rick Warren, Silent Enabler Of Hatred—The Daily Dish," *Atlantic*, November 30, 2009, http://andrewsullivan.theatlantic.com/the_daily_dish/2009/11/rick-warren-silent-enabler-of-hatred/193551/.

82. John L. Allen, Jr., "Why Catholics Aren't Speaking up in Uganda about Anti-Gay Bill," *National Catholic Reporter*, December 16, 2009, https://www.ncronline.org/blogs/ncr-today/why-catholics-arent-speaking-uganda-about-anti-gay-bill.

83. Ibid.

84. Lillian Kwon, "Uganda Pastors Chide Rick Warren; Defend Anti-Gay Bill," *Christian Post*, December 21, 2009, https://www.christianpost.com/news/uganda-pastors-chide-rick-warren-defend-anti-gay-bill-42372/. The task force had members from the National Fellowship of Born Again Churches, Seventh-day Adventist Church, Orthodox Church in Uganda, Roman Catholic Church in Uganda, Islamic Office of Social Welfare in Uganda, and Born Again Faith Federation. On the Catholic response, John L. Allen, Jr., "Anti-Gay Bill in Uganda Challenges Catholics to

Take a Stand," *National Catholic Reporter*, November 27, 2009, https://www.ncronline.org/blogs/all-things-catholic/anti-gay-bill-uganda-challenges-catholics-take-stand.

85. Sarah Pulliam Bailey, "Church of Uganda Recommends Amending Anti-Homosexuality Bill," *CT*, February 9, 2010, http://www.christianitytoday.com/news/2010/february/church-of-uganda-recommends-amending-anti-homosexuality.html.

86. Sarah Pulliam Bailey, "Ugandan Bishop Pleads With American Christians on Anti-Homosexuality Bill," *CT* (web only), December 17, 2009, http://www.ctlibrary.com/ct/2009/decemberweb-only/151-42.0.html.

87. Jodi Jacobson, "Martin Ssempa Responds to Rick Warren on Uganda's Homosexuality Bill," *Rewire*, December 19, 2009, https://rewire.news/article/2009/12/19/updated-martin-ssempa-responds-rick-warren-ugandas-homosexuality-bill/.

88. Jeffrey Gettleman, "David Kato, Gay Rights Activist, Is Killed in Uganda," *NYT*, January 27, 2011.

89. Sarah S. Kilborne, "The Funeral of David Kato: How Uganda's Leading Gay Activist Was Laid to Rest," *Slate*, January 26, 2015, http://www.slate.com/blogs/outward/2015/01/26/david_kato_s_funeral_how_uganda_s_leading_gay_activist_was_laid_to_rest.html.

90. Josh Kron, "Resentment Toward the West Bolsters Uganda's New Anti-Gay Bill," *NYT*, February 29, 2012.

91. "Deadly Intolerance," *Economist*, March 1, 2014, 42.

92. Peter Baker, "Uganda: Anti-Gay Law Draws Sanctions," *NYT*, June 19, 2014; Ty McCormick, "Is the US Military Propping Up Uganda's 'Elected' Autocrat?" *Foreign Policy*, February 18, 2016, http://foreignpolicy.com/2016/02/18/is-the-us-military-propping-up-ugandas-elected-autocrat-museveni-elections/.

93. Auugrah Kumar, "Uganda Court Declares Draconian Anti-Gay Law 'Null and Void,'" *Christian Post*, August 2, 2014, http://www.christianpost.com/news/uganda-court-declares-draconian-anti-gay-law-null-and-void-124201/. See David Smith, "Front: Uganda Scraps Harsh Anti-Gay Law on a Legal Technicality," *Guardian* (UK), August 2, 2014.

94. Elias Biryabarema, "Uganda's Museveni Wants to Water Down Anti-Gay Law," *Reuters UK*, August 9, 2014, http://uk.reuters.com/article/uk-uganda-gay/ugandas-museveni-wants-to-water-down-anti-gay-law-lawmaker-idUKKBN0GC0YG20140812.

CHAPTER 15

1. I use the first names, but not the last names, of the IVCF team. In some cases, I have changed the first name as well. This is at the request of the team leader, who said that some of the students may well want to go back to the Muslim world at some point, and it would be best not to have their history with InterVarsity published.

2. Scott Bessenecker, "Our Vision for the Global Urban Trek," *Global Urban Trek*, 2006, http://globalurbantrek.intervarsity.org/vision-trek. Bessenecker was on InterVarsity's staff as the Global Urban Trek director. He is also editor or author of several important books on evangelical social concern, including Bessenecker, *The New Friars*.

3. InterVarsity, "Vision for the Trek," *Global Urban Trek*, 2013, http://globalurbantrek.intervarsity.org/vision-trek. A good study of InterVarsity is Bramadat, *The Church on the World's Turf*.

4. Stassen and Gushee, *Kingdom Ethics*.

5. See Bessenecker and World Vision International, *Quest for Hope in the Slum Community*.

6. Priest et al., "Researching the Short-Term Mission Movement."

7. Tracy update, "O-h-n Spells 'Cat,'" Global Urban Trek 2006: Cairo July 10, 2006. The original URL is no longer hosted but the posts have all been reposted. See at http://cairotrek. blogspot.com/2006/11/trek-update-o-h-n-spells-cat-retro.html.

8. Tracy, "City of the Sun," Global Urban Trek 2006: Cairo (Sudanese), July 12, 2006, reposted at http://cairotrek.blogspot.com/2006/11/trek-update-city-of-sun-july-12-2006.html.

9. Le Houérou, *Forced Migrants and Host Societies*, 60–71.

10. Mahmoud, "'Conflict Defines Origins.'" On the long history of evangelicalism in Egypt, see Sharkey, *American Evangelicals in Egypt*.

11. The UNHCR reported that 58,535 people had applied for refugee status from 1994 to 2005; Azzam, *Tragedy of Failures*, 11. A 2006 report quotes the SPLA office in Cairo as setting the number at 2.2 million, while the Egyptian government estimated 4 million. Grabska, "Marginalization in Urban Spaces"; Le Houérou, *Forced Migrants and Host Societies*.

12. Kagan, "Frontier Justice"; Grabska, "Marginalization in Urban Spaces."

13. Bayat, *Life as Politics*, 46–47.

14. Seventy-one percent of the people who were considered for refugee status were *not* resettled into a third country. Of the total applicants: 27 percent were rejected; 26 percent were granted refugee status but were not resettled and instead were presumed to be in a process of "local integration"; another 17 percent were not declared refugees but given temporary asylum seeker protection; and 29 percent were resettled elsewhere. The numbers do not equal 100 percent because of rounding. Azzam, *Tragedy of Failures*, 11–12.

15. Daniel Williams, "Egypt Is Uneasy Stop For Sudanese Refugees," *WP*, February 27, 2006; Dan Murphy, "For Sudanese Refugees, a Cycle of Flight," *CSM*, August 30, 2007; Al-Sharmani and Grabska, "African Refugees and Diasporic Struggles in Cairo."

16. Mahmoud, "'Conflict Defines Origins,'" 282.

17. Moulin and Nyers, "We Live in a Country of UNHCR"; Azzam, *Tragedy of Failures*.

18. Myers, *Walking With the Poor*.

19. Tracy, "City of the Sun," July 12, 2006 at http://cairotrek.blogspot.com/2006/11/trek-update-city-of-sun-july-12-2006.html. Rich Mullins was a popular singer/songwriter in the Christian music scene who died in a car crash in 1997.

20. Tracy, "News from the Outside," July 18, 2006 reposted at http://cairotrek.blogspot.com/2006/11/trek-update-news-from-outside-july-18.html.

21. Linhart, "They Were So Alive!"

22. Interview with Paula Fuller, executive vice president for People and Cultures, IVCF, April 18, 2017. Thanks also to Ned Hale, who gathered information about the history of black campus ministries at InterVarsity. On race and racism in evangelical communities, see McGlathery and Griffin, "Becoming Conservative, Becoming White?"; Wadsworth, *Ambivalent Miracles*.

23. McAlister, "US Evangelicals and the Politics of Slave Redemption."

EPILOGUE

1. Daniel Cox, "White Christians Side with Trump," *PRRI,* November 9, 2016, https://www.prri.org/spotlight/religion-vote-presidential-election-2004-2016/.

2. Darren Patrick Guerra, "Actually, Most Evangelicals Don't Vote Trump," *CT*, March 18, 2016, http://www.christianitytoday.com/ct/2016/march-web-only/actually-most-evangelicals-dont-vote-trump.html; Maggie Haberman and Thomas Kaplan, "Evangelicals See Donald Trump

as Man of Conviction, If Not Faith," *NYT*, January 18, 2016; Jonathan Merritt. "Donald Trump Exposes the Split Between Ordinary and Elite Evangelicals," *Atlantic*, February 1, 2016, http://www.theatlantic.com/politics/archive/2016/02/donald-trumps-evangelical-divide/458706/.

3. Kate Shellnut and Sarah Eekhoff Zylstra, "Who's Who of Trump's 'Tremendous' Faith Advisers," *CT* (web only), June 22, 2016, http://www.christianitytoday.com/ct/2016/june-web-only/whos-who-of-trumps-tremendous-faith-advisors.html; Jonathan Merritt, "The Awkward Love Story of Trump and American Evangelicals," *Atlantic*, June 24, 2016, http://www.theatlantic.com/politics/archive/2016/06/trump-and-the-evangelicals-a-match-made-in-well/488552/.

4. Gregory Smith and Jessica Martínez, "How the Faithful Voted: A Preliminary 2016 Analysis," Pew Research Center, November 9, 2016, http://www.pewresearch.org/fact-tank/2016/11/09/how-the-faithful-voted-a-preliminary-2016-analysis/; Jon Huang et al., "Election 2016: Exit Polls," *NYT*, November 8, 2016, http://www.nytimes.com/interactive/2016/11/08/us/politics/election-exit-polls.html. Twenty-five percent of the electorate self-identified as white and either evangelical or born-again.

5. Kevin Porter, "TD Jakes Says Americans Traumatized by Trump's Election," *Christian Post*, November 13, 2016, http://www.christianpost.com/news/td-jakes-says-americans-traumatized-by-trumps-election-protests-spread-nationwide-171464/.

6. Yolanda Pierce, "Watching 81% of my White Brothers and Sisters Vote for Trump Has Broken Something in Me," *Religion Dispatches*, November 15, 2016, http://religiondispatches.org/watching-81-of-my-white-brothers-and-sisters-vote-for-trump-has-broken-something-in-me/. Also Collin Hansen, "Two Concerns for the Religious Right Under Trump," TGC—The Gospel Coalition, November 9, 2016, https://www.thegospelcoalition.org/article/two-concerns-for-the-religious-right-under-president-trump.

7. Emily Lund, "Trump Won. Here's How 20 Evangelical Leaders Feel," *CT* (web only), November 11, 2016, http://www.christianitytoday.com/ct/2016/november-web-only/trump-won-how-evangelical- leaders-feel.html.

8. Kate Shellnutt, "Global Evangelical Leaders: Trump's Win Will Harm the Church's Witness," *CT*, November 15, 2016, http://www.christianitytoday.com/gleanings/2016/november/global-evangelical-leaders-trump-win-will-harm-churchs-witn.html.

9. Daniel Schulz, "What's Behind Trump's 'Impossibly Stupid' Rollback of the Contraception Mandate," *Religion Dispatches*, October 9, 2017, http://religiondispatches.org/whats-behind-trumps-impossibly-stupid-roll-back-of-contraception-mandate/; Kathryn Jean Lopez, "What Now for Religious Freedom? An Interview with Tim Schultz," *National Review*, November 12, 2016, http://www.nationalreview.com/article/442143/religious-freedom-next-steps-following-donald-trumps-election.

10. Dam Arel, "The Biggest Victim under a President Trump? Freedom of Religion," *Hill*, November 23, 2016, http://thehill.com/blogs/pundits-blog/the-administration/307351-the-biggest-victim-under-a-president-trump-freedom-of; Mark Joseph Stern, "Cake Wreck," *Slate*, September 8, 2017, http://www.slate.com/articles/news_and_politics/jurisprudence/2017/09/doj_s_cynical_embarrassing_brief_in_the_supreme_court_s_anti_gay_baker_case.html.

11. Emma Green, "The Religious Liberty Showdowns Coming in 2017," *Atlantic*, December 28, 2016, https://www.theatlantic.com/politics/archive/2016/12/the-religious-liberty-showdowns-coming-in-2017/511400/.

12. Katayoun Kishi, "Anti-Muslim Assaults Reach 9/11-Era Levels, FBI Data Show," Pew Research Center, November 21, 2016, http://www.pewresearch.org/fact-tank/2016/11/21/anti-muslim-assaults-reach-911-era-levels-fbi-data-show/.

13. Jonathan Turley, "Third Time's a Charm for Trump's Travel Ban," *The Hill*, September 25, 2017, http://thehill.com/opinion/international/352215-third-times-a-charm-for-trumps-travel-ban-why-this-one-will-stick; Daniel Burke, "For American Muslims: Shock, Fear and Resolve," *CNN*, November 11, 2016, http://www.cnn.com/2016/11/09/politics/muslims-trump-reaction/index.html; Emma Green, "White Evangelicals Believe They Face More Discrimination than Muslims," *Atlantic*, March 10, 2017, https://www.theatlantic.com/politics/archive/2017/03/perceptions-discrimination-muslims-christians/519135/.

14. Bruce Stokes, "Do Muslims Around the World Really Hate the United States?" *Foreign Policy*, December 15, 2015, https://foreignpolicy.com/2015/12/15/do-muslims-around-the-world-really-hate-the-united-states/.

15. Johnson and Zurlo, "Christian Martyrdom."

16. Michael Gerson, "The Religious Right Carries its Golden Calf into Steve Bannon's Battles," *WP*, October 16, 2017.

BIBLIOGRAPHY

Abrams, Elliott. *The Influence of Faith: Religious Groups and US Foreign Policy.* Lanham, MD: Rowman & Littlefield, 2001.

Achebe, Chinua. *Things Fall Apart.* Orig. 1958. New York: Anchor, 1994.

Adams, Evan. "Youth and Tradition." In *God's Men From All Nations to All Nations,* 139–46. Chicago: InterVarsity Press, 1968.

Adeyemo, Tokunboh, ed. *Africa Bible Commentary: A One-Volume Commentary Written by 70 African Scholars.* Grand Rapids, MI: Zondervan, 2006.

Ad Hoc working group. "Theology Implications of Radical Discipleship." In Douglas, *Let the Earth Hear His Voice,* 1294–96.

Adler, Elizabeth. *Small Beginning: Assessment of the First Five Years of the Programme to Combat Racism.* Geneva: World Council of Churches, 1974.

Ahmad, Attiya. *Everyday Conversions: Islam, Domestic Work, and South Asian Migrant Women in Kuwait.* Durham: Duke University Press, 2017.

Ahmed, Sara. *The Promise of Happiness.* Durham, NC: Duke University Press, 2010.

Aidi, Hisham. "Slavery, Genocide and the Politics of Outrage: Understanding the New 'Racial Olympics.'" *Middle East Report* no. 234 (Spring 2005): 40–56.

Akol, Lam. "Operation Lifeline Sudan: War, Peace, and Relief in Southern Sudan." *Accord: An International Review of Peace Initiatives* no. 16 (2005): 52–55.

Albanese, Catherine. *America: Religions and Religion.* 5th ed. Belmont, CA: Wadsworth, 2012.

Ali, Wajahat, Eli Clifton, Matthew Duss, Lee Fang, Scott Keyes, and Faiz Shakir. "Fear, Inc.: The Roots of the Islamophobia Network in America." Washington, DC: Center for American

Progress, 2011. https://www.americanprogress.org/issues/religion/reports/2011/08/26/10165/fear-inc/.

All Africa Church Conference, and Conference on Christian Education in a Changing Africa. *Christian Education in Africa; Report*. London: Published for All Africa Churches Conference by Oxford University Press, 1963.

Allen, James, Jon Lewis, Leon F. Litwack, and Hilton Als. *Without Sanctuary: Lynching Photography in America*. Santa Fe, NM: Twin Palms Publishers, 2000.

Al-Sharmani, Mulki, and Katarzyna Grabska. "African Refugees and Diasporic Struggles in Cairo." In *Cairo Contested*, edited by Diane Singerman, 455–88. Cairo: American University in Cairo Press, 2011.

AME General Conference of 1976. "Liberation Movements: A Critical Assessment and a Reaffirmation." In *Black Theology: A Documentary History, 1966–1979*, edited by Gayraud Wilmore and James Cone, 250–56.

Ammerman, Nancy Tatom. *Baptist Battles: Social Change and Religious Conflict in the Southern Baptist Convention*. New Brunswick, NJ: Rutgers University Press, 1990.

_____. *Bible Believers: Fundamentalists in the Modern World*. New Brunswick, NJ: Rutgers University Press, 1987.

Anderson, Allan H. *African Reformation: African Initiated Christianity in the 20th Century*. Trenton, NJ: Africa World Press, 2001.

_____. *To the Ends of the Earth: Pentecostalism and the Transformation of World Christianity*. New York: Oxford University Press, 2012.

Anderson, Gerald H. "American Protestants in Pursuit of Mission: 1886-1986." *International Bulletin of Missionary Research* 12, no. 3 (July 1988): 98–135.

Anderson, John. "Conservative Christianity, the Global South and the Battle over Sexual Orientation." *Third World Quarterly* 32, no. 9 (2011): 1589–1605.

Appiah, Kwame Anthony and Martin Bunzi, eds. *Buying Freedom: The Ethics and Economics of Slave Redemption*. Princeton, NJ: Princeton University Press, 2007.

Ariel, Yaakov. *An Unusual Relationship: Evangelical Christians and Jews*. New York: New York University Press, 2013.

_____. *Evangelizing the Chosen People: Missions to the Jews in America, 1880-2000*. Chapel Hill: University of North Carolina Press, 2000.

_____. *On Behalf of Israel: American Fundamentalist Attitudes toward Jews, Judaism, and Zionism, 1865-1945*. Brooklyn, NY: Carlson Pub., 1991.

Asad, Talal. *Formations of the Secular: Christianity, Islam, Modernity*. Stanford, CA: Stanford University Press, 2003.

_____. *Genealogies of Religion: Discipline and Reasons of Power in Christianity and Islam*. Baltimore, MD: Johns Hopkins University Press, 1993.

Assemblies of God. *Unreached People*. Springfield, MO: Verite Productions, 1989.

Atia, Mona. *Building a House in Heaven: Pious Neoliberalism and Islamic Charity in Egypt*. Minneapolis: University of Minnesota Press, 2013.

Augustine of Hippo. *The City of God*. Translated by Marcus Dods. Peabody, MA: Hendrickson Publishers, 2009.

Azoulay, Ariella. *The Civil Contract of Photography*. New York: Zone Books, 2008.

Azzam, Fateh. *A Tragedy of Failures and False Expectations: Report on the Events Surrounding the Three-Month Sit-in and Forced Removal of Sudanese Refugees in Cairo, September-December 2005*. Cairo: American University of Cairo, June 2006.

Baker, Pauline. *The United States and South Africa: The Reagan Years*. New York: Ford Foundation, 1989.

Balbier, Uta. "The World Congress on Evangelism 1966 in Berlin: US Evangelicalism, Cultural Dominance, and Global Challenges." *Journal of American Studies* 44, no. 51 (November 2017): 1171–96.

Balbier, Uta, Hans Krabbendam, Kendrick Oliver, and Axel R. Schäfer. "Introduction: Exploring the Global History of American Evangelicalism." *Journal of American Studies* 44, no. 51 (November 2017): 1019–42.

Balcomb, Anthony O. "Left, Right and Centre: Evangelicals and the Struggle for Liberation in South Africa." *Journal of Theology for Southern Africa* no. 118 (March 2004): 146–60.

_____. "Nicholas Bhengu: The Impact of an African Pentecostal on South African Society." *Exchange* 34, no. 4 (January 1, 2005): 337–48.

Baldwin, Maria T. *Amnesty International and U.S. Foreign Policy: Human Rights Campaigns in Guatemala, the United States, and China*. El Paso, TX: LFB Scholarly Publishing, 2008.

Balfour, Ian, and Eduardo Cadava. "The Claims of Human Rights: An Introduction." *South Atlantic Quarterly* 103, no. 2/3 (Spring 2004): 277–96.

Ball, George. "American Policy in the Congo (January 1962)." In *Footnotes to the Congo Story; an Africa Report Anthology*, edited by Helen A. Kitchen. New York: Walker, 1967.

Balmer, Randall. *Mine Eyes Have Seen the Glory: A Journey into the Evangelical Subculture in America*. 5th ed. New York: Oxford University Press, 2014.

_____. *Thy Kingdom Come: How the Religious Right Distorts the Faith and Threatens America: An Evangelical's Lament*. New York: Basic Books, 2006.

Baraka, Amiri. "Last Days of the American Empire (With Some Instructions for Black People)." In *Home: Social Essays*, 214–35. New York: Akashic Books, 2009.

Barfoot, Charles H. *Aimee Semple McPherson and the Making of Modern Pentecostalism, 1890-1926*. London: Routledge, 2014.

Barnett, Michael. *Empire of Humanity: A History of Humanitarianism*. Ithaca, NY: Cornell University Press, 2011.

Barnett, Michael, and Thomas George Weiss, eds. *Humanitarianism in Question: Politics, Power, Ethics*. Ithaca, NY: Cornell University Press, 2008.

Bassham, Rodger. *Mission Theology, 1948-1975: Years of Worldwide Creative Tension—Ecumenical, Evangelical, and Roman Catholic*. Pasadena, CA: William Carey Library, 1979.

Bayat, Asef. *Life as Politics: How Ordinary People Change the Middle East*. 2nd ed. Stanford, CA: Stanford University Press, 2013.

Baylor Religion Survey. *American Piety in the 21st Century: New Insights into the Depth and Complexity of Religion in the US*. Waco, TX: Baylor University, 2006.

Bayoumi, Moustafa. *This Muslim American Life: Dispatches from the War on Terror*. New York: New York University Press, 2015.

Bays, Daniel H., and Grant Wacker, eds. *The Foreign Missionary Enterprise at Home: Explorations in North American Cultural History*. Tuscaloosa: University Alabama Press, 2003.

Bebbington, David W. *Evangelicalism in Modern Britain: A History from the 1730s to the 1980s.* Rev. ed. London: Routledge, 1988.

Bediako, Kwame. *Christianity in Africa: The Renewal of Non-Western Religion.* Marynoll, NY: Orbis Books, 1996.

Bell, Catherine. *Ritual Theory, Ritual Practice.* New York: Oxford University Press, 1992.

Bender, Courtney. *The New Metaphysicals: Spirituality and the American Religious Imagination.* Chicago: University of Chicago Press, 2010.

Bentley, William H. "Bible Believers in the Black Community." In *The Evangelicals: What They Believe, Who They Are, Where They Are Changing,* edited by David Wells and John D. Woodbridge, 108–21. Grand Rapids, MI: Baker Book House, 1975.

_____. *The National Black Evangelical Association: Reflections on the Evolution of a Concept of Ministry.* Revised. Self-Published, 1978.

Berkley Center for Religion, Peace, & World Affairs. "Proselytism and Religious Freedom in the 21st Century." Conference in Washington, DC, March 2-3, 2010. https://berkley-center.georgetown.edu/events/proselytism-and-religious-freedom-in-the-twenty-first-century.

_____. "Why Religious Freedom? The Origins and Promise of US International Religious Freedom Policy." Conference in Washington, DC, February 24-25, 2008. https://berkleycenter.georgetown.edu/events/why-religious-freedom-the-origins-and-promise-of-us-international-religious-freedom-policy

Berlant, Lauren. "Compassion (and Withholding)." In *Compassion: The Culture and Politics of an Emotion,* edited by L. Berlant, 1–14. New York: Routledge, 2004.

_____. *Cruel Optimism.* Durham: Duke University Press, 2011.

Bernstein, Elizabeth. "The Sexual Politics of the 'New Abolitionism.'" *Differences* 18, no. 3 (Fall 2007): 128–51.

Berry, Malinda Elizabeth, Peter Goodwin Heltzel, and Bruce Ellis Benson, eds. *Prophetic Evangelicals: Envisioning a Just and Peaceable Kingdom.* Grand Rapids, MI: Wm. B. Eerdmans Publishing, 2012.

Bessenecker, Scott. *The New Friars: The Emerging Movement Serving the World's Poor.* Downers Grove, IL: InterVarsity Press Books, 2006.

Bessenecker, Scott, and World Vision International. *Quest for Hope in the Slum Community: A Global Urban Reader.* Waynesboro, GA: Authentic, 2005.

Bhengu, Nicholas. "My Search for the Fullness of God." In *I Will Heal Their Land,* edited by Michael Cassidy, 301–302. Maseru, Lesotho: Africa Enterprise, 1974

Biehl, Jo, and Torben Eskerod. *Vita: Life in a Zone of Social Abandonment.* Berkeley: University of California Press, 2005.

Biko, Stephen. *I Write What I Like: Selected Writings.* Edited by Aelred Stubbs. Chicago: University of Chicago Press, 2002.

Billingsley, Scott. *It's a New Day: Race and Gender in the Modern Charismatic Movement.* Tuscaloosa: University of Alabama Press, 2008.

Birai, Umar M. "Islamic Tajdid and the Political Process in Nigeria." In *Fundamentalisms and the State: Remaking Politics, Economies, and Militance,* edited by Martin Marty, et al., 184–203. Chicago: University of Chicago Press, 1996.

Birnbaum, Karl. "Human Rights and East-West Relations." *Foreign Affairs* 55, no. 4 (July 1977): 783–99.

Bíró, Gáspár. "Interim Report on the Situation of Human Rights in the Sudan." UN General Assembly document A/50/569, October 16, 1995. http://www.un.org/documents/ga/docs/50/plenary/a50-569.htm.

Black, Megan. "Interior's Exterior: The State, Mining Companies, and Resource Ideologies in the Point Four Program." *Diplomatic History* 40, no. 1 (January 2016): 81–110.

Blessing, William L., Timothy Green Beckley, Tim R. Swartz, and Dennis Crenshaw. *Inner Earth People And Outer Space People*. New Brunswick, NJ: Inner Light Publications, 2008.

Blitzer, Wolf. *Between Washington and Jerusalem: A Reporter's Notebook*. New York: Oxford University Press, 1985.

Blumhofer, Edith L. *Restoring the Faith: The Assemblies of God, Pentecostalism, and American Culture*. Urbana: University of Illinois Press, 1993.

Boel, Brent. "Bible Smuggling and Human Rights in the Cold War." In *Transnational Anti-Communism and the Cold War: Agents, Activities, and Networks*, edited by Stéphanie Roulin, Giles Scott-Smith, and Luc van Dongen, 263–75. Basingstoke, UK: Palgrave Macmillan, 2014.

Boger, Gretchen. "American Protestantism in the Asian Crucible, 1919–1939." PhD diss., Princeton University, 2008.

Bonhoeffer, Dietrich. *The Cost of Discipleship*. New York: Macmillan, 1963.

Boogaart, Peter C., and Thomas Arthur Boogaart. "A Critical Review of This Present Darkness." *Reformed Review* 47, no. 1 (1993): 5–16.

Bourdieu, Pierre. *The Field of Cultural Production: Essays on Art and Literature*. New York: Columbia University Press, 1993.

_____. *The Logic of Practice*. Stanford, CA: Stanford University Press, 1990.

Boyd, Lydia. *Preaching Prevention: Born-Again Christianity and the Moral Politics of AIDS in Uganda*. Athens: Ohio University Press, 2015.

Bornstein, Erica. "Developing Faith: Theologies of Economic Development in Zimbabwe." *Journal of Religion in Africa* 32, no. 1 (February 2002): 4–31.

_____. *Disquieting Gifts: Humanitarianism in New Delhi*. Stanford, CA: Stanford University Press, 2012.

_____. *The Spirit of Development: Protestant NGOs, Morality, and Economics in Zimbabwe*. Stanford, CA: Stanford University Press, 2005.

Borstelmann, Thomas. *Apartheid's Reluctant Uncle: The United States and Southern Africa in the Early Cold War*. New York: Oxford University Press, 1993.

_____. *The Cold War and the Color Line: American Race Relations in the Global Arena*. Cambridge, MA: Harvard University Press, 2003.

Borthwick, Paul. *How to Be a World-Class Christian*. Wheaton, IL: Victor Books, 1993.

Bosch, David. "Nothing but a Heresy." In *Apartheid is a Heresy*, edited by John De Gruchy and Charles Villa-Vicencio, 24–38. Grand Rapids, MI: Wm. B. Eerdmans Publishing, 1983.

Bowler, Kate. *Blessed: A History of the American Prosperity Gospel*. New York: Oxford University Press, 2013.

Bowman, Glenn. "The Politics of Tour Guiding: Israeli and Palestinian Guides." In *Tourism and the Less Developed Countries*, edited by David Harrison, 121–34. New York: Halsted Press, 1992.

Boyer, Paul. *When Time Shall Be No More: Prophecy Belief in Modern American Culture*. Cambridge, MA: Belknap Press of Harvard University Press, 1992.

Braekman, E. M. *Histoire Du Protestantisme Au Congo*. Bruxelles: Librairie des Eclaireurs Unionistes, 1961.

Bradley, Mark Philip. *The World Reimagined: Americans and Human Rights in the Twentieth Century*. Cambridge: Cambridge University Press, 2016.

Bradley, Mark Philip, and Patrice Petro. "Introduction." In *Truth Claims: Representation and Human Rights*, edited by Bradley and Petro, 1–10. New Brunswick, NJ: Rutgers University Press, 2002.

Bramadat, Paul. *The Church on the World's Turf: An Evangelical Christian Group at a Secular University*. New York: Oxford University Press, 2000.

Brashler, Peter J. *Change, My Thirty-Five Years in Africa*. Wheaton, IL: Tyndale House Publishers, 1979.

Breman, Christien M. "A Portrait of Dr Byang H Kato." *Africa Journal of Evangelical Theology* 15, no. 2 (January 1, 1996): 135–51.

Brittain, Christopher Craig, and Andrew McKinnon. "Homosexuality and the Construction of 'Anglican Orthodoxy': The Symbolic Politics of the Anglican Communion." *Sociology of Religion* 72, no. 3 (Autumn 2011): 351–73.

Brother Andrew. *God's Smuggler*. New York: New American Library, 1967.

Brown, Wendy. *States of Injury*. Princeton, NJ: Princeton University Press, 1995.

Bryant, David. *In the Gap*. Rev. ed. Ventura, CA: Regal Books, 1984.

Buck, Pearl S. *The Good Earth*. New York: John Day Company, 1931.

Burgess, Richard. *Nigeria's Christian Revolution: The Civil War Revival and Its Pentecostal Progeny (1967-2006)*. Eugene, OR: Wipf & Stock Publishers, 2008.

Bush, Luis. "The Challenge Before Us." In *Proclaim Christ until He Comes*, edited by J. D. Douglas, 58–62.

Bush, Luis, and Beverly Pegues. *The Move of the Holy Spirit in the 10/40 Window*. Seattle, WA: YWAM Publishers, 1999.

Butler, Anthea D. *Women in the Church of God in Christ: Making a Sanctified World*. Chapel Hill: University of North Carolina Press, 2007.

Byrnes, Timothy A. "How 'Seamless' a Garment? The Catholic Bishops and the Politics of Abortion." *Journal of Church & State* 33, no. 1 (Winter 1991): 17–35.

Caleb Project. *Life-Changing Encounters: A Handbook for Short-Term Research Among Unreached Peoples*. Littleton, CO: Caleb Project, 1995.

Campbell, James T. *Middle Passages: African American Journeys to Africa, 1787-2005*. New York: Penguin Press, 2006.

———. *Songs of Zion: The African Methodist Episcopal Church in the United States and South Africa*. New York: Oxford University Press, 1995.

Cantrell, Phillip A. "The Anglican Church of Rwanda: Domestic Agendas and International Linkages." *Journal of Modern African Studies* 45, no. 3 (September 2007): 333–354.

Carby, Hazel V. "'On the Threshold of Woman's Era': Lynching, Empire, and Sexuality in Black Feminist Theory." *Critical Inquiry* 12, no. 1 (Autumn 1985): 262–77.

Carenen, Caitlin. *The Fervent Embrace: Liberal Protestants, Evangelicals, and Israel*. New York: New York University Press, 2012.

Carpenter, Joel. "Propagating the Faith Once Delivered: The Fundamentalist Missionary Enterprise." In *Earthen Vessels*, edited by J. Carpenter and W. Shenk, 92–132.

———. *Revive Us Again: The Reawakening of American Fundamentalism*. New York: Oxford University Press, 1997.

Carpenter, Joel, and W.R. Shenk, eds. *Earthen Vessels: American Evangelicals and Foreign Missions, 1880-1980*. Grand Rapids, MI: Wm. B. Eerdmans Publishing, 1990.

Cassidy, Michael, ed. *I Will Heal Their Land: Papers of the South African Congress on Mission and Evangelism, Durban, 1973.* Maseru, Lesotho: African Enterprise, 1974.

_____. "The Ethics of Political Nationalism." In *One Race, One Gospel, One Task,* vol 2, edited by C. Henry and S. Mooneyham, 312–16.

Castelli, Elizabeth. *Martyrdom and Memory: Early Christian Culture Making.* 2nd ed. New York: Columbia University Press, 2007.

_____. "Praying for the Persecuted Church: US Christian Activism in the Global Arena." *Journal of Human Rights* 4, no. 3 (September 2005): 321–51.

Cati, W. L. *Married to Muhammad.* Lake Mary, FL: Creation House, 2001.

Chang, Eunhye, J. Rupert Morgan, Timothy Nyasulu, and Robert J. Priest. "Paul G. Hiebert and Critical Contextualization." *Trinity Journal; Deerfield* 30, no. 2 (Fall 2009): 199–207.

Chappell, David L. *A Stone of Hope: Prophetic Religion and the Death of Jim Crow.* Chapel Hill: University of North Carolina Press, 2005.

Cheney, Kristen. "Locating Neocolonialism, 'Tradition,' and Human Rights in Uganda's 'Gay Death Penalty.'" *African Studies Review* 55, no. 2 (September 2012): 77–95.

Chesworth, John A. "Fundamentalism and Outreach Strategies in East Africa: Christian Evangelism and Muslim Da'wa." In *Muslim-Christian Encounters in Africa,* edited by Benjamin F. Soares, 159–86. Boston: Brill, 2006.

Church, Frank. *Expressing the Sense of the Congress with Respect to the Treatment of Christians by the Union of Soviet Socialist Republics.* S. Rpt. 96–1016, Senate Committee on Foreign Relations (1980).

Cizik, Richard. "My Journey Toward the 'New Evangelicalism.'" In *A New Evangelical Manifesto,* edited by David Gushee, 26–41.

Clark, Lynn Schofield. *From Angels to Aliens: Teenagers, the Media, and the Supernatural.* New York: Oxford University Press, 2003.

Clark, Nancy L., and William H. Worger. *South Africa: The Rise and Fall of Apartheid.* 2nd ed. New York: Longman, 2011.

Cmiel, Kenneth. "The Emergence of Human Rights Politics in the United States." *Journal of American History* 86, no. 3 (December 1999): 1231–50.

Coffman, Elesha J. *The Christian Century and the Rise of the Protestant Mainline.* New York: Oxford University Press, 2013.

Cohen, Daniel. "Elusive Neutrality: Christian Humanitarianism and the Question of Palestine, 1948–1967." *Humanity Journal* 5, no. 2 (July 2004): 183–210.

Collins-Kreiner, Noga, Nurit Kliot, and Keren Sagi. *Christian Tourism to the Holy Land: Pilgrimage during Security Crisis.* Aldershot, England: Ashgate Publishing, 2006.

Collins, Robert O. *A History of Modern Sudan.* Cambridge: Cambridge University Press, 2008.

Comaroff, Jean. *Body of Power, Spirit of Resistance: The Culture and History of a South African People.* Chicago: University of Chicago Press, 1985.

Comaroff, Jean, and John L Comaroff. *Of Revelation and Revolution,* vol. 2, *The Dialectics of Modernity on a South African Frontier.* Chicago: University of Chicago Press, 1991.

Comhaire, Jean. "Sociétés Secrètes et Mouvements Prophétiques Au Congo Belge." *Africa: Journal of the International African Institute* 25, no. 1 (January 1955): 54–59.

Communist Exploitation of Religion, Hearing before the Senate Judiciary Committee. Senate, 89th Congress, 2 (1966).

Concerned Evangelicals. *Evangelical Witness in South Africa*. Grand Rapids, MI: Wm. B. Eerdmans Publishing, 1987.

Cone, James. *Black Theology and Black Power*. New York: Seabury Press, 1969.

Connolly, William E. "The Complexity of Intention." *Critical Inquiry* 37, no. 4 (Summer 2011): 791–98.

Cookman, Claude. "Gilles Caron's Coverage of the Crisis in Biafra." *Visual Communication Quarterly* 15, no. 4 (December 2008): 226–42.

Coomes, Anne. *The Authorized Biography of Festo Kivengere*. Eastbourne, England: Monarch Books, 1990.

Cooper, Barbara. *Evangelical Christians in the Muslim Sahel*. Bloomington: Indiana University Press, 2006.

Coote, Robert T. "AD 2000 and the 10/40 Window: A Preliminary Assessment." *International Bulletin of Missionary Research* 24, no. 4 (October 2000): 160-66.

———. "Lausanne II and World Evangelization." *International Bulletin of Missionary Research* 14, no. 1 (January 1990): 10–17.

Corten, Andre, and Ruth R. Marshall-Fratani. *Between Babel and Pentecost: Transnational Pentecostalism in Africa and Latin America*. Bloomington: Indiana University Press, 2001.

Cox, Dan. "Pew Forum: Young White Evangelicals: Less Republican, Still Conservative." Pew Forum on Religion & Public Life, September 28, 2007. http://www.pewforum.org/2007/09/28/young-white-evangelicals-less-republican-still-conservative/.

Crane, Johanna Tayloe. *Scrambling for Africa AIDS, Expertise, and the Rise of American Global Health Science*. Ithaca, NY: Cornell University Press, 2013.

C.R.I.S.P. *Congo 1964: Political Documents of a Developing Nation*. Princeton, NJ: Princeton University Press, 1966.

Croft, Stuart. "'Thy Will Be Done': The New Foreign Policy of America's Christian Right." *International Politics* 44, no. 6 (November 2007): 692–710.

Cullather, Nick. *The Hungry World: America's Cold War Battle against Poverty in Asia*. Cambridge, MA: Harvard University Press, 2010.

Cunningham, Loren, and Janice Rogers. *Is That Really You, God?: Hearing the Voice of God*. Seattle: YWAM Publishers, 2001.

Daly, Mary. *The Church and the Second Sex*. London: G. Chapman, 1968.

Daly, M.W. *Imperial Sudan: The Anglo-Egyptian Condominium 1934-1956*. Cambridge: Cambridge University Press, 2003.

———. "Islam, Secularism and Ethnic Identity in the Sudan." In *Religion and Political Power*, edited by Gustavo Benavides and M.W. Daly, 87–98. Albany: State University of New York Press, 1990.

Danforth, John. "The Outlook for Peace in Sudan." Washington, DC: US Department of State, April 26, 2002. https://reliefweb.int/report/sudan/us-dos-danforth-report-outlook-peace-sudan.

Danner, Mark. *Torture and Truth: America, Abu Ghraib, and the War on Terror*. New York: New York Review Books, 2004.

Davis, John. *The Landscape of Belief*. Princeton, NJ: Princeton University Press, 1996.

Davis, John. "The Clinton Model: Sudan and the Failure to Capture Bin Laden." In *Africa and the War on Terrorism*, edited by John Davis, 129–42. Aldershot: Ashgate Publishing, 2013.

Davis, Rochelle. *Palestinian Village Histories: Geographies of the Displaced*. Stanford, CA: Stanford University Press, 2010.

Dayton, Edward R., and Samuel Wilson, eds. *The Future of World Evangelization: Unreached People '84*. Monrovia, CA: MARC, 1984.

DC Talk. *Jesus Freaks: Martyrs—Stories of Those Who Stood for Jesus*. Bloomington, MN: Bethany House Publishers, 1999.

_____. *Jesus Freaks, Volume 2: Stories of Revolutionaries Who Changed their World*. Bloomington, MN: Bethany House Publishers, 2002.

Deal, Elmer, and Mike Randall. *Out of the Mouth of the Lion*. Self-published, 2009.

De Gruchy, John W. "The Church and the Struggle for South Africa." *Theology Today* 43, no. 2 (July 1986): 229–43.

_____. *The Church Struggle in South Africa*. 25th anniversary ed. Minneapolis: Fortress Press, 2005.

de Waal, Alex. *Famine Crimes: Politics & the Disaster Relief Industry in Africa*. Bloomington: Indiana University Press, 1997.

_____. "No Money, No Peace." *Foreign Policy*, December 2, 2015. http://foreignpolicy.com/2015/12/02/no-money-no-peace-south-sudan/

_____. *Sudan: What Kind of State? What Kind of Crisis?* Occasional Paper. London: Crisis States Research Centre and London School of Economics, April 2007.

Diamond, Sara. *Roads to Dominion: Right-Wing Movements and Political Power in the United States*. New York: Guilford Press, 1995.

Diamond, Stephen F. "The PetroChina Syndrome: Regulating Capital Markets in the Anti-Globalization Era." *Journal of Corporation Law* 29, no. 1 (Fall 2003), 39–102.

Dietrich, John. "The Politics of PEPFAR: The President's Emergency Plan for AIDS Relief." *Ethics & International Affairs* 21, no. 3 (Fall 2007): 277–92.

Dillon, Michele. "Religion and Culture in Tension: The Abortion Discourses of the US Catholic Bishops and the Southern Baptist Convention." *Religion and American Culture* 5, no. 2 (1995):159–80.

Dochuk, Darren. *From Bible Belt to Sunbelt: Plain-Folk Religion, Grassroots Politics, and the Rise of Evangelical Conservatism*. New York: W. W. Norton & Company, 2010.

Donnelly, John. "How George W. Bush And Aides Came To 'Think Big' On Battling HIV." *Health Affairs* 31, no. 7 (July 2012): 1389–96.

Douglas, J.D., ed. *Let the Earth Hear His Voice: Official Reference Volume, Papers and Responses; International Congress on World Evangelization, Lausanne, Switzerland*. Minneapolis, MN: World Wide Publications, 1975.

_____, ed. *Proclaim Christ Till He Comes: Calling the Whole Church to Take the Whole Gospel to the Whole World*. Minneapolis, MN: World Wide Publications, 1990.

Dow, Philip. "The Missionary Factor in US Relations with East and Central Africa During the Cold War." PhD diss., University of Cambridge, Clare College, 2011.

Dowdy, Homer E. *Out of the Jaws of the Lion*. London: Hodder & Stoughton, 1965.

Dudziak, Mary L. *Cold War Civil Rights: Race and the Image of American Democracy*. Princeton, NJ: Princeton University Press, 2011.

Dunch, Ryan. "Beyond Cultural Imperialism: Cultural Theory, Christian Missions, and Global Modernity." *History and Theory*, no. 41 (October 2002): 301–25.

Dupont, Carolyn Renée. *Mississippi Praying: Southern White Evangelicals and the Civil Rights Movement, 1945-1975*. New York: New York University Press, 2013.

Duriez, Colin. *Francis Schaeffer: An Authentic Life*. Wheaton, IL: Crossway Books, 2008.

Du Toit, Brian M. "Theology, Kairos, and the Church in South Africa." *Missiology* 16, no. 1 (January 1988): 57–71.

Dunn, James, and Grady C. Cothen. *Soul Freedom: Baptist Battle Cry*. Macon, GA: Smyth & Helwys Publishers, 2000.

Durban-Albrecht, Erin L. "Performing Postcolonial Homophobia: A Decolonial Analysis of the 2013 Public Demonstrations Against Same-Sex Marriage in Haiti." *Women and Performance* 27, no. 2 (2017): 160–75.

Dworkin, Ira. "'American Congo': Booker T. Washington, l'Afrique et L'imaginaire Politique Noir Americain." *Civilisations* 55, no. 1/2 (February 2006): 165–79.

_____. "In the Country of My Forefathers." *Atlantic Studies* 5, no. 1 (April 2008): 99–118.

Edgar, Robert R., ed. *Sanctioning Apartheid*. Trenton, NJ: Africa World Press, 1990.

Edwards, Brian. *Morocco Bound: Disorienting America's Maghreb, from Casablanca to the Marrakech Express*. Durham, NC: Duke University Press, 2005.

Eibner, John. "My Career Redeeming Slaves." *Middle East Quarterly* 6, no. 4 (December 1999): 3–16.

Eighmy, John Lee. *Churches in Cultural Captivity: A History of the Social Attitudes of Southern Baptists*. Knoxville: University of Tennessee Press, 1972.

Elisha, Omri. *Moral Ambition: Mobilization and Social Outreach in Evangelical Megachurches*. Berkeley: University of California Press, 2011.

Ellis, Elward. *What Went Down at Urbana 67*. 1969. https://vimeo.com/42230364.

Elshtain, Jean Bethke. *Just War Against Terror: The Burden of American Power In a Violent World*. New York: Basic Books, 2003.

Engerman, David C. "The Anti-Politics of Inequality: Reflections on a Special Issue." *Journal of Global History* 6, no. 1 (March 2011): 143–51.

_____. *Modernization from the Other Shore: American Intellectuals and the Romance of Russian Development*. Cambridge, MA: Harvard University Press, 2004.

Engerman, David C., Nils Gilman, Michael Latham, and Mark Haefele, eds. *Staging Growth: Modernization, Development, and the Global Cold War*. Amherst: University of Massachusetts Press, 2003.

Erlich, Haggai. *Islam and Christianity in the Horn of Africa: Somalia, Ethiopia, Sudan*. Boulder, CO: Lynne Rienner Publishers, 2010.

Enroth, Ronald, Edward Ericson Jr., and C. Breckinridge Peters. *The Jesus People: Old-Time Religion in the Age of Aquarius*. Grand Rapids, MI: Wm. B. Eerdmans Publishing, 1972.

Epprecht, Marc. *Sexuality and Social Justice in Africa: Rethinking Homophobia and Forging Resistance*. London: Zed Books, 2013.

Epstein, Helen. "God and the Fight Against AIDS." *New York Review of Books* (April 28, 2005): 47–51.

Escobar, Samuel. "Social Concern and World Evangelism." In *Christ the Liberator*, edited by John Stott, 103–12.

_____. *The New Global Mission: The Gospel from Everywhere to Everyone*. Downers Grove, IL: InterVarsity Press, 2003.

Esposito, John L., and Ibrahim Kalin, eds. *Islamophobia: The Challenge of Pluralism in the 21st Century*. New York: Oxford University Press, 2011.

Evangelicals for Human Rights. "An Evangelical Declaration Against Torture: Protecting Human Rights in an Age of Terror." *Review of Faith and International Affairs* 5, no. 2 (Summer 2007): 41–60.

Falwell, Jerry. "Interview." *Transformation* 3, no. 2 (April 1986): 36.

Fancello, Sandra. "Gagner les Nations à Jésus: Entreprises Missionaires et Guerre Spirituelle en Afrique." *Social Sciences and Missions* 20 (2007): 82–98.

Fassin, Didier. "Heart of Humanness: The Moral Economy of Humanitarian Intervention." In *Contemporary States of Emergency: The Politics of Military and Humanitarian Interventions*, edited by Didier Fassin and Mariella Pandolfi, 269–94. Brooklyn, NY: Zone Books, 2010.

_____. *Humanitarian Reason: A Moral History of the Present*. Berkeley: University of California Press, 2011.

Fehrenbach, Heide, and Davide Rodogno, eds. *Humanitarian Photography: A History*. Cambridge: Cambridge University Press, 2014.

Feldman, Keith P. *A Shadow over Palestine: The Imperial Life of Race in America*. Minneapolis: University of Minnesota Press, 2015.

Feldman, Ilana. *Governing Gaza: Bureaucracy, Authority, and the Work of Rule, 1917–1967*. Durham, NC: Duke University Press, 2008.

Feldman, Ilana, and Miriam Ticktin, eds. *In the Name of Humanity: The Government of Threat and Care*. Durham, NC: Duke University Press, 2010.

Feldman, Jackie. "Constructing a Shared Bible Land: Jewish Israeli Guiding Performances for Protestant Pilgrims." *American Ethnologist* 34, no. 2 (May 2007): 351–74.

Ferdinando, Keith. "The Legacy of Byang Kato." *International Bulletin of Missionary Research* 28, no. 4 (October 1, 2004): 169–74.

Ferguson, James. *Global Shadows: Africa in the Neoliberal World Order*. Durham, NC: Duke University Press, 2006.

_____. *The Anti-Politics Machine: Development, Depoliticization, and Bureaucratic Power in Lesotho*. Minneapolis: University of Minnesota Press, 1994.

Field, Connie. *Have You Heard From Johannesburg?* Clarity Films, 2010.

FitzGerald, Frances. *The Evangelicals: The Struggle to Shape America*. New York: Simon & Schuster, 2017.

Foucault, Michel. *Security, Territory, Population: Lectures at the Collège de France, 1977–78*. New York: Palgrave Macmillan, 2007.

_____. *The Government of Self and Others: Lectures at the Collège de France, 1982–1983*. Edited by Arnold I. Davidson. Translated by Graham Burchell. New York: Picador, 2011.

Fox, Richard W. *Jesus in America: Personal Savior, Cultural Hero, National Obsession*. San Francisco: HarperOne, 2005.

Frederick, Marla F. *Between Sundays: Black Women and Everyday Struggles of Faith*. Berkeley: University of California Press, 2003.

_____. *Colored Television: American Religion Gone Global*. Stanford, CA: Stanford University Press, 2016.

Frederickson, George. *Black Liberation: A Comparative History of Black Ideologies in the United States and South Africa*. New York: Oxford University Press, 1996.

Freedom from Religious Persecution Act of 1997: Hearing before the Committee on International Relations, House, 105th Cong., 1 (1997).

Freston, Paul. *Evangelicals and Politics in Asia, Africa and Latin America*. Cambridge: Cambridge University Press, 2004.

Gagnon, Georgette, Audrey Maklin, and Penelope Simons. *Deconstructing Engagement: Corporate Self-Regulation in Conflict Zones—Implications for Human Rights and Canadian Public Policy.* Toronto: Social Science and Humanities Research Council and the Law Commission of Canada, January 2003.

Gaines, Kevin. *American Africans in Ghana: Black Expatriates and the Civil Rights Era.* Chapel Hill: University of North Carolina Press, 2006.

Gardner, Christine J. *Making Chastity Sexy: The Rhetoric of Evangelical Abstinence Campaigns.* Berkeley: University of California Press, 2011.

Gasaway, Brantley W. "An Alternative Soul of Politics: The Rise of Contemporary Progressive Evangelicalism." PhD diss., University of North Carolina at Chapel Hill, 2008.

_____. *Progressive Evangelicals and the Pursuit of Social Justice.* Chapel Hill: University of North Carolina Press, 2014.

Gatu, John. "The Urgency of the Evangelistic Task." In *The New Face of Evangelicalism*, edited by René Padilla, 163–76.

Gerard, Emmanuel, and Bruce Kuklick. *Death in the Congo: Murdering Patrice Lumumba.* Cambridge, MA: Harvard University Press, 2015.

Gifford, Paul. " 'Africa Shall Be Saved' : An Appraisal of Reinhard Bonnke's Pan-African Crusade." *Journal of Religion in Africa* 17, no. 1 (Fall 1987): 63–92.

_____. *Ghana's New Christianity: Pentecostalism in a Globalizing African Economy.* Bloomington: Indiana University Press, 2004.

_____. "Some Recent Developments in African Christianity." *African Affairs* 93, no. 373 (October 1994): 513–34.

_____. *The Religious Right in Southern Africa.* Harare: University of Zimbabwe Publications, 1988.

Gill, Anthol. "Christian Social Responsibility." In *The New Face of Evangelicalism*, edited by René Padilla, 87–102.

Gilman, Nils. *Mandarins of the Future: Modernization Theory in Cold War America.* Baltimore, MD: Johns Hopkins University Press, 2004.

Gilroy, Paul. *The Black Atlantic: Modernity and Double-Consciousness.* Cambridge, MA: Harvard University Press, 1993.

Glasser, Arthur F. "The Mission Board and the Church." In InterVarsity Christian Fellowship, *Commission, Conflict, Commitment*, 145–53.

_____. "The Urgency of the Hour." In *Commission, Conflict, Commitment*, edited by InterVarsity Christian Fellowship, 200–210.

Gleijeses, Piero. *Conflicting Missions: Havana, Washington, and Africa, 1959-1976.* Chapel Hill: University of North Carolina Press, 2003.

_____. *Visions of Freedom: Havana, Washington, Pretoria, and the Struggle for Southern Africa, 1976–1991.* Chapel Hill: University of North Carolina Press, 2013.

Glickman, Harvey. "When and How to Resolve Ethnic Conflicts: Islamism in Sudan's Civil War." *Orbis* 44, no. 2 (Spring 2000): 267–81.

Global Health: Spending Requirement Presents Challenges for Allocating Prevention Funding under the President's Emergency Plan for AIDS Relief. Washington, DC: Government Accountability Office, April 2006.

Gloege, Timothy. *Guaranteed Pure: The Moody Bible Institute, Business, and the Making of Modern Evangelicalism.* Chapel Hill: University of North Carolina Press, 2015.

Goba, Bonganjalo. "The Kairos Document and Its Implications for Liberation in South Africa." *Journal of Law and Religion* 5, no. 2 (January 1, 1987): 313–25.

Goldberg, Michelle. *Kingdom Coming: The Rise of Christian Nationalism.* New York: W.W. Norton & Co., 2006.

Goldman, Shalom L. *Zeal for Zion: Christians, Jews, and the Idea of the Promised Land.* Chapel Hill: University of North Carolina Press, 2009.

Gondola, Didier. *The History of Congo.* Annotated ed. Westport, CT: Greenwood, 2002.

Gouverneur, Joe. "Underground Evangelism: Missions During the Cold War." *Transformation* 24, no. 2 (April 2007): 80–86.

Grabska, Katarzyna. "Marginalization in Urban Spaces of the Global South: Urban Refugees in Cairo." *Journal of Refugee Studies* 19 (2006): 287–307.

Graham, Billy. "Why Lausanne?" In *Let the Earth Hear His Voice*, edited by J. D. Douglas, 22–38.

Graham, Franklin. *The Name.* Nashville, TN: Nelson Books, 2002.

Grant, Kevin. *A Civilised Savagery: Britain and the New Slaveries in Africa, 1884-1926.* New York: Routledge, 2004.

Green, Edward C., Daniel T. Halperin, Vinand Nantulya, and Janice A. Hogle. "Uganda's HIV Prevention Success: The Role of Sexual Behavior Change and the National Response." *AIDS and Behavior* 10, no. 4 (July 2006): 335–46.

Griffith, R. Marie. *Born Again Bodies: Flesh and Spirit in American Christianity.* Berkeley: University of California Press, 2004.

_____. *God's Daughters: Evangelical Women and the Power of Submission.* Berkeley: University of California Press, 1997.

Griffith, R. Marie, and Melani McAlister. "Introduction: Is the Public Square Still Naked?" In *Religion and Politics in the Contemporary United States*, edited by R. M. Griffith and M. McAlister, 1–25. Baltimore, MD: Johns Hopkins University Press, 2008.

Guelich, Robert A. "Spiritual Warfare: Jesus, Paul and Peretti." *Pneuma* 13, no. 1 (1991): 33–64.

Gunn, Jeremy. "American Exceptionalism and Globalist Double Standards: A More Balanced Alternative." *Columbia Journal of Transnational Law* 41 (2002-2003): 137–52.

Gushee, David, ed. *A New Evangelical Manifesto: A Kingdom Vision for the Common Good.* St. Louis, MO: Chalice Press, 2012.

_____. *The Future of Faith in American Politics: The Public Witness of the Evangelical Center.* Waco, TX: Baylor University Press, 2008.

_____. "How to Read 'An Evangelical Declaration Against Torture.'" *Review of Faith and International Affairs* 5, no. 2 (Summer 2007): 61–64.

Guthrie, Stan. *Missions in the Third Millennium: 21 Key Trends for the 21st Century.* Revised and expanded ed. Milton Keynes: Paternoster Press, 2004.

Hackett, Conrad, and Brian J. Grim. "Global Christianity: A Report on the Size and Distribution of the World's Christian Population." Washington, DC: Pew Forum Religion & Public Life, December 2011. http://www.pewforum.org/2011/12/19/global-christianity-exec/.

Hackett, Rosalind, ed. *Proselytization Revisited: Rights Talk, Free Markets, and Culture Wars.* London: Equinox, 2008.

Halperin, Daniel T., and Helen Epstein. "Concurrent Sexual Partnerships Help to Explain Africa's High HIV Prevalence: Implications for Prevention." *Lancet* 364, no. 9428 (July 3, 2004): 4–6.

Hanford III, John V., John Shattuck, and Thomas Farr. "International Religious Freedom: Religion and International Diplomacy." Transcript of discussion at Pew Research Center, Washington DC, May 8, 2007. http://www.pewforum.org/2007/05/08/international-religious-freedom-religion-and-international-diplomacy/.

Hankins, Barry. *Francis Schaeffer and the Shaping of Evangelical America*. Grand Rapids, MI: Wm. B. Eerdmans Publishing, 2008.

Hall, David D. *Lived Religion in America: Toward a History of Practice*. Princeton, NJ: Princeton University Press, 1997.

Halsell, Grace. *Prophecy and Politics: Militant Evangelists on the Road to Nuclear War*. Westport, CT: Lawrence Hill & Co., 1986.

Hannah, John D. *An Uncommon Union: Dallas Theological Seminary and American Evangelicalism*. Grand Rapids, MI: Zondervan, 2009.

Harding, Susan Friend. *The Book of Jerry Falwell: Fundamentalist Language and Politics*. Princeton, NJ: Princeton University Press, 2001.

Haron, Muhammed. "Da'wah Movements and Sufi Tariqahs: Competing for Spiritual Spaces in Contemporary South Africa." *Journal of Muslim Minority Affairs* 25, no. 2 (August 2005): 261–85.

Hartman, Andrew. *A War for the Soul of America: A History of the Culture Wars*. Chicago: University of Chicago Press, 2015.

Harvey, Paul. *Freedom's Coming: Religious Culture and the Shaping of the South from the Civil War through the Civil Rights Era*. Chapel Hill: University of North Carolina Press, 2005.

Hassett, Miranda. *Anglican Communion in Crisis: How Episcopal Dissidents and Their African Allies Are Reshaping Anglicanism*. Princeton, NJ: Princeton University Press, 2007.

Hastings, Adrian. *A History of African Christianity, 1950–1975*. Cambridge: Cambridge University Press, 1979.

Haynes, Jeff. *Religion, Politics and International Relations: Selected Essays*. New York: Routledge, 2011.

Haynes, Stephen R. *The Last Segregated Hour: The Memphis Kneel-Ins and the Campaign for Southern Church Desegregation*. New York: Oxford University Press, 2012.

Heaney, Sharon E. *Contextual Theology for Latin America: Liberation Themes in Evangelical Perspective*. Eugene, OR: Wipf & Stock Pub, 2008.

Hedstrom, Matthew S. *The Rise of Liberal Religion: Book Culture and American Spirituality in the Twentieth Century*. New York: Oxford University Press, 2012.

Heineman, Kenneth. *God Is a Conservative: Religion, Politics, and Morality in Contemporary America*. New York: New York University Press, 1998.

Hendrickson, Francis. "A Study Of The Reactions Of Selected Congo Missionaries Toward Presumed Criticisms Of Missionary Education In Africa." PhD diss. Columbia University, 1964.

Henry, Carl F. "Jesus Christ and the Last Days." In *Prophecy in the Making*, edited by C. F. Henry, 169–86.

⸻, ed. *Prophecy in the Making*. Carol Stream, IL: Creation House, 1971.

Henry, Carl F. and W. Stanley Mooneyham, eds. *One Race, One Gospel, One Task: Official Reference Volumes: Papers and Reports, Volumes 1 & 2*. Minneapolis, MN: World Wide Publications, 1967.

Hearn, Julie. "The 'Invisible' NGO: US Evangelical Missions in Kenya." *Journal of Religion in Africa* 32, no. 1 (February 2002): 32–60.

Hertzke, Allen. *Freeing God's Children: The Unlikely Alliance for Global Human Rights*. Lanham, MD: Rowman & Littlefield, 2004.

Higgs, Catherine. "Silence, Disobedience, and African Catholic Sisters in Apartheid South Africa." *African Studies Review* 54, no. 2 (September 2011): 1–22.

Hiebert, Paul G. "Missions and Anthropology: A Love/Hate Relationship." *Missiology* 6, no. 2 (April 1978): 165–80.

_____. "Missions and the Understanding of Culture." In *Church in Mission, A Sixtieth Anniversary Tribute to J B Toews*, edited by A.J. Klassen, 251–65. Fresno, CA: Board of Christian Literature, Mennonite Brethren Church, 1967.

Hill, Patricia. *The World Their Household: The American Women's Foreign Mission Movement and Cultural Transformation, 1870–1920*. Ann Arbor: University of Michigan Press, 1985.

Hirsch, Alan, and Michael Frost. *The Shaping of Things to Come: Innovation and Mission for the 21st-Century Church*. Ada, MI: Baker Books, 2003.

Hochschild, Adam. *King Leopold's Ghost: A Story of Greed, Terror, and Heroism in Colonial Africa*. Boston: Houghton Mifflin, 1999.

Hocking, William E. *Re-Thinking Missions: A Laymen's Inquiry After One Hundred Years*. New York, Harper and Brothers Publishers, 1932.

Hofer, Katharina. "The Role of Evangelical NGOs in International Development: A Comparative Case Study of Kenya and Uganda." *Africa Spectrum* 38, no. 3 (2003): 375–98.

Hoffman, Elizabeth Cobbs. *All You Need Is Love: The Peace Corps and the Spirit of the 1960s*. Cambridge, MA: Harvard University Press, 2000.

Hoganson, Kristin L. *Consumers' Imperium: The Global Production of American Domesticity, 1865–1920*. Chapel Hill: University of North Carolina Press, 2007.

Hollinger, David A. *After Cloven Tongues of Fire: Protestant Liberalism in Modern American History*. Princeton, NJ: Princeton University Press, 2013.

_____. *Protestants Abroad: How Missionaries Tried to Change the World But Changed America*. Princeton, NJ: Princeton University Press, 2017.

Holvast, Rene. *Spiritual Mapping in the United States and Argentina, 1989–2005: A Geography of Fear*. Boston: Brill Academic Publishers, 2008.

Hopkins, Dwight N. *Black Theology, USA and South Africa: Politics, Culture, and Liberation*. Eugene, OR: Wipf & Stock Publishers, 2005.

Howard, David. "A Personal Encounter with the South Africa Police." *Transformation* 3, no. 2 (April 1986): 21–22.

_____. "The South African Conference on Evangelical Leadership." *Transformation* 3, no. 2 (April 1986): 9–10.

_____. *What I Saw God Do: Reflections on a Lifetime in Missions*. Self-published, CreateSpace, 2013.

Howland, Nina, David Humphrey, and Harriet Schwar, eds. *Foreign Relations of the United States, 1964-1968*, Volume XXIII, Congo 1960–68. Washington: Government Printing Office, 2013.

Huliaras, Asteris. "Evangelists, Oil Companies, and Terrorists: The Bush Administration's Policy Toward Sudan." *Orbis* 50, no. 4 (Fall 2006): 709–24.

Hunt, Keith. *For Christ and the University: The Story of InterVarsity Christian Fellowship-USA, 1940–1990*. Downers Grove, IL: InterVarsity Press, 1992.

Hunt, Lynn. *Inventing Human Rights: A History*. New York: W.W. Norton, 2007.

Hunter, George S. "The Legacy of Donald A. McGavran." *International Bulletin of Missionary Research* 16, no. 4 (October 1992): 158–62.

Hunter, James Davison. *To Change the World: The Irony, Tragedy, and Possibility of Christianity in the Late Modern World*. New York: Oxford University Press, 2010.

Hurd, Elizabeth Shakman. *Beyond Religious Freedom: The New Global Politics of Religion.* Princeton, NJ: Princeton University Press, 2015.

———. *The Politics of Secularism in International Relations.* Princeton, NJ: Princeton University Press, 2007.

Hutchinson, Sharon E. *Nuer Dilemmas: Coping with Money, War, and the State.* Berkeley: University of California Press, 1996.

Hutchison, William R. *Errand to the World: American Protestant Thought and Foreign Missions.* Chicago: University of Chicago Press, 1987.

Immerwahr, Daniel. *Thinking Small: The United States and the Lure of Community Development.* Cambridge, MA: Harvard University Press, 2015.

Inboden, William. *Religion and American Foreign Policy, 1945-1960: The Soul of Containment.* Cambridge: Cambridge University Press, 2008.

InterVarsity Christian Fellowship, ed. *Commission, Conflict, Commitment: Messages from the Sixth International Student Missionary Convention.* Chicago: InterVarsity Press, 1962.

InterVarsity Christian Fellowship, ed. *God's Men From All Nations to All Nations: The Eighth InterVarsity Missions Convention.* Chicago: InterVarsity Press, 1968.

Irvine, Cecilia. *The Church of Christ in Zaire, a Handbook of Protestant Churches, Missions and Communities, 1878–1978.* Indianapolis, IN: Division of Overseas Ministries, Christian Church (Disciples of Christ), 1978.

Jakes, T.D. *Woman, Thou Art Loosed.* Shippensburg, PA: Destiny Image Publishers, 2006.

Janson, Torsten. "Da'wa: Islamic Missiology in Discourse and History." *Svensk Missionstidskrift* 89, no. 3 (January 2001): 359–415.

Jenkins, Philip. *The New Faces of Christianity: Believing the Bible in the Global South.* New York: Oxford University Press, 2006.

———. *The Next Christendom: The Coming of Global Christianity.* New York: Oxford University Press, 2002.

Johanson, Brian. "The South African Congress on Mission and Evangelism." *Journal of Theology for Southern Africa*, no. 3 (June 1973): 57–63.

Johnson, Douglas Hamilton. *The Root Causes of Sudan's Civil Wars.* Indianapolis: Indiana University Press, 2003.

Johnson, Sylvester A. *African American Religions, 1500–2000: Colonialism, Democracy, and Freedom.* Cambridge: Cambridge University Press, 2015.

Johnson, Todd M., and David R. Scoggins. "Christian Missions and Islamic Da'wah: A Preliminary Quantitative Assessment." *International Bulletin of Missionary Research* 29, no. 1 (January 2005): 8–11.

Johnson, Todd M., and Gina A. Zurlo. "Christian Martyrdom as a Pervasive Phenomenon." *Society* 51, no. 6 (December 1, 2014): 679–85.

Johnstone, Patrick, John Hanna, and Marti Smith. *Praying Through the Window III: The Unreached Peoples.* Seattle: YWAM Publishing, 1996.

Jones, Howard O., and Edward Gilbreath. *Gospel Trailblazer: An African American Preacher's Historic Journey Across Racial Lines.* Chicago: Moody Publishers, 2003.

Jok, Jok Madut. "Slavery and Slave Redemption in Sudan." In *Buying Freedom*, edited by Anthony Appiah and Martin Bunzi, 143–57.

Jones, Jeffrey McClain. "Ronald Sider and Radical Evangelical Political Theology (Volumes I and II)." PhD diss., Northwestern University, 1990.

Jones, Tony. *The New Christians: Dispatches from the Emergent Frontier.* Hoboken, NJ: Jossey-Bass, 2008.

Jonsson, John N. "Baptists in Socio-Political Life in South Africa: Historical and Theological Reflections Covering the Past 30 Years." *American Baptist Quarterly* 4, no. 3 (September 1985): 243–56.

_____. "Missions and the Liberation of Human Life as Part of Our Baptist Heritage." *Review & Expositor* 84, no. 4 (September 1987): 667–79.

_____. "When You Put Your Body Where Your Mouth Is: How Falwell Got It Wrong." *Transformation* 3, no. 2 (April 1986): 37–40.

Jubber, Ken. "The Roman Catholic Church and Apartheid." *Journal of Theology for Southern Africa* 15 (June 1976): 25–38.

Kaell, Hillary. "Pilgrimage in the Jet Age: The Development of the American Holy Land Travel Industry, 1948-1978." *Journal of Tourism History* 2, no. 1 (April 2010): 23–38.

_____. *Walking Where Jesus Walked: American Christians and Holy Land Pilgrimage.* New York: New York University Press, 2014.

Kairos Document: Challenge to the Church, A Theological Comment on the Political Crisis in South Africa. Edited by John W. de Gruchy. Grand Rapids, MI: Wm. B. Eerdmans Publishing, 1986.

Kagan, Michael. "Frontier Justice: Legal Aid and UNHCR Refugee Status Determination in Egypt." *Journal of Refugee Studies* 19 (2006): 45–68.

Kalb, Madeleine G. *The Congo Cables: The Cold War in Africa—from Eisenhower to Kennedy.* New York: Macmillan, 1982.

Kalu, Ogbu. *African Pentecostalism: An Introduction.* New York: Oxford University Press, 2008.

_____. "Constructing a Global Pentecostal Discourse: An African Example." In *The Collected Essays of Ogbu Uke Kalu, vol. 1,* edited by Wilhelmina Kelu et al., 35–55.

_____. "Pentecostal and Charismatic Reshaping of the African Religious Landscape." In *The Collected Essays of Ogbu Uke Kalu, vol. 1,* edited by Wilhelmina Kelu et al., 109–32.

Kane, Herbert J. *A Concise History of the Christian World Mission: A Panoramic View of Missions from Pentecost to the Present.* Rev. ed. Grand Rapids, MI: Baker Academic, 1978.

Kansteiner, Walter H. *South Africa, Revolution or Reconciliation?; Revolution or Reconciliation.* 2nd ed. Washington: Institute for Religion and Democracy Press, 1988.

Kaoma, Kapya. *Globalizing the Culture Wars: US Conservatives, African Churches, and Homophobia.* Cambridge, MA: Political Research Associates, November 2009.

_____. "How US Clergy Brought Hate to Uganda." *Gay & Lesbian Review Worldwide* 17, no. 3 (June 2010): 20–23.

Kasongo, Michael. *History of the Methodist Church in the Central Congo.* Lanham, MD: University Press of America, 1998.

Kato, Byang. *Biblical Christianity in Africa: A Collection of Papers and Addresses.* Achimota, Ghana: Africa Christian Press, 1985.

_____. *Theological Pitfalls in Africa.* Kisumu, Kenya: Evangel Publishing House, 1975.

Kearney, Paddy. *Guardian of the Light: Denis Hurley, Renewing the Church, Opposing Apartheid.* New York: Continuum, 2009.

Kelley, Dean M. *Why Conservative Churches Are Growing: A Study in Sociology of Religion.* Atlanta, GA: Mercer University Press, 1977.

Kelu, Wilhelmina, Nimi Wariboko, and Toyin Falola, eds. *The Collected Essays of Ogbu Uke Kalu, vol. 1: Global Discourses, Migrations, Exchanges.* Trenton, NJ: Africa World Press, 2010.

Kemble, Penn, et al. *Slavery, Abduction and Forced Servitude in Sudan*. Khartoum: International Eminent Persons Group, May 22, 2002. https://johnryle.com/?article=slavery-abduction-and-forced-servitude-in-sudan-report-of-the-eminent-persons-group-2002.

Kent, Eliza. *Converting Women: Gender and Protestant Christianity in Colonial South India*. New York: Oxford University Press, 2004.

Keough, Lucy. "Conquering Slim: Uganda's War on HIV/AIDS." Paper presented at the Global Learning Process of Scaling up Poverty Reduction conference, Shanghai, May 25, 2004. https://berkleycenter.georgetown.edu/publications/conquering-slim-uganda-s-war-on-hiv-aids.

Keys, Barbara. *Reclaiming American Virtue: The Human Rights Revolution of the 1970s*. Cambridge, MA: Harvard University Press, 2014.

King, David P. "Heartbroken for God's World: The Story of Bob Pierce, Founder of World Vision and Samaritan's Purse." In *Religion in Philanthropic Organizations : Family, Friend, Foe?* edited by Thomas J. Davis, 71–92. Bloomington: Indiana University Press, 2013.

———. "Seeking a Global Vision: The Evolution of World Vision and American Evangelicalism." PhD diss., Emory University, 2012.

———. "The New Internationalists: World Vision and the Revival of American Evangelical Humanitarianism, 1950-2010." *Religions* 3, no. 4 (2012): 922–49.

———. "World Vision: Religious Identity in the Discourse and Practice of Global Relief and Development." *Review of Faith & International Affairs* 9, no. 3 (September 2011): 21–28.

Kiracofe, Clifford A. *Dark Crusade: Christian Zionism and US Foreign Policy*. New York: I.B. Tauris, 2009.

Kirkpatrick, David C. "C. René Padilla and the Origins of Integral Mission in Post-War Latin America." *Journal of Ecclesiastical History* 67, no. 2 (April 2016): 351–71.

Kivengere, Festo. *I Love Idi Amin: The Story of Triumph Under Fire in the Midst of Suffering and Persecution in Uganda*. Old Tappan, NJ: F.H. Revell Co., 1977.

———, ed. "Personal Revival." In *Commission, Conflict, Commitment*, edited by InterVarsity Christian Fellowship, 27–47.

Klaits, Frederick. *Death in a Church of Life: Moral Passion during Botswana's Time of AIDS*. Berkeley: University of California Press, 2010.

Klein, Christina. *Cold War Orientalism: Asia in the Middlebrow Imagination, 1945–1961*. Berkeley: University of California Press, 2002.

Korey, William. "Jackson-Vanik and Soviet Jewry." *Washington Quarterly* 7, no. 1 (Winter 1984): 116–28.

Kosek, Joseph. *Acts of Conscience: Christian Nonviolence and Modern American Democracy*. New York: Columbia University Press, 2009.

Kovachi, Noam. "Insights Abandoned, Flexibility Lost: Kissinger, Soviet Jewish Emigration, and the Demise of Détente." *Diplomatic History* 29, no. 3 (June 2005): 503–30.

Kruse, Kevin M. *One Nation Under God: How Corporate America Invented Christian America*. New York: Basic Books, 2015.

Kruse, Kevin M. *White Flight: Atlanta and the Making of Modern Conservatism*. Princeton, NJ: Princeton University Press, 2012.

Kuklick, Bruce. *Puritans in Babylon*. Princeton, NJ: Princeton University Press, 1996.

Kumar, Deepa. *Islamophobia and the Politics of Empire*. Chicago: Haymarket Books, 2012.

Kuperus, Tracy. "The Political Role and Democratic Contribution of Churches in Post-Apartheid South Africa." *Journal of Church and State* 53, no. 2 (Spring 2011): 278–306.

Laats, Adam. *Fundamentalism and Education in the Scopes Era: God, Darwin, and the Roots of America's Culture Wars*. New York: Palgrave Macmillan, 2010.

Lagergren, David. *Mission and State in the Congo. A Study of the Relations Between Protestant Missions and the Congo Independent State Authorities with Special Reference to the Equator District, 1885–1903*. Lund, Sweden: Gleerup, 1970.

Lahr, Angela M. *Millennial Dreams and Apocalyptic Nightmares: The Cold War Origins of Political Evangelicalism*. New York: Oxford University Press, 2007.

Lambert, Tony. "Post-Tiananmen Chinese Communist Party Religious Policy." *Religion, State, and Society* 20, no. 3–4 (1992): 391–97.

Landau, Paul S. "An Amazing Distance: People and Pictures in Africa." In *Images and Empires: Visuality in Colonial and Postcolonial Africa*, edited by Paul S. Landau and Deborah D. Kaspin, 1–40. Berkeley: University of California Press, 2002.

_____. *The Realm of the Word: Language, Gender, and Christianity in a Southern African Kingdom*. London: J. Currey, 1995.

Latham, Michael E. *Modernization as Ideology: American Social Science and "Nation Building" in the Kennedy Era*. Chapel Hill: University of North Carolina Press, 2000.

Latour, Bruno. *Reassembling the Social: An Introduction to Actor-Network-Theory*. Oxford: Oxford University Press, 2005.

_____. *We Have Never Been Modern*. Cambridge, MA: Harvard University Press, 1993.

Law, Virginia. *Appointment Congo*. Chicago: Rand McNally, 1966.

Le Houérou, Fabienne. *Forced Migrants and Host Societies in Egypt and Sudan*. Cairo: American University in Cairo Press, 2006.

Lefever, Ernest W. *Amsterdam to Nairobi: The World Council of Churches and the Third World*. Washington, DC: Ethics and Public Policy Center & Georgetown University Press, 1979.

LeGrande, Larry. "Historical & Contemporary Reasons For the Existence of 17,000 Unreached People Groups and Factors Being Employed to Lesson Their Number." MA thesis, Liberty University, 1986.

Leonard, Bill J. *Baptists in America*. New York: Columbia University Press, 2005.

_____. *God's Last and Only Hope: The Fragmentation of the Southern Baptist Convention*. Grand Rapids, MI: Wm. B. Eerdmans Publishing, 1990.

Lesch, Ann M. "Sudan: The Torn Country." *Current History* 98, no. 628 (May 1999): 218–22.

_____. *The Sudan: Contested National Identities*. Oxford, UK: J. Currey, 1998.

Leys, Ruth. "The Turn to Affect: A Critique." *Critical Inquiry* 37, no. 3 (Summer 2011): 434–72.

Lian, Xi. *The Conversion of Missionaries: Liberalism in American Protestant Missions in China, 1907-1932*. University Park, PA: Pennsylvania State University Press, 1997.

Lichtman, Allan J. *White Protestant Nation: The Rise of the American Conservative Movement*. New York: Atlantic Monthly Press, 2008.

Linhart, Terence. "They Were So Alive!: The Spectacle Self and Youth Group Short-Term Mission Trips." *Missiology: An International Review* 34, no. 4 (October 2006): 451–62.

Lively, Scott, and Kevin Abrams. *Pink Swastika : Homosexuality in the Nazi Party*. Keizer: Founders Publishing, 1995.

Livermore, David. *Serving with Eyes Wide Open: Doing Short-Term Missions with Cultural Intelligence*. Grand Rapids, MI: Baker Books, 2006.

Lobban, Richard. "Slavery in the Sudan since 1989." *Arab Studies Quarterly* 23, no. 2 (Spring 2001): 31–39.

Lockman, Zachary. *Contending Visions of the Middle East: The History and Politics of Orientalism.* Cambridge: Cambridge University Press, 2004.

Lodberg, Peter. "Desmond Tutu: Church Resistance to Apartheid and Injustice in Africa." In *Christianity and Resistance in the 20th Century: From Kaj Munk and Dietrich Bonhoeffer to Desmond Tutu*, edited by von Sören Dosenrode-Lynge, 261–75. Boston: Brill, 2009.

Lodge, Tom. *Sharpeville: An Apartheid Massacre and Its Consequences.* New York: Oxford University Press, 2011.

Lofton, Kathryn E. *Oprah: The Gospel of an Icon.* Berkeley: University of California Press, 2011.

_____. "The Preacher Paradigm: Promotional Biographies and the Modern-Made Evangelist." *Religion and American Culture: A Journal of Interpretation* 16, no. 1 (Winter 2006): 95–123.

Long, Kathryn. "In the Modern World, but Not of It: The 'Auca Martyrs,' Evangelicalism, and Postwar American Culture." In *The Foreign Missionary Enterprise at Home*, edited by Daniel Bays and Grant Wacker, 223–36.

LOP 49: Understanding Muslims. Pattaya, Thailand: Lausanne Movement, 2004. https://www.lausanne.org/content/lop/lop-49.

Louw, P. Eric. *The Rise, Fall, and Legacy of Apartheid.* Westport, CT: Praeger, 2004.

Lubin, Alex. *Geographies of Liberation: The Making of an Afro-Arab Political Imaginary.* Chapel Hill: University of North Carolina Press, 2014.

Lugo, Luis, and Alan Copperman. "Tolerance and Tension: Islam and Christianity in Sub-Saharan Africa." Washington, DC: Pew Forum Religion & Public Life, April 2010. http://pewforum.org/executive-summary-islam-and-christianity-in-sub-saharan-africa.aspx.

Luhr, Eileen. "A Revolutionary Mission: Young Evangelicals and the Language of the Sixties." In *American Evangelicals and the 1960s*, edited by Axel Schäfer, 61–80.

_____. *Witnessing Suburbia: Conservatives and Christian Youth Culture.* Berkeley: University of California Press, 2009.

Lund, Christopher Alan. "A Critical Examination of Evangelicalism in South Africa, with Special Reference to the Evangelical Witness Document and Concerned Evangelicals." Master's thesis, University of Cape Town, 1988.

MacDougall, Gay. "Implementation of the Anti-Apartheid Act of 1986." In *Sanctioning Apartheid*, edited by Robert Edgar, 19–57.

MacGaffey, Wyatt. "Cultural Roots of Kongo Prophetism." *History of Religions* 17, no. 2 (November 1977): 177–93.

Maclure, David. "Wholly Available: Missionary Motivation Where Consumer Choice Reigns." *Evangel* 20, no 3 (Autumn 2002): i–iv.

Mahaniah, Kimpianga. "The Presence of Black Americans in Lower Congo from 1878 to 1921." *Global Dimensions of the African Diaspora*, edited by Joseph E. Harris, 268–82. Washington, DC: Howard University Press, 1982.

Mahmoud, Hala W. "'Conflict Defines Origins': Identity Transformations of Sudanese Refugees in Cairo." *Conflict Resolution Quarterly* 28, no. 3 (March 2011): 263–89.

Mahmood, Saba. *Religious Difference in a Secular Age: A Minority Report.* Princeton, NJ: Princeton University Press, 2015.

Malit, Froilan, and Ali Al Youha. *Labor Migration in the United Arab Emirates: Challenges and Responses.* Washington, DC: Migration Policy Institute, September 18, 2013. http://www.migrationpolicy.org/article/labor-migration-united-arab-emirates-challenges-and-responses.

Mansfeld, Yoel. "The Middle East Conflict and Tourism to Israel, 1967-90." *Middle Eastern Studies* 30, no. 3 (July 1994): 646–67.

Markowitz, Marvin D. *Cross and Sword: The Political Role of Christian Missions in the Belgian Congo, 1908-1960*. Stanford, CA: Hoover Institution Press, 1973.

Marr, Timothy. *The Cultural Roots of American Islamicism*. Cambridge: Cambridge University Press, 2006.

Marsden, George. *Fundamentalism and American Culture*. 2nd ed. New York: Oxford University Press, 2006.

_____. *Reforming Fundamentalism: Fuller Seminary and the New Evangelicalism*. Grand Rapids, MI: Wm. B. Eerdmans Publishing, 1995.

_____. *Understanding Fundamentalism and Evangelicalism*. Grand Rapids, MI: Wm. B. Eerdmans Publishing, 1991.

Marsh, Charles. *Wayward Christian Soldiers: Freeing the Gospel from Political Captivity*. New York: Oxford University Press, 2007.

Marshall, Paul A. *Their Blood Cries Out: The Untold Story of Persecution Against Christians in the Modern World*. Dallas: World Publishing, 1997.

Marshall, Ruth. *Political Spiritualities: The Pentecostal Revolution in Nigeria*. Chicago: University of Chicago Press, 2009.

Mart, Michelle. *Eye on Israel: How America Came to View Israel As an Ally*. Albany: State University of New York Press, 2007.

Martin, William. *A Prophet with Honor: The Billy Graham Story*. New York: W. Morrow and Co., 1991.

_____. *With God On Our Side: The Rise of the Religious Right in America*. New York: Broadway, 2005.

Marty, Martin E. *Dietrich Bonhoeffer's "Letters and Papers from Prison": A Biography*. Princeton, NJ: Princeton University Press, 2011.

Massie, Robert Kinloch. *Loosing the Bonds: The United States and South Africa in the Apartheid Years*. New York: Nan A. Talese, 1997.

Massumi, Brian. *Parables for the Virtual: Movement, Affect, Sensation*. Durham, NC: Duke University Press, 2002.

Masuku, Tobias, and Nelus Niemandt. "The Ministry of Beyers Naude to the Victims of Oppression 1960–1994: A Challenge to Christian Mission in Post-Apartheid South Africa." *Verbum et Ecclesia* 33, no. 1 (2012): 1–7.

Mathews, Mary Beth Swetnam. *Doctrine and Race: African American Evangelicals and Fundamentalism between the Wars*. Tuscaloosa: University Alabama Press, 2017.

Maxwell, David. *African Gifts of the Spirit: Pentecostalism & the Rise of Zimbabwean Transnational Religious Movement*. Athens: Ohio University Press, 2007.

Maxwell, David, Martina Santschi, and Rachel Gordon. *Looking Back to Look Ahead? Reviewing Key Lessons from Operation Lifeline Sudan and Past Humanitarian Operations in South Sudan*. London: Secure Livelihoods Research Consortium, October 2014. http://www.secureliveli-hoods.org/publications_details.aspx?resourceid=329.

Maxwell, Melody. "'This Only Christian Women Can Supply': Southern Baptist Women's Roles as Portrayed in the Magazines of Woman's Missionary Union, 1906–2006." PhD diss., International Baptist Theological Seminary of the European Baptist Federation (Czech Republic), 2010.

Mays, Benjamin E. *Born to Rebel: An Autobiography*. Athens: University of Georgia Press, 2003.

Mbali, Zolile. *The Churches and Racism: A Black South African Perspective*. London: SCM Press, 1987.

McAlister, Elizabeth. "Humanitarian Adhocracy: Transnational New Apostolic Missions, and Evangelical Anti-Dependency in a Haitian Refugee Camp." *Nova Religio* 16, no. 4 (May 2013): 11–34.

McAlister, Melani. *Epic Encounters: Culture, Media, and U.S. Interests in the Middle East Since 1945*. 2nd ed. Berkeley: University of California Press, 2005.

_____. "Left Behind and the Politics of Prophecy Talk." In *Exceptional State: Contemporary U.S. Culture and the New Imperialism*, edited by Ashley Dawson and Malini Johar Schueller, 191–220. Durham, NC: Duke University Press, 2007.

_____. "Rethinking the 'Clash of Civilizations': American Evangelicals, the Bush Administration, and the Winding Road to the Iraq War." In *Race, Nation, and Empire in American History*, edited by James T. Campbell, Matthew P. Guterl, and Robert G. Lee, 352–74. Chapel Hill: University of North Carolina Press, 2007.

_____. "US Evangelicals and the Politics of Slave Redemption as Religious Freedom in Sudan." *South Atlantic Quarterly* 113, no. 1 (Winter 2014): 87–108.

_____. "What Is Your Heart For? Affect and Internationalism in the Evangelical Public Sphere." *American Literary History* 20, no. 4 (Winter 2008): 870–95.

McAllister, William. "Politics, Economics and the Problems of Protestant Church Leadership in Africa: The Case of the Unevangelized Fields Mission/Communaute Episcopale Evangelique Au Zaire." PhD diss., University of Aberdeen (United Kingdom), 1986.

McClintock, David W. "The Southern Sudan Problem: Evolution of an Arab-African Confrontation." *Middle East Journal* 24, no. 4 (1970): 466–78.

McGavran, Donald A. "My Pilgrimage in Mission." *International Bulletin of Missionary Research* 10, no. 2 (April 1986): 53–58.

_____. *Understanding Church Growth*. Grand Rapids, MI: Wm. B. Eerdmans Publishing, 1970.

McGirr, Lisa. *Suburban Warriors: The Origins of the New American Right*. Princeton, NJ: Princeton University Press, 2001.

McGlathery, Marla Frederick, and Traci Griffin. " 'Becoming Conservative, Becoming White?' : Black Evangelicals and the Para-Church Movement." In *This Side of Heaven: Race, Ethnicity, and Christian Faith*, edited by Robert Priest and Alvaro L. Nieves, 145–64. New York: Oxford University Press, 2006.

McRoberts, Omar M. *Streets of Glory: Church and Community in a Black Urban Neighborhood*. Chicago: University of Chicago Press, 2005.

Mercer, Charles E. *Rachel Cade*. New York: Putnam, 1956.

Meriwether, James H. *Proudly We Can Be Africans: Black Americans and Africa, 1935-1961*. Chapel Hill: University of North Carolina Press, 2002.

Merson, Michael et al. "The President's Emergency Plan For AIDS Relief: From Successes Of The Emergency Response To Challenges Of Sustainable Action." *Health Affairs* 31, no. 7 (July 2012): 1380–88.

Michener, James. *Hawaii*. New York: Random House, 1958.

Miller, Albert G. "The Construction of a Black Fundamentalist Worldview." In *African Americans and the Bible: Sacred Texts and Social Structures*, edited by Vincent L. Wimbush, 712–27. New York: Continuum, 2001.

Miller, Paul. "Evangelicals, Israel, and US Foreign Policy." *Survival: Global Politics and Strategy* 56, no. 1 (February 2014): 7–26.

Miller, Steven P. *Billy Graham and the Rise of the Republican South*. Philadelphia: University of Pennsylvania Press, 2009.

Milne, David. *America's Rasputin: Walt Rostow and the Vietnam War*. New York: Hill and Wang, 2008.

Miniter, Richard. "The False Promise of Slave Redemption." *Atlantic* (July 1999): 63–70.

Moffett, Samuel H. "Report of Group Discussion." In *One Race, One Gospel, One Task, vol 2*, edited by Carl F. Henry and W. Stanley Mooneyham, 316–17.

Molebatsi, Caesar. *A Flame for Justice*. Oxford: Lion, 1991.

Moore, Rick. "The Genres of Religious Freedom: Creating Discourses on Religion at the State Department." In *History, Time, Meaning, and Memory: Ideas for the Sociology of Religion*, edited by Barbara Denison and John Simpson, 223–53. Leiden, Netherlands: Brill, 2011.

Moreau, A. Scott, ed. *Evangelical Dictionary of World Missions*. Grand Rapids, MI: Baker Academic, 2000.

Moreton, Bethany. *To Serve God and Wal-Mart: The Making of Christian Free Enterprise*. Cambridge, MA: Harvard University Press, 2009.

Morgan, Eric J. "The World Is Watching: Polaroid and South Africa." *Enterprise & Society* 7, no. 3 (2006): 520–49.

Morgan, Michael Cotey. "The United States and the Making of the Helsinki Final Act." In *Nixon in the World: American Foreign Relations, 1969–1977*, edited by Andrew Preston, 164–84. New York: Oxford University Press, 2008.

Moulin, Carolina, and Peter Nyers. "'We Live in a Country of UNHCR'—Refugee Protests and Global Political Society." *International Political Sociology* 1, no. 4 (November 2007): 356–72.

Moyn, Samuel. *Christian Human Rights*. Philadelphia: University of Pennsylvania Press, 2015.

———. *The Last Utopia: Human Rights in History*. Cambridge, MA: Belknap Press, 2010.

M'Timkulu, Donald G. S. "The All Africa Church Conference." *Journal of Modern African Studies* 1, no. 1 (March 1963): 109–10.

Myers, Bryant L. *Walking With the Poor: Principles and Practices of Transformational Development*. Marynoll, NY: Orbis Books, 1999.

Namikas, Lise. *Battleground Africa: Cold War in the Congo, 1960–1965*. Stanford, CA: Stanford University Press, 2013.

Nelson, Jack E. *Christian Missionizing and Social Transformation: A History of Conflict and Change in Eastern Zaire*. New York: Praeger, 1992.

Nelson, Robert Gilbert. *Congo Crisis and Christian Mission*. St. Louis: Bethany Press, 1961.

Nesbitt, Francis Njubi. *Race for Sanctions: African Americans Against Apartheid, 1946–1994*. Bloomington: Indiana University Press, 2004.

Neuhaus, Richard J. *The Naked Public Square: Religion and Democracy in America*. Grand Rapids, MI: Wm. B. Eerdmans Publishing, 1984.

Newman, Mark. *Getting Right with God: Southern Baptists and Desegregation, 1945–1995*. Tuscaloosa: University of Alabama Press, 2001.

Nichols, Alan. *LOP 20: An Evangelical Commitment to Simple Life-Style*. Hoddesdon, UK: Lausanne Committee for World Evangelization, 1980. http://www.lausanne.org/all-documents/lop-20.html.

Noll, Mark A. *God and Race in American Politics: A Short History*. Princeton, NJ: Princeton University Press, 2010.

_____. *The New Shape of World Christianity: How American Experience Reflects Global Faith*. Wheaton, IL: InterVarsity Press Academic, 2009.

_____. *The Scandal of the Evangelical Mind*. Grand Rapids, MI: Wm.B. Eerdmans, 1994.

Noll, Mark A., and Carolyn Nystrom. *Clouds of Witnesses: Christian Voices from Africa and Asia*. Downers Grove, IL: InterVarsity Press, 2011.

Nurser, John S. *For All Peoples and All Nations: The Ecumenical Church and Human Rights*. Washington, DC: Georgetown University Press, 2005.

Ntlha, Moss. "Evangelical Witness in South Africa—the Story of Concerned Evangelicals." *International Review of Mission* 83, no. 328 (January 1994): 139–141.

Nzongola-Ntalaja, Georges. *The Congo: From Leopold to Kabila: A People's History*. London: Zed Books, 2002.

Oha, Obododimma. "Yoruba Christian Video Narrative and Indigenous Imaginations: Dialogue and Duelogue." *Cahiers d'Études Africaines* 42, no. 165 (2002): 121–42.

O'Neill, Kevin Lewis. *Secure the Soul: Christian Piety and Gang Prevention in Guatemala*. Berkeley: University of California Press, 2015.

Padilla, C. René. "Evangelism and the World: Paper as Presented." In Douglas, *Let the Earth Hear His Voice*, edited by J. D. Douglas, 134–46.

_____. "Evangelism and the World: Pre-Circulated Paper." In *Let the Earth Hear His Voice*, edited by J.D. Douglas, 116–33.

_____. "Integral Mission and Its Historical Development." In *Justice, Mercy, and Humility: Integral Mission and the Poor*, edited by Tim Chester, et al., 42–58. Milton Keynes, UK: Paternoster, 2003.

_____. "Introduction." In *The New Face of Evangelicalism*, edited by René Padilla, 8–16.

_____., ed. *The New Face of Evangelicalism: An International Symposium on the Lausanne Covenant*. Downers Grove, IL: InterVarsity Press, 1976.

Padilla, C. René, and Chris Sugden, eds. *Texts on Evangelical and Social Ethics, 1974–1983*, Vol.1. Bramcote & Nottingham: Grove Books Limited, 1985.

Pagels, Elaine H. *The Gnostic Gospels*. New York: Random House, 1979.

Pannell, William E. *My Friend, The Enemy*. Waco, TX: Word Books, 1968.

Pannell, William. "The Religious Heritage of Blacks." In *The Evangelicals: What They Believe, Who They Are, Where They Are Changing*, Rev. ed., edited by David F. Wells and John D. Woodbridge, 96–107. Grand Rapids, MI: Baker Book House, 1975.

Parker, Michael. *The Kingdom of Character: The Student Volunteer Movement for Foreign Missions, 1886-1926*. Pasadena, CA: William Carey Library, 2007.

Patterson, James. "Cultural Pessimism in Modern Evangelical Thought: Francis Schaeffer, Carl Henry, and Charles Colson." *Journal of the Evangelical Theological Society* 40, no. 4 (December 2006): 807-20.

Peagler, Victoria Morongwa. "Blow the Trumpet in Black Zion: A Phenomenological Exploration of the Zionist Christian Church of South Africa." PhD diss., Fuller Theological Seminary, School of Intercultural Studies, 2010.

Peau, Andrew T. Le, and Linda Doll. *Heart, Soul, Mind, Strength: An Anecdotal History of InterVarsity Press, 1947-2007*. Downers Grove, IL: InterVarsity Press, 2006.

Pendleton, Kimberly. "The Other Sex Industry: Narratives of Feminism and Freedom in Evangelical Discourses of Human Trafficking." *New Formations* 91 (2017): 102-15.

Peretti, Frank E. *Piercing the Darkness*. Wheaton, IL: Tyndale Momentum, 2002.

_____. *This Present Darkness*. Wheaton, IL: Crossway, 1986.

Peretz, Pauline. "Nixon et Le Vote Juif: La Campagne Presidentielle de 1972." *Vingtième Siécle*, no. 90 (April–June 2006): 109–20.

Peterson, Derek R. *Ethnic Patriotism and the East African Revival: A History of Dissent, c.1935–1972*. Cambridge: Cambridge University Press, 2014.

Petersen, William J. *Another Hand on Mine: The Story of Dr. Carl K. Becker of the Africa Inland Mission*. New York: McGraw-Hill, 1967.

Pew Research Center. *America's Changing Religious Landscape*. Washington, DC: Forum on Religion and Public Life, May 12, 2015. http://www.pewforum.org/2015/05/12/americas-changing-religious-landscape/.

_____. *A Religious Portrait of African-Americans*. Washington, DC: Forum on Religion and Public Life, January 30, 2009. http://www.pewforum.org/2009/01/30/a-religious-portrait-of-african-americans/.

_____. *Asian Americans: A Mosaic of Faiths*. Washington, DC, Forum on Religion and Public Life, July 19, 2012. http://www.pewforum.org/2012/07/19/asian-americans-a-mosaic-of-faiths-overview/.

_____. *Changing Faiths: Latinos and the Transformation of American Religion*. Washington, DC: Forum on Religion & Public Life, April 2007. http://pewforum.org/surveys/hispanic/.

_____. *Different Faiths, Different Messages*. Washington, DC: US Politics & Policy, March 19, 2003. http://people-press.org/reports/display.php3?ReportID=176.

_____. *Foreign Policy Attitudes Now Driven by 9/11 and Iraq*. Washington, DC: US Politics & Policy, August 18, 2004. http://people-press.org/reports/display.php3?PageID=862.

_____. "Leading Experts and Activists to Participate in Town Hall Meeting on the Role of Evangelicals in Global Human Rights and Bush Administration Foreign Policy." Transcript of Pew Forum on Religion & Public Life event, September 27, 2005. http://pewforum.org/press/index.php?ReleaseID=33.

_____. *Religion in Latin America: Widespread Change in a Historically Catholic Region*. Washington, DC: Religion & Public Life, November 13, 2014. http://www.pewforum.org/2014/11/13/religion-in-latin-america/.

_____. *The Future of World Religions: Population Growth Projections, 2010-2050*. Washington, DC: Religion and Public Life, April 2, 2015. http://www.pewforum.org/2015/04/02/religious-projections-2010-2050/.

_____. *The Shifting Religious Identity of Latinos in the United States*. Washington, DC: Religion and Public Life, May 7, 2014. http://www.pewforum.org/2014/05/07/the-shifting-religious-identity-of-latinos-in-the-united-states/.

_____. *US Needs More International Backing*. Washington, DC: US Politics & Policy, February 20, 2003. http://www.people-press.org/2003/02/20/other-important-findings-and-analyses-3/.

_____. *US Religious Landscape Survey*. Washington: Religion & Public Life, 2008. http://religions.pewforum.org/reports#.

Phares, Walid. "The Sudanese Battle for American Opinion." *Middle East Quarterly* 5, no. 1 (March 1998), 19–31.

Phiri, Isaac. *Proclaiming Political Pluralism: Churches and Political Transitions in Africa*. Westport, CT: Praeger, 2001.

Poiger, Uta. *Jazz, Rock, and Rebels: Cold War Politics and American Culture in a Divided Germany*. Berkeley: University of California Press, 2000.

Poland, Larry W. *How to Prepare for the Coming Persecution*. 3rd ed. New York: Thomas Nelson Inc., 1990.

Pollock, John Charles. *The Siberian Seven*. Waco, TX: Word Books, 1980.

Potter, Ronald C. "The New Black Evangelicals." In *Black Theology*, edited by Gayraud Wilmore and James Cone, 302–9.

Powell, Eve Troutt. *A Different Shade of Colonialism: Egypt, Great Britain, and the Mastery of the Sudan*. Berkeley: University of California Press, 2003

Preston, Andrew. "Evangelical Internationalism: A Conservative Worldview for the Age of Globalization." In *The Right Side of the Sixties: Reexamining Conservatism's Decade of Transformation*, edited by Laura Jane Gifford and Daniel K. Williams, 221–42. New York: Palgrave Macmillan, 2012.

_____. *Sword of the Spirit, Shield of Faith: Religion in American War and Diplomacy*. New York: Knopf, 2012.

_____. "Tempered by the Fires of War: Vietnam and the Transformation of the Evangelical Worldview." In *American Evangelicals and the 1960s*, edited by Axel Schäfer, 189–2010.

Price, Robert M. *The Apartheid State in Crisis: Political Transformation in South Africa, 1975-1990*. New York: Oxford University Press, 1991.

Priest, Robert J. "Anthropology and Missiology: Reflections on the Relationship." In *Paradigm Shifts in Christian Witness: Insights from Anthropology, Communication, and Spiritual Power*, edited by Charles E. Ven Engen, Darrell Whiteman, and J. Dudley Woodberry, 23–32. Marynoll, NY: Orbis Books, 2008.

Priest, Robert, Thomas Campbell, and Bradford A. Mullen. "Missiological Syncretism: The New Animistic Paradigm." In *Spiritual Power and Missions: Raising the Issues*, edited by Edward Rommen, 9–87. Pasadena, CA: William Carey Library, 1995.

Priest, Robert, Terry Dischinger, Steve Rasmussen, and C.M. Brown. "Researching the Short-Term Mission Movement." *Missiology: An International Review* 34, no. 4 (October 2006): 431–50.

Prothero, Stephen R. *American Jesus: How the Son of God Became a National Icon*. New York: Farrar, Straus, and Giroux, 2003.

Quebedeaux, Richard. *The Young Evangelicals; Revolution in Orthodoxy*. New York: Harper & Row, 1974.

Redfield, Peter. *Life in Crisis: The Ethical Journey of Doctors Without Borders*. Berkeley: University of California Press, 2013.

Religious Persecution in the Middle East; Faces of the Persecuted. Hearings Before the Subcommittee on Near Eastern and South Asian Affairs, Senate Committee on Foreign Relations,, 105th Congress (1997).

Reese, Robert. "John Gatu and the Moratorium on Missionaries." *Missiology: An International Review* 42, no. 3 (July 2014): 245–56.

Richardson, Don. *Secrets of the Koran*. Ventura, CA: Regal Books, 2003.

Roach, David Christopher. "The Southern Baptist Convention and Civil Rights, 1954–1995." PhD diss., Southern Baptist Theological Seminary, 2009.

Robert, Dana L., ed. *Gospel Bearers, Gender Barriers: Missionary Women in the Twentieth Century*. Maryknoll, NY: Orbis Books, 2002.

_____. "The Origin of the Student Volunteer Watchword: 'The Evangelization of the World in This Generation.'" *International Bulletin of Missionary Research* 10, no. 4 (October 1986): 146–49.

Robinson, James H. *Africa at the Crossroads*. Philadelphia: Westminster Press, 1962.

Robinson, Shira. *Citizen Strangers: Palestinians and the Birth of Israel's Liberal Settler State*. Stanford, CA: Stanford University Press, 2013.

Rogers, Carol Ann, and Kenneth Swinnerton. "Slave Redemption When It Takes Time to Redeem Slaves." In *Buying Freedom*, edited by Anthony Appiah and Martin Bunzi, 20–36.

Rosenberg, Emily S. *Spreading the American Dream: American Economic and Cultural Expansion, 1890–1945.* New York: Hill and Wang, 1982.

Rubenstein, Mary-Jane. "Anglicans in the Postcolony: On Sex and the Limits of Communion." *Telos* no. 143 (June 2008): 133–60.

Ruble, Sarah E. *The Gospel of Freedom and Power: Protestant Missionaries in American Culture after World War II.* Chapel Hill: University of North Carolina Press, 2012.

Ryle, John, Madut Jok Jok, and Fergus Boyle. *The Sudan Abduction and Slavery Project.* Nairobi: Rift Valley Institute, 2003. http://riftvalley.net/project/sudan-abduction-and-slavery-project#.Wd7eatOGNBw

Sadgrove, Joanna, Robert M. Vanderbeck, Johan Andersson, Gill Valentine, and Kevin Ward. "Morality Plays and Money Matters: Towards a Situated Understanding of the Politics of Homosexuality in Uganda." *Journal of Modern African Studies* 50, no. 1 (March 2012): 103–29.

Sadgrove, Joanna, Robert M. Vanderbeck, Kevin Ward, Gill Valentine, and Johan Andersson. "Constructing the Boundaries of Anglican Orthodoxy: An Analysis of the Global Anglican Future Conference (GAFCON)." *Religion* 40, no. 3 (July 2010): 193–206.

Sa'di, Ahmad H., and Lila Abu-Lughod, eds. *Nakba: Palestine, 1948, and the Claims of Memory.* New York: Columbia University Press, 2007.

Said, Edward W., and Palestine Human Rights Campaign, eds. *A Profile of the Palestinian People.* Chicago: Palestine Human Rights Campaign, 1983.

Salomon, Noah. "The Ruse of Law: Legal Equality and the Problem of Citizenship in a Multireligious Sudan." In *After Secular Law*, edited by Winnifred F. Sullivan, Robert A. Yelle, and Mateo Taussig-Rubbo, 200–20. Stanford, CA: Stanford Law Books, 2011.

Sanneh, Lamin O. "Christian Experience of Islamic Da'wah, with Particular Reference to Africa." *International Review of Mission* 65, no. 260 (October 1976): 410–26.

⎯⎯⎯. *Piety and Power: Muslims and Christians in West Africa.* Maryknoll, NY: Orbis Books, 1996.

⎯⎯⎯. *Translating the Message: The Missionary Impact on Culture.* 2nd ed. Marynoll, NY: Orbis Books, 2008.

Sargent, Daniel J. *A Superpower Transformed: The Remaking of American Foreign Relations in the 1970s.* Oxford: Oxford University Press, 2015.

Sarkela, Sandra, and Patrick Mazzeo. "Rev. James H. Robinson and American Support for African Democracy and Nation-Building, 1950s–1970s." In *Freedom's Distant Shores: American Protestants and Post-Colonial Alliances with Africa*, edited by Drew R. Smith, 37–52. Waco, TX: Baylor University Press, 2006.

Savage, Barbara Dianne. *Your Spirits Walk Beside Us: The Politics of Black Religion.* Cambridge, MA: Belknap Press of Harvard University Press, 2008.

Sawatsky, Walter. *Soviet Evangelicals Since World War II.* Kitchener, Ontario: Herald Pr, 1981.

Schildkrout, Enid. "Though the Lens of Herbert Lang: Belgian Congo Photographs, 1909-1915." *African Arts* 24, no. 4 (October 1991): 70ff.

Schäfer, Axel R, ed. *American Evangelicals and the 1960s.* Madison: University of Wisconsin Press, 2013.

⎯⎯⎯. *Countercultural Conservatives: American Evangelicalism from the Postwar Revival to the New Christian Right.* Madison: University of Wisconsin Press, 2011.

⎯⎯⎯. *Piety and Public Funding: Evangelicals and the State in Modern America.* Philadelphia: University of Pennsylvania Press, 2012.

Schaeffer, Francis A. *Escape from Reason*. Downers Grove, IL: InterVarsity Press, 1968.

_____. "Form and Freedom in the Church: Paper as Delivered." In *Let the Earth Hear His Voice*, edited by J. D. Douglas, 361–67.

_____. "Form and Freedom in the Church: Pre-Circulated Paper." In *Let the Earth Hear His Voice*, edited by J. D. Douglas, 368–79.

_____. *He Is There and He Is Not Silent*. Carol Stream, IL: Tyndale House Publishers Inc., 1972.

_____. *How Should We Then Live? The Rise and Decline of Western Thought and Culture*. Old Tappan, NJ: F. H. Revell Co., 1976.

_____. *The God Who Is There: Speaking Historic Christianity into the Twentieth Century*. Downers Grove, IL: InterVarsity Press, 1968.

_____. *Whatever Happened to the Human Race?* Old Tappan, NJ: F.H. Revell Co., 1979.

Schaeffer, Frank. *Crazy for God: How I Grew Up as One of the Elect, Helped Found the Religious Right*. Boston: Da Capo Press, 2007.

Schenkel, Albert Frederick. "New Wine and Baptist Wineskins: American and Southern Baptist Denominational Responses to Charismatic Renewal, 1960-80." In *Pentecostal Currents in American Protestantism*, edited by Edith Blumhofer, Rusell P. Spittler, and Grant A. Wacker, 152–67. Urbana: University of Illinois Press, 1999.

Schlossberg, Herbert. *A Fragrance of Oppression: The Church and Its Persecutors*. Wheaton, IL: Crossway Books, 1991.

Schreck, Harley, and David Barrett. *Unreached Peoples: Clarifying the Task*. Pasadena, CA: Missions Advanced Research Center, 1987.

Schwartz, Glenn. "Two Awesome Problems: How Short Term Missions Go Wrong." *International Journal of Frontier Missions* 21, no. 1 (Spring 2004): 27–34.

Sehat, David. *The Myth of American Religious Freedom*. New York: Oxford University Press, 2011.

Seiple, Robert and Charles Borchini. "Religion and Security: The New Nexus in International Relations." Presentation at the Pew Research Center Religion & Public Life, Washington, DC, November 10, 2004. http://www.pewforum.org/2004/11/10/religion-and-security-the-new-nexus-in-international-relations/.

Seiple, Robert, and Dennis Hoover. *Religion and Security: The New Nexus in International Relations*. Lanham, MD: Rowman & Littlefield, 2004.

Sellars, Kirsten. *The Rise and Rise of Human Rights*. Stroud: Sutton, 2002.

Shah, Timothy, et al. "Pew Forum: Legislating International Religious Freedom." Panel presentation, Washington, DC, November 20, 2006. http://www.pewforum.org/2006/11/20/legislating-international-religious-freedom/.

Sharkey, Heather J. *American Evangelicals in Egypt: Missionary Encounters in an Age of Empire*. Princeton, NJ: Princeton University Press, 2008.

_____. "American Presbyterians, Freedmen's Missions, and the Nile Valley: Missionary History, Racial Orders, and Church Politics on the World Stage." *Journal of Religious History* 35, no. 1 (March 2001): 24–42.

_____. *Living with Colonialism: Nationalism and Culture in the Anglo-Egyptian Sudan*. Berkeley: University of California Press, 2003.

Sharlet, Jeff. *C Street: The Fundamentalist Threat to American Democracy*. New York: Little, Brown and Company, 2010.

Shea, Nina. *In the Lion's Den: A Shocking Account of Persecuted and Martyrdom of Christians Today and How We Should Respond*. Nashville, TN: Broadman & Holman Publishers, 1997.

_____. "Origins and Legacy of the Movement to Fight Religious Persecution." *Review of Faith and International Affairs* 6, no. 2 (June 2008): 25–33.

Shires, Preston. *Hippies of the Religious Right: From the Countercultures of Jerry Garcia to the Subculture of Jerry Falwell.* Waco, TX: Baylor University Press, 2007.

Showalter, Nathan D. *The End of a Crusade.* Lanham, MD: Scarecrow Press, 1997.

Shriver, Peggy L. "Evangelicals and World Affairs." *World Policy Journal* 23, no. 3 (2006): 52–58.

Simon, Merrill. *Jerry Falwell and the Jews.* Middle Village, NY: Jonathan David Publishers, 1984.

Singh, Nikhil Pal. *Black Is a Country: Race and the Unfinished Struggle for Democracy.* Cambridge, MA: Harvard University Press, 2004.

Sinha, Mrinalini. *Specters of Mother India: The Global Restructuring of an Empire.* Durham, NC: Duke University Press, 2006.

Skinner, Tom. *Black and Free.* Grand Rapids, MI: Zondervan Publishing House, 1968.

_____. *How Black Is the Gospel?* Philadelphia: Lippincott, 1970.

_____. "The U.S. Racial Crisis and World Evangelism." In *Christ The Liberator*, edited by John Stott, 189–210. Downer's Grove, IL: InterVarsity Press, 1971.

Smith, Gayle. "George Bush in Khartoum." *MERIP Reports*, no. 135 (September 1985): 25–26.

Smith, Valene L. "War and Tourism: An American Ethnography." *Annals of Tourism Research* 25, no. 1 (January 1998): 202–27.

Snyder, Sarah B. *Human Rights Activism and the End of the Cold War: A Transnational History of the Helsinki Network.* Cambridge: Cambridge University Press, 2011.

Sontag, Susan. *Regarding the Pain of Others.* New York: Penguin Books Ltd., 2004.

Sookhdeo, Patrick. *A People Betrayed: The Impact of Islamisation on the Christian Community in Pakistan.* McLean, VA: Isaac Publishing, 2002.

_____. *Global Jihad: The Future in the Face of Militant Islam.* McLean, VA: Isaac Publishing, 2007.

_____. *LOP 32: The Persecuted Church.* Pattya, Thailand: Lausanne Committee for World Evagelization, 2004.

Spector, Stephen. *Evangelicals and Israel: The Story of American Christian Zionism.* New York: Oxford University Press, 2008.

Stackhouse, Max. "Why Human Rights Needs God: A Christian Perspective." In *Does Human Rights Need God?*, edited by Elizabeth Bucar and Barbra Barnett, 25–40. Grand Rapids, MI: Wm. B. Eerdmans Publishers, 2005.

Stanley, Brian. "'Lausanne 1974': The Challenge from the Majority World to Northern-Hemisphere Evangelicalism." *Journal of Ecclesiastical History* 64, no. 3 (2013): 533–51.

_____. *The Global Diffusion of Evangelicalism: The Age of Billy Graham and John Stott.* Downers Grove, IL: InterVarsity Press Academic, 2013.

Stassen, Glen H., and David P. Gushee. *Kingdom Ethics: Following Jesus in Contemporary Context.* Downers Grove, IL: InterVarsity Press, 2003.

Stein, Rebecca L. *Itineraries in Conflict: Israelis, Palestinians, and the Political Lives of Tourism.* Durham, NC: Duke University Press, 2008.

Stephens, Randall J. "'It Has to Come from the Hearts of the People': Evangelicals, Fundamentalists, Race, and the 1964 Civil Rights Act." *Journal of American Studies* 50, no. 3 (August 2016): 559–85.

_____. *The Fire Spreads: Holiness and Pentecostalism in the American South.* Cambridge, MA: Harvard University Press, 2010.

Stocking, George W. "Franz Boas and the Culture Concept in Historical Perspective." *American Anthropologist* 68, no. 4 (August 1966): 867–82.

Stott, John, ed. *Christ the Liberator*. Downers Grove, IL: InterVarsity Press, 1971.

———. "The Charge to Suffer for the Gospel." In InterVarsity Christian Fellowship, *In God's Men: From All Nations to All Nations*, 33–50.

———. "The Gospel and the Nations." In Henry, *Prophecy in the Making*, 217–44.

Strober, Gerald S., and Ruth Tomczak. *Jerry Falwell: Aflame for God*. 2nd ed. Nashville, TN: Thomas Nelson, 1979.

Sullivan, Winnifred Fallers. *The Impossibility of Religious Freedom*. Princeton, NJ: Princeton University Press, 2005.

Sutton, Matthew Avery. *Aimee Semple McPherson and the Resurrection of Christian America*. Cambridge, MA: Harvard University Press, 2009.

———. *American Apocalypse: A History of Modern Evangelicalism*. Cambridge, MA: Belknap Press, 2014.

Swartz, David R. "Left Behind: The Evangelical Left and the Limits of Evangelical Politics, 1965-1988." Ph.D diss., University of Notre Dame, 2008.

———. *Moral Minority: The Evangelical Left in an Age of Conservatism*. Philadelphia: University of Pennsylvania Press, 2012.

Synan, Vinson. *The Holiness-Pentecostal Tradition: Charismatic Movements in the Twentieth Century*. Grand Rapids, MI: Wm. B. Eerdmans Publishing, 1997.

Taylor, Joan E. "Golgotha: A Reconsideration of the Evidence for the Sites of Jesus' Crucifixion and Burial." *New Testament Studies* 44, no. 2 (April 1998): 180–203.

Taylor-Robinson, S.D. "Operation Lifeline Sudan." *Journal of Medical Ethics* 28 (2002): 44–51.

Thomson, Alex. *Incomplete Engagement: U.S. Foreign Policy Towards the Republic of South Africa, 1981–1988*. Brookfield, VT: Avebury, 1996.

Thompson, Douglas E. *Richmond's Priests and Prophets: Race, Religion, and Social Change in the Civil Rights Era*. Tuscaloosa: University Alabama Press, 2017.

Thornton, Robert. *Unimagined Community: Sex, Networks, and AIDS in Uganda and South Africa*. Berkeley: University of California Press, 2008.

Tizon, Al. *Transformation after Lausanne: Radical Evangelical Mission in Global-Local Perspective*. Eugene, OR: Wipf & Stock Publishers, 2008.

Torgovnick, Marianna. *Gone Primitive: Savage Intellects, Modern Lives*. Chicago: University of Chicago Press, 1991.

Trinitapoli, Jenny, and Alexander Weinreb. *Religion and AIDS in Africa*. New York: Oxford University Press, 2012.

Tsing, Anna Lowenhaupt. *Friction: An Ethnography of Global Connection*. Princeton, NJ: Princeton University Press, 2004.

Turek, Lauren. "To Bring the Good News to All Nations: Evangelicals, Human Rights, and US Foreign Policy 1969-1994." PhD diss., Univ. of Virginia, 2015.

Turner, John G. *Bill Bright and Campus Crusade for Christ: The Renewal of Evangelicalism in Postwar America*. Chapel Hill: University of North Carolina Press, 2008.

Twain, Mark. *King Leopold's Soliloquy*. Boston: The P.R. Warren Company, 1905.

Tweed, Thomas. *Crossing and Dwelling: A Theory of Religion*. Cambridge, MA: Harvard University Press, 2006.

———. *The American Encounter with Buddhism, 1844-1912: Victorian Culture & the Limits of Dissent*. Chapel Hill: University of North Carolina Press, 2000.

Tyrrell, Ian. *Reforming the World: The Creation of America's Moral Empire*. Princeton, NJ: Princeton University Press, 2010.

Uda, Sasumu. "Biblical Authority and Evangelism-Paper Sent to Participants prior to Congress." In *Let the Earth Hear His Voice*, edited by J. D. Douglas, 79–87.

Uganda Bureau of Statistics. *National Population and Housing Census 2014*. Kampala, 2016. http://www.ubos.org/onlinefiles/uploads/ubos/NPHC/2014%20National%20Census%20Main%20Report.pdf

_____. *Uganda Population and Housing Census 2002*. Kampala, 2003. http://www.ubos.org/2002-census/.

Unreached Peoples: A Preliminary Compilation. Pasadena, CA: Missions Advanced Research Center, 1974.

U.S. Response to Global AIDS Crisis: A Two-Year Review, Hearing Before House Committee on International Relations, H.R. Rep. No. 109-86 (2005).

Valentine, Foy. *Believe and Behave*. Nashville, TN: Broadman Press, 1964.

Van Engen, Charles. "A Broadening Vision: Forty Years of Evangelical Theology of Mission, 1946–1986." In *Earthen Vessels*, edited by Joel Carpenter and W. R. Shenk, 230–34.

Van Voorhis, Bruce. "Food as a Weapon for Peace: Operation Lifeline Sudan." *Africa Today* 36, no. 3/4 (1989): 29–42.

Ver Beek, Kurt Alan. "The Impact of Short-Term Missions: A Case Study of House Construction in Honduras after Hurricane Mitch." *Missiology* 34, no. 4 (October 2006): 477–95.

Von Eschen, Penny. *Race Against Empire: Black Americans and Anticolonialism, 1937-1957*. Ithaca, NY: Cornell University Press, 1997.

Wacker, Grant. *America's Pastor: Billy Graham and the Shaping of a Nation*. Cambridge, MA: Belknap Press of Harvard University Press, 2014.

_____. *Heaven Below: Early Pentecostals and American Culture*. Cambridge, MA: Harvard University Press, 2003.

_____. "The Waning of the Missionary Impulse: The Case of Pearl S. Buck." In *The Foreign Missionary Enterprise at Home*, edited by Daniel Bays and Grant Wacker, 191–205.

Wadsworth, Nancy D. *Ambivalent Miracles: Evangelicals and the Politics of Racial Healing*. Charlottesville: University of Virginia Press, 2014.

Wagner, C. Peter. *Latin American Theology: Radical or Evangelical? The Struggle for the Faith in a Young Church*. Grand Rapids, MI: Wm. B. Eerdmans Publishing, 1970.

_____. ed. *Signs & Wonders Today*. New expanded ed. Altamonte Springs, FL: Creation House, 1987.

_____. "Territorial Spirits and World Missions." *EMQ*, July 1989. https://emqonline.com/node/530.

_____. *Unreached Peoples '79*. Elgin, IL: D.C. Cook Publishers Co., 1978.

_____. *Wrestling with Alligators, Prophets and Theologians: Lessons from a Lifetime in the Church-A Memoir*. Ventura, CA: Gospel Light Publications, 2010.

Wakatama, Pius. *Independence for the Third World Church: An African's Perspective on Missionary Work*. Downers Grove, IL: InterVarsity Press, 1976.

Walker, David. "Evangelicals and Apartheid: An Inquiry into Some Predispositions." *Journal of Theology for Southern Africa*, no. 67 (June 1989): 46–61.

Wallis, Jim. *The Great Awakening: Reviving Faith & Politics in a Post-Religious Right America*. New York: HarperOne, 2008.

Walshe, Peter. *Church Versus State in South Africa: The Case of the Christian Institute*. Maryknoll, NY: Orbis Books, 1983.

_____. *Prophetic Christianity and the Liberation Movement in South Africa*. Pietermaritzburg, South Africa: Cluster Publications, 1995.

Walton, Jonathan. *Watch This! The Ethics and Aesthetics of Black Televangelism*. New York: New York University Press, 2009.

Walvoord, John F. *Israel in Prophecy*. Grand Rapids, MI: Zondervan, 1962.

Wang, Thomas. "By the Year 2000: Is God Trying to Tell Us Something?" In *Countdown to AD 2000: The Official Compendium of the Global Consultation on World Evangelization by AD 2000 and Beyond, Singapore, January 5–8, 1989*, edited by Thomas Wang, xiv–xx. Pasadena, CA: William Carey Library, 1989.

Ward, Kevin. "Same-Sex Relations in Africa and the Debate on Homosexuality in East African Anglicanism." *Anglican Theological Review* 84, no. 1 (Winter 2002): 81–111.

Ward, Kevin and Emma Wild-Wood, eds. *The East African Revival: History and Legacies*. New York: Routledge, 2016.

Washington Office on Africa. *Slavery, War and Peace in Sudan*. Briefing paper. Washington, DC, November 29, 1999.

Watt, David Harrington. *A Transforming Faith: Explorations of Twentieth-Century American Evangelicalism*. New Brunswick, NJ: Rutgers University Press, 1991.

_____. "The Private Hopes of American Fundamentalists and Evangelicals, 1925–1975." *Religion and American Culture* 1, no. 2 (Summer 1991): 155–75.

Weaver, Aaron Douglas. *James M. Dunn and Soul Freedom*. Macon, GA: Smyth & Helwys Publishing, 2011.

Weaver, John. *The New Apostolic Reformation: History of a Modern Charismatic Movement*. Jefferson, NC: McFarland, 2016.

Weber, Hans Ruedi. "South African Travel Diary." *Ecumenical Review* 25, no. 3 (July 1997): 337–41.

Weber, Max. "Science as a Vocation." In *From Max Weber: Essays in Sociology*, 129–58. New York: Oxford University Press, 1958.

_____. *The Protestant Ethic and the Spirit of Capitalism*. Edited by Anthony Giddens. Translated by Talcott Parsons. 2nd ed. New York: Routledge, 2001.

Weber, Timothy P. *On the Road to Armageddon: How Evangelicals Became Israel's Best Friend*. Grand Rapids, MI: Baker Academic, 2004.

Weissman, Stephen R. *American Foreign Policy in the Congo, 1960–1964*. Ithaca, NY: Cornell University Press, 1974.

Welch, Claude E. "Mobilizing Morality: The World Council of Churches and Its Program to Combat Racism, 1969-1994." *Human Rights Quarterly* 23, no. 4 (November 2001): 863–910.

Welsh, David. *The Rise and Fall of Apartheid*. Charlottesville: University of Virginia Press, 2009.

Westad, Odd Arne. *The Global Cold War: Third World Interventions and the Making of Our Times*. Cambridge: Cambridge University Press, 2007.

Westerlund, David, and Ingvar Svanberg. *Islam Outside the Arab World*. New York: Palgrave Macmillan, 1999.

Whiteman, Darrell L. "Anthropological Reflections on Contextualizing Theology in a Globalizing World." In *Globalizing Theology: Belief and Practice in an Era of World Christianity*, edited by Craig Ott and Harold A. Netland, 52–69. Grand Rapids, MI: Baker Academic, 2006.

Whitman, T. Stephen. *The Price of Freedom: Slavery and Manumission in Baltimore and Early National Maryland*. Louisville: University of Kentucky Press, 1997.

Williams, Daniel K. *God's Own Party: The Making of the Christian Right*. New York: Oxford University Press, 2010.

_____. "Jerry Falwell's Sunbelt Politics: The Regional Origins of the Moral Majority." *Journal of Policy History* 22, no. 2 (April 2010): 125–47.

Williams, Ronald Cartell. "Adversarial Diplomacy and African American Politics." PhD diss., University of California, Berkeley, 2011.

Wilmore, Gayraud S. and James H. Cone, eds. *Black Theology: A Documentary History, 1966–1979*. Marynoll, NY: Orbis Books, 1979.

Willis, Alan Scot. *All According to God's Plan: Southern Baptist Missions and Race, 1945-1970*. Lexington: University Press of Kentucky, 2004.

Wilson, J. Christy Jr. *Today's Tentmakers: Self Support—An Alternative Model for Worldwide Witness*. Carol Stream, IL: Tyndale House Publishers, 1979.

Winston, Diane H. "Back to the Future: Religion, Politics, and the Media." *American Quarterly* 59, no. 3 (September 2007): 969–89.

Winter, Ralph. *Frontiers in Mission: Discovering and Surmounting the Barriers to the Missio Dei*. 4th ed. Pasadena, CA: William Carey International University Press, 2008.

_____. *Theological Education by Extension*. Pasadena, CA: William Carey Library, 1969.

Witte, Ludo de. *Assassination of Lumumba*. New York: Verso, 2003.

Worden, Nigel. *The Making of Modern South Africa: Conquest, Apartheid, Democracy*. 5th ed. New York: Wiley-Blackwell, 2012.

World Bank. *A Poverty Profile for the Southern States of Sudan*. Washington, DC: World Bank, March 2011.

World Christian Staff. *30 Days: Muslim Prayer Focus*. Colorado Springs, CO: World Christian Books, 1998.

Worthen, Molly. *Apostles of Reason: The Crisis of Authority in American Evangelicalism*. New York: Oxford University Press, 2013.

Wurmbrand, Richard. *From Suffering to Triumph*. Kregel Pubns, 1993.

_____. *If Prison Walls Could Speak*. Bartlesville, OK: Living Sacrifice Book Co., 1993.

_____. *The Church in Chains*. Rev. ed. London: Hodder & Stoughton, 1974.

_____. *Tortured for Christ*. Darby, PA: Diane Books, 1967.

Wuthnow, Robert. *Boundless Faith: The Global Outreach of American Churches*. Berkeley: University of California Press, 2010.

_____. *Inventing American Religion: Polls, Surveys, and the Tenuous Quest for a Nation's Faith*. New York: Oxford University Press, 2015.

Yoder, John Howard. *The Politics of Jesus*. Grand Rapids, MI: Wm. B. Eerdmans Publishing, 1972.

Young, F. Lionel. "A 'New Breed of Missionaries': Assessing Attitudes Toward Western Missions at the Nairobi Evangelical Graduate School of Theology." *International Bulletin of Missionary Research* 36, no. 2 (April 2012): 90–94.

Young, Shawn David. *Gray Sabbath: Jesus People USA, the Evangelical Left, and the Evolution of Christian Rock*. New York: Columbia University Press, 2015.

Zahar, Marie-Joelle. "A Journey of a Thousand Steps: The Challenges of State and Nation Building in South Sudan." *Middle East Report*, no. 259 (Summer 2011): 36–40.

Ziegler, Mary. *After Roe: The Lost History of the Abortion Debate*. Cambridge, MA: Harvard University Press, 2015.

INDEX